INSIDE THE MIND OF A

DRUG ADDICT

INSIDE THE MIND OF A

DRUG ADDICT

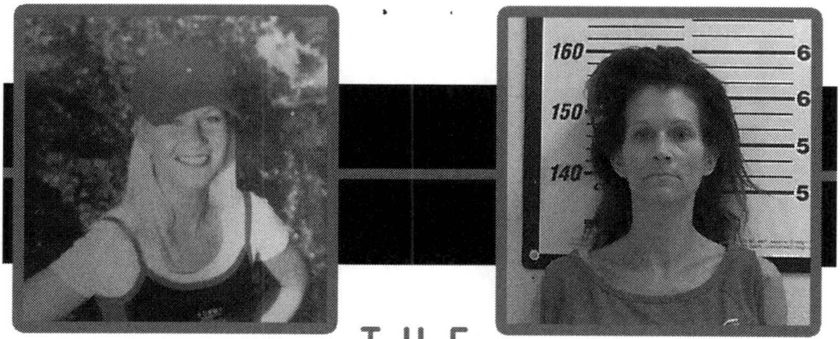

THE NATALIE ALLEN STORY

MICHELLE ROGERS

Inside the Mind of a Drug Addict: The Natalie Allen Story

For information about this title or to order other books and/or electronic media, contact the publisher:

Michelle Rogers
m-t-rogers@q.com

ISBNs:
979-8-9852844-0-9 (softcover)
979-8-9852844-1-6 (eBook)

Printed in the United States of America

Cover and Interior design: 1106 Design

Dedicated to Nat's children: Adison, Mason, and Jala.
Thank you for giving my sister a reason to live as long as she did.

Inside The Mind Of A Drug Addict

"It's not like I woke up one day when I was going out and told myself 'I wanna be a drug addict, I want to completely ruin my entire life and the lives of those around me that love and care about me.' I have definitely learned now that this is a DISEASE, and when I pick up that 1st drug, I cannot stop."

"I wish I had never picked up that 1st drug and ever put myself around the people that I did! My life would be 100% different. Now, I'm fighting every single day of my life to stay clean. It is the hardest thing I have had to go through in my life! I hope I can change someone's life one day after hearing what I've been through in my life because of drugs."

CONTENTS

INTRODUCTION

I HAVE KNOWN I WOULD WRITE this book for years. My sister Natalie (Nat) wanted to share her story and help others while she was alive; it was her dream. Unfortunately, she was never able to fulfill her dream, so I am doing it for her. I tried to start this book in November of 2018, but it didn't feel right; her story was not ready to be shared. Less than two months later, on January 14, 2019, my sister passed away. Now, it's time.

Nat journaled for years and in 2014 after drug court she gave me a stack of journals she wanted me to keep for her, and on many occasions, she shared with me her desire to share her story to help others who struggle with addiction. Her journals start in 2009 and end on January 12, 2019, two days before she lost her battle.

This is my sister's story; it is not mine. These are her words from journals she kept during some of her years of using. The wording is exactly as she wrote it in her journals. Sometimes it makes sense, and other times it doesn't. I will add my insight and thoughts and explanations that will help preface her journal entries. My insight will be italicized, and my thoughts are based on the memories of myself and other family members. I wanted to leave her journal entries as they were to show what was really going on in her mind. The entries are taken from multiple journals she would keep at the same time. I have put them in chronological order, so some dates have more than one entry.

Other than family, names have been changed to protect the privacy of others.

I have learned so much from these journals and have had so many insights into her mind and her behavior during her 23-year addiction.

Nat and I always had a very close bond, which I believe began before our Earth life. I imagine us as spirits in our pre-Earth life in which we made a pact that she would be the stronger spirit. She agreed to take this excruciating trial in life as a way to teach all of us the things we needed to learn. Since she wasn't able to share her story while she was alive, I would step up to do it as a way of honoring her life and possibly saving someone else from the horrific effects of drug abuse. I believe her story will save lives and help other families dealing with drug addiction. It is raw and real. During the last year of her life, she wrote in her journals that she wondered why she was still alive and what her purpose was. Honestly, the rest of the family asked the same question. I believe she lived as long as she did because she was fulfilling her purpose, journaling her life story to help others, even though she didn't know her purpose when she was alive.

CHAPTER 1

FAMILY

I AM THE OLDEST DAUGHTER in our family of four girls. Michelle (me, Shall), Angie (Ang), Natalie (Nat or NaNa), and Emily (Em or Emmy). Nat was born on February 23, 1979. We are each three years apart. We were raised in a loving, supportive, religious home with both parents who are still married. We had a home where people were always welcome. The front door was always open for anyone. Our house was the one where family parties and events took place. We had cousins live with us periodically. We also had a very close extended family.

This picture was taken before our youngest sister, Emily, was born. Nat is about eighteen months old

Nat at three years old

Nat at four years old

Nat at five years old

Nat at nine years old

Nat at ten years old

Nat at eleven years old

The four of us sisters have always been very close. At different stages of our lives, different circumstances had brought us closer than we already were. Even now, all of our children have continued to stay close, as well as our entire family.

My earliest memories of Nat are of her being really hyperactive. The rest of us girls would tease her about taking her "hyper" pills (Ritalin, ADD medication, which she was only on temporarily). When I was asked to babysit my three younger sisters, Nat was always the one who kept me on my toes. As I got older and had friends and boyfriends, she would always be my little sidekick and loved to be with me and my friends. Nat always had so much energy and always made her presence known. She channeled that energy into cheerleading, dance, and gymnastics. Nat made us all so proud with her accomplishments in these activities. She had natural talent and seemed to be able to do anything and do it well, even school.

Nat at twelve years old

In Nat's own words from her Personal Progress Book (a book produced by our church and was given to young girls to keep a record of goals, etc.), this is what she wrote when she was twelve years old:

I feel happy when . . . Me and my sisters get along, and me and my parents get along and when we all are together and we do something together like have family night.

I feel good about myself when . . . I do what is right and live the commandments and help out around the house.

One of my dreams is to . . . get married in the temple and have my husband go on a mission.

One of the best things that happened to me is . . . being a Mormon and going to church and living the commandments.

Things that are important to me . . . My family and friends, my health. That I'm a member of the church.

What are the happiest memories you have of your parents . . . When we go on a trip or a vacation. Being a thoughtful person and being kind to others.

What are some of the things your family does together . . . Going on vacations and we all have a wonderful time being with each other.

Nat at fourteen years old

This shows her innocence and a little of what she imagined her future life would look like. It's incredible to think that four years later, her addiction would begin.

• • •

CHAPTER 2

THE BEGINNING

WHEN NAT WAS A JUNIOR in high school (sixteen years old), she was at a cheer practice and was dropped during a stunt. She ended up with a concussion and was prescribed muscle relaxers and pain pills to help with the pain. She kept complaining of the pain after the prescriptions had run out, so my mom called the doctor to get refills, thinking she was helping her. I believe this is the first time Nat felt "normal" since being on Ritalin *(ADD medication)* from age 5–7. Later that same year, Nat showed up at my house in her cheerleading uniform with her boyfriend, and told me and my husband Tye that she was pregnant and wanted our help telling our parents. She ended up marrying the father on January 26, 1996, a few weeks before her seventeenth birthday and seven months before Adi was born. While she was pregnant, she needed her gallbladder removed and had surgery where she was prescribed

Nat at sixteen years old, just before she was pregnant with Adi. This is what she looked like when she came to my house and told me and my husband that she was pregnant

pain medication. After childbirth, she was once again prescribed pain medication. Her dependency on pain medication began to develop. Not long after, she started drinking.

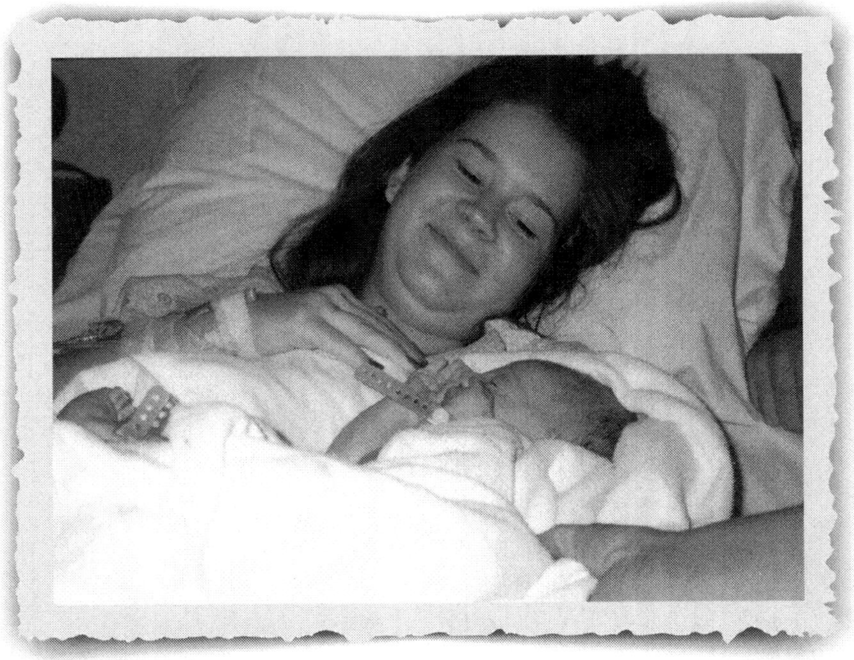

August 1996, Nat and Adi

Eventually Nat and her first husband were able to move into a beautiful, brand-new home. Nat and I were pregnant with our first two children at the same time and by the time both of our babies were born in 1996 (our children were three months apart), we lived a couple miles away from each other and we were inseparable. Our children, Adison (Adi) and Austin, were more like brother and sister than cousins. They were our lives, as well as the focus and joy of our entire family. Nat was a great mom and was always very attentive to Adi. We dressed them alike and would rollerblade around town while pushing the kids in their strollers. We even took Mommy-and-Me gymnastic classes with our babies. Nat was able to be at home and take care of Adi without working outside the home.

Around this time, she got licensed to do nails, which she did out of her home for extra money. She also met some friends in her new neighborhood, as well as couples that she and her husband would hang out with. Around this time, she started spending more time with friends outside of our family. These friends would often drink alcohol together and swap pain pills with each other.

In 1998, she got pregnant with her second child, Mason (Mas), who was born in April 1999. Sure enough, a few months later, I was pregnant with my second child, Kierra. By the time Mas was born, Nat was still able to hold things together, at least on the outside. To our family and others, it looked like she was still an attentive mother. We were still very close, talked almost every day and saw each other often, but I noticed a change in her; she was spending a lot of time on her social life, which slowly started to take her focus off of her children.

Nat and Mas

In an effort to stay in chronological order, I include doctors' notes and other information I received after she passed away. Her journal entries begin in 2009.

• • •

CHAPTER 3

2001–2004

ON JANUARY 2, 2001, I wrote in my journal about our New Year's Eve night. My sisters and I, along with our husbands, had gone to a place called "The Homestead" and danced through the New Year's celebration. I wrote about how I looked over at all my sisters and their husbands while we were all slow dancing and felt so happy. I treasure that memory.

In the spring of 2001, Nat had elective cosmetic surgery and was prescribed pain medication. She was divorced from her first husband later that year when their marriage started to fall apart. Adi was five years old and Mason was two. Our youngest sister, Em, was married that year also, and during this time, Nat lived in an apartment near our parents' home.

During 2002, she dated a man named Bart. He had moved from Utah to Denver, and she would travel back and forth to see him and was living with our parents at the time and working at Yvonne's Salon as a nail tech.

Em and Nat

In 2003, she worked at a beauty salon my husband and I owned as a nail tech. I remember one time in particular, she was trying to do an older woman's nails, but she was so high that she couldn't keep her eyes open. She was slurring her words and falling off her chair. My brother-in-law had to carry her out of the salon and take her to my parents.

She dated many different men and partied until the summer of 2004 when she met Jay at our salon, where she was still working. In November of that year Nat received services at Lakeview Hospital for a CT of her pelvis, a metabolic panel, and a chlamydia screening. The next day she was back in the hospital for a CT of her abdomen and mono screening. I do not know the results of these tests.

• • •

CHAPTER 4

2005–2006

IN 2005 NAT WAS *twenty-six years old, Adi was nine, and Mas was six.*

The children were being raised by their father and my parents. Nat was living at my parents' home, and she came home late one evening raging and yelling as she tried to pull the telephone off of the wall. My parents ended up calling the cops because they could not calm her down. She gave the cops a hard time, and they had to push her to the cement on her stomach so they could handcuff her. My parents were so devastated, as was the rest of the family. This is Nat's first arrest.

Nat was court-ordered to attend and complete psychotherapy and outpatient treatment at Lakeview Hospital. This treatment lasted from Jauary until April when she graduated from Lakeview Lifeworks Substance Abuse Program. She then worked at Garden Day Spa in Bountiful as a nail tech.

ARREST:
One day in jail.
January 2, 2005–January 3, 2005
West Bountiful Police Department
Charged with Abuse of Telegraph Service
Resisting/Interfering with Police
Intoxication

BIRTHDAY CARD FROM ME TO NAT FEBRUARY 23, 2005:

NAT:
HAPPY 26TH!! YOU'RE GETTING UP THERE LITTLE SIS! I HOPE YOU HAVE A GREAT DAY AND KNOW HOW MUCH YOU ARE LOVED BY EVERYONE. YOU HAVE SUCH A SWEET SPIRIT ABOUT YOU THAT PEOPLE LOVE. I CAN'T EVEN BEGIN TO TELL YOU HOW PROUD I AM OF YOU. I THINK ABOUT ALL YOU ARE GOING THROUGH NUMEROUS TIMES A DAY AND EACH TIME I THINK–HOW DOES SHE DO IT? I DON'T KNOW IF I WOULD HAVE THE STRENGTH AND COURAGE TO DO WHAT YOU ARE DOING. I KNOW LIFE SEEMS CRAZY TO YOU RIGHT NOW, BUT I KNOW YOU WILL MAKE IT THROUGH AND I KNOW YOU WILL BE A BETTER PERSON FOR THIS. YOU DESERVE EVERYTHING YOU DREAM OF AND SOMEDAY YOU WILL GET IT–I PROMISE! I HOPE YOU KNOW THAT I LOVE YOU-AND I AM HERE FOR YOU NO MATTER WHAT! PLEASE STAY STRONG, ENJOY YOUR DAY AND HAVE FUN BEING 26!!
I LOVE YOU!
YOUR BIGGEST SIS!

At this time, I knew she was drinking and taking pain pills but I was under the impression she was getting clean.

In 2006, Nat was twenty-seven years old, Adi was ten, Mas was seven.

Nat's third child Jala was born in January, 2006.

Nat and Jay married in June, 2006, and they were legally married until she passed away. Jay is Jala's father. After a few years they stopped living together but were best friends and Jay continued to look out for her until she passed. They lived together on and off throughout the years. She continued drinking and using pills during this time.

Nat met Jennifer in 2006. Jennifer introduced Nat to methadone (a prescription to help with addiction withdrawals from opioids which are narcotic pain killers.) Soon after, Jennifer introduced my sister to Mary and David, a couple who were drug dealers, and they introduced her to meth.

I include information about these drugs because it helps to better understand her behaviors and the effects each drug had on her physically and mentally. Nat suffered from ADD and anxiety during her life, starting at an early age. Knowing this, it's interesting to see how the side effects of the drugs she used significantly enhanced these disorders, as well as added depression and bipolar symptoms, to name a few.

From Davis Behavioral Health:

Methamphetamine is an extremely powerful stimulant. Effects of meth use include: intense rush, euphoria, rapid heartbeat, high blood pressure, abnormal heart rhythms, extreme increase in physical activities, increased body core temperatures, increased wakefulness and decreased appetite. Most people stay awake for days.

Mood symptoms include: anxiety and restlessness, panic, aggression, inability to sit still, racing thoughts, severe depression following methamphetamine binges, euphoria, violent mood swings, delusions of power.

Behavioral symptoms include: risky sexual behavior, increased sexual activity, increase in fighting, violence, avoiding hobbies and activities that were once considered pleasurable, legal problems, borrowing or stealing money, preoccupation with "chasing the next high," pulling away from friends and family, engaging in unsafe activities.

Physical symptoms include: marked weight loss, rapid heart rate, molecular and functional changes in the brain, inability of body to repair damaged tissues, increased libido, malnutrition, insomnia (especially during methamphetamine binge), constriction of the blood vessels in the body, respiratory problems, liver disease and damage, acne or picking scars, loss of elasticity of the skin, "meth mouth" (severe tooth decay, tooth loss and acid erosion), immune system dysfunction, brain damage, seizures, heart attack, stroke.

Psychological symptoms include: marked confusion, memory loss, disorganized lifestyle, paranoia (which can be permanent), psychosis, hallucinations, violence, total break from reality which is an upper and keeps you up for three days straight.

From DrugRehab.com:

Meth can cause severe itching that makes people rub their skin raw. It can also make people hallucinate and scratch imaginary bugs.

To come down from the high of meth, Mary and David introduced Nat to heroin (a depressant or downer), which she smoked and sniffed, and by 2008 she was injecting the drugs using a needle. Heroin (black or blk) was her drug of choice, but she used every drug she could get her hands on.

From Options Behavioral Health Systems:

Heroin "black tar heroin" is sticky like roofing tar or hard like coal. Heroin is usually dissolved, diluted, and injected into veins, muscles, or under the skin. Side effects of heroin include: depression, euphoria, mood swings, anxiety, hostility toward others, agitation and irritability, lying about drug use, avoiding loved ones, weight loss, scabs or bruises as the result of picking at the skin, delusions, disorientation, hallucinations, paranoia, decreased attention to personal hygiene, possession of burned spoons, needles or syringes, missing shoelaces, glass pipes, stashing drugs in various places around the home, car and work, periods of hyperactivity followed by periods of exhaustion, inability to fulfill responsibilities at work or school, increased sleeping, apathy and lack of motivation, decline in occupational or academic performance, slurred speech, shortness of breath, frequent respiratory infections, dry mouth, going "on the nod" (a back and forth state of being conscious and semiconscious) during conversations, forced, pressured speech, track marks on arms and legs, warm, flushed skin, constricted pupils, extreme itching.

Severity of symptoms tend to get worse the longer the drug is abused. The most common effects of heroin addiction may include: liver disease, skin disease and abscesses around injection sites, infections of the valves and lining of the heart, HIV or Hepatitis B and C, chronic pneumonia, clouded mental functioning, collapsed, scarred veins, blood clots leading to stroke, pulmonary embolism and heart attack, kidney disease, risks of contracting chronic illnesses, risks for blood-borne pathogens, respiratory depression, seizures, overdose and death.

Those who are addicted to heroin not only become physically dependent on the substance but are also afraid to quit for fear of the symptoms they may experience. Withdrawal symptoms from heroin can develop as soon as a few hours after sustained use. Some effects of withdrawal include: intense craving for heroin, extreme sweating, nausea and vomiting, severe muscle aches and pains, cramping in the limbs, feelings of heaviness of the body, extreme pain in muscles and bones, insomnia, cold sweats, runny nose, fever, diarrhea, and death that can occur when other medical conditions are present.

Nat also smoked bath salts. She would get severe sore throats and strep-like symptoms from this drug. This drug has been linked to behaviors of cannibalism.

From narconon.com:

Medical personnel who come across someone who is in a full-blown delusion as a result of bath salts may not recognize the effects and may not know what to do. There are more than eighty chemicals that might be included in these small packets. It is a class of stimulants that creates aggression and hallucinations. These substances are contained in small foil packages. Bath salts effects tend to last about three or four hours, but rapid heartbeat, increased blood pressure, and other effects of a stimulant may last longer. High doses have caused intense and extended panic attacks in some people. Since this drug is a stimulant, it tends to disrupt sleep. A person who takes the drug frequently may suffer from sleep-deprivation psychosis. Addiction is also a very likely effect.

Mentally, the user will experience euphoria, alertness, anxiety, and agitation. They will probably not feel hungry. They may have a headache, tense muscles, increased body temperature, nosebleeds and dilated pupils. They may also be dizzy and confused and may grind their teeth. But those are the milder effects. The more serious effects include fits, hallucinations, aggression, suicidal thoughts or attempts and psychotic delusions. Physically, a person can experience liver failure, kidney failure and loss of bowel control, a spontaneous breakdown of muscle fiber that can lead to death. Tragically, one of the effects of bath salts abuse is death, either because of the direct effect of the drug or because of a person's actions.

Crack cocaine is another drug my sister used.

From drugfreeworld.com:

Because it is smoked, the effects of crack cocaine are more immediate and more intense than that of powdered cocaine. Effects include: loss of appetite, increased heart rate, blood pressure and body temperature, contracted blood vessels, increased rate of breathing, dilated pupils, disturbed sleep patterns, nausea, hyperstimulation, bizarre, erratic, sometimes violent behavior, hallucinations, hyperexcitability, irritability, tactile hallucination that creates the illusion of bugs burrowing under the skin, intense euphoria, anxiety and paranoia, depression, panic and psychosis, convulsions, seizures and sudden death from high doses (even one time), liver, kidney and lung damage, disorientation, apathy, confused exhaustion, irritability and mood disturbances, delirium or psychosis and severe depression.

These are just a few of the drugs Nat used. The list could go on and on. Her drug of choice was always heroin, but when she couldn't get it, she would use meth, bath salts, or crack, etc., which were all uppers.

• • •

CHAPTER 5

2007–2008

IN 2007, NAT WAS *twenty-eight years old, Adi was eleven, Mas was eight, and Jala was one.*

In January, 2007, Nat had surgery on her shoulder. Around this time she and Jay were evicted from their apartment and moved from North Salt Lake to Bountiful, Utah.

In November she started seeing a doctor to get a prescription for Suboxone. Suboxone is a prescription used to treat narcotic (opioid) addiction. The following are her medical records from this doctor. When she refers to "doctor" in her journals, this is who she is referring to. I believe this is the year that using drugs was no longer a conscious choice for her; the addiction had taken over.

11-28-2007: Dr. Note–Seen for Suboxone. Uses heroin daily 5–6 balloons. *(A dealer uses unfilled water balloons and puts heroin in them. People buy them in packs of ten or more. The average balloon has one gram of heroin in it. The reason behind this is so one could swallow them if need be, if cops were around, etc., and not need medical attention. People wait to "pass" the balloons so they can use them.)* Prescribed Trazadone *(sleeping medication)* and Paxil *(antidepressant)*. Mom with her. Mom's looking into inpatient vs. outpatient facility for her. Currently having withdrawal symptoms. Hot and cold sweats, stomach upset, anxiety, restless body and muscle aches. 113 lbs. *(I'm including her weight from the doctor because it shows how much she fluctuated in her weight with drugs. Heroin usually made her gain weight and meth made her lose weight.)* Smokes 1 pack per day, no desire to quit. Working doing nails.

In order for someone to take Suboxone, they have to detox off heroin for twenty-four hours prior or they would get violently sick. If they were to use heroin while on Suboxone, they would immediately experience severe withdrawals.

11-30-2007: Dr. Note–110 lbs. Prescribed Suboxone.

12-13-2007: Dr. Note–119 lbs. Denies having cravings. Suboxone.

12-19-2007: Dr. Note–Jay called. She's having panic attacks, hyperventilating, hands and feet tingling, can't breathe, wants anxiety meds. Prescribed Klonopin *(a sedative that treats seizures, panic disorders, and anxiety).*

12-20-2007: Lakeview Hospital emergency evaluation.

12-27-2007: Dr. Note–Natalie called, her daughter is sick can't come in wants Suboxone prescribed.

In 2008, Nat was twenty-nine years old. Adi was twelve, Mas was nine, and Jala was two.

Nat lost custody of all three of her children this year and was evicted once again from her apartment with Jay.

1-2-2008: Dr. Note–110 lbs. Relapsed on heroin December 31. Lots of anxiety, situational problems with husband and family.

1-21-2008: Dr. Note–Natalie canceled appointment. Sick child. Called in Suboxone.

1-24-2008: Dr. Note–Natalie called appointment is Monday can't come has sick child. Called in Suboxone.

1-30-2008: Dr. Note–Natalie did not show for appointment.

2-1-2008: Dr. Note–Missed appointment daughter at PCMC rescheduled for Thurs. Wants Dr. to call in Suboxone.

In February Nat was court-ordered to be drug tested and go to counseling when her two older children were taken away from her and her ex-husband received full custody.

2-4-2008: Dr. Note–Requested letter for judge that she is on Suboxone. Not until seen.

2-7-2008: Dr. Note–Canceled appointment. No $.

2-15-2008: Dr Note–No show.

2-18-2008: Dr. Note–Hasn't had Paxil in 4 days, having anxiety. Says she is taking 12 mg Suboxone but not consistently. *(She told me she would sell her Suboxone for money to get drugs.)* Very emotional, vomiting, dizzy, etc., extremely depressed because children were taken away. Sister Angie was with her. Having suicidal thoughts. Prescribed Suboxone, Klonopin *(antianxiety medication)*, Phenergan shot *(for nausea)* and Paxil.

2-20-2008: Dr. Note–Natalie called. Court is having her do random drug testing can she bring the results here instead of testing 2 times? Yes.

2-25-2008: Dr. Note–116 lbs. Doing better. Denies relapse. Brought in court drug test. Negative. Receiving counseling through drug court.

3-7-2008: Dr. Note–No show for appointment.

3-13-2008: Dr. Note–108 lbs. Forgot to take Suboxone 4 times. Denies relapse. Working on getting kids back. Prescribed Suboxone every few days.

3-31-2008: Dr. Note–Canceled appointment baby ill will reschedule.

In April Nat lost her drivers license due to failure to comply with a citation she had received on April 13th. At the end of that month DCFS (Department of Child and Family Services) opened a case for Jala.

4-17-2008: Dr. Note–Canceled sick flu.

4-28-2008: Dr. Note–DCFS called wants dates Natalie was seen and drug test results.

4-30-2008: Dr. Note–Sent note to DCFS. 5 tests all negative.

I should note here that some addicts use "substitute" urine to cheat drug tests. They use urine that belongs to someone or something else, such as an animal. They use devices to keep it warm or hold it close to their bodies in an armpit or groin area. Nat admitted to me that she had done this to pass drug tests.

In May of 2008, my family and I moved to Saint George, Utah (a four-hour drive from Nat and our families), because after we had come home one evening from a family activity and walked in our house our answering machine was going off—Nat was yelling and cussing at me. One of my young children said to me, "Why is NaNa saying that to you?" I decided at that point that things were starting to affect my family. I could not let go of the idea that I could help "save" Nat from this horrible addiction and protect her children, and it was consuming me. I needed to get away and remove my family from situations like this.

When we lived near my family, I would dream over and over of shaking Nat and trying to get her to listen to me. I cried constantly about her and her children. It was taking a huge toll on me and my ability to function as a wife and mother to my own family. So, we moved two weeks after that incident and have remained in Saint George to this day. I had to walk away from Nat and my family. It took years for me to learn to set boundaries and get over my guilt of feeling like I had abandoned my family, and especially Nat and her children, and the realization that I could not save them. There are many journal entries where Nat is upset with me. I was the one who always broke the news to my family about the severity of her addiction, even when I had to betray her trust to do so. I always had her children's and my entire family's protection, safety, and best interests in mind.

7-8-2008: Dr. Note–Natalie went to court didn't get kids back.

7-9-2008: Dr. Note–No show. Admits to using 3–4 balloons of heroin daily—smoked.

7-28-2008: Dr. Note–Natalie did not show up to Dr. appointment.

Three days after the first arrest, she was arrested again for domestic violence. Nat and Jay were living in North Salt Lake when this arrest

ARREST:
Released same day.
July 26, 2008–July 26, 2008
North Salt Lake Police Department
Charged with Speeding 16–20 mph over
Driving on Suspension/Revocation

ARREST:
In Jail for 2 days.
July 29, 2008–July 31, 2008
North Salt Lake Police Department
Charged with Domestic Violence (witnessed by child)
Damage Property Private

occurred. Nat threw a phone at Jay while he was holding Jala. Jay could not calm her down, so he called the police. Jay did not know she was using at this point.

After her arrest she was court-ordered to parenting classes, drug and alcohol treatment and testing, and a mental heath assessment. She was also given one-and-a-half years of probation. Around this time, I contacted DCFS (Division of Child and Family Services) and reported Nat's drug abuse and my concern for Jala. They visited the home but did not make any further findings. I do believe a case file was opened, though.

7-31-2008: Dr. Note–144 lbs. Just out of jail. Jay was with her. Prescribed Klonopin. Off Suboxone relapsed on heroin. Prescribed Suboxone.

During this time, the family was very concerned for Nat and her children.

The following letter is a plea from our grandmother, who we call Omi, to Nat. At the time, Adi was twelve years old, Mas was nine, and Jala was two.

LETTER FROM OMI, AUGUST 2, 2008:

MY DEAREST NATALIE,

I AM WRITING TO YOU TODAY IN HOPES THAT YOU CAN UNDERSTAND WHY WE ALL NEEDED TO SAY NO TO YOU, EVEN THOUGH IT WAS VERY HARD FOR US BECAUSE WE ALL LOVE YOU VERY MUCH AND WE WOULD ALL, EVERY ONE OF US, HELP YOU IF WE COULD. WE KNOW THAT YOU NEED TO GET PROFESSIONAL HELP, YOU CAN'T DO IT ALONE ANYMORE. *(The family would say no to some of her requests when we knew she was using. She would ask Omi if she could store things at her house in her garage, shower there, live there, etc.)*

NATALIE, THINK ABOUT YOUR CHILDREN WHO NEED YOU NOW MORE THAN EVER. THINK ABOUT WHAT YOU ARE MISSING. NOBODY CAN TURN BACK TIME, BUT YOU CAN START NOW TO

CHANGE YOUR LIFE. YOU NOW HAVE THE OPPORTUNITY TO GET HELP, WHY DON'T YOU TAKE IT? *(The family had offered to get her into a treatment facility.)* HOW LONG DO YOU WANT TO STRUGGLE AND MISS OUT ON ALL THE HAPPINESS YOU CAN HAVE NOW? YOU NEED TO BELIEVE IT IS NEVER TOO LATE. YOU ARE A STRONG MINDED WOMAN. USE THAT STRENGTH FOR YOUR PROGRESS AND GOOD. I TOTALLY BELIEVE IN YOU AND KNOW THAT YOU CAN MAKE IT. DRUGS CANNOT EVER BE MORE IMPORTANT THAN YOUR CHILDREN AND ALL YOUR FAMILY WHO ARE ONE HUNDRED PERCENT COMMITTED TO YOU AND STAND READY TO HELP IF YOU WILL CHOOSE TO ACCEPT THE HELP YOU NEED NOW.

OH NATALIE, DON'T MISS OUT ON LIFE, YOUR LIFE. GET HELP NOW, GO AND TURN YOURSELF IN TO A PLACE WHERE THEY CAN HELP YOU. DO IT FOR YOUR CHILDREN WHO WANT TO BE WITH YOU. IT WON'T TAKE LONG AND YOU CAN BE FREE OF ALL THAT AND HAVE A NORMAL HAPPY LIFE. YOU CAN MAKE IT, I KNOW YOU CAN. I'M NOT SAYING IT WILL BE EASY, BUT YOUR STUBBORN SIDE WILL HELP YOU GET THROUGH IT ALL.

PLEASE LISTEN TO ME JUST THIS ONCE. IF WE DIDN'T CARE FOR YOU AND LOVE YOU SO MUCH, I WOULDN'T WRITE THIS LETTER TODAY. YOU CAN'T EVEN IMAGINE HOW MUCH IT HURTS US ALL, WHEN WE HAVE TO SAY NO TO SOME OF YOUR REQUESTS, BUT WE HAVE TO DO ALL OF IT FOR YOUR OWN GOOD AND SOMEDAY YOU WILL UNDERSTAND.

WE LOVE YOU AND HOPE AND PRAY YOU WILL DO THE RIGHT THING.

WE ALL LOVE YOU AND ARE NOT GIVING UP ON YOU,
OMI AND ALL OF YOUR FAMILY

8-4-2008: Dr. Note–Natalie called Dr. not sleeping, nightmares of jail, needs sleeping pill. Prescribed Ambien *(sleeping medication).*

8-6-2008: Dr. Note–Natalie called Dr. to refill Paxil *(antidepressant)*. Doing well.

8-11-2008: Dr. Note–Natalie called Dr. having panic attacks going to court tomorrow needs Klonopin. Prescribed Klonopin *(antianxiety medication)*.

8-13-2008: Dr. Note–124 lbs. Relapsed on cocaine 3 days ago. Said she found cocaine in her house and used before court. Also using Lortab and Percocet *(prescription pain medications)*. She says she's doing good. Jay is monitoring Ambien and Klonopin. Prescribed Suboxone.

Around this time is when Jay started to put the pieces together and realized Nat was using. She was very good at hiding her addiction. Jay ended up taking Jala (who was two years old) into DCFS to see if she had drugs in her system. Cocaine (784 pc/mg) was found in a hair-follicle test from Jala. DCFS opened the case and ended up taking Jala from Jay and Nat. Jay also lost custody of Jala and went through a six-month period without Jala while he underwent multiple tests and exams to show he was not on drugs. Jay's brother and his wife took Jala in for those six months. Eventually, Jay was cleared and got Jala back. Nat did not live with Jay permanently from there on out. She lost rights to Jala and was living with Mary and David.

8-21-2008: Dr. Note–Wants to refill Klonopin. Husband left her 2 days ago. Not doing well said she is clean. Asked if Xanax *(prescription anxiety medication)* would be better than Klonopin. Prescribed Xanax. Called and canceled appointment for tomorrow. No $ for appointment or medications. Rescheduled for Tuesday when she has $. Said her daughter was taken away and she was evicted from her home. Suboxone. Wants Klonopin. Needs to be seen.

It is so unbelievable to me that she would request medication from this doctor and he would fill it every time, with only two exceptions when he did drug test her. Could the doctor not see that she was using, and her husband was leaving her, and her kids were being taken away from her because of her drug abuse? Yet, he kept giving her medications. Shouldn't he have been reporting her for using prescription drugs that were not prescribed to her, and illegal drugs? It's unreal!

9-2-2008: Dr. Note–123 lbs. Withdrawing from Suboxone—denies relapse. Drug test positive for Suboxone and benzos *(drugs that affect the central nervous system, which she obtained illegally).* Natalie is using Oxycontin and heroin. Looking into drug program with Dave. Mom is monitoring meds. Jay left. Kids gone. Wants to increase Suboxone—hurt her right shoulder. Prescribed Klonopin, Rozerem *(sleeping medication)*, Suboxone.

9-17-2008: Dr. Note–No show for appointment.

During this time period, she started injecting drugs with a needle.

10-6-2008: Dr. Note–Natalie is not consistent with visits. Has not followed up. Says lack of $. Using Oxycontin and heroin. Prescribed Suboxone and Klonopin.

10-23-2008: Dr. Note–Natalie called no $ to come in. Changed appointment to 10-27. Out of subs. Called in enough until 27th.

On October 24th, Nat was served with papers from Woods Cross City for failure to appear in court and intent to issue warrant of arrest for nonappearance.

Up to this point, Nat was either living with Mary and David or in and out of hotels. She was unemployed and had no contact with her children or our family. Around this time, Nat called Ang and asked her to pick her up at a Starbucks in Salt Lake City. When Ang pulled up, Nat was sitting on a curb and looked horrible—she weighed about 90 lbs. Ang was so afraid that Nat was dying that she took her to Lakeview Hospital. Our parents came to the hospital and saw that she was in terrible shape. She detoxed in the hospital and agreed to go to Ascend Recovery treatment facility from the hospital. We were starting to have hope as a family. She was only in Ascend for a short period of time before she was kicked out for using and having heroin hidden in her socks. After this incident, she moved back in with our parents.

I should note here that treatment facilities cannot "force" anyone over age eighteen to stay in their program unless they are court-ordered. If court-ordered and they leave, they will be arrested and sent to jail. Other than that, the only place that can legally "force" an adult to stay is jail, so an adult can walk out of any treatment center.

10-27-2008: Dr. Note–Canceled appointment. In hospital.

On November 4th, Nat was served papers from the City of North Salt Lake for failure to comply (fee payment of $120.00).

11-7-2008: Dr. Note–No show for appointment.

NOVEMBER 23, 2008: Alta View hospital: emergency IV hydration; drug screening; EKG.

Under court order, Nat was required to go to the Bountiful Methadone Clinic daily to "dose," which means they would give her a prescription of methadone to take in their office supervised. Methadone is a drug that stops withdrawal symptoms and is similar to Suboxone.

NOVEMBER 28, 2008: Bountiful Methadone Clinic, 40mg.

DECEMBER 1-11, 2008: Bountiful Methadone Clinic, 40mg (liquid).

12-3-2008: Dr. Note–124 lbs. Anxiety attacks. Using Methadone. Filled out mood questionnaire—possible bipolar disorder. *(Nat was never officially diagnosed with bipolar disorder that we are aware of.)* In Ascend

Recovery Center, used and got kicked out. Going to Methadone Clinic. Not ready to quit using only doing Methadone to try and get kids back. Called in Paxil *(anxiety/depression medication).* Seroquel *(treats bipolar disorder)* given samples.

Nat underwent forensic drug testing also on December 3rd which was ordered by DCFS. I was not able to access those results.

On December 4th the Ogden City Constable's Office put a warrant out for her arrest for failure to comply with court order and order to pay fines.

12-8-2008: Dr. Note–133 lbs. Raspberry tongue got in Ascend Recovery Center *(smoking illegal drugs such as Bath Salts, Meth, and Cocaine causes this).* Told she had infection and treated with antibiotic and numbing meds. No culture done, no fever, sore throat, or other symptoms. Anxiety, depression, opiate dependency, and crystal meth dependency. Called in Seroquel and Rozerem *(sleeping medication).*

12-30-2008: Dr. Note–Refilled Paxil.

• • •

CHAPTER 6

2009

IN 2009, NAT WAS THIRTY YEARS OLD, *Adi was thirteen, Mas was ten, and Jala was three.*

This is where her journals begin.

MONDAY, FEBRUARY 16, 2009, NAT'S JOURNAL:

DEAR JOURNAL,

THIS IS DEFINITELY MY FIRST TIME WRITING IN A JOURNAL AND REALLY BEING SERIOUS ABOUT IT. THE REASON I WANT TO WRITE THINGS DOWN IS SO THAT AFTER TODAY IF I AM HAVING A REALLY SHITTY DAY, ALL I NEED TO DO IS GO BACK TO THE START OF MY JOURNAL AND READ HOW FUCKED UP MY LIFE IS AND THEN WHAT I'M WORRIED ABOUT, OR HAVING A HARD TIME ABOUT, IT WILL NO LONGER BOTHER ME AS MUCH!

I AM DEFINITELY NOT HAPPY IN ANY WAY RIGHT NOW IN MY LIFE. I HAVE LOST EVERYTHING! THE MOST IMPORTANT PEOPLE IN MY LIFE WERE TAKEN AWAY FROM ME. I NEVER THOUGHT IN A MILLION YEARS THIS WOULD HAPPEN TO ME.

DRUGS IS WHAT GOT ME HERE AND WILL KEEP GETTING WORSE AND WORSE IF I DON'T LEAVE THE DRUGS BEHIND ME AND NOT LET DRUGS TAKE OVER MY LIFE.

I HAVE NEVER HAD SUCH A LOW SELF-ESTEEM AS I DO NOW. ACTUALLY AS OF A COUPLE OF MONTHS AGO I HAVE NOT HAD A SELF-ESTEEM AT ALL! I REALLY DO HATE MYSELF RIGHT NOW AND CAN'T LOOK IN THE MIRROR VERY LONG 'CAUSE I THINK I AM THE UGLIEST PERSON RIGHT NOW AND HAVE FELT THIS WAY FOR A LONG TIME NOW.

A high school friend who had used drugs with her told me that Nat had charm and looks and could get anyone to fall in love with her. And if they had money or drugs, they would give it to her freely. Nat was crafty and got people to do anything she wanted. She had a really hard time as the drugs deteriorated and aged her because her looks were something she relied on so heavily.

I HAVE LOST MY WHOLE LIFE, SO I AM GOING TO DO ANYTHING AND EVERYTHING I CAN POSSIBLY DO TO GET MY KIDS BACK, 'CAUSE THEY ARE DEFINITELY MY WHOLE ENTIRE LIFE!!!

I GO TO COURT IN A COUPLE DAYS *(over custody issues with her children and ordered by DCFS),* THEN RIGHT AFTER DCFS WILL BE TAKING ME TO A TREATMENT CENTER CALLED WRC (WOMEN'S RECOVERY CENTER). I ACTUALLY AM NOT MAD ABOUT GOING THERE 'CAUSE I AM COMPLETELY DETERMINED TO GET MY FAMILY BACK AND GOING THERE IS THE FIRST STEP I TAKE.

I'M GOING THROUGH A HORRIBLE CUSTODY BATTLE WITH MY EX AND HE HAS FULL CUSTODY RIGHT NOW. THIS ALL HAPPENED BECAUSE I GOT CAUGHT UP IN THE HORRIBLE DRUG WORLD!

GOING THROUGH ANOTHER COURT BATTLE WITH DCFS TO GET MY LITTLE JALA BACK! IT HASN'T WORKED VERY WELL AT THIS POINT BECAUSE DRUGS WERE STILL IN MY LIFE, BUT NOW THAT I'M CLEAN, AS OF A COUPLE OF DAYS, I AM SO DETERMINED TO GET MY LIFE BACK, WITHOUT DRUGS, AND GET MY FAMILY BACK.

JAY AND I ARE SEPARATED RIGHT NOW AND IT'S KILLING ME SINCE THE DAY I GOT BOOTED OUT OF MY OWN HOUSE BY DCFS! I HAVE SO MUCH GUILT AND PAIN IN MY HEART BECAUSE OF WHAT I HAVE DONE TO MY WONDERFUL HUSBAND AND KIDS. ALL OF THIS IS THE RESULT OF DRUGS! THEY DEFINITELY TOOK ME DOWN AND MY LIFE! WELL, IT'S ABOUT 2:00 A.M. ON WEDNESDAY MORNING AND I REALLY NEED TO GET MY REST BECAUSE I HAVE COURT TOMORROW FOR JALA, THEN I HEAD TO WRC!

Nat did not get Jala back. She left the WRC after two days, then went back to jail after being charged with contempt of court, and returned to the WRC on April 6th, 2009.

ARREST:
Almost a month in jail.
March 11, 2009–April 6, 2009
Davis County
Charged with Contempt of Court

I drove from Saint George to Salt Lake with the intention of visiting Nat in jail, but I couldn't bring myself to go. This letter shows the tremendous hurt, pain, and anger that I was feeling. These feelings persisted until the following year when I read her journals and realized the "real" Nat was still in there. After reading her journals I gained so much empathy for her, and throughout the years, gained a greater understanding about the addiction disease.

LETTER FROM ME TO NAT, SUNDAY, MARCH 15, 2009:

NAT,

IT'S SUNDAY NIGHT AND I AM SITTING HERE AT MOM'S IN THE OFFICE WRITING THIS LETTER TO YOU BECAUSE I CAME UP TO MOM'S TO COME VISIT YOU IN JAIL (I CAN'T BELIEVE I JUST WROTE THAT), BUT AFTER A LOT OF THOUGHT, I HAVE DECIDED THAT I WILL JUST WRITE YOU THIS LETTER AND DELIVER IT TO THE JAIL FOR TWO REASONS. THE FIRST BEING THAT I LOOKED UP YOUR MUGSHOT AND JUST STARED AT THE PICTURE AND COULDN'T HANDLE IT, SO I FIGURE SEEING YOU BEHIND GLASS OR ON A MONITOR WOULD BE EVEN HARDER AND I DON'T THINK I COULD HANDLE THAT RIGHT NOW. SECOND, BECAUSE I DON'T THINK YOU ARE IN A PLACE EMOTIONALLY WHERE WE COULD TALK CLEARLY, AND I DON'T KNOW IF YOU EVER WILL BE. SO, I DECIDED IF I WROTE MY FEELINGS DOWN (WHICH I'VE CONTEMPLATED SEVERAL TIMES) THEN YOU WOULD HAVE SOMETHING TANGIBLE TO READ AND RE-READ AS YOUR HEAD GETS CLEARER (IF IT EVER DOES). THE REALITY I HAVE COME TO OVER THESE PAST YEARS IS THAT MY SISTER NATALIE IS DEAD—I WILL NEVER HAVE HER BACK ON THIS EARTH, BUT PHYSICALLY THERE IS A STRANGE "SHELL" OF HER BODY AND RARELY (VERY RARELY) I GET GLIMPSES WHICH REMIND ME OF MY SISTER WHO WAS MY CLOSEST, MOST-LIKE-ME SISTER, WHO WAS ALWAYS PREGNANT WITH ME AND WORE DUMB JUMPSUITS WITH ME AND WHO LAUGHED AND CHEERED AND CRIED WITH ME ALL THROUGHOUT MY LIFE AND THE ONE WHO IS ON THE CAMCORDER BEING GOOFY. WHEN OUR OLDEST KIDS WERE BABIES AND WE WOULD SANITIZE THEIR TOYS OVER AND OVER AND WOULD ROLLERBLADE AROUND WITH OUR BABIES IN STROLLERS…I COULD GO ON AND ON BECAUSE SHE WAS A HUGE PART OF MY LIFE, BUT SHE'S GONE AND I KNOW THE HARSH REALITY IS GOING TO BE OUR FAMILY PLANNING YOUR

FUNERAL AND COMFORTING YOUR THREE BEAUTIFUL CHILDREN THAT WERE ENTRUSTED TO YOU FROM OUR HEAVENLY FATHER. EVERY TIME MY PHONE RINGS, I WONDER IF IT'S "THE CALL" THAT YOU'RE GONE, AND HOW WILL I HANDLE IT? I DON'T THINK I WILL. I THINK I WILL TRULY LOSE IT.

ON MY DRIVE HERE TODAY, I REMEMBERED YOU SAYING YEARS AGO THAT YOU WOULD NOT BE ABLE TO HANDLE LOSING ONE OF YOUR SISTERS–BUT THAT IS OUR REALITY NOW–WE ARE LOSING YOU. I DON'T THINK YOU ARE CAPABLE OF FULLY UNDERSTANDING EVERYTHING I AM SAYING RIGHT NOW BUT I PRAY THAT THERE IS A TINY PART OF YOU STILL THERE THAT WILL LISTEN.

MASON AND ADI SLEPT OVER WITH US TONIGHT AND I TUCKED MASON IN. HE HAD A LITTLE STUFFED BLACK KITTY HE SLEEPS WITH AND HE SAID IT REMINDS HIM OF HIS KITTY YOU AND JAY HAD. ADI SAYS HE CRIES EVERY NIGHT TO GET TO SLEEP BECAUSE HE MISSES YOU AND JALA AND THE KITTY. HIS HAIR IS BIG AND HE NEEDS A HAIRCUT AND I WONDER IF IT WILL EVER GET DONE. ADI IS GETTING SO OLD AND MATURE–BUT SHE WILL NOT MENTION YOUR NAME. SHE DOES NOT WANT TO TALK ABOUT YOU. SHE IS SUCH A GOOD GIRL WITH SUCH A POSITIVE OUTLOOK. I AM SO PROUD OF HER. I TELL THEM BOTH EVERY CHANCE I GET HOW MUCH I LOVE THEM AND HOW PROUD I AM OF THEM. I HOPE AND PRAY THEY KNOW THAT BUT I ALSO KNOW I CAN'T REPLACE YOU. BUT WE ALL TRY TO FILL IN. I HAVEN'T SEEN JALA FOR A WHILE BUT I HAVE PICTURES OF HER THROUGHOUT MY HOUSE. IT'S STILL SO HARD FOR ME TO COMPREHEND THAT THIS IS OUR FAMILY NOW–THAT ALL THAT CRAZY STUFF OTHER PEOPLE DID–IS NOW US–AND WE LOOK INTO THE EYES OF YOUR THREE CHILDREN AND OUR HEARTS BREAK EVERY DAY BECAUSE THEY DON'T HAVE A MOM. THEY DON'T HAVE YOU TO COMFORT THEM, ESPECIALLY WHEN THEY ARE SAD OR SICK, OR TO TUCK THEM IN. I CAN HARDLY STAND TO THINK ABOUT IT.

I'VE BEEN RESEARCHING (OF COURSE) HEROIN SPECIFICALLY AND WHAT IT IS AND HOW IT IS MADE, HOW IT'S USED, SIDE EFFECTS LONG TERM AND SHORT TERM AND WHAT IS USED TO INJECT IT, HOW OFTEN, ETC. (I THINK IT HELPS ME COPE WHEN I KNOW EVERYTHING I CAN ABOUT THINGS.) THE REALITY OF IT IS THAT NOT EVEN 50% OF HEROIN ADDICTS SURVIVE.

I KNOW YOU ARE IN JAIL BUT YOU WERE FORCED BY THE LAW. YOU HAD THREE CHOICES BEFORE YOU WENT, SUICIDE, JAIL, OR DEATH FROM OVERDOSE. I WAS REALLY SURPRISED YOU ACTUALLY SHOWED UP TO JAIL, TO BE HONEST. I CAN'T REALLY GIVE YOU CREDIT FOR BEING THERE BECAUSE YOUR CRAVING AND ADDICTION DRIVING YOU TO LIVE FOR THE DRUGS IS OBVIOUSLY STRONGER THAN DEATH. SO YOU WENT TO JAIL, AND WHEN YOU'VE SERVED YOUR TIME YOU WILL GET OUT AND MAYBE GO TO TREATMENT AND END UP BACK IN YOUR HELL-HOLE LIFE. I DON'T THINK THERE'S MUCH LEFT OF YOU THAT WANTS TO BE CLEAN, BUT IF THERE IS, THIS IS YOUR CHANCE, NAT. I HAVE A FEELING THIS MIGHT BE YOUR LAST CHANCE AND WITH EVERY OUNCE OF ME, I'M ASKING YOU TO GIVE IT EVERYTHING YOU'VE GOT AND PULL YOURSELF OUT OF THIS.

I CAN'T IMAGINE HOW YOU FEEL (ALTHOUGH I TRY) AND I KNOW THE ODDS ARE AGAINST YOU, BUT I ALSO KNOW MY SISTER NATALIE IS A FEISTY ONE WHO WILL DO EVERYTHING SHE CAN FOR HER CHILDREN AND FAMILY. WE ALL MISS YOU SO MUCH. THERE IS SO MUCH OF OUR FAMILY MISSING WITHOUT YOU AROUND. THIS DEMON THAT YOU ARE FIGHTING IS UGLY BUT I TRULY BELIEVE YOU CAN DO THIS BECAUSE IT'S YOU AND YOU CAN FIGHT FOR YOUR KIDS AND YOUR LIFE BACK.

I PRAY EVERY DAY THAT THE NEXT TIME I SEE YOU I CAN GIVE YOU A HUG AND THAT IT'S NOT IN A COFFIN.

I LOVE YOU AND ALWAYS WILL-

LOVE, YOUR BIGGEST SIS!

Ten days later I received this letter in the mail:

<u>LETTER FROM NAT TO ME, TUESDAY, MARCH 24, 2009</u>:

SHALL,

IT'S TUESDAY MORNING ABOUT 11:30 A.M. AND I JUST RECEIVED YOUR LETTER. THAT WAS BY FAR THE SADDEST LETTER I HAVE EVER READ IN MY LIFE! IT WAS THE HARDEST THING TO GET THROUGH THAT LETTER. I HAVE BEEN IN TEARS FOR ABOUT THIRTY MINUTES NOW. I HAVE BEEN IN HERE, IN THIS HELL HOLE, FOR FOURTEEN DAYS NOW. I'M GOING CRAZY. IT IS THE HARDEST THING I HAVE EVER BEEN THROUGH (BESIDES LOSING MY PRECIOUS BABIES).

IT'S BEEN REALLY HARD SITTING IN HERE WAITING FOR SOMEONE IN OUR FAMILY TO COME VISIT ME. ESPECIALLY YOU! I PRAY EVERY DAY THAT YOU CAN FIND IT IN YOUR HEART, NO MATTER HOW HARD IT IS FOR YOU, TO COME VISIT ME IN HERE. I AM SO ALONE AND MISS MY KIDS SO MUCH THAT IT PHYSICALLY HURTS!

SHALL, I UNDERSTAND COMPLETELY EVERYTHING YOU WERE TELLING ME IN YOUR LETTER. IF IT WOULD HAVE BEEN ANY EARLIER IN THE PAST FEW WEEKS, I PROBABLY WOULDN'T HAVE READ THROUGH THE WHOLE THING AND JUST WOULD HAVE GOTTEN EXTREMELY MAD. BUT AMAZINGLY I FEEL LIKE A COMPLETELY DIFFERENT PERSON AFTER BEING LOCKED UP AND HAVING ALL THE TIME IN THE WORLD TO THINK AND REALLY OPEN UP MY HEART, FINDING MYSELF AGAIN, AND TRULY UNDERSTANDING JUST HOW HORRIBLE MY LIFE HAS TURNED OUT TO BE. I CAN'T EVEN FATHOM ALL THE MISTAKES I HAVE MADE AND ALL THE HORRIBLE AND ROTTEN THINGS I HAVE DONE. YOU AND I BOTH KNOW THIS IS NOT ME! AND FOR THE FIRST TIME IN YEARS, I CAN FINALLY LOOK BACK AND TRULY SEE ALL THE MISTAKES I HAVE MADE AND JUST HOW MANY PEOPLE I HAVE HURT AND HOW LONG I HAVE PUT THE ONES I LOVE IN ALL THIS MISERY AND

PAIN. I HONESTLY FOR A LONG, LONG TIME NOW HAVE FELT THAT NOBODY IN THIS FAMILY HAS CARED AT ALL ABOUT ME AND THAT ALL OF YOU HONESTLY HATED ME AND WANTED ABSOLUTELY NOTHING TO DO WITH ME. ANGIE IS THE ONLY PERSON I THOUGHT THAT HAS NEVER STOPPED LOVING ME AND WOULD ALWAYS SUPPORT ME AND HELP ME GET THROUGH THIS AWFUL NIGHTMARE. BUT I NOW FINALLY REALIZE WHY YOU HAVE ALL PUSHED ME AWAY AND WHY EVERYBODY IN OUR FAMILY HAS COMPLETELY LOST ALL HOPE FOR ME.

THANK YOU SO MUCH FOR BEING THERE FOR MY BEAUTIFUL KIDS. I CAN'T EVEN IMAGINE WHAT THEY ARE GOING THROUGH WITHOUT ME BEING THERE FOR THEM. THINK OF HOW MUCH IT BREAKS YOUR HEART SEEING MY KIDS GO THROUGH THIS. IT BREAKS MY HEART A THOUSAND TIMES MORE, THEY ARE *MY KIDS!* I CAN'T BELIEVE WHAT I HAVE DONE TO THEM AND HOW SELFISH I HAVE BEEN THE PAST COUPLE OF YEARS. THAT IS SO *NOT* ME! MY THREE KIDS ARE MY EVERYTHING, MY WHOLE ENTIRE WORLD AND I HAVE LOST ALL OF THEM AND BROKEN THEIR LITTLE HEARTS. WHAT IN THE *HELL* HAVE I DONE, SHALL? IT IS THE MOST GUT WRENCHING, MOST AWFUL, HORRIBLE FEELING I HAVE EVER HAD IN MY LIFE LAYING HERE EVERY NIGHT ALL ALONE, WITHOUT MY KIDS, KNOWING WHAT I HAVE DONE.

I DON'T PLAN ON GETTING OUT OF HERE ANYTIME SOON, SO I HAVE A LOT OF TIME FOR THINKING. IT SUCKS AND IT'S SO HARD GOING ON EACH DAY KNOWING WHAT I HAVE DONE. SOMETIMES, I JUST DO NOT WANT TO GO ON ANYMORE 'CAUSE IT HURTS MORE THAN YOU COULD EVER IMAGINE.

I'M BACK, SHALL, IT'S ME, AND I AM REALLY, REALLY SCARED! I AM GOING TO REHAB WHEN I GET OUT AND I *AM* GOING TO FINISH IT AND GRADUATE FROM THE WRC AND GET MY WONDERFUL KIDS BACK! THAT IS MY PROMISE TO MYSELF. AND I *WILL* MAKE IT HAPPEN. I NO LONGER WANT TO LIVE MY LIFE WITHOUT MY KIDS. I NEVER DID, BUT DIDN'T KNOW HOW TO GET MY LIFE BETTER. I DO NOW, AND YOU BETTER

TRUST AND BELIEVE THAT THE OLD NATALIE THAT YOU ALL USED TO KNOW AND LOVE IS BACK AND READY TO GET MY LIFE AND KIDS BACK!

EVER SINCE I GOT HERE, I HAVE WENT TO LDS CHURCH THREE TIMES AND HAVE HAD TWO BLESSINGS. IT WAS INCREDIBLE AND I HONESTLY, FOR THE FIRST TIME IN SO MANY YEARS, FELT THE SPIRIT WITH ME. I WISH YOU COULD HAVE BEEN THERE TO HEAR THEM. I GOT A BLESSING THIS LAST SUNDAY AND HE TOLD ME THAT WITH ALL THE EXPERIENCES I HAVE BEEN THROUGH, AND ALL THE AWFUL THINGS THAT HAVE HAPPENED TO ME, THAT I WILL LEARN FROM THEM AND THAT I WILL TEACH MANY PEOPLE SOMEDAY ABOUT THE EFFECTS AND HORRIBLE THINGS I HAVE BEEN THROUGH AND WHAT DRUGS REALLY DO TO PEOPLE'S LIVES. I JUST THOUGHT OF YOU AND HOW MANY TIMES YOU HAVE TOLD ME THAT. I DEFINITELY THINK THAT IS MY NEXT CALLING IN LIFE, JUST AS YOU HAVE TOLD ME THE LAST LITTLE WHILE. I AM *DONE* WITH THAT LIFE, AND TRULY, HONESTLY WANT TO START OVER! I WILL MAKE MY KIDS SO PROUD THAT I AM THEIR MOTHER. THEY WILL NOT, AND NONE OF YOU WILL EVER BE ASHAMED TO CALL ME YOUR SISTER OR THEIR MOM AGAIN! I KNOW THESE ARE JUST WORDS, NOT ACTIONS, BUT YOU WILL SEE AND SO WILL EVERYONE ELSE IN OUR FAMILY! BUT I HONESTLY DON'T CARE WHAT ANYONE ELSE THINKS BUT MY THREE KIDS. I WILL PROVE TO THEM, MYSELF, AND NOBODY ELSE! I REALLY WANT TO HELP PEOPLE THAT ARE GOING THROUGH WHAT I HAVE BEEN THROUGH AFTER I GET MY KIDS' LIVES BACK ON TRACK AND WITH THEIR MOTHER!!! I MISS THEM SO MUCH!!

I CAN GUARANTEE TO YOU THAT YOU WILL NOT GET THAT "CALL" AND THAT YOU WILL HUG YOUR SISTER NATALIE AGAIN AND YOU WILL MOST DEFINITELY NOT SEE ME IN A COFFIN ANYTIME SOON.

PLEASE TAKE CARE OF MY BABIES WHILE I AM AWAY AND PLEASE COME VISIT ME, IF NOT IN HERE (WHICH I REALLY

WISH YOU WOULD), THEN AT THE WRC WHEN I FINALLY GET THERE!

I LOVE YOU WITH ALL MY HEART, SHALL!

NAT

*PLEASE GIVE ALL MY KIDS HUGS AND KISSES FOR ME AND TELL THEM JUST HOW MUCH I MISS AND LOVE THEM! AND PLEASE SEND ME ANY PICTURES THAT YOU CAN OF MY KIDS, I DON'T HAVE ANY.

XOXOXO

Nat was back in WRC on April 6th, 2009, after serving her jail time. Her records from the WRC indicate that she attended multiple classes and therapy sessions each day. She had classes on parenting, drug addiction, dental hygiene, behavioral therapy, healthy sexuality, exercise, relapse prevention, anger, etc. In the reports, she admitted to struggling with memory problems with the number of legal charges she had, how long she had been using, and the effects drug use had on her sexual activity.

MONDAY, APRIL 13, 2009, NAT'S JOURNAL:

I AM AT THE WRC ONCE AGAIN. I CAME HERE ONCE BEFORE BUT WAS WITHDRAWING OFF HEROIN LIKE I NEVER HAVE BEFORE, SO LEFT AFTER TWO DAYS. I THEN WENT TO JAIL, WHICH WAS THE WORST EXPERIENCE I HAVE EVER HAD, THEN CAME STRAIGHT BACK HERE FROM JAIL. I GOT HERE APRIL 6TH, 2009, THE DAY AFTER MASON'S BIRTHDAY. I HAVE BEEN HERE NOW FOR SEVEN DAYS TODAY. I AM 34 DAYS CLEAN NOW. THAT MAKES ME VERY HAPPY CONSIDERING I HAVEN'T BEEN CLEAN FOR THE PAST 2 1/2 YEARS. I HAVE BEEN DOING HEROIN, METH, AND COKE FOR A LONG TIME NOW AND HAVE BEEN SHOOTING UP DRUGS FOR ABOUT 6 MONTHS NOW. I REALLY WANT TO STAY CLEAN NOW SO I CAN GET BACK TO MY FAMILY, BUT ALL THAT RUNS THROUGH MY HEAD DAILY IS

A SHOT OF HEROIN OR METH OR COCAINE. MAINLY HEROIN. I CRAVE IT! THIS PROGRAM OF STAYING CLEAN IS THE HARDEST THING I HAVE EVER HAD TO GO THROUGH BESIDES JAIL.

MY HUSBAND AND MY FAMILY MEAN THE WORLD TO ME AND I WANT AND NEED TO BE THERE FOR THEM. SO, I AM TRYING WITH ALL MY MIND TO BE STRONG. EVERY SINGLE DAY IS A CHALLENGE TO STAY CLEAN. BUT IT REALLY ISN'T TOO BAD HERE. THE GIRLS HERE RIGHT NOW ARE GREAT AND A VERY GOOD SUPPORT.

I PRAY EVERY NIGHT THAT I CAN GET THROUGH THIS TEST HEAVENLY FATHER HAS GIVEN ME AND I CAN MAKE IT HOME AGAIN WITH MY FAMILY!

<u>TUESDAY, APRIL 14, 2009</u>:

IT'S MY SECOND WEEK AT THE WRC AND I'M DOING A *HELL* OF A LOT BETTER THAN I EVER THOUGHT. I GOT MY AUTOBIOGRAPHY DONE *(I have not located this document),* TWENTY PAGES LONG, AND NOW I'M WORKING ON MY STEP 1. THE STEP WORK IS A BITCH TO DO. TODAY IT WAS REALLY GLOOMY AND RAINY OUTSIDE, SO I WAS PRETTY TIRED ALL DAY. IT SUCKS WHEN IT'S RAINING HERE BECAUSE WE ARE STUCK IN THIS BUILDING ALL DAY LONG. OTHER THAN BEING TIRED TODAY, I HAD A PRETTY GOOD DAY UNTIL I GOT ON THE PHONE WITH JAY TONIGHT. HE MOVED INTO A DIFFERENT PLACE TO GET CHEAPER RENT. HE MOVED INTO LINDA'S BASEMENT. *(Jay's friend.)* WHEN I WAS TALKING TO JAY, I COULD HEAR HER TALKING TO JALA AND TELLING HER WHAT TO DO. IT HURTS ME SO MUCH, I FEEL LIKE THIS WOMAN IS TAKING OVER MY LIFE, MY HUSBAND, AND MY PRECIOUS LITTLE JALA. I'M STUCK HERE IN REHAB WHILE SOME WOMAN I DON'T EVEN KNOW IS SPENDING TIME WITH MY FAMILY. IT HURTS!

I JUST WANT TO GET OUT OF HERE SO BAD AND GET BACK TO MY FAMILY. BUT ON THE OTHER HAND, I NEED TO

STAY HERE AND TAKE CARE OF MYSELF OR I WON'T HAVE A FAMILY TO GO HOME TO.

I MISS ALL THREE OF MY KIDS AND MY HUSBAND!!!

WEDNESDAY, APRIL 15, 2009:

WELL, TODAY WAS ANOTHER OKAY DAY AT THE WRC. IT'S REALLY, REALLY TOUGH THOUGH BEING WITHOUT MY KIDS AND MY HUSBAND. IT'S REALLY BEEN HARD STAYING CLEAN TOO. I THINK ABOUT HEROIN EVERY SECOND OF EVERY DAY AND IT SUCKS SO BAD! HOPEFULLY THE CRAVINGS GET BETTER BECAUSE I DO NOT WANT TO THINK ABOUT IT ANYMORE. I DO MISS ROBERT A LOT. I LOVE MY HUSBAND WITH ALL MY HEART, BUT ROBERT WILL ALWAYS HAVE A SPECIAL PLACE IN MY HEART. BUT I THINK HE'S GOING TO FEDERAL PRISON FOR A REALLY LONG TIME. I HOPE AND PRAY FOR HIS SAKE AND HIS GIRLS' SAKE THAT HE WILL NOT BE CONVICTED, I WILL DIE!!! WELL, WE WENT TO GOLD'S GYM TODAY AND NOW I'M SO EXTREMELY TIRED SO I'M GOING TO SLEEP. I'M SO GLAD THAT I AM CLEAN AND SOBER TODAY!!!

Original medical progress reports from the WRC:

Her progress reports from WRC stated that she was in intensive-level treatment. She had a visit with Jay and her kids. Jay asked lots of questions about her use and she answered his questions. Natalie expressed her jealousy of Linda and her feelings about not being there for Jala. She was told to be understanding of her husband's position. Jay was trying to raise Jala, take care of Natalie, get a career going to support all three of them, and understand what Natalie was doing.

When I asked Jay in 2019 about what he thought was going on with her, he said, "I had no idea…I was so naive. I've never been in that world. I took her at her word. She was my wife. I look back…shamefully. I've never experienced that level of manipulation. There was so much good in her, but she was literally two different people, and they were polar opposites. She would shift from one to the other in a split-second. We'd be talking and it would happen. She'd say the most awful things; it was like she was possessed. Her expression would change, her body would shift...her eyes changed to black and she'd be vacant. I brushed it off because I didn't understand. It was way out of my league. There would be glimpses of her and that's what I always held on to."

<u>THURSDAY, APRIL 16, 2009</u>:

STILL IN REHAB AND DOING OKAY. TODAY I WAS PRETTY TIRED AND EMOTIONAL. I MISS JAY AND MY KIDS SO MUCH. I MISS ROBERT ALSO AND AM FREAKING OUT 'CAUSE I HAVE NO IDEA WHETHER HE IS IN FEDERAL PRISON OR NOT. IT'S REALLY HARD HERE TO TRY AND FOCUS ON ME ALL THE TIME RATHER THAN ON ALL THE ONES I LOVE OUT THERE! JAY IS BEING REALLY GOOD TO ME WHEN I CALL HIM AT NIGHT, SO THAT ALWAYS MAKES ME FEEL BETTER. BUT I ONLY GET ONE PHONE CALL A NIGHT FOR ONLY TEN MINUTES. I HAVEN'T TALKED TO ADI OR MAS ALL WEEK 'CAUSE I HAVE BEEN CALLING JAY AND JALA. IT'S KILLING ME. I MISS THEM SO MUCH! I HOPE THEY SHOW UP ON SUNDAY OR MY HEART WILL BREAK!!!

On April 20, 2009, her progress report from the WRC stated that she was feeling okay, but had no visitors the past weekend. Jay was unsure of where their relationship was going, so he didn't visit. Natalie said she was feeling lots of emotions. The group confronted her about interrupting, which she did several times during conversation in 'group.' She admitted to being bossy and a "know-it-all" and acknowledged that she interrupted a lot with Jay. She was asked to work on it and also to request rather than demand from her family. Natalie struggled with self-importance and following directions. She was working on assignments to help her cope with the pain and emotions regarding the damage she had done while using.

On April 22, 2009, her progress note read that she acknowledged that she was raised "a spoiled, rich brat" and didn't want to come to WRC. She admitted to being in other programs before, but that she would always leave and never got much out of them. She didn't like going to them because it felt dirty and beneath her.

On April 26, 2009, her progress note read that her mother brought two of her children in to visit. Natalie said it was bittersweet and she missed her husband.

April 28, 2009, individual psychotherapy progress notes state that Natalie was struck by a group on loving our children. She wanted to discuss ways of expressing her feelings for her children. She had taken notes on things she wanted to tell her kids. Natalie's voice was recorded telling one daughter the ways and reasons she loves her. Natalie had some tears listening to her recorded message. She talked about a routine she once had with her kids, reading from the book *I Love You Forever.* Natalie was to have court on Thursday for DCFS review. She was frustrated with her worker coming to see her. DCFS was reviewing her case to set up a visit. She discussed frustrations with DCFS. She opened up that she was scared about court. She was struggling with communicating with peers and being sarcastic, and the group was now calling her "nasty Natalie." She attended an anger management course that same day. She was in pain about her teeth; several were rotting out and they slowly fell out one by one.

On May 3, 2009, her report read: "Natalie stated she was 'pissed' off at her husband because he keeps going back and forth as to if he wants to keep or end the marriage. She also stated she was upset with her Probation Officer but did not mention why."

Nat was kicked out of the WRC on May 4, 2009. The story she told us was that one of her friends in treatment got some drugs and used, and her counselors figured Nat knew about it. She moved into our parents' house at this time but only stayed for a couple of weeks. She was using immediately after she was out of the WRC.

THURSDAY, MAY 14, 2009, NAT'S JOURNAL:

SO...*I AM OUT!* I MADE IT OUT OF THE WRC!!! I WASN'T EXPECTING AT ALL TO GET OUT SO SOON, BUT EVERYTHING HAPPENS FOR A REASON. IT ACTUALLY WAS NOT A GOOD SITUATION AT ALL. THE REASON I AM ALREADY OUT OF REHAB IS I WAS THE ONLY ONE THERE ALMOST THIRTY DAYS. I DID FINISH THE INTENSIVE PART OF THE PROGRAM, BUT IT'S A NINETY DAY PROGRAM AND I WAS EXPECTED TO BE IN THERE AT LEAST NINETY DAYS, IF NOT LONGER. BUT THINGS OBVIOUSLY DIDN'T TURN OUT THAT WAY. BUT I AM SO NOT COMPLAINING! I AM SO HAPPY I'M NOT QUARANTINED IN THAT DISGUSTING BUILDING ANY LONGER. I HAD DEFINITELY HAD ENOUGH OF THAT PLACE.

I GOT SUSPENDED FOR THIRTY DAYS BECAUSE SUSAN MY CLOSEST FRIEND IN THERE, HAD AN EIGHT HOUR PASS TWO SUNDAYS AGO, LEFT FOR THE DAY WITH HER DAD AND HUSBAND, AND WHEN HER DAD LEFT HER ALONE WITH HER HUSBAND FOR A COUPLE OF HOURS THEY WENT AND GOT SOME DOPE *(heroin).* WHEN SHE CAME BACK THAT NIGHT TO THE WRC, SHE BROUGHT IT WITH HER, SHE WAITED TILL KAREN *(counselor)* UA'D HER *(urine analysis),* THEN SHE WENT BACK INTO HER ROOM, SHE SHOT UP HEROIN AND PASSED OUT AND ACTUALLY DIED. A COUPLE OF GIRLS THAT ARE TRAINED NURSES REVIVED HER. AFTER SHE HAD BEEN GONE ABOUT TWENTY MINUTES IN HER ROOM, I STARTED GETTING A LITTLE CONCERNED BECAUSE ME AND SUSAN NEVER SEPARATED. WE WERE HIP TO HIP SINCE THE DAY I ARRIVED AT THE WRC. SHE HAD ONLY GOTTEN THERE A WEEK PREVIOUS TO MY ARRIVAL. WE ACTUALLY GOT IN TROUBLE A COUPLE OF TIMES, WHICH IS RIDICULOUS BECAUSE A LOT OF GIRLS WERE EXTREMELY JEALOUS AND BUTT HURT BECAUSE ME AND SUSAN WERE ALWAYS TOGETHER AND NEVER LEFT EACH OTHER'S SIDE! WE WERE IN THE MIDDLE OF WATCHING A MOVIE AND I GOT UP TO GO LOOK FOR MY GIRL, AT THIS POINT SHE

HAD BEEN GONE A WHILE. I FINALLY GOT UP AND WENT TO LOOK FOR SUSAN. I OPENED THE DOOR TO HER ROOM, WHICH WAS DIRECTLY ACROSS THE HALLWAY FROM MINE, AND I SAW HER LAYING ON THE GROUND AND HER FACE WAS DARK-DARK BLUE. I KNEW INSTANTLY WHAT HAD HAPPENED. ME AND SUSAN HAD A LOT IN COMMON, THAT'S WHY WE HIT IT OFF SO WELL WHEN WE MET. WE BOTH HAD BEEN THROUGH A LOT OF THE SAME THINGS AND WE BOTH HAD THE SAME DRUG OF CHOICE, WHICH WAS HEROIN. WE BOTH LIKED SHOOTING UP HEROIN AND BOTH HAD A REALLY HARD TIME NOT THINKING ABOUT IT EVERY DAY. SO WHEN I FOUND HER LYING ON THE FLOOR, I KNEW RIGHT AWAY SHE HAD JUST SHOT UP SOME HEROIN.

I WAS IN SHOCK AND I FROZE FOR A MINUTE. I RAN OVER TO SUSAN AND TRIED LIFTING UP HER UPPER BODY AND TRIED TO GET A RESPONSE FROM HER. ABSOLUTELY NOTHING! I SLAPPED HER FACE A COUPLE OF TIMES, SCREAMING AT HER TO WAKE UP. THEN I REALIZED SHE WAS DEAD. SHE HAD NO HEARTBEAT AT ALL AND WAS NOT BREATHING. I THEN RAN DOWN THE HALL, GOT KAREN THE COUNSELOR, AND NANCY THE NURSE AND LILY A NURSE, THEY WERE GIRLS IN THERE LIKE ME WITH AN ADDICTION PROBLEM, BUT THEY WERE TRAINED NURSES. THEY CAME IN, SAW HER, AND NANCY HAD TO BREATH FOR HER FOR TEN MINUTES UNTIL THE PARAMEDICS ARRIVED. THEY REVIVED HER AFTER NANCY SAVED HER LIFE BY GIVING HER CPR, AND SHE WOKE UP BEFORE PUTTING HER ON THE STRETCHER. I WAS COMPLETELY TRAUMATIZED AND WAS A MESS! MY BEST FRIEND ALMOST LOST HER LIFE OVER DOPE!!! AFTER THEY TOOK HER TO THE HOSPITAL, WHICH WAS RIGHT NEXT DOOR, WE HAD A HOUSE MEETING. KAREN (WHICH WAS MY FAVORITE TECH) STARTED YELLING AT ME AND ACCUSING ME OF KNOWING THAT SUSAN BROUGHT HEROIN IN THE WRC AND TOLD ME I WAS SUSPENDED FOR THIRTY DAYS BECAUSE I KEPT A SECRET AND DIDN'T NOTIFY STAFF AND ASKED ME TO PACK UP ALL MY STUFF RIGHT AWAY. I WAS DEFINITELY

IN SHOCK BECAUSE I DIDN'T DO ANYTHING WRONG. I FOUND SUSAN, SAVED HER LIFE, AND I GET KICKED OUT!!! WHAT A FUCKED UP REHAB CENTER AND I AM NOT GOING BACK!

I AM JUST GOING TO TAKE IT ONE DAY AT A TIME AND STAY CLEAN *JUST FOR TODAY!* I KNOW I CAN DO THIS!

SO, SURPRISINGLY, I AM RESIDING NOW AT MY PARENTS' HOUSE (AGAIN) UNTIL THE STATE CAN HELP ME FIND A PLACE OF MY OWN. I'M SO OVERWHELMED EVERY DAY THOUGH WITH ALL THE SHIT I NEED TO TAKE CARE OF. I MISS MY FAMILY SO DAMN MUCH. MY BEAUTIFUL THREE KIDS AND MY HUSBAND WHICH I LOVE AND ADORE SO VERY MUCH!

I GOT TO BE WITH ALL THREE OF MY KIDS LAST SUNDAY FOR MOTHER'S DAY AND IT WAS ONE OF THE BEST DAYS OF MY LIFE! IT COULDN'T HAVE BEEN MORE PERFECT TIMING TO GET KICKED OUT OF REHAB; A COUPLE OF DAYS, ACTUALLY A WEEK, BEFORE MOTHER'S DAY!! HOW ABSOLUTELY PERFECT TIMING WAS THAT?! THE ONLY THING MISSING THAT DAY WAS MY HUSBAND JAY.

<u>FRIDAY, MAY 15, 2009</u>:

TODAY WAS A ROUGH DAY! MY TOOTH HAS BEEN HURTING FOR A WHILE NOW BUT TODAY WAS MUCH WORSE THAN ANY OTHER DAY. I WAS UP ALL NIGHT LAST NIGHT BECAUSE IT HAS BEEN THROBBING SO BAD, SO TODAY I WAS SO TIRED! DAMN DRUGS COMPLETELY ROTTED OUT ALL OF MY TEETH! IT'S HORRIBLE! I FINALLY WENT TO SLEEP AROUND 6:30 A.M. THIS MORNING. WENT TO LUNCH WITH ANGIE AND JAY AND COULDN'T EVEN ENJOY IT BECAUSE OF MY FREAKING TOOTH! I CAME BACK HOME AND TOOK A NAP. I DIDN'T GET ANYTHING DONE THAT I WAS PLANNING ON TODAY AND I'M REALLY FRUSTRATED. I'M HOPING AND PRAYING EVERY NIGHT THAT JAY CAN FORGIVE ME AND WE CAN MAKE OUR MARRIAGE WORK. I KNOW I WILL NEVER HURT HIM AGAIN LIKE I DID THE PAST THREE YEARS. I JUST PRAY HE WILL GIVE ME ANOTHER CHANCE.

A few days later...

<u>MONDAY, MAY 18, 2009</u>:

I DEFINITELY HAD A REALLY BAD WEEKEND! SATURDAY, I WENT WITH MICHAEL TO RUN SOME ERRANDS FOR A COUPLE OF HOURS THEN GOT REALLY SICK TO MY STOMACH SO I CAME HOME AROUND FOUR AND WENT TO BED AFTER THROWING UP.

SUNDAY, I TALKED TO MY FRIEND SANDY IN THE MORNING, SHE WAS IN JAIL WITH ME AND WE HIT IT OFF REALLY WELL. I ENDED UP GOING TO HER HOUSE, HUNG OUT THERE FOR A LITTLE BIT, THEN WE BOTH GOT BORED SO WE WENT TO JOSEPH'S APARTMENT AND CHILLED THERE FOR A BIT. WASN'T VERY FUN AT ALL. I WAS LOOKING FOR A RIDE HOME THE WHOLE TIME I WAS THERE BECAUSE LATELY, SINCE I DON'T HAVE A CAR AND MY LICENSE IS SUSPENDED, IT'S BEEN PRETTY DIFFICULT TO FIND RIDES EVERYWHERE. IN THE MEANTIME, WE SAW OUT THE WINDOW A HUGE FIGHT. THERE WAS BLOOD EVERYWHERE, AND SO MANY PEOPLE CAME OUT TO WATCH LIKE THEY HADN'T EVER SEEN A FIGHT BEFORE. I AM ALREADY ON EXTREMELY THIN ICE WITH MY PARENTS BECAUSE I HAVE COMPLETELY BROKEN THEIR TRUST. IT'S SO NICE STAYING AT MY PARENTS' HOUSE RATHER THAN MARY AND DAVID'S LIKE I HAD BEEN BEFORE I WAS BOOKED IN JAIL. I AM SO GRATEFUL TO BE HERE AND HAVE A NICE ROOF OVER MY HEAD. I MISS MY KIDS AND HUSBAND SO MUCH THAT IT PHYSICALLY MAKES ME SICK! I *WILL* GET MY FAMILY BACK SOON AND I WILL *NEVER* IN A MILLION YEARS LOSE THEM AGAIN!!!!

Nat left my parents' house at this time and lived with random people.

<u>WEDNESDAY, MAY 20, 2009</u>:

ANOTHER ROTTEN DAY FOR ME! BUT AFTER EVERYTHING I HAVE PUT THE ONES I LOVE THROUGH, I GUESS I DESERVE IT! BUT IT REALLY DOES SUCK AND IT MAKES ME WANT TO GO OUT AND USE SO I DON'T HAVE TO FEEL ALL THESE AWFUL EMOTIONS AND SUCH HORRIBLE PAIN. *(Nat was using as soon as she left the WRC. She couldn't handle emotions and wasn't used to feeling emotions because the drugs numbed her; all emotions were awful for her. This is the pattern she followed for dealing with emotions her entire life.)* I GOT TO SEE JALA TODAY BUT NOT LONG ENOUGH AT ALL!! I ONLY GOT TO SPEND ONE HOUR WITH HER AT DCFS *(supervised visits).* THIS DAY COULD NOT GET ANY WORSE. BUT I CAN GET PAST THIS AND LIVE AND LEARN FROM IT, THAT'S ALL I CAN DO. I MISS MY KIDS AND HUSBAND SO MUCH, I DON'T KNOW HOW MUCH LONGER I CAN DEAL WITH THIS EXCRUCIATING PAIN I HAVE TO DEAL WITH ON A DAILY BASIS.

Nat talks a lot about her "bad days." For the most part, she hid her emotions and would put on a happy face when she was around all of us. We never saw her at her worst.

Almost a month later...

<u>MONDAY, JUNE 15, 2009</u>: Bountiful radiology of her abdomen. *(Possibly for an abcess).*

A few weeks later...

<u>7-30-2009:</u> <u>Dr. Note</u>–Natalie paid outstanding Dr. bill. Requested Paxil. Needs to be seen.

A few weeks later...

8-21-2009: Dr. Note–Canceled Dr. appointment, couldn't get off work. *(She wasn't working at this time.)*

Four months after she was kicked out of the WRC, she voluntarily went to a detox center called the VOA (Volunteers of America).

LETTER FROM NAT TO ME, SATURDAY, SEPTEMBER 5, 2009:

HEY SHALL! WELL, IT'S ABOUT 11:45 P.M. AND THIS IS MY FIRST NIGHT HERE *(in the VOA)*. IT'S ABSOLUTELY AWFUL HERE!! I'M THROWN IN A ROOM WITH ABOUT TEN DIFFERENT WOMEN. WE SLEEP ON BUNK BEDS AND THERE IS ONE BATHROOM, ONE SHOWER, AND ONE SINK FOR ALL OF US TO SHARE. IT'S HONESTLY EVEN WORSE THAN I PICTURED IN MY HEAD. I DON'T EVEN CARE, SHALL...AND I AM SO SURPRISED. I AM SO READY TO GET MY LIFE AND MY KIDS BACK. I WOULD ABSOLUTELY DO JUST ABOUT ANYTHING TO GET ADI, MAS, AND JALA BACK WITH ME. IT HAS BEEN WAY TOO LONG THAT I HAVE BEEN WRAPPED UP IN THIS BIG MESS. IT'S GOING TO BE VERY HARD TO BE HERE AND I AM PROBABLY GOING TO CRY EVERY DAY THAT I'M HERE, BUT IT'S GOING TO BE WORTH IT. IT'S DEFINITELY GOING TO BE WORTH IT, THOUGH IT SUCKS SO DAMN BAD! I HONESTLY CANNOT BELIEVE THAT THIS IS MY LIFE RIGHT NOW. IT'S PATHETIC. I AM NOW ON DAY TWO. THIS IS SO EXTREMELY HARD, SHALL. ESPECIALLY KNOWING THAT I DON'T HAVE TO BE HERE. I COULD BAIL WHENEVER I WANTED TO. BUT I JUST KEEP REMINDING MYSELF ABOUT MY BEAUTIFUL KIDS. THEY NEED ME AND IT'S ABOUT TIME I PULL MY SHIT TOGETHER AND BE THERE FOR ALL THREE OF THEM.

I AM SO SICK RIGHT NOW, SHALL. I HAVEN'T HAD MY ASSESSMENT YET TO GET MY SUBOXONE AND I AM NOT DOING

SO GOOD AT ALL. IT IS ABOUT 3:30 P.M. RIGHT NOW AND I HAVEN'T BEEN ABLE TO EAT ALL DAY. I AM LAYING ON MY BED SHIVERING WITH CHILLS, FEELING LIKE I AM ABOUT TO PUKE OR HAVE AN ANXIETY ATTACK. THIS IS DEFINITELY NOT FUN OR EASY. I AM GOING TO HAVE TO DEAL WITH THIS ALL NIGHT LONG AND POSSIBLY THROUGHOUT THE MORNING. THIS IS THE TIME THAT MAKES IT DIFFICULT TO STAY, ESPECIALLY WHEN ONE OF MY DEALERS IS LITERALLY RIGHT AROUND THE CORNER FROM THIS PLACE. I'M TRYING REALLY HARD TO FOCUS AND NOT FORGETTING WHY I'M HERE.

She was out of the VOA before the 10th of September; she left after four days.

FRIDAY, SEPTEMBER 11, 2009, MICHELLE'S JOURNAL:

I JUST GOT OFF THE PHONE WITH NAT, FOR POSSIBLY THE LAST TIME. EVERY TIME I TALK TO HER I THINK IT IS THE LAST TIME I WILL HEAR HER VOICE. I STORE HER MESSAGES ON MY CELL PHONE SO I ALWAYS HAVE HER VOICE AND EVERY TIME MY MOM OR OTHER SISTERS CALL, I THINK THEY ARE CALLING TO SAY SHE'S GONE. OUR CONVERSATION TONIGHT WAS DIFFERENT, ALMOST UNCOMFORTABLE IN THE BEGINNING. IT WAS A RARE OCCASION WHERE SHE WAS ABLE TO HOLD A CONVERSATION AND SHE ACTUALLY LISTENED AND TALKED AND WAS CALM. WE TALKED FOR A WHILE; I KEPT FEELING LIKE IT WAS THAT MOMENT WHEN SOMEONE IS DYING AND INCOHERENT AND THEY COME TO FOR A MINUTE TO SAY GOODBYE BEFORE THEY PASS. ANYWAY, IT'S HARD TO HAVE SMALL TALK WITH SOMEONE WHO IS SHOOTING UP CONSTANTLY AND LYING AROUND HOMELESS WITH NO RESPONSIBILITY OR ANYTHING. SO I ASKED HER IF SHE THOUGHT SHE WAS GOING TO MAKE IT AND SHE SAID SHE DIDN'T KNOW. I ASKED HER IF SHE WAS SCARED AND SHE SAID IT WAS THE MOST SCARED SHE'S EVER BEEN. SHE FELT THIS AWFUL SCARED FEELING FOR THE PAST WEEK. SHE SAID SHE CAN'T EAT—WHEN SHE DOES,

HER THROAT CLOSES OFF. SHE SAID SHE'S REALLY HOMESICK FOR JAY AND HER KIDS AND SHE ACHES TO HOLD THEM. SHE SAID HER AND ADI ARE REALLY CLOSE RIGHT NOW BY PHONE, THEY TALK MULTIPLE TIMES A DAY, BEFORE SCHOOL, DURING SCHOOL, AND AFTER. SHE SAID ADI ASKS HER ADVICE, AND SHE WAS CRYING TELLING ME HOW MUCH THAT MEANT TO HER AND WE TALKED ABOUT WHAT A SPECIAL SPIRIT ADI IS AND WHAT A GOOD GIRL SHE IS. SHE SAID MAS SEEMS TO BE IN HIS OWN WORLD, NOT AS LOVING WHEN SHE SAW HIM YESTERDAY, AND WANTED TO KNOW IF HE WAS ALL RIGHT. I TOLD HER HE'S JUST COPING IN HIS OWN WAY–MAYBE HE'S ANGRY RIGHT NOW. *(Mas was fairly protected from the reality of Nat's addiction and would not know the truth until he was older).* NAT SAID SHE'S JUST TRYING TO STAY ALIVE ALTHOUGH SHE THINKS ABOUT BEING OUT OF HER MISERY OFTEN. SHE KEPT SAYING SHE WANTS TO BE COMFORTABLE. SHE HASN'T BEEN COMFORTABLE IN A LONG TIME AND SHE WANTS TO SLEEP PEACEFULLY. WHY WAS IT HER GOING THROUGH THIS–WHY COULDN'T IT BE ME? IF I COULD, I TOLD HER, I WOULD TRADE PLACES WITH HER–I WOULD. SHE FEELS SO WORTHLESS AS A PERSON, SHE SAYS, AND MY HEART BREAKS BECAUSE SHE'S THE GREATEST PERSON INSIDE AND OUT AND I LOVE HER SO MUCH. I TOLD HER I LOVED HER LIKE I ALWAYS DO BECAUSE I WANT HER TO ALWAYS KNOW THAT. I ALSO TOLD HER THAT SHE IS NOT WORTHLESS–SHE IS STILL MY SISTER NO MATTER WHAT TERRIBLE UNIMAGINABLE THINGS SHE'S DONE. I GUESS THAT'S WHAT IT MEANS TO LOVE UNCONDITIONALLY, NOTHING CAN CHANGE THAT. SHE WAS ALWAYS SO HAPPY AND FUN WHEN WE WERE NEW MOMS TOGETHER. SHE ALWAYS MADE ME FEEL LIKE I WAS THE GREATEST PERSON EVER. WE RAISED OUR BABIES TOGETHER EVERY MINUTE OF EVERY DAY. I MISS HER SO MUCH RIGHT NOW EVEN THOUGH SHE'S ALIVE–IT'S VERY RARE THAT I GET TO HAVE SUCH A CONVERSATION WITH HER. THESE PAST COUPLE OF WEEKS, I AM FINALLY TURNING THIS OVER TO MY HEAVENLY FATHER.

FOR ME TO PRAY TO KEEP HER ALIVE IS SELFISH OF ME. MAYBE SHE'S MEANT TO BE OUR FAMILY'S GUARDIAN ANGEL. WHATEVER IT IS, I AM COMING TO THE REALIZATION THAT MY SISTER IS DYING.

I remember this conversation well. I never asked her where she was. I also remember during this time, Nat telling me that she was sleeping in the streets and that she would take used cigarette butts out of public ashtrays and smoke them because she had no money to buy cigarettes.

We had multiple conversations between September and October, but I do not remember any specifics. She was still living on the streets and in hotels.

Over a month later...

LETTER FROM NAT TO ME, TUESDAY, OCTOBER 27, 2009:

SHALL, IT'S 4:30 A.M. WEDNESDAY MORNING. I COULDN'T SLEEP AT ALL LAST NIGHT, JUST LIKE EVERY OTHER NIGHT. IT'S GETTING REALLY OLD THAT I CAN NEVER SLEEP AT NIGHT. I HAVE VERY GOOD REASONS WHY...I DON'T REMEMBER THE LAST TIME I FELT COMFORTABLE ENOUGH TO FALL ASLEEP. I JUMP FROM HOUSE TO HOUSE ALL THE TIME JUST TO HAVE SOMEWHERE TO GO AND REST MY HEAD. IT'S PATHETIC. THE SAD THING IS, THE ONLY PEOPLE THAT WILL WELCOME ME IN THEIR HOME FOR A COUPLE DAYS AT A TIME IS PEOPLE THAT USE. THAT'S WHY I OBVIOUSLY CAN'T FEEL COMFORT WHATSOEVER. I WOULD GIVE ANYTHING JUST TO HAVE ONE GOOD NIGHT'S REST AT A PLACE WHERE I FEEL COMFORTABLE AND SAFE. I NEVER THOUGHT IN A MILLION YEARS THAT MY LIFE WOULD END UP LIKE THIS, AND I REALLY AM SHOCKED I LET MYSELF GET THIS BAD. ADDICTION IS THE MOST DIFFICULT THING TO TAKE CARE OF. IT HAS HAD SO MUCH CONTROL OVER ME FOR WAY TOO LONG THAT *I AM DONE!* I WANT DRUGS OUT OF MY LIFE, BUT I DON'T HAVE THE

RESOURCES OR THE MONEY TO MAKE THAT HAPPEN. I HAVE NEVER WANTED SOMETHING SO BADLY IN MY ENTIRE LIFE AS I DO NOW. IT'S RIDICULOUS THAT IT'S THIS DIFFICULT TO STOP USING. I HAVE LOST WAY TOO MUCH TIME WITH MY KIDS AND IT MAKES ME SICK. THOSE THREE KIDS ARE DEFINITELY THE ONE AND ONLY REASON THAT I AM ALIVE TODAY. IF IT WEREN'T FOR THEM, I WOULD HAVE BEEN GONE A LONG TIME AGO. SCARY TO SAY BUT I HAVE DEFINITELY HAD SOME EXTREMELY CLOSE CALLS LATELY. I ACTUALLY CAN'T BELIEVE I LIVED THROUGH THEM OR ANY OF MY SITUATIONS. THERE IS OBVIOUSLY A COUPLE GOOD REASONS WHY I AM STILL ALIVE. MY KIDS BEING ONE OF THEM. I DON'T KNOW WHY ELSE BUT I'M SURE I'LL FIGURE IT OUT SOONER THAN LATER. I REALLY HOPE THAT GOING THROUGH WHAT I HAVE GONE THROUGH WILL BENEFIT SOMEONE SOMEDAY.

I HAVE BEEN THINKING A LOT ABOUT IT LATELY AND TALKED TO JAY ABOUT IT AND WE BOTH THINK THE SAME AS YOU ABOUT ME WRITING A BOOK OR TALKING TO PEOPLE SO THAT I CAN HELP WITH ALL THE EXPERIENCES THAT I HAVE HAD. I KNOW FOR A FACT IT WILL HAVE A LOT OF IMPACT ON PEOPLE WHEN THEY HEAR EVERYTHING I HAVE GONE THROUGH. IT'S SOMETIMES OVERBEARING EVEN THINKING ABOUT A LOT OF THINGS THAT HAVE HAPPENED TO ME THAT I HAVE ASKED HEAVENLY FATHER MORE THAN ONCE TO TAKE ME. I JUST DON'T KNOW HOW MUCH MORE OF THIS AWFUL LIFE THAT I CAN TAKE. I DO WRITE EVERY SINGLE DAY, SOMETIMES HOURS AT A TIME AND MORE THAN ONCE A DAY. I WRITE TO MY KIDS DAILY AND EVERY COUPLE OF DAYS I WRITE ABOUT THINGS THAT ARE GOING ON WITH ME. SOME THINGS ARE SO HORRID THAT I COULDN'T EVEN WRITE IT DOWN.

ALL I WANT IS MY HUSBAND AND KIDS BACK, NOTHING ELSE, JUST THEM. WHY DOES IT HAVE TO BE SO HARD TO GET MY OWN CHILDREN BACK? I DEFINITELY TOOK SO MUCH FOR GRANTED. BUT I HAVE LEARNED SO MUCH, MICHELLE. I

AM LUCKY AND VERY GLAD THAT I KNOW THE THINGS ABOUT ME THAT I DO NOW AND ABOUT MY LIFE. *(I often wondered if something happened to her in her younger years. She told me once that in the WRC, they did so many workbooks, steps and therapy, and that she was the only one that the therapists had ever known that didn't have something traumatic happen to them as a child. A part of me wonders if something did happen and she kept it to herself.)* THAT'S ONE THING I AM GRATEFUL FOR AFTER GOING THROUGH ALL THIS HELL IS WHAT I HAVE UNCOVERED ABOUT MYSELF AND LEARNING ALL THE THINGS I DID. I WOULD NEVER HAVE KNOWN THE THINGS I DO NOW IF I WOULDN'T HAVE MADE ALL THESE HORRIBLE MISTAKES. I KNOW IT SOUNDS STRANGE, BUT I DO BELIEVE THAT YOU CAN TURN ALMOST EVERY EXPERIENCE INTO A POSITIVE ONE IF YOU REALLY DIG DEEP.

I WISH I HAD BETTER NEWS FOR YOU, SHALL, BUT I AM STILL STUCK IN THE SAME HOLE JUST TRYING TO PRY MYSELF OUT OF IT EACH DAY. PRAY FOR ME PLEASE. I AM DOING MY BEST TO GET MY LIFE BACK. THANK YOU FOR ALL YOUR HELP BY MAKING ALL THE PHONE CALLS THAT YOU DID AND TRYING SO HARD TO FIGURE SOMETHING OUT FOR ME. *(I was calling rehabs and facilities to try and get her off the street.)* I APPRECIATE IT MORE THAN YOU KNOW.

PLEASE KEEP IN TOUCH WITH ME, SHALL, I NEED YOU!

NAT

A few days later…

<u>LETTER FROM NAT TO ME, TUESDAY, NOVEMBER 3, 2009</u>:

SHALL,

I TALKED TO YOU TODAY OVER TEXTING AND I DON'T KNOW EXACTLY WHY, BUT EVERY TIME I AM IN TOUCH WITH YOU, A LOT OF PEACE COMES OVER ME AND I HAVEN'T FELT PEACE IN SO, SO LONG.

YOU ASKED ME WHAT YOU SHOULD DO...WELL, I DON'T HAVE ANY IDEA WHAT THE ANSWER TO THAT IS. I HAVE A HARD ENOUGH TIME EVERY SINGLE DAY TRYING TO FIND SOMEWHERE TO TAKE A SHOWER AND SOMEWHERE TO SLEEP THAT NIGHT. I SLEEP AT A DIFFERENT PLACE EVERY SINGLE NIGHT AND IT'S ABSOLUTELY HORRIBLE. I HAVE BEEN HOMELESS FOR SO LONG NOW. I JUST WANT TO FEEL THE PEACE AND COMFORT OF HAVING MY OWN HOME. I HAVE BEEN SO DEPRESSED AND HAVE WANTED TO DIE FOR WAY TOO LONG NOW. I HONESTLY CAN'T TAKE IT ANYMORE!!! THE ONLY TIME I EVER HAVE A SMILE ON MY FACE IS MONDAYS WHEN I SEE ALL MY KIDS. *(This was her visitation day at my mom's.)* IT'S ABSOLUTELY PURE HEAVEN TO ME. I AM SO HAPPY WHEN I'M WITH MY KIDS, THE WHOLE WORLD BLOCKS OUT AND I AM ON TOP OF THE WORLD!

AFTER GOING TO THE VOA AND THEM NOT HELPING ME IN ANY WAY AT ALL, I FEEL LIKE THERE IS NO HOPE FOR ME ANYMORE. IT'S THE WORST FEELING IN THE WORLD. I HAVE ABSOLUTELY NO IDEA HOW TO TAKE THE FIRST STEP, SHALL! I FEEL LIKE THE WORLD IS SO TOTALLY AGAINST ME, AND IN A WAY, IT IS BECAUSE OF THE WRONG CHOICES I MADE. I WISH EVERY DAY THAT I COULD TURN BACK TIME. I WOULD HAVE LIVED MY LIFE COMPLETELY DIFFERENT AND MADE COMPLETELY DIFFERENT CHOICES. I WANT THIS NIGHTMARE OVER! I WANT MY FAMILY BACK AND MY LIFE BACK! WHY IS IT SO DAMN HARD TO HAVE THAT??? I DON'T KNOW WHAT TO DO AND I RACK MY BRAIN EVERY MINUTE OF EVERY DAY TO TRY AND FIGURE OUT A SOLUTION TO THIS BIG MESS.

I HAVE ABSOLUTELY NOBODY TO SUPPORT ME. I AM GOING THROUGH THIS 100% ON MY OWN AND I NEED SOME ADVICE AND SOME IDEAS BECAUSE RIGHT NOW, I HAVE NO HOPE. SOMETHING NEEDS TO CHANGE AND FAST, SHALL, OR I WILL NO LONGER BE HERE.

I CAN'T IMAGINE WHAT THAT WOULD DO TO MY POOR KIDS! I CAN'T EVEN THINK ABOUT WHAT I HAVE PUT THEM

THROUGH, LET ALONE LEAVING THEM FOR GOOD. THEY ARE MY WHOLE ENTIRE HEART, WITHOUT THEM I AM NOTHING, I AM NOT ME WHATSOEVER!

ANYTHING YOU CAN DO TO HELP ME, SHALL, WILL HELP TREMENDOUSLY. I NEED A COMPLETE TURN AROUND AND I HAVE NEVER WANTED ANYTHING IN MY LIFE SO BADLY!

PLEASE KEEP IN TOUCH WITH ME AS MUCH AS YOU POSSIBLY CAN, IT HELPS ME MORE THAN YOU KNOW!

NAT

I don't remember if she mailed these letters to me or if she kept them in her journals. At this point, I think most of the family was burned out. We didn't see her during this time. She was terrified of us seeing her that way: sick, thin, and high. She was also "on the run" during this time, meaning she was hiding from people. The entire family didn't back away completely until years later. Up until then, she always had somebody in the family trying to help her. It seemed that one person would get burned out and another would be right there, ready to help until they, too got burned out, and so on. The only time she was clean was when we all backed away at the same time.

NOVEMBER 13, 2009: LDS Hospital Emergency Salt Lake City. *(Abscess removal in hip.)*

LETTER FROM NAT TO ME, SATURDAY, NOVEMBER 14, 2009:

SHALL,

HOW IS EVERYTHING? THE KIDS OKAY? I MISS YOU ALL SO VERY MUCH! I'M JUST LAYIN' HERE IN BED AT THOMAS' HOUSE IN SO MUCH PAIN BECAUSE I HAD THAT STUPID SURGERY YESTERDAY. *(Nat had an abscess, which she got often. It is an infection or bacteria from a needle in the skin. Treatment usually requires that it be opened and drained.)* I GOT MY HIP CUT OPEN AND DRAINED AND IT WAS SO AWFUL. I AM SO

SICK OF THIS, SHALL. I AM SO UNHEALTHY AND IT SCARES ME SO BAD!

THANK YOU SO MUCH FOR CHECKING INTO PLACES FOR ME STILL. I HONESTLY HAVE NOBODY TO TURN TO OR TO ASK FOR HELP. I'M SORRY THAT I AM ALWAYS ASKING YOU TO HELP ME. I JUST HAVE NO IDEA WHAT TO DO AND NO RESOURCES TO FIND ANYTHING OUT. I FEEL LIKE I AM A BURDEN ON EVERYONE ALL THE TIME. I HATE MYSELF SO VERY MUCH FOR EVER GETTING TO THIS POINT. HOW ON EARTH DID I POSSIBLY GET HERE??? I KNOW I AM SMARTER THAN THIS AND SO MUCH BETTER THAN THIS, BUT RIGHT NOW I FEEL COMPLETELY WORTHLESS. I CAN'T BELIEVE THAT DRUGS HAD THIS MUCH POWER OVER ME! IT'S SO EXTREMELY SCARY!

I HAVEN'T EVEN BEEN TO YOUR HOUSE YET *(in Saint George).* I WANT TO COME STAY WITH YOU SO BAD BUT I COMPLETELY UNDERSTAND WHY YOU DON'T WANT ME THERE YET. *(I had tried to put off having her know where I lived because I wanted to protect my family. I must have said something to her about her waiting to come and visit and made up another reason why.)* I JUST HOPE I CAN COME THERE SOON AND BE WITH ALL OF YOU.

I AM SO SAD. IT'S GOING TO BE THANKSGIVING AND CHRISTMAS SOON AND I DON'T THINK I AM EVEN GOING TO BE ABLE TO BE WITH MY FAMILY OR KIDS. I AM SO EXTREMELY HOMESICK ALL THE TIME. IT'S AN AWFUL, PHYSICAL PAIN THAT NEVER EVER GOES AWAY UNTIL I AM HOME FOR GOOD WITH MY THREE KIDS. I CAN'T EVEN EXPLAIN HOW AWFUL THIS LIFE IS AND HOW MUCH PAIN I AM ALWAYS IN. THIS IS DEFINITELY NOT ME, AND I HAVE KNOWN THAT FOR A VERY LONG TIME NOW. I JUST DON'T KNOW HOW IN THE HELL TO GET OUT! I WISH I KNEW WHAT TO DO.

I felt so bad for her and wanted to help, but I lived in Saint George, which was a very good thing; that is exactly why I lived where I did. I did make a lot of phone calls for her, trying to find rehabs and programs, but sometimes

I felt helpless and had to let it go. After so many years, my family and I were so numb to her ever-changing emotions. Maybe it was our way of coping.

TUESDAY, NOVEMBER 17, 2009: LDS Hospital Emergency Salt Lake City. *(Repacking of abscess.)*

WEDNESDAY, NOVEMBER 18, 2009, NAT JOURNALING TO SHALL:

JAY AND JALA WERE JUST HERE VISITING *(she was still living at different "friends" homes and got to see the kids and Jay during weekly visits at my parents' home).* GOSH, IT'S LIKE THE HIGHLIGHT OF MY DAY WHEN I GET TO SEE MY KIDS! SO, I REALLY DON'T HAVE ANYONE TO TALK TO EVER OR TO VENT TO SO I DECIDED THAT WHEN I NEEDED TO VENT, I WOULD JUST WRITE TO YOU (MICHELLE), KINDA LIKE A JOURNAL. I JUST HOPE YOU DON'T EVER JUDGE ME OR FEEL ANY DIFFERENT TOWARDS ME AFTER READING ALL THIS. I AM A BIT CRAZY THOUGH AND I'M SURE YOU WILL AGREE AFTER READING THE FIRST PAGE OF MY LITTLE JOURNAL TO YOU. YOU WOULD REALLY BE SURPRISED HOW MUCH IT CALMS ME AND SETTLES ME DOWN EVERY TIME I SIT AND WRITE TO YOU AND MY KIDS.

SHALL, I AM COMPLETELY IN LOVE WITH JAY AND HONESTLY ALWAYS HAVE BEEN. I TOOK HIM FOR GRANTED AND NOW I HAVE THE HARDEST TIME LOOKING AT MYSELF IN THE MIRROR EVER, KNOWING WHAT I'VE DONE TO HIM AND MY THREE WONDERFUL, MOST AMAZING CHILDREN. I AM SO SCARED THAT I HAVE LOST MY HUSBAND, SHALL. HE IS SLIPPING SLOWLY AND SLOWLY OUT OF MY LIFE. I KNOW HE STILL LOVES ME BUT I ALSO KNOW HE DOES NOT AT ALL TRUST ME, NOT EVEN A LITTLE BIT, AND I DON'T KNOW IF HE EVER WILL. IT LITERALLY BREAKS MY HEART. I HAVE NO IDEA WHAT TO DO AND I HAVE NO IDEA WHAT THE FIRST STEP IS TO TAKE TO TRY AND GET MY HUSBAND BACK. I KNOW WITHOUT A DOUBT

IN MY MIND THAT IF I HAD MY HUSBAND BACK BY MY SIDE SUPPORTING ME AND LOVING ME I WOULD HAVE THAT MUCH MORE STRENGTH TO FIGHT TO GET MY KIDS BACK, MY LITTLE FAMILY! I REALLY FEEL LIKE I'M DYING SLOWLY EVERY DAY WITHOUT THEM AND DON'T KNOW THE RIGHT THING TO DO TO GET THEM ALL BACK BEFORE IT'S TOO LATE. I AM SERIOUSLY SO SCARED EVERY DAY, SHALL, THAT MY BODY IS JUST GOING TO SHUT DOWN AND I WILL NEVER BE ABLE TO SEE MY THREE BEAUTIFUL KIDS, MY HUSBAND, MY THREE ABSOLUTELY AMAZING, LOVING SISTERS, MY HELPFUL MOTHER AND FATHER, AND ALL MY SILLY BUT AWESOME NIECES AND NEPHEWS THE NEXT DAY. BEING THIS TERRIFIED EVERY SINGLE DAY LITERALLY WEARS ME OUT. WELL, IT'S ABOUT 2:15 A.M. AND I THINK I MIGHT JUST BE ABLE TO FALL ASLEEP NOW. I LOVE YOU, SHALL, AND WILL MOST LIKELY TALK (WRITE) TO YOU TOMORROW BECAUSE WRITING TO YOU ALMOST EVERY DAY IS THE ONE AND ONLY THING I HAVE TO LOOK FORWARD TO EACH DAY.

NOVEMBER 19, 2009: LDS Hospital Emergency Salt Lake City. *(Repacking of abscess.)*

LETTER FROM NAT TO ANG, THURSDAY, NOVEMBER 19, 2009:

ANG,

HEY, HOW ARE YOU? YOU CLEANING YOUR HOUSE TODAY? I'M SURE YOU ARE. SO, I WANTED TO SEE IF I COULD POSSIBLY STOP AGAIN TO SAY HI BECAUSE I WILL MOST LIKELY BE IN THE AREA. HOW ARE THE KIDS? I MISS THEM SO VERY MUCH! I HAVE NOT BEEN ABLE TO TALK TO YOU IN SUCH A LONG TIME, SO I REALLY DON'T KNOW IF I AM ALLOWED BY YOU OR YOUR HUSBAND TO STOP IN FOR A FEW.

YOU LOOKED GREAT WHEN I SAW YOU LAST MONDAY AT YOUR HOUSE. I ALWAYS TELL EVERYONE THAT COMES IN CONTACT WITH ME JUST HOW BEAUTIFUL MY SISTERS ARE, ESPECIALLY YOU. EVERYONE THAT SEES YOU OR THAT HAS SEEN YOUR PICTURE SAYS THAT YOU AND I LOOK EXACTLY ALIKE! THAT MAKES ME FEEL SO GOOD BECAUSE I THINK YOU ARE ONE OF THE PRETTIEST WOMEN I HAVE EVER KNOWN. AND I DON'T KNOW WHAT YOU DO BUT YOU STAY SO THIN ALL THE TIME. YOU HAVE SUCH A GREAT FIGURE AND SUCH A BEAUTIFUL FACE.

THANK YOU SO MUCH FOR TAKING CARE OF JALA ON FRIDAY. I HOPE SHE WAS GOOD FOR YOU. I THINK BECAUSE SHE IS IN PRESCHOOL AND DAYCARE NOW, SHE HAS DEFINITELY LEARNED TO FEND FOR HERSELF AT TIMES AND JUST HOW TO GET EXACTLY WHAT SHE WANTS. IT BREAKS MY HEART SO VERY MUCH THAT SHE IS IN DAYCARE ALL DAY LONG EVERY DAY. AND SHE IS IN THERE SIX DAYS A WEEK. I HATE IT SO BAD AND IT STRESSES ME OUT MORE THAN YOU COULD POSSIBLY IMAGINE. I CAN'T EVEN STAND THINKING ABOUT IT OR I WILL GO COMPLETELY CRAZY. WHAT SHE REALLY NEEDS IS HER MOMMY, MASON, AND HER ADI. THAT WOULD DEFINITELY MAKE HER A HAPPIER LITTLE GIRL, I KNOW IT. I DID NOT PLAN OR EVER WANT ANY OF MY KIDS IN THE POSITION THAT THEY ARE IN NOW. THEY DON'T OR EVER DID DESERVE ANY OF THIS. IT'S BEEN WAY TOO LONG TOO. I JUST DON'T KNOW HOW OR THE FASTEST WAY TO GO ABOUT GETTING THE POLICE OFF OUR BACKS AT THIS POINT. WE *(she and Mary)* ARE CONSTANTLY RUNNING, RUNNING, RUNNING. *(Nat had two warrants out for her arrest.)* THIS LIFE HAS MADE ME FEEL MORE WORTHLESS THAN I EVER HAVE BEFORE IN MY ENTIRE LIFETIME. I AM SO NOT THIS PERSON AND WE ALL KNOW IT. I JUST DON'T KNOW HOW EXACTLY TO GET OUT. I NEED HELP. I CANNOT DO THIS ON MY OWN, THE DOCTORS ALL TOLD ME THAT. BUT I DON'T EXPECT ANY OF YOU TO HELP

ME IN ANY WAY. I JUST WANT YOUR SUPPORT AND LOVE AND THEN MAYBE I WILL FEEL LIKE I'M WORTH SOMETHING.

ANG, I KNOW ACTIONS SPEAK MUCH, MUCH LOUDER THAN WORDS BUT I HAVE CHANGED AND AM WORKING EVERY DAY TRYING TO FIGURE OUT A PLACE TO LIVE AND GET MY LIFE SOMEWHAT BACK ON TRACK. I AM LOOKING AROUND FOR JOBS TOO RIGHT NOW, BUT THEY CAN FIND OUT WHETHER YOU HAVE BEEN IN JAIL IN THE PAST SIX MONTHS OR NOT, AND IF YOU HAVE, THEY WON'T EVEN TAKE A LOOK AT YOUR RESUME. IT IS SO FREAKING DIFFICULT, ANG. I BELIEVE I HAVE PAID FOR THE MISTAKES I MADE WITH YOU *(I don't know what those are)* AND JUST IN GENERAL WITH ALL THE MANY, MANY CONSEQUENCES I HAVE HAD TO FACE. YES, I HAVE DEFINITELY LEARNED MY LESSON AND NEVER WANT THIS HORRIBLE LIFE BACK AGAIN ONCE IT'S GONE. YOU SHOULD FEEL SO LUCKY, ANG. YOU HAVE GOT EVERYTHING A GIRL COULD POSSIBLY EVER ASK FOR. I WOULD GIVE ANYTHING IN THIS WORLD TO BE WHERE YOU, SHALL, AND EMILY ARE AND I KNOW JUST HOW TO BE THE HAPPIEST I HAVE EVER BEEN NOW AND KNOW EXACTLY WHAT I NEED TO DO TO START MY LIFE OVER AGAIN AND MAKE A FRESH NEW START. I LITERALLY PRAY FOR THAT EVERY NIGHT AND TO GET ALL MY KIDS BACK LIVING WITH ME AGAIN UNDER THE SAME ROOF VERY, VERY SOON.

I DON'T KNOW IF YOU HEARD OR NOT THAT I HAD TO GET SURGERY A COUPLE OF DAYS AGO. YEP, HAD AN ABSCESS ON MY HIP FROM BEING TOTALLY GHETTO. I JUST CAN'T BELIEVE EVERYTHING ALWAYS HAPPENS TO ME. I NEED A DAMN BREAK. I AM SO SAD AND GETTING SADDER EVERY DAY BECAUSE THE HOLIDAYS ARE COMING UP AND I HAVE ABSOLUTELY NOBODY TO SHARE THEM WITH. I HONESTLY

HAVE NO IDEA WHAT I AM GOING TO DO, AND I'M TERRIFIED BECAUSE I DON'T WANT TO BE ON THE STREETS, COLD, ON THANKSGIVING AND CHRISTMAS. I GET ANXIETY JUST THINKING ABOUT IT NOW.

I MISS ALL OF YOU SO MUCH AND I TRULY HOPE YOU CAN TRUST ME WHEN I SAY THAT WE WILL ALL BE TOGETHER AGAIN SOMEDAY REALLY SOON.

OK, HONEY, I NEED TO LAY DOWN BECAUSE MY HIP'S KILLING ME RIGHT NOW AND I NEED SOME HELP.

I HOPE WE CAN GET TOGETHER SOMETIME REALLY SOON AND GO TO LUNCH OR DINNER OR SOMETHING.

LOVE YOU SO MUCH, ANG!

NAT

P.S. GIVE SPARKY SPARKS *(Angie's dog)* A HUG FOR ME.

As I read these letters now, I see how severely she manipulated Ang and me. Nat did end up spending Thanksgiving with all of us at my parents' home. After the visit, I told my family that she was still using. She had told me she was using confidentially, but I had an obligation to tell the family for the safety of her children and everyone else. This was so hard for me to do, knowing that she would no longer be allowed to visit her kids at my parents' house. I knew the consequences that would follow, and that the kids would suffer, but I had to do it anyway.

NOVEMBER 22, 2009: LDS Hospital Emergency Salt Lake City. *(Repacking of existing Abscess.)*

NOVEMBER 24, 2009: LDS Hospital Emergency, home care services. IV infusion therapy on Bactrim *(antibiotic)*, Clindamycin *(antibiotic)*, Keflex *(antibiotic)*, and Lortab *(pain medication)*. *Nat continued these home-care services through November 30, 2009.*

A couple of weeks later...

MONDAY, DECEMBER 7, 2009, NAT JOURNALING TO SHALL:

IT'S ABOUT 3:00 A.M. AND I HAVE BEEN SO UPSET THAT I COULDN'T EVEN PICK UP A PEN AND WRITE UNTIL NOW. I DIDN'T SEE YOU TOO LONG AGO BECAUSE IT WAS THANKSGIVING, AND I WAS SO EXCITED TO SEE THE PERSON THAT I ADMIRE THE MOST IN THIS WORLD...YOU. BUT I DON'T KNOW WHY, SHALL, BUT EVERY TIME, YOU STIR THINGS UP AND MAKE EVERYTHING SO MUCH WORSE FOR ME. JUST WHEN I THOUGHT MY LIFE COULDN'T POSSIBLY GET ANY WORSE THAN IT ALREADY IS, IT DEFINITELY DOES BY FAR, AND THE MAJORITY OF THE TIME, IT'S YOU THAT CAUSED IT. WHY, SHALL? I LOOK UP TO YOU AND COMPLETELY ADMIRE YOU MORE THAN ANYONE IN THIS WORLD AND I ALWAYS HAVE, ALWAYS! SO YOU CAN'T EVEN POSSIBLY COMPREHEND KNOWING THE HURT AND PAIN THAT I FEEL WHEN FINDING OUT THAT YOU WERE THE ONE THAT TALKED TO MOM AND JAY ABOUT SOME THINGS THAT I CONFIDED TO YOU WITH WHEN WE SPOKE LAST OVER THANKSGIVING. SHALL, YOU CAN KEEP ON TELLING ME OVER AND OVER THAT YOU DO THESE THINGS BECAUSE YOU WANT TO HELP, WHEN WE BOTH KNOW THAT IT TURNS INTO SOMETHING THAT DIDN'T NEED TO BE. IT STIRS EVERYBODY UP IN THE FAMILY AND LITERALLY TURNS THEM AWAY FROM ME AND IT PUTS ME AND YOU FURTHER APART THAN WE ALREADY WERE. I WILL OWN UP TO MY MISTAKES, MICHELLE, AND I DEFINITELY PAY FOR THOSE MISTAKES EVERY DAY OF MY LIFE AND IT'S KILLING ME. IT HURTS ME MORE THAN YOU COULD POSSIBLY KNOW, KNOWING THAT EVERYTHING I HAVE EVER COME TO YOU WITH, CONFIDED IN YOU, VENTING TO YOU AND ON MORE THAN A FEW OCCASIONS CRYING TO YOU, THAT NOT ONCE, HONESTLY, NOT ONE TIME HAVE YOU EVER KEPT WHAT I SAID TO YOU BETWEEN JUST ME AND YOU, LIKE I HAD ALWAYS ASKED. AND I DON'T KNOW WHY, BECAUSE I

HONESTLY DO NOT TRUST YOU TO KEEP WHAT I TELL YOU TO YOURSELF, BUT YOU, ONLY YOU, ARE THE ONLY PERSON I EVER FEEL COMPLETELY COMFORTABLE OPENING UP TO AND BEING THE REAL ME WITHOUT HOLDING ANYTHING BACK WHATSOEVER. YOU NEVER HAVE JUDGED ME, I HOPE, AND YOU HAVE ALWAYS BEEN THE ONE AND ONLY PERSON IN MY LIFE THAT I HAVE ALWAYS WANTED TO BE EXACTLY ALIKE. I THINK YOU ARE THE CLOSEST TO PERFECT PERSON THAT I HAVE EVER MET OR BELIEVE THAT LIVES IN THIS WORLD. BUT WHEN I HEAR THAT YOU HAVE STIRRED THINGS UP ABOUT ME TO MOM, JAY, AND WHOEVER ELSE, I LOSE FAITH IN YOU AND START TO WONDER WHY I HAVE ALWAYS PUT YOU ON SUCH A VERY HIGH PEDESTAL MY ENTIRE LIFE. I HAVE BEEN IN TEARS NON-STOP THE PAST COUPLE OF DAYS BECAUSE OF THE THINGS I FOUND OUT AND KNOWING WHAT YOU TOLD MOM AND JAY ABOUT ME. THIS IS NOT HELPING ME, SHALL, AND I KNOW THAT YOU KNOW THAT IT WOULDN'T AND THAT IT WOULD START MORE PROBLEMS WITHIN THE FAMILY. JUST PLEASE EXPLAIN WHY! I KNOW THAT YOU THINK I AM SO FAR GONE RIGHT NOW, SHALL, AND THAT I CAN'T COMPREHEND MUCH, BUT I AM ABSOLUTELY NOT STUPID AND I KNOW MORE THAN YOU THINK I DO AND AM HONESTLY TRYING A HELL OF A LOT MORE THAN YOU THINK OR BELIEVE THAT I AM. THERE REALLY IS NOT A LOT THAT I CAN DO ON MY OWN WITHOUT TRANSPORTATION, LOTS OF MONEY, AND STRENGTH AND SUPPORT. EVERY SINGLE TIME I FEEL LIKE I AM ACTUALLY GETTING SOMEWHERE, I GET PUSHED RIGHT BACK DOWN INTO MY HELL HOLE. AND PLEASE DON'T TAKE WHAT I AM SAYING AS IF I AM TRYING TO BLAME YOU OR OTHER PEOPLE FOR MY PROBLEMS. THAT IS SO NOT WHERE I AM GOING WITH THIS IN THE LEAST. ALL I KNOW, SHALL, IS THAT THE ONE THING THAT HAS KEPT ME GOING AND SOMETIMES PUTS A GREAT BIG SMILE ON MY FACE IS THE COUPLE OF HOURS A WEEK ON MONDAYS THAT I GET TO SPEND WITH ALL THREE OF MY AMAZING, WONDERFUL CHILDREN. NOW THAT HAS BEEN

TAKEN AWAY FROM ME AND IT DOESN'T MAKE ANY SENSE TO ME AT ALL BECAUSE I AM DOING A HECK OF A LOT BETTER TODAY THAN I WAS A MONTH OR TWO MONTHS AGO. I WAS JUST BARELY ALLOWED BACK INTO MOM AND DAD'S HOUSE, JUST IN THE LAST COUPLE OF MONTHS STARTED BUILDING SOMEWHAT OF A RELATIONSHIP WITH EMILY, AND JAY HAS GOTTEN A LOT CLOSER TO ME, BEEN THERE TO HELP ME WHENEVER I NEED HIM AND WANTING TO FINALLY BE AROUND ME AND ENJOY MY COMPANY, AND IN THE LAST WEEK, SURPRISINGLY TO ME, MOM WON'T ALLOW ME IN HER HOME ANYMORE, EMILY WON'T TALK TO ME AGAIN, AND JAY TOLD ME HE BASICALLY HAS NO TIME FOR ME IN HIS LIFE. THIS HAS LITERALLY BROUGHT ME TO THE POINT OF DEATH. I WAS SUPPOSED TO SEE MY KIDS TONIGHT AND COULDN'T. JAY WON'T TALK TO ME AND I HAVE NEVER IN MY LIFE FELT THIS MUCH PHYSICAL, EMOTIONAL, AND MENTAL HURT AND PAIN AS I AM RIGHT NOW. I AM SO BAD TODAY, SHALL, THAT THIS TIME IT WILL HAVE TO TAKE A MIRACLE TO MAKE ME FIGHT TO LIVE FOR MY LIFE. HOW IN THE HELL DID MY LIFE GET TO BE SO EXTREMELY HORRIBLE? EVERY TIME I GET HOPE AND I AM ON MY WAY UP IN MY LIFE, I GET TORN DOWN EVERY SINGLE TIME. BUT EACH TIME I GET PUSHED BACK DOWN, IT GETS FURTHER AND FURTHER AWAY FROM EVER HAVING A CHANCE AGAIN WITH MY KIDS AND MY HUSBAND. I DON'T THINK, ACTUALLY, I KNOW THAT YOU HAVE ABSOLUTELY NO IDEA HOW HARD I TRY OR WHAT I ACTUALLY GO THROUGH EACH DAY OF MY LIFE RIGHT NOW TO GET WHERE I WANT TO BE! I WISH JUST FOR ONE DAY THAT YOU COULD WALK AND SPEND ONE DAY IN MY SHOES AND EXPERIENCE MY LIFE AND FEEL WHAT I FEEL, SEE WHAT I SEE, AND STRIVE THE WAY I STRIVE. BUT YOU NEVER WILL BECAUSE YOU NEVER MADE THE AWFUL MISTAKES THAT I HAVE MADE AND NEVER WERE AS STUPID AS I WAS TO DO THE HORRIBLE THINGS LIKE I DID TO GET ME TO WHERE I AM TODAY.

I ASK GOD ALMOST EVERY NIGHT, "HAVEN'T I HAD ENOUGH? ISN'T IT ABOUT TIME I CAUGHT MY BREAK?" BUT EVERY DAY ALWAYS GETS WORSE AND WORSE AND I DON'T KNOW HOW TO BREAK IT OR GET RID OF THIS HORRIFYING NIGHTMARE I HAVE BEEN LIVING FOR WAY TOO LONG NOW. I KNOW ALL THE HORRIBLE MISTAKES THAT I HAVE MADE IN MY LIFE AND I KNOW WITHOUT A DOUBT IN MY MIND THAT I WILL NEVER REPEAT THEM. I KNOW ALL THE PEOPLE THAT I HAVE HURT, AND MOST IMPORTANT, I DO REALIZE WHAT I HAVE DONE TO MY THREE CHILDREN. I HAVE TO LIVE WITH THAT GUILT FOR THE REST OF MY LIFE, AND MOST OF THE TIME, IT IS COMPLETELY OVERBEARING WHERE IT TAKES MY BREATH AWAY, LITERALLY. WHEN I THINK ABOUT WHAT I HAVE DONE TO MY KIDS AND WHAT I HAVE PUT THEM THROUGH, I ABSOLUTELY DO NOT WANT TO LIVE ONE MORE DAY, BUT WHAT WOULD THAT DO TO THEM THEN? EITHER WAY, WITH ALL THAT I HAVE DONE AND BEEN THROUGH, IT WILL DEFINITELY BE A CHALLENGE FOR ME TO MAKE IT THROUGH EACH DAY TILL THE NEXT.

SHALL, I DON'T KNOW HOW YOU CAN HELP, BUT PLEASE HELP ME. HELP ME GET MY LIFE BACK WITH MY KIDS AND POSSIBLY MY HUSBAND. I CAN'T DO THIS ALONE, I ABSOLUTELY DO NOT HAVE ENOUGH STRENGTH OR WISDOM OR EVEN COURAGE TO WALK EACH DAY ALONE LIKE I HAVE BEEN FOR THE PAST THREE YEARS.

WELL, I VENTED ENOUGH TONIGHT, OR SHOULD I SAY MORNING. DEFINITELY NOT LOOKING FORWARD TO THIS DAY AT ALL. I WILL ACTUALLY BE SHOCKED IF I MAKE IT THROUGH ONE MORE DAY. I HOPE YOU ARE PRAYING FOR ME, SHALL, BECAUSE GOD KNOWS I NEED ALL THE HELP THAT I CAN POSSIBLY GET. XOXO

This letter was so hard for me to read.

The next day...

TUESDAY, DECEMBER 8, 2009:

IT'S ABOUT 2:00 A.M. AND I AM SO EXTREMELY TIRED BUT CANNOT FOR THE LIFE OF ME FALL ASLEEP. I HAVE BEEN IN TEARS, HONESTLY FOR ABOUT THREE HOURS NOW. I DEFINITELY GOT SOME NEWS THAT LITERALLY MADE ME FALL TO THE FLOOR AND WEEP. MASON CALLED ME AT ABOUT 10:00 P.M. TO TELL ME GOODNIGHT BEFORE HE WENT TO SLEEP. I HAVE NOT TALKED TO EITHER MASON OR ADI FOR THE PAST COUPLE OF DAYS AND I WAS NOT LOOKING FORWARD TO IT LIKE I USUALLY AM. I KNEW ONCE I GOT ON THE PHONE WITH EITHER ONE OF THEM THAT I WOULD NOT BE ABLE TO STOP CRYING, AND THEY DON'T NEED TO HEAR THEIR MOTHER SOBBING. LAST NIGHT, I WAS SUPPOSED TO BE AT MOM'S HOUSE FOR MY VISIT WITH MY KIDS. WHEN I WAS ON THE PHONE WITH MY SWEET MASON TONIGHT, HE SOUNDED SO SAD, IT TORE ME APART. HE DIDN'T ASK WHERE I WAS LAST NIGHT AND DIDN'T WANT TO TALK ABOUT THE NIGHT AT ALL. THE OTHER LINE RANG WHEN I WAS ON THE PHONE WITH MAS AND IT WAS MY BEAUTIFUL ADISON. I GOT OFF THE PHONE WITH MASON AND TALKED TO ADI FOR A BIT. SHE WAS NOT DOING GOOD AT ALL. SHE TOLD ME HOW CUTE JALA WAS LAST NIGHT WITH THEM AND HOW SHE WOULDN'T LET GO OF ADI ALL NIGHT LONG UNTIL JAY CAME TO GET HER. I KNEW JALA WOULD HAVE A HARD TIME THERE LAST NIGHT BECAUSE ME AND HER HAVE BEEN SPENDING A LOT OF TIME TOGETHER LATELY, AND I HONESTLY CAN'T REMEMBER THE LAST TIME I SPENT A MONDAY NIGHT WITHOUT MY KIDS. OTHER THAN THEIR MOM NOT BEING THERE WITH THEM, ADISON HAD A GREAT NIGHT WITH HER BABY SISTER. BUT THEN ADISON TOLD ME SOMETHING THAT PUT US BOTH IN TEARS. SHE TOLD ME THAT MOM TOLD HER THE REASON

I WAS NOT THERE WITH THEM WAS BECAUSE I WAS STILL ON HEAVY DRUGS.

A couple of weeks later...

Christmas Day, she was still living with random people.

<u>FRIDAY, DECEMBER 25, 2009</u>:

MY FAVORITE SIS,

WE HAVE DEFINITELY ALWAYS KNOWN THAT. I JUST GOT OFF THE PHONE WITH YOU AND BESIDES THE FACT THAT I WAS EXTREMELY UPSET BECAUSE OF WHAT YOU WERE TALKING ABOUT, I ALSO FELT SO HAPPY BECAUSE I HAVE NOT TALKED TO YOU LIKE THAT, AND FOR THAT LONG, IN A VERY, VERY LONG TIME. IT WAS LIKE WE WERE "US" AGAIN. I MISS OUR RELATIONSHIP THAT WE HAD, SHALL. I HONESTLY DON'T THINK THERE HAS EVER BEEN TWO SISTERS THAT WERE AS CLOSE AS WE WERE. AND IT WAS ALWAYS LIKE THAT. WE HAVE HAD OUR STUPID FIGHTS, DISAGREEMENTS, AND ARGUMENTS, BUT NOBODY WILL EVER OR COULD EVER FILL YOUR PLACE. YOU HAVE ALWAYS BEEN THE CLOSEST PERSON TO ME AS FAR BACK AS I CAN REMEMBER. I HAVE ALWAYS IDOLIZED YOU AND WANTED TO BE A GREAT AND WONDERFUL PERSON LIKE YOU ARE. I STILL TO THIS VERY DAY ABSOLUTELY LOVE TO BE JUST LIKE YOU. I REALLY DO THINK, SHALL, THAT YOU ARE THE CLOSEST TO PERFECT PERSON THAT I HAVE EVER KNOWN. I HAVE ALWAYS LEARNED SO MUCH FROM YOU AND ONLY TOOK YOUR ADVICE WHEN I TALKED TO YOU.

SHALL, I KNOW I HAVE DONE AND SAID SOME THINGS TO YOU *(I believe she was apologizing for getting upset with me earlier, after I told my family she was using)* THAT YOU WILL PROBABLY NEVER FORGET, BUT IN ALL HONESTY, I DIDN'T MEAN THEM,

'CAUSE I HAVE ALWAYS THOUGHT THE ABSOLUTE WORLD OF YOU AND THINK YOU ARE THE MOST AMAZING WOMAN I HAVE EVER CAME ACROSS. I STRIVE TO BE MORE LIKE YOU. THE FUNNY THING IS THAT WE HAVE THE CLOSEST PERSONALITIES IN THE FAMILY AND THINK SO VERY MUCH ALIKE BUT HAVE TWO TOTALLY COMPLETELY DIFFERENT LIVES. YOU ARE TRULY THE ONE AND ONLY PERSON IN MY LIFE THAT I ACTUALLY EVER EVEN LISTENED TO OR TOOK ADVICE FROM, OR EVEN CARED ABOUT YOUR OPINION. YOU HAVE TAUGHT ME SO MUCH, SHALL, AND JUST BECAUSE I HAVEN'T APPLIED ANYTHING YOU HAVE EVER TOLD ME IN MY LIFE DOESN'T MEAN I NEVER WILL. PLEASE DON'T GIVE UP ON ME JUST QUITE YET, MY LIFE IS ABOUT TO DO A 180 AND I WANT YOU BY MY SIDE, SUPPORTING ME, TEACHING ME, AND LOVING ME JUST AS YOU ALWAYS HAVE IN MY LIFE. YOU HAVE BEEN THE ONE PERSON IN MY LIFE THAT HAS TRULY MADE THE BIGGEST IMPACT ON ME. BELIEVE IT OR NOT, YOU ARE REALLY THE ONLY PERSON IN MY LIFE THAT I HAVE EVER LISTENED TO OR EVEN SLIGHTLY TRUSTED.

SHALL, I REALLY HOPE WITH ALL MY HEART THAT YOU CAN FORGIVE ME FOR ALL THAT I HAVE PUT YOU THROUGH. IT WAS NEVER, EVER INTENTIONAL AND I REALLY HOPE YOU BELIEVE THAT. I HAVE ALWAYS CARED SO MUCH ABOUT HOW YOU LOOK AT ME OR THINK OF ME.

I JUST PRAY EVERY DAY THAT WE CAN BE BACK THE WAY WE ALWAYS WERE OR EVEN CLOSER. YOU MEAN SO MUCH TO ME, SHALL, AND MY LIFE WOULD NEVER BE OKAY WITHOUT YOU IN IT. YOU WOULD BE SURPRISED HOW BIG OF A PART YOU PLAY IN MY LIFE.

I HONESTLY TRY HARD SOMETIMES TO FIND AT LEAST ONE OF YOUR FLAWS AND I NEVER CAN. I THINK YOU ARE A COMPLETELY BEAUTIFUL, FLAWLESS PERSON INSIDE AND OUT, AND I WANT TO BE LIKE YOU SOMEDAY AND HAVE PEOPLE LOOK UP TO ME THE WAY PEOPLE DO YOU. I FEEL SO EXTREMELY LUCKY TO HAVE YOU IN MY LIFE, LET ALONE YOU BEING MY

SISTER. EVERY TIME I SEE YOU, YOU ARE MORE BEAUTIFUL AND MORE AMAZING AND ALWAYS GIVE ME HOPE IN MY LIFE. YOU HAVE NO IDEA WHAT THAT DOES FOR ME BECAUSE I VERY RARELY HAVE ANY MORE HOPE IN MY LIFE ANYMORE. IT'S SAD WHAT I HAVE BECOME.

THANK YOU SO MUCH, SHALL, FOR NEVER FULLY GIVING UP ON ME. I DON'T KNOW WHAT I WOULD DO WITHOUT YOU. YOU ARE SUCH AN INSPIRATION TO ME, AND I LOVE YOU WITH ALL MY HEART.

MERRY CHRISTMAS TOO, BY THE WAY!

I LOVE YOU, SHALL, LOVE ME

It's really hard to know which parts were her true feelings and which were merely manipulations. I always believed we had such a special bond, but I question that sometimes when I reread these letters because it's hard not to think that everything she said to me was manipulation. I do know from her actions throughout her life, though, that family meant so much to her, and anytime I needed someone, she was the first one there.

• • •

CHAPTER 7
2010

IN 2010, NAT TURNED *thirty-one, Adi fourteen, Mas eleven, and Jala four.*

MONDAY, JANUARY 25, 2010, MICHELLE'S JOURNAL:

NAT CAME TO MY HOUSE IN SAINT GEORGE FOR THE FIRST TIME TODAY SINCE WE MOVED HERE ONE AND A HALF YEARS AGO. MY COUSIN BROUGHT HER HERE TO SEE IF SHE COULD LIVE IN A DRUG FREE ENVIRONMENT VISITING THE METHADONE CLINIC DAILY AND SEEING A THERAPIST. *(The methadone clinic is where she would go daily to dose. Methadone is like Suboxone; it helps take away withdrawal symptoms.)* SO...SHE'S MADE HERSELF AT HOME IN OUR SPARE BEDROOM, WHICH I'M SO HAPPY TO BE ABLE TO PROVIDE FOR HER. IT ALMOST FEELS LIKE WE'RE YOUNG AGAIN. I MISS MY SISTER SO MUCH IT'S INDESCRIBABLE AND IT'S HARD TO GET THESE GLIMPSES OF THE OLD HER AND KNOW IT WILL BE SHORT LIVED. I AM TAKING HER TO THE METHADONE CLINIC IN THE MORNING AND THEN TO SEE THE PHYSICIAN TO GET HER A FULL PHYSICAL AND LAB WORK. SHE JUST WENT TO BED AFTER SHE TOOK A BATH AND WE SAT AT THE COMPUTER LOOKING UP SIDE EFFECTS AND SYMPTOMS OF HIV AND HEPATITIS. SHE BELIEVES SHE HAS

EITHER OR BOTH. SHE HAS ALL THE SYMPTOMS OF BOTH AND SHE'S SO SCARED. SHE TOLD ME SHE'S HAD DARK SPOTS ALL OVER HER BODY FOR A COUPLE OF DAYS, ON HER BACK, BETWEEN HER BOOBS, AND NECK. SHE SAID THEY WOULD BE GONE IN THE MORNING. SHE'S HAD LUMPS ON HER THROAT—ABSCESSES, ETC. SHE'LL GO FROM HAPPY AND UPBEAT TO EXHAUSTED IN MINUTES. I WONDER WHAT SHE'S ON BESIDES METHADONE. MY MIND IS CONSTANTLY RACING. IT'S HARD TO STAY FOCUSED ON MY HUSBAND AND KIDS AND NORMAL ROUTINE OF THINGS AND TAKE CARE OF HER AND MAKE SURE MY CHILDREN AND HOME ARE SAFE. TWO WEEKS SEEMS LIKE A LONG TIME TONIGHT.

This is the only picture I have of the time she stayed at my house to get clean. This is her and my daughter Kierra on the couch

TUESDAY, JANUARY 26, 2010, MICHELLE'S JOURNAL:

I'VE EXPOSED MY IMMEDIATE FAMILY (TYE AND KIDS) TO THIS AWFUL DRUG WORLD. I HAVE HER DRUG DEALER'S DRIVER'S LICENSE, GREEN CARD, AND SOCIAL SECURITY CARD THAT HE LEFT IN HER WALLET. WON'T HE BE LOOKING FOR THEM? FOR HER? HOW DO I GET IT TO HIM? MAIL? NO RETURN ADDRESS? WENT TO METHADONE CLINIC WITH HER THIS MORNING, SAW A DIFFERENT WORLD AT CLINIC, SAW A SICK GIRL, TALKED TO NAT'S COUNSELOR, WATCHED HER TAKE MEDICINE, TALKED TO STRANGERS WAITING THEIR TURN AT WINDOW COMPARING DOSES. TOOK HER TO PHYSICIAN TO GET PHYSICAL AND PAP, HER COLON IS ABOUT TO RUPTURE, HER LYMPH NODES ARE ALL SWOLLEN. DOCTOR'S FIRST CONCERN IS COLON, HAS YEAST AND ANOTHER BACTERIAL INFECTION AND POSSIBLE CHLAMYDIA AND OTHER STD. NAT FREAKED OUT ABOUT STD AND STARTED THROWING UP IN TRASH. ASKED DR. ABOUT SAFETY IN HOME FOR MY KIDS WITH HER POSSIBLY HAVING HIV & HEP C. KIERRA WANTS TO BORROW HER CLOTHES, THEY SMELL LIKE SMOKE—I THINK I SMELL LIKE SMOKE—HARD TO KEEP THAT AWAY. I'M TRYING HARD TO TREAT HER WITH RESPECT BUT ALSO LAY BOUNDARIES. I THINK SHE HAS DRUGS HERE. SHE CLAIMS SHE'S JUST TIRED AND CAN BARELY KEEP HER EYES OPEN. I DON'T BELIEVE ANYTHING SHE SAYS, LOTS OF LIES. THIS IS TOO BIG OF A JOB FOR ONE PERSON TO TAKE CARE OF HER. ENDLESS POCKETBOOK, THAT IS WHAT I FEEL LIKE. THIS IS MONEY MY HUSBAND HAS WORKED SO HARD FOR AND I'M STRESSING HIM OUT FINANCIALLY AND HE DOESN'T NEED THAT. AFTER DOCTOR, I TOOK HER TO LAB, THEY COULDN'T GET VEINS FOR HIV AND HEP C TESTS SO WE HAVE TO GO BACK BEFORE FIVE TODAY. SHE WAS COMPLAINING BECAUSE HE POKED HER TWO TIMES, AND

IN MY MIND, I'M THINKING–YOU DO THIS EVERY DAY, ALL DAY TO GET DRUGS, SO WHY IS THIS SO BAD? TOOK HER TO SCHOOL TO TEACH MY CLASS, SHE PUT ON SUNGLASSES AND SAT THERE FALLING ASLEEP, COULD HARDLY WALK, TOOK MY KEYS AND WENT TO CAR, SO I HAD TO LEAVE–TOLD HER IN THE CAR THAT I HAVE TO CONTINUE WITH MY SCHEDULE, SHE NEEDS TO COME WITH ME. WHAT'S THE DIFFERENCE IN HER FROM YESTERDAY TO TODAY? SHE CLAIMS IT'S ALL SLEEP RELATED. I'M NOT BUYING IT. I'M EXHAUSTED. SHE NEEDS SO MUCH MORE HELP AND FINANCIAL AID THAN I CAN GIVE. I DON'T KNOW WHAT TO DO. SHE'S DOWNSTAIRS SLEEPING, I CAN'T LEAVE HER ALONE, WE ARE SUPPOSED TO GO TO LAB AND PHARMACY TO CLEAR COLON. I'M MISSING MY KIDS AND HUSBAND. I FEEL LIKE I AM NEGLECTING THEM–SO HARD TO BALANCE. CALLED DAVEY *(therapist)*–HOPEFULLY HE WILL VISIT WITH ME TONIGHT.

I FEEL REGRET FOR LETTING HER KNOW WHERE I LIVE AND HAVING HER HERE, BUT AN OBLIGATION AT THE SAME TIME–I DON'T KNOW WHICH WAY TO GO.

THURSDAY, JANUARY 28, 2010, MICHELLE'S JOURNAL:

YESTERDAY, THE SAME PATTERN HAPPENED IN THE AFTERNOON–WENT TO TEACH–SHE USED THE BATHROOM AND THEN STARTED GETTING SLEEPY AND SAT AT THE COUNTER AND FELL ASLEEP, THEN WENT TO THE COUCH AND FELL ASLEEP, THEN WENT DOWNSTAIRS FOR A FEW HOURS AND SLEPT AND WOKE UP–ATE–WENT BACK TO BED. DURING THE AFTERNOON, BEFORE SLEEPING, SHE LOWERED HER HAT TO COVER HER EYES AND WAS ASKING ME IF I WAS OK AND TRYING REALLY HARD NOT TO SEEM TIRED. I WAS VERY FRUSTRATED THAT NIGHT, SO I SAT ONLINE LOOKING AT HEROIN SIGNS, AND SHE HAS ALL OF THEM. THEN CALLED A DRUG HOTLINE TO SEE IF METHADONE COULD BE MAKING HER THAT WAY–THEY SAID POSSIBLY AND TO GET UA *(Urine Analysis)* TEST. SO

THIS MORNING WE WENT TO THE METHADONE CLINIC. SHE HAD TO MEET WITH THE DOCTOR AND FILL OUT PAPERWORK. TYSON WASN'T FEELING WELL SO I LEFT HER THERE AND TOOK HIM TO GET CHECKED AT HIS DOCTOR. I CAME BACK AND MET WITH THE PROGRAM DIRECTOR WHILE SHE FILLED OUT MORE PAPERWORK. I TOLD HIM THE PATTERNS OF BEHAVIOR I WAS SEEING, AND HE TOLD ME THE UA TEST WOULD TELL US IF SHE WAS USING AND WE'D FIND OUT IN A FEW DAYS AND WAS AWARE OF MY CONCERNS AND WOULD TRY TO WORK WITH HER TOMORROW IN A SESSION TO TALK. HER HIV AND HEP C TESTS CAME BACK NEGATIVE–WHICH IS NOT NECESSARILY THE CASE–SHE HAS TO BE RECHECKED IN SIX MONTHS BECAUSE IT MAY NOT SHOW UP IN THE BLOOD YET. I'M NOT CONVINCED SHE'S CLEAN. I ALSO TALKED TO DAVEY AND HE'S CONVINCED SHE'S USING. IF UA TEST IS POSITIVE, I'M SENDING HER HOME. AUSTIN AND KIERRA ARE BOTH HAVING A HARD TIME. KIERRA SEEMS EXTRA MOODY AND AUSTIN SAYS HE DOESN'T LIKE THE FEELING OF OUR HOME WITH HER HERE. THEY BOTH CONSTANTLY ASK WHERE SHE IS AND IF SHE'S OKAY. I THINK WE ARE ALL JUST NERVOUS ABOUT HER STAYING ALIVE. SHE SEEMS HAPPY BUT DOESN'T HAVE A TON OF EMOTION. SHE'S VERY DETACHED.

<u>LETTER FROM NAT TO ME, MONDAY, FEBRUARY 1, 2010</u>:

SHALL,

I CAN'T EVEN PUT INTO WORDS HOW GRATEFUL I AM TO YOU AND TYE FOR GIVING ME THIS CHANCE TO COME DOWN AND STAY WITH YOU AND YOUR FAMILY. IT FEELS SO AMAZING TO BE GENUINELY CARED ABOUT LIKE I HAVE BEEN THE PAST WEEK BY ALL OF YOU. HONESTLY, I HAVE NOT FELT THIS LOVED BY ANYONE IN SUCH A LONG TIME. SHALL, I DON'T WANT YOU TO THINK THAT JUST BECAUSE I WAS HERE FOR SUCH A SHORT PERIOD OF TIME THAT IT DIDN'T DO ANY GOOD. I HAVE NEVER IN MY LIFE FELT THIS MOTIVATED

EVER. I KNOW THAT THIS WEEK HAS DEFINITELY CHANGED ME AND MY LIFE.

SO, WE FINALLY DECIDED THAT I AM LEAVING THURSDAY AND I AM REALLY HAVING A HARD TIME. I AM REALLY, REALLY SAD. I HAVE BEEN SO COMFORTABLE AND HAVE HAD SO MUCH FUN, WHICH I DIDN'T THINK WAS POSSIBLE WITHOUT DRUGS. I HAVE LEARNED SO MUCH ABOUT LIFE AND MYSELF IN JUST THE PAST WEEK. I HONESTLY DON'T KNOW WHAT TO SAY OR DO TO SHOW YOU HOW MUCH I APPRECIATE EVERYTHING YOU AND YOUR HUSBAND HAVE DONE FOR ME.

I AM HAVING A VERY HARD TIME KNOWING THAT I AM FOR SURE GOING THROUGH ANOTHER DIVORCE, BUT I AM SO VERY THANKFUL THAT I WAS HERE WITH YOU WHEN I FOUND OUT. I HANDLED IT SO MUCH BETTER THAN I EVER THOUGHT I WOULD, AND I KNOW IT'S BECAUSE I WAS HERE WITH YOU AND LISTENED TO YOU AND TOOK YOUR ADVICE. THIS ONE IS GOING TO BE VERY ROUGH FOR ME, BUT I WILL GET THROUGH IT, I KNOW NOW THAT I AM STRONG ENOUGH.

I WISH THERE WAS SOMETHING I COULD DO FOR YOU GUYS, BUT I KNOW THE ONLY THING THAT YOU WOULD LIKE IS TO HAVE YOUR SISTER BACK AND TO STAY CLEAN. I WILL DO MY VERY, VERY BEST, SHALL, AND REALLY THINK BEFORE I EVER PICK UP AGAIN, IF THERE IS A NEXT TIME. PRAY FOR ME ALWAYS, PLEASE.

I LOVE YOU SO MUCH!

ME

We never found out the results of her UA because she left before they came back. Jay had called her while she was staying with me and said he wanted a divorce, but it never happened.

<u>TUESDAY, FEBRUARY 2, 2010, MICHELLE'S JOURNAL</u>:

TODAY IS TUESDAY. IT'S BEEN ONE WEEK AND A DAY SINCE NAT CAME. I WROTE A COUPLE OF THINGS I REMEMBERED THE

LAST COUPLE OF DAYS. THE FIRST NIGHT SHE WAS HERE, WE HAD PRAYERS AND SCRIPTURE STUDY BEFORE BED AND AUSTIN SAID THE PRAYER AND THANKED HEAVENLY FATHER FOR LETTING NANA SPEND SOME TIME WITH US. SHE STARTED CRYING. SHE WOULD ALSO (2X) MAKE EXCUSES TO RUN BACK IN THE HOUSE WHEN WE WERE LEAVING SOMEWHERE, ONCE FOR SMOKES AND ONCE FOR SUNGLASSES. SHE HAS COME UP WITH EXCUSES EVERY DAY IN THE AFTERNOON FOR WHY SHE ACTS DIFFERENT. DAY 1-FALLING ASLEEP EVERYWHERE WAS BECAUSE OUR COUSIN WHOM SHE WAS STAYING WITH BEFORE SHE CAME DIDN'T LET HER GET ANY SLEEP EVER. DAY 2-SHE SAYS SHE'S COMING OFF METH. DAY 3-METHADONE TOO STRONG (60MG). DAY 4-UPPED HER TO 70MG OF METHADONE AND TOLD THE CLINIC SHE WAS HAVING MAJOR WITHDRAWALS BY 4:00 EVERY DAY (SHE WAS SLEEPING AT THAT TIME EVERY DAY) SO IT CONTRADICTED WHAT SHE WAS TELLING ME. SO, I CALLED CLINIC, SHE STILL CLAIMS SHE IS CLEAN. SHE STARTED GETTING REALLY ENERGETIC THIS DAY AND EVERY DAY AFTER. ENDLESS ENERGY. ASKED ME ONE DAY IF HER EYES LOOKED WEIRD. SATURDAY MORNING, SHE GOT 70MG AT 12:00, SHE STARTED SAYING SHE WAS SICK. WE CAME HOME FROM GETTING KIERRA AND SHE RAN RIGHT DOWNSTAIRS AND CLAIMS SHE THREW UP BUT NOT THE METHADONE OR IT WOULD HAVE BEEN PINK, SO SHE MUST HAVE ABSORBED IT ALREADY SHE SAID. SHE LOOKED GAUNT AND HER EYES LOOKED DIFFERENT. SHE MADE EXCUSES FOR IF HER UA COMES BACK DIRTY, THEN IT WAS TYLENOL WITH CODEINE AND MORPHINE SHE GOT FROM OUR COUSIN. SHE SAYS SHE'S BEEN COMPLETELY CLEAN SINCE SHE HAS BEEN HERE, FOR THE FIRST TIME IN FIFTEEN YEARS. I'VE BEEN CONFRONTING HER ABOUT PROSTITUTION AND WHEN SHE STARTED USING AT FIFTEEN AND MENTAL ISSUES-TOLD HER I READ HER JOURNAL AT MOM'S-SHE WASN'T UPSET. SUNDAY BEFORE CHURCH, SHE SAID SHE WAS GOING TO PUKE-SAID SHE WAS OVER MEDICATED. I TOLD HER SHE HAD TO GO, TO GET UP AND GET READY. ONCE SHE

WAS THERE, SHE WAS FINE. SAID SHE TOOK THE METHADONE TOO LATE–10:00–I TOLD HER THE OTHER DAY SHE DIDN'T TAKE IT UNTIL 11:30 SO IT COULDN'T BE THAT. WE CAME HOME AND WATCHED HOME VIDEOS. SHE SEEMED DETACHED EMOTIONALLY AND KEPT GOING OUT. THAT NIGHT, WE HAD A LONG TALK, I TOLD HER AGAIN THAT I THINK SHE'S USING IN MY HOUSE AND GAVE HER ANOTHER OPPORTUNITY TO COME CLEAN–SHE DENIED IT. STARTED FROM AGE FIFTEEN AND WE DISCUSSED HOW SHE ENDED UP THIS WAY. 15–CHEERLEADER, DROPPED, GOT MUSCLE RELAXERS. 16–DRINKING AND PILLS, PREGNANT AND GALLBLADDER SURGERY–GOT PAIN PILLS. DR. KEPT GIVING THEM TO HER, PERCOCET. DRINKING AND PILLS CONTINUED UNTIL, SHE CLAIMS, FIVE YEARS AGO. MET KENNEDY IN LAYTON HOUSE, SHE SWAPPED MORPHINE AND PERCOCET WITH HER. USED WHILE SHE WAS PREGNANT WITH JALA (METHADONE, I THINK), WHICH SHE GOT FROM JENNIFER, SHE SWAPPED FOR PERCOCET, THEN TO GET OFF METHADONE MARY AND DAVID TOLD HER TO TAKE METH–GAVE HER SOME–SUPPLIED HER, THEN TO COME DOWN OFF METH, SHE WOULD USE HEROIN–HAS USED HEROIN, COCAINE, METH, PILLS, AND ANYTHING SHE CAN GET. LIVED WITH SUPPLIERS AND DEALERS AND SOLD HERSELF FOR THE DRUGS. SAID SHE BECAME A SUPPLIER AND GOT STUFF FROM HER HEROIN DEALER AND SUPPLIED PEOPLE. THAT'S WHAT SHE WOULD DO ALL DAY AND NIGHT–RUN DRUGS TO AND FROM PEOPLE–HITCHED RIDES WITH WHOEVER, NEVER SLEPT. MONDAY, WE HAD A GOOD DAY. SHE HAD TONS OF ENERGY, HELPED OUT A LOT. LATER THAT DAY, SHE SHOWED ME HER WRISTS AND SAID SHE SHAVED AND THEY LOOKED WORSE. THEY LOOKED LIKE NEW TRACK MARKS TO ME. WENT WITH TYE TO PICK UP KIERRA AND DIDN'T REMEMBER HIS TRUCK FROM TWO DAYS PREVIOUS. TODAY, TUESDAY, WENT TO CLINIC, STILL NO UA RESULTS, I'M ANXIOUS TO GET THEM AS PROOF OF HER USING. TOLD COUNSELOR THAT IT WOULD PROBABLY SHOW POSITIVE FOR MORPHINE BECAUSE SHE TOOK STUFF AT OUR COUSIN'S, AND

HE SAID NO IT SHOULDN'T BECAUSE SHE TOOK IT THREE DAYS BEFORE BEING HERE AND THE TEST ONLY GOES BACK THREE DAYS. SHE SAID, "OH, THAT'S RIGHT," THEN TALKED ABOUT ACCURACY OF UA AND SAID SHE'S PROBABLY DIGGING HER OWN GRAVE BY ADMITTING PEOPLE BUY URINE TO PASS UAS AND JAY'S GOING TO ASK IF I WATCHED HER GIVE UA AND WANTED TO KNOW WHY NOBODY WATCHED HER. DAVEY TOLD ME URINE SELLS ON THE STREET–EVEN WITH TRACES OF METHADONE–SO PEOPLE CAN PASS UAS, AND WOMEN PUT IT IN BALLOONS OR GLOVES AND PUT IT IN THEM SO IT'S BODY TEMP, AND GIVE UAS. SICK! WE TALKED ABOUT HER MENTALLY BEING A FIFTEEN-YEAR-OLD BECAUSE HER BRAIN NEVER HAD A CHANCE TO DEVELOP PAST THEN. SHE DIDN'T LIKE HEARING THAT. I HAD HER SHOW HER WRISTS–HE SAID THEY LOOKED THE SAME AS WHEN SHE GOT HERE. I DISAGREE. SHE DENIED SLEEPING THE FIRST 4-5 DAYS. TOLD US TO COME UP WITH A PLAN SO SHE COULD GO BACK THIS WEEKEND. I TOOK HER TO VOLUNTEER CLINIC TO GET TWO TEETH PULLED–INFECTION–SHE'S RESTING IN THE THEATRE ROOM.

Nat decided she needed to go back home on Thursday the 4th. I'm sure she was running low on her supply. I was very eager for her to go. I was exhausted! My husband drove her home, and she asked to be dropped off at I-15 and 1300 South in Salt Lake on the side of the road.

TUESDAY, FEBRUARY 23, 2010, MICHELLE'S JOURNAL:

TODAY IS NAT'S BIRTHDAY. I JUST TEXTED HER AND TOLD HER I LOVED HER AND WISHED HER A HAPPY 31ST BIRTHDAY. I AM SO HEAVY HEARTED TODAY FOR SOME REASON. JUST THINKING ABOUT HER AND 31 YEARS OF LIFE AND 16 OF IT ON DRUGS, IT'S UNBELIEVABLE. I FEEL SO SAD FOR HER KIDS (I ALWAYS DO) BUT EVEN MORE TODAY ON THEIR MOM'S BIRTHDAY. THIS IS A VERY DIFFICULT TRIAL FOR ALL OF US–WATCHING SOMEONE YOU LOVE DESTROY THEIR LIFE AND

THROW AWAY THE BEST THINGS IN LIFE FOR DRUGS. I PRAY FOR HER AND HER CHILDREN EVERY DAY.

Nat moved into Linda's house (Jay's friend), where Jay and Jala were living, and she was going to Stevens-Henager College; she wanted to be a nurse. She had received a grant to pay for school, and also received a laptop from the school, which she was supposed to return when she left. Instead, she sold it. I don't recall how she ended up living with Jay and Jala again. She was still using heavily but able to hide it from Jay. My family and I moved back from Saint George in May of 2010 and stayed until the following April, then returned to live in Saint George.

Five months later...

FRIDAY, JULY 30, 2010, NAT'S JOURNAL:

IT'S FRIDAY AND I AM LAYING DOWN WITH THE SWEETEST LITTLE GIRL IN THE WORLD, MY PRINCESS JALA. WE HAVE HAD A PRETTY GOOD DAY SO FAR. ME, JAY, AND JALA JUST GOT BACK FROM WALMART SHOPPING. I'M A LITTLE (ACTUALLY MORE THAN I WANT TO ADMIT) DEPRESSED THIS WEEKEND. MY WHOLE FAMILY, SHALL, TYE, ANGIE, RANDY, MOM, & DAD, ALL WENT TO IDAHO, TAKING MY TWO KIDS ALONG WITH THEM TO STAY AT EMILY'S BECAUSE IT'S JASA'S *(Em's daughter)* BAPTISM TOMORROW. I WAS NOT INVITED. IT DOESN'T SURPRISE ME AT ALL THAT I WASN'T INVITED, BUT IT IS ABSOLUTELY KILLING ME INSIDE THAT I AM NOT THERE FOR JASA'S SPECIAL DAY. I WOULD NOT HAVE MISSED THAT FOR ANYTHING.

I AM HOPING AND PRAYING EVERY SINGLE DAY AND NIGHT THAT ONE DAY MY FAMILY WILL FORGIVE ME.

A couple of days later....

SUNDAY, AUGUST 1, 2010:

TODAY WAS A VERY RELAXING DAY. IT WASN'T BAD AT ALL. AS LONG AS I AM WITH AT LEAST ONE OF MY BEAUTIFUL KIDS THEN I AM SOMEWHAT OKAY. BUT EVERY SINGLE DAY, WITHOUT FAIL, I HAVE A PIT IN MY STOMACH AND FEEL LIKE SOMETHING IS MISSING AND I FEEL COMPLETELY OFF. IT WON'T EVER GO AWAY TILL I HAVE ALL THREE OF MY KIDS BACK LIVING WITH ME IN THE SAME HOME. I WILL NEVER BE OKAY UNTIL THEY ARE ALL WITH ME IN THE SAME HOME UNDER THE SAME ROOF. YA, JUST SAID THE SAME THING TWICE BECAUSE MY CHILD IS NOT LIKING ME WRITING AND NOT PLAYING WITH HER. I AM JUST NOT HAPPY AT ALL IN MY LIFE RIGHT NOW. I AM TEMPORARILY LIVING WITH JAY AND JALA RIGHT NOW, BUT NOT FOR LONG, AND I AM SO STRESSED BECAUSE I HAVE NO HOME AND NO IDEA WHERE I AM GOING TO LIVE. I DON'T HAVE MY HUSBAND ANYMORE, BEEN SEPARATED FOR OVER A YEAR, AND DON'T HAVE ANY OF MY KIDS (OR HAVE ANY RIGHTS TO THEM). IT LITERALLY BREAKS MY HEART AND TEARS MY INSIDES APART. I WANT MY FAMILY BACK MORE THAN ANYTHING IN THIS WORLD AND I WILL DO ABSOLUTELY ANYTHING AND EVERYTHING TO GET THEM BACK.

MONDAY, AUGUST 2, 2010:

TODAY WASN'T SO EXCITING. JAY AND JALA WENT TO HIS PARENTS' HOUSE AND I WENT SHOPPING AT WALMART WITH MY ANNOYING FRIEND ANTHONY (NOT SO MUCH A FRIEND). GOT A BUNCH OF STUFF FOR JALA AND ADI'S NOTEBOOKS THAT SHE NEEDED FOR SCHOOL. SAW CHRISTOPHER TODAY FOR ABOUT TWENTY MINUTES. POOR GUY. HE'S GETS OUT OF JAIL IN TWO DAYS, THEN GETS SHIPPED BACK TO HONDURAS. HE IS

PLANNING ON COMING BACK IN TWO WEEKS AFTER HE IS IN HONDURAS, BUT IF HE GETS CAUGHT BACK HERE, HE WILL GO TO PRISON FOR TWENTY YEARS. SAD. GOTTA FIND A PLACE TO LIVE THIS WEEK AND I AM SO EXTREMELY STRESSED OUT. WHAT IF I CAN'T FIND SOMEWHERE TO LIVE? I HOPE AND PRAY THAT I WILL. *(Jay told her she couldn't live there permanently; this was just temporary).*

TUESDAY, AUGUST 3, 2010:

TODAY WAS ONE OF THE BEST DAYS I HAVE HAD IN A VERY LONG TIME. WOKE UP NEXT TO MY BABY GIRL AND I WAS SUPPOSED TO HAVE SCHOOL TODAY BUT DECIDED TO STAY HOME WITH MY LITTLE GIRL. I CAN MISS ONE DAY, IT'LL BE OKAY. I JUST HAVE A HELL OF A LOT OF MAKEUP WORK TO DO. MY MOM CAME TO PICK ME AND JALA UP TO TAKE ME TO DOSE AT THE CLINIC *(methadone)* AND ADI AND MAS CAME ALONG FOR THE RIDE. *(I recently asked my mom what Mas thought about going to the methadone clinic and she said Nat just told him she had to go get medicine to keep her from getting sick).* WE CAME BACK HOME (JALA & I) AND WE GOT READY AND MY MOM CAME BACK A COUPLE HOURS LATER TO PICK US UP AND WE HUNG OUT ALL DAY AND NIGHT AT MY MOM'S WITH ADI AND MAS. JAY MET US THERE RIGHT WHEN WE GOT THERE AND HUNG OUT OVER THERE WITH US. DIDN'T GET TO SPEND MUCH TIME WITH MASON AND JALA BECAUSE I WAS WITH ADI THE WHOLE TIME DOING HER NAILS AND TALKING WITH HER. IT WAS REALLY NICE. IT'S GOING TO BE REALLY HARD WHEN I LEAVE HERE (WHICH WILL PROBABLY BE NEXT WEEK) BECAUSE I WON'T BE LIVING WITH JALA ANYMORE. SHE JUST GOT USED TO HAVING ME BACK AGAIN AND IT'S GOING TO BE REALLY HARD FOR HER TO BE WITHOUT HER MOMMY AGAIN. I CAN'T EVEN THINK ABOUT IT OR I WILL BREAK DOWN. I PRAY THINGS WILL WORK OUT FOR THE VERY

BEST FOR ME, MY KIDS, AND JAY. I WANT US ALL BACK TOGETHER AND ALL HAPPY.

WEDNESDAY, AUGUST 4, 2010:

I WENT TO SCHOOL TODAY FROM 8:30 TO 2:15. MY FIRST CLASS IS MED AND MY SECOND IS ENGLISH. THEY ARE BOTH PRETTY HARD, BUT I WILL GET THROUGH IT. STILL LIVING AT LINDA'S HOUSE WITH JAY AND JALA, AND OTHER THAN BEING AROUND LINDA AND HER KIDS, I ABSOLUTELY LOVE IT BECAUSE I GET TO BE WITH MY BABY GIRL. I'M REALLY STRESSED OUT, THOUGH, EVERY SINGLE DAY BECAUSE I NEED TO LEAVE HERE WITHIN TWO DAYS AND I HAVE ABSOLUTELY NO IDEA WHERE I AM GOING TO GO. I HAVE NO FRIENDS AND NO FAMILY. I FEEL ALL ALONE ALL THE TIME. MY LIFE IS ABSOLUTELY NOT A HAPPY ONE RIGHT NOW. I WISH I COULD BE WITH MY KIDS AND HAVE A PLACE TO CALL HOME FOR ONCE. I'M SO EXTREMELY HOMESICK AND WISH I HAD AT LEAST ONE PERSON I COULD TALK TO AND CONFIDE IN. THE ONE AND ONLY PERSON I THOUGHT I COULD TRUST COMPLETELY WENT BEHIND MY BACK AND SIDED WITH SOMEONE ELSE. JAY WAS THE ONE AND ONLY PERSON THAT HAS STAYED BY MY SIDE AND THAT I COULD TALK TO AND TRUST. NOW, WE ARE FIGHTING ONCE AGAIN, AND HE IS BELIEVING LINDA OVER ME. I DON'T HAVE ANY REASON TO LIE TO JAY OR BETRAY HIM. I HAVE ALREADY DONE THAT ONCE BEFORE AND I WILL REGRET THAT TILL THE DAY I DIE. I REALLY HOPE THIS LIFE GETS BETTER.

FRIDAY, AUGUST 6, 2010:

IT'S ABOUT 2:00 IN THE AFTERNOON AND SO FAR, TODAY HAS BEEN AN OKAY DAY. HOPEFULLY, I WILL STILL BE SAYING THAT BY TONIGHT. BEEN TALKING TO LINDA MOST OF THE DAY, SHE LITERALLY DRIVES ME CRAZY, BUT SHE

IS DEFINITELY HELPING ME OUT SO MUCH BY GIVING ME A PLACE TO STAY. I REALLY AM THANKFUL FOR THAT BECAUSE MY OWN FAMILY WOULDN'T EVER GIVE ME A PLACE TO STAY, LET ALONE ANY OF MY FRIENDS. *(My parents let her live with them multiple times, and the minute they would find out she was using, they would kick her out.)* OH WAIT, I DON'T HAVE ANY FRIENDS. AND I HONESTLY DON'T. THIS IS THE VERY FIRST TIME IN MY LIFE WHERE I ABSOLUTELY HAVE ZERO FRIENDS. WHEN I SAID MY KIDS AND JAY WERE ALL I HAVE, I TRULY MEANT IT. SOMETIMES I FEEL LIKE I DON'T HAVE THOSE FOUR EITHER. WELL, LATELY I DON'T HAVE JAY TO CONFIDE IN. HE PRETTY MUCH BETRAYED ME AND PUT ME ON THE SIDE WAY BEHIND HIS FRIENDS. THAT IS ABSOLUTELY NOT WHAT I DESERVE AND NOT HOW I WANTED TO BE TREATED. I LOVE JAY, MORE THAN ANYONE BESIDES MY KIDS, BUT I WILL NOT CHASE HIM OR BE WITH ANYONE THAT DOESN'T WANT TO BE WITH ME. JAY HAS DEFINITELY SHOWN ME TIME AND TIME AGAIN SINCE I HAVE BEEN LIVING WITH HIM AND LINDA THAT HE DOES NOT LOVE ME ANYMORE AND THAT HE HAS PUSHED ME SO FAR ASIDE THAT I DON'T REALLY EVEN EXIST IN HIS "PERFECT LITTLE WORLD." MAKES ME REALLY SAD BUT ALSO OPENS MY EYES. SOMETHING I NEEDED TO SEE, AND EVEN THOUGH IT'S GOING TO BE ONE OF THE HARDEST THINGS I WILL EVER HAVE TO DO, I HAVE TO LET HIM GO AND I NEED TO MOVE ON WITH MY LIFE WITHOUT HIM.

I AM LITERALLY ALWAYS, ALWAYS UNHAPPY. EVERY DAY JUST KEEPS GETTING WORSE AND WORSE. I AM GOING ABSOLUTELY NOWHERE IN MY LIFE AND DON'T HAVE A SINGLE PERSON IN MY WORLD THAT GIVES A SHIT. I'M REALLY NOT JUST FEELING SORRY FOR MYSELF, MY LIFE RIGHT NOW IS A DEAD END. I REALLY DON'T WANT TO REMEMBER THIS FEELING, BUT I AM HOPING AND PRAYING THAT IT GETS BETTER. IF IT DOESN'T, I AM TRULY HONESTLY SCARED ABOUT WHAT MIGHT HAPPEN TO ME. I HAVE NO FUTURE IF I DON'T GET ANY OF MY KIDS BACK, AND IT DOESN'T LOOK TOO PROMISING

CONSIDERING THE TWO MEN I HAVE TO FIGHT TO GET THEM BACK.

SATURDAY, AUGUST 7, 2010:

TOMORROW IS ADISON'S 14TH BIRTHDAY! I CAN'T BELIEVE MY BABY GIRL IS GOING TO BE FOURTEEN! TIME FLIES WAY TOO, TOO FAST. I HAVE NOT HAD ENOUGH TIME WITH HER AND IT LITERALLY BREAKS MY HEART. WELL, ALL I CAN DO NOW IS WORK MY HARDEST TO GET MY KIDS BACK AND SPEND ALL THE TIME THAT I CAN TILL THEY ARE OLD ENOUGH TO HAVE A FAMILY OF THEIR OWN. I LOVE ALL THREE OF MY KIDS MORE THAN ANYTHING IN THIS WHOLE ENTIRE WORLD. RIGHT NOW, I OWE MY EX ALMOST $8,000 IN CHILD SUPPORT. HOW IN GOD'S NAME AM I EVER GOING TO COME UP WITH THAT AND FIGHT HIM IN COURT TO GET MY KIDS BACK? I DON'T EVEN HAVE AN ATTORNEY ANY LONGER 'CAUSE ONE DROPPED ME 'CAUSE I COULDN'T PAY HER. LIFE IS HARD AND SOMETIMES I JUST DON'T WANT TO GO ON. BUT THERE ARE THREE BEAUTIFUL KIDS THAT ARE STOPPING ME FROM DOING ANYTHING STUPID.

SUNDAY, AUGUST 8, 2010:

IT'S ADISON'S BIRTHDAY! ME, JAY, AND JALA WENT TO GRANDMA'S HOUSE 'CAUSE ADI AND KIERRA WERE HAVING THEIR BIRTHDAY DINNER THERE AND IT WAS GREAT AT FIRST, THEN ADI LEFT FOR A MINUTE TO PRACTICE SOMETHING FOR CHURCH AND ALL THE GIRLS WENT UPSTAIRS (MY SISTERS) AND STARTED TALKING ABOUT HOW MUCH FUN THEY HAD THIS YEAR AND ALL THE VACATIONS THEY WENT ON. NONE OF THEM EVEN ACKNOWLEDGED THAT I WAS IN THE ROOM, I GUESS 'CAUSE WHILE THEY WERE ON THEIR VACATIONS, I WAS TRYIN' TO FIND A PLACE TO LAY MY HEAD AT NIGHT. SOMETIMES I JUST FEEL LIKE I SHOULD GO TO HONDURAS

WITH CHRISTOPHER 'CAUSE HE KEEPS ASKING ME TO AND I HAVE NOTHING OR NOBODY HERE TO STOP ME. I HONESTLY DO NOT THINK MY FAMILY OR MY SISTERS ARE EVER GOING TO COME AROUND. I AM STUCK ALL ALONE AND I AM EXTREMELY SCARED!

MONDAY, AUGUST 9, 2010:

YESTERDAY WAS MY BABY'S BIRTHDAY. SHE TURNED FOURTEEN YEARS OLD. SHE IS TALLER THAN ME AND ABSOLUTELY BEAUTIFUL. I'M DEFINITELY GOING TO HAVE MY HANDS FULL WHEN I FINALLY GET MY INCREDIBLE KIDS BACK WITH ME. YESTERDAY WAS DEFINITELY NOT THE WAY I HAD HOPED OR PLANNED. ADI, MAS, AND JALA HAD A GREAT TIME AND EXCELLENT DAY, BUT I WISH MINE HAD BEEN BETTER. I HARDLY GOT TO SEE MY DAUGHTER (ADISON) ON HER BIRTHDAY AT ALL. TO START THE DAY OFF, I DIDN'T HAVE THE MONEY I WAS PLANNING ON GETTING SO I COULDN'T EVEN BRING ADI HER BIRTHDAY PRESENT THAT SHE WAS SO EXCITED TO GET ALL WEEK. I'M STILL NOT GOING TO HAVE THE MONEY FOR HER BIRTHDAY PRESENT FOR ANOTHER COUPLE OF DAYS. WHAT KIND OF MOTHER AM I?

BUT ONE THING THAT DID MAKE ME HAPPY WAS THAT JAY CAME TO ADI'S BIRTHDAY DINNER AND STAYED WITH ME ALL AFTERNOON. THAT REALLY MEANT A LOT TO ME. AND LITTLE MISS JALA ABSOLUTELY LOVES AND ADORES HER BROTHER AND SISTER, ADI AND MAS, MORE THAN ANYBODY IN THIS WORLD. I LOVE MY KIDS!

IT'S ABOUT 12:00 A.M. AND LAYING IN BED WITH JAY AND JALA. *(She was still living with Jay at Linda's).* HAD A PRETTY GOOD DAY TODAY ACTUALLY. I WENT WITH JALA AND JAY TO THE FARMINGTON POOL AND WE ALL HAD A BLAST. THEN

AFTER WE WENT TO MICHAEL'S AND GOT STUFF FOR CREATIVE TIMES. JAY IS MAKING THINGS FOR JALA AND THEY ARE SO CUTE. HE ALREADY MADE HER A DOLL HOUSE AND NOW HE IS MAKING A BRIDGE. THEY ARE AWESOME. SAW ADI AND MAS FOR JUST ABOUT AN HOUR AT MY MOM'S. I MISS THEM. THEY ARE TWO ABSOLUTELY AMAZING KIDS. I AM GOING TO FIGHT LIKE HELL VERY SOON TO GET THEM BACK, ATTORNEY OR NOT. THEY ARE MY EVERYTHING.

The next day...

TUESDAY, AUGUST 10, 2010:

WELL, TODAY SUCKED, AS ALWAYS. I GOT UP, WENT TO SCHOOL, CAME HOME, WAS LITERALLY LINDA'S MAID UNTIL ONE, LAID DOWN ABOUT A HALF HOUR AGO. IT'S ABOUT 11:00 P.M., JAY WAS GONE THE ENTIRE NIGHT AT VOLLEYBALL IN OGDEN WITH ALL HIS BROTHERS. JALA STAYED HERE WITH ME. SHE WAS TIRED FROM BEING AT LAGOON ALL DAY AND I WAS REALLY BUSY CLEANING AND DOING HOMEWORK SO I REALLY CAN'T BLAME HER. I JUST FEEL SO BAD THAT I WAS SO UPTIGHT ALL NIGHT AND WORRIED AND THINKING ABOUT WHAT AND WHO JAY WAS WITH WHEN HE REALLY DOESN'T HAVE AN INTEREST IN ME. I HONESTLY NEED TO COMPLETELY FORGET ABOUT HIM AND TRY AND MOVE ON. BUT RIGHT NOW, HE IS ALL I HAVE. I DON'T KNOW WHAT TO DO, I STILL HAVE NO IDEA WHERE I AM GOING TO GO AFTER I LEAVE LINDA'S AND I AM SCARED TO DEATH. I HAVE ABSOLUTELY NOBODY IN MY LIFE THAT GIVES A DAMN ABOUT ME AND I HAVE NEVER BEEN THIS WAY BEFORE IN MY ENTIRE LIFE. I ALWAYS HAD PEOPLE FIGHTING ABOUT WANTING TO BE AROUND ME. NOW, I AM ALL ALONE AND HAVE NOBODY TO HELP ME. I HOPE THIS LIFE GETS BETTER.

Three days later...

FRIDAY, AUGUST 13, 2010:

WELL, MY DAYS ARE MOSTLY THE SAME LATELY. I WAKE UP, DOSE *(methadone)* (WHICH I AM SO, SO SICK OF), CLEAN THE HOUSE, BE LINDA'S SLAVE, TAKE CARE OF MY LITTLE PRINCESS, WHICH I DON'T GET TO PLAY WITH A LOT DURING THE DAY 'CAUSE I AM SLAVING OVER LINDA, THEN EAT DINNER, BATHE, THEN GO TO BED. I HONESTLY DON'T DO MUCH OF ANYTHING EVER. IT'S GETTING REALLY FRUSTRATING. I AM SO EXTREMELY LONELY AND BORED. I HONESTLY HAVE NEVER EVER BEEN THIS ALONE AND THIS BORED. I HAVE ALWAYS HAD PEOPLE AROUND ME, GOSH, I EVEN ALWAYS HAD PEOPLE, OTHER GIRLS, EVEN WANT TO BE EXACTLY LIKE ME. THEY WOULD EVEN GO TO LENGTHS AND RUIN MY LIFE AND BECOME JUST LIKE ME BECAUSE THEY WERE SO VERY JEALOUS OF ME AND WANTED TO TAKE MY LIFE OVER. AND NOT TO MENTION ALL THE GUYS I HAVE ALWAYS TRIED TO JUGGLE BECAUSE THERE WERE ALWAYS SO MANY MEN WHO WANTED TO BE WITH ME. NOW, I HAVE ABSOLUTELY NOBODY. I DON'T CARE ABOUT MEN BECAUSE THAT GOT OLD REALLY FAST, BUT IT WOULD BE VERY NICE TO HAVE AT LEAST ONE FRIEND TO TALK TO. THIS SUCKS SO BAD. I LOVE SPENDING TIME WITH JALA DURING THE DAY, IF I COULD REALLY PAY ALL MY ATTENTION TO HER, OTHER THAN THAT MY LIFE LITERALLY SUCKS. I ABSOLUTELY HATE MY LIFE RIGHT NOW. I HOPE AND PRAY EVERY DAY AND NIGHT THAT THINGS WILL GET BETTER.

SATURDAY, AUGUST 14, 2010:

JUST SITTIN' HERE NEXT TO MY BABY GIRL JALA AND JAY, RELAXIN' ON A SATURDAY AFTERNOON. I REALLY SHOULD BE DOING MY HOMEWORK, 'CAUSE I HAVE A LOT OF IT, BUT

INSTEAD I'M WRITING IN MY JOURNAL, COLORING WITH JALA, AND WATCHING MOVIES WITH JAY. AFTER ALL, I HAVE DONE HOMEWORK EVERY NIGHT THIS WEEK AT LEAST 3 TO 4 HOURS AT A TIME. I'M A LITTLE BURNED OUT AND MY BRAIN JUST CAN'T FUNCTION ANYMORE! ADI AND MAS ARE IN YELLOWSTONE WITH THEIR DAD AND I MISS ADI AND MAS SO VERY, VERY MUCH. MY 3 KIDS ARE 100% EVERYTHING TO ME AND NOTHING WILL EVER, EVER CHANGE THAT. EVERY DAY, I FEEL SO LONELY AND ALWAYS FEEL LIKE THERE IS SOMETHING MISSING. WELL, THERE IS, ADI, MASON, AND EVEN THOUGH I'M LIVING WITH JAY AND JALA RIGHT NOW, I KNOW IT'S NOT GOING TO BE VERY MUCH LONGER AND I AM DREADING THAT DAY MORE THAN ANYTHING IN THIS WORLD. THAT DAY IS DEFINITELY GOING TO BE ONE OF THE WORST DAYS OF MY LIFE, WATCHING THE ONE THING THAT PUTS A SMILE ON MY FACE EVERY DAY, WALK AWAY FROM ME. MY BABY GIRL JALA. I CAN'T EVEN THINK ABOUT IT WITHOUT CRYING. I AM PRAYING THAT THINGS IN MY LIFE WILL GET BETTER SOON. IT'S NOW 10:00 PM. SATURDAY NIGHT AND WE ARE ALL THREE LAYING IN BED WHILE JAY READS BEDTIME STORIES TO OUR LITTLE MISS JALA. SHE IS DEFINITELY THE MOST BEAUTIFUL LITTLE GIRL IN THIS ENTIRE WORLD, BESIDES ADISON, OF COURSE. MY KIDS ARE LITERALLY THE MOST BEAUTIFUL KIDS EVER. THEY ARE MY WHOLE ENTIRE LIFE AND ALWAYS WILL BE. I JUST WISH I HAD A HUSBAND (MY HUSBAND) TO SPEND EACH DAY WITH AND GO TO SLEEP AT NIGHT WITH. I STILL ABSOLUTELY LOVE JAY, BUT WE JUST CAN'T EVER SEEM TO GET ALONG. WE'LL JUST SEE WHAT HAPPENS.

<u>SUNDAY, AUGUST 15, 2010</u>:

IT IS NOW ABOUT 9:00 P.M. SUNDAY NIGHT. TODAY WAS AN OKAY DAY. I HAVE TO STUDY A LOT TONIGHT BECAUSE I HAVE A BIG EXAM TOMORROW IN SCHOOL. I GET REALLY NERVOUS EVERY TIME I HAVE ONE OF THESE. BUT, I HAVE

PASSED EACH ONE SO FAR. I HONESTLY CAN'T BELIEVE IT EITHER! CHRISTOPHER CALLED ME TODAY AND HE HAS BEEN IN ARIZONA FOR ABOUT A WEEK NOW. HE IS HAPPY HE IS FINALLY GETTING OUT OF JAIL. BLESS HIS HEART, HE JUST SHOULD NOT EVEN HAVE BEEN THERE. HE DEFINITELY LEARNED SOMETHING ABOUT CROSSING THE BORDER AND NOT BEING LEGALLY HERE. IT SUCKS FOR PEOPLE LIKE THEM (IMMIGRANTS), THEY DEFINITELY HAVE IT HARD. HE IS STILL BEGGING ME TO GO TO HONDURAS WITH HIM AND I WOULD, BUT I CAN'T LEAVE BOUNTIFUL AT ALL BECAUSE I NEED TO DOSE AT THE CLINIC EVERY STINKING MORNING. I *HATE* IT SO STINKIN' BAD. BUT IT'S BETTER THAN BEING ON HEROIN, THAT'S FOR SURE. WELL, BETTER GET STUDYING.

MONDAY, AUGUST 16, 2010:

HAD SCHOOL TODAY AND HAD A BIG EXAM AND I KICKED ASS. TOTALLY PASSED. I AM SO EXTREMELY PROUD OF MYSELF. I JUST HOPE I DO THAT WELL ON ALL MY OTHER EXAMS. IF I STUDY THEM, THEN I KNOW I WILL. DIDN'T DO MUCH OF ANYTHING ELSE AFTER SCHOOL 'CAUSE I WASN'T FEELING SO WELL. OF COURSE, JAY WAS NOT HAPPY WITH ME, DON'T ASK ME WHY. SO, WE DIDN'T GET ALONG THE WHOLE NIGHT. I ABSOLUTELY HATE FIGHTING WITH HIM. I HAVE ACCEPTED THAT WE ARE NOT GETTING BACK TOGETHER, IT SUCKS BUT IT'S REALITY.

TUESDAY, AUGUST 17, 2010:

IT'S ABOUT 4:00 TUESDAY AFTERNOON AND JALA AND I JUST GOT HOME FROM SWIMMING WITH LINDA AND HER KIDS. IT WAS A FUN DAY SO FAR. I SWAM WITH JALA BASICALLY THE WHOLE TIME AND SHE FOUND OUT TODAY THAT SHE WON'T DROWN WITH A LIFE JACKET ON! IT TOOK HER A MINUTE TO

LET GO OF ME, BUT ONCE SHE DID, IT WAS ALL GOOD! SHE SWAM ALL BY HERSELF FROM THAT POINT ON. JUMPED IN THE POOL ALONE AND EVERYTHING. SHE HAD LOTS OF FUN AND NOW SHE IS RIGHT NEXT TO ME IN BED, OUT COLD! PRECIOUS LITTLE THING. I LOVE HER SO MUCH! TONIGHT IS DEFINITELY BETTER THAN LAST NIGHT, THAT'S FOR SURE! NOW JUST SITTING DOWN WITH JAY WATCHING A MOVIE. I'M JUST HOPING WE GET ALONG LONG ENOUGH. ADI AND MAS ARE FINALLY COMING HOME FROM YELLOWSTONE!

IT'S NOW 10:00 P.M. WE JUST GOT HOME FROM DONNA'S HOUSE, WHICH IS RIGHT ACROSS THE STREET FROM LINDA'S HOUSE, WHERE I AM LIVING RIGHT NOW. ME AND JAY HUNG OUT WITH DONNA AND HER HUSBAND, WHICH IS A COP, WHILE JALA AND HER LITTLE GIRL PLAYED TOGETHER. IT WAS NICE ACTUALLY TALKING WITH A FRIEND. HOPEFULLY I WILL SEE MORE OF HER, I NEED A FRIEND!

WEDNESDAY, AUGUST 18, 2010:

WOKE UP TODAY, WENT TO SCHOOL (WHICH I WASN'T FEELING GOOD THE ENTIRE TIME), CAME HOME, CLEANED UP AROUND THE HOUSE, THEN WENT SWIMMING WITH JAY, JALA, LINDA AND HER KIDS. IT WAS ACTUALLY A GOOD TIME, WE ALL HAD A LOT OF FUN. AFTER SWIMMING, JAY AND I MADE DINNER AND IT WAS AWESOME. WE MADE SPAGHETTI AND MEATBALLS AND SOUR CREAM SALAD. I HAVE NOT HAD A MEAL LIKE THAT IN WHO KNOWS HOW LONG. IT WAS FANTASTIC AND JAY AND I HAD A GOOD TIME MAKING DINNER TOGETHER. IF WE GOT ALONG LIKE WE DID TONIGHT, EVERY OTHER DAY, WE WOULD BE A PERFECT COUPLE AND HAVE AN AWESOME MARRIAGE. TOO BAD WE CAN'T HAVE THAT,IT WOULD BE A DREAM COME TRUE FOR ME BECAUSE THEN I WOULD HAVE MY FAMILY BACK. AND THAT IS ABSOLUTELY ALL I WANT IN MY LIFE. I WILL JUST KEEP PRAYING.

Six days later...

TUESDAY, AUGUST 24, 2010:

TODAY WAS HONESTLY ONE OF THE BEST DAYS I HAVE HAD IN A VERY LONG TIME. LAST NIGHT, JAY AND I GOT INTO THE BIGGEST AND WORST FIGHT THAT WE HAVE EVER HAD. BUT AFTER WE CALMED DOWN AND ACTUALLY REALIZED HOW WE WERE TREATING EACH OTHER, IT OPENED BOTH OF OUR EYES. TODAY, ALL DAY LONG, WE BOTH TREATED EACH OTHER WITH NOTHING BUT KINDNESS AND RESPECT. THAT FIGHT, ODDLY ENOUGH, WAS DEFINITELY MEANT TO HAPPEN TO CHANGE THE BOTH OF US AND SHOW US HOW TO TREAT EACH OTHER. I DEFINITELY DO NOT WANT TO EVER HAVE ANOTHER FIGHT LIKE LAST NIGHT, BUT IT WAS A BLESSING IN DISGUISE THAT WE BOTH NEEDED.

WEDNESDAY, AUGUST 25, 2010:

JUST ANOTHER SHITTY DAY FOR NATALIE! LATELY, I JUST CAN'T SEEM TO STAY AWAY FROM THEM. IT REALLY, REALLY SUCKS! HAD SCHOOL TODAY AND HAD MY FINAL EXAM AND I PASSED IT. I THOUGHT I WOULD BE A LITTLE MORE EXCITED THAN I AM. I JUST DON'T HAVE ANYONE TO SHARE MY GOOD NEWS WITH AND IT MAKES ME REALLY DEPRESSED. I AM HOPING AND PRAYING THAT THIS LIFE GETS BETTER. AND THE ONLY THING THAT I KNOW WITHOUT A DOUBT IN MY MIND IS THAT ONCE I HAVE ALL 3 OF MY PRECIOUS KIDS BACK LIVING WITH ME, I WILL BE HAPPIER THAN I EVER HAVE BEEN BEFORE IN MY LIFE. IT WILL BE MY HEAVEN. GOING TO PRAY NOW.

FRIDAY, AUGUST 27, 2010:

THIS IS THE LAST THURSDAY I HAVE FREE, STARTING NEXT WEEK I HAVE TWO MED CLASSES. *STAY CLEAN!*

Almost two weeks later...

Nat moved back in with our parents; they believed she was clean.

MONDAY, SEPTEMBER 6, 2010:

WELL I CAN'T EVEN BELIEVE IT MYSELF, I'M STILL IN SHOCK! I AM OUT OF BITCH LINDA'S HOUSE AND BACK AT MY LOVELY PARENTS' HOUSE AT THIRTY-ONE YEARS OLD. JAY AND I ARE NOT AT ALL ON GOOD TERMS RIGHT NOW AND I AM MISSING MY BABY GIRL LIKE CRAZY. JAY AND I GOT INTO A HUGE FIGHT A COUPLE OF DAYS AGO AND THEY BOTH TOLD ME I HAD TO LEAVE. I HAVE ABSOLUTELY NOBODY AND NOWHERE TO GO. SO I BROKE DOWN AND CALLED MY DAD. I LITERALLY BEGGED HIM TO GIVE ME ONE LAST CHANCE AND LET ME COME HOME. HE TOLD ME MOM WOULD ABSOLUTELY NOT LET ME, AND HE TOLD ME TO GO TO A HOMELESS SHELTER. I LITERALLY ALMOST PUT A KNIFE TO MY THROAT. I WOULD MUCH RATHER DIE THAN EVER PUT MYSELF IN A HOMELESS SHELTER. I CAN'T IMAGINE WHAT MY KIDS WOULD THINK OF ME THEN. I CALLED ANGIE, MY ONE AND ONLY WHOLE-HEARTED SISTER, AND SHE WAS HONESTLY MY VERY LAST RESORT. SHE WAS INCREDIBLE TO ME. SHE TOLD ME THERE WAS ABSOLUTELY NO WAY SHE WAS LETTING ME GO TO A HOMELESS SHELTER. SHE TALKED TO RANDY AND THEY CALLED MY MOM AND DAD AND TALKED THEM INTO LETTING ME COME BACK HOME. WITHOUT THEM, I WOULD LITERALLY BE DEAD RIGHT NOW OR ON THE STREET DYING. THEY WERE MY MIRACLE.

THURSDAY, SEPTEMBER 9, 2010:

TODAY WAS AN OKAY DAY. GOT UP, WENT TO SCHOOL, CAME HOME AND LOOKED FOR JOBS ONLINE, THEN AT 7:00 P.M. WENT WITH MY MOM AND SHALL TO A RELIEF SOCIETY MEETING *(a function in our church).* IT WAS AWESOME! I ABSOLUTELY LOVED THE TALK AND IT REALLY MADE ME THINK AND, OF COURSE, VERY, VERY EMOTIONAL. I ABSOLUTELY LOVE MY MOTHER!

IN COLLEGE, IN MY COMMUNICATIONS CLASS, I HAD TO DO AN ASSIGNMENT WHERE I HAD TO ASK AS MANY PEOPLE AS I COULD QUESTIONS ABOUT ME. I HAD TO ASK THEM WHAT TRAITS THEY THOUGHT I HAD…THIS IS WHAT PEOPLE SAID ABOUT ME…

JAY SAID, WHEN WATCHING MOVIES WITH ME, IT'S FUNNIER WATCHING ME THAN THE MOVIE BECAUSE I REALLY GET INTO THEM, HE ALSO SAYS THAT I AM A CLOSET ROCK FAN (AND I DON'T WANT ANYONE TO KNOW THAT) AND I AM AN OCD FREAK WITH PERSONAL HYGIENE AND MY HOME. HE SAYS I AM VERY SELFLESS (NOW) WHICH IS COMPLETE OPPOSITE OF HOW I USED TO BE, AND I PUT OTHERS AROUND ME FIRST. A LOT OF PEOPLE TOLD ME THAT I DO NOT HOLD GRUDGES AND IN A GENERAL SETTING I'M A VERY NICE AND FUN PERSON. JAY AND A COUPLE OTHER PEOPLE ALSO SAID THAT PEOPLE ARE DRAWN TO ME. I USUALLY COME ACROSS AS SELF-RELIANT AND POSITIVE, BUT AT MOST TIMES, AN EASILY DISTRACTED YOUNG GIRL. I WAS REALLY NERVOUS ABOUT ASKING OTHER'S WHAT THEY THOUGHT OF ME, BUT AFTER I WAS THROUGH, I WAS EMOTIONAL AND VERY HAPPY!

FRIDAY, SEPTEMBER 10, 2010:

I AM ABSOLUTELY GOING TO FIND A JOB TODAY! IT'S NOW 12:33 FRIDAY MORNING AND I AM GOING TO HAVE AN AWESOME

DAY TODAY! SO FAR THIS TIME AROUND, LIVING AT MY PARENTS' HAS BEEN INCREDIBLY WELL! I AM SO THANKFUL TO BE HERE AROUND MY MOM AND DAD IN A NICE HOME RATHER THAN A HOMELESS SHELTER! I CAME SO VERY, VERY CLOSE TO GOING TO THE HOMELESS SHELTER.

Ten days later...

MONDAY, SEPTEMBER 20, 2010:

MY DAD'S BIRTHDAY. IT'S 4:00 A.M. MONDAY MORNING, LAYING IN BED DOWNSTAIRS AT MY PARENTS' HOUSE (WHICH IS STILL GOING VERY, VERY WELL). I AM ACTUALLY VERY THANKFUL AND HAPPY TO BE LIVING HERE AGAIN. I GET PLENTY OF PRIVATE SPACE SINCE I AM THE ONLY ONE LIVING HERE BESIDES MY MOM AND DAD. IT'S ALWAYS SO CLEAN AND COMFORTABLE SINCE MY MOTHER IS AN OCD CLEAN FREAK, JUST AS HER DAUGHTERS ARE. I GET TO SEE MY OLDER KIDS (ADI AND MAS) A HELL OF A LOT MORE, I DON'T HAVE TO PAY A DIME TO LIVE HERE EVEN THOUGH I WANT TO HELP WITH FOOD AND STUFF. NOW THAT I GOT A JOB, I CAN. I START MY NEW JOB AT THE CHOCOLATE FACTORY AS THE MANAGER AT THE SALT LAKE AIRPORT. I START SEPTEMBER 27TH, NEXT WEEK. I AM SO EXCITED 'CAUSE I HAVE NOT HAD A SALARY PAYING JOB IN A VERY LONG TIME, AND IGGY'S (RESTAURANT/ BAR) IN CENTERVILLE PRETTY MUCH JUST HIRED ME TODAY. I'M WAY EXCITED BECAUSE IT'S WALKING DISTANCE FROM MY HOME AND ALSO CROWDED WITH LOTS OF FUN PEOPLE. I WILL ENJOY IT, I KNOW IT. THE ONLY DOWNFALL ABOUT ME GETTING BACK INTO THE BUSY JOB STATE IS THAT I WON'T BE WITH MY PRECIOUS JALA EVERY DAY ANYMORE.

Six days later...

SUNDAY, SEPTEMBER 26, 2010:

WELL, I ABSOLUTELY LOVE LIVING AT MY MOM'S HOUSE. IT'S ABOUT 2:00 IN THE AFTERNOON AND EVERYONE IS HERE. EMILY, SHALL, AND ANGIE. I ABSOLUTELY LOVE IT. I HAVEN'T BEEN WITH ALL MY FAMILY IN SO LONG.

FRIDAY, OCTOBER 1, 2010:

THE LAST FEW DAYS HAVE DEFINITELY NOT BEEN SO GOOD. I DID GET MY BADGE TODAY, THOUGH, TO START WORK AT THE AIRPORT NEXT WEEK AT THE CHOCOLATE FACTORY. I'M WAY EXCITED! I CAN'T WAIT UNTIL I ACTUALLY START WORKING (NOT TRAINING) WORKING!!! BUT, ON THE DOWNSIDE, I HAVE TO QUIT SCHOOL. I HAVE PUT A LOT OF HARD WORK INTO SCHOOL, BUT I JUST CAN'T DO THAT, WORK, KIDS, AND HAVE A LIFE OF MY OWN, IT JUST WOULDN'T WORK. I'M HAVING A REALLY HARD TIME WITH MY FAMILY RIGHT NOW. ANYTHING AND EVERYTHING I DO IS JUST NOT GOOD ENOUGH FOR THEM.

She only worked at the Chocolate Factory a couple times and then quit to work at Iggy's.

Two weeks later...

WEDNESDAY, OCTOBER 13, 2010:

TODAY I HAD AN ABSOLUTELY FABULOUS DAY. I GOT TO STAY AT HOME ALL DAY LONG WITH MY LITTLE PRINCESS JALA. I STARTED WORKING AT THE AIRPORT A COUPLE WEEKS AGO, SO I HAVEN'T BEEN ABLE TO STAY AT HOME WITH JALA ALL DAY LIKE I USUALLY AM AND IT'S REALLY STARTING TO AFFECT

HER AND ME. SHE'S MY BABY, I AM NOT HAVING ANY MORE KIDS, SO MY TIME WITH JALA IS PRECIOUS TIME.

OKAY, MY LIFE IS GETTING BETTER AND BETTER WITH EACH DAY THAT GOES BY, AND EXTREMELY BETTER THAN IT HAS BEEN FOR A VERY LONG TIME NOW. SO WHY AM I NOT OPENING MY EYES WIDER AND GROWING UP AND PUTTING A FINAL STOP TO THE ONE THING THAT RUINED MY LIFE COMPLETELY, TOOK MY KIDS AND MY FAMILY AWAY, AND MANY, MANY TIMES ALMOST KILLED ME? I AM ABSOLUTELY BETTER THAN I EVER HAVE BEEN WITH IT AND DROPPED ALL MY FRIENDS ALL TOGETHER SO I WOULD NOT BE TEMPTED IN ANY WAY OR BE AROUND BAD INFLUENCES AND PEOPLE THAT BRING ME DOWN. THERE IS JUST ONE PROBLEM, I AM MY OWN WORST INFLUENCE AND THE HARDEST PERSON ON MYSELF. I HONESTLY DON'T BELIEVE I CAN EVER FORGIVE MYSELF FOR WHAT I DID TO MYSELF, MY KIDS, MY FAMILY, AND MY HUSBAND AND IT SCARES ME TO DEATH BECAUSE I THINK IT'S GOING TO KILL ME.

WELL, THIS IS IT, I ABSOLUTELY CANNOT LIVE LIKE THIS ANYMORE AND NOBODY CARES ENOUGH ANYMORE TO HELP ME THROUGH ALL THIS SO IT'S ALL UP TO ME NOW, CHANGE MY WAYS TODAY AND WORK ON MYSELF EVERY DAY TO REALIZE I DO NOT NEED DRUGS IN MY LIFE ANY LONGER AND GET RID OF THEM FOR GOOD TODAY AND NO LATER OR SAY GOODBYE TO MY KIDS, BECAUSE IF I DON'T QUIT NOW, I NEVER WILL, AND I WILL DIE SOON. I HAVE HAD ENOUGH, IT'S UP TO ONLY ME NOW.

A week later...

WEDNESDAY, OCTOBER 20, 2010:

THIS MORNING WAS ABSOLUTELY HORRIBLE. JAY AND I GOT IN A HUGE FIGHT AND I WAS REALLY UPSET BECAUSE WE HAVE BEEN DOING REALLY GOOD LATELY. *(She never says what the fights are about; I am sure most of them are related to her using).* WELL, HE TOOK OFF AND TOOK JALA WITH HIM, SO SHE COULDN'T STAY WITH ME ANYMORE *(at our parents').* I WAS ABSOLUTELY FURIOUS. I AM SO SICK OF THESE TWO MEN (MY EX AND JAY) HAVING TOTAL CONTROL OVER MY BABIES. THAT WILL CHANGE VERY, VERY SOON. I WENT TO WORK AT THE AIRPORT AT ABOUT 6:30 AND GOT HOME AROUND MIDNIGHT. I AM HOPING TOMORROW WILL BE BETTER.

FRIDAY, OCTOBER 22, 2010:

SLEPT OVER AT JAY'S LAST NIGHT AND WATCHED MOVIES WITH HIM TILL 2:00 A.M. IT WAS AN OKAY NIGHT. DIDN'T WORK TODAY SO I GOT TO SPEND TIME WITH MY PRINCESS JALA ALL DAY TODAY. ANGIE CAME AND GOT US AROUND NOON AND MICHELLE SHOWED UP AT THE SAME TIME, ASKING ME IF I WOULD MIND TAKING ABOUT 45 MIN SUNDAY AND LETTING HER VIDEO RECORD ME TALKING ABOUT MY DRUG ADDICTION FOR AUSTIN'S SCHOOL. SHE THOUGHT I WAS GOING TO GET MAD AT HER FOR ASKING ME TO DO THAT, BUT I DIDN'T AT ALL. I TOLD HER I WOULD BE HAPPY TO DO IT BECAUSE I WOULD LOVE TO TELL MY STORY AND WHAT I HAVE BEEN THROUGH AND EXPERIENCED THE PAST TEN YEARS. I WANT MY STORY TO BENEFIT OTHER PEOPLE AND HOPEFULLY CHILDREN THAT REALLY LISTEN TO ME WILL LEARN FROM MY MISTAKES. I'M EXCITED TO DO IT. WENT TO ANGIE'S AFTER, SHALL CAME OVER AND HUNG OUT ALL DAY, THEN ADISON SHOWED UP AND WE ALL WENT TO THE TRAINING TABLE FOR DINNER. IT WAS A GOOD NIGHT SO FAR. AFTER DINNER, WE WENT TO THE MALL AND I BOUGHT ADI A HALLOWEEN COSTUME (REFEREE). IT'S DARLING. ADI WAS GOING TO SLEEP OVER WITH ME AND JALA AT ANGIE'S TONIGHT BECAUSE RANDY IS OUT OF TOWN AND JAY IS AT HIS BROTHER'S HALLOWEEN PARTY.

I asked Nat if I could video record her telling her story so I could show it to my son's school for Red Ribbon Week, which is a week they spend in the schools talking about drugs. She eagerly agreed.

Six days later...

THURSDAY, OCTOBER 28, 2010:

HAVEN'T WRITTEN IN A WHILE AND I THINK IT'S BECAUSE I FEEL ASHAMED AND FEEL LIKE THERE IS REALLY NOTHING GOOD ABOUT MY LIFE TO WRITE DOWN. I AM SO SICK AND TIRED OF WRITING DOWN NOTHING BUT NEGATIVE THINGS ALL THE TIME AND I WANT TO WRITE POSITIVE THINGS THAT MAKE ME HAPPY AND PROUD. WELL, I HAVE BEEN DOING LOTS BETTER AND I GOT A GOOD JOB AND STILL LIVE WITH MY MOM AND DAD, WHICH IS ABSOLUTELY AWESOME. I AM SO GRATEFUL TO HAVE THIS CHANCE HERE TO START OVER MY LIFE. I JUST CAN'T DO IT ALL ALONE. I SPEND MOST OF MY DAYS AND NIGHTS AT JAY'S PLACE AND STILL WANT TO BE WITH HIM, BUT HE WON'T TAKE ME BACK QUITE YET. MY TEETH ARE CONSTANTLY HURTING ALL THE TIME *(they were rotting and falling out from drug use)* AND I REALLY NEED TO WAKE UP, NAT, AND REALIZE WHAT I HAVE DONE TO MY BODY AND FINALLY TRY AND FIX IT.

I want to point out here that Nat always remembered everyone's birthdays in the family, including nieces and nephews, and she would always call or be with us to celebrate, until now. Even birthday phone calls stopped. Both of my sons have birthdays the first week of November and this year she didn't remember either.

A few days later…

WEDNESDAY, NOVEMBER 3, 2010:

WELL, A LOT HAS HAPPENED AND I CAN'T SAY IT HAS BEEN GOOD AT ALL. ACTUALLY, I HAVE BEEN THROUGH PROBABLY THE MOST TRAUMATIZING NIGHT I HAVE EVER, EVER HAD. HALLOWEEN NIGHT STARTED OUT ABSOLUTELY WONDERFUL, ME, JAY AND JALA, ADI AND MAS WERE UP AT SHALL'S HOUSE HANGIN' OUT TOGETHER ON HALLOWEEN. I WAS ON CLOUD NINE BECAUSE I HAD ALL THREE OF MY KIDS THERE AND MY HUSBAND. I WAS HAPPIER THAN I HAVE BEEN IN A VERY LONG TIME. WE ATE DINNER AND THE KIDS DRESSED UP JAY LIKE A WOMAN AND MADE A HAUNTED HOUSE THAT ACTUALLY THEY ALL PUT ON FOR TWO NIGHTS IN A ROW FOR ABOUT FOUR TO FIVE HOURS, AND LUCKILY, MANY CHILDREN CAME AND ABSOLUTELY LOVED IT. THE KIDS HAD A GREAT HALLOWEEN. BUT IT WAS ALL RUINED IN A SPLIT SECOND. ALL THREE OF MY KIDS WANTED TO RIDE HOME WITH GRANDMA, OF COURSE, SO WE LET THEM AND I DROVE HOME WITH JAY. WE LEFT ABOUT 10 P.M. AND THE ROADS WERE PACKED WITH PEOPLE. I GOT HOME AND WENT DOWN TO MY ROOM AND HEARD MY PHONE RING. MY PHONE HAD BEEN RINGING ALL NIGHT LONG, BUT THIS WAS THE ONLY RING I HEARD. I DIDN'T EVEN THINK TO AND I USUALLY DO, I IMMEDIATELY PICKED UP MY PHONE. IT WAS MASON TELLING ME THAT A DRUNK DRIVER HAD HIT THEM ON THE FREEWAY, AND THEY SPUN THREE TIMES AND ADI GOT HIT AND COULDN'T BREATHE. MY STOMACH DROPPED SO FAST, I FELT LIKE I COULD NOT EVEN TAKE ANOTHER BREATH. WELL, JAY HAD ALREADY LEFT SO I WENT UPSTAIRS AND FOUND MY DAD, HEARING THE NEWS HE DROPPED THE PHONE AND WE BOTH TOOK OFF IN HIS TRUCK. IT HAPPENED DIRECTLY IN FRONT OF LAGOON *(an amusement park)* AND WAS A SIX CAR PILEUP BECAUSE OF ONE DRUNK DRIVER. THEY DID SPIN THREE TIMES, GOT HIT BY TWO DIFFERENT CARS A NUMBER

OF TIMES AND ENDED UP FACING ONCOMING TRAFFIC ON THE FREEWAY. MY MOM'S EXPEDITION IS COMPLETELY TOTALED, BUT IT WAS A MIRACLE, JALA WAS OKAY, MAS WAS OKAY, MY MOM WAS OKAY, BUT ADI HAD TO GO TO THE HOSPITAL. SHE BRUISED HER LUNGS AND RIB ON HER RIGHT SIDE PRETTY BAD. MY KIDS AND MY MOM WERE DEFINITELY WATCHED OVER BY ANGELS THAT NIGHT.

• • •

CHAPTER 8

2011

IN 2011, NAT TURNED *thirty-two, Adi fifteen, Mas twelve, and Jala five.*

Five months later…

TUESDAY, APRIL 12, 2011:

I AM SO LOST, MORE THAN I THINK I HAVE BEEN IN A VERY LONG TIME. I AM IN A GOOD PLACE RIGHT NOW AT MY PARENTS' HOUSE, HAVE A GOOD JOB, SEE ADI AND MAS A LOT MORE NOW, AND HAVE MY BABY GIRL EVERY SINGLE DAY. EVERYTHING I HAVE EVER WANTED, BUT STILL NOT HAPPY AND FEEL LIKE I AM STANDING STILL, NOT GOING ANYWHERE IN MY LIFE. I WORK MY BUTT OFF EVERY DAMN DAY AND IT'S NOT ENOUGH, NEVER IS. STILL WANT MY HUSBAND BACK AND MY THREE KIDS BUT HONESTLY DON'T KNOW IF IT'S GOING TO HAPPEN. BUT I WILL NEVER STOP TRYING. I AM JUST AFRAID TO FALL AGAIN.

A month later...

FRIDAY, MAY 13, 2011:

IT'S FRIDAY, ABOUT 1:30 A.M., AND I'M JUST SETTLING IN BED AFTER A LONG NIGHT AT WORK. I HAVE WORKED AT IGGY'S NOW FOR ABOUT FIVE MONTHS *(eight months)* AND SO FAR, I ABSOLUTELY LOVE IT! IT'S VERY HARD WORK AND I AM ON MY FEET SOMETIMES FOR 12 HOURS A DAY. I HAVE NEVER WORKED SO HARD AT A JOB BEFORE AND IT'S NICE TO ACTUALLY MAKE MY OWN MONEY SINCE I HAVEN'T BEEN ABLE TO DO THAT FOR A VERY LONG TIME. LIVIN' AT MY PARENTS' HOUSE STILL AND I AM ACTUALLY TOTALLY FINE WITH IT. I HAVE BEEN HERE FOR ABOUT 7/8 MONTHS AND USUALLY BY NOW I WOULD BE GOING CRAZY TRYING TO GET OUT AND FINDING MY OWN PLACE TO LIVE. BUT, I HAVE BEEN THROUGH SO DAMN MUCH THE PAST 6/7 YEARS THAT I AM SO EXTREMELY GRATEFUL TO HAVE A PLACE TO LIVE. AND, A NICE PLACE TO LIVE LIKE THIS! I HONESTLY DON'T KNOW WHAT I WOULD DO IF MY PARENTS DIDN'T COME AROUND AND GIVE ME ANOTHER CHANCE. I AM DOING PRETTY GOOD, STILL ON METHADONE, WANT TO GET OFF MORE THAN ANYTHING BUT CAN'T RIGHT NOW. I PAY $400 MONTHLY BEING ON THIS SHIT, IT'S KILLING ME. BUT RIGHT NOW, IT'S JUST NOT A GOOD TIME TO TRY AND GET OFF. GOING TO BED, HAVE ANOTHER LONG WORKDAY TOMORROW.

A few weeks later...

TUESDAY, JUNE 7, 2011:

GETTING READY TO SLEEP AND THOUGHT I WOULD READ A COUPLE OF PAGES AND SEE HOW DIFFERENT MY LIFE IS TODAY COMPARED TO THEN. NIGHT AND DAY DIFFERENCE. I AM NOT EVEN CLOSE TO THE SAME PERSON THAT I WAS WHEN I WROTE

IN THIS JOURNAL BEFORE. I HAD MOST DEFINITELY FALLEN OFF MY ROCKER, I WAS CRAZY. BUT THAT'S WHAT DRUGS DO TO YA. THEY COMPLETELY FUCK YOU UP, MAKE YOU A DIFFERENT EVIL PERSON AND TAKE EVERYTHING THAT YOU HAVE AWAY. I AM A VERY LUCKY PERSON AND I REALLY DO NEED TO TELL MYSELF THAT ON A DAILY BASIS. THE MAJORITY OF PEOPLE THAT LIVED THEIR LIFE THE WAY I DID FOR THAT LONG OF A TIME DOING THE THINGS (DRUGS) I DID USUALLY END UP DEAD. I WAS DOWN THAT ROAD MORE TIMES THAN I CAN COUNT. EVERYONE, INCLUDING MYSELF, GAVE UP ON ME. WE ALL KNEW I WAS GOING TO DIE. I REALLY DO NEED TO BE MORE THANKFUL FOR HAVING THE STRENGTH THAT I DID AND THE DRIVE THAT I DID THAT GOT ME OUT ALIVE. I HONESTLY NEVER EVER THOUGHT THAT I WOULD BE BACK IN MY PARENTS' HOUSE IN THE BASEMENT AT THIRTY-TWO YEARS OLD WRITING IN MY JOURNAL REMINDING MYSELF THAT I AM A BETTER PERSON THAN I AM GIVING MYSELF CREDIT FOR LATELY. I KNOW I DID MY SHARE OF ABSOLUTELY UNFORGETTABLE, HORRIBLE THINGS TO MYSELF AND THE PEOPLE I LOVE, BUT I AM A CHANGED PERSON. I AM NOWHERE NEAR THE HORRIBLE PERSON THAT I WAS FOR SUCH A LONG TIME. THIS HAS DEFINITELY BEEN A CHALLENGE FOR ME AND THE ABSOLUTE HARDEST THING I HAVE EVER HAD TO FACE IN MY LIFE, IS GETTING OVER THE GUILT, SHAME, AND TRULY FORGIVING MYSELF FOR WHAT I DID TO MYSELF AND TO THE PEOPLE I LOVE. I AM DEFINITELY NOT THERE YET AND AM SOMETIMES REALLY FINDING IT HARD TO BELIEVE THAT I CAN ACTUALLY EVER REALLY FORGIVE MYSELF. THAT PERSON THAT I WAS FOR SO LONG SCARES ME TO DEATH BECAUSE IT IS NOT EVEN CLOSE TO BEING THE KIND OF PERSON THAT I REALLY AM. DON'T GET ME WRONG, I AM PROUD OF MYSELF FOR GETTING THIS FAR. I REALLY NEVER THOUGHT IN A MILLION YEARS THAT I COULD EVER GET OUT OF THAT TRASHY HOLE I WAS IN AND ACTUALLY TURN MY LIFE AROUND AGAIN AND BECOMING THAT PERSON

THAT I HAD LOST A LONG TIME AGO. WELL, I DID IT, I FOUGHT HARDER THAN I EVER HAVE IN MY LIFE BEFORE AND CHANGED MY LIFE. I AM WITH MY BABY JALA EVERY SINGLE DAY, WORKING AT IGGY'S AT NIGHT, AND ON MY WAY TO GETTING MY OTHER TWO KIDS BACK IN THE SAME HOME AS ME AGAIN. I SHOULD BE HAPPY RIGHT? NOT TODAY. I HAVE BEEN IN TEARS ALL DAY BECAUSE LAST NIGHT I RELAPSED. I AM SO MUCH STRONGER NOW AND NOWHERE NEAR THE SAME EVIL WOMAN THAT I WAS WHEN I WAS USING BUT I FUCKED UP AND IT WAS THE WORST EXPERIENCE THAT I HAVE HAD IN A VERY LONG TIME, THAT I KNOW I WILL NEVER DO IT AGAIN. I HAVE DONE AWESOME AND HAVE STAYED STRONG FOR A LONG TIME NOW BUT LAST NIGHT THAT DEVIL'S VOICE CAME INTO MY HEAD AGAIN AND I GAVE IN. WELL, I AM ACTUALLY VERY, VERY THANKFUL IT TURNED OUT THE WAY IT DID AND THAT I HAD ONE OF THOSE DAYS THAT I DON'T EVER WANT TO RELIVE AGAIN. AS HARD AS I AM BEING ON MYSELF TODAY, I AM THANKFUL IT HAPPENED BECAUSE NOW I KNOW THAT MY PAST WON'T BE HAUNTING ME ANY LONGER BECAUSE AFTER TODAY, I WILL NEVER PUT MYSELF IN THAT SITUATION AGAIN. I LIKE WHERE I AM RIGHT NOW, IN MY COZY BED IN MY PARENTS' HOUSE AND FEEL MORE COMFORTABLE AND MORE LOVED THAN I HAVE FELT IN YEARS. REMEMBER THIS SITUATION AND THIS FEELING…I WILL FROM THIS DAY FORWARD STAY CLEAN!!

I DON'T TAKE TIME OUT OF MY LIFE MUCH ANYMORE TO SIT DOWN AND WRITE. AND THE PAST FIVE MONTHS I HAVE BEEN WORKING MY ASS OFF AT IGGY'S. I LITERALLY WORK ALMOST EVERY STINKIN' DAY! IF I HAVE A DAY OFF DURING THE WEEK, I'M LUCKY IT HASN'T REALLY EVER BOTHERED ME BECAUSE I DO ENJOY MY JOB, BUT I AM DEFINITELY GETTING WORN OUT. THEY MADE ME CLOSE LAST WEEK WHICH IS A BIG COMPLIMENT TOWARDS ME BECAUSE I HAVE NOT BEEN THERE THAT LONG. BUT PAYNE CAME TO ME THE OTHER DAY TELLING ME HOW GRATEFUL HE IS THAT I AM THERE AND FOR

MAKING HIM LOOK GOOD BY MAKING ME A CLOSER BECAUSE I DID AN AWESOME JOB! THAT REALLY MADE ME FEEL SO MUCH BETTER ABOUT MYSELF, CONSIDERING IT HAS BEEN AN EXTREMELY LONG TIME THAT I HAVE HEARD ANYBODY WAS PROUD OF ME.

Same day, different journal:

HAD AN AWFUL DAY TODAY. I HAVE BEEN DOING SO WELL FOR A LONG TIME NOW AND HAVE MADE A LOT OF PROGRESS IN MY LIFE THAT I HONESTLY THOUGHT WOULD NEVER HAPPEN AND HAVE FINALLY STARTED MAKING SOMETHING OF MY LIFE AND GOING IN THE RIGHT DIRECTION NOW AND IN ONE NIGHT I FUCK IT ALL UP! I DON'T KNOW WHY BUT I RELAPSED LAST NIGHT, AND I HAVE NEVER IN MY ENTIRE LIFE FELT THAT MUCH GUILT AND SADNESS ALL DAY TODAY THAT I CAN HONESTLY TELL MYSELF, IT WILL *NEVER* HAPPEN AGAIN! IT SHOWED ME LAST NIGHT HOW EASY IT IS TO FALL BACK INTO MY LIFE THAT TOOK ME DOWN AND MADE ME LOSE EVERYTHING! AFTER LAST NIGHT, THAT OLD LIFE THAT I HATED SO MUCH THAT KEEPS HAUNTING ME AND TAUNTING ME, WILL ALL GO AWAY AND NEVER BE A THREAT AGAIN!

A week later…

TUESDAY, JUNE 14, 2011:

WELL, NOT TOO EXCITING OF A DAY. EMILY WAS HERE THE LAST COUPLE DAYS, SO I HAD ALL MY KIDS FOR THE LAST THREE DAYS, WHICH WAS AWESOME! *(Whenever Emily or I were in town, we tried to all be together as a family.)* SHE LEFT TODAY SO JALA AND I JUST TOOK IT EASY TODAY, THEN I HAD TO GO TO WORK. I GOT CUT REALLY EARLY BECAUSE IT WAS SO SLOW, SO NOW I AM HOME WAITING FOR JAY AND JALA TO GET OUT OF A MOVIE THAT THEY WENT TO SEE AND THEY ARE

PICKING ME UP TO STAY THE NIGHT OVER THERE. I STAY AT JAY'S ABOUT HALF THE TIME I SLEEP AT MY OWN HOUSE. I DON'T KNOW WHY WE DON'T JUST GET BACK TOGETHER! HE IS TOO SCARED, WHICH I DON'T BLAME HIM AT ALL, BUT I AM A DIFFERENT PERSON NOW AND HE KNOWS THAT, AND HE SPENDS ALL OF HIS TIME WITH ME AND HIS DAUGHTER! THAT WOULD BE MY DREAM COME TRUE, TO GET MY FAMILY BACK, BUT MY DREAMS DON'T SEEM TO EVER HAPPEN! I AM WORKING ON IT, THOUGH! IT'S REALLY NOT BAD STAYING HERE AT MY PARENTS, BUT I AM WORKING HARD TO GET MY SHIT TOGETHER TO GET MY KIDS BACK AND GET MY OWN PLACE. IT'S TAKEN A LONG TIME, BUT I WILL GET THERE! I KNOW I WILL!

Four months later...

10-19-2011: Dr. Note–Natalie is abusing Heroin and Methadone. 124 lbs., taking Rozerem *(sleeping medication)*, Methadone, Seroquel *(anti-psychotic medication)*, Paxil *(antidepressant)*, Buprenorphine *(treats pain and addiction and helps with withdrawals, same as Suboxone; I don't know why he prescribed both)*, and Suboxone.

10-26-2011: Dr. Note–Natalie called Dr., can't sit still, shaking. Dr. prescribed Carbidopa/Levodopa *(medication for Parkinson's disease, which she did not have)*. Needs to be seen if shaking doesn't stop. Dad called Dr. to say she was in ER yesterday for IV fluids. She took Suboxone 18 hours out from Methadone and had major withdrawals. Dad wanted to know when she could take her Suboxone. Hospital gave her nausea medication, Clonidine *(treats high blood pressure, ADHD, and cancer pain)* and Diazepam *(treats anxiety, muscle spasms, and seizures)*.

A few weeks later...

11-16-2011: Dr. Note–120 lbs. Took Buprenorphine too early and made her sick but got 16 mg, then ran out and used Heroin yesterday.

A few weeks later...

12-7-2011: Dr. Note–Canceled appointment.

12-28-2011: Dr. Note–Canceled appointment, got called into work.

• • •

CHAPTER 9

2012

IN 2012, NAT TURNED *thirty-three, Adi sixteen, Mas thirteen, and Jala six.*

1-9-2012: Dr. Note–116 lbs. Natalie has a hard time financially. Her friend gave her Suboxone for 2 months, holidays were hard but she's doing better, denies relapse. Prescribed Suboxone, Buprenorphine and Amitriptyline *(medication for nerve pain and depression).*

Nat was still living at our parents' home. My parents cosigned and put a deposit down on a brand-new Mazda car for her, and she was responsible for the monthly payment. They believed she was clean.

TUESDAY, JANUARY 24, 2012:

OBVIOUSLY, MY PRECIOUS BABY GIRL GOT AHOLD OF MY LITTLE BOOK AND DECIDED TO PUT STICKERS ON EVERY PAGE. SHE IS SO DAMN CUTE! JALA JUST TURNED 6 LAST WEEK AND I WAS SO SAD. MY BABY GIRL IS GROWING UP WAY TOO FAST! SHE HAD A REALLY GOOD BIRTHDAY. WE CELEBRATED IT ALL WEEK LONG. WE HAD EVERYONE OVER AT GRANDMA'S HOUSE TO DO CAKE AND OPEN PRESENTS. SHE IS DEFINITELY MY LITTLE HANDFUL! I HAD THE DAY OFF YESTERDAY, WHICH

IS NOT VERY OFTEN, SO ME, JALA, AND GRANDMA WENT TO SPARKLING NAILS AND GOT OUR NAILS AND TOES DONE. I LOVE DAYS LIKE THAT BECAUSE I DON'T GET THEM VERY OFTEN. I CLOSE THURSDAY-SUNDAY AND OPEN ON TUESDAY. I WORK ALL THE DAMN TIME. I HAVE REALLY ENJOYED MY JOB AT IGGY'S BUT NOW I AM GETTING A LITTLE BURNED OUT. I AM THE ONLY PERSON THERE THAT HAS FOUR CLOSING SHIFTS AND CLOSING GETS VERY TIRING AND TAKES A LOT OUT OF ME. I AM MAKING PRETTY DECENT MONEY. I AVERAGE AROUND $100 TO $150 A NIGHT (CLOSING) AND ABOUT $100 TO $130 OPENING. I JUST NEED TO BUDGET MY MONEY RIGHT *(most, if not all of her money was spent on her addiction)* AND THEN I CAN START LOOKING FOR A PLACE OF MY OWN. HOW WONDERFUL WOULD THAT BE? I REALLY NEED A PLACE OF MY OWN. I REALLY APPRECIATE ALL THAT MY PARENTS HAVE DONE FOR ME BY TAKING ME IN, BUT I FEEL LIKE SUCH A LOW LIFE LOSER ALL THE TIME. HOPEFULLY IT WILL HAPPEN SOONER THAN LATER. SO, I HAVE BEEN ASKED OUT THIS PAST WEEK MORE THAN I EVER HAD BEFORE. I AM THINKING ABOUT IT BECAUSE JAY JUST WON'T COMMIT TO ME. I DON'T BLAME HIM AT ALL. I JUST WISH HE WOULD GIVE ME ANOTHER CHANCE AND I COULD HAVE MY FAMILY BACK. THAT IS ALL I WANT! IS THAT TOO MUCH TO ASK FOR? I KNOW I PUT MY KIDS AND JAY THROUGH HELL AND BACK BUT IS IT THAT UNREASONABLE TO ASK FOR A SECOND CHANCE? I JUST DON'T KNOW WHAT IN THE HELL TO DO. I WANT TO MOVE ON WITH MY LIFE, BUT I DON'T WANT TO DATE AND GO THROUGH ALL THAT BULLSHIT AGAIN. AND, I DON'T KNOW HOW IT'S POSSIBLE TO GO OUT ON DATES WITH OTHER MEN WHEN MY HEART IS WITH ONE MAN ALREADY. I JUST WANT TO BE HAPPY FOR A CHANGE. I WORK MY ASS OFF AND DON'T EVER HAVE ANY FUN TIME FOR ME. I NEVER DO ANYTHING ANYMORE. ALL I DO IS WORK TO PAY MY BILLS AND SPEND TIME WITH MY KIDS. BUT I DON'T GET ENOUGH TIME WITH ADI AND MAS JUST QUITE YET. HOPEFULLY THINGS CAN START TO CHANGE

FOR THE BETTER. I'M TRYING TO WRITE MORE, I REALLY NEED TO.

Same day, different journal:

Jala's picture she drew for Nat

TODAY, I WORKED AND MADE VERY LITTLE MONEY AND WORKED MY ASS OFF. THAT'S THE RESTAURANT BUSINESS. I AM PRETTY DEPRESSED LATELY. I FEEL LIKE I'M STANDING STILL AND NOT GOING ANYWHERE IN MY LIFE. I WANT TO WORK THINGS OUT WITH MY HUSBAND, BUT HE JUST CAN'T COMMIT TO ME QUITE YET. I DON'T BLAME HIM AFTER EVERYTHING I PUT HIM THROUGH, BUT HOW LONG DO I WAIT? I HAVE BEEN WORKING MY ASS OFF AT IGGY'S FOR THE PAST YEAR AND HAVE NOTHING TO SHOW FOR IT BUT MY NEW CAR. IT IS SO HARD LIVING AT MY PARENTS' BEING 32, ALMOST 33 YEARS OLD. I FEEL LIKE THE BIGGEST LOSER AND I'M GOING CRAZY FEELING LIKE I WILL BE HERE FOR THE REST OF MY LIFE. COME HELL OR HIGH WATER, I WILL BE OUT OF MY PARENTS' HOUSE SOMEDAY, I JUST PRAY IT'S SOONER THAN LATER. THIS PAST WEEK, I HAVE BEEN ASKED OUT AT LEAST 3 TIMES BY DECENT MEN. I HAVE ABSOLUTELY NO DESIRE TO DATE ANYONE. I WISH I DID, BUT MY HEART IS STILL WITH JAY AND I AM SO EXHAUSTED ALL THE TIME. I AM JUST NOT HAPPY AT ALL WITH MYSELF RIGHT NOW. I NEED TO BE STRONG AND BE PROUD OF WHAT I HAVE DONE WITH MY LIFE SO FAR. BUT IT'S JUST NOT ENOUGH FOR ME. I DESERVE A BETTER LIFE THAN THIS. AND I KNOW I AM A BETTER PERSON THAN JUST WAITS TABLES AT A RESTAURANT DOWN THE STREET. I JUST DON'T KNOW HOW TO BETTER THINGS, MY SITUATION. I WANT TO BE HAPPY AND THE BOTTOM LINE IS, I WON'T BE TILL I

CHANGE MY LIFE, GET MY KIDS BACK AND MY HUSBAND AND HAVE A FAMILY AGAIN. THAT IS WHAT I WANT MORE THAN LIFE ITSELF, TO HAVE MY LITTLE FAMILY BACK. ME, JAY, ADI, MAS, AND JALA. THAT'S ALL I NEED.

WEDNESDAY, JANUARY 25, 2012:

I WAS GOING TO GO BACK AND READ THROUGH THIS *(journal)*, BUT I AM WAY TOO SCARED. I AM A TOTALLY DIFFERENT PERSON THAN I WAS A YEAR AGO AND STILL CHANGING FOR THE BETTER. I'M STILL NOT QUITE THERE YET, BUT IN A LOT BETTER PLACE NOW THAN I HAVE BEEN IN A VERY, VERY LONG TIME. I STILL HAVE A WAY TO GO, THOUGH.

I HAVE BEEN WORKING AT IGGY'S FOR OVER A YEAR NOW AND AM THE MAIN CLOSER. DOING GREAT OVER THERE BUT GETTING VERY BURNED OUT WITH IT. IT TAKES A LOT OF ENERGY THAT I REALLY DON'T HAVE. STILL LIVING AT MY PARENTS' HOUSE AND STILL FEEL LIKE A HUGE LOSER BECAUSE OF IT, BUT I AM VERY, VERY GRATEFUL THAT I HAVE THE CHANCE TO HAVE A GOOD RELATIONSHIP WITH MY MOM AND DAD AND A WONDERFUL PLACE TO LAY MY HEAD AT NIGHT. BUT THINGS REALLY DO NEED TO CHANGE. I NEED TO GET MY KIDS AND MY FAMILY (HUSBAND) BACK TO EVEN START TO FEEL HAPPY AGAIN. I DON'T EVEN KNOW WHAT IT FEELS LIKE TO BE HAPPY ANYMORE. I WANT THAT FEELING AGAIN AND HOPE I GET IT SOON. I WISH MYSELF LUCK THIS WEEK TO START AND CHANGE MY LIFE SO I CAN FEEL HAPPINESS AGAIN.

A few days later...

SATURDAY, JANUARY 28, 2012:

SO, I JUST GOT DONE READING SOME OF THESE PAGES IN FRONT OF THIS BOOK AND HOW FREAKING DEPRESSING THEY

ALL ARE. I AM IN A TOTALLY DIFFERENT SPOT THAN I WAS A YEAR AGO AND IN A MUCH BETTER PLACE IN MY LIFE. I HAVE A GREAT JOB AND A WONDERFUL PLACE TO LIVE (MY PARENTS') AND GET TO SEE MY KIDS ALL THE TIME. YA, A WHOLE HELL OF A LOT BETTER THAN HOW THINGS WERE A YEAR AGO. IT WAS REALLY HARD READING THROUGH THIS BOOK AND REMEMBERING, VERY CLEARLY, ALL THOSE HORRIBLE TIMES AND HOW AWFUL AND DISGUSTING MY LIFE WAS. IT'S STILL NOT AT ALL OR EVEN CLOSE TO WHERE I WANT IT TO BE, BUT AT LEAST RIGHT NOW I AM COMPLETELY INDEPENDENT AND GETTING TREATED LIKE AN ACTUAL PERSON RIGHT NOW RATHER THAN BEING 100% INVISIBLE TO THE PEOPLE I LOVE THE MOST.

I AM WORKING REALLY, REALLY HARD RIGHT NOW, HARDER THAN I THINK I HAVE EVER WORKED BEFORE IN MY LIFE. I WORK AT IGGY'S AND HAVE BEEN THERE A LITTLE OVER A YEAR NOW, GOT MYSELF A BRAND NEW CAR THAT I ABSOLUTELY LOVE ABOUT FOUR MONTHS AGO. BUT STILL NOT AT ALL WHAT I WANT OUT OF MY LIFE AND AM SO EXTREMELY UNHAPPY EVERY SINGLE DAY OF MY LIFE BUT TRYING TO PUT A SMILE ON MY FACE FOR MY KIDS AND PEOPLE AROUND ME. I DON'T KNOW WHAT ELSE TO DO TO MAKE MY LIFE BETTER AND HAPPY. I THINK I NEED TO DO WHAT I HAVEN'T DONE IN A VERY, VERY LONG TIME, IS TURN MYSELF TO HEAVENLY FATHER AND ASK HIM TO GUIDE ME AND START DOING THE THINGS I KNOW I NEED TO DO AND GETTING CLOSER TO THE CHURCH. I DON'T KNOW WHEN THE LAST TIME WAS THAT I TURNED MY LIFE OVER TO HEAVENLY FATHER AND HAVE DONE WHAT IS RIGHT SO I THINK NOW IS THE TIME TO DO IT, AND I HAVE A GOOD FEELING THAT MY LIFE WILL START TURNING AROUND FOR THE BETTER AND I CAN FINALLY START TO FEEL SOME KIND OF HAPPINESS. THIS IS THE ONLY THING THAT FEELS RIGHT TO DO, AND THE ONLY THING LEFT I HAVE TO TRY. I AM PRAYING THAT I CAN DO THIS AND THAT MY LIFE WILL TURN AROUND FOR THE BETTER AND I CAN FINALLY OPEN MY

EYES TO WHAT I AM SUPPOSED TO BE DOING. 'CAUSE GOD KNOWS I AM A LOST SOUL RIGHT NOW AND THINGS NEED TO CHANGE!

Same day, different journal:

WOW! TODAY WAS AN ABSOLUTELY CRAZY DAY AT WORK. IT WAS SO BUSY THAT WE HAD PEOPLE WAITING FOR OVER AN HOUR. I'M GETTING REALLY UPSET WITH MY JOB LATELY. AND IT'S NOT MY JOB ITSELF, 'CAUSE I REALLY DON'T MIND IT, BUT IT'S THE PEOPLE THAT COME IN. SOME PEOPLE JUST REALLY SHOCK ME. I THOUGHT I WAS GOING TO MAKE A LOT MORE THAN I WALKED WITH TONIGHT. IT REALLY UPSET ME BECAUSE I WORK REALLY HARD AT MY JOB AND DESERVE A LOT BETTER TIPS THAN PEOPLE ARE LEAVING. ON A GOOD NOTE, ADI AND HER BOYFRIEND DAKOTA CAME IN TO SEE ME TONIGHT AND EAT, THEY CAME IN WITH 2 MORE OF DAKOTA'S FRIENDS. THEY HAD FUN! I WALKED OUT WITH $145, BUT I HONESTLY THOUGHT I WAS GOING TO BE MAKING CLOSE TO $200 TONIGHT BECAUSE OF HOW OUT-OF-CONTROL CROWDED IT WAS AND I TURNED A BUNCH OF TABLES. HOPEFULLY IT WILL GET BETTER 'CAUSE I'M NOT LEAVING THERE ANYTIME SOON. I AM THEIR MAIN CLOSER. I DO REALLY LIKE MY JOB, THOUGH, IT GETS VERY OVERWHELMING AND STRESSFUL, BUT I DO ENJOY IT. I HAVE BEEN AT IGGY'S OVER A YEAR NOW. IT IS LIKE MY SECOND HOME NOW! SOMEBODY ASKED ME LAST NIGHT AT WORK IF I WAS MARRIED TO MY JOB? I HONESTLY DON'T HAVE TIME TO DO ANYTHING ANYMORE. I CLOSE THURSDAY–SUNDAY, OPEN TUESDAY, AND AM WITH MY KIDS MONDAY AND WEDNESDAY. I REALLY NEED TO START MAKING TIME FOR MYSELF BEFORE I GO CRAZY! BY THE TIME PEOPLE WERE SAT TONIGHT, THEY WERE ALL SO UNPLEASANT. I DEAL WITH MORE SOBER FACED, UNPLEASANT PEOPLE THAN I DO CHEERFUL AND HAPPY PEOPLE. HOW SAD IS THAT? IT IS REALLY HARD BEING A SERVER, PUTTING A

HAPPY FACE ON ALL THE TIME NO MATTER WHAT AND BENDING OVER BACKWARDS FOR PEOPLE AND CATERING TO THEIR EVERY WANT AND DESIRE. THE MAJORITY OF THE TIME, THEY DON'T TIP US WHAT WE DESERVE, NOT EVEN 1/2 OF WHAT WE DESERVE. IT'S GETTING A LOT HARDER FOR ME TOO, AS TIME GOES ON. I HAVE BEEN AT IGGY'S FOR A LITTLE OVER A YEAR NOW AND I THOUGHT I WOULD GET USED TO THE CHEAP, DEMANDING DUMBASS PEOPLE THAT COME IN ALL THE TIME, BUT I'M NOT. IT'S GETTING ACTUALLY WORSE FOR ME EVERY DAY THAT GOES BY, I JUST CAN'T BELIEVE HALF THE PEOPLE IN THIS WORLD AND HOW ABSOLUTELY SELFISH THEY ARE. SOMETIMES, I GET SO CLOSE TO SAYING SOMETHING TO THE CUSTOMER OR JUST WALKING OUT. I WOULD NEVER DO THAT BECAUSE I NEED THIS JOB MORE THAN ANYTHING, BUT IT DOES GO THROUGH MY MIND MORE THAN 10 TIMES A NIGHT. I'M REALLY UPSET LATELY AND DON'T KNOW WHAT TO DO ABOUT IT, I ACTUALLY SHOULD SAY REALLY DEPRESSED. I WORK 5 NIGHTS A WEEK (ALL WEEKENDS) AND THE DAYS I HAVE OFF I SPEND WITH MY KIDS. WHICH, DON'T GET ME WRONG, THERE IS ABSOLUTELY NOTHING MORE I WOULD RATHER DO THAN BE WITH MY KIDS, BUT I NEED A BREAK FOR ME, DO SOMETHING FOR ME. I DON'T EVEN KNOW THE LAST TIME I WENT OUT WITH ANYONE BESIDES MY KIDS AND HAD FUN. THE ONLY PERSON I HANG OUT WITH IS JAY AND I LOVE THAT BECAUSE I LOVE HIM, BUT WE DON'T GO DO ANYTHING. WE JUST STAY AT HIS HOUSE AND WATCH MOVIES. MY LIFE IS GOING NOWHERE AND IT'S REALLY CREEPING AND STRESSING ME OUT. I DON'T KNOW WHETHER TO MOVE ON WITHOUT JAY, WHICH I REALLY DON'T WANT TO DO, OR JUST KEEP BEING PATIENT AND SEEING WHAT HAPPENS BETWEEN US. I AM SO CONFUSED AND SO SAD AND FEEL LIKE I AM ALL ALONE AND IN A BIG HOLE THAT I JUST CANNOT SEEM TO CLIMB OUT FROM. I AM SO THANKFUL FOR HOW MY LIFE IS RIGHT NOW VS. HOW IT WAS A COUPLE YEARS AGO, EVEN LAST YEAR, BUT I NEED TO MOVE AND CAN'T SEEM TO KEEP UP OR MOVE

FORWARD. I STILL HAVE A WHOLE HELL OF A LOT TO WORK ON, BUT IT IS SO DIFFICULT RIGHT NOW. I DON'T HAVE ANY FRIENDS TO TALK TO OTHER THAN FRIENDS AT WORK, BUT NONE OF THEM ARE PEOPLE I WANT TO LET INTO MY LIFE FURTHER THAN WORK. I AM SERIOUSLY SO FUCKING LONELY THAT IT IS KILLING ME. I NEVER WANTED MY LIFE TO BE LIKE THIS AND I AM DOING EVERYTHING I CAN TO CHANGE IT, BUT IT'S JUST NOT ENOUGH. I DON'T KNOW IF GETTING MORE INVOLVED WITH THE CHURCH IS THE RIGHT ANSWER OR NOT. I HAVE BEEN GOING WITH MY KIDS EVERY SO OFTEN TO CHURCH AND IT'S BEEN GOOD. I THINK I MIGHT START GETTING MORE INVOLVED WITH MY RELIGION AND SEE IF HEAVENLY FATHER CAN HELP ME OUT OF THIS RUTT OR NOT. WISH MYSELF LUCK!

Adi and Nat

<u>TUESDAY, JANUARY 31, 2012</u>:

WATCHIN' *FROSTY THE SNOWMAN* WITH MY SWEET BABY GIRL. IT'S MOMENTS LIKE THIS THAT I ABSOLUTELY TREASURE. SHE IS NOW SIX AND I AM FREAKING OUT. MY BABY GIRL IS GROWING UP WAY TOO FAST. SHE IS AN AMAZING LITTLE GIRL. I AM SO VERY PROUD OF ALL THREE OF MY KIDS. THEY ARE TRULY INCREDIBLE KIDS. I COULDN'T ASK FOR BETTER CHILDREN. THAT'S WHY IT MAKES ME LITERALLY ILL KNOWING THAT I GOT THEM TAKEN FROM ME. I WOULD GIVE ANYTHING TO TAKE THAT TIME PERIOD ALL BACK AND DO IT DIFFERENTLY SO MY KIDS WOULD STILL BE WITH ME.

I'M WORKIN' ON IT, EVERY DAY, TRYING TO GET THEM BACK WITH ME. I'M IN A MUCH, MUCH BETTER PLACE NOW THAN I HAVE BEEN IN YEARS. BUT, I STILL HAVE A LOT OF STUFF TO FIX IN MY LIFE. I WILL DO IT! MY KIDS ARE MY ABSOLUTE EVERYTHING AND THEY ARE GROWING UP WAY TOO FAST TO WASTE ANY TIME. ADI IS FIFTEEN AND MAS IS TWELVE. ADI HAS A BOYFRIEND (DAKOTA) THAT SHE HAS HAD FOR A WHILE NOW. HE SEEMS LIKE A GOOD KID, BUT IT STILL FREAKS ME OUT. SHE IS STILL MY BABY GIRL.

WISHING MYSELF LUCK, ALL THE LUCK IN THE WORLD TO GIVE ME STRENGTH AND COURAGE EACH DAY TO GET MY LIFE BACK WITH MY KIDS AND MY HUSBAND THE WAY IT SHOULD BE. I WILL GET THERE, I KNOW I WILL!!

ANOTHER DAY AT WORK, WHICH WAS A TIRING BUT OKAY DAY BECAUSE I MADE DECENT MONEY TODAY. I OPENED TODAY AND WALKED WITH $165 TODAY. I WAS EXCITED BECAUSE IT'S BEEN REALLY SLOW LATELY AND TIPS HAVE BEEN ABSOLUTELY HORRIBLE. I AM EXTREMELY EXHAUSTED TODAY, THOUGH, BECAUSE I STAYED OVER AT THE HOSPITAL LAST NIGHT WITH SHALL BECAUSE SHE HAD BACK SURGERY. IT SUCKED SO BAD BECAUSE I HAD TO TRY AND SLEEP IN A CHAIR THAT BARELY RECLINED. I GOT NO SLEEP LAST NIGHT, BUT I WOULD DO IT AGAIN IN A HEARTBEAT BECAUSE IT WAS FOR MY SISTER. STILL HAVING A HARD TIME. I JUST WANT TO BE HAPPY AND UNTIL I GET MY KIDS, MY HUSBAND, AND MY OWN PLACE TO LIVE. IT'S HARD TO STAY HOPEFUL BECAUSE I KNOW IT'S A LONG WAY OFF. I NEED MORE STRENGTH AND TO STAY POSITIVE AND IT'S VERY HARD FOR ME TO DO THAT. I JUST KEEP THINKING TO MYSELF, HOW DID I LET MY LIFE TURN OUT LIKE THIS, AND AM I EVER GOING TO BE ABLE TO TURN IT AROUND AND HAVE THE LIFE I HAVE ALWAYS WANTED FOR ME AND MY THREE KIDS. I LOOK AT MY THREE SISTERS AND WOULD GIVE ANYTHING TO HAVE WHAT THEY HAVE. I HOPE AND PRAY THAT I WILL HAVE THAT SOMEDAY. I WISH MYSELF GOOD LUCK.

THURSDAY, FEBRUARY 2, 2012:

I HAVE ABOUT THREE JOURNALS RIGHT NOW AND I ALWAYS SEEM TO LOSE THEM, SO I FIGURE THREE WILL HELP ME OUT A LITTLE MORE. I LIKE TO GO BACK AND READ AND USUALLY IT MAKES ME VERY HAPPY BECAUSE I HAVE COME A VERY LONG WAY THAN WHERE I WAS LAST YEAR. I AM VERY, VERY GRATEFUL FOR WHAT I HAVE NOW AND THE SUPPORT FROM MY FAMILY THAT I HAVE BEEN WANTING FOR YEARS AND YEARS NOW, BUT I AM NOT WHAT I KNOW I AM CAPABLE OF. STILL, I WANT AND NEED MORE AND IT'S KILLING ME THAT I DON'T HAVE IT ALL YET. I AM LITERALLY WORKING MY ASS OFF AT IGGY'S AND HAVE BEEN A LITTLE OVER A YEAR NOW AND I AM HONESTLY GETTING SO BURNED OUT. I DON'T EVER TAKE ANY TIME FOR MYSELF AND NEVER EVER HAVE ANY KIND OF FUN. IT'S REALLY GETTING TO ME. I AM SO EXTREMELY DEPRESSED AND HONESTLY HAVE NOBODY TO TALK TO. MY SISTERS ARE THE ONLY PEOPLE I OPEN UP TO AND CONFIDE IN, BUT THEY DON'T NEED TO WORRY ABOUT ME RIGHT NOW AND THEY COULDN'T HELP ANYWAY WITH WHAT I NEED. I NEED TO DIG MYSELF OUT OF THIS DARK HOLE ALL BY MYSELF. I AM THE ONLY ONE THAT CAN TURN MY LIFE AROUND AND MAKE WHAT I WANT HAPPEN. IT'S JUST SO FUCKING HARD. I NEED MORE STRENGTH AND MORE FAITH. I KNOW I CAN DO THIS, IT'S JUST TAKING A LOT LONGER THAN I THOUGHT. THE MORE TIME I TAKE, THE FURTHER DOWN THIS YUCKY HOLE I AM GETTING. I BETTER PULL MY ASS OUT SOON AND VERY SOON. GOOD LUCK, NAT! YOU CAN DO THIS! ONE OF THESE DAYS, HOPEFULLY SOON, I AM GOING TO WRITE HOW PROUD OF MYSELF I AM AND HOW HAPPY I AM. I AM JUST PRAYING IT WILL BE SOMETIME SOON.

It makes me so sad knowing she felt she had to pull out of this on her own. I often wonder what would have happened if she would have just opened up to our family and told the truth and asked for help. Instead, all of us had to guess how she was doing and try to help her without knowing what was really going on in her head and in her life.

DAYS ARE JUST PASSIN' AND PASSIN' WAY TOO FAST FOR ME TO KEEP UP. I AM GETTING VERY, VERY IMPATIENT THE PAST FEW WEEKS WITH MY DULL LIFE. NOTHING IS CHANGING. I GO TO WORK, ALMOST EVERY DAY, TILL REALLY, REALLY LATE, WHICH GIVES ME NO TIME TO HAVE ANY FUN AT ALL, THEN RAISIN' MY BABY GIRL, WHICH I WILL NEVER COMPLAIN ABOUT THAT. I ABSOLUTELY ADORE MY LITTLE PRINCESS, BUT I FEEL LIKE I AM NOT GIVING HER THE LIFE SHE DESERVES. SHE NEEDS TO GO PLAY, DO FUN THINGS AND ENJOY LIFE. ALL SHE DOES IS GO TO SCHOOL AND HANG OUT WITH ME UNTIL I GO TO WORK, WHICH IS USUALLY ONLY A COUPLE OF HOURS BY THE TIME SHE GETS OUT OF SCHOOL AND I HAVE TO GO TO WORK. IT BREAKS MY HEART, EVERY TIME I AM LEAVING FOR WORK, SHE CRIES. IT JUST BREAKS ME. I JUST WANT TO GIVE HER MORE. I WANT AND NEED THINGS TO CHANGE. I KEEP SAYING THAT, BUT I'M NOT GETTING ANYWHERE. I DON'T KNOW WHAT THE HELL TO DO. WHY IS LIFE SO DAMN DIFFICULT? WHY CAN'T WE ALL JUST BE HAPPY AND GET THE THINGS IN LIFE THAT WE WANT AND DESERVE?

Same day, different journal:

DAYS JUST KEEP PASSING AND PASSING AND I'M STILL STUCK IN THE SAME DAMN PLACE. IS LIFE GOING TO GET BETTER FOR ME? I KEEP ASKING MYSELF THAT, AND I AM HOPING I WILL SEE A LIGHT OF HAPPINESS SOMETIME SOON. I AM REALLY NOT IN A GOOD PLACE RIGHT NOW. AND I HONESTLY HAVE NOBODY TO TALK TO. I DON'T HAVE ANY FRIENDS, WELL, AT LEAST SOMEONE I CAN TRUST AND CONFIDE IN AND MY SISTERS ALL HAVE ENOUGH ON THEIR PLATES TO WORRY AND HEAR ALL MY MANY PROBLEMS. MY SISTERS OR JAY ARE REALLY THE ONLY PEOPLE THAT I TRUST, BUT I CAN'T GO

TO ANY OF THEM RIGHT NOW. I NEED TO GET OUT OF THIS DARK HOLE AND START TO STRAIGHTEN MY LIFE UP ALL ON MY OWN. I KNOW I AM THE ONLY ONE THAT CAN MAKE THIS HAPPEN AND TURN MY LIFE AROUND, BUT I AM HAVING THE HARDEST DAMN TIME. THINGS ARE 100% BETTER NOW THAN THEY HAVE BEEN IN YEARS, OR AS LONG AS I CAN REMEMBER, BUT THAT DOESN'T HELP ME AT ALL RIGHT NOW. I KNOW HOW MY LIFE CAN BE AND THAT I CAN HAVE ALL THE HAPPINESS IN THE WORLD, IT'S JUST SO HARD FOR ME TO GET WHERE I WANT AND NEED TO BE. DON'T GET ME WRONG, I AM SO EXTREMELY HAPPY THAT I HAVE MY PARENTS' SUPPORT AND THIS HOME THEY ARE LETTING ME LIVE THERE AND I AM SO GRATEFUL THAT I HAVE CUSTODY OF JALA AGAIN. *(To be clear, she didn't have custody of Jala, but Jay let them be alone together.)* I GET TO SEE ADI AND MAS A LOT MORE, BUT IT'S NOT AT ALL GOOD ENOUGH FOR ME. I WANT TO MOVE OUT, BE WITH MY HUSBAND AGAIN, AND HAVE RIGHTS BACK TO MY OLDER KIDS. THAT SEEMS LIKE A LONG SHOT AND IT SCARES ME TO DEATH THAT IT WON'T HAPPEN AND IT'S LITERALLY KILLING ME. I AM SO STRESSED ABOUT ALL THESE THINGS I AM STRIVING FOR THAT I AM SICK ALL THE TIME, AND BELIEVE ME, IT SUCKS BECAUSE I AM WORKING MY ASS OFF AT WORK AND I AM SO BURNED OUT. I NEED A BREAK AND A SHOULDER TO UNLOAD AND CRY ON. GOOD LUCK, NAT. I REALLY AM TRYING MY BEST TO WRITE EVERY NIGHT, BUT BY THE TIME I GET HOME FROM WORK, IT'S USUALLY 1 OR 1:30 IN THE MORNING AND I AM ABSOLUTELY EXHAUSTED.

I should explain here that one of the reasons she was so miserable was that she was using and trying to keep it from the family and Jay while she was living in my parents' home. All her work money went to supply her habit. She was depressed and exhausted from trying to live two lives, and her body was so damaged from the drugs.

It is the same throughout all of her journals that she thought she just had to be stronger and have more willpower to get clean. Drug addiction is a disease, and she needed a lot more than just willpower.

TUESDAY, FEBRUARY 7, 2012:

GOT OFF WORK A COUPLE OF HOURS AGO, NOW JUST SITTIN' WITH MY FAVORITE GIRL (JALA) WHILE WE WIND DOWN AND GET READY FOR BED. SHE IS WATCHING *TWILIGHT* AND COLORING IN HER NEW STRAWBERRY SHORTCAKE COLORING BOOK. SHE IS SUCH AN AMAZING, BEAUTIFUL LITTLE GIRL. I'M GETTING HER INTO DANCE IN THE NEXT COUPLE OF WEEKS AND I'M SO EXCITED TO START WATCHING HER DANCE.

ADI HAS HER VALENTINE'S DANCE THIS SATURDAY AND SHE IS GOING WITH HER BOYFRIEND DAKOTA. THEY HAVE BEEN TOGETHER FOR A COUPLE OF MONTHS NOW, SEEMS LIKE A PRETTY GOOD KID AND TREATS ADI REALLY GOOD. ADI, ME, GRANDMA, & JALA WENT TO BUY ADI'S DRESS YESTERDAY AT CAROLINE'S, JUST UP THE STREET. IT IS ABSOLUTELY BEAUTIFUL ON HER. SHE HAS SUCH A PERFECT, CUTE LITTLE FIGURE ANYWAYS. I'M PAYING FOR HER DRESS THIS TIME BECAUSE HER DAD PAID LAST DANCE, AND APPARENTLY WE ARE TAKING TURNS BUYING HER DRESSES, WHICH SEEMS FAIR, BUT DANG THEY ARE SO EXPENSIVE. JAY AND I HAD THE MOST INCREDIBLE NIGHT THE OTHER NIGHT. HE PAMPERED ME FOR ABOUT 2 1/2 HOURS, MASSAGED MY LEGS, MY FEET, TICKLED MY BACK AND BODY AND LEANED OVER ALL NIGHT KISSING MY CHEEK AND FOREHEAD. I CAN'T REMEMBER THE LAST TIME HE TREATED ME THAT WAY. HOPEFULLY THIS IS A START FOR US AND WE CAN GIVE US ANOTHER TRY. I HOPE!

The next day...

WEDNESDAY, FEBRUARY 8, 2012:

IT'S ABOUT 3:30 A.M. AND I HAVE MY SWEET LITTLE PRINCESS LAYING WITH ME IN BED. I CAN'T SLEEP, I HAVE WAY TOO MUCH GOING ON THROUGH MY HEAD RIGHT NOW. I HAVE A DATE TONIGHT WITH SOMEONE I MET AT WORK, HIS NAME IS PAUL. I DON'T KNOW IF I SHOULD GO OR NOT. JAY TOLD ME TO DATE. I DON'T KNOW WHAT IN THE HELL TO DO. I LOVE HIM SO MUCH, BUT HOW LONG DO I WAIT? I'M GETTING OLDER, MY BIRTHDAY IS IN TWO WEEKS, I AM GOING TO BE THIRTY-THREE. THAT IS SO OLD! I DON'T HAVE TIME TO MESS AROUND. GOOD LUCK, NAT.

FRIDAY, FEBRUARY 10, 2012:

MY BABY BOY JUST GOT HERE 'CAUSE IT'S MY WEEKEND. *(She only had Mas because she was living with my parents and they had him quite often; If she had been on her own, she would not have had him because she had to have supervised visits.)* HE SURE DOES PUT A BIG SMILE ON MY FACE! I LOVE MY WONDERFUL KIDS! ADI HAS THE VALENTINE'S DANCE TOMORROW NIGHT. I AM HEADING TO WORK HERE IN ABOUT AN HOUR AND IT'S GOING TO BE ANOTHER LONG, LONG NIGHT. I HOPE I MAKE GOOD MONEY TONIGHT BECAUSE I REALLY, REALLY NEED IT. I AM CHANGING MY LIFE FOR THE GOOD AND I KNOW I WILL RECEIVE BLESSINGS FOR IT AND FINALLY BEGIN TO FEEL HAPPINESS.

SO, I MET THIS ABSOLUTELY AMAZING MAN AT WORK A COUPLE WEEKS AGO WITH HIS KIDS. HE IS HONESTLY THE MOST POLITE, KIND PERSON I HAVE EVER MET. SO ARE HIS KIDS. LAST NIGHT HE CAME TO SEE ME AT WORK AND BROUGHT ME A KEVA JUICE. AFTER WORK, I WENT BY HIS HOUSE AND WE TALKED FOR A COUPLE HOURS. HE IS SUCH AN AMAZING MAN. I THINK I AM GOING TO START SEEING HIM IF JAY DOESN'T COMMIT TO ME SOMETIME SOON. AND I

HONESTLY DON'T THINK HE WILL. AND AS MUCH AS IT HURTS THINKING THIS, I THINK IT'S ABOUT TIME TO MOVE ON AND STOP HOPING FOR JAY TO COME AROUND. JAY AND I HAD AN AMAZING NIGHT THE OTHER NIGHT, BUT HE ISN'T ACTING ANY DIFFERENT NOW TOWARDS ME AND I CAN'T KEEP PUTTING MY LIFE ON HOLD AND WAITING AROUND PATIENTLY FOR HIM. I LOVE HIM SO MUCH, BUT I HONESTLY DON'T THINK HE WILL EVER COME AROUND AND FULLY COMMIT TO ME AGAIN. THAT HURTS, BUT I HAVE TO FACE REALITY. I WISH MORE THAN ANYTHING THAT JAY AND I COULD WORK THINGS OUT AND BE A FAMILY AGAIN WITH JALA, BUT THAT IS, SAD TO SAY, JUST WISHFUL THINKING. SO, I THINK I MIGHT LOOK INTO DIVORCE PAPERS AND GIVE THIS NEW PAUL GUY A TRY.

SATURDAY, FEBRUARY 11, 2012:

SO, PAUL CAME BY AGAIN TO MY WORK WITH HIS DAUGHTER AND BROUGHT ME A KEVA JUICE. I AM THINKING ABOUT HIM A LOT AND IT'S KINDA SCARING ME. I REALLY NEED TO GET DIVORCE PAPERS OR JUST KEEP WAITING FOR JAY, PATIENTLY, WHICH I HAVE BEEN DOING FOR A LONG TIME NOW AND I JUST DON'T KNOW WHAT TO DO. I WISH I HAD AN ANSWER. THIS IS WAY TOO HARD TO FIGURE OUT ALL ALONE. I HAVE ALL THREE OF MY BABIES HERE WITH ME TONIGHT. IT BRINGS SO MUCH HAPPINESS TO MY HEART TO HAVE AND BE AROUND MY WONDERFUL, BEAUTIFUL, AND ABSOLUTELY AMAZING KIDS. I LOVE THEM. WELL, SHOULD GO TO SLEEP NOW OR AT LEAST TRY. GOOD LUCK, NAT!

Six days later…

FRIDAY, FEBRUARY 17, 2012:

WELL, IT'S ABOUT 3:00 A.M. JUST GOT HOME FROM WORK A COUPLE HOURS AGO AND THEN HAD TO GO PICK UP MY SLEEPY

BABY GIRL TO STAY THE NIGHT WITH ME BECAUSE JAY IS GOING TO VEGAS, ALONG WITH EVERYBODY ELSE. JAY *(he went separately with some friends),* MY MOM AND DAD, SHALL & TYE, ANGIE & RANDY, ETC. ARE ALL GOING TO VEGAS THIS WEEKEND, AND GUESS WHAT I GET TO DO? YEP, YEP, WORK! I JUST PRAY THAT ALL THIS HARD WORK WILL BLESS ME SOON AND I WILL GET TO GO ON VACATION AND ACTUALLY DO SOMETHING FUN, SOMETHING FOR ME! SO, I AM STILL TALKING TO THIS NEW GUY PAUL AND HE IS STILL ABSOLUTELY AMAZING, BUT I HAVE ONLY GONE OUT WITH HIM A COUPLE TIMES, SO IT'S TOO EARLY TO REALLY KNOW HIM. ALMOST EVERY SINGLE NIGHT, HE BRINGS ME A KEVA JUICE TO WORK BECAUSE HE KNOWS I CAN'T EAT TILL LATE AND IT REALLY HOLDS ME OVER. MY MOM AND DAD BROUGHT MY SWEET JALA IN TONIGHT TO EAT AND PAUL DROPPED BY WITH ANOTHER KEVA WHILE MY PARENTS WERE THERE, AND HE WENT OVER AND INTRODUCED HIMSELF AND MET JALA. IT WAS THE CUTEST THING EVER! I'M JUST SO CONFUSED! GOOD LUCK!

Two days later...

SUNDAY, FEBRUARY 19, 2012:

IT'S ABOUT 2:30 P.M. AND I'M JUST GETTIN' READY TO TAKE MY LITTLE PRINCESS TO KAILEE *(Angie's daughter)* SO SHE CAN WATCH HER WHILE I GO INTO WORK. YEP, ANOTHER WORKING DAY FOR ME. HOPEFULLY I CAN MAKE SOME GOOD MONEY TODAY 'CAUSE I AM DESPERATELY NEEDING IT. I CLOSE TONIGHT SO WON'T BE HOME UNTIL AROUND 10:00 P.M., WHICH IS A LITTLE LATE TO MAKE ANY GREAT PLANS. JAY AND EVERYONE ELSE GETS HOME FROM VEGAS TOMORROW AND THEN MAYBE I CAN GET A BIT OF A BREAK. JALA AND I HAVE ACTUALLY HAD A LOT OF FUN TOGETHER THIS WEEKEND, EVEN THOUGH I HAD TO WORK ALL WEEKEND, WE STILL MADE

TIME TO BE TOGETHER AND HANG OUT. THAT'S THE FUNNEST TIMES EVER FOR ME TO BE WITH MY BABY GIRL.

I KNOW I HAVE MADE WRONG CHOICES IN MY LIFE AND SOME OF THEM A LOT WORSE THAN A LOT OF PEOPLE MAKE, BUT I AM WORKING MY ASS OFF TO PUT MY LIFE BACK TOGETHER AND IT JUST IS NOT MOVING QUITE FAST ENOUGH FOR ME. I REALLY NEED TO RECEIVE A BLESSING SO THAT I HAVE HOPE AND IT WILL SHOW ME THAT PEOPLE DO RECEIVE BLESSINGS AND HAPPINESS. I KNOW THAT I HAVE BEEN BLESSED A LOT THE PAST YEAR, BUT I THINK I HAVE EARNED IT. I KNOW THERE IS A LOT I STILL NEED TO WORK ON AND MAKE BETTER CHOICES. I NEED SOME SORT OF FUN AND HAPPINESS IN MY LIFE. I NEED SOME ANSWERS. THAT IS WHAT I DEFINITELY NEED, ANSWERS! I KNOW I NEED TO WORK HARDER EACH DAY ON TRYING TO GET MY LIFE THE WAY I KNOW IT WILL BE GOOD FOR ME AND MY PRECIOUS KIDS. I DEFINITELY NEED TO MAKE BETTER CHOICES EACH DAY, BUT I PRAY I WILL START TO FEEL SOME HAPPINESS AND HOPEFULLY GET MY HUSBAND AND KIDS BACK UNDER THE SAME ROOF AS ME. GOOD LUCK, NAT!

WELL, JUST GOT HOME FROM WORK AND FOR THE TIME I WAS THERE, I DIDN'T DO TOO BAD. EVERYONE IS STILL OUT OF TOWN, INCLUDING JAY. THEY ALL GET BACK MONDAY MORNING. KAILEE HAS BEEN WATCHING JALA ALL WEEKEND FOR ME SO THAT I CAN WORK. I REALLY NEED TO TAKE A BREAK AND GET THE HELL OUT OF HERE FOR A WEEKEND. I THINK I DESERVE IT BY NOW. UNFORTUNATELY, THE ONLY PERSON I WOULD WANT TO GET AWAY WITH IS JAY. PAUL IS DEFINITELY GROWING ON ME, THOUGH. HE BROUGHT ME IN ANOTHER KEVA JUICE AGAIN AT WORK TONIGHT. HE IS TRULY A PERFECT MAN, BUT MY HEART AND MIND ARE STILL ON JAY, BUT I AM TRYING SO HARD TO CHANGE THAT! I'M LOOKING AT MY SWEET BABY GIRL RIGHT NOW, SHE JUST FELL ASLEEP, MY PERFECT AND ABSOLUTELY BEAUTIFUL LITTLE GIRL. I

COULDN'T ASK FOR A MORE PERFECT DAUGHTER. GOOD LUCK, NATALIE!

Nat was still living with my parents, and the family thought she was clean.

Same day, different journal...

I'M LOOKING AT MY BEAUTIFUL BABY GIRL RIGHT NOW WHILE SHE'S SLEEPING, AND SHE IS THE MOST AMAZING AND PERFECT LITTLE GIRL A MOTHER COULD EVER ASK FOR. SHE MAKES MY HEART SMILE! I DON'T KNOW HOW I DID IT, BUT ADI AND MAS ARE JUST AS ABSOLUTELY AMAZING, PERFECT CHILDREN. I AM SO EXTREMELY PROUD OF ALL THREE OF MY KIDS. I HONESTLY HAVE NO IDEA HOW I BECAME SO VERY LUCKY TO HAVE SUCH AMAZING, GOOD CHILDREN. THEY SERIOUSLY ARE THE HIGHLIGHT OF MY LIFE AND MY ABSOLUTE WHOLE ENTIRE WORLD. JUST CAME OUTSIDE TO SMOKE AND IT IS LIGHTLY SNOWING BUT LOOKS LIKE IT HAS BEEN 'CAUSE THERE IS ABOUT AN INCH OF SNOW ON OUR FRONT PORCH. YAY, I LIKE THE SNOW! PAUL BROUGHT ME IN A KEVA JUICE AGAIN TONIGHT AT WORK. I CAN'T EVEN COUNT HOW MANY TIMES HE HAS DONE THIS FOR ME. HE IS REALLY TRYING HARD WITH ME. I REALLY LIKE IT, IT'S GREAT TO FINALLY FEEL WANTED BY SOMEBODY. BUT JAY IS STILL HERE, HOLDING TIGHT ONTO MY HEART. WELL, I AM JUST GOING TO TAKE IT A DAY AT A TIME AND WHATEVER HAPPENS, HAPPENS. I WILL HAVE TO SEE HOW JAY ACTS TOWARDS ME WHEN HE GETS HOME FROM VEGAS. THE LAST TIME WE TALKED, REALLY TALKED, WAS LAST WEEK, THE NIGHT BEFORE VALENTINE'S DAY, AND JAY TOLD ME THAT HE WAS NOT DONE AND THAT HE WANTS TO START TAKING ME OUT MORE ON DATES AND SPENDING MORE TIME WITH ME SO WE CAN SLOWLY TRY AND POSSIBLY GET OUR FAMILY BACK TOGETHER. I HOPE AND PRAY EVERY DAY THAT GOD WILL BLESS ME FINALLY AND GIVE ME BACK MY FAMILY, MY HUSBAND, KIDS, ALL OF US TOGETHER!

MONDAY, FEBRUARY 20, 2012:

IT'S ABOUT 1:00 A.M. AND I JUST GOT HOME FROM PICKING UP MY LITTLE PRINCESS A COUPLE HOURS AGO FROM ANGIE'S HOUSE. KAILEE DID SUCH AN AMAZING JOB WATCHING JALA FOR ME WHILE I WAS AT WORK. SHE WATCHED JALA FRIDAY, SATURDAY, AND SUNDAY FOR ME WHILE I WAS AT WORK. SHE TOTALLY SAVED ME THIS WEEKEND AND JALA HAD SO MUCH FUN. MY PARENTS GOT HOME LAST NIGHT, SO DID ANGIE, DON'T KNOW ABOUT SHALL, BUT JAY COMES HOME TOMORROW. HE IS LEAVING VEGAS AROUND 9:00 A.M., SO HE SHOULDN'T BE TOO LATE. JALA IS SO EXCITED TO SEE JAY, THEY HAVEN'T BEEN APART FOR THIS LONG IN A VERY, VERY LONG TIME ACTUALLY. I CAN'T REMEMBER THE LAST TIME JAY AND JALA WERE APART FROM EACH OTHER FOR MORE THAN A DAY. THEY HAVE A SPECIAL BOND BETWEEN THE TWO OF THEM. THEY GOT EXTREMELY CLOSE BECAUSE I WAS GONE FOR THE LONGEST TIME AND ALL THEY HAD WAS EACH OTHER. I AM TRYING TO CREATE A RELATIONSHIP AND A BOND WITH JALA THAT IS VERY TIGHT AND SPECIAL. I WAS AWAY FROM HER FOR WAY TOO LONG AND I DON'T WANT HER TO EVER REMEMBER HER MOTHER BEING GONE AND NOT AROUND. IT BREAKS MY HEART TO EVEN THINK THAT SHE MIGHT HAVE THAT MEMORY OF ME NOT BEING THERE WHEN SHE WAS GROWING UP. BUT, I AM HERE NOW AND I AM NEVER, EVER GOING ANYWHERE AND I AM GOING TO CREATE SOME UNFORGETTABLE MEMORIES WITH HER AND MY OTHER KIDS THAT WILL BE SO SPECIAL TO THEM AND THEY WILL NEVER, EVER FORGET. I'M HERE TO STAY. WELL, BELIEVE IT OR NOT, I REALLY SHOULD BE LAYING DOWN NEXT TO MY BEAUTIFUL BABY GIRL AND FALLING ASLEEP, SINCE IT'S 1:30 A.M., INSTEAD I'M OUTSIDE ON THE PORCH SMOKING AND COMPLAINING. WHY CAN'T I JUST BE HAPPY? I USED TO BE A FUN ENERGETIC PERSON THAT EVERYONE ALWAYS WANTED TO BE AROUND. LATELY, NOW ALL I AM IS A MISERABLE, STRESSED, UNHAPPY, NOT

WANTING TO DO ANYTHING AT ALL PERSON. HOW ON EARTH DID I BECOME LIKE THIS? WELL, I NEED TO PULL MYSELF TOGETHER AND BECOME THE PERSON THAT I KNOW I AM. FUN LOVING, ENERGETIC, GOOD MOTHER, THAT PEOPLE WOULD DO ANYTHING TO BE AROUND. IT DOESN'T TAKE MUCH, NAT, AND I KNOW WHAT I HAVE TO DO, I'M JUST SO SCARED. I HAVE SAID THIS MANY, MANY TIMES BEFORE. I KNOW WHAT I NEED TO DO, I NEED TO TAKE THAT BIG STEP AND JUST FUCKING DO IT! *(Get clean.)* I KNOW I WILL RECEIVE MANY BLESSINGS, MY LIFE WOULD BE GOING IN THE RIGHT DIRECTION AND I WILL FINALLY BE HAPPY! THE ONE THING I WANT AND CRAVE MORE THAN ANYTHING! PURE AND COMPLETE HAPPINESS. I DESERVE IT! I HONESTLY CANNOT REMEMBER THE LAST TIME I FELT FREE, HAPPY, AND POSITIVE. I NEED THESE THINGS IN MY LIFE AND QUICK, OR I WON'T MAKE IT. MY KIDS ALSO DESERVE TO SEE THEIR MOTHER HAPPY AND POSITIVE AND DOING THE RIGHT THINGS. I WANT TO BE AN EXAMPLE TO ALL THREE OF MY KIDS THAT THEY WILL STRIVE TO BE LIKE THEIR MOTHER WHEN THEY ARE OLDER. TURN IT AROUND, NAT, AND THIS IS ONLY THE BEGINNING OF A GREAT AND WONDERFUL LIFE, IT IS SO NOT THE END, LIKE I HAVE BEEN LIVING IT OUT TO BE.

I AM EXTREMELY STRESSED OUT LATELY FINANCIALLY. I HAVE PEOPLE KEEP TELLING ME THAT IT IS JUST MONEY AND THAT I SHOULDN'T LET IT GET ME THIS UNHAPPY AND THIS COMPLETELY STRESSED OUT. I REALLY AM LETTING IT TEAR ME APART, I CAN'T EAT, SLEEP, OR KEEP A SMILE ON MY FACE. I HAD TO REALIZE THAT I AM DOING MY ABSOLUTE BEST AND THAT'S ALL I CAN DO. I JUST GOT SO, SO BEHIND ON ALL MY BILLS THIS MONTH AND I CAN'T SEEM TO GET BACK ON TOP OF THINGS. IT'S MY BIRTHDAY THURSDAY, SO I TOOK THE DAY OFF, NOW I'M SCARED THAT I SHOULDN'T 'CAUSE I REALLY, REALLY NEED THE MONEY. KEEP SMILING, NAT! I AM HONESTLY DOING EVERYTHING I CAN AND THERE

IS NOTHING ELSE I CAN DO, IT'S JUST MONEY, IT'S NOT HAPPINESS. I HAVE MY KIDS AND LOTS OF PEOPLE THAT WANT TO BE AROUND ME RIGHT NOW. I NEED TO REMEMBER THAT WHEN I AM FEELING REALLY DOWN, IT'S NOT THE END OF THE WORLD AND I KNOW I CAN GET ON TOP OF THINGS AND GET EVERYTHING TAKEN CARE OF. I AM THE ONLY PERSON THAT CAN MAKE ME HAPPY, SO KEEP SMILING, LIFE IS GREAT!

TUESDAY, FEBRUARY 21, 2012:

WATCHING MOTLEY CRUE AT JAY'S RIGHT NOW 'CAUSE HE JUST GOT HOME FROM VEGAS AT THE MOTLEY CRUE CONCERT. HE WAS GONE FOR ABOUT 4 DAYS AND I WAS REALLY CURIOUS TO SEE HOW HE WAS TOWARDS ME WHEN HE GOT HOME. I WAS HOPING FOR SOMETHING THAT I DEEP DOWN KNEW I WAS NOT GOING TO GET FROM HIM. DIDN'T ACT EXCITED TO SEE ME AT ALL. A LITTLE EXCITEMENT WOULD HAVE BEEN NICE, BUT ABSOLUTELY NOTHING AT ALL. WHY DO I KEEP PUTTING MYSELF THROUGH THIS TORTURE? JAY IS NOT GOING TO CHANGE, AND I HAVE GOT TO STOP HOPING AND PRAYING THAT HE MIGHT COME BACK TO ME. I HAVE THIS ABSOLUTELY AMAZING MAN THAT IS HEAD OVER HEELS INTO ME AND WOULD DO ABSOLUTELY ANYTHING FOR ME. HE IS THE TYPE OF GUY THAT GIRLS CHOOSE EVERY DAY. HE IS ABSOLUTELY DARLING AND HAS A HEART OF GOLD. I REALLY NEED TO WAKE UP. IF I LET THIS GUY (PAUL) GO, I KNOW I WILL REGRET IT AND I HAVE NO DOUBT IN MY MIND THAT IF I GIVE HIM A CHANCE THAT WE COULD HAVE SOMETHING GREAT. SO, I STILL HAVE A NEEDLE STUCK IN MY LEG AND I THINK IT TRAVELED AND STARTED AN INFECTION. THE INSIDE OF MY THIGH IS COMPLETELY SWOLLEN AND BRIGHT RED, AND IT HURTS LIKE A BITCH TO WALK ON. I DON'T HAVE THE MONEY OR THE COURAGE TO GET IT LOOKED AT. I AM A COMPLETE

MESS! MY BODY IS ALWAYS FUCKED UP ONE WAY OR THE OTHER. IT SUCKS SO BAD. AND DRUGS TOTALLY AGED ME. I LOOK A LOT OLDER THAN I REALLY AM AND THAT MAKES ME FEEL REALLY UGLY. I JUST HAVE A HORRIBLE SELF-ESTEEM LATELY. I AM TRYING TO GET SOME CONFIDENCE BACK LIKE I USED TO HAVE BUT AFTER EVERYTHING I HAVE DONE, IT IS IMPOSSIBLE TO FEEL GOOD ABOUT MYSELF. I JUST NEVER EVEN FEEL WORTHY OR GOOD ENOUGH FOR ANYONE. HOW SAD IT THAT?

I don't remember hearing anything about the needle stuck in her leg or what ended up becoming of that.

IT'S ABOUT 3:00 A.M. AND I AM WRITING IN MY JOURNAL 'CAUSE I CANNOT FOR THE LIFE OF ME FALL ASLEEP. I HATE HOW I STRESS OUT SO MUCH OVER MONEY. I KNOW HOW TO STOP MY FINANCIAL PROBLEMS AND I KNOW WHY I GOT THIS BAD BEHIND THIS MONTH, BUT I WON'T FIX IT! I AM SO SCARED AND HAVE NOT HAD THE STRENGTH TO DO WHAT I NEED TO DO TO MAKE MY LIFE CHANGE FOR THE BETTER AND QUIT PUTTING MYSELF IN THIS FINANCIAL HOLE. MY CELL PHONE JUST GOT SHUT OFF THIS MORNING AND THEY TOOK MY FOOD STAMPS AWAY LAST WEEK. I AM SO SCREWED RIGHT NOW, WORSE THAN I HAVE BEEN IN A LONG TIME, AND I HAVE NO IDEA HOW I AM GOING TO GET BACK ON TOP OF THINGS. I NEED HELP IN A BAD WAY AND AM TOO PRIDEFUL AND EMBARRASSED TO ASK ANYONE IN MY FAMILY FOR HELP. GOOD LUCK, NAT, IT WILL ALL WORK OUT. KEEP THE FAITH.

<u>WEDNESDAY, FEBRUARY 22, 2012</u>:

IT'S MY BIRTHDAY TOMORROW AND I AM NOT THE LEAST BIT EXCITED FOR IT. IT'S JUST ANOTHER DAY NOW THAT I AM AN OLD FART! I DON'T KNOW WHAT I AM GOING TO DO YET. I

TOOK WORK OFF, SO HOPEFULLY I WILL END UP DOING SOMETHING FUN AND SOMETHING THAT I WILL REMEMBER 'CAUSE THE PAST ABOUT 5 YEARS ARE HORRIBLE BLANKS OF MY BIRTHDAYS. I AM PRAYING THIS YEAR WILL BE MUCH, MUCH BETTER. PAUL AND JAY BOTH ASKED ME TO DO SOMETHING THAT DAY AND I HAVE ABSOLUTELY NO IDEA WHO I WANT TO GO WITH. I KEEP GOING BACK AND FORTH AND BACK AND FORTH. WELL, WHATEVER I DECIDE, I HOPE IT WILL BE A FANTASTIC DAY. I THINK I DESERVE IT, ACTUALLY, MAYBE I DON'T. I DON'T KNOW ANYMORE. *MY HEART AND INTENTIONS ARE CLEAN AND PURE, BUT MY ACTIONS AND CHOICES SAY MUCH DIFFERENT.* I AM TRYING, BUT LIKE JAY ALWAYS SAYS, YOU EITHER DO OR YOU DON'T, THERE IS NO TRY. I JUST DON'T KNOW HOW TO DO IT, HOW TO CHANGE MY LIFE. I AM WORKING MY ASS OFF AT WORK AND I WAS REWARDING MYSELF IN MY MIND BECAUSE OF IT, BUT IT'S NOT ENOUGH. I CAN DO BETTER. I CAN MAKE BETTER CHOICES AND PUT MY KIDS FIRST AND STOP BEING SO SELFISH. CHANGE IT, NAT! I KNOW YOU CAN DO IT, YOU JUST NEED TO *DO IT,* MAKE THAT MOVE, MY LIFE WILL BE THE BEST IT COULD EVER BE. I CHALLENGE MYSELF, MAKE IT HAPPEN AFTER THIS WEEKEND IS OVER! I CAN DO IT AND I KNOW I AM STRONG ENOUGH TO DO WHATEVER IT IS I NEED TO DO TO MAKE MY LIFE BETTER FOR MY KIDS AND ME. GOOD LUCK, NAT, YOU CAN DO IT!!!

THURSDAY, FEBRUARY 23, 2012:

IT'S MY BIRTHDAY TODAY AND I AM HOPING AND PRAYING THAT THIS YEAR I WILL HAVE A MUCH BETTER ONE THAN THE PAST COUPLE YEARS. I JUST WOKE UP AND THERE WAS AN ENVELOPE ON MY DRESSER FROM MY MOM AND DAD WITH $400, TELLING ME THEY GOT MY CAR PAYMENT THIS MONTH. *(At this time my parents believed she was clean and were willing to help her financially.)* WHAT A BIRTHDAY PRESENT! I AM IN SHOCK AND WANT TO CRY! THEY ARE SO EXTREMELY GOOD TO

ME, I DON'T FEEL WORTHY ENOUGH. SHALL IS PICKING ME UP IN ABOUT AN HOUR AND TAKING ME TO BENIHANA'S FOR LUNCH. MY ABSOLUTE FAVORITE RESTAURANT IN THE WORLD. IT WILL BE JUST ME AND HER AND MY MOM, ANGIE FLEW TO CALIFORNIA THIS MORNING AND EM IS NOT HERE. I AM EXCITED WE WILL HAVE A LOT OF FUN!

Me, mom, Kierra, Adi and Nat at Benihana's

SO, I HAVE HAD A GREAT DAY! ADI, SHALL AND MOM TOOK ME TO LUNCH AT BENIHANA'S, THEN WENT HOME AND SPENT TIME WITH THE KIDS. MY PARENTS DID WAY MORE FOR ME THAN THEY EVER SHOULD HAVE. THEY PAID MY CAR PAYMENT AND INSURANCE BECAUSE THEY KNEW I WAS STRUGGLING THIS MONTH. I NEED TO SHAPE UP AND FAST. MY PARENTS HAVE DONE ENOUGH FOR ME, I AM ABSOLUTELY GRATEFUL, BUT I FEEL SO TERRIBLY BAD AT THE SAME TIME. I KNOW HOW TO GET MY SHIT TOGETHER SO I WON'T HAVE TO STRUGGLE

LIKE THIS ANYMORE, OR PUT MY PARENTS IN THAT KIND OF SITUATION AGAIN, BUT I AM BEYOND TERRIFIED. IT SCARES ME TO DEATH, BUT ONCE I DO THIS, MY LIFE WILL GET MUCH BETTER AND I WILL FINALLY FEEL SOME HAPPINESS. THIS HAS DEFINITELY BEEN AN INCREDIBLE BIRTHDAY, IT'S BEEN AWESOME!

A couple of days later...

SATURDAY, FEBRUARY 25, 2012:

SITTING HERE AT ABOUT 11:30 AT NIGHT. MY BIRTHDAY WAS INCREDIBLE. WENT TO BENIHANA'S WITH SHALL AND MY MOM, THEN THAT NIGHT PAUL SURPRISED ME AND HAD A ROOM AT THE ANNIVERSARY INN FOR ME AND HIM AND HE WAS ABSOLUTELY AMAZING ALL NIGHT LONG. HE IS TOTALLY GETTING ME OVER JAY. I NEVER THOUGHT IT COULD HAPPEN OR AT LEAST THIS FAST. HE IS EVERYTHING I NEED AND WANT OUT OF A MAN AND MUCH MORE. I THINK I AM FALLING FOR THIS GUY. I CAN'T STOP THINKING ABOUT HIM AND HE MAKES ME SO HAPPY. I NEVER THOUGHT I COULD EVER FIND SOMEONE THAT I DESERVE AND GET TREATED BETTER THAN A PRINCESS, UNTIL PAUL. HE IS SO MUCH MORE THAN I EVER WANTED. LITERALLY PERFECT FOR ME IN EVERY WAY. I AM GOING TO FINALLY GET THIS DIVORCE DONE AND MOVE ON, AND THE WAY IT'S GOING RIGHT NOW, IT WILL BE WITH PAUL. HE KEEPS A SMILE ON MY FACE ALL DAY LONG. I NEVER THOUGHT I COULD EVER HAVE THESE FEELINGS AGAIN AND IT IS AWESOME. I FEEL LIKE I AM IN HEAVEN, I HAVEN'T BEEN THIS HAPPY IN GOD KNOWS HOW LONG!

SUNDAY, FEBRUARY 26, 2012:

IT'S ABOUT 2:30 ON SUNDAY AND I AM JUST ABOUT TO GET READY FOR WORK. YAY, ANOTHER WORKDAY! WELL, I HAVE

GOT TO CHANGE MY LIFE. THIS IS JUST NOT WORKING FOR ME. I HAVE TO GET RID OF A FEW PEOPLE IN MY LIFE AND MY LIFE WILL CHANGE DRAMATICALLY FOR THE BETTER. I THOUGHT I WAS TRYING, BUT I'M NOT TRYING HARD ENOUGH. I MAKE ENOUGH MONEY TO PAY MY BILLS AND PAY MY EX, AND I HAVE NOT BEEN USING MY MONEY WISELY, SO I GOT IN A BIND THIS LAST MONTH AND MY MOM AND DAD PAID FOR MY CAR PAYMENT, INSURANCE, AND MY PHONE BILL, WHICH WAS $300. THEY DON'T NEED MY FINANCIAL MISTAKES FALLING BACK ON THEM. THAT'S WHAT MY DAD CAME DOWN AND TOLD ME LAST NIGHT, AND IT'S TRUE. THEY DON'T DESERVE ALL THIS ADDED FINANCIAL STRESS BECAUSE OF ME. I KNOW WHAT I NEED TO DO, I JUST NEED TO DO IT. I AM REALLY STRESSED OUT, FRIDAY ORS *(Office of Recovery Services for child support)* CALLED AND TOLD ME IF I DON'T START PAYING MY EX, THEY WILL TAKE LEGAL ACTION, WHICH MEANS JAIL. I AM FREAKING OUT! I TOLD THEM I WOULD MAKE A PAYMENT AND THEY SAID NO LATER THAN WEDNESDAY. I AM SO SCARED, THAT IS DEFINITELY GOING TO BE THE VERY FIRST THING I PAY EACH MONTH. I CANNOT GO BACK TO JAIL AGAIN. MAKE LOTS OF MONEY AND HAVE A FABULOUS DAY TODAY, NAT, TRY NOT TO TAKE ALL YOUR WORRIES TO WORK, IT WILL ALL WORK OUT!

A couple of weeks later...

3-14-2012: Dr. Note–109 lbs. Dr. told her to be more consistent with taking Suboxone or no more treatment. Says she's too busy for counseling. Denies relapse. Prescribed Suboxone.

A month later...

4-19-2012: Dr. Note–105 lbs. Working at Iggy's, relationship stage. Says mom had heart attack last week. *(Our mother never had a heart attack).*

Ran out of meds and got from a friend. Dr. said this is addictive behavior. She is not committed to only taking her meds and stop giving hers to anyone else. Continue on Suboxone. *(She was using and would sell her Suboxone to get money for heroin, etc.)*

A month later...

FRIDAY, MAY 18, 2012:

I HAVE NOT WRITTEN FOR A LONG TIME BECAUSE MY LIFE HAS BEEN ABSOLUTELY CRAZY, CRAZY! BETWEEN WORKING SIX DAYS A WEEK AND BEING IN THE HOSPITAL OVER AND OVER AGAIN THE LAST LITTLE WHILE, I HAVE NOT HAD A CHANCE TO BREATHE. SO, GOT AN INFECTION ABOUT A MONTH AGO THAT IS PRETTY DAMN SERIOUS. I HAVE NOT BEEN ABLE TO WORK FOR TWO WEEKS NOW, LAST NIGHT WAS MY FIRST NIGHT BACK, AND THAT WAS VERY CHALLENGING TRYING TO LIVE THE PAST COUPLE WEEKS WITH NO MONEY COMING IN. THANK YOU TO MY AMAZING PARENTS. IF IT WAS NOT FOR THEM, I REALLY DON'T KNOW IF I WOULD HAVE MADE IT THROUGH. *(Our parents still thought she was clean.)* SO, AFTER A BUNCH OF TESTING AT LDS HOSPITAL, THEY FINALLY FIGURED OUT THAT I HAVE MRSA. IT IS A VERY HORRIBLE DEADLY STAPH INFECTION AND IF YOU DON'T CATCH IT FAST, YOU EITHER LOSE PARTS OF YOUR BODY OR YOU DIE. YA, WE ALL HAVE BEEN FREAKING OUT A BIT. THE PAST FEW DAYS ARE THE FIRST DAYS IN PROBABLY TWO AND A HALF MONTHS THAT I FELT OKAY. I AM GOING TO HAVE THIS DISEASE THE REST OF MY LIFE NOW AND IT CAN ATTACK AT ANY GIVEN MOMENT. IT'S SO SCARY. I AM SO THANKFUL I WENT TO THE HOSPITAL WHEN I DID, BECAUSE THINGS COULD HAVE WENT A LOT WORSE. I'M ON TWO ANTIBIOTICS AND HOPEFULLY IT WILL HELP LIKE IT SHOULD. YA, WHAT A PAST COUPLE MONTHS I HAVE HAD.

A LOT HAS BEEN GOING ON LATELY, SO I AM MAD AT MYSELF FOR NOT TAKING 5/10 MIN. OUT OF MY DAY TO WRITE IN MY JOURNAL. A LOT OF GREAT THINGS HAVE HAPPENED THE PAST COUPLE OF MONTHS, AND ALSO SOME HORRIBLE THINGS HAVE HAPPENED TOO. I AM TRULY BLESSED, THOUGH, BECAUSE AS I WAS GOING THROUGH ALL THE HORRIBLE STUFF, I HAD AN ABSOLUTELY AMAZING, LOVING MAN RIGHT BY MY SIDE HELPING ME THROUGH IT ALL. I HAVE ONLY KNOWN PAUL FOR A LITTLE LESS THAN 3 MONTHS, BUT I AM TRULY IN LOVE WITH THIS MAN. I KNEW IT AFTER BEING WITH HIM A COUPLE TIMES. I HAVE NEVER IN MY LIFE MET ANYONE LIKE HIM. MY DIVORCE IS ALMOST FINAL WITH JAY *(they never divorced)* AND I CAN'T BELIEVE HOW MUCH MY HEART HAS CHANGED. I LOVE JAY AND ALWAYS WILL, TO AN EXTENT, BUT WE ARE SO NOT GOOD TOGETHER. I DON'T KNOW QUITE HOW TO RESPOND TO PAUL BECAUSE HE IS SO WONDERFUL TO ME. PAUL & I TALK ABOUT GETTING MARRIED EVERY DAY AND I KNOW IT'S FAST, BUT I HAVE NEVER FELT THIS WAY BEFORE ABOUT ANY MAN. I ABSOLUTELY LOVE HIM. MY KIDS LOVE HIM, AND MY FAMILY LOVES HIM, EVEN MY DAD, THAT'S GOT TO TELL YA SOMETHING!

Paul had no idea she was using, although he did know she had a history of drug use. She lived a completely separate life that Paul didn't know about. She would go on her drug runs after work and in the middle of the night while he was asleep. I often wonder what he thought, especially when she got abscesses.

<u>5-21-2012:</u> <u>Dr. Note</u>–Natalie did not show for her Dr. appointment.

<u>TUESDAY, MAY 29, 2012</u>:

WELL, A HELL OF A LOT HAS HAPPENED AND CHANGED IN THE PAST COUPLE MONTHS, AND YEARS. I AM SO EXTREMELY HAPPY RIGHT NOW BUT SO EXTREMELY STRESSED TOO. I FOUND

THE MAN OF MY DREAMS AND I HAVE NEVER BEEN SO HAPPY (RELATIONSHIP WISE), BUT EVERYTHING ELSE IS STILL A BIG MESS. GOING THROUGH MY SECOND DIVORCE, STILL TRYING TO GET MY KIDS BACK AND STILL LIVING WITH MY PARENTS AT THE PRESENT TIME. I AM VERY, VERY THANKFUL THAT I HAVE THIS NICE HOME TO LIVE IN, BUT I AM THIRTY-THREE YEARS OLD AND FEEL LIKE A COMPLETE LOSER! HOPEFULLY SOMETIME SOON, I CAN MOVE OUT OF HERE AND BE ON MY OWN WITH MY KIDS. PAUL AND I HAVE TALKED ABOUT MARRIAGE A LOT. ACTUALLY EVERY DAY, AND I WANT TO DO IT, BUT AM SO SO SCARED AT THE SAME TIME. HE TREATS ME LIKE AN ANGEL AND I ABSOLUTELY ADORE HIM, BUT THIS WILL BE MARRIAGE #3! WORK IS STILL GOING OKAY, I WORK 6 DAYS A WEEK AND AM REALLY, REALLY BURNED OUT, BUT I AM SO GRATEFUL TO HAVE THIS JOB. I AM REALLY DOING GOOD THERE. THERE IS A COUPLE OF THINGS I REALLY NEED TO CHANGE IN MY LIFE IN ORDER FOR ME TO BE HAPPY AND FOR EVERYTHING TO WORK OUT. WISHING MYSELF THE MOST LUCK TO CHANGE THEM, RIGHT AWAY!

THERE IS ALWAYS SO MUCH GOING ON THAT I NEVER KNOW JUST WHAT TO WRITE. SHALL AND TYE MOVED BACK TO SAINT GEORGE A COUPLE WEEKS AGO AND THAT WAS REALLY HARD. SHE CAME DOWN TODAY AND IS STAYING THE REST OF THE WEEK! PAUL FINALLY MET HER ON MOTHER'S DAY, AND OF COURSE, SHALL ABSOLUTELY LOVED HIM! I REALLY FELL HARD AND FAST FOR PAUL. I NEVER IN A MILLION YEARS THOUGHT THAT I WOULD EVER GET OVER JAY, BUT I HAVE. I FINALLY FOUND SOMEONE THAT TREATS ME LIKE A PRINCESS AND LIKE THE MOST IMPORTANT PERSON IN THE WORLD. I HAVE ALWAYS DREAMED OF HAVING A MAN LIKE THIS AND I FINALLY FOUND HIM. HE IS ABSOLUTELY EVERYTHING I HAVE HOPED AND PRAYED FOR. HE IS SO AMAZING! I DON'T KNOW HOW TO ACT SOMETIMES BECAUSE HE IS GOOD TO ME. I DEFINITELY NEED TO BE CAREFUL WITH THIS ONE BECAUSE I DON'T WANT TO LOSE HIM. I CANNOT TREAT HIM AT ALL

LIKE THE LAST TWO MEN I MARRIED. I NEED TO BE FAITHFUL AND TREAT HIM AS HE TREATS ME, ABSOLUTELY WONDERFUL! I KNOW IT'S STILL NEW, BUT IT FEELS SO RIGHT. I REALLY AM IN LOVE WITH HIM. I HAVE HAD MY KIDS A LOT MORE LATELY THAN I HAVE IN THE PAST FOUR YEARS. ADI IS HERE ALMOST EVERY SINGLE DAY. I LOVE IT. THEY ALL WANT MY ATTENTION AT THE SAME TIME, AND THEY WANT ALL OF ME, IT'S KIND OF DIFFICULT JUGGLING THREE KIDS, AND NOW TWO OTHER KIDS *(Paul has two children).* I REALLY ADORE PAUL'S KIDS, BUT THIS IS SOMETHING I KNOW LATER WILL BE VERY DIFFICULT FOR ME.

5-30-2012: Dr. Note–Says she is doing well, denies any problems. Prescribed Suboxone and Buprenorphine.

SATURDAY, JUNE 2, 2012:

IT'S ABOUT 1:30 A.M. AND I JUST GOT HOME FROM WORK A LITTLE BIT AGO. I DO LIKE MY JOB, BUT TONIGHT IT REALLY SUCKED! I HAD THE WORST PEOPLE TONIGHT. I GO OUT OF MY WAY TO BE THE BEST SERVER THAT I CAN, AND PEOPLE JUST DON'T GIVE A SHIT. NOBODY KNOWS HOW TO TIP ANYMORE. OH WELL, SOME NIGHTS ARE REALLY GREAT AND OTHER NIGHTS, I JUST WANT TO KILL EVERYONE! SHALL AND TYE SLEPT OVER TONIGHT *(at my parents')* 'CAUSE THEY ARE LEAVING IN THE MORNING, SO THAT MADE ME HAPPY TO KNOW THEY WERE HERE WHEN I GOT HOME. I HATE IT WHEN SHALL LEAVES, I MISS HER SO MUCH. SHE WILL ALWAYS BE THE ONE PERSON THAT I ALWAYS LOOK UP TO AND ADMIRE AND TRY TO BE LIKE SOMEDAY. SHE IS AS PERFECT AS ANYONE COULD POSSIBLY GET. HAVEN'T SEEN MY MAN VERY MUCH THIS WEEK, AND I AM GOING CRAZY! I HAVE HAD MY KIDS ALL WEEK EXCEPT FOR LAST NIGHT, SO I GOT TO SEE HIM FOR ONE NIGHT AND IT WAS ABSOLUTELY AMAZING! EVERY SECOND WITH PAUL MAKES ME FEEL AS IF I WERE

IN HEAVEN. I ABSOLUTELY LOVE HIM AND ADORE HIM. YEP, I DEFINITELY WANT TO MARRY THIS MAN SOMETIME SOON. BETTER GET MY DIVORCE OVER FIRST. IT SHOULD BE OVER VERY SOON. WE BOTH HAVE TO TAKE THE PARENTING CLASS, THEN OUR DIVORCE WILL BE FINAL. I AM HONESTLY THE HAPPIEST I HAVE EVER BEEN WITH PAUL! I WILL KEEP HIM!

While we were staying at my parents, I had a dream that Nat had drugs hidden in between her mattresses, so Adi and I went to her room to look while she was at work. We found a lockbox in between the mattresses of her bed, and we opened it and found her drugs and needles. We brought it upstairs and showed my parents. My mom flushed the drugs down the toilet and they kicked her out.

A month later...

MONDAY, JULY 9, 2012:

THE ONE THING THAT I HAVE BEEN SO SCARED ABOUT HAPPENED, AND NOW MY LIFE HAS BEEN TURNED UPSIDE DOWN! MY SISTER, THE ONE THAT *ALWAYS* KNOWS, WENT IN MY ROOM WHILE I WAS AT WORK AND FOUND MY LITTLE RED BOX THAT HAS MY SYRINGES, HEROIN, AND METH IN IT. I HAVE BEEN SO SCARED LATELY THAT THEY WOULD FIND OUT I WAS USING AGAIN, AND THEY DID! I DID THIS TO MYSELF, ONCE AGAIN! FUCKED MY LIFE UP, REALLY GOOD THIS TIME. I TOLD PAUL JUST THAT I WAS KICKED OUT, NOT USING, AND HE WAS NOT OKAY, BUT IS STILL STAYING BY MY SIDE, HE IS HONESTLY THE GREATEST MAN I HAVE EVER MET. MY PARENTS, OF COURSE, KICKED ME OUT AND JAY WON'T LET ME SEE JALA AT ALL, AND ADI SAID SHE NEVER WANTED TO SPEAK TO ME AGAIN, ALONG WITH SOME OTHER EXTREMELY HEARTBREAKING WORDS. *(I can only imagine how hurt and angry Adi was after we found the drugs in her mom's room and knowing she had been lied to for so long. It broke my heart.)* I DEFINITELY DID IT THIS

TIME. I AM LIVING WITH PAUL RIGHT NOW AND IT IS GOING JUST FINE, OTHER THAN I MISS MY KIDS AND MY FAMILY. I WENT TO SEATTLE LAST WEEK WITH PAUL AND HIS KIDS, AND IT WAS GREAT AT FIRST, THEN TURNED INTO A DISASTER. I GOT SO SICK THE LAST THREE DAYS WE WERE THERE AND HAD TO LEAVE A DAY EARLY. PAUL WAS UPSET! I THOUGHT FOR SURE HE WAS DONE WITH ME, BUT TO MY SURPRISE, ONCE AGAIN, THIS AMAZING MAN IS STILL HERE, TREATING ME LIKE A QUEEN. I NEED TO CHANGE THINGS, AND RIGHT AWAY, OR I AM GOING TO LOSE MY LIFE FOR GOOD. I KNOW I CAN DO THIS, I AM STRONG AND CAN DEFINITELY FIGHT FOR WHAT I WANT! GOOD LUCK AND DON'T WASTE ANOTHER DAY!!

July 11, 2012: Dr. Note–105 lbs. Relapsed on Heroin five weeks ago. Couldn't afford Suboxone. Used once—feels bad—back on track says she's doing well. Prescribed Suboxone and Buprenorphine.

WEDNESDAY, JULY 11, 2012:

WELL, TODAY WAS A VERY SHITTY DAY, TO SAY THE LEAST! I DON'T WORK ON WEDNESDAYS BECAUSE THAT IS THE ONE DAY EVERY SINGLE WEEK THAT I GET TO BE WITH ALL THREE OF MY BEAUTIFUL KIDS! BUT, NOT TODAY. I HAVE NOT BEEN OR SEEN MY KIDS IN ALMOST A MONTH NOW! I AM IN TEARS EVERY SINGLE DAY RIGHT NOW. I DID THIS TO MYSELF, I GOT MYSELF INTO THIS MESS, HURT SO MANY PEOPLE THAT WERE VERY SPECIAL/IMPORTANT TO ME, SO NOW IT'S ABOUT TIME TO DIG MYSELF OUT OF THIS DARK HELL HOLE. IT'S SO TIME! I AM TAKING MARY TO COURT IN THE MORNING AND WE FIND OUT HER SENTENCING. IT'S GOING TO BE THREE TO TEN YEARS IN PRISON FOR HER. IT TOOK QUITE A WHILE, BUT MARY IS GETTING PUNISHED FOR ALL THE THINGS SHE HAS DONE THAT ARE NOT RIGHT. IT'S GOING TO BE SAD, WEIRD, AND GOOD THAT SHE IS GOING TO BE GONE. I REALLY NEEDED HER OUT OF MY LIFE, AND I COULD NEVER

DO IT. MAYBE THIS WAS A BLESSING IN DISGUISE FOR ME AND AN ANSWER TO MY PRAYERS BY GETTING HER AWAY FROM ME. THIS IS THE HARDEST THING BY FAR FOR ME TO DO. GETTING RID AND AWAY FROM ALL THE PEOPLE IN MY LIFE THAT USE WAS DEFINITELY THE HARDEST THING FOR ME TO DO. I STILL HAVEN'T DONE IT, AND IT'S THE ONE THING AND THE MOST IMPORTANT THING FOR ME TO DO TO START A CLEAN LIFE. A CLEAN LIFE IS THE ONE THING I WANT MORE THAN ANYTHING AND THE HARDEST THING I HAVE EVER HAD TO FACE AND DEAL WITH IN MY LIFE. I KNOW I CAN DO THIS. I AM STRONG AND I AM DEFINITELY A FIGHTER! I WILL GET THROUGH THIS AND COME OUT ON TOP!

Five days later...

MONDAY, JULY 16, 2012:

STILL MADLY IN LOVE WITH PAUL AND IT MAKES ME SO HAPPY! EVEN THOUGH MY LIFE COULDN'T BE MORE UPSIDE DOWN AND FUCKED UP, I AM STILL UNUSUALLY HAPPY, BUT SO, SO SAD AT THE SAME TIME. IT'S THE STRANGEST FEELING, SOMETIMES I DON'T KNOW HOW I FEEL BECAUSE THEY ARE BOTH SUCH STRONG FEELINGS, AND TIMES. STILL LIVING WITH MY MAN, AND FOR THE MOST PART, IT'S GOING GREAT. BUT THE OTHER NIGHT, IT WAS NOT SO GREAT. WE GOT INTO A HUGE FIGHT AND HE WANTED ME TO LEAVE, WHICH WAS AN AWFUL TIME FOR ME. WE ENDED UP WORKING THINGS OUT LIKE WE ALWAYS DO, AND WE ARE BETTER THAN EVER NOW. ACTUALLY, YESTERDAY HE CAME INTO THE BATHROOM WHILE I WAS SHOWERING AND HANDED ME A RING, AN AWESOME RING, AND SAID, "HAPPY SIX MONTH ANNIVERSARY." SWEETEST THING EVER! I NEVER EVEN KNEW HOW LONG WE HAVE BEEN DATING. I HAVE NOT SEEN ADI OR MAS IN OVER A MONTH AND I HAVE NOT EVEN TALKED TO ADI REALLY ON THE PHONE EITHER. SHE HAS BEEN SO HURT AND ANGRY WITH ME THAT

SHE WOULD NOT EVEN TALK TO ME. BUT TO MY SURPRISE, WHILE I WAS AT WORK TODAY, SHE CALLED ME ABOUT EIGHT TIMES. I CALLED HER WHEN I GOT OFF AND SHE WANTED ME TO PICK HER UP AND GRAB SOME FOOD. I DID AND WE TALKED, AND IT WAS WONDERFUL! IT WAS SO GOOD TO SEE MY BABY GIRL! I MISS HER SO DAMN MUCH! IN TWO DAYS, WEDNESDAY, I GET TO SPEND THE DAY WITH ALL THREE OF MY AWESOME KIDS. I AM SO EXCITED, I CAN HARDLY WAIT!!

TUESDAY, JULY 17, 2012:

WELL, MY LIFE COULDN'T BE MORE TURNED UPSIDE DOWN THAN IT IS RIGHT NOW. I AM THE SADDEST I HAVE EVER BEEN RIGHT NOW. I LITERALLY WANT TO DIE. I LOST MY KIDS AGAIN, AND MY FAMILY. I HAD FINALLY EARNED ALL THEIR TRUST BACK AND IT TOOK A VERY, VERY LONG TIME, AND NOW I FUCKED UP ONCE AGAIN AND LOST IT AGAIN. I CAN'T SEE MY KIDS NOW AND I AM LITERALLY IN TEARS EVERY SINGLE DAY. HOW DID I DO THIS AGAIN. ALL I KNOW IS THAT I BETTER CHANGE THINGS AND QUICK, 'CAUSE I AM NOT GOING TO BE WITHOUT MY BEAUTIFUL KIDS ANY LONGER. THEY NEED THEIR MOTHER BACK AND I AM GOING TO BRING MYSELF BACK TO THEM BETTER THAN EVER!

I don't know what she is talking about in this entry. The day before, she was so excited to be able to see her kids, and the day after this entry, she saw them.

WEDNESDAY, JULY 18, 2012:

WELL, TODAY WAS AN ABSOLUTELY AWESOME DAY! I GOT TO SPEND THE ENTIRE DAY WITH ALL THREE OF MY INCREDIBLE KIDS. IT WAS FABULOUS! I GET TO SPEND THE DAY TOMORROW WITH JALA BEFORE I HAVE TO GO TO WORK. SHE IS HAVING A TOUGH TIME WITHOUT ME AND IT BREAKS MY HEART INTO A

MILLION LITTLE PIECES. I NEED TO GET THINGS FIXED AND FAST. JALA, ADI, AND MAS ARE ALL GROWING UP WAY TOO FAST AND I DON'T HAVE MUCH TIME LEFT. IT WAS REALLY HARD LEAVING THEM TODAY.

THURSDAY, JULY 19, 2012:

JUST GOT HOME FROM CLOSING AT WORK. I LIKE IT THERE MOST OF THE TIME (IGGY'S), IT'S THE CUSTOMERS I GET FURIOUS WITH! PEOPLE JUST DON'T KNOW HOW TO TIP ANYMORE. IT'S VERY SELDOM THAT I WALK AWAY AT THE END OF MY SHIFT WITHOUT GETTING ANGRY AT A BUNCH OF TABLES BECAUSE THEY LEFT ME NOTHING. PAYNE SAYS I WILL GET USED TO IT BUT I HAVE BEEN WORKING THERE FOR OVER A YEAR AND A HALF NOW AND I AM MORE ANGRY THAN EVER LATELY.

I AM SITTING HERE WATCHING MY MAN BREAK DANCE, HE THINKS HE IS PRETTY GOOD! HE IS JUST THE CUTEST THING EVER (PAUL). WE HAVE BEEN DATING FOR ABOUT 4 MONTHS NOW AND ARE TALKING ABOUT GETTING MARRIED. I REALLY HAVE NEVER FELT SO SURE ABOUT ANYTHING IN MY LIFE, LIKE I HAVE WITH "US." WE ARE AN ABSOLUTELY PERFECT FIT! I SURE DO LOVE HIM.

TODAY WAS AN AWESOME DAY!! AND I USUALLY DON'T EVER SAY THAT, AT LEAST NOT LATELY. I GOT TO BE WITH ALL THREE OF MY AMAZINGLY WONDERFUL KIDS AND THEY REALLY ARE ABSOLUTELY AMAZING! IT WAS REALLY NICE, BUT WHEN IT WAS TIME TO LEAVE THEM, IT WAS NOT ALL THAT GREAT. JALA WOULD NOT STOP CRYING AND TO SEE THE DISAPPOINTED LOOK ON MASON AND ADI'S FACES ABSOLUTELY KILLED ME! HOW DID I LET THIS HAPPEN AGAIN?!? I AM A STRONGER PERSON THAN THIS AND MY KIDS MEAN MORE TO ME THAN I HAVE BEEN SHOWING THEM. TIME IS GOING BY WAY TOO FAST AND IF I DON'T TURN MY LIFE AROUND REAL SOON, I AM NOT GOING TO LIKE WHAT COMES NEXT. JALA IS NOW SIX,

MASON NOW THIRTEEN, AND ADISON NOW SIXTEEN. I HAVE NO MORE TIME LEFT WITH ADI, WHICH BREAKS MY HEART, BUT I STILL HAVE A LITTLE TIME WITH MASON AND JALA. MY KIDS ARE MY LIFE, THEY MEAN THE ABSOLUTE WORLD TO ME, SO HOW DID I EVER LET ALL THIS SHIT HAPPEN? THIS LIFE IS NOT ME!! I AM MUCH BETTER THAN ALL THIS AND MUCH, MUCH BETTER THAN ALL THE HORRIBLE PEOPLE I HAVE BEEN TALKING TO THE PAST COUPLE MONTHS/YEARS. NOW I FINALLY FOUND A PERFECT MAN, PAUL, AND I WILL NOT FUCK THINGS UP WITH HIM. I HAVE GONE THROUGH A BUNCH OF LOSERS AND WAITED MY WHOLE LIFE FOR THIS MAN. I WILL CHANGE MY LIFE, KEEP PAUL AROUND FOREVER, AND GET MY KIDS AND MY FAMILY BACK…WATCH!!

<u>FRIDAY, JULY 20, 2012</u>:

I SAW MY BABY GIRL AGAIN TODAY AND IT WAS GREAT. BUT EVERY TIME I NEED TO LEAVE, IT IS THE ABSOLUTE WORST FEELING IN THE WORLD. I CAN'T TAKE BEING AWAY FROM MY KIDS ANYMORE. I NEED TO CHANGE THINGS AND I NEED TO DO IT FAST. LIFE IS TOO SHORT, AND MY KIDS ARE GOING TO BE OUT OF OUR HOUSE AND OUT OF OUR CONTROL IN NO TIME. I DON'T HAVE ANY MORE TIME TO SPARE, NONE AT ALL!

<u>SUNDAY, JULY 22, 2012</u>:

I CLOSED LAST NIGHT AT WORK AND GOT HOME REALLY LATE, I AM A BIT TIRED TODAY. WE ARE GOING TO THE MOVIES NOW AND I REALLY WISH MY KIDS WERE GOING WITH US. I MISS THEM SO BAD THAT IT PHYSICALLY HURTS. TODAY HAS JUST BEEN AN AWFUL DAY, I MISS MY KIDS SO MUCH. I KNOW WHAT I NEED TO DO, I JUST NEED TO DO IT!

WELL, TODAY WAS SUPPOSED TO BE A GREAT DAY 'CAUSE I DIDN'T HAVE TO WORK AND I GOT TO SEE MY MAN ALL DAY, IT DIDN'T END UP BEING A GOOD DAY AT ALL. ACTUALLY,

HORRIBLE! PAUL AND I GOT IN A HUGE FIGHT AND HE ALWAYS, WELL, THE TIMES WE HAVE GOTTEN IN OUR REALLY BIG FIGHTS WHICH HAVE ONLY BEEN A FEW, HE DOES IT RIGHT IN FRONT OF HIS KIDS. HE FREAKS OUT ON ME AND I LOOK LIKE A COMPLETE IDIOT IN FRONT OF HIS KIDS. YA, I DESERVED A COUPLE OF LASHES OUT AT ME BECAUSE I DID SOME FUCKED UP THINGS, BUT WHY IN FRONT OF HIS KIDS? HE TOLD ME THAT I JUST HAVEN'T REALLY BEEN HOME LATELY. WELL, IT'S PROBABLY TRUE. WHEN HE HAS HIS KIDS, I DON'T HARDLY SEE HIM AT ALL. I AM GLAD HE IS SO GOOD TO HIS KIDS, BUT HE IS A TAD BIT OVERBOARD. IT'S ALL ABOUT THEM ALL THE TIME, AND YA, I PROBABLY HAVEN'T BEEN VERY FUN TO BE AROUND BECAUSE I WANT TO BE WITH MY KIDS TOO! I ABSOLUTELY LOVE HIS KIDS, THEY ARE GREAT KIDS, BUT PAUL IS ABSOLUTELY OBSESSED WITH THEM AND IT'S REALLY HARD TO BE AROUND ALL THREE OF THEM TOGETHER, BECAUSE IT'S LIKE I DON'T EVEN EXIST. I WANT MY KIDS!!

THURSDAY, JULY 26, 2012:

TODAY WAS AN OKAY DAY OTHER THAN I HAVE BEEN SICK ALL DAMN DAY *(when she says "sick," it's almost always drug related),* BUT I GOT TO BE WITH ADI AND JALA FOR THE MAJORITY OF THE DAY AND THAT ALWAYS MAKES ME THE HAPPIEST. I DIDN'T GO INTO WORK TONIGHT BECAUSE I FEEL SO SHITTY. HOPEFULLY I FEEL BETTER TOMORROW 'CAUSE I CAN'T MISS MY FRIDAY NIGHT SHIFT. THAT IS MY BIGGEST SHIFT. STILL LIVING AT PAUL'S.

SUNDAY, JULY 29, 2012:

WELL, TODAY STARTED OUT PRETTY SHITTY BECAUSE PAUL AND I WERE FIGHTING PRETTY BAD. MY MOM AND DAD HAD ALL MY KIDS TODAY, EVEN JALA, AND THEY ALL WANTED ME

TO COME OVER SO BAD. I DID THIS TO MYSELF, NOW I NEED TO GET MYSELF OUT OF IT, AGAIN. WHEN AM I GOING TO LEARN? THIS IS NOT WHAT I WANT OUT OF MY LIFE. NOW I NEED TO CHANGE IT, AND QUICK. LIFE IS TOO SHORT, AND TIME GOES BY WAY TOO FAST TO NOT MAKE THINGS RIGHT.

MONDAY, JULY 30, 2012:

I JUST GOT HOME FROM WORK ABOUT TWO HOURS AGO AND I AM JUST RELAXIN' WITH MY HONEY. WE HAVE BEEN THROUGH SOME SHIT LATELY, BUT WE MAKE IT THROUGH IT EVERY TIME AND COME OUT EVEN STRONGER. WELL, I HOPE WE GET THROUGH IT STRONGER. I JUST DON'T KNOW HOW MUCH MORE OF THIS I CAN TAKE. WHEN HE GETS MAD, HE IS *MAD!* AND THERE IS NO WAY TO GET HIM IN A BETTER PLACE AT THAT POINT. I JUST NEED TO GET AWAY, 'CAUSE IT GETS WORSE FROM THEN ON. ADI TURNS 16 NEXT WEEK AND I AM FREAKING OUT ABOUT IT. I HAVE HAD NO TIME WITH HER. WHAT THE *HELL* AM I DOING? MY KIDS ARE MY WHOLE LIFE AND SO MUCH MORE, SO HOW IN THE HELL DID I GET IT THIS WAY? I DON'T EVEN KNOW WHAT STEP TO TAKE FIRST.

TUESDAY, JULY 31, 2012:

JUST GOT HOME FROM WORK ABOUT AN HOUR AGO. WORK WAS OKAY, I AM JUST REALLY BURNED OUT. I AM REALLY EXCITED BECAUSE I GET TO SEE ALL THREE OF MY BEAUTIFUL KIDS TOMORROW. I LOVE WEDNESDAYS. I NEED WEDNESDAYS EVERY DAY, THOUGH. I AM REALLY GETTING SCARED, I NEED TO DO SOMETHING AND FAST. ADI TURNS 16 NEXT WEDNESDAY AND I AM FREAKING OUT. I HAVE LOST WAY TOO MUCH TIME WITH ADI. I WANT TO GET SOME TIME BACK, BUT I DON'T KNOW HOW. I KNOW MY BABY JALA IS REALLY GOING THROUGH A ROUGH TIME WITHOUT ME. WE WENT FROM BEING TOGETHER EVERY DAY ALL DAY LONG TO SEEING EACH OTHER ONE DAY

A WEEK. YA, SHE ISN'T DOING SO GOOD. I HEAR HER VOICE WHEN I TALK TO HER ON THE PHONE AND I SEE HER POOR LITTLE FACE WHEN I AM ABOUT TO LEAVE. IT BREAKS MY HEART INTO A MILLION LITTLE PIECES. I NEED TO GET MY SHIT TOGETHER AND RAISE THAT PRECIOUS LITTLE GIRL LIKE I SHOULD. WHAT IN THE *HELL* IS WRONG WITH ME? WHY DID I CHOOSE THIS LIFE OVER MY THREE PRECIOUS KIDS? BECAUSE I DIDN'T CHOOSE, IT TOOK OVER ME AND I HAVE NOT HAD THE STRENGTH TO FIGHT IT AWAY. WELL, I KNOW I HAVE THE STRENGTH NOW, AND I NEED TO FIGHT *NOW,* OR I AM GOING TO DIE!

WEDNESDAY, AUGUST 1, 2012:

TODAY WAS A FANTASTIC DAY 'CAUSE I GOT TO BE WITH ALL THREE OF MY KIDS! I ABSOLUTELY LOVE WEDNESDAYS. ADI'S BIRTHDAY IS COMING UP NEXT WEEK AND SHE IS GOING TO BE SIXTEEN. I AM FREAKING OUT. WHAT DO I GET HER AND WHAT DO I DO? I NEED TO DO SOMETHING INCREDIBLE BECAUSE SHE ALREADY GOT A CAR. SHE IS SO EXCITED. I AM SO HAPPY FOR HER. MY BDAY GIRL IS TURNING 16!!

THURSDAY, AUGUST 2, 2012:

JUST GOT HOME FROM WORK A LITTLE BIT AGO, MADE NO MONEY TONIGHT. $56.00, THAT IS ABSOLUTELY AWFUL! TODAY WAS A PRETTY GOOD DAY, THOUGH. WELL, IT IS ALWAYS A GOOD DAY WHEN I GET TO SEE MY BEAUTIFUL KIDS. ME, ADI, JALA, SHALL, GRANDMA, AND TYSON ALL WENT SWIMMING AT THE REC CENTER BEFORE I HAD TO GET READY FOR WORK. JUST STAYED FOR A COUPLE OF HOURS, BUT IT WAS TOTALLY WORTH IT. JALA ABSOLUTELY LOVES SWIMMING. SHE PRETTY MUCH TAUGHT HERSELF AND SHE IS REALLY GOOD, GOES UNDER WATER AND EVERYTHING. IT IS THE CUTEST THING EVER. AFTER SWIMMING, HAD TO GO TO WORK, CLOSED TONIGHT AND

IT WAS SO SLOW. THE OLYMPICS HAVE BEEN ON, SO IT HAS BEEN PRETTY CROWDED AND BUSY, BUT UNFORTUNATELY, NOT TONIGHT. IT WAS A PRETTY BORING NIGHT. I AM EXCITED BECAUSE TOMORROW I GET TO SPEND MORE TIME WITH MY KIDS. HOPEFULLY, I GET TO SEE MY BABY BOY, 'CAUSE I DIDN'T GET TO SEE HIM TODAY. HE IS A LITTLE BUSY BODY. ALWAYS OUT WITH HIS FRIENDS DOING FUN THINGS. HARD TO FIND TIME WITH HIM 'CAUSE HE IS ALWAYS PLAYING.

FRIDAY, AUGUST 3, 2012:

CLOSED AT WORK TONIGHT AND DIDN'T MAKE MUCH MONEY AT ALL. HOPEFULLY TOMORROW WILL BE A LOT BETTER. SPENDING THE DAY WITH MY KIDS TODAY, I AM SO EXCITED. SHALL HAS BEEN HERE ALL WEEK AND WE HAVE BEEN TALKING A LOT. ME, SHALL, ADI, JALA, GRANDMA, AND TYSON ALL WENT TO THE REC CENTER AND WENT SWIMMING, IT WAS WAY FUN. I HOPE SHALL AND I CAN GET BACK TO THE WAY WE WERE. I MISS ALL MY SISTERS SO MUCH. ANGIE IS OKAY RIGHT NOW, BUT EMILY WON'T TALK TO ME OR SEE ME. I DON'T THINK SHE IS GOING TO FORGIVE ME THIS TIME *(after finding out she was still using).*

MONDAY, AUGUST 6, 2012:

JUST GOT OFF WORK ABOUT AN HOUR AGO AND DIDN'T HAVE A VERY GOOD DAY AT ALL. SO, THE PLANS FOR ADI'S BIRTHDAY ON WEDNESDAY ARE ME AND PAUL AND POSSIBLY MY MOM ARE GOING TO TAKE ADI TO LUNCH AND THEN SHOPPING. I AM SO EXCITED FOR HER. I CAN HARDLY STAND IT. MY LITTLE GIRL HAS GROWN UP! I HAVE MISSED SO MUCH TIME WITH HER THAT IT KILLS ME. I MISS MY KIDS SO DAMN MUCH! WHY CAN'T LIFE BE EASIER? WHY ME, WHY MY LIFE? I

JUST WANTED TO RAISE MY KIDS AND HAVE A FAMILY. WHY DID EVERYTHING GET SO FUCKED UP? NOW, IT'S GONNA BE HELL TO TRY AND FIX IT. I DON'T EVEN KNOW HOW, AND IT STRESSES ME OUT MORE THAN ANYONE COULD POSSIBLY IMAGINE. I WANT MY LIFE BACK WITH MY KIDS!

TUESDAY, AUGUST 7, 2012:

JUST GOT HOME FROM WORK ABOUT AN HOUR AGO. IT WASN'T VERY BAD TONIGHT. IT WENT BY PRETTY FAST. I AM SO EXCITED FOR ADI'S BIRTHDAY TOMORROW. SHE IS 16! I CAN'T BELIEVE IT! WE ARE GOING TO HAVE AN AWESOME DAY TOMORROW. PAUL TOOK THE DAY OFF AND WE ARE TAKING HER TO LUNCH AND SHOPPING. IT'S GOING TO BE AN INCREDIBLE DAY. JAY BROUGHT JALA IN TO SEE ME AT WORK TONIGHT, I WAS ON TOP OF THE WORLD. BUT MY SWEET LITTLE PRINCESS WAS SICK. GOD, I HATE THIS! I JUST WANT TO BE WITH MY BABIES. THEY ALL NEED ME AND WANT TO BE WITH ME. THEY ARE MY KIDS! AND I AM GOING TO GET THEM BACK AND VERY, VERY SOON. I WILL MAKE DAMN SURE OF THAT!

WEDNESDAY, AUGUST 8, 2012:

IT WAS MY BABY GIRL'S BDAY TODAY. ADI TURNED SWEET 16 TODAY! I AM FREAKING OUT. MY KIDS NEED TO STOP GROWING. TIME GOES BY WAY TOO STINKIN' FAST. IT WAS A GREAT DAY, THOUGH. ADI, ME, PAUL, AND MOM WENT TO CITY CREEK AND TOOK ADI SHOPPING, THEN WENT TO EAT AT ELMATADOR. THE BDAY GIRL GOT TO CHOOSE WHERE SHE WANTED TO EAT. IT WAS WAY FUN. AFTER SHOPPING, I WENT TO JAY'S APARTMENT AND STAYED WITH MY OTHER BABY GIRL WHILE JAY WENT TO WORK. JALA HAS BEEN REALLY SICK SINCE LAST NIGHT, SO WE DIDN'T WANT HER TO LEAVE THE HOUSE. IT WAS SO SAD, SHE WAS SO SICK.

THURSDAY, AUGUST 9, 2012:

JUST GOT HOME FROM WORK ABOUT AN HOUR AGO AND I KICKED ASS TONIGHT. I WAS SO UPSET BECAUSE THEY TOOK ME OFF THURSDAY CLOSES, WHICH I HAVE NO IDEA WHY. I AM THE HARDEST WORKER THERE BY FAR. I HAVE NOT HAD A SHIFT THAT WASN'T AN OPENING/CLOSING SHIFT IN ABOUT A YEAR. SO, I WAS REALLY UPSET TONIGHT WHEN I WENT TO WORK. IT FELT SO WEIRD THAT I WASN'T CLOSING, BUT IT TURNED OUT TO BE A KICK ASS NIGHT. I WAS THERE FOR ABOUT 2 1/2 HOURS AND MADE MORE THAN THE CLOSERS AND EVERYBODY ELSE THERE THAT HAD BEEN THERE FOR 6 HOURS OR MORE. I MADE $120.00 TONIGHT. IT WAS AWESOME! BEFORE I WENT TO WORK, I WAS WITH ALL MY BABIES AT MY MOM'S, AND THEN JALA WANTED TO COME HOME WITH ME WHILE I GOT READY. I ABSOLUTELY LOVED IT. BRINGING MY BABY GIRL HOME WITH ME *(to Paul's)* FOR A COUPLE HOURS MEANT THE WORLD TO ME. I ABSOLUTELY LOVED HAVING HER HERE. WELL, PAUL AND I ARE NOW GONNA TALK BUSINESS BEFORE WE GO TO BED. WE ARE OPENING A WINDSHIELD REPAIR BUSINESS TOGETHER!

FRIDAY, AUGUST 10, 2012:

TODAY WAS AN OKAY DAY BUT A VERY, VERY SHITTY NIGHT AT WORK. I SWEAR, WORK IS JUST GETTING WORSE AND WORSE EACH DAY. I TOOK JALA OVER HERE AGAIN TO BE WITH ME WHILE I GOT READY FOR WORK AND PAUL BROUGHT HIS KIDS AND LUNCH OVER BEFORE I WENT INTO WORK. JALA HAD A BLAST PLAYING WITH THE KIDS. THEY ARE CUTE TOGETHER. THEN, RIGHT BEFORE WORK, WE ALL WENT TO TAKE JALA BACK TO MY MOM'S AND ANGIE AND RANDY AND THEIR KIDS AND ADI AND MAS WERE THERE, SO OF COURSE, THEY ALL

HUNG OUT TOGETHER AND HAD A BLAST. ADI GOT A GUITAR FOR HER BIRTHDAY BUT HAS NO IDEA HOW TO PLAY IT. PAUL BROUGHT HIS GUITAR AND STAYED HERE AFTER I LEFT FOR WORK AND SHOWED ADI HOW TO PLAY. THEY LOOK SO CUTE TOGETHER WITH BOTH THEIR GUITARS DOWNSTAIRS AT MY MOM'S. I MISS MY SISTERS SO VERY MUCH. I CAN'T STAND IT! I AM SO SAD BECAUSE I JUST DON'T THINK EM WILL GET OVER THIS ONE THIS TIME. I HOPE AND PRAY THAT SHE DOES.

SUNDAY, AUGUST 12, 2012:

GOT HOME FROM WORK A BIT AGO AND NOW ME AND PAUL ARE JUST GOING TO WATCH A MOVIE AND GRAB SOME DINNER. I NEVER WORK ON SUNDAYS, BUT A GIRL JUST CALLED AND ASKED IF I WOULD COVER HER SHIFT. I COULDN'T SAY NO 'CAUSE SHE ALWAYS HELPS ME OUT. I HATE CLOSING ON SUNDAYS. I AM JUST HATING WORK ALL TOGETHER, BUT I HAVE TO KEEP THIS JOB UNTIL PAUL AND I START UP OUR OWN BUSINESS, WHICH I AM ECSTATIC ABOUT. SO, JAY TOLD ME EARLIER TODAY THAT MY MOM HAS JALA TONIGHT TO SLEEP OVER AND TO TAKE HER TO CHURCH IN THE MORNING. IT'S SO SAD THAT I CAN'T EVEN GO OVER THERE WHILE THEY HAVE MY KIDS. *(Something must have happened in the previous two days that made it so she could not be around her kids, but she ended up at my mom's three days later.)* MASON IS THERE TOO, BUT NOT ADI. NOW THAT SHE IS 16, THAT GIRL WILL NOT STAY PUT. I HOPE MY BABY GIRL IS OKAY OVER THERE WITHOUT ME. SHE USUALLY HAS A HARD TIME WHEN I'M NOT THERE. IT LITERALLY MAKES ME PHYSICALLY ILL THINKING THAT SHE COULD BE CRYING OR JUST WANTING ME AND I AM NOT THERE. I CAN'T EVEN THINK ABOUT IT OR I JUST WANT TO KILL MYSELF. HOW IN THE HELL DID I LET IT GET LIKE THIS?!?

MONDAY, AUGUST 13, 2012:

I OPENED TODAY AT WORK AND IT SUCKED! I AM A LITTLE BURNED OUT. I HAVE NOT HAD A DAY OFF SINCE WEDNESDAY, AND I WON'T AGAIN TILL THIS NEXT WEDNESDAY. I AM JUST REALLY, REALLY GETTING BURNED OUT OF IGGY'S. I HAVE BEEN THERE FOR ALMOST TWO YEARS NOW. I AM SO TIRED OF IT. I REALLY MISS MY SISTERS, SO MUCH THAT SOMETIMES IT PHYSICALLY HURTS. ON ADI'S BIRTHDAY, ME AND MOM WERE DRIVING HOME AND I LOST IT. I CRIED THE WHOLE WAY HOME. I MISS MY DAD SO MUCH. I REALLY DON'T KNOW IF HE IS EVER GOING TO LET THIS ONE GO. MY MOM SAYS HE IS, BUT MY MOTHER IS THE MOST POSITIVE PERSON I KNOW. SHE LOOKS AT THE GOOD IN EVERYTHING. I WISH I WAS LIKE THAT. I REALLY AM VERY NEGATIVE. PEOPLE TELL ME THAT ALL THE TIME, BUT I NEVER NOTICED IT UNTIL RECENTLY. I REALLY AM. I SAY MORE NEGATIVE THINGS DURING A DAY THAN POSITIVE, A LOT MORE. THAT MAKES ME REALLY SAD. I AM DEFINITELY GOING TO WORK ON THAT.

TUESDAY, AUGUST 14, 2012:

TODAY WAS AN OKAY DAY. I OPENED AT WORK AND EVERY DAY THERE IS JUST GETTING WORSE AND WORSE. I DON'T GET WHY IT KEEPS GETTING BAD THERE. I STILL LIVE WITH PAUL AND IT IS GOING ABSOLUTELY WONDERFUL. I GET SO EXCITED TO SEE HIM EVERY NIGHT WHEN I GET OFF WORK. HE IS AN AMAZING GUY AND I FEEL VERY LUCKY AND PROUD TO BE WITH HIM, AND I JUST HOPE I DON'T FUCK THIS ONE UP LIKE I DO EVERY RELATIONSHIP I AM IN.

WEDNESDAY, AUGUST 15, 2012:

TODAY HAS BEEN AN AWESOME DAY. I SPENT THE DAY AT MY MOM'S WITH JALA AND ADI. THEN CAME HOME AND ME AND MY

MAN ARE LISTENING TO MUSIC AND TALKING AND DANCING. I AM GETTING OLD. I AM 33 AND THAT FREAKS ME OUT! I NEVER THOUGHT I WOULD EVER GET THIS OLD. I HAVEN'T DONE HALF OF WHAT I ALWAYS WANTED TO DO, AND MY LIFE IS ABSOLUTELY NOT HOW I PICTURED IT AND I WISH I COULD TAKE BACK THE MAJORITY OF THE PAST 10-15 YEARS. HOW SAD IS THAT? I HAD BIG PLANS FOR MYSELF, MY LIFE, AND FOR MY PRECIOUS KIDS, AND NOTHING TURNED OUT AT ALL LIKE I WANTED OR PLANNED. I JUST SURE HOPE ALL THIS SHIT THAT I HAVE GONE THROUGH AND AM STILL GOING THROUGH HAS A PURPOSE 'CAUSE IT ALL MAKES ME SICK AND SO MAD AT MYSELF.

JUST GOT HOME FROM WORK ABOUT AN HOUR AGO, IT WAS AN OKAY NIGHT. I HAD TO TEACH MELISSA HOW TO CLOSE AND IT SUCKED TEACHING SOMEONE ALL THAT STUFF. BUT WE GOT OUT FAST, YAY! I AM REALLY STARTING TO FREAK OUT A BIT. I AM NOT GETTING ANY BETTER AT ALL. I GOT OFF EVERYTHING FOR ABOUT A YEAR *(she was never clean that long),* THEN SAW MARY AGAIN AND EVERYTHING WENT TO SHIT FROM THAT POINT AGAIN. WHAT IN THE HELL AM I DOING? I ALREADY LOST MY KIDS ONCE, AND NOW AGAIN. HOW COULD I LET THIS HAPPEN AGAIN? I AM SO DISAPPOINTED IN MYSELF, I CAN HARDLY STAND IT. MARY AND DAVID ARE BOTH IN JAIL RIGHT NOW, WHICH IS A GOOD THING, BUT I STILL MISS THEM LIKE CRAZY. THEY WERE MY ONLY FAMILY FOR A LONG TIME. EVEN THOUGH THEY ARE THE ONES THAT GOT ME INTO ALL THIS SHIT, THEY STILL BOTH HOLD A SPECIAL PLACE IN MY HEART. DAVID KEEPS CALLING ME TO COME SEE HIM 'CAUSE HE WILL BE LOCKED UP FOR A LONG, LONG TIME, MANY YEARS. MARY WILL BE OUT IN 30 DAYS, HER AND ANDREW. IF SHE FOUND OUT I WENT TO SEE HIM, SHE WOULD GO APE SHIT ON ME. BUT I FEEL BAD, I LOVE DAVID TO DEATH, MARY TOO, AND I DON'T WANT TO START UP SHIT WITH MARY. I REALLY NEED TO COMPLETELY GET

THEM OUT OF MY LIFE IF I WANT TO GET ANY BETTER AND GET MY KIDS BACK, BUT IT IS SO HARD!

There is such a conflict in her here. She knew she needed to stay away from Mary and David, but she kept going back, she said she loved them and felt they were family. They had a long history together.

THURSDAY, AUGUST 16, 2012:

WELL, IT IS 4:15 A.M. RIGHT NOW, THURSDAY MORNING, AND I CANNOT SLEEP FOR THE LIFE OF ME AND I REALLY NEED TO BECAUSE I HAVE TO WORK TOMORROW NIGHT. I DON'T CLOSE, THOUGH, SO IT WON'T BE TOO BAD. THEY TOOK MY THURSDAY CLOSES AWAY, THEY ARE REALLY BEING MEAN TO ME RIGHT NOW, ESPECIALLY THE GM, HE WAS ALWAYS SO GOOD TO ME. *(I think everyone at work was slowly realizing she was using; she had also used with coworkers.)* I AM HAVING A HARD TIME AT WORK LATELY. PAYNE SAYS IN THE PAST 3/4 MONTHS I HAVE COMPLETELY CHANGED AND EVERYONE HAS NOTICED IT. *(It was obvious in her appearance that she was using.)* I HAVE NO IDEA WHAT I AM DOING ANY DIFFERENT. I WORK MY ASS OFF AT WORK. I AM BY FAR THE HARDEST WORKER THERE. SO, WHY IN THE HELL AM I GETTING TREATED LIKE SHIT? IT JUST DOESN'T MAKE ANY SENSE TO ME. OH WELL, PAUL SAYS HE WANTS OUR BUSINESS TO BE GOING NO LATER THAN NEXT MONTH, AND IF THAT HAPPENS, THEN GOODBYE IGGY'S! YAY! I HOPE THIS BUSINESS GOES LIKE PAUL SAYS IT WILL. HE SAYS I WILL BE MAKING 3/4 GRAND A MONTH. WOULDN'T THAT BE NICE?

WAS WITH MY BABIES YESTERDAY, EXCEPT MY BOY 'CAUSE HE IS ON A CAMPOUT FOR 7 DAYS, AND IT WAS A WONDERFUL DAY. I LOVE MY GIRLS SO MUCH. ADI IS SO GROWN UP, 16 YEARS OLD, I STILL CAN'T BELIEVE IT!

FRIDAY, AUGUST 17, 2012:

WELL, EVEN THOUGH I GOT ZERO SLEEP LAST NIGHT, I AM GOING TO HAVE A FANTASTIC DAY BECAUSE I AM GOING TO BE WITH JALA ALL DAY UNTIL I GO TO WORK. I'M HERE AT JAY'S RIGHT NOW 'CAUSE HE HAS TO GO TO WORK. I LOVE MY BABY GIRL.

NOW I HAVE JALA OVER AT MY FRIEND MELISSA'S HOUSE PLAYING WITH HER LITTLE GIRL THAT IS EXACTLY JALA'S AGE. NOW WE CAME TO MCDONALD'S AND THE KIDS ARE PLAYING. YEP, I DEFINITELY HAD A FANTASTIC DAY! BUT WHAT IN THE HELL AM I DOING? JALA OR I SHOULD NOT BE HANGING AROUND THEM! I NEED TO GET MY PRIORITIES STRAIGHT. JALA HAD A BLAST WITH HER DAUGHTER, BUT THEY ARE YOUR TYPICAL TWEEKERS! I WOULD NEVER IN A MILLION YEARS PUT JALA IN HARM OR PUT HER AROUND DRUGS, BUT THESE ARE NOT THE KIND OF PEOPLE I NEED TO BE AROUND! I REALLY, REALLY NEED TO CHANGE MY LIFE AND VERY FAST BEFORE SOMETHING BAD HAPPENS. I REALLY NEED TO TAKE MY OWN ADVICE AND START FACING MY WORST FEAR EVER, GETTING CLEAN. I KNOW I CAN DO IT, I JUST GET SO SCARED OF GETTING SICK, I HONESTLY CANNOT HANDLE THAT PART VERY WELL AT ALL. PLEASE, GOD, GIVE ME THE STRENGTH AND THE TOOLS I NEED TO GET MYSELF BETTER AND GET MY LIFE BACK.

SATURDAY, AUGUST 18, 2012:

JUST GOT HOME FROM WORK A LITTLE BIT AGO AND TONIGHT SUCKED! PAUL AND I GOT IN THE BIGGEST FIGHT YESTERDAY AND I COMPLETELY LOST IT! I HAVE NOT UNLEASHED ON HIM YET AND YESTERDAY I DID. I HAD TO DROP OFF JALA BACK TO JAY 'CAUSE WE WERE FIGHTING SO STINKIN' BAD. BUT WE MADE IT THROUGH ONCE AGAIN. IF WE GOT PAST

ALL THAT WE HAVE, THEN WE CAN GET THROUGH ABSOLUTELY ANYTHING. I'M STILL A LITTLE BIT UPSET, THOUGH. HE SAID SOME THINGS THAT I WILL NEVER FORGET. I WILL TRY BUT I DON'T THINK I WILL.

Jala still has a memory of being in the hallway at Nat and Paul's and seeing Paul grab Nat's arm and throw her into the bedroom; she heard screaming and slapping sounds.

SUNDAY, AUGUST 19, 2012:

WELL, TODAY WASN'T THE MOST EXCITING DAY. SAT AT THE HOSPITAL FOR TWO HOURS WAITING FOR A DR. AND THEY TOOK SO LONG, SO I LEFT. I HAVE ANOTHER ABSCESS! WHEN AM I GOING TO LEARN? I REALLY WANT TO CHANGE MY LIFE BUT AM SO DAMN SCARED AND HAVE NO IDEA HOW TO DO IT. I CAN'T LOSE MY JOB, AND I NEVER HAVE A COUPLE DAYS OFF IN A ROW EVER. HOW AM I EVER SUPPOSED TO GET CLEAN? IT'S SO DAMN FRUSTRATING. I CAN'T LOSE PAUL OR ANYTHING ELSE, LIKE MY JOB. I NEED TO GET THINGS FIGURED OUT. I THINK MY MRSA IS BACK AND I AM PRETTY MUCH FREAKIN' OUT 'CAUSE IT'S DANGEROUS STUFF. *(MRSA is a staph infection that is resistant to some antibiotics. It leads to Sepsis and the last stage being Septic which causes organ failure and leads to death.).* I AM SITTING HERE ON MY BED RIGHT NOW WATCHING *Burlesque*. I OPEN TOMORROW AND I AM SO SCARED 'CAUSE MY ABSCESS IS ON MY HIP FLEXOR AND IN A VERY PAINFUL SPOT. I AM DEFINITELY GOING TO BE HURTING TOMORROW.

HAVEN'T TALKED TO ADI OR MAS FOR A WHILE. MAS IS ON A CAMPOUT AND HAS BEEN GONE SINCE LAST SUNDAY AND I MISS HIM SO MUCH. ADI HAS BEEN IN SAINT GEORGE FOR THE PAST COUPLE DAYS. I MISS THEM!

MONDAY, AUGUST 20, 2012:

I KNOW THIS SOUNDS VERY BAD, BUT I FEEL LIKE I AM COMPETING WITH PAUL'S KIDS THE MAJORITY OF THE TIME. I ABSOLUTELY LOVE THEM TO DEATH AND AM SO HAPPY THEY ARE PART OF MY LIFE NOW, BUT THERE COMES A POINT WHERE YOU NEED TO LET GO OF YOUR CHILDREN A LITTLE BIT. HE IS THE MOST AMAZING FATHER THAT I HAVE EVER SEEN, BUT GIVE THE KIDS A LITTLE ROOM TO BREATHE ON THEIR OWN. THEY ARE NOT BABIES ANYMORE. THEY ARE HIS EVERYTHING, WHICH IS AWESOME TO A POINT. WHEN THEY ARE AROUND, I DON'T EXIST AT ALL. HE DOESN'T EVEN KNOW I AM HERE! HE ALWAYS WANTS TO BE AROUND THEM, SO WE HAVE THEM EVERY WEEKEND! EVERY FRIDAY NIGHT AND EVERY WEEKEND! WHEN WILL PAUL AND I EVER HAVE TIME TOGETHER ALONE? I JUST DON'T KNOW IF I CAN COMPETE. I KNOW IT SOUNDS SILLY 'CAUSE IT'S HIS KIDS, BUT HE WOULD PUSH ME ASIDE ANY TIME FOR THEM. I HAVE AN ABSCESS AND HAD TO GO TO THE HOSPITAL, AND PAUL WENT GOLFING WITH HIS KIDS AND LET ME GO ALONE! AND YES, I DID TELL HIM I DIDN'T MIND GOING UP TO THE HOSPITAL ALONE, BUT COME ON, HE WAS THERE THE TIMES BEFORE. HE KNOWS JUST HOW PAINFUL IT IS AND WHAT GOES ON, AND HE SHOULD HAVE JUST WENT WITH ME. WHAT GUY IN THEIR RIGHT MIND WOULD LET HIS WOMAN GO TO THE HOSPITAL ALONE AND GO PLAY GOLF WITH THE TWO MOST IMPORTANT PEOPLE IN HIS LIFE? YA, NOBODY IS PERFECT, AND I KNOW THAT, BUT THERE IS COMMON SENSE! WHEN I HAVE TO WORK AS HARD AS I DO TO EVEN BE NOTICED WHEN THEY ARE AROUND, IT WILL DEFINITELY GET TO ANYONE, WHETHER YOU WANT IT TO OR NOT, AND I CAN'T TALK TO HIM ABOUT IT OR HE WOULD *FREAK!* I WISH I MEANT 1/2 AS MUCH TO HIM AS HIS KIDS DO.

WELL, I JUST GOT UP TO LDS HOSPITAL AGAIN. I HAVE 2 ABSCESSES AND THEY ARE SO DAMN PAINFUL. I HAD TO OPEN AT WORK THIS MORNING AND IT WAS SO STINKIN' HARD

BECAUSE I COULD HARDLY WORK. I CAN'T BELIEVE I KEEP DOING THIS TO MYSELF. PAUL AND I ARE FIGHTING RIGHT NOW SO HE DOESN'T EVEN KNOW I CAME UP. DEBORAH BROUGHT ME UP. SHE AND HER HUSBAND ARE BEING SO GOOD TO ME. THEY JUST GAVE ME $280 TO HELP ME WITH MY CAR PAYMENT. I AM SO BEHIND ON ALL MY BILLS, IT IS STRESSING ME OUT SO STINKIN' BAD. I AM SO GRATEFUL THAT DEBORAH BROUGHT ME HERE AND IS STAYING WITH ME, BUT I WISH PAUL WAS WITH ME SO BAD! I REALLY DON'T WANT TO LOSE HIM, BUT I FEEL LIKE I AM AT A LOSS. I HAVE NO IDEA HOW TO MAKE THINGS BETTER BETWEEN US. I DIDN'T TELL ANYONE OTHER THAN ADI AND OF COURSE DEBORAH THAT I WAS COMING TO THE HOSPITAL. I FEEL SO EMBARRASSED THAT THIS HAPPENED TO ME, ONCE AGAIN. I CAN'T EVEN COUNT HOW MANY TIMES I HAVE BEEN UP HERE FOR THIS, YOU WOULD THINK I WOULD LEARN. JUST TALKED TO PAUL AND HE IS REALLY UPSET I CAME UP HERE WITHOUT HIM. I HONESTLY HAVE NO IDEA WHAT TO DO NEXT WITH HIM. I REALLY, REALLY HOPE WE CAN GET THROUGH THIS.

<u>TUESDAY, AUGUST 21, 2012</u>:

I CLOSE AT WORK TONIGHT AND I AM DEFINITELY NOT LOOKING FORWARD TO IT. THEY ARE ALL TREATING ME LIKE SHIT! I HONESTLY HAVE NO IDEA WHY. I AM BY FAR THE HARDEST WORKER THERE. THEY ALWAYS TREATED ME SO GOOD AND NEVER WOULD MAKE ME FEEL BAD, NOW THE PAST COUPLE OF MONTHS THAT IS ALL THEY DO. I REALLY JUST DON'T KNOW WHAT IN THE HELL TO DO! I HAVE AN ABSCESS STILL AND AM GOING TO WORK IN EXCRUCIATING PAIN, I SHOULD NOT BE BUT I CANNOT LOSE MY JOB. I AM WISHING MYSELF GOOD LUCK FROM THIS POINT ON, IT IS GOING TO GET MUCH, MUCH BETTER. THINKING POSITIVE!

WEDNESDAY, AUGUST 22, 2012:

IT'S ABOUT 6:00 P.M. AND I JUST GOT HOME FROM THE HOSPITAL. IT WAS THE WORST THING. I AM SICK OF PUTTING MYSELF THROUGH ALL THIS SHIT. I AM IN SO MUCH PAIN. IT WAS SUCH HORRIBLE, HORRIBLE PAIN, BUT THE BEST EXPERIENCE I HAVE EVER HAD AT A HOSPITAL. MY NURSE REMEMBERED ME FROM 6 MONTHS AGO WITH MY HIP AND SHE IS ABSOLUTELY DARLING, AND THE DOCTOR WAS A WOMAN AND SHE WAS ABSOLUTELY AMAZING TO ME. SHE TREATED ME SO GOOD, WAS SO PROFESSIONAL AND DID NOT JUDGE ME WHATSOEVER. SO, WHEN I GOT HOME PAUL WAS VERY UPSET BECAUSE I DIDN'T TELL HIM I WAS GOING. HE REALLY WANTED TO BE THERE. THEN HE ASKED ME WHEN "REALLY" WAS THE LAST TIME I USED ANY DRUGS. I HATE LYING TO HIM, BUT I CANNOT TELL HIM. SOME THINGS ARE JUST BETTER LEFT UNSAID. IT DOES NOT MAKE ME A BAD PERSON OR A LIAR. *(I wonder why Paul thought she was getting abscesses when she denied using.)*

TODAY HAS BEEN AN ALL TOGETHER SHITTY FUCKING DAY! GOT UP, TOOK ADI TO HER SCHOOL TO CHANGE HER SCHEDULE 'CAUSE SHE GOT HER FIRST JOB AT PARADISE CAFE, THEN CAME HOME AND GOT READY FOR MY DR. APPT., WENT TO THE DOCTOR, THEN HAD TO GO BACK TO THE HOSPITAL TO GET MY ABSCESS CHECKED. MOST LIKELY GOING TO HAVE TO GET MY ARM CUT OPEN TOO. I WILL KNOW IN THREE DAYS. AFTER THE HOSPITAL, I WENT TO MY MOM'S, ATE, HUNG OUT WITH JALA FOR ABOUT AN HOUR WHILE DOING LAUNDRY. NOW I AM HOME FIGHTING WITH PAUL, ONCE AGAIN. I HONESTLY HAVE NO IDEA HOW TO KEEP HIM HAPPY. HE IS A LOST CAUSE. NO MATTER WHAT I DO, IT'S JUST WRONG OR NOT GOOD ENOUGH, AT LEAST LATELY. I JUST DON'T KNOW WHAT TO DO ANYMORE ABOUT ANYTHING. JAY AND PAUL MET TONIGHT AT MY MOM'S AND IT ACTUALLY WENT REALLY GOOD. JAY SAYS HE REALLY

LIKES PAUL AND IS SO SORRY FOR ANYTHING NEGATIVE HE HAS EVER SAID ABOUT HIM.

THURSDAY, AUGUST 23, 2012:

TODAY HAS BEEN A PRETTY GOOD DAY SO FAR. WOKE UP, PAUL MADE ME BREAKFAST, HUNG OUT WITH HIM FOR A MINUTE, THEN HAD TO GO GET JALA. JALA AND I WENT TO A COUPLE OF STORES, THEN WE WENT BACK TO MINE AND PAUL'S PLACE SO I COULD GET READY, AND NOW I AM AT MCDONALD'S WATCHING MY BABY GIRL PLAY. I LOVE HER! SHE IS AN AMAZING LITTLE GIRL, VERY SMART TOO! I HAVE TO GO TO WORK HERE IN ABOUT AN HOUR AND I AM SO NOT LOOKING FORWARD TO IT. THE MANAGERS HAVE ALL ABSOLUTELY LOVED ME AND TREATED ME SO GOOD SINCE THE DAY I STARTED UNTIL NOW. I DON'T KNOW WHAT CHANGED BECAUSE I WORK JUST AS HARD OR HARDER, BUT THEY DON'T SEEM TO GIVE A SHIT. THEY DO NOT LIKE ME RIGHT NOW. I AM WISHING MYSELF GOOD LUCK AT WORK!

I AM SO UNHAPPY RIGHT NOW! MY JOB IS GOING TO SHIT, I AM BEHIND ON ALL MY BILLS, AND I AM SO SICK FROM THIS MRSA SHIT. I HAVE TO GO BACK TO THE HOSPITAL IN THREE DAYS AND THEY WILL NEED TO SEE IF I NEED MY ARM CUT OPEN OR NOT. I AM REALLY SICK OF BEING CUT OPEN. AND I AM SO SICK RIGHT NOW, NAUSEATED AND FEELING LIKE I AM GOING TO FAINT. MASON'S FIRST FOOTBALL GAME IS THIS NEXT COMING SATURDAY (IN 2 DAYS) AND I COULDN'T BE MORE EXCITED. I ABSOLUTELY LOVE TO WATCH MY BABY BOY PLAY. FOOTBALL IS SO STINKIN' CUTE. ADI GOT A JOB AT PARADISE CAFE AND SHE STARTS TOMORROW. I AM SO EXTREMELY PROUD OF HER. THIS WILL KEEP HER OUT OF ANY TROUBLE, AND GIVE HER MONEY AS SHE IS LEARNING RESPONSIBILITY. I CAN'T BELIEVE MY BABY GIRL IS 16 YEARS OLD! WHERE DID THE TIME AND DAYS GO? IT SEEMS LIKE YESTERDAY ME AND SHALL WERE IN UGLY JUMPSUITS

OR TAKING AUSTIN AND ADI SWIMMING OR SOMEWHERE FUN AT THE AGE OF 2 OR 3. I WANT THOSE TIMES BACK, INSTEAD WE FACE THESE PROBLEMS EVERY DAY AND IT SUCKS. HOPEFULLY, PAUL AND I CAN GET THIS BUSINESS OFF THE GROUND SOON AND WE CAN START MAKING SOME GOOD MONEY 'CAUSE I AM SO SICK OF BEING STRAPPED!

GOT HOME FROM WORK ABOUT 8:30 TONIGHT. IT SUCKED SO BAD. KENNETH BROUGHT ME IN THE OFFICE AND TALKED TO ME ABOUT WHY I GOT MY CLOSING SHIFTS TAKEN AWAY. IT IS THE STUPIDEST REASON I HAVE EVER HEARD! HE SAID THAT WHENEVER I AM AT WORK, I ACT LIKE I WANT TO LEAVE AND I DON'T WANT TO BE THERE! ARE YOU KIDDING ME? I HAVE NEVER BEEN LATE, ALWAYS HAD MY SHIFTS COVERED, AND NEVER GOTTEN WRITTEN UP FOR ANYTHING, WHAT IN THE HELL? THEY ARE JUST TRYING TO FIND REASONS TO GET RID OF ME, AND IT'S KILLING ME BECAUSE ALL THE OTHER MANAGERS LOVE ME. WELL, PAUL'S DAD JUST FLEW IN FROM WASHINGTON, SO I AM GOING TO SPEND SOME TIME WITH THE BOYS, BYE!

<u>FRIDAY, AUGUST 24, 2012</u>:

I AM AT THE DOCTOR RIGHT NOW AND I'M A LITTLE NERVOUS BECAUSE I HAVE AN ABSCESS ON MY ARM THAT IS VERY NOTICEABLE AND I DON'T WANT TO TELL HIM THAT I HAVE BEEN USING. WELL, HE IS DEFINITELY GOING TO FIND OUT. WELL, ONE OF MY NIGHTMARES CAME TRUE, I TALKED TO PAYNE LAST NIGHT AND THEY TOOK ALL OF MY CLOSES AWAY. I WAS IN TEARS FOR A WHILE LAST NIGHT. I WON'T MAKE ANY MONEY IF I AM NOT CLOSING. I AM SO UPSET. I DON'T KNOW WHAT IN THE HELL I AM GOING TO DO. I AM ALREADY BEHIND ON ALL MY BILLS AND MAKING LESS MONEY NOW. I WILL LITERALLY BE SCRAPING BY.

I AM GETTING REALLY SCARED WITH HOW SICK I ALWAYS AM. BEFORE I LEFT WORK ON MONDAY, PAYNE SAID HE HOPES

I MAKE IT OUT OF THE HOSPITAL ALIVE. HE ALWAYS SAID THAT HE DOESN'T THINK I AM GOING TO MAKE IT PAST 35. WHO SAYS THAT TO SOMEONE? *(It was very noticeable in her appearance that she was deteriorating from drug use.)* BUT, IT REALLY DID MAKE ME THINK I NEED TO CHANGE MY LIFE AND SOON OR I REALLY WON'T MAKE IT MUCH LONGER. THEY JUST WEIGHED ME AT THE DOCTOR, AND I WEIGH 99LBS, I AM 33 YEARS OLD, THAT IS NOT GOOD OR HEALTHY AT ALL.

Nat and my son Austin

TODAY IS GOING TO BE A GOOD DAY! WELL, I WAS SUPPOSED TO GO TO MY MOM'S TODAY TO BE WITH JALA AND ADI AND MAYBE MAS, AND I CAN'T NOW BECAUSE EMILY CAME DOWN FROM IDAHO AND SHE DOESN'T WANT TO BE AROUND ME. *(This was always so hard for my mom because she wanted all of her girls together, but sometimes the anger and frustration were so intense that we couldn't.)* SO I CAN'T COME OVER. IT BREAKS MY HEART. I MISS MY SISTERS SO BAD! MY LIFE IS JUST NOT THE SAME WITHOUT MY THREE SISTERS IN IT AND RIGHT NOW, THEY'RE NOT. I HAVEN'T TALKED TO SHALL OR ANGIE FOR AT LEAST A MONTH, AND EMILY ABOUT THREE/FOUR MONTHS NOW. EMILY AND I WERE JUST GETTING CLOSE AGAIN, JUST LIKE ME AND MY DAD WERE, THEN I HAVE TO GO AND FUCK THINGS UP AGAIN. WHAT IN THE HELL AM I DOING? I HONESTLY DON'T KNOW IF THEY ARE GOING TO EVER FORGIVE ME THIS TIME. I DON'T KNOW IF I CAN HANDLE MY SISTERS WRITING ME OFF AGAIN.

SO FAR, IT HAS BEEN A FANTASTIC DAY! I'M AT HOME RIGHT NOW WITH PAUL, HIS DAD, JALA, AND HIS KIDS. WE JUST GOT DONE EATING LUNCH AND I HAVE TO GO TO WORK

IN A COUPLE HOURS. TONIGHT IS MY LAST CLOSING SHIFT, AT LEAST FOR A WHILE. I HAVE TO PROVE TO THE MANAGERS THAT I WANT TO BE THERE. EVEN THOUGH I DON'T. I HONESTLY DIDN'T THINK THEY WOULD SEE RIGHT THROUGH ME LIKE THEY HAVE. I AM DEFINITELY NOT GOING TO WORK MY ASS OFF TONIGHT, SHOW THEM THAT THEY ARE ABSOLUTELY STUPID FOR TAKING MY CLOSING SHIFTS AWAY. SO, JAY AND PAUL MET THE OTHER DAY AND IT WENT REALLY, REALLY WELL. JAY LETS ME TAKE JALA WHENEVER I WANT NOW AND RESPECTS PAUL A LOT. NEVER IN A MILLION YEARS DID I EVER THINK THOSE TWO WOULD BE CIVIL TO EACH OTHER. IT WAS PAUL THAT WENT UP TO JAY AND INTRODUCED HIMSELF, AND I AM SO GLAD HE DID. HE IS SUCH AN AWESOME GUY! JALA, PAUL'S DAUGHTER, AND ME ARE IN MINE AND PAUL'S ROOM WATCHING MICHAEL JACKSON WHILE THEY ARE DANCING. IT IS THE CUTEST THING EVER. THEY ARE HAVING SO MUCH FUN. I WISH I DIDN'T HAVE TO LEAVE THEM TO GO TO WORK. MY BABY GIRL IS BY FAR THE CUTEST LITTLE GIRL IN THE ENTIRE WORLD. WISHING MYSELF GOOD LUCK AT WORK TONIGHT!

SATURDAY, AUGUST 25, 2012:

WELL, LAST NIGHT AT WORK WENT BETTER THAN I THOUGHT IT WAS GOING TO. IT WAS MY LAST CLOSING SHIFT, AT LEAST FOR NOW. I KNOW I CAN GET THEM BACK, I JUST THINK THIS MIGHT BE GOOD FOR ME RIGHT NOW. IT WILL GIVE ME A LITTLE BIT OF A BREAK AND MORE TIME WITH PAUL. I WORK IN THE BAR TONIGHT AND I USUALLY MAKE NO MONEY AT THE BAR, BUT I LIKE IT 'CAUSE IT'S A CHANGE OF PACE, I NEED CHANGE, OR I GET REALLY BORED. IT'S MASON'S FIRST FOOTBALL GAME TONIGHT, WELL, TODAY AT 1:00, AND I AM SO EXCITED! I WAIT ALL YEAR FOR HIS FOOTBALL GAMES! HE IS THE CUTEST LITTLE BOY EVER! I LOVE TO WATCH HIM IN HIS LITTLE FOOTBALL UNIFORM, HE

IS ABSOLUTELY ADORABLE! HE KICKS ASS TOO! HE WANTS TO BE A PROFESSIONAL FOOTBALL PLAYER WHEN HE GROWS UP AND HAS WANTED TO FOR YEARS. I THINK IT'S A DEFINITE POSSIBILITY. HE PUTS HIS HEART AND SOUL INTO FOOTBALL AND HE IS AWESOME. I REALLY HOPE I DIDN'T RUIN MY KIDS' LIVES. I KNOW THEY COULD HAVE HAD IT BETTER, ME AROUND, BUT I KNOW IT HAS NOT BEEN HORRIBLE. I AM ACTUALLY VERY GRATEFUL FOR MY EX AND JAY. THEY TOOK RESPONSIBILITY FOR MY KIDS WHEN I DIDN'T AND THEY BOTH DO A PRETTY GOOD JOB RAISING MY KIDS. IT'S MY OWN FAULT, NOW CHANGE!

IT'S ABOUT 2:30 A.M. AND I AM SITTING HERE WRITING AND WATCHING PAUL SLEEP. HE ALWAYS GOES TO BED WAY, WAY EARLIER THAN ME. DON'T EVER WAKE THIS MAN UP, THOUGH. I LEARNED THAT THE HARD WAY, AND I WILL ABSOLUTELY NEVER LET THAT HAPPEN AGAIN. I HAVE DEFINITELY SEEN THE BAD SIDE OF PAUL. IT'S PRETTY DAMN SCARY. HE TRIES REALLY HARD, THOUGH, AND THE GOOD DEFINITELY OUTWEIGHS THE BAD, BUT I CAN'T EVEN PUT INTO WORDS HOW SCARED I GET WHEN HE GETS ANGRY. I'M NOT SCARED THAT HE IS GOING TO HIT ME OR BE PHYSICAL WITH ME, I AM TERRIFIED OF THE MENTAL ABUSE AND WHEN HE IS UPSET OR ANGRY, HE DEFINITELY ABUSES ME MORE WAYS THAN ONE MENTALLY. I HONESTLY DOUBT HE WOULD AGREE WITH THAT, BUT SOMETIMES HE CAN'T SEE PAST HIS ANGER, IT COMPLETELY TAKES OVER HIM MENTALLY. HE IS NOT EVEN THE SAME PERSON WHEN HE GETS THAT WAY. I DO LOVE HIM WITH ALL MY HEART, BUT I DON'T KNOW IF I CAN TAKE ONE MORE FIGHT WITH THIS MAN. HE GETS EVIL. I COME 2ND.

SUNDAY, AUGUST 26, 2012:

TODAY IS GOING TO BE AN AWESOME DAY. I REALLY WISH I COULD GO TO MY MOM'S TODAY WITH ALL MY SISTERS AND

EVERYBODY, BUT I CAN'T. I HOPE EMILY AND MY DAD GET OVER THIS SOON. MASON'S GAME WAS SO FUN YESTERDAY. PAUL, ME, MY MOM, JALA, ADI, KAILEE, JUSTIN AND EMMY, AND JASA ALL WENT! EMILY WOULD NOT EVEN LOOK AT ME. SHE WOULDN'T EVEN LET HER KIDS NEAR ME EITHER. MY DAD CAME FOR A MINUTE BUT THEN HE HAD TO LEAVE BECAUSE FRIDAY HE CUT HIS FINGER WITH A SAW, SO HE WASN'T FEELING SO GOOD. PAUL TALKED TO HIM THE WHOLE TIME HE WAS THERE. I KNOW I HAVE MY FAULTS, BUT I WOULD NEVER WRITE ANYONE OFF IN MY FAMILY, NO MATTER WHAT THEY DID. PAUL IS BEING INCREDIBLE TO ME. HE ADMITTED TO ME THAT HE HAS BEEN THE CAUSE OF ALL OF OUR FIGHTS LATELY AND HE IS SO SORRY AND HE WILL TRY A LOT HARDER. MY FAVORITE FLOWERS ARE WHITE, SO HE BROUGHT ME HOME A DOZEN WHITE FLOWERS TODAY, AND THEY ARE REALLY LITTLE BECAUSE HE KNOWS I LIKE SMALL THINGS. *(When Nat passed away and we were going through her apartment, she had drawers full of mini items like tableware etc..)* HE IS DOING AWESOME LATELY, GIVING ME THE WORLD, TREATING ME LIKE A PRINCESS. I LOVE THIS GUY! NOTHING IS GOING TO TEAR US APART AND I AM GOING TO TRY MY HARDEST WITH THIS ONE AND CHANGE MY WAYS!

IT'S BEEN A GOOD DAY SO FAR. WOKE UP, GOT STARBUCKS, THEN CAME HOME TO GET READY. WE ARE NOW AT KEVIN'S (PAUL'S DAD) MOM'S PLACE IN MURRAY VISITING AT AN OLD FOLKS' HOME. OUR DRIVE OUT HERE WAS SO FUN. PAUL AND I HAVE SUCH A BLAST TOGETHER WHEN WE ARE BY OURSELVES. I AM NOT GOING TO FUCK THIS ONE UP. I FOUND THE MAN OF MY DREAMS AND I AM NEVER LETTING HIM GO. HE IS MY KNIGHT IN SHINING ARMOR. HE IS SO PROTECTIVE OF ME, I ABSOLUTELY LOVE IT. IF ANYONE TREATS ME BAD OR THERE IS A CHANCE I COULD GET HURT, PAUL WILL STEP IN AND TAKE CARE OF IT FOR ME. I LOVE THAT HE TAKES CARE OF ME THE WAY HE DOES. HE WILL NEVER LET ANYTHING HAPPEN TO ME. IT'S VERY COMFORTING.

WELL, DEFINITELY TIME FOR A NEW JOURNAL. IT'S AMAZING TO SEE WHAT I HAVE GONE THROUGH THE PAST 2-3 YEARS. SO MUCH HAS CHANGED. IT'S THE SAME AND IT'S CHANGED SO MUCH. IT MAKES ME KINDA SAD READING SOME OF THESE PAGES, BUT ON THE OTHER HAND, I AM SO GRATEFUL FOR WHAT I HAVE NOW. IT'S BEEN A CRAZY, CRAZY PAST COUPLE YEARS. I AM GLAD AND ACTUALLY THANKFUL FOR EVERYTHING I DID GO THROUGH 'CAUSE IT DEFINITELY MADE ME THE PERSON I AM TODAY. I KNOW THAT SOUNDS CRAZY BUT I HAVE LEARNED SO DAMN MUCH AND I WOULDN'T CHANGE ANYTHING. I AM SO MUCH MORE HUMBLE AND NOT AS JUDGMENTAL AS BAD AS I USED TO BE. I AM A MUCH BETTER PERSON, EVEN THOUGH I STILL HAVE A BUNCH OF ISSUES TO RESOLVE, AND I KNOW I CAN CHANGE THEM IF I PUT MY MIND TO IT, 110% INTO IT AND I KNOW I HAVE A SHOT. I KNOW HOW TO MAKE MY LIFE BETTER AND GET EVERYTHING I EVER WANTED, AND IT IS THE HARDEST THING I WILL EVER HAVE TO FACE. BUT I KNOW I CAN DO IT, I HAVE BEFORE A BUNCH OF TIMES AND I AM MUCH STRONGER NOW AND KNOW EXACTLY WHAT TO DO. SO, I JUST NEED TO DO IT. I HAVE THE LOVE OF MY LIFE AND 3 BEAUTIFUL AMAZING KIDS THAT ARE WAITING VERY PATIENTLY FOR ME. I NEED TO GET MY HEAD OUT OF MY ASS AND STRAIGHTEN THIS SHITTY LIFE OUT. I KNOW I CAN!

MONDAY, AUGUST 27, 2012:

BE POSITIVE, THINK POSITIVE! THAT IS MY NEW GOAL. TOO MANY PEOPLE INCLUDING PAUL TELL ME DAILY HOW NEGATIVE I AM AND THAT I NEED TO BE MORE POSITIVE AND HOPEFUL. I KNOW IF I DO THIS, MY LIFE WILL CHANGE FOR THE BETTER. I HAVE A COUPLE REALLY BIG THINGS TO CHANGE IN MY LIFE, AND IF I DO, THEN I KNOW I WILL BE MUCH, MUCH HAPPIER. BUT IT'S GOING TO BE THE HARDEST THING I WILL EVER HAVE TO DO OR FACE, BUT IF/WHEN I GET

THROUGH IT, I WILL BE A MUCH BETTER PERSON AND BE IN A MUCH BETTER PLACE IN MY LIFE. IT'S CRAZY WHEN I AM DOING THE WRONG THINGS IN MY LIFE, EVERYTHING GOES WRONG, ABSOLUTELY EVERYTHING DOES. WHEN I CHANGE IT, AND DO THE RIGHT THINGS IN MY LIFE, EVERYTHING SEEMS TO FALL INTO PLACE AND GO RIGHT! THE HARD PART IS, I NEED TO BE ABSOLUTELY READY TO CHANGE, AND RIGHT NOW, I AM NOT. I WANT TO BE READY, BUT UNFORTUNATELY, I AM NOT. I HAVE NO IDEA WHAT IT'S GOING TO TAKE TO MAKE ME READY, BUT ALL I KNOW IS THAT IF I DON'T CHANGE SOON, I WON'T BE AROUND TO HAVE A LIFE AT ALL. I WEIGH 99LBS RIGHT NOW AND I'M 33 YEARS OLD! THAT IS NOT GOOD AT ALL. I'M STARTING TO LOOK LIKE A CRACK WHORE! I DO NOT LIKE THE WAY I LOOK RIGHT NOW, I'M WAY TOO SKINNY AND MY FACE HAS AGED SO MUCH FROM DRUGS, IT'S PATHETIC! WHY DID I EVER HAVE TO TRY DRUGS AND BRING THEM INTO MY LIFE? THEY WILL BE THE DEATH OF ME IF I DON'T DO SOMETHING ABOUT IT VERY, VERY SOON. I WANT TO SEE MY BABIES GROW UP!

TUESDAY, AUGUST 28, 2012:

IT'S ABOUT 12:30 AT NIGHT AND I AM SITTING HERE EATING CHINESE FOOD. HOW MUCH BETTER CAN IT GET? ACTUALLY, IT COULD GET A LOT BETTER. I COULD HAVE MY KIDS WITH ME AND PAUL. IT WILL HAPPEN IF I PULL MY HEAD OUT OF MY ASS. ADI GETS HER DRIVER'S LICENSE TOMORROW. I AM SO SUPER EXCITED FOR HER BUT AT THE SAME TIME SO SUPER SAD THAT SHE IS THIS GROWN UP ALREADY. TIME FLIES. SERIOUSLY, WHERE DID ALL THESE YEARS GO? I WANT THEM BACK! I NEED MORE TIME WITH ADI. IT LITERALLY MAKES ME PHYSICALLY ILL KNOWING HOW MUCH TIME I LOST WITH MY BABY GIRL. I CAN NEVER GET THOSE YEARS BACK EVER. I DO NOT WANT TO GO THROUGH THAT WITH JALA OR MAS! THE SAME THING IS HAPPENING WITH MAS. I DON'T WANT IT

TO HAPPEN TO JALA TOO. THEY ARE MY WORLD, MY BABIES! NOTHING OR NOBODY IS MORE IMPORTANT THAN THEY ARE. I REALLY DON'T KNOW HOW TO SHOW IT, THOUGH, OBVIOUSLY. I OPENED TODAY AND IT WAS AN OKAY DAY. I MADE $85 AND I TALKED TO PAYNE AND SETTLED SOME THINGS, HE WAS BEING NICE. NOW, HOPEFULLY, I CAN GET MY CLOSES BACK.

IT'S GOING TO BE SO WEIRD NOT CLOSING TONIGHT AND JUST WORKING. I HOPE I AT LEAST MAKE A LITTLE BIT OF MONEY. THIS WEEK IS GOING TO BE A LOT DIFFERENT 'CAUSE I AM GOING TO BE HOME A LOT EARLIER EVERY NIGHT RATHER THAN ONE IN THE MORNING. THIS MIGHT ACTUALLY BE NICE. I WILL BE ABLE TO DO THINGS WITH MY HONEY NOW, AND HAVE A LIFE OUTSIDE OF IGGY'S. THIS IS A GOOD THING...THAT PLACE WAS DEFINITELY WEARING ME OUT. IT'S TIME FOR ME TO HAVE A BREAK AND SPEND MORE TIME WITH MY HONEY AND MY THREE BEAUTIFUL KIDS. IT MAKES ME SAD BECAUSE I SPEND MORE TIME WITH PAUL'S KIDS THAN I DO MY OWN KIDS. I FREAKING HATE IT! IT'S NOT FAIR ONE BIT! I NEED TO SEE MY KIDS MORE THAN ONE TIME A WEEK. I MISS THEM! I MISS MY SISTERS AND MY FAMILY SO MUCH. I HAVE NEVER GONE THIS LONG WITHOUT TALKING TO MY SISTERS. IT'S KILLING ME! I NEED MY SISTERS IN MY LIFE, IT'S JUST NOT COMPLETE WITHOUT THEM. THEY ARE, BESIDES MY KIDS, THE MOST IMPORTANT PEOPLE IN MY LIFE. I JUST FEEL SO GUILTY AND STUPID! WHY AND HOW DID I DO THIS TO MYSELF...AGAIN? THANK GOD I HAVE PAUL, OR I WOULD NOT AT ALL BE AMONG THE LIVING. I WOULD BE ON THE STREETS AND COMPLETELY BROKEN. HE HELPS ME LIVE LIFE AND MAKES ME WANT TO BE A MUCH BETTER PERSON. BE GRATEFUL FOR WHAT YOU DO HAVE AND QUIT FOCUSING ON WHAT YOU DON'T.

WEDNESDAY, AUGUST 29, 2012:

STILL THINKING AND BEING POSITIVE. SAY GOOD THINGS ABOUT OTHERS, DON'T JUDGE, AND BE THE VERY BEST PERSON THAT I CAN BE. LIVE FOR JUST TODAY. TODAY WAS AN OKAY DAY. WOKE UP, WENT AND PICKED UP JALA, THEN WENT TO MOM'S TO START LAUNDRY, SAW ADI AND MAS FOR A MINUTE, THEN WENT TO MCDONALD'S, THEN WENT AND HUNG OUT AT MELISSA'S HOUSE UNTIL MY MAN GOT HOME. KEVIN AND LAURA CAME OVER AND WE TALKED FOR A BIT, THEN PAUL AND I WENT TO BREWVIE'S AND I GOT SO SICK BECAUSE I DRANK A RED BULL VODKA AND MY ANTIBIOTICS THAT I AM ON MADE ME SO SICK. I AM NOT SUPPOSED TO DRINK WITH THAT MEDICATION, BUT I DIDN'T KNOW THAT. IT SUCKED SO BAD. I CAME HOME AND THREW UP SO MUCH IT WAS AWFUL. I BETTER BE OKAY BY TOMORROW 'CAUSE I HAVE MISS JALA ALL DAY UNTIL I GO TO WORK. IT ACTUALLY HAS BEEN REALLY NICE NOT CLOSING. I GET HOME AROUND 9:30 OR EARLIER AND IT IS A LOT LESS WORK. THIS DEFINITELY WAS A GOOD THING FOR ME. MY FRIEND AMY HAD A MISCARRIAGE THE OTHER DAY. SHE WENT INTO THE HOSPITAL, HAD NO IDEA SHE WAS PREGNANT, AND HAD TO HAVE A D&C. HOW SAD IS THAT? MARY IS OUT OF JAIL. I CAN'T BELIEVE SHE HASN'T TRIED TO GET AHOLD OF ME. I AM GLAD!

THURSDAY, AUGUST 30, 2012:

SITTING HERE WITH MY LITTLE PRINCESS JALA. I HAVE TO WORK TODAY AT 5:00 AND HOPEFULLY I MAKE GOOD MONEY 'CAUSE I HAVE BEEN BEHIND ALL MONTH LONG. I HAVEN'T TALKED TO MY SISTERS IN WEEKS, MAYBE EVEN A MONTH. NOTHING AT ALL. IT'S NOT NORMAL AT ALL FOR US NOT TO TALK. I MISS THEM ALL SO VERY MUCH. HOPEFULLY THEY CAN FORGIVE ME SOMETIME SOON. I PRAY THAT IT IS SOMETIME VERY, VERY SOON. WELL, TAKING JALA TO MCDONALD'S AGAIN

TODAY. IT'S THE ONLY THING THAT I KNOW FOR SURE THAT SHE WILL EAT. SHE IS SO SUPER DUPER SKINNY, SO IF THERE IS SOMETHING I KNOW SHE WILL EAT, THEN I AM GOING TO GET IT FOR HER. ADI GOT HER LICENSE A COUPLE DAYS AGO AND SHE GOT HER JEEP. IT'S SO CUTE. SHE IS GETTING SO OLD, I DON'T WANT MY KIDS TO GET ANY OLDER, THEY ARE ALL GROWING UP WAY, WAY TOO FAST. THEY ALL START SCHOOL ON MONDAY, AND THEY ARE ALL EXCITED. I HOPE THEY ALL HAVE A GREAT YEAR AT SCHOOL. I HOPE TONIGHT IS A GOOD NIGHT AT WORK. I PRAY IT IS.

WELL, IT WAS AN OKAY NIGHT AT WORK. I GOT CUT AND I WAS HOME AT 9:00 P.M. NOW I AM WATCHING A MOVIE WITH MY BABY. HE TOLD ME TODAY THAT HE FOUND ME A RING. I AM SO EXCITED. I WANT NOTHING MORE THAN TO BE HIS WIFE.

FRIDAY, AUGUST 31, 2012:

LAST DAY OF AUGUST! TODAY IS GOING TO BE A GOOD DAY. I CAN FEEL IT. I SURE HOPE NEXT MONTH IS A LOT BETTER THAN THIS LAST MONTH WAS. I CAN'T WAIT UNTIL WE GET MARRIED. I AM SO EXTREMELY EXCITED! HE IS SO MUCH DIFFERENT THAN ANY OTHER MAN I HAVE EVER BEEN WITH. WE FIT, ABSOLUTELY PERFECT TOGETHER.

WELL, JUST GOT HOME FROM WORK ABOUT AN HOUR AGO AND IT IS 1:00 A.M. IT WAS MY FIRST FRIDAY NOT CLOSING AND I STILL GOT HOME WAY TOO LATE. IT'S NICE BEING ABLE TO COME HOME EARLY (MOST NIGHTS), BUT WHILE I AM THERE, I WOULD MUCH RATHER BE A CLOSER. THE SHITTY PART ABOUT THE WHOLE THING IS THAT THEY STILL HAVEN'T GIVEN ME A REASON WHY THEY TOOK MY CLOSES. KENNETH SAID IT WAS BECAUSE I ACTED LIKE I DIDN'T WANT TO BE THERE. WHAT KIND OF STUPID FUCKED-UP REASON IS THAT? I WANTED TO COME HOME EARLY TONIGHT TO SPEND TIME WITH MY BABY, BUT FUCK THAT IDEA. WHEN I GOT HOME,

HE WAS ALREADY ASLEEP. I HAVE MASON'S FOOTBALL (2ND) GAME IN THE MORNING. I AM SO EXCITED. TODAY WAS A GOOD DAY, THOUGH. I SPENT THE DAY WITH MY BABY GIRL, AND WE HAD A GREAT DAY TOGETHER.

WELL, IT'S THREE A.M. RIGHT NOW AND I AM SO HUNGRY AND TIRED AND SO MAD AT MYSELF. I WANT TO CHANGE MY LIFE FOR ME AND MY KIDS AND PAUL, AND I CAN'T SEEM TO FIND THE WILL POWER OR STRENGTH TO DO IT. I KNOW I CAN FIGHT THIS, I JUST DO AND DON'T WANT TO. *I NEED HELP.*

I can only imagine how hard the battle was within her.

SATURDAY, SEPTEMBER 1, 2012:

MY DAY OFF, YAY! TODAY IS ALREADY GONNA BE A GREAT DAY BECAUSE I DON'T HAVE TO GO TO STUPID WORK! SO, WE STILL HAVE PAUL'S KIDS. WE HAVE THEM EVERY WEEKEND. I LIKE IT, BUT I NEVER SEE PAUL ALONE ANYMORE, I MISS MY MAN! WE WENT TO HOLLYWOOD CONNECTION AND IT ACTUALLY WAS VERY FUN. WE WENT ROLLERSKATING AND HAD SUCH A FUN TIME. I REALLY CANNOT WAIT TO MARRY THIS MAN! I AM SO GLAD I HAVE HIM. HE IS SITTING RIGHT NEXT TO ME RIGHT NOW FALLING ASLEEP. HIS KIDS ARE AWESOME, THEY ARE REALLY GOOD KIDS. IT'S JUST HARD WHEN THEY ARE AROUND BECAUSE THEY TAKE ALL OF PAUL'S ATTENTION. IT'S GOOD HE IS SO GOOD TO THEM, BUT I WANT SOME OF HIS ATTENTION TOO. KIERRA *(my daughter)* TEXTED ME TODAY AND I STARTED CRYING. SHE SAID SHE CRIES EVERY DAY 'CAUSE SHE MISSES ME SO MUCH. SO I TEXTED SHALL 'CAUSE I HAVEN'T TALKED TO HER IN FOREVER AND I MISS HER SO MUCH. SHE TEXTED ME RIGHT BACK AND SAID SHE IS ALWAYS HERE FOR ME AND ALWAYS HAS TIME TO TALK. I MISS MY SISTERS SO MUCH IT PHYSICALLY HURTS. I HOPE THEY COME AROUND. *(It was really hard to watch my children suffer from Nat's drug abuse. They loved her so much and were heartbroken when she wasn't around. She was the funnest aunt and had an incredible connection with all of the nieces and nephews.)*

Same day, same journal:

TODAY WAS AN OKAY DAY, I GUESS. WOKE UP AND WENT TO MASON'S FOOTBALL GAME, THEN CAME HOME, GOT READY, THEN WENT TO WORK. YAY, WHAT AN UNEVENTFUL SATURDAY. I ABSOLUTELY LOVE TO GO TO MASON'S FOOTBALL GAMES, HE IS SO STINKIN' GOOD. THAT WAS THE HIGHLIGHT OF MY DAY. WORK SUCKED AGAIN. I WORKED THE BAR AGAIN AND MADE NO $ AGAIN. I SHOULD QUIT, BUT I DON'T HAVE A CHOICE RIGHT NOW. PAUL REALLY WANTS ME TO, BUT I REALLY CAN'T. IF HE STARTED PAYING FOR EVERYTHING FOR ME, THEN THAT WOULD BE AN ABSOLUTELY DIFFERENT STORY. WHEN WE ARE TOGETHER, HE TOTALLY PAYS FOR EVERYTHING, WON'T EVER LET ME GET ANYTHING, BUT I DO PAY FOR MY DR. APPTS., MY CAR PAYMENT, CAR INSURANCE, ETC. SO, I NEED THIS STUPID JOB FOR ANOTHER MINUTE OR SO. SO, WE HAVE HIS KIDS EVERY STINKIN' WEEKEND. I HAVE BEEN OKAY WITH IT UNTIL NOW. WHEN THEY ARE AROUND, NOBODY ELSE EXISTS IN PAUL'S WORLD. I'M NOT COMPETING WITH HIS KIDS AT ALL, IT JUST REALLY SUCKS WHEN THEY ARE AROUND LATELY BECAUSE IT'S ALL ABOUT THEM!

Same day, different journal:

MASON'S 2ND FOOTBALL GAME TODAY! I ABSOLUTELY LOVE GOING TO MASON'S FOOTBALL GAMES AND HE ALWAYS PLAYS HIS LITTLE HEART OUT. HE WANTS TO BE A PROFESSIONAL FOOTBALL PLAYER WHEN HE GROWS UP AND HAS WANTED TO EVER SINCE HE STARTED FOOTBALL. IF HE KEEPS GOING THE WAY HE IS, HE HAS A DAMN GOOD SHOT OF HAVING HIS

DREAMS COME TRUE! I AM SO EXTREMELY PROUD OF HIM. I COULDN'T ASK FOR A BETTER SON. HE IS EVERYTHING AND MUCH, MUCH MORE THAT A MOTHER WANTS AS A CHILD. I CAN COUNT ON ONE HAND THE NUMBER OF TIMES MASON HAS UPSET ME IN HIS LIFETIME. HE IS EVERY MOTHER'S DREAM COME TRUE. HE MAKES MY HEART HAPPY. I WISH I COULD HAVE BEEN THE MOTHER FOR HIM THAT HE ALWAYS WANTED AND THE MOTHER I SHOULD HAVE BEEN. HE DESERVES IT! IT BREAKS MY HEART WHAT I HAVE DONE TO HIM. NOW, I NEED TO GET MY SHIT TOGETHER AND MAKE IT UP TO HIM, HE DESERVES AT LEAST THAT! THEY ALL THREE DESERVE SO MUCH MORE FROM ME. PULL YOUR HEAD OUT OF YOUR ASS, NAT, AND *FIGHT!!!* MASON WON! I AM SO PROUD OF MY BOY! HE IS SUCH A GOOD LITTLE FOOTBALL PLAYER!

MONDAY, SEPTEMBER 3, 2012:

WOW, IT WAS HELLA BUSY AT WORK TODAY. I OPENED AND RIGHT AT ELEVEN, I HAD A 12 TOP *(a table of 12)* AND IT JUST KEPT GOING FROM THEN ON TILL 5:30 P.M. I DIDN'T MAKE HALF OF WHAT I THOUGHT I WAS GOING TO MAKE, THOUGH. I LOVE IT WHEN IT'S BUSY LIKE THAT. IT MAKES TIME FLY! WHEN I GOT OFF, I TOOK A TRIP TO BRIAN'S *(a dealer),* UNFORTUNATELY, THEN MET UP WITH ADI AND GOT SOME MAKEUP. PAUL IS HONESTLY PERFECT TO ME, IN EVERY WAY. WHY DID IT TAKE THIS LONG TO FIND HIM? WELL, I AM NOT DISAPPOINTED THAT I MARRIED JAY OR MY EX, OR I WOULDN'T HAVE MY BEAUTIFUL KIDS. HE IS RIGHT NEXT TO ME SLEEPING AGAIN. I AM ALWAYS AWAKE WAY LONGER AT NIGHTS AND HE GETS UP AT LEAST THREE HOURS EARLIER THAN ME EVERY SINGLE MORNING. I DO NOT DO MORNINGS! AND TOMORROW IS THE FIRST DAY OF SCHOOL FOR THE KIDS, AND JALA HAS MRS. MECHAM, MY KINDERGARTEN TEACHER! HOW COOL IS THAT? ADI HAS HER JEEP TO DRIVE TO SCHOOL,

AND SHE WILL DROP MY SWEET BOY OFF ON HER WAY. I HOPE THEY HAVE A GOOD YEAR!

TUESDAY, SEPTEMBER 4, 2012:

IT WAS THE KIDS' FIRST DAY OF SCHOOL TODAY. ADI IS A JUNIOR AT BOUNTIFUL HIGH, MAS IS IN 8TH GRADE AT BOUNTIFUL JUNIOR HIGH, AND JALA IS IN FIRST GRADE AT WEST BOUNTIFUL. THEY ARE ALL GROWING UP WAY TOO DAMN FAST. THEY ARE ALL THREE SUCH AMAZING, FANTASTIC KIDS. I COULDN'T ASK FOR BETTER CHILDREN. THEY ARE THE BEST! WELL, WORK SUCKED TONIGHT, IT WAS SO SLOW! I'M SITTING HERE WITH MY BABY RIGHT NOW WATCHING A MOVIE. I LOVE HIM SO MUCH. IT WAS SO CUTE TODAY. I TOOK JALA TO HER FIRST DAY OF SCHOOL, SHE WAS SO CUTE. SHE WOULDN'T HOLD MY HAND BECAUSE SHE THOUGHT THE OTHER KIDS MIGHT SEE! SHE IS GETTING WAY TOO OLD, IT'S KILLING ME! SO, I TALKED TO SHALL TODAY AND I HAVE NOT TALKED TO HER IN A LONG TIME, WAY TOO LONG. SHE IS MY BEST FRIEND IN THE WHOLE WORLD AND ALWAYS HAS BEEN. SO, I HEARD TODAY, 'CAUSE I TALKED TO CATHERINE, THAT MARY GOT OUT OF JAIL, WENT BACK TO THE HOUSE HER AND ROBERT WERE STAYING AT. IT GOT RAIDED. SHE IS BACK IN JAIL. SHE IS NOW FINALLY GETTING WHAT SHE DESERVES, JAIL TIME.

WEDNESDAY, SEPTEMBER 5, 2012:

I GET TO BE WITH ALL THREE OF MY BEAUTIFUL KIDS TODAY! IT WAS A GOOD DAY. DIDN'T GET TO SEE ADI AND MAS MUCH BECAUSE THEY GOT HOME FROM SCHOOL, ATE DINNER WITH ME AT MY MOM'S, THEN WENT TO YOUNG WOMEN'S AND YOUNG MEN'S *(church activities).* JALA LOVES SCHOOL. I PICK HER UP EVERY DAY AND I LOVE IT! I LOVE MY BABY GIRL. I DIDN'T SEE MY BABY MUCH AT ALL TODAY. I RAN ERRANDS WITH AMY TODAY AND ENDED UP OVER AT SAMUEL'S HOUSE.

ONLY STAYED THERE FOR A FEW. I THINK I AM GOING TO SMOKE WITH HIM IN THE MORNING TO START MY DAY OFF. I CAN'T EVER HIT *(find a vein to shoot up in)* ANYMORE AND I ACTUALLY GET IT, THAT'S DEFINITELY A RED FLAG, HUGE SIGN! SO, I'M THINKING ABOUT GOING AND SEEING DAVID TOMORROW. I SHOULD GO TO SEE MARY, I THINK I WILL. I CAN'T BELIEVE SHE ENDED UP BACK IN JAIL RIGHT AFTER SHE GOT OUT! THEY ARE DEFINITELY WATCHING HER. THAT'S FOR DAMN SURE. I DO MISS HER, THOUGH, SHE REALLY WAS MY VERY BEST FRIEND. I FEEL BAD FOR HER, BUT SHE HAS DONE THIS WAY TOO LONG AND ALWAYS HAS SOMEBODY THAT HAS HAD HER BACK, SO SHE NEVER GOT IN TROUBLE, EVER! EVERYBODY ELSE THAT SHE WAS WITH DID! I AM SO GLAD I HAVE PAUL AND MY THREE WONDERFUL KIDS. WHAT MORE COULD I POSSIBLY ASK FOR? WHY DID I EVER GET INTO THE LIFE I DID? WHY CAN'T I GET OUT OF IT? I REALLY WANT TO!

THURSDAY, SEPTEMBER 6, 2012:

TODAY IS GOING TO BE A FANTASTIC DAY!

WELL, IT WAS AN OKAY DAY, BUT WORK SUCKED! I CAN'T KEEP GOING LIKE THIS. I AM MAKING NO MONEY RIGHT NOW WITHOUT HAVING MY CLOSING SHIFTS. THEY SAID I WAS GOING TO GET MY CLOSING SHIFTS BACK SOON, BUT HASN'T HAPPENED YET. I AM NOT DOING OKAY WITHOUT THOSE SHIFTS. SO, PAUL IS GOING TO WASHINGTON IN A COUPLE OF WEEKS AND WE HAVE NOT BEEN APART EVER SINCE WE MET. I AM NOT GOING TO BE OKAY WITHOUT HIM. I NEED MY BABY. I WANT TO GO SEE MICHELLE AND STAY WITH HER, BUT I CAN'T MISS WORK. THAT JOB IS REALLY BRINGING ME DOWN LATELY. THEY ALL TREAT ME BAD NOW AND I HAVE HORRIBLE SHIFTS. PAUL REALLY WANTS TO START THIS BUSINESS AND I REALLY WANT TO GET THIS STARTED TOO, BUT I AM VERY SCARED. VERY, VERY SCARED. WHAT IF IT DOESN'T WORK OUT? WE CAN'T AFFORD TO LOSE MONEY. I DON'T KNOW HOW

MUCH PAUL MAKES, IT MUST BE OKAY BECAUSE HE ALWAYS HAS MONEY, I JUST HAVE NO IDEA HOW MUCH. IT BUGS ME! EITHER WAY, I LOVE HIM MORE THAN ANYTHING AND I COULD CARE LESS HOW MUCH HE MAKES. BUT I JUST WANT TO KNOW, I AM SO VERY CURIOUS. HE TAKES CARE OF ME, THOUGH, IF I REALLY NEED SOMETHING, HE ALWAYS TAKES CARE OF IT. HE IS HONESTLY THE MAN OF MY DREAMS.

FRIDAY, SEPTEMBER 7, 2012:

I HAVE A GREAT LIFE, 3 BEAUTIFUL KIDS, A HOT, SWEET, CARING MAN THAT I WANT TO MARRY. TONIGHT IS GOING TO BE MUCH BETTER AT WORK AND I AM GOING TO MAKE LOTS OF MONEY.

WELL, IT WAS AN OKAY NIGHT, I GUESS. I HAD ONE TABLE THAT WAS A 6 TOP AND THEY LEFT ME $40 ON A $40 CHECK. THEY WERE AWESOME. I DIDN'T EXPECT IT AT ALL! THE REST OF MY TABLES ABSOLUTELY SUCKED AND LEFT ME ABSOLUTELY HORRIBLE TIPS. WELL, IT'S ONLY 11:00 P.M. AND I GOT HOME AND PAUL AND BOTH HIS KIDS WERE ALREADY ASLEEP, SO I AM GOING TO BE SO DAMN BORED! I AM SO EXCITED FOR MASON'S GAME TOMORROW. I LOVE HIS FOOTBALL GAMES. MY MOM HAS ALL MY KIDS THIS WEEKEND, SO PAUL AND I ARE PLANNING ON TAKING JALA TO HOLLYWOOD CONNECTION ON SUNDAY WITH HIS KIDS. THAT WILL BE SO FUN. JALA WILL LOVE IT! I LOVE TO SEE MY LITTLE PRINCESS HAPPY!

SATURDAY, SEPTEMBER 8, 2012:

MASON'S 3RD FOOTBALL GAME! I LIVE TO WATCH THESE GAMES!! HE IS SUCH AN AWESOME LITTLE FOOTBALL PLAYER AND I AM NOT JUST SAYING THAT 'CAUSE HE'S MY BOY, HE IS A REALLY GOOD PLAYER AND IF HE KEEPS IT UP, HIS DREAM OF BECOMING A PROFESSIONAL FOOTBALL PLAYER WHEN HE

GROWS UP, JUST MIGHT COME TRUE. I LOVE MY BOY!! AND, MY SWEET MAN PAUL COMES TO EVERY SINGLE ONE OF HIS GAMES WITH ME. HOW STINKIN' SWEET IS THAT? WELL, THEY LOST THEIR GAME, BUT THEY ALL PLAYED REALLY, REALLY GOOD. PAUL WAS SO UPSET 'CAUSE HE COULDN'T GO. KIERRA TEXTED ME AGAIN TODAY SAYING HOW MUCH SHE MISSED ME AND LOVED ME. I LOVE THAT GIRL! I REALLY DON'T LIKE IT THAT THEY MOVED BACK TO ST. GEORGE. I MISS THEM ALL SO DAMN MUCH! I AM JUST NOT MYSELF OR COMPLETE IN ANY WAY NOT HAVING SHALL AROUND. SHE IS MY BEST FRIEND AND THE ONE PERSON I LOOK UP TO AND ADMIRE THE MOST. ME AND HER WILL ALWAYS BE CONNECTED LIKE NO ONE ELSE, WE HAVE A BOND THAT NOBODY OR NOTHING COULD EVER BREAK. WE HAVE ALWAYS BEEN THAT WAY AND WE ALWAYS WILL. BETTER GET SOME REST SINCE MY BABY AND I ARE GOING TO WENDOVER TOMORROW! *(A city in Nevada where gambling is legal.)*

SUNDAY, SEPTEMBER 9, 2012:

WENT TO WENDOVER TO WATCH THE BRONCOS PLAY AGAINST THE STEELERS AND IT WAS A BLAST! WE HAD A SUITE THERE AND HAD A LOT OF FUN, BUT WE ATE AT THE BUFFET FOR LUNCH AND PAUL GOT FOOD POISONING, POOR THING! BY THE MIDDLE OF THE GAME, HE WAS PUKING SO BAD AND WAS FOR A COUPLE DAYS AFTER THAT! I DIDN'T WANT TO COME BACK, THOUGH. I HATE REALITY SOMETIMES. IT IS SO HARD TO BE AN ADULT AT TIMES. IT'S SO, SO MUCH BETTER TO BE A KID! WORK IS GOING ABSOLUTELY AWFUL! I SWITCHED WITH MELISSA SO I COULD STAY HOME WITH PAUL THE NEXT DAY BECAUSE HE WAS SO SICK AND THAT DID NOT TURN OUT WELL AT ALL. THEY WERE TREATING ME SO BAD WHEN I WENT INTO WORK TONIGHT AND THEY TOLD ME I WASN'T GETTING MY CLOSING SHIFTS BACK, WHAT IN THE HELL DID I DO WRONG? THEY CAN'T EVEN GIVE ME A STRAIGHT ANSWER. I DON'T

KNOW WHAT TO DO! PAUL CAME IN TO TALK TO PAYNE, AND LUCKILY, HE WAS GONE OR SHIT WOULD HAVE HIT THE FAN! PAUL WANTS ME TO DO A LAWSUIT AGAINST THEM BECAUSE OF ALL THAT THEY ARE DOING TO ME! THEY HAVE NO GROUNDS AT ALL TO BE TREATING ME THIS WAY!

WEDNESDAY, SEPTEMBER 12, 2012:

WELL, TODAY STARTED OUT PRETTY SHITTY, BUT TURNED OUT PRETTY DAMN GOOD! CLEANED THE HOUSE, THEN PICKED UP MISS JALA FROM SCHOOL, THEN WENT TO MOM'S, PUT SOME LAUNDRY IN, ATE DINNER WITH THE MISSIONARIES *(for our church),* MY MOM, MY DAD, MASON AND HIS TWO FRIENDS, AND JALA. THEN CAME HOME, GOT READY, AND THEN ME AND PAUL MET HIS BROTHER RAYMOND AT THE STATE FAIR. IT WAS THE FIRST TIME I HAD EVER MET HIS BROTHER AND I DON'T KNOW EXACTLY WHAT I THINK OF HIM YET. HE HAD HIS GIRLFRIEND WITH HIM, AND SHE WAS FROM NEW JERSEY AND I WANTED TO KILL HER! SHE WAS A STUCK UP BITCH! SHE WAS COMPLAINING THE WHOLE TIME HERE SAYING HOW MESSED UP THIS STATE IS. I'M NOT ALWAYS HAPPY WITH UTAH BUT I STILL THINK IT'S A GREAT STATE. WE WENT TO DINNER AND THEN CAME HOME AND WATCHED A MOVIE AND NOW HE IS SITTING HERE WATCHING ME WRITE IN MY JOURNAL. HOW STINKIN' SWEET IS HE? I LOVE HIM. HE IS BY FAR THE BEST THING THAT HAS EVER HAPPENED TO ME SINCE MY KIDS. I AM NEVER, EVER LETTING THIS MAN GO!

THURSDAY, SEPTEMBER 13, 2012:

WELL, WORK JUST KEEPS GETTING BETTER AND BETTER! I CAME IN AND ASKED TO TALK TO THE GM AND HE SAID NOT RIGHT NOW BUT LATER. I TOLD HIM TO LET ME KNOW WHEN HE WAS READY AND THEN HE LEFT AFTER A COUPLE HOURS. HE WON'T EVEN TALK TO ME! WHAT KIND OF MANAGEMENT ARE

THEY? THEY ARE SO EXTREMELY MEAN TO ME NOW, AND FOR ABSOLUTELY NO REASON AT ALL. I GOT HOME AND RAYMOND, PAUL'S BROTHER, AND HIS GIRLFRIEND HAD JUST LEFT. THEY WERE WAITING FOR ME, BUT I GOT HOME AT LIKE 11:30 P.M. PAUL IS JUST A TOTALLY DIFFERENT PERSON TO ME WHEN HIS KIDS ARE AROUND. I HAVE NO IDEA WHY, BUT OH WELL, I HOPE IT GETS A LITTLE BETTER. I HONESTLY FEEL LIKE I AM IN AN UPSIDE-DOWN SPIRAL EVERY DAY. I HAVE TOO MUCH GOING ON ALL THE TIME. I HAVE NO MONEY 'CAUSE I AM MAKING NO MONEY AND I CAN'T GET MY STINKIN' BILLS CAUGHT UP AND I AM RUNNING FROM EVERYTHING. I AM SUCH A WRECK RIGHT NOW AND CANNOT GET A HOLD ON THINGS OR MY LIFE! THE ONLY THING I AM HAPPY ABOUT RIGHT NOW IS PAUL AND I. WE ARE AWESOME TOGETHER AND I CAN'T WAIT TO MARRY THIS MAN! I HOPE HE ASKS ME TO MARRY HIM SOON. *(She was still married to Jay.)* I AM PRAYING IT IS SOMETIME SOON. I MISS MY SISTERS AND MY KIDS SO MUCH IT PHYSICALLY HURTS. I CAN'T EVEN THINK ABOUT IT LONG ENOUGH OR I WILL GO ABSOLUTELY CRAZY! I NEED MY KIDS, AND MY SISTERS BACK!

FRIDAY, SEPTEMBER 14, 2012:

TODAY WAS AN OKAY DAY. I GOT TO SPEND THE DAY WITH MY LITTLE MISS JALA AND THAT IS ALWAYS MY FAVORITE THING. MY MORNING STARTED OUT WITH PAUL WAKING ME UP WITH A STARBUCKS DRINK AND THEN ADI CAME BY THIS MORNING BEFORE SCHOOL. WE TALKED FOR ABOUT 30 MIN. IT WAS AWESOME!

SO, I JUST GOT HOME FROM WORK ABOUT AN HOUR AGO AND IT WAS FINE. I JUST GOT OFF THE PHONE WITH SHALL AND KIERRA AND TYSON. I MISS THEM ALL SO, SO MUCH. MY LIFE IS JUST NOT THE SAME WITHOUT SHALL HERE, WHERE I CAN SEE HER EVERY DAY. NO MATTER WHAT IS HAPPENING IN OUR LIVES, SHALL AND I ARE ALWAYS CONNECTED.

BESIDES MY KIDS, SHE IS THE MOST IMPORTANT PERSON TO ME. BESIDES PAUL, TOO, OF COURSE. I CAN'T WAIT TO SEE HER OR KIERRA. THAT LITTLE GIRL HAS MY HEART, JUST LIKE MY KIDS DO. I MISS THEM LIKE CRAZY. EMILY STILL IS NOT TALKING TO ME AND WON'T FOR A LONG TIME, IF SHE EVER WILL, AND ANGIE IS ALWAYS BUSY. I NEED SHALL HERE SO BAD. I NEED MY BEST FRIEND TO TALK TO. I DON'T HAVE ANYONE TO TALK TO RIGHT NOW. I DON'T REALLY HAVE ANY GIRLFRIENDS 'CAUSE GIRLS ALWAYS FUCK ME OVER FOR SOME REASON. AND THERE IS ONLY CERTAIN THINGS I CAN OPEN UP AND TALK TO PAUL ABOUT. I FEEL REALLY LONELY LATELY THAT WAY.

<u>SATURDAY, SEPTEMBER 15, 2012</u>:

SMILE! TODAY IS GOING TO BE A FANTASTIC DAY! YA, AT LEAST I WAS HOPING IT WAS GOING TO BE. PAUL AND I GOT INTO A HUGE FIGHT THIS MORNING AND WE HAVE NOT FOUGHT LIKE THAT IN A VERY, VERY LONG TIME. I ABSOLUTELY HATE FIGHTING WITH HIM. I LOVE THIS MAN AND I DON'T KNOW WHY I SAY HURTFUL THINGS SOMETIMES TO HIM. I SPEAK BEFORE I THINK, A LOT! THIS WAS NOT A FIGHT I EVER WANT TO REPEAT. HE CAN REALLY THROW SOME LOW BLOWS! THIS MAN DEFINITELY KNOWS HOW TO FIGHT. BUT SO DO I, I DON'T EVER WANT TO SEE US BOTH AT OUR WORST, AGAINST EACH OTHER, IT WOULD BE REALLY, REALLY BAD. I THINK WE CAN GET THROUGH THIS, THOUGH. WE HAVE BEEN ABLE TO EVERY OTHER TIME, WITH FLYING COLORS. I PRAY WE GET THROUGH THIS. MASON'S GAME WAS TODAY, AND THEY LOST. BUT THEY PLAYED REALLY GOOD. HE IS SUCH AN AWESOME LITTLE FOOTBALL PLAYER. I LOVE HIM! I ABSOLUTELY LOVE PAUL'S KIDS BUT EVERY TIME WE FIGHT, HE HAS TO EVERY TIME BRING HIS KIDS UP AND EVERYTHING IS ALWAYS ABOUT THEM, WHICH IT SHOULD BE, BUT WHERE ARE MY KIDS? WE DON'T SEE OR TALK ABOUT OR EVEN SPEND HALF AS MUCH

TIME WITH MY KIDS LIKE WE DO HIS. I REALLY HOPE ONE DAY MY KIDS WILL BE JUST AS IMPORTANT TO HIM AS HIS KIDS ARE. DON'T GET ME WRONG, HE IS FABULOUS WITH MY KIDS, WHEN HE ACTUALLY SEES THEM.

MONDAY, SEPTEMBER 17, 2012:

IT WAS NOT A BAD DAY AT ALL TODAY. I OPENED AT WORK, THAT WASN'T VERY FUN, BUT GOT HOME, HANGING OUT WITH MY MOM FOR A BIT. I MISS HER SO MUCH. I NEED TO STOP ALL THIS SHIT AND QUIT BEING SO DAMN SELFISH! I NEED TO GET MY KIDS BACK. HOW ON EARTH DID I LET THEM GO IN THE 1ST PLACE? OR LET THEM GET TAKEN FROM ME? WHAT KIND OF MOTHER LETS THAT HAPPEN? AN ABSOLUTE HORRIBLE ONE! I AM HELL-A-SICK OF THIS LIFE ANYWAYS! IT'S BEEN WAY TOO LONG NOW WITHOUT MY BEAUTIFUL KIDS AND WAY TOO LONG FUCKING UP MY BODY! WHY DID I DO THIS TO MYSELF? IT IS THE HARDEST THING IN THE ENTIRE WORLD TO OVERCOME. BUT I HAVE DONE IT, I KNOW I CAN DO IT AGAIN, BUT I NEED THE WILL POWER TO DO IT AND I JUST DON'T HAVE IT! HOW DO I GET IT? I AM JUST SO LOW LATELY. I CAN'T GET OUT OF THIS HOLE. I LOVE MY KIDS AND LOVE PAUL AND THAT SHOULD BE ENOUGH TO FIGHT, WHY AM I NOT???

TUESDAY, SEPTEMBER 18, 2012:

IT'S ABOUT 1:15 A.M. RIGHT NOW AND I AM TRIPPIN' BIG TIME! MY FRIEND MELISSA FROM WORK JUST GOT OFF A BIT AGO AND WANTED ME TO COME OVER AND SMOKE A BOWL WITH HER. WELL, HER HUSBAND FREAKED OUT ON HER AND SHE CALLED ME AND LET ME LISTEN TO HIM TOTALLY EMOTIONALLY ABUSE HER WHILE I WAS ON SPEAKER. IT FREAKED ME OUT SO BAD! I THOUGHT FOR SURE HE WAS GOING TO HURT HER. LUCKILY, HE DIDN'T, BUT I FELT REALLY, REALLY BAD FOR HER. WELL, UNFORTUNATELY, SHE WAS NOT THE ONLY

ONE THAT HAD A SHITTY, SHITTY NIGHT. PAUL AND I GOT INTO THE WORST FIGHT WE HAVE EVER GOTTEN IN. IT WAS ABSOLUTELY HORRIBLE. HE SAID WE WERE DONE FOR GOOD THIS TIME. I WENT ABSOLUTELY CRAZY! I CRIED SO BAD THAT I COULD NOT EVEN BREATHE. IT DIDN'T FAZE HIM AT ALL! WELL, AFTER A VERY, VERY LONG, HORRIBLE NIGHT, WE ENDED UP LAYING DOWN TOGETHER AT LIKE 6:00 A.M. AND WOKE UP AND THINGS WERE BETTER BUT THEY ARE NOT AT ALL THE SAME. I AM VERY SAD TO SAY THIS, BUT I DON'T THINK THEY EVER WILL BE AGAIN. I AM DEFINITELY QUESTIONING HIS LOVE FOR ME NOW. I ABSOLUTELY HATE THAT FEELING. I MADE SUCH A FOOL OF MYSELF LAST NIGHT AND MY SELF-ESTEEM IS JUST COMPLETELY AWAY. I FEEL LIKE A COMPLETE LOSER AND NOW I AM COMPLETELY PARANOID AND FRUSTRATED 'CAUSE I DON'T KNOW WHAT IS GOING TO HAPPEN WITH US NOW. I NEED TO KNOW!!!

WEDNESDAY, SEPTEMBER 19, 2012:

RAYMOND'S GIRLFRIEND CAME OVER LAST NIGHT AND WE HAD A GOOD TIME TOGETHER, UNTIL THEY LEFT. I ASKED PAUL IF WE WERE OKAY AS HE WAS LYING DOWN TO GO TO BED AND HE FREAKED! SAID HE DIDN'T DO ANYTHING WRONG AND HE KNOWS THIS ISN'T GOING TO GET BETTER. I STAYED CALM WHILE HE FREAKED OUT ON ME AND SAID THE MOST HORRIBLE THINGS TO ME. I DID ABSOLUTELY NOTHING WRONG LAST NIGHT AND HE IS DOING A FANTASTIC JOB TO TRY AND PUSH ME AWAY! HE IS DEFINITELY DOING JUST THAT! I REALLY DON'T KNOW HOW MUCH MORE OF THIS I CAN TAKE! NOBODY SHOULD CRY THE WAY I DO ALMOST EVERY NIGHT THE LAST WEEK! IT'S JUST NOT RIGHT. I TOLD HIM I WOULD NEVER GIVE UP AND WOULD FIGHT FOR US TILL THE END BUT THERE COMES A CERTAIN POINT THAT YOU JUST CAN'T DO IT ANY LONGER. IT'S COMING, AND IT'S COMING FAST! THERE IS ONLY SO MUCH I CAN TAKE! I LOVE THIS MAN BUT I WON'T

PUT MYSELF THROUGH THIS KIND OF ABUSE, IT'S JUST NOT FAIR! I AM DOING EVERYTHING I POSSIBLY CAN, BUT IT'S JUST NOT ENOUGH! I HOPE WE CAN WORK THROUGH THIS BUT I AM NOT GOING TO LET SOMEONE WALK ALL OVER ME LIKE THIS AND MAKE ME ABSOLUTELY CRAZY! I AM DOING THE VERY BEST THAT I CAN!

WELL, I FOUND OUT WHY PAUL HAS BEEN SO ANGRY THE PAST FEW DAYS AND BEEN LASHING OUT AT ME. HE FOUND OUT THAT HIS BROTHER RAYMOND, THAT IS IN TOWN RIGHT NOW, THAT HE HASN'T SEEN IN 4 YEARS, JUST GOT OUT OF REHAB FOR HEROIN. PAUL IS VERY UPSET BECAUSE HE SAID RAYMOND WATCHED PAUL HELP HIS OTHER BROTHER THROUGH IT. I DON'T BLAME HIM AT ALL FOR BEING UPSET. HIS DAD AND NOW BOTH OF HIS BROTHERS HAVE ALL BEEN HEROIN ADDICTS! HOW SAD IS THAT? AND NOW HIS GIRLFRIEND, WHAT ARE THE ODDS OF THAT? PAUL DOESN'T EVEN LIKE HEARING THE WORD HEROIN.

SUNDAY, SEPTEMBER 23, 2012:

IT'S ABOUT 2:20 A.M. RIGHT NOW AND I AM STARING AT THE MOST BEAUTIFUL LITTLE GIRL RIGHT NOW! THIS IS THE 1ST TIME IN A LONG TIME THAT I HAVE BEEN ABLE TO KEEP MY PRINCESS OVERNIGHT AND SLEEP WITH HER. IT WAS A PERFECT NIGHT BECAUSE PAUL IS GONE FOR 5 DAYS (WASHINGTON) AND IT'S REALLY HARD BEING ALONE IN THIS HOUSE, HAVING MY BABY JALA WITH ME IS ABSOLUTELY WONDERFUL. I LOVE MY LITTLE PRINCESS! I ABSOLUTELY HATE BEING ALONE WITHOUT PAUL. I AM WANTING HIM BACK HERE SO BAD! RAYMOND AND HIS GIRLFRIEND CAME OVER TONIGHT AND WERE SUPPOSED TO STAY OVER BUT THEY WOULDN'T. I GET SO SCARED OVER HERE BY MYSELF AND I CAN'T FIND ANYONE TO STAY WITH ME, SO I FINALLY CALLED PATRICK AND HIM AND HIS FRIEND CAME TO GET ME AND WE ARE KICKING IT NOW. *(I wonder if she took Jala with her.)* BUT NOW I WANT

TO GO BACK HOME. I DON'T FEEL COMFORTABLE ANYWHERE BUT MY OWN HOUSE, EVEN THOUGH I AM SCARED!

TUESDAY, SEPTEMBER 25, 2012:

WELL, TODAY HAS BEEN AN AWFUL DAY. PAUL IS STILL OUT OF TOWN, HE COMES HOME TOMORROW NIGHT AND I AM SO EXCITED TO SEE HIM! DEBORAH CAME OVER TODAY, SO DID RAYMOND AND HIS GIRLFRIEND, AND WE WERE ALL TALKING ON THE PORCH. WE CAME IN AND THE BIRD WAS *DEAD!* I FREAKED OUT! PAUL AND HIS KIDS LOVED THAT BIRD. DEBORAH DID CPR ON THE BIRD FOR ABOUT 20 MIN, ABSOLUTELY NOTHING! PAUL JUST CALLED AND I DIDN'T EVEN DARE TO TELL HIM. THIS JUST STARTED MY HORRIBLE DAY! THEN I WENT TO WORK AND MADE ABSOLUTELY NO MONEY. I MADE $25, THAT IS IT! I GOT CUT EARLY AND I CAME HOME AND HAD JAY BRING JALA OVER. HE HAD KELLIE *(his girlfriend at the time)* IN THE CAR WITH HIM AND I FREAKED OUT! I DON'T KNOW WHY. IT BLEW UP FROM THERE, AND JAY AND I GOT INTO THE BIGGEST FIGHT. POOR LITTLE JALA WAS SCREAMING AND SOBBING. IT WAS THE SADDEST THING EVER! I WILL NOT FIGHT LIKE THAT AGAIN. THE PERSON THAT SUFFERED THE MOST WAS POOR JALA! I HAVE NOT FOUGHT LIKE THAT WITH JAY IN A VERY, VERY LONG TIME. WELL, JALA ENDED UP STAYING THE NIGHT AND IT WAS AWESOME. I ABSOLUTELY LOVE HAVING MY BABY GIRL WITH ME. I AM GOING TO TRY AND HAVE HER MORE OFTEN. I MISS PAUL SO MUCH IT PHYSICALLY HURTS. HE COMES HOME TOMORROW, THOUGH, AND I AM SO DAMN EXCITED! I HOPE TOMORROW WILL BE A MUCH BETTER DAY.

WEDNESDAY, SEPTEMBER 26, 2012:

WOKE UP NEXT TO MY BABY GIRL TODAY AND IT STARTED MY DAY OUT SO GOOD! I LOVE MY LITTLE PRINCESS! I GET TO

BE WITH ALL 3 OF MY KIDS TODAY AND I AM SO EXCITED! AND...MY BABY COMES HOME TONIGHT! I CAN'T WAIT TO SEE HIM, I CAN HARDLY STAND IT!

WELL, IT'S ABOUT 10:20 P.M. RIGHT NOW AND I AM WAITING FOR MY BABY TO GET HERE. HIS PLANE LANDED AT 10, SO HE SHOULD BE HERE ANYTIME. I CAN'T WAIT! RACHEL CAME AND SPENT THE DAY WITH ME TODAY. SHE JUST LEFT ABOUT A HALF HOUR AGO. SHE IS REALLY A SWEET GIRL. IT WAS FUN. WE PICKED JALA UP, THEN WENT TO MY MOM'S AND HUNG OUT WITH ADI AND MAS FOR A LITTLE BIT, THEN ATE DINNER WITH EVERYONE AND TOOK JALA TO JAY. HE APOLOGIZED TO ME FOR LAST NIGHT AND TOLD ME HE WANTS ME HAPPY AND THAT HE LOVES ME. IT MADE ME FEEL BETTER THAT HE APOLOGIZED FOR LAST NIGHT, BUT IT STILL HURTS THAT JALA HAD TO SEE THAT. IT'S NOT ERASED OUT OF HER HEAD AND I AM NOT OKAY, AND SORRY DOESN'T MAKE IT ANY BETTER. MY BABY JUST CALLED ME, AND HE IS ON HIS WAY HOME. I'M GETTING BUTTERFLIES JUST THINKING ABOUT IT! I LOVE THIS MAN, I MISSED HIM MORE THAN I THOUGHT I WOULD.

THURSDAY, SEPTEMBER 27, 2012:

IT'S ABOUT 10:30 P.M. RIGHT NOW AND PAUL AND I ARE GETTING READY TO GO TO BREWVIE'S AND WATCH A MOVIE WITH RACHEL AND RAYMOND. WORK ABSOLUTELY SUCKED TONIGHT. I MADE $10.00. THAT IS PATHETIC! MASON ASKED ME AGAIN LAST NIGHT IF AND WHEN I WAS GOING TO GET THEM BACK. IT BREAKS MY HEART BECAUSE I HONESTLY HAVE NO IDEA IF I WILL GET THEM BACK, ACTUALLY, WHY DID I SAY THAT...I MEANT I DON'T KNOW *WHEN* I AM GOING TO GET THEM BACK...BUT IT WILL HAPPEN, IT WILL! I GET JALA THIS WEEKEND A LOT BECAUSE I WANT TO SPEND A LOT OF TIME WITH HER BEFORE SHE LEAVES NEXT WEEK TO CALIFORNIA. IT'S SO STINKIN' CUTE, SHE IS SO SUPER

EXCITED TO GO SEE ALL THE PRINCESSES @ DISNEYLAND. I AM GOING TO MISS HER, THOUGH, SHE IS GOING TO BE GONE FOR 10 DAYS. RAYMOND AND RACHEL ARE LEAVING TO LA NEXT WEEK, ACTUALLY A COUPLE DAYS, AND I AM GOING TO BE SUPER SAD. I ABSOLUTELY LOVE THAT GIRL! SHE HAS BEEN SO SUPER FUN SINCE SHE HAS BEEN HERE. I HOPE THAT AFTER SHE LEAVES THAT I GET TO SEE HER REALLY SOON. SHE IS DARLING. WE WENT TO BREWVIE'S TONIGHT AND WE HAD TO LEAVE BECAUSE RAYMOND ALMOST GOT IN A FIGHT WITH SOME GUYS THAT WERE TRYING TO TALK TO ME AND RACHEL. SO WE WENT TO THE PIE, ATE SOME AMAZING PIZZA, THEN CAME HOME. IT WAS AN OKAY NIGHT, I GUESS.

<u>SATURDAY, SEPTEMBER 29, 2012</u>:

WELL, WORK JUST KEEPS GETTING MORE AND MORE MISERABLE EACH DAY THAT I GO IN! IT WAS SO GREAT WHEN I STARTED, AND ALL THE MANAGERS ABSOLUTELY LOVED ME, AND FOR A VERY LONG TIME, AT LEAST OVER A YEAR, THEN ALL OF A SUDDEN THEY STARTED HATING ME. NOW, I AM GETTING AWFUL SHIFTS AND AWFUL SECTIONS. THEY CUT ME VERY 1ST EVERY SINGLE NIGHT AND NONE OF THE MANAGERS TALK TO ME AT ALL ANYMORE AND I CAN FEEL THE TENSION EVERY TIME I WALK IN THAT RESTAURANT NOW. IT SUCKS! I USED TO LOVE GOING INTO WORK, NOW I CAN'T WAIT TO GET OUT OF THERE 'CAUSE I KNOW THEY ALL JUST HATE ME AND ARE WAITING FOR ME TO MAKE THE WRONG MOVE SO THEY CAN WRITE ME UP AND FIRE ME. WELL, I AM *NOT* ABOUT TO LET THAT HAPPEN. I AM JUST GOING TO KEEP ON DOING MY BEST AND SHOVE IT IN THEIR FACE. HOPEFULLY IT GETS BETTER, IF NOT, I HAVE TO MOVE ON AND FIND SOMETHING ELSE.

WELL, I HONESTLY CANNOT HANDLE ANY MORE OF THESE STUPID FIGHTS ME AND PAUL ARE GETTING IN. THEY ARE SO STUPID AND DO NOT NEED TO HAPPEN. I REALLY DO TRY

MY HARDEST WITH HIM AND IT'S JUST NOT GOOD ENOUGH. I KNOW I HAVE SOME ISSUES AND PROBLEMS BUT NOWHERE NEAR LIKE PAUL DOES. AND SERIOUSLY, I LOVE HIS KIDS TO DEATH, BUT *EVERY* TIME THEY ARE HERE, I AM COMPLETELY OUT OF THE PICTURE. I CAN DEAL WITH THAT, BUT THESE FIGHTS AND THE DISRESPECT I AM GETTING FROM HIM, I DON'T KNOW HOW MUCH MORE OF THIS I CAN TAKE. HE DOESN'T REALIZE I AM VERY, VERY CLOSE TO LEAVING, OR MAYBE HE JUST DOESN'T CARE! MASON'S GAME WAS TODAY, AND RACHEL WENT AND IT WAS AN ADVENTURE, DEFINITELY! IT WAS GREAT SITTING WITH ADI BECAUSE I NEVER GET TO SEE HER AS MUCH AS I WOULD LIKE. JALA SLEPT OVER LAST NIGHT AND IT WAS GREAT! I LOVED WAKING UP NEXT TO MY LITTLE PRINCESS. SHE CAME WITH US TO THE GAME AND SPENT THE DAY WITH US, I COULDN'T HAVE HAD IT ANY OTHER WAY! I LOVE BEING WITH MY KIDS! THEY ARE ABSOLUTELY EVERYTHING TO ME! I WISH THEY WERE IN MY LIFE A LOT MORE. ADI CAME OVER TONIGHT AFTER WORK AND BROUGHT US ALL SOME COOKIES. IT WAS THE CUTEST THING EVER! IT WAS SUCH A SURPRISE, HER STOPPING BY, AND IT MADE MY WHOLE ENTIRE NIGHT. IT'S ABOUT MIDNIGHT RIGHT NOW AND I AM GOING TO BED 'CAUSE I OPEN IN THE MORNING, YAY!

SUNDAY, SEPTEMBER 30, 2012:

HAD TO OPEN TODAY AND YEP, IT SUCKED ONCE AGAIN! HARDLY MADE ANY MONEY AT ALL, MAYBE TOOK HOME $50, THAT JUST SUCKS! WHEN I GOT OFF WORK, RACHEL PICKED ME UP AND WE WENT BACK TO THEIR CONDO, HUNG OUT A LITTLE BIT, THEN CAME HOME AND HUNG OUT. RACHEL TOLD ME SOME VERY INTERESTING NEWS. I AM ACTUALLY TRIPPIN' OUT BAD!! SHE TOLD ME THAT PAUL USED TO BEAT THE KIDS' MOM HORRIBLY BAD AND HE USED TO BEAT HIS KIDS!! I DON'T KNOW WHAT TO BELIEVE, I DON'T IMAGINE RACHEL WOULD LIE TO ME,

BUT I KNOW PAUL (I THOUGHT) AND I KNOW HE HAS A REALLY BAD TEMPER, BUT I JUST DON'T SEE HIM BEATING ANYONE, ESPECIALLY HIS KIDS, HE IS SO DAMN GREAT WITH HIS KIDS, ACTUALLY TOO GREAT. I DON'T KNOW WHAT THE HELL TO THINK. I FEEL SO ALONE AND COMPLETELY BETRAYED, PAUL TOLD ME HE COULD NEVER HIT A GIRL AND HE NEVER HAS! I HAVE NO IDEA WHAT TO THINK. BUT WHY IN THE HELL WOULD SHE LIE TO ME? SHE HAS BEEN AWESOME TO ME AND I REALLY DON'T THINK THAT SHE WOULD MAKE SOMETHING LIKE THAT UP. I AM SO EXTREMELY SCARED NOW. WHAT IN THE HELL DO I DO? I THOUGHT I KNEW EVERYTHING ABOUT THIS GUY, AND I DON'T!

THURSDAY, OCTOBER 4, 2012:

I WOKE UP FROM THE SWEETEST LETTER FROM PAUL THAT MADE MY ENTIRE DAY! HE HAS ONLY WRITTEN ME A CARD, MAYBE ONE LETTER THE WHOLE TIME WE HAVE BEEN TOGETHER, SO IT MEANT THE WORLD TO ME. WE HAVE NOT BEEN GETTING ALONG VERY WELL LATELY AND THIS IS WEIRD, ESPECIALLY FOR US, SO PAUL HAS BEEN TREATING ME LIKE A QUEEN THE PAST COUPLE OF DAYS. WHEN HE IS GOOD TO ME, IT IS BEING TREATED LIKE I HONESTLY WAS ROYALTY! HE REALLY IS AN AMAZING MAN. I HAVE ABSOLUTELY HAD IT WITH HIS BROTHER AND RACHEL LATELY. THEY HAVE BEEN HERE A MONTH NOW AND THEY ARE STARTING TO CAUSE A LOT OF PROBLEMS BETWEEN ME AND PAUL. I HONESTLY DON'T THINK ANYTHING THAT RACHEL WAS TELLING ME ABOUT PAUL WAS TRUE AT ALL. BUT WHO THE HELL KNOWS. THEY ARE BOTH JUST DRIVING ME *NUTS!* IT WAS ABSOLUTELY GREAT HAVING THEM AROUND AT FIRST, BUT NOW THEY ARE WITH US EVERY STINKIN' DAY AND PAUL AND I NEVER GET ANY TIME ALONE ANYMORE. THEY REALLY JUST NEED TO GO BACK TO

LA. SHALL CALLED ME TODAY, TELLING ME HOW MUCH SHE MISSED ME AND LOVED ME. I WAS MAD AT HER FOR A MINUTE, BUT IT'S ONLY BECAUSE I KNOW SHE IS RIGHT. SHE IS THE ONE AND ONLY PERSON THAT CAN SEE RIGHT THROUGH ME! I CANNOT EVER KEEP ANYTHING FROM MICHELLE. WE ARE SO SUPER CLOSE THAT WE CAN HONESTLY FEEL AND SEE WHAT EACH OTHER IS GOING THROUGH. SHE IS AND ALWAYS WILL BE MY INSPIRATION!

FRIDAY, OCTOBER 5, 2012:

TODAY WAS AN OKAY DAY, I GUESS. WOKE UP AND SPENT THE MORNING WITH MY BABY, THEN GOT READY AND WENT TO PATRICK'S HOUSE FOR A COUPLE HOURS, THEN WENT TO WORK. WORK WAS NOT GOOD, AS ALWAYS NOW. I ABSOLUTELY HATE BEING THERE, IT SUCKS SO BAD. I WANT TO QUIT SO BAD BUT I CAN'T. I NEED TO MAKE MONEY FOR MYSELF. I ABSOLUTELY HAVE TO. JUST GOT HOME A COUPLE HOURS AGO AND PAUL AND I FINISHED A MOVIE THAT WE STARTED A WHILE AGO. THEN I GOT IN THE BATH, AND NOW I'M WRITING WHILE MY BABY IS ASLEEP RIGHT NEXT TO ME. I REALLY DO LOVE THIS MAN. JALA AND JAY ARE IN DISNEYLAND RIGHT NOW AND SHE HAS CALLED ME EVERY DAY TELLING ME WHO SHE MET IN DISNEYLAND AND JUST HOW MUCH FUN SHE IS HAVING. I AM SUPER GLAD SHE GOT TO GO, BUT I WISH I WAS THE ONE WHO TOOK HER. OH WELL, SOMEDAY SOON, I HOPE! I CAN'T WAIT TILL SHE GETS BACK, THOUGH. I MISS HER SO MUCH! SO, I WENT TO MY MOM'S TODAY AND ADI WAS SITTING IN HER JEEP CRYING AND WOULDN'T OPEN THE DOOR SO I COULD TALK TO HER. I JUST STOPPED BY TO GRAB THE REST OF MY LAUNDRY AND I HAD TO GO HOME AND CHANGE FOR WORK, SO I COULDN'T SIT THERE AND BEG HER TO TALK TO ME. I HAVE NO IDEA WHAT WAS WRONG WITH HER, BUT I REALLY WANT TO FIND OUT. SHE IS *MY GIRL!*

<u>WEDNESDAY, OCTOBER 10, 2012</u>:

PAUL AND I JUST GOT HOME FROM GOING TO ADI'S EVENING OF EXCELLENCE *(an activity for the young women in our church)* AT MY MOM'S CHURCH. ADI DID A SOLO AND IT WAS AMAZING, AS ALWAYS! THAT GIRL HAS A SET OF LUNGS ON HER! SHE HAS THE MOST INCREDIBLE VOICE, I LOVE TO HEAR HER SING! SO, PAUL AND I ARE DOING AWESOME! YA, WE HAVE DEFINITELY HAD OUR BUMPS IN THE ROAD, BUT WE MADE IT THROUGH ALL OF THEM AND ARE THAT MUCH CLOSER AND STRONGER BECAUSE OF IT. I LOVE THIS MAN WITH ALL MY HEART! JALA GOT HOME FROM DISNEYLAND TODAY. IT WAS SO GREAT SEEING HER. I MISSED HER SO MUCH! SHE WAS REALLY CLINGY TODAY, DID NOT WANT ME OUT OF HER SIGHT. SHE SAID SHE CRIED FOR ME A LOT. HOW SAD IT THAT? MY KIDS ARE ABSOLUTELY AMAZING! I LOVE THEM MORE THAN ANYTHING IN THIS WORLD. I HAVE SUCH A HARD TIME TRYING TO FIGURE OUT WHY I MADE THE CHOICES THAT I HAVE. IT COMPLETELY FUCKED MY WORLD UP AND MY KIDS, NOT TO MENTION MY FAMILY. I WISH I COULD TAKE BACK SO MUCH OF ALL THE BAD AND HORRIBLE MISTAKES THAT I HAVE MADE. I HAVE PUT SO MANY PEOPLE THROUGH HELL AND BACK.

<u>THURSDAY, OCTOBER 11, 2012</u>:

THIS MONTH/YEAR HAS FLOWN! TIME GOES BY WAY TOO FAST. AND ALL I KNOW IS THAT I AM IN THE SAME BOAT THAT I HAVE BEEN IN FOR WAY TOO LONG NOW. WHY CAN'T I OPEN MY EYES AND REALIZE WHAT THE FUCK I AM DOING? WHY CAN'T I STOP? AND I KEEP WRITING THIS SAME THING OVER AND OVER IN EVERY JOURNAL THAT I HAVE, WHICH IS ABOUT EIGHT OF THEM. I HAVE EVERY MEANS TO STOP, WHICH I MEAN, I HAVE A DR., I GET SUBOXONE EVERY MONTH, BUT I JUST WON'T DO IT. I AM TELLING MYSELF NOW, NEXT MONTH, WHEN I GET MY SUBS, I AM GOING TO USE THEM!

I AM TRULY GIVING MYSELF A DEADLINE, AND THIS IS IT! I AM DONE HURTING THE PEOPLE I LOVE AND MYSELF. WHY I DIDN'T DO THIS A LONG TIME AGO, I HAVE NO IDEA. I GUESS I AM JUST A SELFISH BITCH. BUT I AM OVER IT, OVER BEING SELFISH, I LOVE MY KIDS, PAUL, AND MYSELF WAY TOO MUCH TO BE KILLING MYSELF. AND THAT IS SO WHERE IT'S LEADING, AND IF I DON'T STOP NOW, I THINK DEATH IS THE NEXT THING COMING. TIME TO STOP NOW, NAT! IT'S NOW OR NEVER!

WELL, TODAY HAS BEEN A RELAXING DAY. HAD AN AWESOME MORNING WITH MY BABY, THEN HAD PAUL'S DAUGHTER FOR THE REST OF THE DAY. SHE GOT SICK AT SCHOOL, SO PAUL PICKED HER UP AND SHE SPENT THE DAY WITH ME. WE HUNG OUT AT THE HOUSE FOR A WHILE AND THEN WE WENT TO WALMART, GOT SOME BOWS AND HEADBANDS, THEN WE WENT TO PICK UP JALA, AND NOW WE'RE BACK AT THE HOUSE AND I'M GETTING READY FOR WORK. JALA IS GOING TO STAY WITH PAUL AND HIS DAUGHTER FOR A BIT WHILE I AM AT WORK. DON'T KNOW WHAT IS GOING TO HAPPEN AT WORK WHEN I GET THERE BECAUSE I WAS SUPPOSED TO HAVE A DR. NOTE 'CAUSE I DIDN'T GO IN THE PAST FEW DAYS 'CAUSE I WAS SICK AND MY DR. WOULDN'T GIVE ME A NOTE UNLESS HE SEES ME. WELL, I DON'T HAVE INSURANCE AND IT WOULD HAVE COST ME $70, JUST TO SEE HIM. NOT WORTH IT! HOPEFULLY, I WILL JUST GET A WRITE UP 'CAUSE I HAVE NEVER IN THE PAST TWO YEARS OF WORKING THERE EVER HAD A WRITE UP, NEVER BEEN LATE, IN TROUBLE OF ANY KIND, OR EVER BEEN WRITTEN UP. I'M VERY CURIOUS TO SEE WHAT THEY ARE GOING TO DO. I'M PRAYING THAT I STILL HAVE A JOB. I REALLY NEED MY JOB! I NEED MY CLOSING SHIFTS BACK BUT THAT'S NOT GOING TO HAPPEN NOW. I'M WISHING MYSELF ALL THE LUCK IN THE WORLD.

IT'S ABOUT 12:00 AND I JUST GOT HOME FROM WORK ABOUT AN HOUR AGO. IT SUCKED SO BAD! THEY GAVE ME A WRITE UP, MY VERY FIRST ONE, AND THEY TOOK ALL MY

OPENS AWAY AND MY BAR SHIFT. AND THEY ONLY HAVE ME ON 5 DAYS A WEEK NOW INSTEAD OF 6. AT LEAST I DIDN'T GET FIRED, BUT MAYBE GETTING FIRED WOULD HAVE BEEN A LOT EASIER TO HANDLE THAN ALL THIS SHIT. I JUST DON'T KNOW WHY THEY HATE ME SO MUCH. WHILE I WAS CLEANING MY SECTION, ANGIE WALKED THROUGH THE DOOR. I IMMEDIATELY STARTED SOBBING 'CAUSE I MISS HER SO MUCH. I HAVE NOT SEEN OR TALKED TO ANGIE IN MONTHS OR EVEN LONGER. WE HUGGED FOR A LONG TIME; IT WAS SO GREAT TO SEE HER! SHALL IS COMING OUT TOMORROW WITH KIERRA AND ANGIE SAID WE SHOULD ALL GET TOGETHER AND HAVE A GIRLS' NIGHT OUT. I WOULD LOVE THAT! I THINK KIERRA IS GOING TO STAY WITH ME ONE NIGHT, YAY!! I'M SO EXCITED!

<u>FRIDAY, OCTOBER 12, 2012</u>:

IT'S 1:30 A.M. AND I AM SITTING HERE WRITING IN MY JOURNAL 'CAUSE I CANNOT GO TO SLEEP WITH EVERYTHING I HAVE ON MY MIND. STRESS IS GOING TO KILL ME, I REALLY NEED TO LEARN HOW TO DEAL WITH IT. JAY IS BEING ABSOLUTELY AWESOME TO ME LATELY. SO, I'M SITTING HERE WITH MY PRINCESS JALA AND PAUL'S DAUGHTER. I GO INTO WORK IN ABOUT AN HOUR AND I AM SO NOT LOOKING FORWARD TO IT. WE HAVE PAUL'S KIDS TONIGHT, TOMORROW NIGHT, AND THE NEXT NIGHT SO I AM GOING TO KEEP JALA ONE OF THOSE NIGHTS. I JUST DON'T KNOW HOW SHE WILL DO HERE. SHE IS NOT USED TO IT AT ALL. I HOPE SHE WILL BE OKAY BECAUSE I WANT TO START TAKING HER A LOT MORE OVERNIGHT. SHE NEEDS TO BE WITH ME A LOT MORE, NOT JUST JAY ALL THE TIME. I MISS HER ALONG WITH MY OTHER TWO KIDS. I MISS MASON BAD! I GET TO SEE JALA AND ADI A LOT, BUT I *NEVER* SEE MAS, IT IS ABSOLUTELY KILLING ME! I NEED MY BOY! IT MAKES ME SUPER SAD!!! WORK SUCKED TONIGHT, AS ALWAYS! I HAD TO SIGN MY FIRST

WRITE UP FOR BEING SICK AND NOT HAVING A DR. NOTE. HOW FUCKED UP IS THAT? IT'S NOT LIKE I DID SOMETHING WRONG. I HAVEN'T EVEN BEEN IN TROUBLE *EVER* SINCE THE DAY I STARTED THERE, IT'S BEEN TWO STINKIN' YEARS! THEY MAKE ME FEEL LIKE I DID SOMETHING WRONG. I AM SO SICK OF THE PEOPLE AT MY JOB. SHALL AND KIERRA CALLED ME TONIGHT WHILE I WAS AT WORK AND KIERRA TEXTS ME LOTS. SHE IS GOING TO STAY WITH ME AT MY HOUSE TOMORROW NIGHT. I AM SO SUPER EXCITED!

SATURDAY, OCTOBER 13, 2012:

TODAY IS GOING TO BE AN AWESOME DAY! IT IS DEFINITELY GOING TO BE A GREAT DAY BECAUSE I HAVE JALA TONIGHT AND KIERRA IS STAYING OVER ALSO, I AM SUPER, SUPER EXCITED!

SO, IT'S ABOUT 3:30 A.M. IN THE MORNING AND I AM LITERALLY GOING TO SUFFOCATE PAUL IF HE DOES NOT STOP BREATHING THE WAY HE DOES WHEN HE IS ASLEEP. HE IS ABSOLUTELY KILLING ME. AND I AM NOT GOING TO WAKE HIM UP 'CAUSE IF I DO, I AM JUST SETTING MYSELF UP FOR PURE *HELL!* I LOVE THIS MAN TO DEATH, BUT HE IS THE MOST ANNOYING, LOUDEST SLEEPER THAT I HAVE EVER HEARD! I HAVE A BIG DAY TODAY, I REALLY NEED MY SLEEP AND IT DOESN'T LOOK LIKE I AM GOING TO GET MUCH. I HAVE TO WAKE UP AT 7:00 A.M. AND GO TO JAY'S AND STAY WITH JALA TILL SHE WAKES UP 'CAUSE JAY HAS TO WORK. THEN COME HOME AND GET READY TO GO TO MASON'S FOOTBALL GAME (YAY!), THEN COME HOME AND GET READY TO GO TO WORK. TOMORROW NIGHT WILL BE MY LAST BAR SHIFT. I AM WAY SAD ABOUT THAT. I DON'T CARE TOO MUCH ABOUT LOSING MY OPENINGS, BUT I AM UPSET THEY TOOK MY BAR SHIFT. THEY ARE DEFINITELY OUT TO GET ME, BUT I AM NOT ABOUT TO LET THEM WIN! I AM GOING TO STAY STRONG, GO INTO WORK EVERY DAY WITH A BIG SMILE ON MY FACE

AND ACT LIKE NOTHING IS BOTHERING ME. THEY CAN ALL KISS MY ASS! I AM DONE TRYING SO HARD THERE! IT GOT ME NOWHERE, SO I WILL JUST DO MY OWN THING NOW. IF THEY FIRE ME, THEN THEY FIRE ME. I HAVE DONE MY VERY BEST THERE FOR TWO YEARS AND EVERYONE KNOWS IT, THEY JUST NEED A REALITY CHECK! I AM THEIR *BEST* EMPLOYEE, BY FAR!

SUNDAY, OCTOBER 14, 2012:

IT'S ABOUT 12:30 SUNDAY MORNING RIGHT NOW AND PAUL, JALA, AND HIS KIDS ARE ALL FAST ASLEEP WHILE I AM AWAKE JUST STRESSING ABOUT LIFE AS I ALWAYS DO. KIERRA WAS SUPPOSED TO SLEEP OVER HERE TONIGHT, BUT SURPRISE, SURPRISE, SHE AT THE LAST MINUTE DECIDED TO STAY WITH ADI AND KAILEE AT GRANDMA'S. COULD BE PARTIALLY TRUE, BUT I KNOW THE REAL REASON IS BECAUSE HER PARENTS DIDN'T WANT HER TO STAY OVER HERE WITH *ME!* I COULD BE TRIPPIN' BUT I HIGHLY DOUBT IT! TONIGHT WAS MY LAST BAR SHIFT. IT WAS SAD, BUT A GREAT NIGHT, THOUGH.

Nat carried her journal with her in her purse and wrote at work and other places.

SO, HERE OPENING AND THINGS ARE FINE. WE ARE SO EXTREMELY SLOW, THOUGH, IT SUCKS! I HAVE ONLY HAD THREE TABLES AND IT'S 1:00. I AM DEFINITELY NOT GOING TO MAKE ANY MONEY IF IT STAYS LIKE THIS!

IT'S ABOUT 8:00 P.M. NOW AND PAUL AND I ARE AT LIQUID JOE'S LISTENING TO HIS FRIEND'S BAND PLAY. ALEXANDER AND HIS BAND, THEY ARE ACTUALLY PRETTY GOOD. WE ARE GOING TO DINNER HERE IN A FEW. I ABSOLUTELY LOVE BEING WITH MY MAN, I AM SO CONTENT AND HAPPY THE MAJORITY OF THE TIME!

MONDAY, OCTOBER 15, 2012:

IT'S ABOUT 12:15 MONDAY MORNING AND HERE I AM ONCE AGAIN WIDE AWAKE WHILE PAUL IS PRETTY MUCH COMATOSE NEXT TO ME, SNORING LOUDER THAN ALL *HELL!* SO, WE ENDED UP HAVING A PRETTY GOOD NIGHT. WE WERE ONLY AT LIQUID JOE'S FOR ABOUT AN HOUR, THEN WENT TO EAT AT EMPIRE AND WE HAD A REALLY GOOD, DEEP TALK THAT REALLY NEEDED TO HAPPEN BETWEEN US. I TOLD HIM EXACTLY HOW I FELT, AND HE TOTALLY LISTENED AND TOOK IT WAY BETTER THAN I THOUGHT.

WELL, TODAY WENT AWESOME AT WORK! IT WAS THE FIRST SHIFT THAT I HAVE HAD NOT AS AN OPENER AND WORKING DURING THE DAY. I MADE MORE MONEY TODAY THAN I HAVE IN MONTHS DURING THE DAY, ALMOST $100.

WEDNESDAY, OCTOBER 17, 2012:

WELL, TODAY STARTED OUT PRETTY GOOD, I GUESS. I SLEPT IN REALLY LATE 'CAUSE I HAVEN'T SLEPT VERY GOOD THE PAST FEW NIGHTS. WOKE UP AROUND 1:00, THEN WENT AND GOT ADISON SO SHE COULD KEEP MY CAR THIS AFTERNOON. THEN WENT TO PICK UP JALA AND WENT TO MY MOM'S AND HUNG OUT WITH JALA. WANTED TO SPEND TIME WITH MASON ALSO BUT HE HAD A FRIEND OVER AGAIN. BUT, JUST KNOWING MASON WAS THERE MADE ME VERY HAPPY. AT HOME NOW WITH JALA, AND I'M GOING TO DROP HER OFF IN A COUPLE HOURS, THEN PAUL AND I ARE GOING OUT! YAY!! WE ARE GOING TO DINNER, THEN TO THE LED ZEPPELIN MOVIE AT THE GATEWAY. I'M SO, SO SUPER EXCITED!

WELL, THERE DEFINITELY WAS A GOOD REASON WHY I WAS EXCITED! WE HAVE SO MUCH FUN TOGETHER. HE TOOK ME TO THE GATEWAY, AND WE ATE AT "BOUT TIME," WHICH IS SUPER YUMMY. THEN WHEN WE WERE DONE EATING, WE WENT TO THE LED ZEPPELIN MOVIE THAT I DIDN'T LIKE AT ALL

BUT AFTER THREE SONGS WE LEFT (PRETTY MUCH FIFTEEN MINUTES INTO THE MUSIC).

THURSDAY, OCTOBER 18, 2012:

IT'S ABOUT 2:00 A.M. AND I AM SO NOT TIRED AT ALL! I WOKE UP AT 2:00 THIS AFTERNOON, SO I GOT PLENTY OF SLEEP. SO DAVID KEEPS CALLING ME FROM JAIL AND IT IS STRESSING ME OUT SO BAD! IF I DON'T ANSWER, THEN CATHERINE CALLS ME. IT'S GETTING A BIT OUT OF CONTROL. HE WANTS ME TO COME SEE HIM! HE KEEPS SENDING ME LETTERS IN THE MAIL. IF MARY ONLY KNEW.

JUST GOT HOME FROM WORK, AND OF COURSE, IT SUCKED SO BAD! WE HAD A WAY FUN DAY TODAY, THOUGH. SHALL, TYE, ANGIE, RANDY, ME, MY MOM, MASON, JALA, AND THIMNA *(a relative of ours from Germany, who was living with us at the time)* AND HER BOYFRIEND ALL WENT TO PARK CITY, ATE LUNCH THERE, THEN WENT DOWN THE ALPINE SLIDE AND THE NEW ROLLER COASTER. IT WAS A BLAST! POOR ADI COULDN'T

Nat and Kierra in Park City

Nat and me in Park City

COME 'CAUSE SHE GOT ALL FOUR OF HER WISDOM TEETH OUT. POOR BABY! YA, ALL IN ALL, IT WAS A GOOD DAY! NOW, I'M SITTING HERE WITH MY BABY AND HAVING A GREAT NIGHT. HE HAS BEEN SO INCREDIBLY GOOD TO ME LATELY! I LOVE HIM SO, SO MUCH!

FRIDAY, OCTOBER 19, 2012:

JUST GOT HOME FROM WORK A LITTLE BIT AGO AND I TRIED TO GET OUT OF THERE FAST BECAUSE JALA WAS HERE WITH PAUL ALL NIGHT. PAUL WAS SO SUPER GOOD WITH JALA. HE IS ABSOLUTELY AMAZING. IT WAS KAILEE'S THRILLER PERFORMANCE IN LOGAN, AND I COULDN'T GO BECAUSE OF WORK. I AM SO SUPER SICK OF MY JOB. I LITERALLY *HATE* ALL THE PEOPLE THERE WITH A PASSION! I HOPE PAUL AND I WILL START OUR BUSINESS SOON AND IT WILL DO *GREAT!*

She talked about doing business with Paul, but it never happened.

SATURDAY, OCTOBER 20, 2012:

SITTIN' HERE AT MASON'S GAME, ME AND JALA, AND OF COURSE, THEY ARE WINNING AGAIN! THEY ARE UNDEFEATED THIS YEAR. THEY ARE GOING TO THE PLAYOFFS AND MASON IS SO SUPER EXCITED! I WORK TODAY AT 5:00 AND I AM NOT LOOKING FORWARD TO IT 'CAUSE LAST NIGHT I MADE HARDLY ANYTHING. IT'S NOT EVEN WORTH IT LATELY. IT BETTER GET BETTER OR I AM DEFINITELY LEAVING THERE AND I AM NEVER LOOKING BACK. IT IS NOT EVEN WORTH MY TIME ANYMORE. I REALLY DON'T KNOW WHAT TO DO BECAUSE I REALLY NEED A JOB BUT I DON'T WANT TO TAKE THIS ABUSE ANYMORE! POOR ADI, I HAVEN'T EVEN SEEN HER SINCE SHE GOT HER WISDOM TEETH OUT. SHE SAYS SHE IS DOING OKAY BUT I DON'T THINK SHE REALLY IS.

SUNDAY, OCTOBER 21, 2012:

SO, WE TOOK JALA TO HOLLYWOOD CONNECTION BECAUSE WE THOUGHT SHE WOULD LOVE IT AND IT WAS A COMPLETE DISASTER! THERE WERE HALLOWEEN DECORATIONS ALL OVER THE PLACE AND SHE LITERALLY FREAKED OUT! JAY HAD TO COME GET HER AND NOW PAUL AND I ARE FIGHTING. WE HAVE NOT FOUGHT IN SUCH A LONG TIME AND I DIDN'T THINK WE WOULD AGAIN THIS BAD, BUT WE ARE! I REALLY DO NOT KNOW HOW TO MAKE THIS MAN HAPPY! I TRY AND TRY AND IT'S JUST NOT GOOD ENOUGH, I DON'T KNOW WHAT TO DO ANY-MORE! SO, I GOT A LETTER FROM DAVID IN THE MAIL TODAY AND IT MADE ME TOTALLY CRY! HE SAID THAT I WAS ALWAYS ON HIS MIND AND THAT IT HAS BEEN SIX MONTHS SINCE HE HAS SEEN ME. I CAN'T BELIEVE IT HAS BEEN THAT LONG! HE ALSO SAID HE KNOWS HOW MUCH I AM STRUGGLING RIGHT NOW AND THAT WHEN HE GETS OUT, HE WILL DO WHATEVER IT TAKES TO GET ME CLEAN BECAUSE HE KNOWS I WILL BE SO MUCH HAPPIER! HE SAYS IT WILL PROBABLY BE A COUPLE WEEKS/MONTHS AT THE MOST TILL HE GETS OUT AND HIS JOB IS SECURE, SO HE WANTS ME TO TAKE CARE OF ALL OF HIS $ BECAUSE HE SAID IT WILL BE EASIER THAT WAY. DAVID WILL ALWAYS HOLD A SPECIAL PLACE IN MY HEART, ALWAYS, ALWAYS. I DO WANT TO GET CLEAN *BAD!*

LETTER FROM DAVID TO NAT:

HEY BABY, HOW ARE YOU DOING? I HOPE EVERYTHING IS AS GOOD AS CAN BE FOR YOU. DO YOU KNOW IT HAS BEEN ALMOST SIX MONTHS SINCE I HAVE SEEN YOU? I MISS THE HELL OUT OF YOU. I KNOW YOU ARE STRUGGLING RIGHT NOW, BUT IT WILL SOON GET BETTER. MY PO *(Parole Officer)* IS GOING TO RECOMMEND DRUG COURT, OR ANOTHER TREATMENT. (YEA) THAT MEANS I COULD BE OUT IN A COUPLE WEEKS. A COUPLE MORE MONTHS AT THE MOST. I CAN'T WAIT. THE

FIRST THING IS TO GET A PLACE TO LIVE. MY JOB IS PRETTY MUCH SECURED STILL. SO I WILL TURN THE INCOME OVER TO YOU. IT IS JUST EASIER FOR ME THAT WAY. THAT WAY, IF YOU NEED TO STAY HOME TO KICK OR QUIT YOUR JOB, YOU CAN. I JUST WANT YOU TO GET CLEAN, I DON'T CARE WHAT IT COST OR WHAT WE HAVE TO DO. YOU DESERVE TO BE SO MUCH BETTER AND HAPPIER. JUST KEEP YOUR HEAD UP, BABE. SORRY THIS IS SO SHORT, I JUST WANTED TO TOUCH BASE WITH YOU TO LET YOU KNOW THAT YOU ARE ALWAYS ON MY MIND. COME AND VISIT ME.

ALL MY LOVE,

DAVID

SORRY THIS IS SO SLOPPY, I AM ON MY BUNK WRITING.

David is Mary's husband. They are the ones that started her on heavy street drugs years ago. I'm not sure what her relationship with David was…

MONDAY, OCTOBER 22, 2012:

TODAY JUST PLAIN OUT SUCKED! GOT UP, WENT TO WORK, GOT CUT AT 2:00 'CAUSE IT WAS SO SUPER SLOW, ONLY MADE $20. THIS SUCKS! AND, WE KNOW WHERE IT ALL GOES… TO GET ME WELL *(which means getting drugs so she wouldn't start to get sick.)* I CHASE *(try to find drugs)* EVERY DAMN DAY AND IT'S GETTING REALLY, REALLY OLD! GOT SOME DINNER WITH PAUL, CHINESE, THEN WATCHED A MOVIE. I REALLY NEED TO CUT BACK, I AM STARTING TO LOSE ALL MY DAMN TEETH! THE ONES IN THE FRONT ARE ALL VERY LOOSE AND I AM FREAKING OUT! I AM GOING TO BE TOOTHLESS IN THE NEXT COUPLE YEARS. I DON'T KNOW WHY I HAVE DONE THIS TO MYSELF! I THINK LIFE IS EXTREMELY PRECIOUS AND WE ONLY HAVE A SHORT, TOO SHORT TIME DOWN HERE ON EARTH. WHY HAVE I DONE ALL THESE HORRIBLE THINGS TO MYSELF AND THE PEOPLE I LOVE THE MOST? WHY CAN'T I STOP? WHAT AM I AFRAID OF? I HAVE BEEN DOING THIS SHIT FOR

SO LONG NOW THAT IT FEELS NORMAL *(meaning she rarely got high at this point; now, she was using just to feel "normal" and not get sick).* HOW FUCKED UP IS THAT? IT IS SO FAR FROM NORMAL AND I AM FUCKING UP MY BODY AND MY LIFE, MORE THAN I ALREADY HAVE. I DON'T KNOW HOW TO STOP! I KNOW HOW AND I KNOW WHAT I NEED TO DO, BUT WHEN IT COMES DOWN TO IT, I JUST DON'T HAVE THE WILL POWER! I NEED TO GET MORE MOTIVATION AND MORE SELF-ASSURANCE AND THEN I CAN DO THIS, NOT JUST FOR ME, BUT FOR THE MOST IMPORTANT PEOPLE IN MY LIFE...ADI, MAS, JALA, & PAUL! THEY WILL GIVE ME THE STRENGTH THAT I NEED, 'CAUSE GOD KNOWS I CAN'T DO IT ALONE! GET CLEAN, NATALIE, YOU CAN DO IT!

TUESDAY, OCTOBER 23, 2012:

WELL, I ACTUALLY ENJOYED WORK TONIGHT, WEIRD, HUH? AND THEY CUT ME EARLY WITHOUT ME EVEN ASKING, I MADE $11, BUT IT WAS A GOOD NIGHT FOR ME, SO I DON'T CARE! SO, I KEEP THINKING ABOUT DAVID'S LETTER, AND IT MAKES ME SUPER SAD! I REALLY DO WANT OFF ALL THIS SHIT, BUT HOW? I DON'T HAVE MY SUBOXONE AND I REALLY DON'T HAVE THE TIME TO KICK ON MY OWN, IT'S KIND OF EXCUSES, BUT THEY ARE BOTH REALLY TRUE. WITHOUT EITHER OF THOSE, I CAN'T GET OFF. I NEED TO SET A TIME OR MAKE A DATE AND JUST DO IT! BUT, I DON'T WANT TO LOSE PAUL OVER IT AND I REALLY NEED TO KEEP MY JOB. THEY ARE NOT A BIT HAPPY WITH ME RIGHT NOW, SO I HONESTLY CANNOT TAKE ANY MORE TIME OFF WITHOUT GETTING FIRED! AND TO BE COMPLETELY HONEST, I WON'T SET MYSELF A DATE OR TIME AND ACTUALLY GO THROUGH WITH IT! I NEED MORE MOTIVATION AND I NEED TO TURN MY LIFE AROUND SO I CAN GET CLEAN, WILLINGLY, AND STAY THAT WAY! I'VE DONE IT BEFORE SO I KNOW I CAN DO IT AGAIN, IT'S JUST GOING TO BE A LOT HARDER THIS TIME AROUND BECAUSE MY *HABIT*

IS *HUGE!* BUT, MARK MY WORDS, I WILL GET CLEAN ON MY OWN WITHOUT ANYONE TELLING ME I HAVE TO OR PUTTING ME ON A GUILT TRIP OR ULTIMATUM! I WILL DO IT COMPLETELY ON MY *OWN,* I WILL PROVE TO MYSELF THAT I AM MUCH, MUCH STRONGER THAN I THINK AND TO EVERYONE IN MY LIFE THAT EVER HAD ANY DOUBTS IN ME! I'M COMING, EVERYBODY!

It must have been exhausting for her trying to live two completely separate lives and feeling like she needed to get clean on her own.

WEDNESDAY, OCTOBER 24, 2012:

AT THE DENTIST RIGHT NOW WITH PAUL. HE IS IN A LOT OF PAIN! I AM FREAKING OUT RIGHT NOW BECAUSE HE JUST TOLD ME I NEED TO RIP ALL MY TEETH OUT AND GET DENTURES, 'CAUSE THEY ARE ALL ROTTED OUT! I AM SERIOUSLY FREAKING OUT! I WANT THE SCREW-IN ONES, BUT THEY ARE $2,000 PER TOOTH. WHO IN THE HELL CAN AFFORD THAT? I CAN'T EVEN BELIEVE IT HAS COME DOWN TO THAT. IT'S GOING TO BE SO MUCH MONEY REGARDLESS OF WHAT I DO, 'CAUSE THEY HAVE TO EXTRACT THE REST OF MY TEETH, THEN GIVE ME DENTURES. I AM WAY TOO YOUNG TO BE LOSING ALL MY TEETH, I AM ONLY 33 YEARS OLD AND I HAVE TO GET DENTURES, HOW FUCKING SAD IS THAT?

I ONLY MADE $50 TONIGHT, WHICH IS ACTUALLY A LOT BETTER THAN LATELY, BUT NOT WORTH MISSING MASON'S FIRST CHOIR CONCERT FOR. HE TOLD ME ABOUT IT LAST NIGHT AND I HAD NO TIME TO FIND SOMEONE TO WORK FOR ME. I WANTED TO GO SO BAD, THOUGH. HE IS MY WHOLE HEART! I LOVE THAT BOY MORE THAN ANYTHING IN THIS WORLD. OH, SO PAUL HAD THREE TEETH THAT WERE BAD ALL IN A ROW. THEY ALL NEED ROOT CANALS. HOW SAD, I KNOW HE WON'T GO GET THEM FIXED, SO HE WILL BE IN PAIN FOR A LONG TIME. HE NEVER COMPLAINS EITHER.

THURSDAY, OCTOBER 25, 2012:

WELL, I AM HAVING A HARD TIME RIGHT NOW BECAUSE THE DENTIST SAID I NEED TO GET DENTURES. I AM NOT READY FOR ALL THIS SHIT! I DON'T HAVE THE MONEY FOR IT AND I AM WAY TOO YOUNG TO BE GOING THROUGH ALL THIS. WHY IN THE HELL DID I PUT MYSELF THROUGH ALL THIS BULLSHIT? I KNOW I HAVE TO FACE MY CONSEQUENCES BUT THERE ARE WAY TOO DAMN MANY!

IT'S ABOUT 11:45 P.M. RIGHT NOW AND I JUST GOT HOME FROM WORK, TOOK ADI SOME SWEATS AND A PHONE CHARGER TO MY MOM'S 'CAUSE SHE IS SLEEPING THERE TONIGHT AND HEAVEN FORBID IF HER PHONE DIES! SHE WOULD BE FREAKING OUT! HAD TO HURRY BACK TO THE HOUSE BECAUSE PAUL IS GOING TO PAINT A BUILDING THROUGHOUT THE NIGHT FOR WORK AND THEY CAN ONLY DO IT BETWEEN MIDNIGHT AND 5:00 A.M. PAUL'S KIDS ARE HERE SO I HAVE TO STAY AND WATCH THEM. HIS DAUGHTER IS SICK AND WAS HOME ALL DAY WITH ME AGAIN. THIS IS THE SECOND TIME IN THE PAST COUPLE WEEKS THAT SHE HAS STAYED HOME FROM SCHOOL AND I HAVE HAD TO TAKE CARE OF HER WHILE PAUL WAS WORKING. IT DOESN'T BOTHER ME AT ALL EXCEPT FOR THE FACT IF I EVER ASK PAUL TO PICK OR TAKE JALA SOMEWHERE, HE GETS BUGGED, SO I DON'T HAVE HIM DO IT! HOW FUCKED UP IS THAT? I AM ALWAYS DOING THINGS FOR HIS KIDS, ALL THE TIME, WAY, WAY MORE THAN MY OWN KIDS AND THE KIDS ARE STARTING TO NOTICE IT. THAT MAKES ME MAD! *NOBODY COMES BEFORE MY 3 KIDS!!!*

Same day, different journal:

I HAVE REALLY MADE A MESS OF MY LIFE, JUST TO GET HIGH! HOW WORTH IT WAS IT? NOT WORTH LOSING THE THREE MOST IMPORTANT PEOPLE IN MY LIFE, ADI, MAS, AND JALA, LOSING MY FAMILY, MY SISTERS, MOM AND DAD, LOSING ALL MY TEETH, IMMUNE SYSTEM SHOT TO HELL AND THE RESPECT OF EVERYONE AROUND ME, INCLUDING MYSELF! MY SELF-ESTEEM IS PRETTY MUCH COMPLETELY GONE TOO! HOW WORTH IT WAS IT, NAT?!?

FRIDAY, OCTOBER 26, 2012:

TODAY WAS PRETTY MUCH HECTIC AS ALWAYS LATELY. PAUL WOKE ME UP EARLY, THEN HE WENT AND GOT HIS DAUGHTER BECAUSE SHE STAYED HOME FROM SCHOOL TODAY BECAUSE SHE SAID SHE WAS SICK...AGAIN. STAYED THE DAY WITH HER, THEN PICKED UP LITTLE MISS PRINCESS AT 1:25 'CAUSE IT WAS EARLY OUT TODAY. CAME BACK TO THE HOUSE AND THE GIRLS COLORED AND DREW FOR A COUPLE HOURS WHILE I GOT READY FOR WORK. JALA HAD A ROUGH DAY TODAY. SHE WAS CRYING FOR NO REASON AT ALL AND KEPT SAYING TO ME THAT I HATE HER AND I LOVE PAUL MORE THAN HER. HOW SAD IS THAT? I DON'T EVER WANT ANY OF MY KIDS TO EVER THINK THEY ARE SECOND TO ME, ESPECIALLY BECAUSE OF PAUL. I AM GOING TO WORK HARDER THAN I EVER HAVE BEFORE THE NEXT LITTLE WHILE TO LET HER KNOW JUST HOW MUCH SHE IS LOVED AND THAT SHE IS THE MOST IMPORTANT PERSON IN MY LIFE AND ALWAYS WILL BE. I LOVE MY THREE KIDS MORE THAN ANYTHING, MORE THAN LIFE ITSELF!

SATURDAY, OCTOBER 27, 2012:

I LOVE SATURDAYS! NUMBER ONE REASON IS BECAUSE MASON HAS HIS FOOTBALL GAMES ON SATURDAYS AND HE HAS MADE IT TO THE PLAYOFFS THIS YEAR. THEIR TEAM IS SO FAR UNDEFEATED! HE IS PLAYING SO GOOD THIS YEAR AND HE

ABSOLUTELY LOVES IT! HE GOES OUT ON THE FIELD AND WILL DIRECT ALL THE OTHER PLAYERS WHERE TO GO, IT IS THE CUTEST THING ON EARTH! ANOTHER REASON WHY I LOVE SATURDAYS IS BECAUSE MY MAN IS USUALLY HOME WITH ME AND SLEEPS IN WITH ME. WHAT MORE COULD I POSSIBLY ASK FOR? OUT IN MAGNA NOW AT MASON'S GAME AND I HAD TO COME OUT HERE BY MYSELF 'CAUSE PAUL WOULDN'T LEAVE HIS DAUGHTER. SHE HAS A COMMON COLD! THAT IS ALL! SHE WAS FINE YESTERDAY AND WAS ABSOLUTELY FINE THIS MORNING. SO, I AM PRETTY UPSET, TO SAY THE LEAST. THERE IS NO REASON PAUL COULDN'T COME WITH ME THIS MORNING. I'M OKAY, THOUGH, ADI IS SITTING WITH ME ON MY LAP AND I LOVE IT! IT'S ACTUALLY OKAY THEY DIDN'T COME, 'CAUSE I GET SOME ALONE TIME WITH MY BEAUTIFUL DAUGHTER! MASON IS SUCH A GOOD LITTLE FOOTBALL PLAYER. HE IS STILL THE SMALLEST ONE ON HIS TEAM, JUST AS HE IS EVERY YEAR, HE IS AWESOME, THOUGH! DON'T QUITE KNOW WHAT I AM DOING THE REST OF THE DAY. I WORK AT 5:00, AND I'M NOT LOOKING FORWARD TO IT AT ALL. EVERYONE AT WORK IS ACTING COMPLETELY DIFFERENT TO ME LATELY. IT'S BEEN THAT WAY FOR A WHILE BUT LAST NIGHT WAS ABSOLUTELY HORRIBLE! I DON'T KNOW WHAT HAPPENED!

SUNDAY, OCTOBER 28, 2012:

AT MY MOM'S RIGHT NOW WITH ALL 3 OF MY KIDS AND I AM IN HEAVEN! I WAS SO SUPER MAD THIS MORNING 'CAUSE I WAS ON CALL FOR WORK AND SOMEONE CALLED IN SICK SO, OF COURSE, HAD TO GO IN AND COVER. I WAS SO MAD 'CAUSE I WANTED TO RELAX TODAY AND SPEND TIME WITH MY KIDS. I WAS ONLY THERE FOR A COUPLE HOURS, BUT THAT WAS A COUPLE HOURS I COULD HAVE SPENT WITH MY KIDS. WORK ALREADY TAKES THE MAJORITY OF MY TIME, BUT WHEN IT MESSES WITH MY TIME WITH MY KIDS, THEN I GET REALLY SAD AND UPSET. I DON'T GET HALF THE TIME WITH MY KIDS

AS I WANT. I NEED TO SEE THEM WAY, WAY MORE. GETTING MY HAIR DONE BY MY MOM RIGHT NOW 'CAUSE MY ROOTS WERE TERRIBLE! JALA HAS HAD A ROUGH TIME LATELY BECAUSE SHE MISSES ME SO MUCH. HOW SAD IS THAT? IT BREAKS MY HEART TO KNOW THAT MY BABY GIRL WANTS TO BE WITH ME AND I HARDLY GET ANY TIME WITH HER. IT JUST SUCKS! THE ONLY DAY I HAD OFF THIS WEEK WAS WEDNESDAY, AND I AM SO SUPER BURNED OUT. THEN ANOTHER SIX DAYS AGAIN THIS WEEK, BOO-HOO!!! JALA JUST LEFT AND I HATE SEEING HER GO!

MONDAY, OCTOBER 29, 2012:

JUST GOT MY LITTLE PRINCESS OUT OF THE BATHTUB AND WE ARE GETTING READY TO TAKE HER BACK TO JAY. I HAVE HAD HER SINCE SHE GOT OUT OF SCHOOL AND I ALREADY HAVE TO GIVE HER BACK TO JAY AND I HATE IT! SO, I AM WORKING WITH PAUL NOW AND I SURPRISINGLY LIKE IT SO FAR. HOW CRAZY IS THAT? NATALIE LIKING HARD LABOR! *(Windshield repair.)* NEVER THOUGHT I WOULD EVER SAY THAT! WELL, AND BEING WITH MY MAN ALL DAY WHILE WORKING ISN'T EXACTLY ROUGH FOR ME! WE HAD SUCH A GREAT DAY TOGETHER. GOT A LOT DONE WITH MY MAN TODAY, THEN CAME HOME TO MY LITTLE GIRL, WHAT MORE COULD I POSSIBLY ASK FOR?

I'M AT ALEXANDER'S HOUSE WHILE PAUL PRACTICES WITH HIS NEW BAND. MY DAY WASN'T ALL THAT BAD! WENT TO WORK AT 11:00, GOT OFF ABOUT 2:30, THEN WENT HOME, GOT IN THE BATH, THEN MET UP WITH SAMUEL *(drug dealer)* FOR A MINUTE, THEN MY BABY TOOK ME OUT TO DINNER. IT WAS REALLY GOOD BUT WE BOTH ATE WAY, WAY TOO MUCH! WE WENT TO A CHINESE BUFFET AND IT WAS HEAVENLY! WE WERE AT SAMUEL'S FOR A COUPLE HOURS AND IT WAS FINE, BUT I AM SURE GLAD WE ARE HOME NOW! PAUL IS PLAYING PLAYSTATION BOXING, IMAGINE THAT? WHILE I AM WRITING IN MY JOURNAL. I AM QUITE STRESSED OUT LATELY. I DON'T

KNOW HOW TO PRIORITIZE MY TIME VERY WELL AND IT IS HURTING A LOT OF PEOPLE THAT I CARE ABOUT THE MOST! ESPECIALLY MY SWEET LITTLE PRINCESS! SHE IS CONSTANTLY CRYING FOR ME LATELY AND I SEEM TO NEVER HAVE ENOUGH TIME WITH HER! THIS SUCKS. NOT TO MENTION ADI AND MAS. I NEVER GET TO SEE MY MASERS, HE IS ALWAYS BUSY WITH FOOTBALL OR WITH HIS FRIENDS. THAT'S GREAT HE HAS SO MANY FRIENDS AND IS ALWAYS HAVING FUN, I WOULDN'T HAVE IT ANY OTHER WAY, BUT I MISS HIM SO DAMN MUCH! I NEED MORE TIME WITH MY BOY, WITH ALL MY KIDS. THEY ARE *MY KIDS* AND SOMETIMES IT FEELS LIKE THEY AREN'T! THINGS NEED TO CHANGE!

TUESDAY, OCTOBER 30, 2012:

IT'S ABOUT 4:00 P.M. AND I JUST CALLED IN TO WORK AND HAD TO HAVE SOMEONE COVER FOR ME BECAUSE JALA IS REALLY, REALLY SICK. SHE HAS BEEN THROWING UP ALL NIGHT LONG. SO, I AM AT MY MOM'S RIGHT NOW DOING LAUNDRY AND LETTING JALA LAY DOWN FOR A BIT. I FEEL SO TERRIBLY BAD FOR HER. I SLEPT SUPER GOOD LAST NIGHT AND SLEPT UNTIL 10:00 A.M. I GOT A LOT OF REST! SO, I CLEANED THE WHOLE HOUSE TODAY. YAY! I HATE, HATE, HATE DIRTY HOUSES OR ANYTHING DIRTY! I AM A LITTLE BIT OF AN OCD FREAK! BUT, IN WAYS, THAT IS DEFINITELY A VERY GOOD THING. PAUL IS GOING TO BE EXCITED I AM NOT WORKING TONIGHT. HE IS ALWAYS ASKING ME TO GET WORK OFF! WATCHING A MOVIE WITH MY BABY RIGHT NOW EATING IN-N-OUT. IT'S GREAT! I DON'T SEE HIM QUITE AS MUCH AS I WANT. I COULD BE WITH THIS GUY 24/7, WE HAVE SO MUCH FUN TOGETHER! I LOVE HIM WITH ALL MY HEART.

WEDNESDAY, OCTOBER 31, 2012:

IT'S *HALLOWEEN* TODAY! AND MY SWEET LITTLE JALA IS SO SICK. SHE HAS BEEN THROWING UP ALL NIGHT LONG. I DON'T THINK SHE WILL MIND IF SHE DOESN'T MAKE IT TRICK-OR-TREATING, BUT TO BE SICK ON HALLOWEEN, WHEN YOU'RE SICK THAT IS JUST SO SAD! IT MAKES ME SICK THAT I CAN'T BE WITH HER. I MEAN, I COULD, BUT I WOULDN'T WANT PAUL GOING OVER TO HIS EX'S HOUSE, SO I NEED TO RESPECT HIM AND DO THE SAME AS I ASK. I ASKED MASON IF HE WAS GOING TRICK-OR-TREATING TONIGHT OR IF HE WAS TOO OLD TO BE DOING THAT KIND OF STUFF NOW AND HE SAID, I DON'T KNOW WHAT ME AND MY FRIENDS ARE DOING! HOW CUTE IS THAT! HE THINKS HE IS SO OLD! SO, I'M FREAKING OUT EVEN MORE TODAY ABOUT MY TEETH, ONE OF MY FRONT TEETH (I MEAN VERY FRONT) IS FALLING OUT. RIGHT WHERE EVERYONE COULD SEE THE MINUTE I OPEN MY MOUTH. I AM GOING TO LOOK LIKE THE BIGGEST TRAILER TRASH DRUGGIE!

AT MY MOM'S RIGHT NOW, IT'S ABOUT 4:00 AND ADI IS SHOWING ME HER NEW CAR. IT'S SO STINKIN' CUTE! IT'S A WHITE NISSAN SENTRA WITH BLACK TINTED WINDOWS. IT FITS HER ABSOLUTELY PERFECT!

11-1-2012: Dr. Note–103 lbs. She is stable working a lot making progress and denies relapse or misuse of meds, claims she's been going to treatment programs. *(She was not in any treatment program at this time.)* Prescribed Suboxone.

THURSDAY, NOVEMBER 1, 2012:

YAY! PUMPKIN PIE SEASON!! JUST FOUND OUT THAT PAYNE IS GOING TO LEAVE OUR IGGY'S AND GO BE THE GM IN OREM. THAT'S DEFINITELY GOING TO MAKE PAUL'S LIFE A LOT EASIER! SO, LAST NIGHT ENDED UP ABSOLUTELY HORRIBLE.

WE WENT TO MY MOM'S TO SEE THE KIDS IN THEIR COSTUMES, PAUL ENDED UP PLAYING FOOTBALL WITH MASON AND HIS FRIENDS FOR ABOUT AN HOUR, IT WAS SO CUTE! BUT, THEN WE WENT INSIDE TO SHOW MY MOM JALA WHEN SHE GOT THERE AND I ACCIDENTALLY CALLED PAUL JAY! OOPS! THAT WAS SO NOT GOOD. WE FOUGHT ALL NIGHT LONG TILL THIS MORNING. I DON'T BLAME HIM AT ALL FOR BEING ANGRY. I WOULD HAVE FREAKED OUT TOO, ESPECIALLY SINCE HE IS JUST RECENTLY MY EX. *(They never divorced.)* PAUL HAS A LOT OF ISSUES WITH JAY. HE HONESTLY BELIEVES THAT ME AND JAY STILL HAVE SOMETHING GOING ON. SO NOT TRUE! I HOPE HE GETS OVER THIS SOON. I AM AT MY DR. APPOINTMENT AND WHEN I LEFT, WE AGREED TO START OVER, START FRESH AND FORGET ABOUT ALL THE HORRIBLE FIGHTS WE HAVE BEEN THROUGH. I HAVE FAITH IN US! WE ARE DOING AWESOME TODAY. I PRAY WE STAY THIS WAY. WE BOTH HAVE A LOT ON OUR PLATES, BUT IF WE WORK TOGETHER, I KNOW WITHOUT A DOUBT IN MY MIND THAT WE WILL MAKE IT THROUGH JUST FINE. WE ARE REALLY PERFECT TOGETHER!

FRIDAY, NOVEMBER 2, 2012:

TODAY HASN'T BEEN TOO THRILLING, JUST BEEN CLEANING/LAUNDRY AND DISHES. PICKED UP JALA AT 1:25 'CAUSE IT WAS EARLY OUT AND NOW WE ARE JUST HANGING OUT AT HOME WITH PAUL'S DAUGHTER AND WE ARE GOING TO GET A YOGURT HERE IN THE NEXT FEW MINUTES. I CALLED INTO WORK SICK BECAUSE I JUST DIDN'T FEEL LIKE GOING TONIGHT. I AM MOST LIKELY GOING TO GET A WRITEUP, BUT I REALLY DON'T CARE ANYMORE. I DON'T THINK I'LL BE THERE MUCH LONGER ANYWAYS!

SITTIN' HERE WITH PAUL'S DAUGHTER, JUST GOT DONE DOING HER NAILS. JALA HAD A VERY HARD TIME TONIGHT

BECAUSE SHE IS VERY JEALOUS OF HER AND THAT I AM AROUND AND WITH HER A LOT. THAT MAKES ME SO SAD! I JUST TRY TO REASSURE HER EVERY DAY THAT SHE IS MY LITTLE PRINCESS! FINALLY WENT TO BED AROUND 2:00 AND HAD TO WAKE UP AT 7:30 A.M. TO PICK UP JALA SO JAY COULD WORK THIS MORNING (SATURDAY MORNING). HE IS AN AWESOME FATHER TO MISS JALA.

SATURDAY, NOVEMBER 3, 2012:

TODAY HAS STARTED OFF TO BE A GREAT DAY. JUST GOT BACK FROM MASON'S GAME AND THEY WON! IT WAS AN INCREDIBLE, INCREDIBLE GAME! HE WAS SO SUPER, SUPER EXCITED! NOW, GETTING READY FOR WORK AND TAKING MY CAR INTO MAZDA TO GET AN OIL CHANGE! YAY, HOW FUN! IT WAS JUST AWESOME SEEING HOW EXCITED AND HAPPY MASON WAS TODAY. I FEEL SO BAD, THOUGH, TYSON IS GETTING BAPTIZED *(a church ordinance)* NEXT WEEKEND (SATURDAY) AND I WAS SO PLANNING ON GOING, BUT THIS NEXT GAME OF MASON'S IS A HUGE ONE BECAUSE IF THEY LOSE, THEY ARE DONE, OUT OF THE PLAYOFFS, AND NOBODY WILL BE HERE BECAUSE THEY ARE ALL GOING TO BE IN SAINT GEORGE. SO, I REALLY NEED TO BE THERE FOR HIM. I REALLY HOPE MICHELLE UNDERSTANDS. AUSTIN IS BAPTIZING TYSON, HOW SWEET IS THAT? I WISH I COULD BE THERE, ESPECIALLY SINCE SHALL'S KIDS ARE LIKE MY OWN, BUT MY BOY COMES FIRST. ALWAYS WILL! SO, WORK IS GOING TO SUCK TONIGHT BECAUSE I BAILED OUT ON WORK LAST NIGHT AND THEY ALREADY HATE ME AS IT IS, I AM SERIOUSLY SCREWED! I LIKE A LOT OF THE PEOPLE THERE, BUT DEFINITELY NOT WORTH STAYING THERE AND GETTING TREATED LIKE SHIT ALL THE DAMN TIME. I REALLY AM JUST DONE WITH THAT PLACE. BUT, I NEED TO MAKE SURE I AM TAKEN CARE OF BEFORE I COMPLETELY BAIL.

SUNDAY, NOVEMBER 4, 2012:

GOING TO WENDOVER TODAY WITH MY BABY! HE GOT US A SUITE AND I AM SO EXCITED TO GET AWAY, WE DEFINITELY NEED IT! SO, I AM SUPER PISSED OFF RIGHT NOW! LAST NIGHT, I WENT INTO WORK AND THEY SENT ME HOME 'CAUSE I DIDN'T HAVE A DR. NOTE. THEY COULD HAVE WRITTEN ME UP OR SOMETHING BUT NOPE, THEY SENT ME HOME AND TOLD ME NOT TO COME BACK TILL I HAVE A DR. NOTE. WELL, I CAN'T GET A DR. NOTE! I REALLY WAS SICK, NOT ENOUGH TO BAIL ON WORK, BUT THEY DON'T KNOW THAT. THE BRIGHT SIDE TO ALL THIS IS I GET A WHOLE WEEKEND OFF AND MY BABY IS TAKING ME AWAY TO WENDOVER, SO NOW I DON'T NEED TO FIND ANYONE TO WORK FOR ME NOW, YAY! HEADING TO WENDOVER NOW AND I'M SO GLAD TO GET AWAY.

The next day...

MONDAY, NOVEMBER 5, 2012:

IT'S ABOUT 11:00 P.M. RIGHT NOW AND IT'S BEEN KIND OF A LONG DAY. WE GOT UP THIS MORNING, THEN DROVE HOME FROM WENDOVER, THEN PAUL WENT TO WORK. I WENT SHOPPING AND GOT A COUPLE THINGS, DID LAUNDRY, THEN CHASED *(looked for drugs)* FOR A BIT, THEN CAME HOME. WE WATCHED A MOVIE. SO, I WAS PLANNING ON GETTING FIRED TODAY AND I WAS REALLY OKAY WITH IT, THEN I TALKED TO PAYNE AND HE TOLD ME TO GET A DR. NOTE TO RELEASE ME BACK TO WORK, THEN TO COME BACK. I HONESTLY DON'T KNOW WHAT TO DO! I DON'T LIKE WORKING MY ASS OFF THERE AND GETTING NO MONEY AND GETTING TREATED LIKE TOTAL DOG SHIT AND IT'S REALLY BAD, NOT JUST BY THE MANAGERS BUT FROM THE SERVERS THERE TOO, BUT I DO NOT WANT TO

QUIT, THEN I WILL BE SCREWED! I KNOW I DON'T MAKE A LOT THERE, BUT I AM ABLE TO TAKE CARE OF MYSELF AND IF I QUIT OR GET FIRED, I WILL HAVE TO RELY ON PAUL. I HONESTLY DON'T KNOW IF I CAN COMPLETELY DO THAT RIGHT NOW. HE ALREADY TAKES CARE OF ME RIGHT NOW AS IT IS, BUT I HAVE MY OWN SPENDING MONEY TOO SINCE I WORK. THIS IS A VERY TOUGH DECISION TO MAKE BECAUSE THE MORE I WORK THERE, THE MORE AND MORE MY SELF-ESTEEM KEEPS DROPPING. I NEED TO MAKE A DECISION AND QUICK!

TUESDAY, NOVEMBER 6, 2012:

WELL, I GO TO WORK AT 5:30 TONIGHT AND I AM DEFINITELY NOT LOOKING FORWARD TO IT! I DON'T EVEN WANT TO KNOW WHAT EVERYBODY HAS BEEN SAYING ABOUT ME SINCE I HAVEN'T BEEN TO WORK FOR FOUR DAYS. DOING LAUNDRY AGAIN AND GETTING MY BABY GIRL AT 3:25, THEN TO GET READY FOR WORK. I'M REALLY NERVOUS ABOUT GOING IN BECAUSE I REALLY DON'T WANT TO DEAL WITH EVERYONE'S SHIT. I HOPE IT GOES SOMEWHAT OKAY. I KNOW THERE IS AT LEAST ONE NEW MANAGER THERE RIGHT NOW AND I'M HOPING THEY LIKE ME!

WELL, I AM SUPER PISSED! MY DOCTOR WOULD NOT WRITE ME A NOTE UNLESS I WAS SEEN. I DON'T HAVE $100 TO GO HAVE HIM WRITE ME A NOTE, SO I CALLED WORK, AND I HAVE TO CALL PAYNE IN THE MORNING. I REALLY STILL HOPE I HAVE MY JOB. I REALLY CAN'T LOSE IT RIGHT NOW, EVEN THOUGH I HATE IT THERE. I CAN'T LOSE IT RIGHT NOW! I AM OFFICIALLY FREAKING OUT! BUT, THE POSITIVE SIDE OF THIS DAY, SINCE I DON'T GO INTO WORK, I GOT TO KEEP JALA WITH ME AND PAUL WAS HOME, SO I GOT TO HANG OUT WITH MY TWO FAVORITE PEOPLE IN THE WORLD! PAUL IS SO DANG CUTE WITH JALA. HE HAS BEEN PLAYING WITH HER FOR THE PAST TWO HOURS.

WEDNESDAY, NOVEMBER 7, 2012:

I ALREADY KNOW TODAY IS GOING TO BE A GREAT DAY BECAUSE IT'S WEDNESDAY AND IT'S THE DAY I GET TO BE WITH ALL MY KIDS. WHAT COULD BE BETTER? ABSOLUTELY NOTHING!

WELL, JUST GOT BACK FROM ALL-A-DOLLAR WITH PAUL AND HEADED DOWN TO PICK UP JALA IN A FEW MINUTES. ON MY WAY, I AM GOING TO CALL PAYNE, I PRAY I STILL HAVE A JOB. I'M WISHING MYSELF ALL THE LUCK IN THE WORLD. WELL, DEFINITELY HAD SOME GOOD LUCK! I CALLED PAYNE AND TOLD HIM THERE IS NO WAY I COULD GET A DR. NOTE. HE TOLD ME THAT THEY DIDN'T WANT TO LOSE ME AND THAT HE WOULD JUST WRITE ME UP FOR ONE SHIFT. I MISSED SIX SHIFTS, SO THAT ROCKS! TODAY IS MY, NO TOMORROW IS MY FIRST DAY BACK AND I'M HOPING IT GOES WELL. PAUL'S NOT TOO THRILLED ABOUT ME GOING IN TOMORROW, BUT I DON'T CARE WHAT ANYONE SAYS RIGHT NOW OR HOW PEOPLE ARE TREATING ME THERE. I NEED MY JOB RIGHT NOW AND THAT IS THE BOTTOM LINE. I HAD AN AWESOME DAY WITH MY KIDS TODAY. PAUL AND I HAD DINNER AT MY MOM'S WITH ALL THE KIDS AND PAUL HELPED JALA LEARN TO ADD ALL BY HERSELF. HOW SWEET IS THAT? IT MELTS MY HEART TO SEE MY KIDS AROUND PAUL BECAUSE HE IS ABSOLUTELY AMAZING WITH THEM, ABSOLUTELY AMAZING!

THURSDAY, NOVEMBER 8, 2012:

IT'S ABOUT 1:00 RIGHT NOW AND I GO INTO WORK TODAY AFTER BEING GONE FOR ALMOST A WEEK AND I'M A LITTLE NERVOUS. I HAVE NOT MET THE TWO NEW MANAGERS AND I HOPE I MAKE A GOOD IMPRESSION ON THEM. IT WILL BE A GOOD NIGHT, I KNOW IT! SITTING HERE AT ANTHONY'S RIGHT NOW, WAITING FOR HIM TO GET HOME AND DOING MY LAUNDRY. HE DRIVES ME ABSOLUTELY CRAZY, BUT HE IS KIND OF A GOOD FRIEND TO HAVE. HE DOES ALMOST ANYTHING

AND EVERYTHING THAT I WANT. I DON'T THINK THERE HAS BEEN A TIME WHERE HE HAS TOLD ME NO. I KNOW THAT'S REALLY MEAN OF ME, USING HIM LIKE THAT, BUT HE LIKES IT AND NEVER COMPLAINS, SO WHY NOT? PLUS, I DON'T HAVE ANYONE ELSE THAT I COULD JUST GO UP TO AND ASK FOR MONEY. PAUL DOES TAKE REALLY GOOD CARE OF ME, BUT I WON'T ASK HIM FOR MONEY! AND, ANTHONY MAKES PRETTY DECENT MONEY, SO HE CAN SHARE.

WELL, JUST GOT HOME FROM WORK A LITTLE BIT AGO. I REALLY DON'T KNOW WHY I WENT BACK. I REALLY DON'T LIKE IT THERE, ESPECIALLY THE PEOPLE. BUT, ONE OF MY REGULARS CAME IN, HE IS THIS EIGHTY-YEAR-OLD MAN THAT LOVES ME AND COMES IN JUST FOR ME. HE GOES TO GOLD'S GYM EVERY NIGHT AND THEN COMES TO EAT. IT'S SO SWEET. IT'S PEOPLE LIKE THAT, THAT MAKE ME STAY, AND OF COURSE, THE MONEY. I DIDN'T WANT TO BE DONE THERE UNTIL I HAD SOMETHING ELSE, BUT AFTER I WENT BACK IN, I DON'T GIVE A FUCK!

FRIDAY, NOVEMBER 9, 2012:

WELL, IT'S JUST BARELY FRIDAY. IT'S ONLY 12:10. I CAN'T SLEEP 'CAUSE I JUST GOT IN THE BATH AND HAD TO KILL THREE SPIDERS. THEY ARE MY WORST FEAR EVER, SO I NOW FEEL LIKE THIS HOUSE IS INFESTED! JUST GOT HOME A LITTLE BIT AGO FROM WORK AND IT WAS ACTUALLY AN OKAY NIGHT. I MADE $75 AND I GOT ALONG WITH EVERYONE, FOR THE MOST PART. I GOT JALA FROM SCHOOL AND ME, PAUL'S DAUGHTER, AND JALA WENT GROCERY SHOPPING AT WALMART AND IT WAS A COMPLETE NIGHTMARE! WHENEVER JALA IS AROUND PAUL'S KIDS, SHE IS A COMPLETELY DIFFERENT CHILD. I KNOW SHE IS JUST JEALOUS, BUT I TRY TO COMFORT HER AND LET HER KNOW THAT SHE IS MY BABY AND MY FAVORITE PERSON IN THE WORLD. IT JUST DOESN'T CUT IT. I GIVE HER ALL THE ATTENTION TOO, BUT IT DOESN'T

CHANGE A THING. I HONESTLY DON'T KNOW WHAT TO DO AT THIS POINT. I CAN'T GET THROUGH TO HER, AND HIS DAUGHTER IS TAKING IT PERSONAL AND IT'S JUST A BIG MESS. I NEED TO BE A BETTER MOM TO ALL MY KIDS, A MUCH, MUCH BETTER PARENT. I FEEL REALLY BAD A LOT THAT I AM MY KIDS' MOM. THEY DESERVE SO MUCH BETTER THAN ME. THEY DESERVE THE BEST BECAUSE THEY ARE AMAZING KIDS. I WOULDN'T CHANGE THEM FOR THE WORLD! BUT, I DO BET THEY WISH THEY HAD A DIFFERENT MOM, A BETTER MOM.

SATURDAY, NOVEMBER 10, 2012:

IT'S MASON'S LAST FOOTBALL GAME! THIS IS DEFINITELY GOING TO BE A VERY STRESSFUL GAME. THIS GAME WILL EITHER WIN THEIR TEAM THE CHAMPIONSHIP OR BREAK THEM. EITHER WAY, THEY PLAYED ABSOLUTELY AMAZING THIS YEAR, OTHER THAN ONE LOSS IN PRE-SEASON, WHICH DOESN'T EVEN COUNT. THEY ARE UNDEFEATED! HOW *AWESOME* IS THAT? MASON IS ON TOP OF THE WORLD RIGHT NOW AND HE IS THE ONE PERSON THAT DESERVES ALL THE GLORY AND BLESSINGS IN THE WORLD! THAT KID IS AN ANGEL, AN ANGEL THAT GLOWS AND LIGHTENS AND BRIGHTENS THE WORLD AROUND HIM. I AM SO PROUD TO CALL THAT BOY MY SON! I COULDN'T ASK FOR A BETTER CHILD. HE, BY FAR, EXCEEDS THE DEFINITION OF BEST CHILD! I LEARN SO MUCH FROM HIM, IT'S UNBELIEVABLE! I LEARN A THING OR TWO FROM ALL MY KIDS, BUT MASON, I DON'T NEED TO SAY ANYMORE, HE IS JUST GOD SENT! HE IS MY HEAVEN! I FEEL SO BAD, THOUGH, TYSON IS GETTING BAPTIZED BY AUSTIN TODAY AND WE CAN'T BE THERE. I HOPE SHALL UNDERSTANDS AND IF NOT, THEN ONE DAY SHE CAN FORGIVE ME. SHE KNOWS THAT HER KIDS MEAN THE WORLD TO ME, JUST LIKE MY OWN AND I WOULD NEVER MISS ANY OF THEIR IMPORTANT TIMES IN THEIR LIFE, BUT THIS WAS A HARD ONE FOR ME. I COULD NOT MISS MASON'S

LAST GAME! THIS GAME IS *HUGE!* AND THEY ARE GOING TO TAKE THE CHAMPIONSHIP!

SUNDAY, NOVEMBER 11, 2012:

WELL, DEFINITELY HAS NOT BEEN THE GREATEST DAY. I HAVE FELT REALLY SICK THE PAST FEW DAYS AND IT HAS DEFINITELY GOT ME DOWN. I COULDN'T GO IN TO WORK LAST NIGHT AND THAT PRETTY MUCH JUST COST ME MY JOB. PAUL SAID THIS JOB IS JUST NOT WORTH IT, AND TO LET HIM TAKE CARE OF ME. WELL, I THINK I MIGHT DO THAT 'CAUSE PAYNE WANTS A DR. NOTE AND I CAN'T AFFORD TO SEE THE DR. AND GO GET ONE.

Nat at my mom's with an IV in her neck

MONDAY, NOVEMBER 12, 2012:

DEFINITELY NOT A GOOD START FOR A NEW JOURNAL. I AM SITTING HERE IN A ROOM AT LDS HOSPITAL, WAITING TO GET AN ULTRASOUND, WITH A DAMN IV IN MY NECK! IT IS SO NOT FUN!! WELL, OTHER THAN BEING TOTALLY FUCKING RETARDED, THIS LITTLE TRIP TO THE ER WASN'T ALL THAT BAD. MY IUD WAS SHIFTED A LITTLE. SO, I JUST NEED TO MAKE AN APPOINTMENT WITH DR. HURST AND GET IT TAKEN OUT, AND I AM EXTREMELY BACKED UP. THE DR. SAID I AM SO BACKED UP THAT IT'S CLOSE TO SURGERY. OH, HELL NO!! CAN YOU IMAGINE...TELLING MY WORK, "I CAN'T COME IN FOR A WHILE 'CAUSE I HAVE TO GET SURGERY, SURGERY ON MY BOWELS, 'CAUSE I CAN'T SHIT!" THAT WOULD DEFINITELY BE A FIRST! ANYWAYS, THE DR. GAVE ME THIS DRINK THAT I WILL NEED TO DO IN THE NEXT COUPLE DAYS AND IT SHOULD COMPLETELY CLEANSE ME OUT. DOESN'T THAT JUST SOUND PLEASANT? I'M SCARED, I HATE DOING THINGS LIKE THIS. PAUL IS OUT PICKING UP SOME CHINESE 'CAUSE I WAS CRAVING IT. WE ARE GOING TO RELAX TONIGHT, EAT CHINESE, WATCH A MOVIE, AND SNUGGLE. IT DOESN'T GET ANY BETTER THAN THIS! ACTUALLY, IT DEFINITELY CAN... WE COULD HAVE ALL THE KIDS WITH US, THEN IT WOULD BE IDEAL!! BEFORE I WENT TO THE HOSPITAL TODAY, I TOOK ADI TO LUNCH 'CAUSE SHE DIDN'T WANT TO GO TO SEMINARY *(a religious class held at school),* WHICH I SHOULDN'T HAVE BEEN OKAY WITH, BUT I WAS. I'M SELFISH, I WANTED HER WITH ME! I WILL TAKE ANY OF MY KIDS EVERY CHANCE I GET! I DON'T GIVE A FUCK WHAT'S GOING ON, IF I HAVE A CHANCE TO BE WITH ANY OF THEM, I AM SO GOING TO TAKE IT! ANYWAYS, WHILE WE WERE EATING AT PARADISE CAFE WHERE ADI WORKS, SHE TOLD ME THAT KIERRA CALLED HER SOBBING THE OTHER DAY BECAUSE SHE THOUGHT I WAS GOING TO DIE. SHE SAID MASON MENTIONED THAT A COUPLE DAYS AGO ALSO. ADI SAID SHE WAS REALLY SCARED. THAT

BREAKS MY HEART IN A MILLION LITTLE PIECES! THAT IS THE *LAST* THING MY KIDS SHOULD BE THINKING ABOUT (WORRIED ABOUT). THE ONLY STRESS A 13 AND 16-YEAR-OLD SHOULD BE HAVING RIGHT NOW IS BREAK-UPS AND FIGHTS WITH THEIR FRIENDS. NOT IF THEIR MOM/AUNT IS GOING TO DIE! I NEED TO CHANGE THINGS AND *FAST*, MY KIDS/NIECE SHOULD NOT HAVE TO WORRY ABOUT THINGS LIKE THAT! I DON'T STOP AND THINK AS OFTEN AS I SHOULD, JUST HOW MUCH THE CHOICES I MAKE EVERY DAY IN MY LIFE AFFECT THOSE AROUND ME! *WAKE UP, NAT!* IT'S *NEVER* TOO LATE TO CHANGE AND MAKE A DIFFERENCE IN MY LIFE! (OR MY SWEET KIDS' LIVES) *OPEN YOUR EYES!*

<u>TUESDAY, NOVEMBER 13, 2012</u>:

STILL FEELING REALLY SICK TODAY! I REALLY NEED TO TAKE A BIG SHIT! IT HURTS SO STINKIN' BAD! JUST WAITIN' TO PICK JALA UP RIGHT NOW, THEN GOING TO MOM'S AND DRINKING THIS DRINK THAT WILL HELP ME SHIT! IT IS SO EXTREMELY DISGUSTING! SITTING HERE WITH JALA RIGHT NOW AT MY MOM'S BECAUSE IT IS HER PARENT TEACHER CONFERENCE TODAY AND I CAN'T GO. THIS WILL BE THE VERY 1ST ONE THAT I HAVE MISSED OF HERS. SO, JAY IS GOING TO PICK HER UP IN THE NEXT FEW MINUTES. I FEEL SO BAD I CAN'T GO. WE ARE WATCHING *MAX & RUBY* RIGHT NOW. THAT IS ONE OF JALA'S FAVORITE SHOWS. SHE IS ONE OF THE BEST THINGS THAT HAS EVER HAPPENED TO ME! SHE IS THE MOST PRECIOUS THING IN MY ENTIRE LIFE! JAY AND I ARE, OF COURSE, FIGHTING REALLY BAD BECAUSE HE SAYS I NEVER ANSWER MY PHONE. I AM HAPPY WITH A FEW THINGS IN MY LIFE, BUT THE REST JUST PLAIN OUT SUCKS! I NEED MY KIDS WITH ME MORE, PAUL NEEDS TO TREAT ME AS GOOD AS HE DOES HIS KIDS. DON'T GET ME WRONG, THE MAN IS ABSOLUTELY AMAZING TO ME AND TREATS ME LIKE A PRINCESS, BUT WHEN IT COMES TO ME OR THE KIDS, THE KIDS

WILL *ALWAYS* COME 1ST AND HE DEFINITELY HAS SHOWN IT OVER AND OVER AGAIN! I REALLY DO THINK HE IS THE BEST FATHER I HAVE EVER SEEN, BUT HIS RELATIONSHIP WITH HIS DAUGHTER IS A LITTLE OVER THE TOP! HE CODDLES HER LIKE NO OTHER AND SHE COULD *NEVER* DO WRONG! HE WOULD RATHER BE WITH THEM MOST OF THE TIME, ACTUALLY, ALL THE TIME...WAY, WAY OVER ME!

WEDNESDAY, NOVEMBER 14, 2012:

STILL SICK TODAY AND IT REALLY SUCKS! I JUST WANT TO FEEL BETTER INSTEAD OF BEING SICK ALL THE DAMN TIME! IT'S GETTING VERY, VERY OLD! SAW ADI AND MAS TODAY, NO, JALA AND MAS, ADI WAS OFF DOING HER OWN THING WITH HER FRIENDS. I HAD TO COME HOME EARLIER THAN I WANTED TO BECAUSE I NEEDED TO FINISH THAT DISGUSTING DRINK AND REST A BIT. JALA WAS CRYING WHEN I LEFT AGAIN. I NEED HER AND THE OTHER TWO KIDS WITH ME EVERY DAY. NOT THIS COUPLE DAYS A WEEK THING. MY MOM SHOWED ME PICTURES OF SHALL AND EVERYONE OVER THE WEEKEND FOR TYSON'S BAPTISM. THEY WERE SWEET PICTURES, IT JUST MAKES ME REALLY SAD BECAUSE I WANTED TO BE THERE MORE THAN ANYTHING! I STILL CAN'T BELIEVE I MISSED IT! OKAY, I AM OFFICIALLY FREAKING THE FUCK OUT! I JUST LOST ONE OF MY FRONT BOTTOM TEETH. ONE OF THE FIRST ONES THAT YOU SEE WHEN I SMILE! WHAT IN THE FUCK AM I GOING TO DO? I DON'T HAVE THE MONEY TO GET DENTURES, DON'T KNOW IF I EVER WILL, BUT I *CANNOT* GO OUT IN PUBLIC LOOKING LIKE THIS! I LOOK LIKE A *TRAILER TRASH WHORE!* I AM BEATING MYSELF UP LIKE THIS AND TALKING SO NEGATIVELY ABOUT MYSELF, BUT COME ON, I DID THIS TO MYSELF AND I HAVE BEEN DEFINITELY PAYING THE CONSEQUENCES OF ALL MY MANY BAD AND HORRIBLE CHOICES. I HONESTLY HAVE NO IDEA WHAT I AM GOING TO DO ABOUT MY TEETH OR ANYTHING ELSE I AM GOING THROUGH. I AM

GOING THROUGH A LOT RIGHT NOW, BUT KEEP YOUR HEAD HIGH, *NAT,* THINGS WILL ALL WORK OUT!!

Around this time Nat ended up getting the rest of her teeth removed and a full set of dentures.

THURSDAY, NOVEMBER 15, 2012:

JUST ANOTHER DAY! CALLED PAYNE TODAY AND HE SAYS HE WANTS ME TO COME BACK, SO I'M GOING BACK TO WORK TOMORROW NIGHT. I'M SURE THERE HAS BEEN A LOT OF TALK ABOUT ME, BUT OH WELL! I GOT TO NOT CARE WHAT PEOPLE THINK AND SAY ABOUT ME. SO, PAUL TOLD ME OUR LAST FIGHT THAT HE WAS SICK OF WAITING AROUND FOR ME ALL THE TIME AND THAT I NEVER HAVE ANY TIME FOR HIM. SO, HE SAID THAT HE WAS GOING TO DO HIS OWN THING AND GO ABOUT HIS LIFE. WELL, HE DEFINITELY HAS. THIS WHOLE WEEK, HE HAS BEEN DOING HIS OWN THING. TODAY, HE GOT UP AT 6:00 A.M. AND HE WON'T BE HOME TILL ABOUT 9/10 P.M. AND USUALLY HE COMES HOME IN THE MIDDLE OF THE DAY TO SAY HI IF HE HAS SOMETHING GOING ON THAT NIGHT, AND HE DIDN'T. I HAVEN'T REALLY SEEN HIM AT ALL THIS WEEK, INCLUDING WHEN I WAS IN THE HOSPITAL. I WAS THERE ALL DAY LONG AND EVEN IF I SAID I DIDN'T NEED HIM THERE, HE SHOULD HAVE KNOWN THAT I DID! IF HE WAS IN THE HOSPITAL, I WOULD BE RIGHT THERE NO MATTER WHAT! SITTING HERE WITH JALA RIGHT NOW AT MY MOM'S, WAITING FOR JAY TO COME. MY MOM JUST TOOK ME GROCERY SHOPPING AND ADI AND JALA CAME. JALA AND I HAVE HAD A GREAT DAY TOGETHER. SHE IS BEING A LITTLE ANGEL! SHE SAW ME AND PAUL'S DAUGHTER IN A PICTURE ON MY LONG MIRROR IN MY ROOM AND SHE WAS DEVASTATED! I TOLD HER I WAS GOING TO THROW THEM AWAY, I DO NOT WANT MY ANGEL TO EVER THINK THAT PAUL'S DAUGHTER (OF ALL PEOPLE) MEANS MORE TO ME THAN HER! SHE IS MY LIFE,

ALONG WITH ADI AND MAS. NOBODY WILL EVER TAKE THEIR PLACE OR COME BEFORE THEM. THEY ARE MY EVERYTHING AND ALWAYS WILL BE, NO MATTER WHAT! I HAVE THE 3 *BEST* CHILDREN IN THE ENTIRE WORLD!!

FRIDAY, NOVEMBER 16, 2012:

IT'S ABOUT 2:00 P.M. RIGHT NOW AND I AM RIGHT DOWN IN BED WITH THE WORST TUMMY ACHE EVER! I FINISHED THAT DRINK AND NOW I FINALLY TOOK A HUGE SHIT AND I DON'T THINK IT HELPED ME FEEL BETTER QUITE YET. I FEEL SICK NOW AND I WAS SUPPOSED TO WORK TONIGHT BUT HAD TO CALL IN AGAIN! TALKED TO A NEW MANAGER, AND TOLD HIM TO TELL PAYNE I WASN'T GOING TO BE IN TILL TOMORROW NIGHT! THEY ARE SO *NOT* GOING TO BE HAPPY WITH ME, EVEN THOUGH I DON'T THINK THEY HAVE BEEN FOR A LONG TIME NOW. I DON'T CARE, I AM DOING WHAT I CAN! ACTUALLY, I CAN'T COMPLAIN RIGHT NOW. EVEN THOUGH I AM NOT FEELING SO GREAT, I HAVE THE MOST BEAUTIFUL ANGEL RIGHT NEXT TO ME. SHE IS LAYING DOWN WITH ME RIGHT NOW 'CAUSE I CAN'T DO MUCH, AND WE ARE WATCHING *THE WILD THINGS,* SUCH A CUTE SHOW. I USED TO READ THIS BOOK WHEN I WAS LITTLE ALL THE TIME! AND, I COULDN'T BE HAPPIER RIGHT NOW, HAVE MY LITTLE PRINCESS NEXT TO ME, RESTING IN BED AND NOT DOING A DAMN THING! IT'S VERY NICE, I MUST SAY. I THINK PAUL'S DAUGHTER WILL BE HERE SOON, THAT WILL GIVE JALA SOMEONE TO PLAY WITH. SO, LAST NIGHT ANTHONY WENT WITH ME TO MEET BRIAN @ 3:00 A.M. AND HE WAS TELLING ME THAT A COUPLE DIFFERENT GROUP OF GUYS TOLD HIM THAT THERE WAS QUITE A BIT OF PEOPLE THAT WERE REALLY UPSET WITH ME...AND PAUL! HOW DOES ANYONE EVEN KNOW WHO PAUL IS? HE SHOULD BE OUT OF THE PICTURE. I DON'T KNOW HOW HIS NAME GOT OUT THERE OR WHY ON EARTH ANYONE WOULD BE ANGRY WITH ME, BUT IT'S SCARING THE LIVING SHIT OUT OF ME!

SATURDAY, NOVEMBER 17, 2012:

AT PAUL'S FIRST KARATE TOURNAMENT AND HE DID ABSOLUTELY AMAZING. HE ALWAYS TOLD ME HE FOUGHT REALLY GOOD AND THAT HE HAS NEVER LOST A FIGHT AND I TOTALLY BELIEVE IT NOW. I NEVER DOUBTED HIM, BUT I REALLY WANTED TO SEE FOR MYSELF HOW GOOD HE REALLY WAS. THE MAIN GUY OVER ALL THE KARATE WAS ROOTING FOR PAUL, IT WAS AWESOME! THE LAST GUY HE FOUGHT, HE LOST BY ONE POINT AND I REALLY THINK IT WASN'T RIGHT. WELL, WE JUST FOUND OUT THAT HE WAS A COP, NOW PAUL WANTS TO KILL HIM. HE GOT SECOND PLACE INSTEAD OF FIRST BECAUSE OF THAT GUY. THAT REALLY PISSED HIM OFF, BUT HE DID FABULOUS! I AM SO SUPER EXCITED TO FIND OUT WHEN THE NEXT TOURNAMENT IS AND GO WATCH IT. IT MAKES ME FEEL SO PROTECTED THAT HE CAN FIGHT SO GOOD, BUT AT THE SAME TIME, IT SCARES THE LIVING SHIT OUT OF ME WHEN WE FIGHT 'CAUSE HE GETS GOING AND HE BLACKS OUT AND GETS EVIL, HE COULD DO ANYTHING AND NOT EVEN KNOW IT. I HONESTLY DON'T THINK HE WOULD OR EVEN COULD EVER HURT ME, BUT THERE IS ALWAYS A FIRST TIME. I DON'T WANT TO EVER BE ON THE OTHER END WHEN HE IS REALLY, REALLY MAD, HE IS DEFINITELY NOT THE SAME PERSON AT ALL. HE HAS TWO PERSONALITIES, FOR SURE. WHEN HE IS JUST HIM, THE MAN I FELL IN LOVE WITH, IT'S PERFECT, EVERYTHING IS PERFECT, BUT WHEN HE IS MAD, HE IS A COMPLETELY DIFFERENT PERSON, AN ULTIMATE *EVIL* PERSON, BUT I LOVE HIM! PAUL'S REALLY GOOD FRIEND CAME, AND I HAVE ALWAYS HAD A BIG ISSUE WITH HER BECAUSE THEY ARE ALWAYS TALKING AND I KNOW HOW MUCH HE CARES ABOUT HER. WELL, SHE IS LIKE HIS LITTLE SISTER, THAT IS TRULY HOW THEIR RELATIONSHIP IS. ANYWAYS, SHE CAME AND SAT WITH ME AND PAUL WASN'T FIGHTING FOR A WHILE, SO HER AND I WENT TO THE HOUSE FOR A MINUTE. SHE ABSOLUTELY LOVED OUR LITTLE SHACK, THEN WE WENT TO THE BANK AND

THEN TO WALMART (ACTUALLY TARGET) AND WE HAD SO MUCH FUN TOGETHER. I CAN SEE HOW PAUL IS FRIENDS WITH HER, SHE IS A LOT OF FUN. BUT SHE IS VERY, VERY YOUNG AND YOUNG GIRLS LIKE TO CAUSE LOTS OF DRAMA! SHE ALREADY HAS A LITTLE BIT WITH PAUL. WELL, WE GOT BACK A COUPLE HOURS LATER AND HE STILL WASN'T GONNA FIGHT FOR ABOUT AN HOUR OR SO, SO WE GRABBED HIS SON AND WE WENT TO NOODLES & COMPANY RIGHT DOWN THE STREET. WE GOT BACK TO THE KARATE TOURNAMENT AND PAUL STARTED FIGHTING A COUPLE MINUTES LATER. HE HAD NOBODY IN HIS DIVISION, 'CAUSE HE WAS A BEGINNER (WHITE BELT), SO HE HAD TO FIGHT BROWN AND BLACK BELTS, WHICH ARE WAY MORE ADVANCED AND ABOVE HIM. HE WON ALL OF THEM BUT ONE, AND HE SHOULD HAVE WON THAT ONE TOO. HE WAS ABSOLUTELY INCREDIBLE! I WAS SO PROUD OF HIM! MY MAN CAN FIGHT! HE TOOK SECOND PLACE IN THE KARATE TOURNAMENT. WE LEFT, CAME HOME, GOT READY FOR MY FIRST NIGHT BACK AT WORK, THEN WENT TO WORK.

SUNDAY, NOVEMBER 18, 2012:

THIS MORNING WAS PRETTY SHITTY! I AM SO TIRED 'CAUSE I SLEPT OVER AT MY MOM'S AND DAD'S HOUSE BECAUSE MY MOM HAD ALL THREE OF THEM *(her kids)* THIS WEEKEND! IT TURNED OUT TO BE A COMPLETE NIGHTMARE! I GOT OVER THERE AROUND 10:45 P.M. (AFTER WORK) AND JALA WAS SCREAMING AND HER POOR FACE WAS BRIGHT RED! ADI WAS GONE WITH HER FRIENDS AND WAS COMING HOME ANY MINUTE, AND MASON, BLESS HIS LITTLE HEART, WAS LAYING NEXT TO JALA TRYING TO CALM HER DOWN AND HELP HER FEEL BETTER. JALA RAN TO ME WITH TEARS ROLLING DOWN HER FACE AND SHE SAID SHE HAD A HEADACHE. I ASKED HER IF HER TUMMY HURT AND IMMEDIATELY AFTER HER SAYING YES, SHE THREW UP ALL OVER THE FLOOR, ALL OVER HER, AND OF COURSE, ALL OVER ME. THAT WAS MY GREETING WHEN I

GOT TO MY MOM'S LAST NIGHT. MY HEART BROKE FOR POOR JALA, 'CAUSE I DIDN'T KNOW JUST HOW LONG SHE HAD BEEN FEELING LIKE THAT. WELL, LITTLE MISS JALA FELL ASLEEP IN ABOUT 5 MINUTES.

MASON'S NOTE TO NAT IN HER JOURNAL:

DEAR MOM,

I LOVE YOU AND I WANT YOU TO GET US BACK. THANK YOU FOR COMING TO ALL OF MY GAMES. I LOVE TO SEE YOU THERE SUPPORTING ME. I REALLY CAN'T WAIT FOR CHRISTMAS. IT WILL BE *AWESOME* (JUST LIKE ME). SO I WILL BE PATIENTLY WAITING FOR BOTH THINGS, IT WILL HAPPEN SOMEDAY.
YOUR BOY,
MAS

MONDAY, NOVEMBER 19, 2012:

SO, MASON WROTE ME THAT NOTE IN CHURCH YESTERDAY. (*NAT WOULD GO TO CHURCH WITH MAS FOR HOLIDAYS OR WHEN HE ASKED HER TO GO.*) I STARTED SOBBING IN THE MIDDLE OF SACRAMENT *(a specific meeting in our Church)* AFTER I READ IT. THAT BOY IS SERIOUSLY THE SWEETEST, KINDEST, BEST, MOST CARING, WITH THE BIGGEST HEART IN THE WORLD LITTLE BOY. I WOULD NOT CHANGE ONE THING ABOUT HIM OR CHANGE HIM FOR THE WORLD! HOW DID HE END UP SO ABSOLUTELY PERFECT AND WONDERFUL? I NEED TO THANK GOD EVERY DAY FOR MY THREE CHILDREN, BUT ESPECIALLY FOR MASON. I LEARN SO MUCH FROM THAT KID. TODAY WAS ACTUALLY A FUN DAY.

GETTING READY ABOUT 10:30 A.M. TO GO MEET PAUL AT HIS WORK *(at the airport doing windshield repair)* 'CAUSE HE WANTS TO SHOW ME WHAT HE DOES SO I CAN LEARN IT AND MAKE WAY MORE MONEY THAN I DO NOW, AND I CALLED WORK

AND HAD TO GO IN. I WASN'T TOO BUGGED, THOUGH, 'CAUSE THEY GAVE ME NO DAYS THIS WEEK EXCEPT SATURDAY AND A COUPLE ON CALLS SO I WAS FINE GOING IN. ONLY MADE $23 BUT I WAS ONLY THERE FOR A COUPLE HOURS. CAME HOME, MARIA CALLED AND WE WENT TO ALL-A-DOLLAR, THEN WENT OUT TO MEET PATRICK, THEN CAME HOME. PAUL WAS PRETTY UPSET WITH ME WHEN HE CAME HOME AND I WAS GONE AND MARIA'S CAR WAS IN THE DRIVEWAY, BUT WE TALKED AND HE WAS FINE REALLY FAST. WE WENT AND ATE AT EMPIRE, WENT TO K-MART FOR A MIN, THEN CAME HOME. IT WAS A GOOD DAY, I NEED A LOT MORE DAYS LIKE THIS!

IT'S THANKSGIVING IN 2 DAYS AND I AM SO SUPER EXCITED TO BE ABLE TO SHARE THE HOLIDAY WITH PAUL AND FOR PAUL TO FINALLY MEET THE ALLEN SIDE *(our dad's side of the family)* AND SHOW HIM OFF TO EVERYONE 'CAUSE I AM SO PROUD AND LUCKY HE IS MINE!!

<u>TUESDAY, NOVEMBER 20, 2012</u>:

I CAN SAY IT AGAIN TODAY, IT WAS A PRETTY DAMN GOOD DAY. NO COMPLAINTS! HOW GREAT IS THAT? GOT UP, AMY CAME BY FOR A MINUTE, THEN I GOT READY, PICKED LITTLE MISS JALA UP FROM SCHOOL AND SHE WAS CUTE AS CAN BE. SHE WAS SUPPOSED TO GO WITH JOYCE *(her babysitter)* TODAY, BUT SHE WANTED TO STAY WITH ME. I ABSOLUTELY LOVE THAT! SHE HAS BEEN REALLY, REALLY CLINGY LATELY. I KIND OF LIKE IT, OKAY, I REALLY LIKE IT! LOVE THAT LITTLE GIRL! LEFT HER WITH MY MOM, CAME HOME AFTER SPENDING THE AFTERNOON WITH HER, MET MY MAN AND WE WENT TO DINNER. HE TOOK ME TO PF CHANG'S AND IT WAS AWESOME! I AM WAKING UP AND GOING WITH PAUL IN THE MORNING TO LEARN WHAT HE DOES JUST IN CASE ANYTHING AT ALL HAPPENS. *(I don't know what she means by this; I believe there was a lot more to Paul than she talks about in her journals.)*

I WILL BE TAKEN CARE OF BECAUSE APPARENTLY THIS CAN AND WILL MAKE ME LOTS OF MONEY. I AM EXCITED, BUT KIND OF NERVOUS AT THE SAME TIME. OH WELL, GOOD LUCK TOMORROW, NAT! WELL, SINCE I'M GETTING UP AT THE FUCKING CRACK OF DAWN IN THE MORNING, I BETTER GET SOME REST! I REALLY NEED TO TAKE THIS VERY SERIOUSLY BECAUSE LIFE THROWS CURVE BALLS ALL THE DAMN TIME, WE NEVER KNOW WHAT'S COMING OUR WAY AND I NEED TO BE PREPARED FOR ANYTHING!

WEDNESDAY, NOVEMBER 21, 2012:

IT'S THE DAY BEFORE THANKSGIVING, BOY, TIME FLIES! THIS YEAR HAS GONE BY SO STINKIN' FAST! TODAY WAS A GOOD DAY, EVEN THOUGH I AM VERY SICK. I LOST MY VOICE, GOT THE WORST STINKIN' HEADACHE, AND I AM SO NAUSEATED. I HATE IT! I GOT TO BE WITH ALL MY KIDS TODAY, AND AS USUAL, THAT'S MY FAVORITE TIME EVER! I AM SO STRESSED FOR CHRISTMAS, 3 KIDS AND NOT A VERY GOOD JOB, SO IT STRESSES ME OUT SO BAD EVERY SINGLE YEAR! I WISH I COULD GET A LITTLE HELP FROM SOMEONE, BUT THAT'S NOT HOW IT WORKS, NOBODY HELPS ME ANYMORE. MY MOM HELPS ME A LOT, WHICH IS AWESOME! LIKE THE OTHER DAY, SHE TOOK ME GROCERY SHOPPING AND BOUGHT ME LOTS OF GROCERIES FOR MY HOUSE, BUT I FEEL SO BAD, 'CAUSE MY MOM AND DAD HAVE DONE SO MUCH FOR ME SO I HATE ASKING THEM, I HATE ASKING ANYONE FOR HELP! I LIKE TO BE SO INDEPENDENT BUT IT'S NOT WORKING TOO WELL LATELY SINCE I HAVE MADE NO MONEY! I LIKE TAKING CARE OF MYSELF AND IT MAKES ME FEEL SO GOOD, BUT HAVEN'T BEEN ABLE TO MUCH LATELY, OKAY FOR A LONG TIME NOW 'CAUSE I CHOOSE THE WRONG WAY TO SPEND MY MONEY AND LOST EVERYTHING PRETTY MUCH. THAT'S WHAT DRUGS DO TO YA!

THURSDAY, NOVEMBER 22, 2012:

HAPPY TURKEY DAY! PAUL AND I SLEPT IN WAY LATE BECAUSE WE BOTH ARE NOT FEELING SO HOT. GOT UP AROUND 12:45, SUPPOSED TO BE AT MY MOM'S BY 1:00 BUT WE GOT THERE AT 2:00, NOT TOO BAD CONSIDERING WE STOPPED AT WALMART TO GET PIES. I HAVE THE STINKIN' FLU SO BAD AND IT SUCKS! MY BODY ACHES AND MY THROAT IS ON FIRE! BUT I STILL HAD AN AWESOME DAY! AFTER EATING, I LAID ON THE COUCH FOR A COUPLE HOURS WITH MAS UNTIL HE WENT TO PLAY FOOTBALL WITH PAUL. IT WAS SO NICE TO SPEND SOME ONE ON ONE WITH MY BOY, WE DON'T GET THAT VERY OFTEN. PAUL AND TYE WERE GETTING ALONG AWESOME! THEY HAVE NEVER REALLY TALKED BUT THEY WERE WATCHING FOOTBALL FOR HOURS TOGETHER. HE GETS ALONG WITH MY FAMILY SO WELL, IT WAS SO MEANT TO BE! PAUL WENT AND GOT HIS KIDS AFTER A LITTLE BIT, AND OF COURSE, THEY FIT RIGHT IN. THEY TOOK OFF PLAYING WITH ALL THE KIDS. HIS DAUGHTER TOLD ME TONIGHT THAT SHE FEELS AT HOME WHEN SHE IS OVER THERE NOW, HOW STINKIN' SWEET IS THAT? CAME HOME AROUND 7:30 P.M., HIS DAUGHTER AND I CAME INTO MY BED AND WROTE FOR A LITTLE BIT TILL WE BOTH FELL ASLEEP. WOKE UP AROUND 11:30, THOUGHT IT WOULD BE A GOOD IDEA TO VISIT BRIAN, AND NOW I JUST GOT BACK. I LOVE MY BED! ESPECIALLY WITH THE HOTTEST MAN ALIVE IN IT WITH ME! GOODNIGHT!

FRIDAY, NOVEMBER 23, 2012:

JUST GOT BACK FROM THE PARK WITH PRINCESS JALA, AND PAUL'S KIDS. PAUL IS AT WORK AND I HAVE THE KIDS, WHICH DOESN'T BOTHER ME AT ALL, BUT IF I ASK HIM TO DO SOMETHING FOR MY KIDS, HE ACTS COMPLETELY PUT OUT! JUST CAME TO THE CAR WASH AND HIS SON IS CLEANING MY CAR, YAY! IT WAS A FILTHY MESS AND I NEVER HAVE

ANY TIME TO CLEAN IT ANYMORE. DON'T KNOW IF I HAVE TO WORK TONIGHT OR NOT, I'M ON CALL AND I AM PRAYING I DON'T HAVE TO! NOPE, DON'T HAVE TO GO IN! YAY! BUT I DON'T KNOW WHAT TO DO, PAUL CAME HOME FREAKING OUT 'CAUSE HE THOUGHT I WAS WITH JAY, AND PAUL WON'T BELIEVE ME! WHEN HE IS MAD, HE TURNS INTO A DIFFERENT PERSON, AN EXTREMELY EVIL, EVIL PERSON! I CAN USUALLY DEAL WITH IT BECAUSE IT ONLY LASTS FOR A MINUTE AND NOT VERY OFTEN, BUT THIS TIME IT WAS TOO MUCH. HE FREAKED OUT ON ME FOR NO REASON AND I SHOULDN'T HAVE TO DEAL WITH THIS AT ALL, BUT I LOVE HIM WITH ALL MY HEART AND HE PUTS UP WITH ALL MY SHIT, SO IF I HAVE TO DEAL WITH THIS, THEN I WILL! I REALLY WOULD DEAL WITH THIS, I WOULD DO ANYTHING FOR THIS GUY! I JUST HOPE WE GET THROUGH THIS AND WE CAN MOVE ON AND THINGS WILL SETTLE DOWN A BIT! I DON'T WANT TO LOSE HIM, THIS IS THE FIRST MAN I REALLY WOULD TAKE ALL THIS SHIT FOR! SO, I'M SITTIN' AT ANTHONY'S RIGHT NOW FOR A FEW MINUTES SO HE CAN COOL OFF A BIT. I REALLY HOPE WHEN I GET BACK HOME THAT HE HAS COOLED DOWN AND WE CAN TALK CIVIL AND GET OUR MARRIAGE BACK ON TRACK. *(They were not married).*

IT'S ABOUT 10:30 P.M. AND IT WAS AN OKAY DAY TILL TONIGHT! PAUL AND I ARE FIGHTING PRETTY BAD, ACTUALLY WORSE THAN I THINK WE EVER HAVE. I WILL NOT GIVE UP, THOUGH, I WON'T. THIS IS THE MAN I LOVE, EVEN THOUGH I DON'T UNDERSTAND HIM THE MAJORITY OF THE TIME, WE FIT! WE REALLY DON'T FIGHT VERY OFTEN AT ALL, BUT WHEN WE DO, WATCH OUT, IT'S REALLY BAD! WE BOTH EVEN STARTED PACKING ALL MY STUFF, WE HAVE NEVER DONE THAT BEFORE! I HONESTLY DON'T KNOW WHAT TO DO! I DO EVERYTHING I CAN FOR THIS GUY, I DON'T KNOW WHAT I AM DOING WRONG. I HAVE NEVER IN MY LIFE TRIED SO HARD WITH SOMEONE LIKE I DO PAUL, AND I KNOW IT'S BECAUSE I REALLY DO LOVE THIS GUY. I KNOW FOR A FACT I DO, AND IT'S GREAT

TO KNOW WITHOUT A DOUBT IN MY MIND THAT I AM TRULY IN LOVE, BUT BEING IN LOVE IS SO EXTREMELY DIFFICULT AND YOU GET HURT ALL THE DAMN TIME. BUT IT'S DEFINITELY WORTH IT. LIKE THE OTHER NIGHT, I WAS GETTING READY IN THE BEDROOM AND HE TURNED SOME MUSIC ON, CAME AND GOT ME, AND WE SLOW DANCED IN THE LIVING ROOM. I SERIOUSLY ALMOST STARTED CRYING! IT WAS BY FAR THE SWEETEST, MOST ROMANTIC THING ANY MAN HAS EVER DONE FOR ME. I CANNOT LOSE HIM! I NEED TO CHANGE THINGS AND QUICK. HE IS ON THE COUCH RIGHT NOW GOING TO SLEEP AND I AM IN THE BEDROOM ON THE BED, I CANNOT SLEEP WITHOUT HIM EVER!

<u>SATURDAY, NOVEMBER 24, 2012</u>:

TODAY IS GOING TO BE A *FANTASTIC* DAY! WELL, IT'S ABOUT 1:00 P.M. AND I HAVE BEEN CRYING ALL DAMN MORNING BECAUSE OF MINE AND PAUL'S FIGHT LAST NIGHT. HE ALWAYS SEEMS TO FIGHT WITH ME EVERY TIME THE KIDS ARE HERE! IT EMBARRASSES ME SO STINKIN' BAD! I LOOK LIKE A FOOL EVERY TIME WE FIGHT BECAUSE I JUST TAKE IT, AND THE KIDS SEE THAT. WHAT HURT THE VERY MOST WAS LAST NIGHT, ALL 3 OF THEM WERE IN THE OTHER ROOM LAUGHING AND HAVING A GREAT TIME WHILE I SAT IN OUR BEDROOM SOBBING. HE DIDN'T CARE ONE BIT! THIS WENT ON FOR ABOUT 3 HOURS. HOW MUCH MORE OF THIS CAN I REALLY TAKE? WELL, I AM FINALLY OFFICIALLY DONE WITH IGGY'S! I BLEW THEM OFF TONIGHT, WHICH I DON'T KNOW WAS THE SMARTEST THING TO DO, BUT I DID IT...I AM GOING TO GIVE PAUL MY ALL, AND KICK BUTT AT THIS NEW JOB WITH HIM. IT'S GOING TO PAY ME A LOT MORE THAN IGGY'S! I MEAN, *A LOT* MORE! I WASN'T MAKING ANYTHING AT IGGY'S ANYWAYS! I AM REALLY SCARED, BUT I THINK THIS WILL BE A GREAT THING! THEY WERE TREATING ME AWFUL THERE

ANYWAYS AND EVERY TIME I LEFT THERE, I FELT LIKE A PIECE OF SHIT! SO, THAT WAY I AM GLAD I LEFT. I FEEL BAD, JUST NOT SHOWING UP, ACTUALLY, I DON'T, THEY HAVE BEEN TREATING ME LIKE SHIT FOR WAY TOO LONG NOW! YA, I'M GLAD I'M GONE, BUT I WILL MISS A LOT OF PEOPLE. I WORKED THERE FOR 2 1/2 YEARS AND GOT CLOSE TO A LOT OF PEOPLE! I AM DOING THE RIGHT THING, I NEED TO GET MY LIFE GOING WITH PAUL, AND THIS IS THE 1ST WAY!!!

The next day...

SUNDAY, NOVEMBER 25, 2012:

SO, I HAD A GOOD DAY YESTERDAY! PAUL, ME, AND HIS KIDS ALL WENT TO SALT LAKE AND PAUL SHOWED ME WHERE WE COULD HAVE OUR WEDDING. IT WAS AWESOME! IT WOULD HAVE BEEN MUCH BETTER IF MY KIDS WERE THERE, BUT IT WAS STILL FUN. CAME HOME, PAUL MADE US DINNER, THEN WE WATCHED A MOVIE. AFTER THE MOVIE, PAUL FELL ASLEEP, SO HIS SON AND I WERE IN THE BATHROOM POPPING HIS ZITS, HIS DAUGHTER WAS WATCHING, AND THE DOORBELL RANG. WE ALL FREAKED OUT 'CAUSE NOBODY KNOWS WHERE WE LIVE, WE LIKE IT THAT WAY. BUT IT WAS MY BABY GIRL, ADI! WHAT AN AWESOME SURPRISE! I ALMOST STARTED CRYING! I REALLY NEEDED THAT! IT WAS SO GOOD TO SEE MY BABY GIRL! SHE CAME OVER AND BROUGHT ME MY COOKIES THAT I LOVE AND A SALAD FROM HER WORK, HOW SWEET IS THAT? I LOVE THAT GIRL!

SO, THIS WEEKEND HAS NOT BEEN THE BEST 'CAUSE WE HAVE BEEN FIGHTING PRETTY BAD, BUT WE ALWAYS COME OUT ON TOP, AND EACH TIME WE SEEM TO GET EVEN STRONGER! I HOPE HE CAN GET HIS ANGER, TEMPER UNDER CONTROL, 'CAUSE I REALLY CAN'T DEAL WITH MUCH MORE!

Same day, different journal:

> TODAY IS GOING TO BE A GREAT DAY 'CAUSE I KNOW I AM NOT WORKING AT THAT HOLE ANYMORE AND I AM GOING TO BE WITH MY ABSOLUTE FAVORITE MAN IN THIS WORLD ALL DAY, WHAT MORE COULD I POSSIBLY ASK FOR? WE WENT BOWLING AND HAD A GREAT TIME AND NOW WE ARE JUST GETTING HOME RELAXIN', GETTING READY TO TAKE THE KIDS HOME. THEY WERE REALLY GREAT THIS WEEKEND, THEY USUALLY ARE, BUT THIS WEEKEND HELPED ME A LOT, 'CAUSE NOW I KNOW HIS DAUGHTER IS NOT JUST MANIPULATING THE 2 OF US, SHE REALLY DOES LOVE ME A LOT, SHE STILL MANIPULATES PAUL A LOT BUT HE HAS TO FIGURE THAT OUT ON HIS OWN, IF HE EVER WILL. MAYBE HE ALREADY DOES, HE JUST DOESN'T CARE. I AM VERY NERVOUS FOR CHRISTMAS, NOW THAT I QUIT MY JOB, NOT THAT IT PAID ME MUCH ANYWAYS, BUT IT'S JUST A SCARY, SCARY FEELING TO BE WITHOUT THE JOB THAT I HAVE HAD FOR THE PAST COUPLE YEARS! I NEEDED TO GET OUT OF THERE, THOUGH, *BAD,* REALLY, REALLY BAD! PAUL'S PLAYING THE GUITAR RIGHT NOW. WE ARE ALL WATCHIN THE BIRD CAUSE IT TILTS IT'S HEAD SO CUTE EVERY TIME HE PLAYS. IT'S A STINKIN CUTE BIRD. I MISS MY KIDS SO FREAKIN' MUCH! IT'S REALLY HARD TO HAVE PAUL'S KIDS AROUND AND NOT MINE! I DON'T GET HALF THE TIME WITH MY KIDS THAT I WANT TO! I LOVE THE HOLIDAYS, THOUGH, 'CAUSE I GET TO SEE THEM A LOT MORE! SO, I AM SUPER STRESSED, PAUL JUST TOOK ME YESTERDAY TO SEE THIS PLACE TO SEE IF I LIKE IT FOR OUR WEDDING. WELL, I AM NOT DIVORCED YET! HE WILL *FREAK THE FUCK OUT* IF HE KNOWS IT'S NOT DONE YET! HE WILL THINK I AM DRAGGING IT ON, ON PURPOSE! I JUST NEED TO GO TO THAT CLASS, THEN IT WILL BE DONE! THE CLASS IS ALMOST $100, THOUGH, AND OF COURSE, I JUST QUIT MY JOB, BUT I NEED TO GET ON IT BEFORE PAUL FINDS OUT!

MONDAY, NOVEMBER 26, 2012:

NATALIE...YOU ARE GOING TO HAVE AN AWESOME DAY TODAY! WELL, DIDN'T START OUT TOO GREAT. WOKE UP REALLY SICK AND COULDN'T GO IN WITH PAUL TODAY. I REALLY WAS LOOKING FORWARD TO GOING WITH HIM TODAY. SO, I HAD JALA LAST NIGHT AND IT DIDN'T GO VERY WELL. ME AND HER WERE GREAT AND HAD A FANTASTIC TIME, BUT PAUL AND HER DID NOT HIT IT OFF TOO WELL LAST NIGHT AND I THOUGHT THAT WAS VERY WEIRD BECAUSE HE HAS ALWAYS BEEN REALLY GOOD TO MY KIDS, I MEAN EXTREMELY GOOD TO MY KIDS. IT UPSET HER SO BAD THAT SHE WAS HYPERVENTILATING. IT WAS THE SADDEST THING I HAVE EVER SEEN. SO, THEN I STARTED CRYING. IT WASN'T EVEN REALLY THAT BIG OF A DEAL, HE JUST SAID, "JALA, COME HERE NOW," AFTER HE HAD ALREADY BEEN ASKING HER TO COME HERE, BUT IT UPSET JALA REALLY BAD AND HE DIDN'T EVEN TRY TO COMFORT HER! IT BOTHERS ME VERY MUCH BECAUSE THERE IS *NO WAY IN HELL* THAT HE WOULD EVER TALK TO HIS DAUGHTER THAT WAY, AND I WOULD *NEVER* TALK TO HIS KIDS THAT WAY. SO, WHAT GIVES HIM THE RIGHT TO TALK TO MY BABY LIKE THAT? AND HOW MUCH FURTHER WILL IT GO NOW?

RIGHT NOW, IT'S ABOUT 2:00 IN THE MORNING. YEP, I'M UP! IT'S THE ONLY TIME I GET TO DO THE THINGS I WANT TO DO BECAUSE PAUL IS ASLEEP. HE DOESN'T WAKE UP FOR ANYTHING, MOST OF THE TIME. NOT THAT HE IS CONTROLLING OR ANYTHING, WE JUST ALWAYS HAVE SOMETHING GOING ON DURING THE DAY, THEN WE LIKE TO SPEND TIME TOGETHER AT NIGHT, WHICH I CAN'T GET MY LITTLE ERRANDS *(drug runs)* DONE WHEN I AM WITH HIM. SO, I HAVE TO GO LATE AT NIGHT WHEN HE IS ASLEEP. HOW SAD IS THAT? ACTUALLY, HE IS A BIT CONTROLLING, HE LIKES ME THERE, WITH HIM, ALL THE TIME! WHICH, AT FIRST, I ABSOLUTELY LOVED IT, BUT NOW IT'S GETTING A LITTLE BIT OLD! I DO NEED MY

OWN SPACE SOMETIMES OR I WILL GO COMPLETELY CRAZY! DID LAUNDRY ALL DAY, THEN MARIA CAME OVER WITH DIANE AND AARON, WENT TO PICK UP JALA, THEN TOOK THEM TO ALL-A-DOLLAR. NOW, JALA AND I ARE SITTING HERE AT OUR FAVORITE CHINESE PLACE WAITING FOR FOOD FOR US. GOING TO HAVE A CHILL NIGHT TONIGHT, I REALLY DON'T WANT TO DO ANYTHING. STILL NOT FEELING SO GREAT. SO, PAUL IS A LITTLE BIT HURT 'CAUSE HIS BEST FRIEND AND I ARE REALLY CLOSE. WE TALK MORE THAN THEY DO NOW, AND HE IS A LITTLE HURT. HE IS ACTUALLY KINDA FUNNY. SAW TIA AT ALL-A-DOLLAR, SHE WORKS THERE NOW, AND SHE TOLD ME THAT MARY IS BACK IN JAIL. NOT SURPRISING AT ALL! I KNEW SHE WOULD GO BACK. I REALLY NEED TO CUT ALL TIES WITH ALL OF THEM, DAVID TOO. I JUST DON'T NEED THEM IN MY LIFE. ALL THEY DO IS CAUSE LOTS OF PROBLEMS!!!

11-28-2012: Dr. Note–110 lbs. Denies relapse, doing well, quit Iggy's, working with fiance Paul. *(I do not recall them ever getting engaged.)* Prescribed Suboxone.

THURSDAY, NOVEMBER 29, 2012:

TODAY, ACTUALLY IT WAS WEDNESDAY MORNING, WAS A FANTASTIC DAY AT THE BEGINNING! THEN IT TURNED INTO A *NIGHTMARE!* I GOT UP, HAD MY DR. APPOINTMENT SO ADI CAME WITH ME 'CAUSE SHE DIDN'T WANT TO GO TO SEMINARY, WHICH I THOUGHT WAS JUST FINE…AFTER THE DR., WE WENT TO LUNCH (ROBINTINO'S), JUST ME AND ADI. IT WAS A *BLAST!* WHENEVER I AM WITH ANY OF MY KIDS, I HAVE NOTHING BUT A WONDERFUL TIME! AFTER LUNCH, I HAD TO RUN SOME ERRANDS SO ADI SAID SHE WOULD PICK JALA UP FOR ME. I GOT TO MY MOM'S AROUND 4:45 AND ADI AND MY MOM WERE GONE. MAS WAS WATCHING JALA, AND OF COURSE, SHE WAS *FREAKING OUT* 'CAUSE MOMMY WASN'T THERE. WELL,

COME TO FIND OUT, MY MOM WAS WITH ADI IN THE ER! YEP, I FREAKED THE FUCK OUT! I GUESS ADI HAS BEEN HAVING TERRIBLE MIGRAINES THE PAST FEW MONTHS AND SHE KEEPS BLACKING OUT BECAUSE OF THEM AND IN CONSTANT PAIN. I RUSHED UP THERE, STAYED FOR ABOUT AN HOUR UNTIL HER DAD CAME. DON'T KNOW RESULTS YET, SHE WAS GOING IN FOR AN MRI WHEN I WAS LEAVING. GOT THE RESULTS LATE TONIGHT...SHE HAD LOTS OF FLUID IN HER SINUS, WHICH CAUSES A LOT OF PRESSURE AND PAIN (MIGRAINES). HOW SAD IS THAT? SITTING DOWN TO WATCH A MOVIE WITH MY BABY! GOOD NIGHT!

SO, JALA HAS A REALLY HARD TIME WITH PAUL'S DAUGHTER. SHE IS VERY, VERY JEALOUS AND THINKS I WANT TO BE AROUND HER MORE THAN I DO HER. I TRY AND EXPLAIN IT TO HER, BUT SHE THINKS WHAT SHE WANTS, AND SHE IS ALWAYS RIGHT! SHE IS THE SWEETEST LITTLE GIRL EVER, BUT SHE HAS A LOT OF MOMENTS THAT SHE FREAKS OUT! SHE IS CONSTANTLY RIGHT NEXT TO ME AND WON'T LEAVE MY SIDE. IT'S SWEET AND ALL AND I LOVE TO BE WITH MY LITTLE GIRL, BUT SHE DEFINITELY WEARS ME OUT SOMETIMES. BUT I *LOVE HER!* SO, I HAVE ANOTHER DAMN ABSCESS! LDS HOSPITAL IS GOING TO KNOW ME BY NAME NOW. I WAS JUST IN THERE ABOUT TWO WEEKS AGO WITH STOMACH PROBLEMS. I AM GOING TO WAIT, THOUGH, AND SEE IF IT WILL GO DOWN AT ALL. IT MOST LIKELY WON'T, BUT I DO NOT WANT TO GO BACK TO THE HOSPITAL! I ALWAYS HAVE TO GO ALONE 'CAUSE I DON'T WANT PAUL TO KNOW WHY I HAVE AN ABSCESS!

FRIDAY, NOVEMBER 30, 2012:

TODAY HAS BEEN AN OKAY DAY, PICKED UP JALA AT 1:25 (EARLY OUT) AND THEN WE CAME HOME, GOT PAUL'S DAUGHTER, THEN I TOOK THEM TO GET AN ICE CREAM AND WENT TO ALL-A-DOLLAR TO GET ADI STUFF TO ASK DAKOTA TO THE DANCE. MADE US DINNER, THEN WE TOOK JALA TO JAY

'CAUSE SHE DIDN'T WANT TO SLEEP OVER. I WISH SHE WOULD JUST GET USED TO IT HERE SO SHE WOULD STAY WITH ME MORE, BUT RIGHT NOW, SHE IS A LITTLE SHY AROUND PAUL AND HIS KIDS. BUT I HATE IT WHEN WE HAVE HIS KIDS, BUT NOT ANY OF MY KIDS, IT REALLY SUCKS! I WANT MY KIDS, NOT THEM! JUST TOOK JALA TO JAY AND PAUL'S SON TO A PARTY AND PAUL AND HIS DAUGHTER ASKED ME TO WATCH A MOVIE WITH THEM, BUT WHEN I GOT IN THERE, SHE WAS LAYING ON PAUL AND THERE WAS NO ROOM FOR ME TO EVEN SIT. SHE ASKED ME IF I WANTED TO SIT DOWN, BUT I SAID NO, THEY *BUG* ME SO BAD TOGETHER! THEY ACT LIKE THEY ARE BOYFRIEND/GIRLFRIEND AND WHEN THEY ARE HERE, I ALWAYS FEEL LIKE I AM IN THE WAY! I KNOW I NEED TO GET USED TO IT, AND THEY ARE AWESOME KIDS, AND TREAT ME SO GOOD, BUT THE WAY THEY ACT WITH PAUL, DRIVES ME NUTS! WHY DOES IT HAVE TO BE LIKE THIS? I FINALLY FOUND THE MAN OF MY *DREAMS,* BUT ALL HE CARES ABOUT IS SPENDING TIME WITH HIS DAMN KIDS! I AM SO NOT TRYING TO COMPETE WITH THEM, THEY ARE KIDS, BUT REALLY, WHEN THEY ARE AROUND, I DON'T EVEN EXIST TO PAUL! I DON'T KNOW IF THAT WILL EVER CHANGE. AND I CAN'T SAY ANYTHING TO HIM THAT WOULD PISS HIM OFF. AND WHAT COULD I SAY? STOP PAYING SO MUCH ATTENTION TO YOUR DAMN KIDS? HE IS A GREAT FATHER, BETTER THAN MOST, BUT THERE NEEDS TO BE SOME BOUNDARIES WITH HIS KIDS, ACTUALLY. THEY ARE ALL OVER EACH OTHER, EVEN IN PUBLIC, AND HIS SON IS HIS SIZE, MAYBE EVEN A LITTLE BIGGER, AND PEOPLE LOOK AT THEM LIKE THEY ARE GAY. IT'S WAY WORSE WITH HIS DAUGHTER, WAY WORSE! THOSE 2 ARE ALL OVER EACH OTHER, IT'S WAY INAPPROPRIATE! EVEN RACHEL SAID SOMETHING ABOUT IT WHEN SHE WAS HERE, SHE WAS LITERALLY APPALLED! IT ACTUALLY PISSED HER OFF ALMOST ABOUT AS BAD AS I GET. I AM JUST FED UP! I WOULD BE FINE IF HE GAVE ME SOME ATTENTION WHEN THEY WERE HERE, JUST *SOME* ATTENTION! I KNOW IT SOUNDS

RIDICULOUS AND THAT'S WHY I WON'T SAY ANYTHING TO PAUL, 'CAUSE HE WON'T EVEN TRY TO SEE MY SIDE OF IT, 'CAUSE IT'S ABOUT HIS KIDS, SO HE WON'T EVEN DISCUSS THAT WITH ME. I JUST GOT OFF THE PHONE WITH JAY, I AM SITTING IN MY CAR SMOKING AND HE TOLD ME THAT HE HAD BEEN CRYING ALL NIGHT 'CAUSE HE THINKS I WANT TO BE WITH PAUL AND HIS KIDS MORE THAN MY OWN KIDS! ARE YOU FUCKING KIDDING ME? HE ALSO SAID THAT HE IS SO DEPRESSED AND MISERABLE 'CAUSE I HAVE PAUL AND HE HAS NOBODY. HE IS A GREAT FATHER AND JALA IS VERY LUCKY TO HAVE HIM AS A DAD.

SATURDAY, DECEMBER 1, 2012:

SITTIN' HERE IN THE HOSPITAL AGAIN…ALL ALONE, BY MY CHOICE, THOUGH, I WOULDN'T LET PAUL COME BECAUSE I DIDN'T WANT HIM TO HEAR WHY I HAVE AN ABSCESS. I JUST NEED TO QUIT THIS SHIT FAST! I THINK I WOULD HAVE LEARNED BY NOW. THIS ABSCESS IS BY FAR THE BIGGEST ONE I HAVE EVER HAD. IT IS ON MY HIP AGAIN AND IT HURTS TO GET CUT OUT, *BAD!* DEFINITELY A NICE WAY TO START MY CHRISTMAS HOLIDAY. WHY DO I PUT MYSELF THROUGH ALL THIS? IS IT REALLY WORTH IT? NOT AT ALL! I AM GOING TO GIVE MYSELF A DEADLINE AND THAT WILL BE IT! NO MORE! WHAT BETTER TIME THAN THE BEGINNING OF THE YEAR? OKAY, NAT, BE DONE AND BE CLEAN BY MY BIRTHDAY, FEBRUARY 23. THAT GIVES ME PLENTY OF TIME TO MENTALLY AND PHYSICALLY PREPARE TO GO THROUGH SOME SERIOUS WITHDRAWALS. IT HAS TO BE DONE SOMETIME, OR IT WILL KILL ME! I KNOW I HAVE SAID THIS BEFORE, BUT IT'S GETTING PRETTY BAD NOW AND IT HAS BEEN LONG ENOUGH. IN FACT, IT'S BEEN A SUPER LONG TIME OF USING AND I AM NOT ABOUT TO LET DRUGS KILL ME! I WANT TO WATCH JALA GROW UP AND RAISE HER TOO AND POSSIBLY RAISE MORE OF MY SWEET SON! GOOD LUCK!

SUNDAY, DECEMBER 2, 2012:

WELL, IT'S 3:00 A.M. SUNDAY MORNING AND I JUST GOT DONE PAINTING MY TOENAILS. PAUL TOOK JALA AND I TO A HOCKEY GAME TONIGHT, IT WAS A LOT OF FUN. WOULD HAVE BEEN A LOT FUNNER IF I WASN'T IN SO MUCH DAMN PAIN FROM MY STUPID HIP. I NEVER GOT IT TAKEN CARE OF YESTERDAY BECAUSE THEY WERE SO BUSY, AND AFTER WAITING FOR ALMOST THREE HOURS, I JUST LEFT. BUT LAST NIGHT, I WAS IN SUCH HORRIBLE PAIN WE HAD TO LEAVE THE HOCKEY GAME EARLY 'CAUSE I COULDN'T SIT THERE ANY LONGER. WE HAD AMAZING SEATS TOO! WE WERE THIRD ROW FROM THE BOTTOM AT THE GRIZZLIES HOCKEY GAME! I HAVE NEVER BEEN TO A PROFESSIONAL HOCKEY GAME BEFORE. I JUST ALWAYS WATCHED JOSE AND POB *(two friends from high school)* PLAY AND THAT WAS THE EXTENT OF IT. IT WAS A LOT OF FUN AND I WOULD LOVE TO GO TO ANOTHER ONE. I DON'T REALLY KNOW WHAT QUITE TO DO, PAUL IS REALLY COMING DOWN HARD ON JALA LATELY. I MEAN SHE DESERVES IT 100%, BUT WHAT GIVES HIM THE RIGHT TO SPEAK TO MY BABY LIKE HE HAS LATELY? TONIGHT, JALA WAS SO SCARED TO GO TO THE HOCKEY GAME 'CAUSE SHE HAD NO IDEA WHAT IT WAS WHEN WE GOT THERE. SHE WAS LITERALLY SHAKING FROM FEAR. PAUL LOOKED AT HER AND SAID STERNLY, "JALA, YOU NEED TO STOP NOW, YOU'RE A BIG GIRL, NOT A BABY ANYMORE." I WAS IN COMPLETE SHOCK!

MONDAY, DECEMBER 3, 2012:

WELL, I'M NOT LIKING THIS NO MONEY THING. PAUL TAKES REALLY GOOD CARE OF ME, THOUGH. I JUST ABSOLUTELY HATE ASKING HIM FOR MONEY. HE USUALLY JUST GIVES IT EVERY DAY, BUT THERE ARE SOME DAYS HE FORGETS, AND I HATE TO ASK. THAT'S WHAT I GET FOR QUITTING MY JOB. IT'S ABOUT 3:00 P.M. AND I AM BACK UP AT THE HOSPITAL.

YAY, I AM BY MYSELF 'CAUSE I DON'T WANT PAUL TO HEAR ANYTHING THAT I TELL THE DR. AND THEY HAVE TO NUMB ME UP AND DRAIN IT, AGAIN, THIS ONE IS BY FAR THE BIGGEST ABSCESS I HAVE EVER HAD. I LET IT GO WAY, WAY TOO LONG AND IT'S ABOUT TO POP OPEN ON ITS OWN! IT'S BIGGER THAN THE SIZE OF A GOLF BALL, ACTUALLY, IT'S WAY BIGGER THAN THAT, ABOUT THE SIZE OF A TENNIS BALL, AND THAT'S NO EXAGGERATION! IT'S DEFINITELY GOING TO HURT BAD! AND THE DR. IS NOT VERY NICE AT ALL. I'M SO STINKIN' SCARED. I HOPE IT GOES BETTER THAN I AM EXPECTING. THEY ARE TAKING FOREVER. I HAVE ALREADY BEEN HERE FOR ABOUT AN HOUR AND A HALF AND IT DIDN'T LOOK LIKE THERE WAS TOO MANY PEOPLE. I AM JUST A VERY, VERY IMPATIENT PERSON! AND, I AM SCARED PAUL IS GOING TO SHOW UP, THEN I'M SCREWED! SOME GIRL IS SOBBING IN THE NEXT ROOM OVER, SAYING HURRY, DR. HURRY! I WONDER WHAT'S GOING ON WITH HER, SHE IS HYSTERICAL RIGHT NOW. SO, ANTHONY IS DEFINITELY OUT OF MY LIFE FOR GOOD THIS TIME! HE WAS SO SUPER MEAN TO ME LAST NIGHT AND I WILL NOT TAKE THAT ABUSE FROM ANYONE! ESPECIALLY A LOSER LIKE HIM!

TUESDAY, DECEMBER 4, 2012:

I AM IN SO MUCH DAMN PAIN TODAY. SO, THIS ABSCESS HAS DEFINITELY BEEN BY FAR THE MOST PAINFUL. I'M SUPPOSED TO GO BACK IN TOMORROW MORNING AND GET THE PACKING OUT AND GET IT CHECKED, BUT I AM LITERALLY TERRIFIED! I CAN'T EVEN TOUCH ANYWHERE NEAR THAT AREA. I KNOW THIS IS A LESSON TO ME, BUT DID IT REALLY NEED TO BE THIS PAINFUL, THIS BAD? PAUL IS REALLY SICK TODAY, HE HAS BEEN THROWING UP EVERYTHING HE EATS, HE CAN'T KEEP ANYTHING DOWN. IT IS SO SAD, HE IS SITTING HERE WITH ME ASKING ME IF I NEED ANYTHING. HE IS SO GOOD TO ME! I TOLD HIM I WATCHED (WANTED TO WATCH) MY 50

CENT MOVIE AND HE SAID NO 'CAUSE IT MAKES HIM JEALOUS. HE DOESN'T WANT ANY MAN (EVEN 50 CENT) AROUND HIS WOMAN. I SAID, HONEY, I DON'T THINK 50 CENT WILL EVER BE AROUND ME, AND HE SAID, "JUST IN CASE," HOW CUTE IS THAT? WELL, WE ARE GETTING READY TO WATCH A MOVIE AND I'M EXCITED TO BE WITH MY BABY. I LOVE HIM SO, SO MUCH. I'M A LITTLE HURT, THOUGH, HE JUST TOLD ME THAT HIS EX CALLED HIM TODAY AND I AM FREAKING OUT! I WAS WAITING FOR THIS DAY, BUT I DIDN'T WANT IT TO COME! I AM NOT GETTING MAD AT HIM, BUT I AM REALLY, REALLY HURT. I LOVE THIS MAN WITH ALL MY HEART!

WEDNESDAY, DECEMBER 5, 2012:

HAVE TO GO IN TODAY AND GET MY PACKING TAKEN OUT AND GET IT CHECKED. IT HURTS LIKE A BITCH SO I AM NOT LOOKING FORWARD TO IT. IT'S ABOUT 2:00 P.M. AND I AM JUST SITTIN' AT MY MOM'S DOING LAUNDRY UNTIL I PICK MY BABY GIRL UP FROM SCHOOL. I CAN'T WAIT TO SEE HER 'CAUSE I HAVEN'T SEEN HER SINCE SATURDAY NIGHT WHEN PAUL AND I TOOK HER TO THE GRIZZLIES HOCKEY GAME! SHE WAS SO SCARED AT FIRST BUT ENDED UP LOVING IT.

SO, I DIDN'T GO IN TODAY *(to the hospital).* I WAS SUPPOSED TO, BUT I AM JUST WAITING TILL TOMORROW, WHEN DEBORAH CAN TAKE ME. IT'S ABOUT 11:00 P.M. NOW AND I CAN'T EVEN WALK! THIS IS VERY, VERY BAD! THIS IS SO BY FAR THE ABSOLUTE WORST ABSCESS I HAVE EVER, EVER HAD. PAUL AND I BOTH LOOKED AT IT WHEN I WAS CHANGING MY GAUZE AND WE BOTH THINK IT IS LOOKING WORSE, NOT BETTER. *(I wonder what Paul thought was causing her abscesses.)* AND IT FEELS TEN TIMES WORSE THAN IT DID WHEN I WENT INTO THE HOSPITAL. THIS IS AWFUL, I DON'T KNOW WHAT TO DO. I JUST DID A SHOT *(of drugs)* AND IT DID ABSOLUTELY NOTHING! I AM TOLERABLE TO ABSOLUTELY EVERYTHING. I NEED THIS PAIN TO GO AWAY! I DON'T HAVE A SLIGHT CLUE

HOW TO DO IT. THIS IS WHAT I GET, THOUGH, BUT NOT BEING ABLE TO WALK REALLY, REALLY SUCKS! AND PAUL IS REALLY MAD AT ME RIGHT NOW 'CAUSE OF SOMETHING I SAID, HE IS NOT HELPING ME AT ALL, I AM LITERALLY FUCKED!

THURSDAY, DECEMBER 6, 2012:

WELL, I HAVE TO GO BACK UP TO THE DAMN HOSPITAL. I HOPE AND PRAY THEY SAY THAT EVERYTHING IS HEALING OKAY.

THAT WAS ONE OF THE WORST EXPERIENCES I HAVE EVER HAD! SO, IT'S NOT HEALING, THEY HAD TO REMOVE THE PACKING, IT HURT LIKE A BITCH, THEN HE HAD TO PUT MORE PACKING IN, WHICH HURT LIKE A BITCH! NOW, IT'S ABOUT 10:00 P.M. AND I CAN'T SLEEP 'CAUSE I AM HURTING SO BAD. THIS HAS HONESTLY BEEN THE WORST EVER. *(She was so immune to pain medications, and even the drugs she used wouldn't take the pain away. That's a scary thought that pain medications had absolutely no effect on her.)* I CAN'T EVEN WALK NOW! JALA CAME OVER TONIGHT AND SHE WAS BEING SO STINKIN' SWEET. SHE WAS HOLDING MY HAND TRYING TO HELP ME WALK. IT WAS THE CUTEST THING EVER! PAUL'S DAD CAME IN TODAY AND IS STAYING UNTIL NEXT TUESDAY. I LOVE HAVING HIM HERE. IT KEEPS PAUL ENTERTAINED, HE IS AN AWESOME, AWESOME GUY! I REALLY LIKE HIM A LOT. BUT, WHEN ANY PART OF PAUL'S FAMILY IS AROUND, I DON'T EVEN EXIST. AT TIMES IT'S GOOD, 'CAUSE I NEED TO BE ALONE AND PAUL FREAKS OUT EVERY TIME I WANT TO LEAVE. LIKE NOW, I REALLY NEED TO GO SEE BRIAN OR SAMUEL *(to get more drugs)* AND I KNOW IF I TELL HIM I AM LEAVING, HE IS GOING TO FLIP A BITCH, BUT HE KNOWS HOW MUCH PAIN I AM IN, SO HOPEFULLY HE WILL LET ME GO. *(Interesting…Did Paul know that she got drugs from them?)* NOT THAT HE CONTROLS ME OR ANYTHING, I JUST DON'T WANT TO FIGHT, I HATE FIGHTING WITH THIS GUY, HE IS THE DEVIL WHEN HE IS MAD! PEOPLE ARE LITERALLY AFRAID OF

HIM. IT'S GOOD FOR ME 'CAUSE I FEEL VERY PROTECTED, BUT *BAD* FOR ME 'CAUSE WHEN HE FIGHTS WITH ME, HE IS ABSOLUTELY RUTHLESS, HE IS HONESTLY WORSE THAN THE DEVIL HIMSELF!

FRIDAY, DECEMBER 7, 2012:

TODAY BETTER BE A BETTER DAY THAN YESTERDAY! YESTERDAY WAS AWFUL! I HAVE NOT BEEN IN THAT MUCH PAIN IN A VERY, VERY LONG TIME.

WELL, IT WAS NOT BETTER, IT WAS 20X WORSE. SO, MY HIP WAS NOT GETTING BETTER AT ALL, IT WAS SO PAINFUL AND DOUBLED ITS SIZE AND THE PAIN. WENT BACK UP TO LDS, DEBORAH TOOK ME BECAUSE PAUL WAS WORKING AND I COULDN'T GET AHOLD OF HIM. THE DR. CAME IN, LOOKED AT IT, AND HE SAID IT WAS NOT HEALING AT ALL AND THAT THEY HAD TO OPEN IT UP A LOT MORE. I LOST IT AT THAT POINT. I ENDED UP GETTING PUT OUT AND THEY CUT ME OPEN *BIG!* I DIDN'T FEEL A THING, THOUGH, BUT I DID AFTER. THEY GOT A JAR FULL OF PUSS (INFECTION) OUT OF ME, HOW SICK IS THAT? SO, RIGHT NOW, I HAVE AN OPEN HIP, THEY LEFT IT OPEN SO IT COULD DRAIN ALL OUT, AND BOY OH BOY, DOES IT HURT. PAUL ENDED UP COMING TO THE HOSPITAL AND DEBORAH LEFT, AND HE HAS BEEN RIGHT HERE FOR ME, WHATEVER I NEED. HE HAS BEEN ABSOLUTELY WONDERFUL TO ME. HE ACTUALLY PICKS ME UP AND CARRIES ME INTO THE BATHROOM WHEN I NEED TO PEE, WHAT DEVOTION! I AM SO UPSET, THOUGH, THIS WAS MY WEEKEND WITH ALL MY KIDS AND I AM LAYING HERE IN BED, NOT BEING ABLE TO MOVE AT ALL. SO, I CAN'T SEE MY KIDS THIS WEEKEND AND IT WAS ADI'S CHRISTMAS DANCE ON SATURDAY, AND I COULDN'T HELP HER OR SEE HER OFF LIKE WE WERE PLANNING. I AM SO FUCKING LIVID! TOMORROW IS GOING TO BE MUCH BRIGHTER!

Five days later...

WEDNESDAY, DECEMBER 12, 2012:

WELL, IT HAS NOT BEEN A GOOD MONTH AT ALL. I KNOW IT'S ONLY THE BEGINNING OF THE MONTH, BUT THIS DECEMBER HAS TOTALLY SUCKED SO FAR. I PRAY TO GOD IT GETS BETTER, 'CAUSE I'M LOSING IT AND *FAST!* I HAVE BEEN IN THE HOSPITAL PRETTY MUCH EVERY DAY FOR THE PAST NINE DAYS BECAUSE OF THIS STUPID ABSCESS! YEAH, STUPID, STUPID ME! TONIGHT WAS THE LAST NIGHT, HOPEFULLY. THEY TOOK THE PACKING OUT AND THERE IS A GAPING HOLE IN MY HIP, BUT THEY SAID IT WOULD HEAL ON ITS OWN, FROM THE INSIDE OUT. THEY SAID IT WOULD TAKE ABOUT TWO WEEKS TO START TO CLOSE UP, THAT'S HOW BIG IT WAS! IN THE MEANTIME, MY SWEET BOY HAD SURGERY ON HIS MOUTH, AND I HAD ABSOLUTELY NO CLUE UNTIL AFTERWARDS. I WAS SOBBING WHEN I FOUND OUT. HE IS OKAY, BUT IT BREAKS MY STINKIN' HEART THAT I WAS NOT THERE FOR HIM, I FELT AWFUL! PLEASE GET BETTER AND HAPPIER, YOUR KIDS NEED IT AND THEY NEED YOU DESPERATELY!

THURSDAY, DECEMBER 13, 2012:

WELL, IT HAS BEEN A CRAZY, CRAZY START TO THIS MONTH, FOR SURE. I HAVE BEEN IN THE HOSPITAL MORE THIS MONTH THAN I HAVE BEEN OUT! AND, NOW WE ARE BACK IN THE HOSPITAL, BUT NOT FOR ME, SURPRISE, SURPRISE! PAUL AND I WERE FIGHTING REALLY BAD LAST NIGHT AND HE PUNCHED A COUPLE WALLS AND BROKE HIS STINKIN' HAND. IT IS MANGLED PRETTY DAMN BAD! I FEEL BAD FOR HIM, BUT THEN AGAIN, I DON'T! HE WAS NOT BEING FAIR AT ALL LAST NIGHT. SO, I HATE TO SAY THIS, BUT HE DESERVES THIS. HE WAS ABSOLUTELY OUT OF CONTROL LAST NIGHT.

THEN, OF COURSE, ALL MORNING AND ALL DAY TODAY HE HAS BEEN COMPLETELY APOLOGETIC. I JUST DON'T KNOW WHAT THE HELL TO BELIEVE ANYMORE FROM THIS GUY! HE CAN BE THE MOST AMAZING, SWEETEST MAN ON EARTH TO ME, BUT WHEN HE'S MAD, THE ABSOLUTE CRUELEST HUMAN BEING I HAVE EVER BEEN AROUND. BUT DON'T GET ME WRONG, HE TREATS ME BETTER THAN I EVER COULD BE TREATED BY ANYONE. IT DEFINITELY OVERPOWERS ALL THE ROUGH TIMES. ADI HAS JALA RIGHT NOW. SHE IS WATCHING HER FOR ME WHILE I AM AT LDS *(hospital)* WITH PAUL. THEY JUST GOT DONE TAKING X-RAYS, SO WE WILL KNOW IN A MINUTE WHAT'S GOING TO HAPPEN WITH HIS HAND. IT'S HIS RIGHT HAND TOO! I AM DEFINITELY GOING TO HAVE TO HELP HIM OUT NOW! IT'S DEFINITELY HIS TURN TO BE TAKEN CARE OF, ODDLY ENOUGH!

SATURDAY, DECEMBER 15, 2012:

IN WENDOVER RIGHT NOW WITH MY BABY AND WE JUST GOT DONE AT THE JIMMY JAYSON CONCERT. IT WAS SURPRISINGLY SO MUCH FUN. PAUL STARTED SINGING TO ME AND I TOTALLY STARTED CRYING. IT WAS THE SWEETEST THING HE HAS EVER DONE. HE CAN DEFINITELY BE THE MOST ROMANTIC GUY EVER. I AM SO IN LOVE WITH THIS MAN. I KNOW FOR A FACT THIS IS SO TRUE LOVE. THIS MAN IS FOR SURE THE *REAL DEAL.* AND, I AM NEVER, EVER LETTING HIM GO. COMING TO WENDOVER WAS SO SUCH A GREAT IDEA. WE TALKED THE ENTIRE WAY OUT HERE AND I TOLD HIM OPENLY EXACTLY HOW I FELT. I HAVE BEEN WANTING TO TELL HIM ALL THAT I TOLD HIM TODAY FOR SUCH A LONG TIME NOW, BUT NEVER GOT THE CHANCE, 'CAUSE I WAS NERVOUS ABOUT THE REACTION. HIS REACTION WAS EXACTLY WHAT I WANTED! BETTER THAN I EVER THOUGHT IT WOULD BE. THIS TRIP AND THIS WEEKEND REALLY NEEDED TO HAPPEN FOR ME AND PAUL. I THINK FROM THIS DAY FORWARD, THINGS ARE GOING TO BE VERY, VERY DIFFERENT. NO MORE DISRESPECT!

SUNDAY, DECEMBER 16, 2012:

OKAY, NOW I AM STARTING TO FREAK OUT *BAD!* I HAVE NO CHRISTMAS SHOPPING DONE FOR ANYONE AND I HAVE ABOUT A WEEK, ACTUALLY LESS. STILL HAVEN'T PAID NOVEMBER CAR PAYMENT AND PAUL IS ABSOLUTELY GOING TO SHIT HIS PANTS WHEN I TELL HIM 'CAUSE I HAD TOLD HIM IT WAS ALREADY TAKEN CARE OF, AND NOW HE IS GOING TO HAVE TO COME UP WITH $600 FOR NOVEMBER AND DECEMBER CAR PAYMENT! AND I KNOW HE WILL PAY IT 'CAUSE HE DRIVES THE MAZDA MORE THAN I DO, BUT HE IS LITERALLY GOING TO SHIT! I AM REALLY FUCKED THIS MONTH AND HAVE NOBODY TO HELP ME. IT'S HARD ENOUGH TAKING MONEY FROM PAUL DAILY, BUT ALL THIS, MY BILLS, CHRISTMAS, I DON'T KNOW HOW HE IS GOING TO REACT TO ALL THIS. STILL IN WENDOVER, HAD A BLAST. I REALLY DON'T WANT TO GO HOME BACK TO REALITY, CAN'T WE JUST STAY A BIT LONGER? OR WIN LOTS OF MONEY AS WE ARE WALKING OUT THE DOOR! I JUST WENT AND GAMBLED FOR THE FIRST TIME SINCE WE HAVE BEEN HERE AND LOST $30 IN A HALF HOUR! WHAT THE FUCK IS UP WITH THAT? THIS TRIP HAS JUST BEEN SO MUCH FUN, WE SO NEEDED THIS, HE HAS BEEN SO SUPER GOOD TO ME, I PRAY TO GOD IT STAYS THIS WAY! I AM LITERALLY IN HEAVEN RIGHT NOW, I DON'T WANT THIS FEELING TO *EVER* GO AWAY! FIRST TIME IN A VERY, VERY LONG TIME THAT I FEEL HARDLY ZERO STRESS! I NEED THIS WAY MORE OFTEN TO KEEP ME GOING AND TO KEEP A SMILE ON MY FACE!

MONDAY, DECEMBER 17, 2012:

STILL IN WENDOVER, BUT LEAVING TODAY! I DON'T WANT TO LEAVE AND GO BACK TO REALITY! CHRISTMAS IS ALMOST HERE, AND I AM NOT EVEN CLOSE TO BEING READY. WE ARE SITTING HERE WATCHING SF AND PATRIOTS, THEY ARE IN OVERTIME AND I JUST TALKED TO MASON AND HE IS

FREAKING OUT 'CAUSE PATRIOTS ARE HIS ABSOLUTE FAVORITE TEAM AND SF IS WINNING RIGHT NOW AND THERE IS ONLY FOUR MINUTES LEFT! LOOK AT ME, I DON'T LIKE WATCHING FOOTBALL, BUT MY BABY BOY IS OBSESSED WITH THE NEW ENGLAND PATRIOTS, SO OF COURSE, I AM GOING TO FOLLOW THEM. I AM NOW INTO THE DENVER BRONCOS AND NEW ENGLAND PATRIOTS, GO FIGURE. I HATED WATCHING FOOTBALL FOR SO, SO LONG...TILL NOW! SO, MASON'S TEAM (PATRIOTS) LOST, NOT BY MUCH, BUT THEY LOST. IT WAS SO SAD TO HEAR MASON'S UPSET VOICE. HE DOES NOT MISS ONE GAME *EVER!* HE IS PROBABLY THE PATRIOTS' BIGGEST FAN! GOT HOME FROM WENDOVER TODAY ABOUT 1:30, DROPPED PAUL OFF AT WORK, WENT TO BRIAN'S, PICKED UP MY SWEET BABY GIRL, CAME HOME FOR ABOUT AN HOUR, THEN WENT BACK OUT TO PICK PAUL UP AT 5:30, DROPPED HIM OFF AT HOME 'CAUSE HE HAS A NASTY SINUS INFECTION HE HAS BEEN FIGHTING FOR ABOUT A MONTH NOW, SO HE WAS NOT DOING VERY GOOD. TOOK PRINCESS JALA TO JAY AT 7:00, WENT BACK OUT TO BRIAN'S FOR A MINUTE, THEN WENT TO SEE MY PRETTY GIRL AT WORK (ADI), GOT FOOD FOR PAUL, AND I WENT TO TARGET AND GRABBED A COUPLE LITTLE CHRISTMAS PRESENTS, THEN CAME HOME. IT'S ABOUT 3:45 A.M., GOODNIGHT!

TUESDAY, DECEMBER 18, 2012:

TODAY WAS AN AWESOME DAY AND IT'S SO NICE TO SAY THAT ESPECIALLY WHEN I AM REALLY STRESSED OUT LATELY 'CAUSE OF THE *BIG DAY, CHRISTMAS!* BUT, IT LOOKS LIKE WE ARE GOING TO BE JUST FINE. I HAVE $700 COMING TO ME TOMORROW *(from a friend who owed her money for drugs)* AND PAUL HAS ABOUT $416 THOUSAND *(... really?)* COMING ANY DAY NOW. WE ARE GOING TO BE JUST FINE. THAT'S SUCH A *GREAT* FEELING! TODAY HAS BEEN A GREAT DAY...AGAIN! IT FEELS SO GOOD TO SAY THAT! WENT TO LUNCH AT ROBINTINO'S WITH ADI AND HER FRIEND, CAME HOME AND MY BABY WAS

ALREADY HOME. TALKED TO HIM FOR A MINUTE, THEN WENT TO THE BANK WITH DEBORAH 'CAUSE SHE OWED ME MONEY AND I GOT $700 FROM HER! YAY! THAT DEFINITELY HELPED A WEEK BEFORE CHRISTMAS! THE KIDS DIDN'T ASK FOR MUCH... WE JUST HAVE A LOT OF DAMN KIDS TOGETHER AND IT ADDS UP VERY FAST! TAKING ADI TOMORROW AFTER SCHOOL TO NORDSTROM'S TO BUY HER UGG BOOTS...$200 AND THAT IS ALL SHE IS GETTING. PAUL IS BUYING HIS SON AN IPAD, WHICH IS ALMOST $400. JUST BETWEEN THE TWO OLDER KIDS WE ARE ALREADY AT $600, AND THAT IS ONLY ONE GIFT EACH! I REALLY HOPE WE CAN MAKE THIS ALL WORK. I TALKED TO SHALL FOR ABOUT AN HOUR TONIGHT, IT WAS REALLY NICE. I MISS HER SO STINKIN' MUCH, IT PHYSICALLY HURTS AT TIMES. WELL, IT'S ABOUT 4:00 IN THE MORNING, I THINK IT'S ABOUT TIME TO GET SOME SLEEP!

WEDNESDAY, DECEMBER 19, 2012:

IT'S ABOUT 2:00 P.M. AND I AM GETTING MY HAIR DONE AT WALMART 'CAUSE I WAS VERY DESPERATE! MY ROOTS WERE SO STINKIN' BAD AND WE HAVE FAMILY PICTURES IN THREE DAYS. I HOPE IT WORKS OUT GOOD HERE, THOUGH. PAUL CAME WITH ME TO KEEP ME COMPANY, HOW SWEET IS THAT? I GOT KIND OF A BUSY DAY TODAY...DOING LAUNDRY, ALMOST DONE WITH MY HAIR, THEN PICKING UP JALA FROM SCHOOL, GOING TO OMI'S TO PICK UP CHRISTMAS TREE AND DECORATIONS, IN AND OUT OF MOM'S WITH KIDS AND LAUNDRY, THEN TAKING PAUL TO ALEXANDER'S TO PRACTICE FOR A COUPLE HOURS. IT'S A CRAZY DAY TODAY 'CAUSE I HAVE BEEN DOWN FOR TOO DAMN LONG! WELL, I AM SITTING HERE AT MY MOM'S WITH MASON AND JALA JUST TRYING TO RELAX! ADI, ME, JALA, AND MAS JUST GOT BACK FROM DINNER, WE WENT TO PARADISE CAFE AND IT WAS GREAT 'CAUSE THEY WERE WITH ME, BY MYSELF, IT WAS WONDERFUL! *(She hardly ever had Adi and Mas alone because her ex petitioned the court to have her supervised when she was with them. This was a rare occasion for her.)* MY THREE KIDS ARE MY ENTIRE LIFE! JALA IS HAVING A ROUGH DAY TODAY, THOUGH, IT BREAKS MY STINKIN' HEART. JAY IS DATING A GIRL FOR ABOUT TWO WEEKS NOW AND JALA IS HAVING A ROUGH TIME WITH IT. SHE IS NOT THE ONLY GIRL IN DADDY'S LIFE NOW AND SHE HAS BEEN SINCE THE DAY SHE WAS BORN. JALA IS JAY'S WHOLE LIFE, HE HAS NOTHING BUT HER, AND HE DOES CHERISH THAT TOO. HE IS A GREAT FATHER! HE IS 100% DEVOTED TO HIS LIFE WITH JALA, THEY ARE SUPER, SUPER TIGHT, SOMETIMES MAKES ME VERY JEALOUS, OKAY, ALL THE TIME!

Family pictures. Ang, Em, Me, and Nat

THURSDAY, DECEMBER 20, 2012:

I HAD AN INCREDIBLE DAY TODAY! IT WAS HONESTLY ONE OF THE BEST DAYS I HAVE HAD IN A VERY, VERY LONG TIME

AND IT WAS ALL THANKS TO MY BABY GIRL, ADISON! SO, WE HAVE BEEN TRYING TO GO TO LUNCH FOR THE PAST MONTH NOW AND FINALLY WAS ABLE TO TODAY! SHE CAME AND PICKED ME UP AROUND 11:00 THIS MORNING AND WE WENT OUT TO CITY CREEK NORDSTROM'S, THEN TO THE GATEWAY SO SHE COULD SHOW ME THE $200 UGG BOOTS THAT SHE WANTED FOR CHRISTMAS. IT WAS SO MUCH FUN...JUST ME AND ADI. WE TALKED A WHOLE BUNCH, STUFF THAT I HAVE WANTED TO TALK TO HER ABOUT FOR A VERY, VERY LONG TIME, JUST NEVER HAD THE GUTS TO BRING IT UP, AND I WAS VERY AFRAID OF WHAT HER RESPONSE WAS GOING TO BE. ADI HAS BEEN SO ANGRY AND NEGATIVE TOWARDS ME FOR QUITE A WHILE NOW, WHICH I *DO NOT* BLAME HER AT ALL, BUT TODAY WAS A RESPONSE FROM HER THAT COMPLETELY TOOK THE BIGGEST BURDEN I HAVE EVER HAD OFF MY SHOULDERS. IT WAS SUCH A WONDERFUL FEELING! I HAVE NEVER HAD THAT QUITE OF AN INTENSE CONVERSATION WITH ANYONE BEFORE, BUT IT TURNED OUT AWESOME! I ASKED HER IF, WHEN SHE LOOKED BACK ON HER CHILDHOOD, WAS ALL THAT SHE COULD REMEMBER WAS ME LEAVING AND RUINING HER LIFE...SHE COMPLETELY SHOCKED ME BY SAYING..."MOM, YOU NEED TO REMEMBER THAT I WAS WITH YOU TILL I WAS 12/13 YEARS OLD AND YOU WERE AN AWESOME MOM AND WHAT I REMEMBER GROWING UP WAS ALWAYS BEING WITH AUNT SHALL, YOU, AND AUSTIN, EVERY SINGLE DAY DOING FUN THINGS." SHE SAID, "YOU RAISED ME, MOM. AND WHEN I LOOK BACK ON MY CHILDHOOD, ALL I CAN REMEMBER WAS GOOD TIMES, BECAUSE IT WAS ALL THE TIME, AND WHEN I THINK ABOUT GROWING UP, I GET SUCH A GREAT FEELING BECAUSE I HAVE SO MANY GREAT MEMORIES TO REMEMBER. I NEVER THINK OF ANYTHING BAD, JUST ALL THE GOOD TIMES, WHICH WAS EVERY DAY." SHE TOLD ME THAT I RAISED HER AND WAS ALWAYS A GREAT MOM AND WAS ALWAYS WITH HER AND I WAS THERE THE YEARS SHE NEEDED ME THE MOST. SHE ALSO SAID, "AND NOW IS WHEN I NEED YOU MORE THAN EVER 'CAUSE ALL THE IMPORTANT THINGS

IN MY LIFE ARE COMING FAST...GRADUATION, MARRIAGE, ETC. AND YOU ARE HERE, MOM, EVERY DAY WHENEVER I NEED YOU." *(I asked Adi about this and she remembers saying these things to help her mom feel better, but she does not have much recollection of the year 2012 other than this.)* I HAVE NEVER IN MY LIFE HEARD SUCH WONDERFUL WORDS THAN I DID TODAY FROM MY DAUGHTER. THE GUILT I WAS HAVING AND HOLDING ON TO FOR SO MANY DAMN YEARS NOW ALMOST COMPLETELY WENT AWAY. I HAVE BEEN HURTING FOR SO MANY YEARS NOW BECAUSE I THOUGHT I RUINED MY KIDS' LIVES AND WHEN THEY LOOKED BACK ON THEIR CHILDHOOD, ALL THEY SAW WAS THE HORRIBLE LIFE I PUT THEM THROUGH. WELL, THEY DON'T, AT LEAST ADI DOESN'T. IT HELPED ME MORE THAN I EVER THOUGHT! I NEEDED TO HEAR THAT FROM HER SO STINKIN' BAD! I REALLY THINK I NEED TO TALK TO MASON NOW ABOUT THE SAME THING. HIS IS MOST LIKELY GOING TO BE THE RESPONSE THAT HAS BEEN WEIGHING SO HEAVILY ON MY SHOULDERS FOR SO MANY YEARS. WELL, IF IT IS, THEN I NEED TO FIX IT AND FAST! TIME GOES BY *WAY TOO FAST* NOW AND I DON'T WANT TO WASTE ANOTHER MINUTE WITHOUT MY BABY BOY! I NEED TO MAKE GOOD AND HAPPY MEMORIES FOR HIM TO HOLD IN HIS HEART FOR THE REST OF HIS LIFE!

One week later...

<u>THURSDAY, DECEMBER 27, 2012</u>:

WELL, THIS WAS DEFINITELY THE WORST CHRISTMAS I HAVE EVER HAD! WE HAD FIVE KIDS TO SHOP FOR AND THE ONLY ONES THAT WERE HAPPY WERE PAUL'S KIDS. WE GOT ADI THE WRONG SIZE OF BOOTS, FORGOT MASON'S BIG GIFT, AND TOTALLY FORGOT TO GET JALA'S PRESENTS THAT I HAD HIDDEN AWAY. I COMPLETELY RUINED THIS CHRISTMAS! ADI IS NOT TALKING TO ME AT ALL, AND I DIDN'T EVEN GET VERY MUCH TIME WITH MY FAMILY OR MY KIDS BECAUSE WE

ALWAYS REVOLVE OUR TIME AND SCHEDULES AROUND PAUL'S KIDS. IT'S STARTING TO REALLY GET ON MY NERVES. PAUL FOUGHT WITH ME REALLY BAD CHRISTMAS DAY AND CHRISTMAS EVE. IT WAS ABSOLUTELY HORRIBLE! ON A POSITIVE NOTE, THOUGH, PAUL GOT ME MY KITTY FOR CHRISTMAS, SHE IS THE SWEETEST THING I HAVE EVER SEEN, SHE IS THE MOST FRIENDLY KITTY I HAVE EVER MET. WE REALLY NEEDED HER BAD! I LOVE HER. I AM PRAYING THAT THINGS GET BETTER BETWEEN PAUL AND I BECAUSE THEY ARE NOT GOING WELL RIGHT NOW AT ALL AND I HONESTLY DON'T KNOW HOW MUCH MORE I CAN HANDLE! I DO LOVE HIM WITH ALL MY HEART, BUT HE HAS MORE PROBLEMS AND ISSUES THAN I THOUGHT. HE IS REALLY SICK AND NEEDS HELP.

Three days later...

SUNDAY, DECEMBER 30, 2012:

IT'S 8:00 P.M. RIGHT NOW AND I AM SITTING HERE IN WENDOVER AT THE PEPPERMILL HOTEL WITH PAUL AND HIS KIDS. HIS DAUGHTER AND I ARE ON THE BED IN OUR ROOM WATCHING TV AND RELAXING WHILE HIS SON AND HIM ARE DOWNSTAIRS IN THE CASINO BETTING ON THE FOOTBALL GAME. I MISS MY KITTY ALREADY! THIS IS THE VERY FIRST TIME I HAVE LEFT HER AND I AM SO NOT OKAY WITH IT. SHE IS THE BEST CAT I HAVE EVER HAD. SHE IS SUCH A PEOPLE PERSON. SHE CLIMBS ALL OVER US INSTEAD OF RUNNING AWAY LIKE ANY OTHER CAT. SHE IS IN LOVE WITH PAUL, SHE HAS TO SLEEP ON HIS HEAD EVERY NIGHT OR IN BETWEEN HIS LEGS UNDER THE BLANKETS. IT'S THE CUTEST THING EVER! SO, ADI WAS SO UPSET WITH ME ON CHRISTMAS, SHE WANTED THESE $200 UGG BOOTS FROM NORDSTROM'S AND WE GOT THEM FOR HER, BUT THE WRONG SIZE. I FELT SO BAD AND THEY WERE SOLD OUT EVERYWHERE AFTER CHRISTMAS, SO SHE COULDN'T EVEN WEAR THEM AFTER SHE GOT THEM.

SHE DIDN'T TALK TO ME TILL YESTERDAY. SHE WAS SO MAD AT ME. BUT, SHE CAME OVER LAST NIGHT TO SEE THE KITTY AND SHE FELL IN LOVE WITH HER, JUST LIKE EVERYBODY ELSE DOES. I HATE FIGHTING WITH ADI, IT IS THE WORST THING IN THE WORLD. WE WERE GOING TO BRING JALA WITH US TO WENDOVER, BUT SHE DIDN'T WANT TO COME. SHE SAID SHE DOESN'T WANT TO BE AROUND PAUL. SHE REALLY DOES NOT LIKE HIM RIGHT NOW. I HOPE EVENTUALLY SHE WILL, 'CAUSE I LOVE HIM SO MUCH!

MONDAY, DECEMBER 31, 2012:

IT'S 2:00 A.M. MONDAY MORNING AND WE ARE IN WENDOVER. JUST GOT BACK FROM BURGER KING ABOUT AN HOUR AGO AND EVERYBODY IS ASLEEP EXCEPT ME, OF COURSE! I REALLY HATE MORNINGS, ALWAYS HAVE AND AM ALWAYS UP LATE AT NIGHT. I HAVE ALWAYS BEEN A NIGHT PERSON. PAUL IS TOTAL OPPOSITE! HE LOVES MORNINGS AND IS ALWAYS UP NO LATER THAN 7:00 A.M. USUALLY AND IS NEVER UP PAST 11:00 P.M. AND THAT'S PUSHING IT! OKAY, SO THIS TRIP WAS WAY FUN, BUT I AM FREAKING THE FUCK OUT NOW! I HAVE NEVER LEFT MY KITTY BEFORE, THIS IS THE FIRST TIME, AND SHE'S ALL I CAN THINK ABOUT, I PRAY SHE IS OKAY. SO, AFTER MY PARENTS KICKED ME OUT ABOUT 8/9 MONTHS AGO BECAUSE OF WHAT MICHELLE FOUND UNDER MY MATTRESS, MY DAD HAS NOT SPOKEN TO ME. I WAS JUST SO SAD BECAUSE HIM AND I BECAME VERY, VERY CLOSE SINCE I MOVED IN WITH THEM. WELL, PAUL FOUND THIS BOOK AT BARNES AND NOBLE THAT WAS CALLED "DADDY'S GIRL" AND IT MADE ME SOB WHEN I READ IT (JUST A SHORT LITTLE BOOK). WELL, HE *(our dad)* HAS FOUR GIRLS AND THAT BOOK WAS ABSOLUTELY AMAZING. SO, PAUL GOT IT FOR ME TO GIVE TO HIM FOR CHRISTMAS. WELL, AFTER GETTING IT, HE CAME INTO THE KITCHEN AND GAVE ME A HUG. I BAWLED MY EYES OUT. AFTER THAT, A COUPLE DAYS LATER, I WENT

TO DO MY LAUNDRY OVER THERE AND HE TALKED TO ME! I COULDN'T BE HAPPIER, I NEEDED MY DADDY BACK! I LOVE MY FATHER WITH ALL MY HEART.

• • •

CHAPTER 10

2013

IN 2013, NAT TURNED *thirty-four, Adi seventeen, Mas fourteen, and Jala seven.*

TUESDAY, JANUARY 1, 2013:

IT'S A BRAND NEW YEAR! (TIME TO MAKE SOME BIG CHANGES!) I KNOW EXACTLY WHAT I NEED TO DO, BUT IT IS GOING TO BE THE *HARDEST* THING I WILL EVER DO! I KNOW I AM STRONG ENOUGH, I JUST HOPE I HAVE THE COURAGE TO DO IT AND QUIT MAKING LAME ASS EXCUSES. MY WHOLE ENTIRE LIFE DEPENDS ON THIS! AND NOT TO MENTION, EVERYONE THAT IS IN MY LIFE! I DESERVE THIS AND SO DO MY THREE KIDS! I KNOW I CAN DO IT, I JUST PRAY TO GOD THAT I WILL! I AM SUPPOSED TO GO WITH MY SISTERS AND MY MOM NEXT WEEK TO ZIONS FOR A GIRLS (SISTERS) GET TOGETHER. SINCE WE HAVEN'T IN YEARS, AND WE ARE ALL DRIFTING FARTHER AND FARTHER AWAY FROM EACH OTHER. BUT, IF I DON'T MAKE THIS HUGE COMMITMENT AND CHANGE, THEN THERE IS NO WAY I WILL BE ABLE TO GO! I REALLY CAN'T DO THAT! MY SISTERS AND MY MOM AND ALL OUR RELATIONSHIPS DEPEND ON THIS, BESIDES, THEY ARE DOING THIS TRIP FOR *ME!*

1-2-2013: Dr. Note–113 lbs. denies relapse, stable. Prescribed Suboxone. *(Nat kept getting prescribed Suboxone and other medications from this doctor. She would sell the Suboxone and continue to use heroin and other drugs. I don't understand why this doctor kept prescribing medications to her even when she told him she was using. Also, when he says here that she's stable and denies relapse, there are no notes of a drug test having been taken.)*

WEDNESDAY, JANUARY 2, 2013:

IT'S ABOUT 1:00 WEDNESDAY MORNING AND THE PAST COUPLE OF DAYS WITH PAUL HAVE BEEN AWESOME! HE HAS BEEN ABSOLUTELY INCREDIBLE TO ME, PLEASE, PLEASE STAY THIS WAY! WHEN HE IS BEING LIKE THIS, WE ARE BOTH SO STINKIN' HAPPY. NEW YEAR'S EVE SUCKED, THOUGH! PAUL FELL ASLEEP AT 9:30 P.M. AND ME AND HIS KIDS STAYED UP AND THAT WAS BORING. OH WELL, AT LEAST WE ARE SAFE AND WE SPENT IT TOGETHER! SO, I AM ALWAYS WITH HIS KIDS AND IT'S NICE EVERY SO OFTEN, BUT NOT ALL THE DAMN TIME! AND I WOULDN'T MIND IT AS MUCH IF I GOT TO SEE MY KIDS EVERY SO OFTEN, BUT I NEVER DO. IT'S ALWAYS REALLY BOTHERED ME, BUT LATELY IT'S STARTING TO PISS ME OFF! I SEE MY BABY GIRL JALA A LOT, BUT ADI AND MAS HARDLY EVER! THEY ARE GROWING UP SO FAST AND I DON'T HAVE MUCH TIME WITH THEM LEFT. I'M SPENDING ALL MY DAMN TIME WITH PAUL'S KIDS AND IT'S REALLY STARTING TO BUG! I REALLY DO LOVE THESE KIDS, THEY ARE GREAT KIDS, BUT MY KIDS NEED MY TIME RIGHT NOW, NOT THESE TWO. AND WHEN WE DO HAVE THEM, WHICH IS *ALL THE TIME*, I AM WITH THEM MORE THAN PAUL IS. PAUL IS ALWAYS BUSY DOING THINGS AND THEY ARE ALWAYS STUCK WITH ME. IT NEVER BOTHERED ME BEFORE BUT NOW IT IS!

SITTING HERE AT THE DR. OFFICE WAITING TO BE SEEN FOR MY MONTHLY VISIT FOR SUBOXONE. ADI HAD TO COME GET ME 'CAUSE PAUL TOOK THE CAR, AND IT WAS SO GREAT

SEEING HER. TODAY IS MY *FAVORITE* DAY OF THE WEEK 'CAUSE I GET TO SEE ALL MY WONDERFUL, BEAUTIFUL, AMAZING KIDS! THEY ARE SERIOUSLY THE *BEST* KIDS, AND I'M NOT JUST SAYING THAT 'CAUSE THEY ARE MINE, PEOPLE TELL ME THAT ALL THE TIME! I DON'T KNOW HOW THEY TURNED OUT SO DAMN GOOD, ESPECIALLY WHAT THEY ALL HAVE BEEN THROUGH WITH ME, BUT THEY ARE ALL MIRACLES! SO, PAUL IS FREAKING ME OUT! HE SAT ME DOWN THIS MORNING TO TALK TO ME ABOUT IN CASE THEY TAKE HIM TO JAIL. *(This is the only time Nat mentioned this and I have no idea what it means).* THEY ARE COMING FOR HIM REALLY SOON. HE HAS PUT A LOT IN IT AND IN ME AND IN THE KIDS IN CASE THEY TAKE HIM TO JAIL AND HE HAS DONE A LOT, ON THE BUSINESS THING FOR US, SO I CAN KEEP IT GOING AND HAVE SOMETHING GOOD TO FALL BACK ON. BUT I WILL DIE IF THEY TAKE HIM. I CAN'T BE WITHOUT HIM FOR MORE THAN ONE DAY, I PRAY TO GOD HE CAN GET THINGS WORKED OUT SO HE NEVER HAS TO LEAVE ME (FOR JAIL!). WHY IN THE *HELL* DO DOCTORS TAKE SO DAMN LONG ALL THE TIME? I NEED TO GET MY DIVORCE DONE AND I NEED TO DO IT *ASAP,* 'CAUSE PAUL WANTS TO GET MARRIED HERE REALLY SOON, ESPECIALLY SINCE HE MIGHT BE GOING AWAY FOR A WHILE. I HAVE A GOOD FEELING THAT EVERYTHING IS GOING TO WORK OUT. I NEED TO THINK POSITIVE AND BE THANKFUL FOR THE THINGS THAT I DO HAVE, NOT NEGATIVE, LIKE I USUALLY AM. THAT HAS GOTTEN ME ABSOLUTELY NOWHERE! I AM IN A BETTER PLACE NOW!

THURSDAY, JANUARY 4, 2013:

THIS NOT HAVING MONEY THING IS ABSOLUTELY KILLING ME. IT IS THE HARDEST THING IN THE WORLD TO KEEP ASKING PAUL FOR MONEY, ESPECIALLY WHEN I NEED IT *EVERY DAY, NO MATTER WHAT!* SO, MASON ASKED ME ON THE PHONE LAST NIGHT WHEN I WAS GOING TO GET HIM BACK. I HAD

NO IDEA WHAT TO SAY, SO I PROMISED HIM I WOULD THIS YEAR! NOW, I REALLY NEED TO MAKE IT HAPPEN. HE SAID HE TRUSTED ME AND THAT HE BELIEVES THAT I AM GOING TO KEEP MY PROMISE! *(Throughout the years, Mason continued to believe his mon was going to get him back.)* IT'S ABOUT 1:15 AND I AM JUST PICKING UP MY LITTLE SWEETHEART FROM SCHOOL. PAUL AND I ARE FIGHTING AGAIN 'CAUSE HIS DAUGHTER GOT HURT YESTERDAY AND JALA WANTED TO KNOW WHAT WAS WRONG WITH HER AND PAUL SNAPPED AT HER AND I GOT MAD AND LEFT FOR ABOUT 5/6 HOURS. IT SUCKED! I DON'T LIKE FIGHTING WITH HIM 'CAUSE IT GETS BLOWN UP EVERY TIME AND HE TELLS ME BYE. I REALLY DON'T KNOW WHAT TO DO ANYMORE. I KISS HIS ASS ALL THE TIME! HE IS VERY GOOD TO ME, BUT WHEN WE ARE FIGHTING, HE IS COMPLETELY EVIL! A TOTALLY DIFFERENT PERSON. AND WHEN IT COMES TO MY KIDS, I AM VERY, VERY PROTECTIVE. THEY ARE MY LIFE. THE THING THAT PISSES ME OFF THE MOST IS I WOULD NEVER TREAT HIS KIDS LIKE THAT! I AM SO GOOD TO THEM, BUT I GUESS WITH THIS RELATIONSHIP, IT'S HIS WAY OR NO WAY. I GOT HOME FROM PICKING UP JALA AND HE TOLD ME HE LOVED ME, BUT THERE IS STILL SO MUCH TENSION BETWEEN US, I HATE IT SO BAD!

FRIDAY, JANUARY 5, 2013:

SO, I AM THINKING ABOUT DOING NAILS AGAIN ON THE SIDE. A COUPLE APPOINTMENTS A DAY, THAT WOULD HELP US SO MUCH, ESPECIALLY SINCE I CAN'T STAND NOT MAKING MY OWN MONEY! PAUL IS AWESOME, THOUGH, AND GIVES ME MONEY EVERY DAY, BUT NOT ENOUGH TO COVER EVERYTHING I NEED. I AM SUPPOSED TO BE GOING OUT OF TOWN NEXT WEEKEND TO ZION'S NATIONAL PARK FOR A SISTERS TRIP AND MOM AND SHALL GAVE US THE WEEKEND PAID FOR WITH FACIALS AND MASSAGES AND I ALREADY COMMITTED TO GOING 'CAUSE

IT'S PRETTY MUCH FOR ME! BUT HOW IN THE HELL DO I DO IT? I HAVE NO MONEY, ESPECIALLY TO STOCK UP FOR WHAT I NEED FOR THE TRIP. I HAVE TO MAKE IT WORK, I CAN'T LET MY SISTERS DOWN OR MY MOM! I ALREADY GAVE MY SUBS OR I WOULD KICK RIGHT BEFORE AND TAKE MY SUBS, BUT THIS MONTH'S ARE ALREADY GONE *(meaning she would have used her Suboxone to get clean before the trip, but she had already sold them).* I REALLY NEEDED THE MONEY FOR CHRISTMAS AND STUFF AND NOW I FUCKED MYSELF...AGAIN! THINGS WILL ALL WORK OUT, STAY POSITIVE, NAT. JALA SLEPT OVER LAST NIGHT AND I ABSOLUTELY LOVED HAVING HER HERE. WENT TO LUNCH WITH ADI YESTERDAY AT CUTLER'S AND IT WAS SO NICE TO JUST SIT AND CHAT WITH HER FOR A BIT. I LOVE THAT GIRL, EVEN THOUGH SHE HAS DEFINITELY BEEN ON ONE LATELY!

SATURDAY, JANUARY 6, 2013:

WELL, TODAY WAS A PRETTY GREAT DAY! GOT UP EARLY AND PAUL'S DAUGHTER AND I MET MASON AT CHURCH 'CAUSE HE REALLY WANTED ME THERE. WHEN WE GOT HOME, WE HUNG OUT FOR A BIT, THEN WE ALL (PAUL AND HIS KIDS AND I) WENT TO MY MOM'S TO HANG OUT WITH MAS FOR A WHILE. THEN CAME HOME, PAUL MADE US DINNER, AND WE WATCHED *21 JUMP STREET,* THE FUNNIEST SHOW I HAVE SEEN IN A VERY LONG TIME. THEN, CLOSE TO THE END, I WENT OUT TO SMOKE, AND OF COURSE, WHEN I CAME IN PAUL WAS ASLEEP, SO I WENT TO SEE PATRICK *(to get drugs)* AND HE MAKES ME SO STINKIN' MAD! HE SCREWS ME EVERY SINGLE TIME I SEE HIM. BUT IT'S COMING TO AN END, DEFINITELY! THERE IS NOBODY TO GO TO ANYMORE. I KEEP PISSING PEOPLE OFF, LIKE BRIAN, AND THEN THEY WON'T MEET ME. I GUESS THAT'S A GOOD THING. I DIDN'T SEE ADI TODAY, I GUESS SHE WON'T GO TO CHURCH ANYMORE.

SUNDAY, JANUARY 7, 2013:

IT'S GOING TO BE AN AWESOME WEEK! IT'S ABOUT 7:00 P.M. RIGHT NOW AND I AM SITTING HERE NEXT TO JALA WATCHING POPEYE. GETTING READY TO MEET JAY AT IN-N-OUT BURGER 'CAUSE JALA IS HUNGRY. IT WAS A VERY UNINTERESTING DAY, THAT'S FOR SURE, ALL I DID WAS CLEAN, THEN WHEN PAUL GOT HOME, WENT AND MET UP WITH SAMUEL *(to get drugs)* FOR ABOUT 45 MINUTES. THEN CAME HOME AND HUNG OUT WITH MY BABY GIRL. WELL, JUST GOT BACK FROM IN-N-OUT BURGER WITH JAY AND JALA. JAY BOUGHT ME DINNER AND IT WAS REALLY NICE TO SIT THERE WITH HIM AND JALA AND JUST TALK AS FRIENDS. JALA WAS IN HEAVEN, IT MAKES ME SO SUPER SAD BECAUSE JALA WANTS US BACK TOGETHER SO STINKIN' BAD. HE IS AN AMAZING FATHER AND I HONESTLY COULDN'T ASK FOR A BETTER FATHER FOR JALA, BUT AS FAR AS ME AND HIM GO, THERE IS PRETTY MUCH NOTHING THERE ANYMORE. MY HEART IS TAKEN FOREVER BY ONE MAN THAT I LOVE WITH ALL MY HEART AND SOUL!

WELL, TWO DAYS TILL I GO ON THE TRIP WITH MY MOM, ANGIE, SHALL, AND EMILY. I AM REALLY, REALLY NERVOUS 'CAUSE I DON'T KNOW IF I CAN GET THE CASH TO GET WHAT I NEED TO GO. I CAN'T BE THAT FAR AWAY AND NOT HAVE WHAT I NEED! I LITERALLY HAVE ONE DAY TO FIGURE THIS ALL OUT. I'M SCARED TO DEATH! IT'S ABOUT 2:00 A.M. TUESDAY MORNING, AND OF COURSE, I AM UP WRITING AND PAUL (POOR GUY) IS SOUND ASLEEP. HE WORKED SO HARD TODAY. HE LEFT ABOUT 7:00 A.M. THIS MORNING, THEN GOT HOME ABOUT 4:00 AFTER PICKING JALA UP FOR ME. THEN HE WATCHED JALA FOR ABOUT AN HOUR WHILE I RAN SOME ERRANDS. HE IS SUCH AN AMAZING GUY. I REALLY DO BELIEVE THAT HIS TEMPER IS GETTING MUCH, MUCH BETTER AND HE WILL REALLY SOON LEARN HOW TO CONTROL IT SO I AM NOT PUT THROUGH ALL THAT SHIT AGAIN. HE IS TRYING REALLY HARD, I CAN SEE IT EVERY DAY, AND HE IS DOING IT FOR

ME!! OH, BY THE WAY...TODAY IS GOING TO BE A *WONDERFUL* DAY, I WILL GET EVERYTHING DONE THAT I WANT TO AND BEFORE I GO TO BED TONIGHT I WILL HAVE A SMILE ON MY FACE.

TODAY HAS NOT BEEN A GOOD DAY AT ALL! I DIDN'T HAVE MY CAR, WHICH I AM NOT HAPPY ABOUT NOW, BUT TRIED TO CHILL WITH SAMUEL AND IT DIDN'T QUITE WORK OUT. JUST DROPPED JALA OFF WITH JAY AND PAUL AND I ARE SITTING AT ORCHARD BOWL AT THE BAR 'CAUSE WE JUST DROPPED HIS SON OFF AT KARATE AND THIS WAS RIGHT AROUND THE CORNER SO WE ARE JUST WAITING TO PICK HIM BACK UP. WE PLAYED GOLF AND POOL AND THAT WAS FUN, NOW WE HAVE TO GO!

MONDAY, JANUARY 8, 2013:

SO, I HAVE TO HAVE EVERYTHING READY BY TONIGHT FOR THE TRIP. I AM REALLY STRESSED OUT 'CAUSE I HAVE A TON TO DO! I'M EXCITED TO GO ON THIS TRIP, IF I HAVE EVERYTHING READY, IF NOT, I WILL BE FREAKING OUT. IT ALL BETTER WORK OUT, AT LEAST FOR MY SISTERS AND MY MOM. I'M PRAYING IT ALL WORKS OUT!

IT'S ABOUT 12:10 NOW AND I AM DOING LAUNDRY AT ANTHONY'S AND WAITING FOR SAMUEL OR BRIAN TO TEXT ME BACK ABOUT MEETING HIM. I AM COMPLETELY OUT AND GETTING SICKER BY THE MINUTE. I HAVE SO MUCH TO DO TODAY, PLUS SPEND TIME WITH MY KIDS. I DON'T KNOW HOW I AM GOING TO PULL THIS ALL OFF, BUT I NEED TO, I HAVE NO CHOICE!

OKAY, NOW IT'S 1:00 IN THE MORNING AND I'M STILL WAITING TO HEAR FROM SAMUEL OR BRIAN. I HONESTLY DON'T KNOW WHAT PAUL THINKS WHEN I LEAVE THIS LATE AT NIGHT. I TOLD HIM I WAS GOING TO MY MOM'S TO SWITCH THE LAUNDRY. I LOVE HIM SO MUCH! THIS MORNING HAS BEEN A VERY SHITTY MORNING.

I HAVE NOT HAD ANY BLK *(heroin)* ALL DAY AND IT'S 1:00 P.M. AND I'M WAITING FOR PAUL TO GET BACK WITH THE CAR. I AM SO SICK RIGHT NOW AND HE WON'T ANSWER HIS FREAKING PHONE!! I HAVE REALLY HAD IT WITH HIM TAKING MY CAR! I HAVE TO TAKE HIS DAUGHTER TO WET SEAL IN THE GATEWAY BECAUSE WE GAVE HER A GIFT CERTIFICATE FOR CHRISTMAS. WELL, TODAY ENDED UP BEING ONE OF THE WORST DAYS OF MY LIFE!!! I HOPE TOMORROW IS MUCH BETTER!

Nat did end up getting the supply of drugs she needed for the trip.

TUESDAY, JANUARY 9, 2013:

LEAVING FOR ST. GEORGE TODAY TO GO HAVE A VACATION WITH MY SISTERS AND MY MOM. SHALL GOT US GIRLS A THREE DAY SUITE AT ZION'S NATIONAL PARK FOR CHRISTMAS. I AM EXCITED BUT SCARED AT THE SAME TIME BECAUSE I DON'T KNOW HOW IT'S GOING TO TURN OUT. ESPECIALLY WITH EMILY THERE. SO, MY MOM FLEW DOWN TO ST. GEORGE LAST NIGHT, SO I AM DRIVING WITH ANGIE AND EMILY. THIS IS GOING TO BE A VERY, VERY INTERESTING CAR RIDE. I HOPE AND PRAY THIS RIDE DOWN, THE RIDE BACK AND THE TRIP ITSELF GOES OKAY. I AM LOOKING FORWARD TO IT BUT AT THE SAME TIME VERY, VERY NERVOUS.

SO, WE ARE HERE! THE RIDE WAS ACTUALLY OKAY, EMILY TALKED TO ME A LOT, IT WAS REALLY NICE. THIS IS GOING TO BE A VERY, VERY GOOD WEEKEND. WE ARE ALL GETTING FACIALS RIGHT NOW, IT'S ABOUT 6:00 P.M., WHEN WE ARE ALL DONE, WE ARE GRABBING SOMETHING TO EAT, THEN GOING TO SHALL'S TO HANG OUT.

SO, WE GOT DONE WITH GETTING THE FACIAL AND WE WENT TO DINNER AND MY MOM JUST TOLD US ALL THAT SHE WAS QUITTING HER JOB. SHE HAS BEEN AT WEST BOUNTIFUL ELEMENTARY FOR 27 YEARS AND SHE IS RETIRING (QUITTING).

My mom was the secretary for 27 years at the elementary school by the home we grew up in. Jala went to that school as well so she could be there with my mom.

<u>WEDNESDAY, JANUARY 10, 2013</u>:

WELL, THE TRIP WITH THE GIRLS HAS BEEN WONDERFUL SO FAR. EMILY AND I ARE TOTALLY TALKING AND IT'S BEEN GREAT. I KNOW SHE IS STILL NOT COMPLETELY OKAY WITH ME AND I DON'T KNOW IF SHE EVER WILL BE, BUT AT LEAST SHE IS COMMUNICATING WITH ME. WE HAVEN'T TALKED IN SO LONG THAT IT'S SO NICE TO BE HEARING HER VOICE AGAIN! I AM PRAYING THE REST OF THE TRIP GOES SMOOTHLY AND I WILL BE HAPPY AND CONTENT WHEN WE LEAVE. WE SLEPT AT SHALL'S LAST NIGHT AND MY MOM AND EMILY SLEPT IN THE ROOM I USED TO LIVE IN *(she's referring to the one time she stayed with me when I thought she was trying to get clean)* AND ANGIE AND I SLEPT IN THE THEATRE ROOM. IT WAS REALLY ACTUALLY NICE 'CAUSE I HAVEN'T SEEN OR TALKED TO ANGIE IN A VERY LONG TIME. I LOVE HER! WE JUST GOT BACK TO ZION'S AND THE ROOMS ARE ABSOLUTELY INCREDIBLE. THERE IS FOUR KING SIZE BEDS, TWO TVS, A FRIDGE, A HUGE BATHROOM, AND ALL FIVE GIRLS! WE ARE TRYING TO FIND BRIDESMAIDS TO WATCH 'CAUSE EMILY HAS NOT SEEN IT YET. I GUESS THE SNOW IS REALLY, REALLY BAD IN BOUNTIFUL THAT NOBODY IS SUPPOSED TO GO OUT ON THE ROADS. PAUL HAS BEEN SENDING ME THE CUTEST PICTURES OF HIM AND THE CAT! THIS TRIP REALLY HAS BEEN AWESOME, I HOPE IT STAYS THAT WAY! I AM SO GLAD I CAME. I WAS THINKING ABOUT NOT GOING A COUPLE TIMES, BUT I AM SO GLAD I DID! WE WATCHED 21 JUMP STREET AND WENT TO SLEEP. I AM SO SURPRISED BUT ME AND EM HAVE TOTALLY BEEN GETTING ALONG. I KNOW SHE WOULD NOT BE OKAY WITH ME IF IT WAS JUST ONE-ON-ONE, BUT WITH ALL FOUR OF US HERE, IT'S BEEN GREAT FOR US. I JUST REALLY HOPE

THAT ME AND HER CAN CONTINUE TALKING EVEN AFTER OUR VACATION IS OVER.

THURSDAY, JANUARY 11, 2013:

THIS HAS BEEN A GREAT TRIP! WE REALLY NEED TO DO THIS MORE OFTEN. WE ARE TALKING ABOUT DOING THIS EVERY YEAR. I WOULD BE SO HAPPY IF WE DID THIS EVERY YEAR. SO, ME, SHALL, ANG, EMILY, AND MOM ARE SITTING AT MEME'S CAFE EATING BREAKFAST IN ZION'S. SLEPT IN THE SAME BED WITH SHALL LAST NIGHT AND WE SLEPT PRETTY GOOD. ANGIE WAS IN THE BED NEXT TO US, AND MOM AND EM WERE IN ANOTHER ROOM CONNECTED TO OURS. TALKING ABOUT SEEING A MOVIE AFTER BREAKFAST. THIS HONESTLY HAS BEEN THE BEST VACATION EVER!

All of us girls

IT'S ABOUT 8:00 P.M., AND IT REALLY HAS BEEN AN AWESOME DAY! WE GOT UP, WENT TO BREAKFAST, THEN CAME BACK, GOT READY (KIND OF), WENT TO WALGREEN'S AND GOT A BUNCH OF CANDY FOR THE MOVIE WE WERE GOING TO AND GOT A BUNCH OF LIP-GLOSSES, THEN WENT TO THE MOVIE (LES MISERABLES), WHICH I DIDN'T LIKE AT FIRST BUT THEN GOT ABSOLUTELY INCREDIBLE. IT WAS A VERY LONG MOVIE, 2 HOURS 45 MINUTES. THEN AFTER THE MOVIE WE CAME BACK UP TO ZION'S AND WENT TO ALL THE LITTLE SHOPS, GOT JALA A PRESENT FOR HER BIRTHDAY NEXT WEEK. OH, AND I FORGOT WE WENT TO FAMILY DOLLAR AND ALL FOUR OF US GIRLS GOT ON THE LITTLE CAROUSAL AND GOT PICTURES. AFTER THE SHOPS, WE WENT TO DINNER AT A VERY NICE RESTAURANT AND HAD A VERY GOOD MEAL! NOW, WE ARE BACK AT THE HOTEL WATCHING TV AND FALLING ASLEEP!

Me and Nat

I remember Nat spending a lot of time in the bathroom on this trip. There was one night that we went to a store and tried on cowboy hats and she stayed back at the hotel because she wasn't feeling good.

SUNDAY, JANUARY 13, 2013:

IT'S ABOUT 8:00 P.M. AND I JUST GOT HOME A COUPLE HOURS AGO FROM MY TRIP WITH MY SISTERS AND MY MOM. WE WENT TO ZION'S NATIONAL PARK FOR THREE DAYS AND ABSOLUTELY VEGGED! THAT WAS SHALL'S CHRISTMAS PRESENT TO ALL OF

US. SHE PAID FOR THE ENTIRE WEEKEND, PAID FOR EVERYTHING. WE ALL HAD A LOT OF FUN! WE DEFINITELY NEEDED IT. EMILY AND I WERE GREAT BUT THE SECOND WE GOT HOME, SHE TURNED BACK INTO THE SAME HATEFUL PERSON TO ME. I TRIED SAYING BYE TO HER AND GAVE HER A HUG AND TOLD HER I LOVED HER…AND NOTHING, SHE DID NOTHING! IT DOESN'T SURPRISE ME AT ALL, I JUST THOUGHT THIS TRIP HAD HELPED, APPARENTLY I WAS WRONG. AMY CALLED ME WHILE I WAS GONE AND TOLD ME SAMUEL HAD BEEN SHOT AND WAS IN THE HOSPITAL, AS SOON AS HE GETS OUT OF SURGERY HE IS GOING STRAIGHT TO JAIL. HOW SAD IS THAT? HE WAS A DICK, BUT HE WAS STILL MY FRIEND. IT'S TIME TO STOP, IT REALLY IS. IT WAS SO GOOD TO COME HOME TO MY MAN. I MISSED HIM SO DAMN MUCH! ADI HAS NOT CALLED ME AT ALL. WE GOT INTO A FIGHT LAST WEDNESDAY AND I HAVEN'T HEARD A THING FROM HER SINCE. IT BREAKS MY HEART. BUT I GUESS I JUST NEED TO GIVE HER TIME AND SPACE RIGHT NOW. JUST GETTING READY FOR BED NOW AND I AM SO DANG EXCITED TO BE ABLE AND GET A GOOD NIGHT'S SLEEP IN MY BED NEXT TO MY MAN! I SLEEP LIKE A BABY WHEN I AM NEXT TO HIM. I CANNOT SLEEP WITHOUT HIM. IT DEFINITELY SHOWED THIS PAST WEEKEND! BUT I DID HAVE A WONDERFUL TIME AND I CAN'T WAIT TO DO IT AGAIN NEXT YEAR. *I LOVE MY SISTERS!*

MONDAY, JANUARY 14, 2013:

WELL, SO FAR, TODAY HAS BEEN AN AWESOME DAY. ADI JUST CAME AND GOT ME AND WE WENT SHOPPING AT WALMART, AND I GOT HER A DAY PLANNER SO SHE CAN WRITE DOWN ALL OF HER HOMEWORK AND SHE GOT JALA SOME CUTE HELLO KITTY THINGS FOR HER BIRTHDAY. WE DIDN'T EVEN TALK ABOUT OUR LAST FIGHT, SHE DIDN'T EVEN BRING IT UP AND I SURE AS HELL DID NOT WANT TO BRING IT UP! IT WOULD JUST CAUSE MORE PROBLEMS. BUT WE ARE FINE AND I LOVE

HER AND I KNOW SHE IS JUST A TEENAGER TRYING TO GET THROUGH HER AWFUL HIGH SCHOOL LIFE, AS SHE PUTS IT. SO, I GOT A CALL FROM MY MOM, JALA IS SICK IN THE OFFICE AND I NEED TO COME AND GET HER. HOW SAD IS THAT? I HATE IT WHEN MY BABY IS SICK. SHE GETS SICK A LOT, TOO, IT BREAKS MY HEART! I JUST GAVE HER SOME CHILDREN'S TYLENOL AND IT SEEMED TO WORK AND PRETTY DAMN FAST. HER FEVER WAS SO BAD WHEN SHE FIRST GOT HERE AND NOW IT'S ALMOST GONE. SHE HAS A BROKEN BLOOD VESSEL IN HER EYE TOO, HALF HER EYE IS BLOODY RED. I FEEL SO STINKIN' BAD FOR HER! I DON'T LIKE IT WHEN ANY OF MY KIDS ARE SICK, I FEEL SO HELPLESS. WE ARE WATCHING THE PROM RIGHT NOW, DISNEY'S "PROM." WE ARE FINANCIALLY IN A VERY TIGHT SPOT RIGHT NOW. I DON'T THINK PAUL HAS EVER HURT LIKE THIS BEFORE FOR MONEY AND I THINK IT'S BECAUSE OF ME. HE COMPLETELY SUPPORTS ME, AND I AM DEFINITELY NOT CHEAP. AND HE JUST BOUGHT CHRISTMAS FOR FIVE KIDS WHEN HE IS ONLY USED TO TWO. WHAT DO I DO, THOUGH? I *WILL NOT* GO BACK TO SERVING, AND I THOUGHT ABOUT DOING NAILS AGAIN, BUT I SOLD ALL MY STUFF AND TO GET STARTED, IT WILL BE AT LEAST $400 TO $500 FOR ALL THE SUPPLIES. THAT'S THE VERY CHEAPEST. GOOD LUCK, NAT!

TUESDAY, JANUARY 15, 2013:

TODAY IS GOING TO BE A GREAT DAY, 'CAUSE I AM GOING TO MAKE SURE OF IT! AND SO FAR, IT HAS BEEN ABSOLUTELY TERRIBLE. PAUL AND I GOT INTO *ANOTHER* FIGHT LAST NIGHT AND LAST NIGHT WAS THE VERY FIRST NIGHT I SLEPT ON THE COUCH 'CAUSE I JUST DIDN'T WANT THE FIGHT TO CONTINUE. WELL, THAT REALLY, REALLY PISSED HIM OFF! AND THEN I SAID SOMETHING SO STUPID. I ASKED HIM IF HE THINKS WE SHOULD TAKE A BREAK. I HAVE BEEN HEARING ABOUT THAT ALL DAMN DAY! WELL, THE TWO TIMES THAT I

HAVE HEARD FROM HIM, HE SAYS HE HAS DOUBTS ABOUT US, BUT, I DO TOO! I DON'T THINK I CAN TAKE MUCH MORE OF THIS FIGHTING AND THE DEGRADING FROM HIM WHEN WE ARE. I LOVE HIM, THERE IS NO DOUBT ABOUT THAT, BUT I JUST DON'T KNOW IF LOVE IS ENOUGH WITH THIS RELATIONSHIP. JALA STAYED HOME FROM SCHOOL TODAY, SO WE HUNG OUT AT MY MOM'S ALL DAY AND I DID LAUNDRY.

MY MOM JUST BROUGHT US BACK HOME 'CAUSE I WANTED TO SEE MY KITTY. I HAVE TEXTED PAUL A COUPLE TIMES, BUT NO RESPONSE AT ALL. I AM REALLY WORRIED. ME AND JALA ARE JUST SITTING HERE WATCHING POPEYE RIGHT NOW. I LOVE BEING WITH MY BABY GIRL, THOUGH, SO THAT HAS PUT A POSITIVE SIDE TO THIS NOT SO GOOD DAY! I'M PRAYING THAT WHEN PAUL GETS HOME, HE WILL HAVE A SOFT HEART AND WE CAN WORK THINGS OUT. *PLEASE, PLEASE, PLEASE!!!*

WELL, TONIGHT WAS ONE OF THE WORST NIGHTS OF MY LIFE! WE FOUGHT FOR ABOUT TWO HOURS, THEN I FELL ASLEEP ON THE COUCH AND WHEN I WOKE UP AT 5:00 A.M., HE WAS BRINGING ALL MY STUFF OUT OF THE ROOM INTO THE LIVING ROOM AND TOLD ME TO STAY IN THERE AND NOT COME INTO THE BEDROOM. FINALLY, I WENT IN, LAID IN BED WITH HIM, AND WE WORKED THINGS OUT. I KNOW, PRETTY FUCKED UP. I HAVE BEEN TEXTING HIM TODAY AND HE ISN'T RESPONDING TO ME AT ALL. RELATIONSHIPS ARE HARD!

WEDNESDAY, JANUARY 16, 2013:

SITTIN' HERE WITH JALA WATCHIN' HER PLAY THE WII. IT'S HER BIRTHDAY TOMORROW AND I AM SO STRESSED ABOUT WHAT TO DO! ADI IS PICKING HER UP FROM SCHOOL, ACTUALLY CHECKING HER OUT FOR LUNCH. HOW CUTE IS THAT? I THINK I AM GOING TO HAVE A BIRTHDAY DINNER FOR HER ON SUNDAY, 'CAUSE SHALL WILL BE HERE AND IT'S JUST A LOT EASIER FOR EVERYONE. SHE IS GETTING SO BIG, SHE IS THE MOST BEAUTIFUL GIRL I HAVE EVER SEEN! MASON

IS IN THE OTHER ROOM PLAYING PLAYSTATION, OR I MEAN X-BOX, WITH "HIS FRIENDS" AND ADI IS UPSTAIRS WATCHING MY MOM MAKE DINNER. SO, MY MOM RETIRED YESTERDAY FROM BEING AT THAT SCHOOL FOR 27 YEARS. SHE GAVE THEM HER TWO WEEKS YESTERDAY. THIS WILL BE GOOD FOR HER, SHE NEEDS A BREAK BEFORE SHE HAS A HEART ATTACK. IT WORRIES ME REALLY BAD BECAUSE SHE IS CONSTANTLY GOING, NEVER, EVER STOPS TO TAKE A BREAK, AND SHE IS 58 YEARS OLD! MY MOM IS ABSOLUTELY INCREDIBLE, THOUGH. I WISH I HAD THE ENERGY OR BE AT LEAST HALF AS GOOD A MOM AS SHE IS! WORDS DO NOT EVEN COME CLOSE TO DESCRIBING HER AND HOW ABSOLUTELY AMAZING SHE IS. I NEED HER AROUND A LOT LONGER, A LOT LONGER! WELL, IT'S ABOUT 8:30 P.M. AND PAUL IS ASLEEP RIGHT NOW, SO I AM GONNA LAY DOWN WITH HIM AND HOPEFULLY GET SOME SLEEP OF MY OWN!!

Eight days later...

THURSDAY, JANUARY 24, 2013:

IT'S ABOUT 11:45 P.M. AND I AM SITTIN' HERE WAITING FOR MY BABY TO GET HOME FROM THE BAR. HE WENT TO SUPPORT HIS FRIEND'S BAND OR SOMETHING LIKE THAT, I TRUST HIM 100% SO I AM FINE WITH IT. PLUS, IT GAVE ME TIME TO GO SHOPPING. I LOVE WALMART LATE AT NIGHT, NOBODY IS THERE. *(Adi remembers Nat telling her that she would often shoplift from Walmart and Smith's late at night.)* I HAVEN'T WRITTEN FOR A LONG TIME 'CAUSE I HAVEN'T HAD THE TIME OR THE ENERGY! PAUL AND I HAVE NOT BEEN GETTING ALONG AT ALL, AND THE PAST COUPLE DAYS HAVE BEEN ABSOLUTELY WONDERFUL! IT'S LIKE WHEN WE WERE FIRST DATING. WE ARE DOING *FANTASTIC!* I JUST PRAY IT STAYS LIKE THIS 'CAUSE I AM A BIT FED UP AND IF HE EXPLODES ON ME EVEN ONE MORE TIME BAD, I AM *WALKIN'!* I

DESERVE A LOT BETTER THAN TO BE TREATED LIKE TRAILER TRASH! I FINALLY REALIZED THAT, AND THANK GOD THAT I DID! I LOVE HIM, BUT I *WILL NOT* BE TREATED BAD! SO, I HOPE HE ASKS ME TO MARRY HIM ON VALENTINE'S DAY OR MY BIRTHDAY. I HOPE, I HOPE, I HOPE! WELL, HE JUST GOT HOME AND I MISSED HIM BAD! I LOVE MY KITTY MORE THAN ANYTHING, MY LITTLE MACY! SO, I HAVE HAD JALA A LOT LATELY AND I LOVE IT. MY MOM'S RETIREMENT PARTY IS TOMORROW AT THE SCHOOL. 27 YEARS AT THAT SCHOOL AND NOW SHE IS DONE. WELL, IT'S ABOUT 4:30 A.M. NOW AND I'M STILL WIDE AWAKE! WELL, I THINK I BETTER GET SOME SLEEP.

She seemed to be all over the place with her thoughts.

FRIDAY, JANUARY 25, 2013:

TODAY HAS ACTUALLY BEEN AN AWESOME DAY. EMILY IS DOING MY HAIR. I AM SO EXCITED! SHE IS GOING TO CUT AND DYE IT AND IT WILL GIVE ME AND HER A CHANCE TO TALK! BUT, ALL IN ALL, IT'S BEEN A WONDERFUL DAY SO FAR. IT'S ABOUT 9:00 P.M. AND I AM GOING TO GET MASON AND PAUL'S SON RIGHT NOW. I GOT MY BOY NOW AND I'M HAPPY! EVEN THOUGH HIM AND PAUL'S SON ARE TOTALLY MAKING FUN OF ME RIGHT NOW. WE ARE HOME NOW, ME, JALA, AND PAUL'S KIDS STAYED AT MY MOM'S HOUSE TO SPEND THE NIGHT WITH MASON. HOW STINKIN' CUTE ARE ALL MY WONDERFUL KIDS! IT'S MIDNIGHT NOW AND WE JUST GOT BACK, AND THE KIDS ARE JUST *FINALLY* LOOKIN' LIKE THEY ARE GOING TO ZONK ANY MINUTE NOW!

SATURDAY, JANUARY 26, 2013:

IT'S ABOUT 1:00 P.M. AND PAUL AND I ARE TAKING JALA AND HIS KIDS TO GATEWAY. I AM TAKING THE GIRLS TO THE

CHILDREN'S MUSEUM AND PAUL IS TAKING HIS SON TO THE PLANETARIUM. MY MOM MADE US ALL BREAKFAST THIS MORNING AND GAVE ALL US GIRLS OUR DVD OF ALL OUR FAMILY PICTURES. I ABSOLUTELY LOVE THEM! THEY ALL TURNED OUT REALLY, REALLY GOOD. I ACTUALLY COULDN'T BELIEVE THAT *ALL* THE KIDS SMILED IN ALMOST ALL OF THEM, NO FUNNY FACES, WELL, EXCEPT FOR A COUPLE OF THEM! TYSON USUALLY MAKES SILLY, SILLY FACES AND HE DIDN'T, I WAS SO IMPRESSED! PAUL STILL WANTS ME TO GAIN 10LBS, BUT THERE IS NO WAY IN HELL! I HAVE ALREADY GAINED LIKE 15LBS IN THE PAST FIVE MONTHS. THERE IS ABSOLUTELY NO WAY I AM PURPOSELY GOING TO GAIN MORE POUNDS. I AM NOW SITTING HERE AT THE CHILDREN'S MUSEUM WHILE PAUL AND HIS SON ARE OUT SHOPPING OR DOING WHO KNOWS WHAT! WHY AM I ALWAYS THE ONE STUCK WITH THE KIDS *ALL THE TIME?* I DON'T MIND IT 'CAUSE I LOVE TO BE WITH JALA AND MOST OF THE TIME HIS DAUGHTER IS FINE TOO, BUT PAUL IS NEVER, EVER WITH ANY OF THE KIDS. I AM! I SPEND WAY MORE TIME WITH HIS KIDS THAN HE DOES! THAT IS SO WRONG ON SO MANY LEVELS. HE WORKS A LOT AND I AM TOTALLY FINE WITH THAT, BUT HE GOES WITH HIS FRIENDS A LOT TO GRAB A DRINK A COUPLE OR THREE TIMES A WEEK. I WOULDN'T CARE, BUT IF I HAVE *HIS* KIDS, THEN IT REALLY, REALLY BOTHERS ME. WE HAVE BEEN GETTING ALONG REALLY GOOD LATELY. HIS DAUGHTER KEEPS TELLING ME THAT SHE THINKS HE IS GOING TO ASK ME TO MARRY HIM ON VALENTINE'S DAY! I WOULD BE TOTALLY FINE WITH THAT.

SUNDAY, JANUARY 27, 2013:

OKAY, WELL THINGS ARE GOING TO CHANGE AND FAST! PAUL AND I WERE DOING GOOD, THEN HE FLIPS OUT! AND THERE WAS ABSOLUTELY *ZERO* REASON FOR HIM TO GET MAD AT ME YESTERDAY! I REALLY AM ON MY LAST STRAW WITH HIM. HE THINKS I AM JUST GOING TO SIT BACK AND TAKE IT AND I

WON'T LEAVE...WELL, HE IS WRONG! I AM SO SUPER CLOSE TO LEAVING, SO, SO CLOSE! JALA WAS SO STINKIN' GOOD TODAY AND ALL DAY YESTERDAY, SHE IS SO POLITE TO EVERYBODY. SHE IS THE SWEETEST, MOST CARING LITTLE GIRL I HAVE EVER SEEN AND SHE'S MINE! I HONESTLY DON'T REMEMBER THE LAST TIME WE HAD THIS MUCH SNOW. WE ARE LITERALLY STUCK AT HOME! MY CAR WOULDN'T EVEN MAKE IT UP THE DRIVEWAY, SO IT'S STUCK AT THE BOTTOM IN THE GUTTER, THERE IS PROBABLY FOUR FEET OF SNOW OUT THERE RIGHT NOW. SO, WE TRIED WATCHING A MOVIE TOGETHER AND GOT HALFWAY THROUGH IT AND STARTED FIGHTING AGAIN! SO NOW HE IS BACK IN HIS SON'S ROOM AND I AM OUT IN THE LIVING ROOM, WHY? WHAT DID I DO TO DESERVE THIS? I DON'T KNOW WHAT TO DO ANYMORE. I LOVE HIM WITH ALL MY HEART AND DON'T EVER WANT TO BE WITHOUT HIM, BUT I CAN'T TAKE ALL THIS FIGHTING ANYMORE AND ALL MY CRYING, IT'S TOTALLY WEARING ON ME. WHAT DO I DO? I FINALLY FOUND TRUE LOVE AND WE CAN'T SEEM TO PULL IT TOGETHER. I WANT TO KNOW IF HE REALLY *LOVES* ME. I THOUGHT HE DID, BUT NOW I REALLY WONDER!

MONDAY, JANUARY 28, 2013:

WELL, I HAD A TON TO DO TODAY AND I DON'T THINK I AM GOING TO BE ABLE GET ANY OF THEM DONE 'CAUSE OF THIS DAMN SNOWSTORM WE HAD YESTERDAY AND ALL NIGHT. I HONESTLY HAVE NEVER SEEN THIS MUCH SNOW HERE. WE PROBABLY GOT OVER 5/6 FEET IN THE PAST 24 HOURS. HOW ABSOLUTELY CRAZY IS THAT? IT'S ABOUT 6:45 P.M. RIGHT NOW AND PAUL JUST GAVE ME THIS GLASS ROSE WITH A LETTER. OF COURSE, I STARTED CRYING, IT WAS THE PERFECT TIME FOR THAT. I REALLY NEEDED HIM TO TELL ME OR SHOW ME THAT HE STILL LOVES ME. HE DOES, I'M JUST SO INSECURE ALL THE TIME THAT I NEED CONSTANT REASSURANCE, WHICH REALLY, REALLY SUCKS! I REALLY NEED TO GET BETTER

SELF-ESTEEM. IT'S SO NOT ATTRACTIVE TO HAVE BAD SELF-ESTEEM, ESPECIALLY FOR A GIRL! I KNOW WHY, THOUGH, IT'S FROM ALL THE MANY, MANY BAD AND HORRIBLE CHOICES I HAVE MADE IN MY LIFE! I NEED TO GET OVER THEM AND NOT MAKE THE SAME MISTAKES. I NEED TO FORGIVE MYSELF OR I WILL NOT BE GOING ANYWHERE IN MY LIFE. PAUL AND I ARE EATING AT THIS NACHO, MEXICAN RESTAURANT IN NORTH SALT LAKE RIGHT UP THE STREET FROM JAY'S HOUSE AND WE CAME HERE TO TALK, BUT NOT DOING MUCH TALKING. *(It sounds like she had her journal with her at dinner.)* I REALLY NEED TO DIG DEEP AND OPEN MY EYES A LITTLE OR A LOT MORE TO REALLY UNDERSTAND WHAT I AM DOING WRONG WITH US. I HONESTLY REALLY WANT TO UNDERSTAND, SO I CAN FIX IT! I LOVE THIS MAN, I CAN'T FUCK THIS ONE UP. I HAVE FUCKED UP ABSOLUTELY EVERYTHING IN MY LIFE, FOR THE PAST 34 YEARS, VERY, VERY BADLY AND PAUL IS THE ONE THING I DID RIGHT, THE ONE THING ALONG WITH MY KIDS THAT TRULY MAKES ME HAPPY. THE ONE THING THAT I WOULD GO THROUGH HELL AND BACK FOR. SO PLEASE SHOW ME WHAT I AM DOING WRONG AND HELP ME FIX IT BEFORE I LOSE THE MAN THAT HOLDS MY ENTIRE HEART!

TUESDAY, JANUARY 29, 2013:

YOU KNOW, I HAVE DONE SOME PRETTY STUPID, STUPID SHIT IN MY LIFE, BUT THIS FEELS LIKE THE SHITTIEST. I KNOW IT ISN'T, BUT I FEEL SO COMPLETELY LOW AND STUPID RIGHT NOW. *(I don't know what this was about.)* THIS DEFINITELY DID NOT HELP MY SELF-ESTEEM AT ALL, AND I NEEDED A LOT OF WORK ON THAT. WELL, PAUL AND I HAVE BEEN DOING WORSE THAN WE EVER HAVE AND WE CAN'T SEEM TO GET OUT OF IT. I KNOW I'VE SAID IT'S BEEN REALLY BAD BEFORE, BUT THIS TOPS IT ALL…IT'S *BAD, VERY BAD!* I JUST PRAY TO GOD THAT I DON'T LOSE THE ONE MAN I AM TRULY IN LOVE WITH! HE IS IN THE KIDS' BEDROOM AGAIN

TONIGHT FOR THE FIFTH NIGHT IN A ROW, AND IT'S 4:30 A.M. AND I STILL CANNOT SLEEP! I NEVER CAN ANYMORE WITHOUT PAUL. I JUST PUT A LETTER UNDER HIS DOOR THAT I WROTE HIM ASKING HIM TO FORGIVE ME FOR ALL THE PAIN AND HURT I HAVE CAUSED HIM AND ASKING HIM TO GIVE ME ANOTHER CHANCE, A NEW START, FORGETTING EVERYTHING WE HAVE PUT EACH OTHER THROUGH. I HONESTLY HAVE *NO IDEA* WHAT HIS RESPONSE IS GOING TO BE, PLEASE GOD, DON'T TAKE THE ONE MAN THAT MAKES ME THE HAPPIEST WOMAN ON EARTH AWAY FROM ME. I TOLD HIM I WOULD CHANGE AND I WOULD FIX ANYTHING AND EVERYTHING THAT I NEEDED TO. PAUL AND I WERE BROUGHT TOGETHER WHEN NEITHER ONE OF US WAS EXPECTING IT, AND FOR A REASON. WE ARE MEANT TO BE TOGETHER, I KNOW, I FEEL IT AND I BREATHE IT! THAT ONLY MAKES SENSE TO ME. I WANT TO MARRY THIS MAN AND STAY FAITHFUL AND TRUE TO ONLY HIM. THERE IS NOT ONE THING THAT I DON'T LIKE ABOUT THIS MAN, HE IS ABSOLUTELY PERFECT IN MY EYES. I CAN'T LOSE HIM! *WON'T!!!* GOOD LUCK, NAT!!!

WEDNESDAY, JANUARY 30, 2013:

I'M SITTING HERE IN THE CENTERVILLE COURTHOUSE 'CAUSE I GOT A DAMN OVERNIGHT PARKING TICKET IN FRONT OF MY HOUSE. I WAS ONLY PARKED THERE 'CAUSE THERE WAS A HUGE SNOWSTORM AND I COULDN'T PULL IN MY DRIVEWAY. I KEPT SLIDING DOWN AND COULDN'T MAKE IT IN. IT'S ONLY A $30 TICKET, BUT I BETTER NOT HAVE TO PAY IT! THIS IS ABSOLUTELY RIDICULOUS! I PLED NOT-GUILTY, SO I HAVE TO COME BACK NEXT WEEK AND SEE THE PROSECUTOR! HOW ABSOLUTELY LAME IS THAT? A BIG WASTE OF MY TIME! SO, PAUL HAS BEEN SLEEPING IN HIS KIDS' ROOM FOR THE PAST WEEK. WE CANNOT SEEM TO GET ALONG AT ALL. I DON'T KNOW WHAT IN THE HELL IS HAPPENING. EVERYTHING I DO IS WRONG AND HE GETS MAD AT ME! I AM TRYING SO HARD

AND ALL WE ARE DOING IS GOING BACKWARDS! I WANT THE PAUL I FELL IN LOVE WITH TO COME BACK! I DON'T KNOW WHAT TO DO ANYMORE, I LOVE HIM, BUT I CAN'T LIVE LIKE THIS ANYMORE. NOBODY COULD! I AM SO SICK OF BEING SCARED ALL THE TIME OF FIGHTING WITH HIM OR LEAVING HIM. I DON'T WANT TO FOCUS THIS MUCH ON A MAN. I WANT TO FOCUS ON MY KIDS, MY KIDS ARE WHERE I WANT TO PUT ALL MY ATTENTION AND TIME AND ENERGY INTO, NOT A MAN! I HAVE HAD ENOUGH OF THOSE, I NEED TIME WITH MY KIDS. I REALLY THOUGHT THIS TIME IT WOULD BE DIFFERENT AND THAT I MET THE MAN OF MY DREAMS. IN A LOT OF WAYS, HE IS THAT GUY, BUT HE ALSO CAN BE THE MAN OF MY NIGHTMARES. I HAVE CRIED EVERY SINGLE NIGHT FOR THE PAST WEEK, AT LEAST SEVEN DAYS, AND IT DOESN'T EVEN PHASE HIM. AM I THAT BLIND AND STUPID THAT I AM IN LOVE WITH A MAN THAT TREATS ME WORSE THAN I HAVE EVER BEEN TREATED AND I DON'T EVEN SEE IT?

THURSDAY, JANUARY 31, 2013:

SO, TODAY HAS BEEN AN OKAY DAY, PICKED UP JALA, THEN CAME HOME 'CAUSE PAUL'S DAUGHTER WALKED OVER, THEN WENT TO MY MOM'S FOR A BIT, NOW JUST CAME HOME. I AM GOING TO MAKE DINNER TONIGHT FOR EVERYONE, SO I NEED TO GO GET SOME GROCERIES. I HAVE BEEN OUT OF BLK *(heroin)* ALL DAMN DAY AND I AM REALLY, REALLY HAVING A ROUGH TIME. I ABSOLUTELY *HATE* THIS FEELING. I REALLY NEED TO DO SOMETHING, AND I KNOW I WILL, I JUST NEED TO DO IT SOON! PAUL CALLED ME TODAY AND TOLD ME THAT WE ARE GOING TO SAN DIEGO FOR A WEEK THE BEGINNING OF MARCH. I AM SO SUPER EXCITED! WE NEED A VACATION, BAD!

IT'S 2:00 A.M. AND I AM JUST BARELY GETTING PAUL TO FINALLY COME TO BED WITH ME. HE HAS NOT SLEPT IN THE SAME BED WITH ME FOR OVER A WEEK. WE HAVE BEEN FIGHTING PRETTY DAMN BAD. THE SAD THING IS THAT HALF

THE TIME WE ARE NOT EVEN KNOWING WHAT WE ARE FIGHTING ABOUT. THOUGHT I WAS GOING TO BE ABLE TO FINALLY SLEEP 'CAUSE HE WAS FINALLY IN BED WITH ME, AND I FOUND OUT THAT HE HAS BEEN LOOKING FOR AN APARTMENT/ CONDO IN PARK CITY, BY *HIMSELF!* MAKES A WHOLE HELL OF A LOT BETTER SENSE NOW WHY HE HAS BEEN TRYING TO FIGHT WITH ME SO MUCH LATELY, 'CAUSE IN HIS MIND, HE HAS ALREADY MOVED ON! NOW I HAVE *ANOTHER* THING TO WORRY ABOUT WITH HIM. JUST WHEN I THOUGHT WE WOULD BE OKAY AND I COULD COMPLETELY FOCUS ON MY KIDS, I FIND THIS SHIT OUT! I AM SO SICK OF ALL THE *BULLSHIT!*

Two days later…

<u>SATURDAY, FEBRUARY 2, 2013</u>:

IT'S ABOUT 11:45 P.M. SATURDAY NIGHT AND I AM SITTIN' HERE IN BED WITH PAUL RIGHT NEXT TO ME, SNORING SO DAMN BAD! DOESN'T REALLY BOTHER ME ANYMORE BECAUSE I AM SO USED TO IT. ACTUALLY, WHEN I DON'T HEAR HIM SNORE, IT REALLY BOTHERS ME 'CAUSE I DON'T THINK HE'S THERE. I HAD A VERY DULL DAY. PAUL TOOK HIS KIDS SNOWBOARDING UP AT THE CANYONS AND I STAYED HOME 'CAUSE I REALLY WASN'T UP TO IT TODAY. I HAD A LOT I HAD TO GET DONE TODAY AND I DIDN'T DO ANY OF THEM. PAUL AND I ARE GOING TO SAN DIEGO IN ABOUT THREE AND A HALF WEEKS AND I AM SO STINKIN' EXCITED! WE DEFINITELY NEED A VACATION TOGETHER. WE ARE GOING TO SEE HIS LITTLE BROTHER GREGORY THAT HE HAS NOT SEEN IN FIVE YEARS. SAD, HUH? WELL, WE ARE STOPPING IN VEGAS ON THE WAY THERE FOR A NIGHT OR TWO AND PAUL ASKED ME IF I WOULD GET MARRIED THERE IN VEGAS WHILE WE WERE THERE…BY ELVIS, AND LATER ON AFTER WE GET BACK, WE CAN HAVE A NICE GET TOGETHER OR RECEPTION FOR ALL THE FAMILY AND FRIENDS OF OURS. HE HASN'T OFFICIALLY

ASKED ME YET, SO I BETTER NOT GET MY HOPES UP, 'CAUSE IF HE DOESN'T SOON, VERY SOON, I WILL BE ABSOLUTELY CRUSHED! BUT BAD NEWS, MINE AND JAY'S DIVORCE IS NOT FINALIZED YET AND PAUL THINKS IT IS! I NEED TO GET ON THAT AND *FAST!*

SUNDAY, FEBRUARY 3, 2013:

IT'S ABOUT 7:30 P.M. AND I AM AT PAUL'S FRIEND'S HOUSE WITH PAUL AND HIS KIDS WATCHING THE SUPERBOWL, BUT OF COURSE, I AM NOT REALLY WATCHING IT, I LOVE THE COMMERCIALS, THOUGH. BEYONCE DID THE HALF TIME AND I DIDN'T EVEN WATCH IT 'CAUSE I DON'T REALLY LIKE HER. SO, PAUL AND I ARE NOW GETTING ALONG A LOT BETTER. BUT EVERY SINGLE TIME I SAY THAT, SOMETHING HAPPENS, BUT I AM GOING TO STAY POSITIVE, VERY, VERY POSITIVE. HE SAID HE FINALLY REALIZED HOW HE HAS BEEN TREATING ME AND HE IS NOT GOING TO TREAT ME LIKE THAT ANYMORE. I REALLY WANT TO BELIEVE HIM, I PRAY THAT HE IS TELLING ME THE TRUTH AND HE DOESN'T TREAT ME LIKE THAT AGAIN. BECAUSE HE IS ABSOLUTELY PERFECT TO ME, OTHER THAN HIS TEMPER! IF HE DIDN'T HAVE HIS TEMPER, HE WOULD BE THE ULTIMATE PERFECT MAN! SO, WE ALL WOKE UP LIKE AT NOON TODAY, VERY, VERY LAZY DAY! I LOVE SUNDAYS JUST BECAUSE OF THAT REASON. SO, I'M STARTING TO DO NAILS AGAIN. I HAVE NOT GOT MY KIT YET OR MY LIGHT, BUT THIS WEEK I AM PROBABLY GOING TO GET IT. I AM ACTUALLY REALLY EXCITED TO GET STARTED AND DO IT AGAIN. I AM GOING TO DO NAILS MOBILE, GO TO PEOPLE'S HOMES. I BET WOMEN WOULD LOVE THAT BECAUSE THEY WON'T NEED TO LEAVE THEIR HOME OR THEIR KIDS. HOPEFULLY IT WORKS OUT, 'CAUSE I NEED TO MAKE SOME MONEY AND REALLY FAST! I CAN'T HANDLE THIS MOOCHING THING ANY LONGER. I ASKED MARIA TO TALK TO PAYNE AT IGGY'S AND ASKED HIM IF I WANTED, COULD I GET MY JOB BACK. HE

TOLD HER IF I CLEANED UP AND CAME AND TALKED TO HIM, THEN I PROBABLY COULD. SCREW THAT, I AM ABSOLUTELY *NOT GOING BACK!*

MONDAY, FEBRUARY 4, 2013:

IT'S 1:00 A.M. AND MY MAN IS PASSED OUT NEXT TO ME IN BED WHILE I SIT HERE WIDE AWAKE (LIKE ALWAYS). I REALLY NEED TO START GOING TO BED WITH HIM EVERY NIGHT, INSTEAD OF STAYING AWAKE 3, 4, 5 HOURS PAST AFTER PAUL GOES TO BED. IT'S REALLY THE ONLY TIME I HAVE WITH HIM TOO, SO I REALLY NEED TO START GOING TO BED EARLY WITH HIM AND HAVE A NORMAL SLEEP SCHEDULE! SO, LAST NIGHT WAS A LOT OF FUN AT PETER'S HOUSE. I REALLY LIKE ALL OF PAUL'S FRIENDS, THEY ARE ALL SO MUCH FUN AND SUPER NICE. HE HAS A LOT OF CLOSE FRIENDS TOO, I MEAN A LOT! THAT ACTUALLY SAYS A LOT ABOUT PAUL. I KNOW HE HAS HIS MOMENTS, BUT PAUL IS AN AWESOME GUY AND I AM VERY LUCKY TO HAVE HIM! MY MOM AND DAD ARE GONE. MY MOM'S LAST DAY AT THE SCHOOL WAS THURSDAY AND NOW SHE IS A *FREE, RETIRED* WOMAN! SO, SATURDAY MY DAD DECIDED TO TAKE HER TO VEGAS UNTIL NEXT THURSDAY TO CELEBRATE HER RETIREMENT. THAT IS A LONG TIME IN VEGAS. I HOPE THEY HAVE A GOOD TIME THOUGH, MY MOM DESERVES IT. SO DOES MY DAD, HE WORKS HIS BUTT OFF. BEFORE THEY LEFT, THOUGH, MY MOM WAS BEING SO RUDE TO ME. I HAVE NO IDEA WHY. I TOLD HER I WAS GOING TO DO MY LAUNDRY THERE WHILE THEY WERE GONE, AND SHE FREAKED OUT ON ME! SHE SAID NOBODY'S COMING IN THIS HOUSE WHILE WE ARE GONE. WELL, EVERYONE IN THE FAMILY KNOWS ALL CODES TO THE DOORS SO THEY CAN GET IN, AND I DON'T KNOW ANY OF THEM BUT THE GARAGE CODE. WELL, THE NIGHT BEFORE THEY LEFT, I SAW MY DAD CHANGING THE GARAGE CODE, HOW AWFUL IS THAT? THEY DON'T WANT ME TO HAVE ANY ACCESS IN THEIR HOUSE AT ALL, BUT EVERYONE

ELSE CAN, EVEN ALL THE KIDS. IT MAKES ME FEEL SO BAD AND DEFINITELY LIKE TRAILER TRASH! *(My parents always had a reason when they changed the codes.)*

TUESDAY, FEBRUARY 5, 2013:

IT'S BEEN A BUSY DAY! GOT UP, MET UP WITH DEBORAH, WENT HOME, GOT READY, WENT AND PICKED UP JALA, THEN WENT BACK HOME, LET THE KIDS PLAY FOR A BIT, THEN TOOK PAUL'S DAUGHTER HOME AND JALA AND I MET UP WITH ADI AT LAYTON HILLS MALL, GOT SOME MAC MAKEUP FOR ADI AND ME, THEN WENT TO PAC SUN TO SHOP FOR DAKOTA 'CAUSE IT'S HIS 18TH BIRTHDAY AND ADI AND I GOT A COUPLE THINGS, CAME HOME, THEN WENT TO MCDONALD'S FOR US, THEN TOOK JALA HOME AND GOT JAY FOOD, THEN MET UP WITH MY BABY AT ORCHARD BOWL AND THE BAR 'CAUSE HE TOOK HIS SON TO KARATE. SO, NOW I'M SITTING HERE WITH MY MAN FOR A BIT. MAS JUST CALLED ME A COUPLE HOURS AGO AND HE TOLD ME HOW MUCH HE MISSED ME AND THAT HE WAS GOING TO CALL ME EVERY DAY AFTER SCHOOL AND EVERY NIGHT. I LOVE THAT KID! HE IS MY HEART! I DON'T KNOW IF I GET TO SEE MY BABY BOY TOMORROW OR NOT 'CAUSE MY MOM AND DAD ARE IN VEGAS AND I HAVE NO IDEA WHEN THEY ARE COMING BACK. *(She could only see Adi and Mas under supervision at our parents' house; she saw Adi a lot more than Mas because Adi could drive.)* IT MAKES ME SO SAD WHEN I CAN'T SEE MY KIDS WHEN I AM SUPPOSED TO. IT LITERALLY MAKES THE REST OF MY WEEK ABSOLUTELY AWFUL. I LOVE MY 3 KIDS MORE THAN LIFE ITSELF AND I *DO NOT* GET ENOUGH TIME WITH THEM AT ALL. I HAVE JALA EVERY SINGLE DAY, EVERY OTHER WEEKEND, AND SOMETIMES WEDNESDAY NIGHTS TOO, SO I GET TO BE WITH HER A LOT AND ACTUALLY GET TO BE HER MOM. ADI CALLS ME AT LEAST TWO TIMES A WEEK TO GO TO LUNCH AND WE GO SHOPPING A LOT TOGETHER, SO I SEE HER A LOT TOO, BUT MASON I

NEVER GET TO SEE, AND I LOVE THAT BOY MORE THAN LIFE ITSELF! I NEED TO FIGURE SOMETHING OUT SO I CAN SEE MY BOY MORE!

2-6-2013: Dr. Note–116 lbs. Prescribed Suboxone

WEDNESDAY, FEBRUARY 6, 2013:

SO, TODAY WAS AN AWESOME DAY. ADI CAME TO PICK ME UP AND WE WENT TO LAYTON HILLS MALL, ATE LUNCH, SHOPPED AT PAC SUN AND GOT SOME AWESOME, AWESOME DEALS, THEN WENT TO BATH & BODY WORKS, THEN HOME, PICKED UP JALA, THEN WENT TO COURT FOR MY STUPID OVERNIGHT PARKING TICKET, THEN CAME HOME, GOT DINNER WITH MY MAN, THEN WATCHED SOME VERY INTENSE GREY'S ANATOMY, CRIED AND CRIED, AND NOW GOING TO BED. WE HAD AN AWESOME NIGHT TOGETHER. I LOVE THIS MAN SO MUCH, EXCEPT I THINK HE'S GETTING IRRITATED WITH ME BECAUSE THE PAST FOUR OR FIVE NIGHTS OR EVEN LONGER, AS SOON AS HE FALLS ASLEEP, I LEAVE FOR AT LEAST A COUPLE HOURS. THE NEXT DAY, HE'LL ASK (NOT PRY AT ALL) WHERE I WENT IN THE MIDDLE OF THE NIGHT, AND I TELL HIM THE STORE, EVERY SINGLE NIGHT, REALLY, HE'S NOT STUPID! I KNOW I SHOULDN'T DO THAT, AND IT LOOKS REALLY STINKIN' *BAD,* BUT WHAT OTHER TIME DO I GO? I HAVE JALA TILL 7 P.M. EVERY SINGLE DAY AND AFTER THAT, I DON'T WANT TO TAKE TIME AWAY FROM PAUL, I BARELY SEE HIM AS IT IS! SO, I FIGURE THE VERY BEST TIME TO GO IS WHEN HE IS ASLEEP, ALWAYS FORGETTING HOW INCREDIBLY BAD AND STUPID THAT LOOKS! I *DO NOT & CAN'T* FUCK THINGS UP WITH THIS ONE! HE IS MY TRUE LOVE AND I HAVE BEEN WAITING MY ENTIRE LIFE FOR HIM!

Adi remembers Nat taking her to buy all new makeup for the both of them during that time. Nat opened a credit card to pay for everything. This bill *went to collections in the amount of $1,300. After Nat received notice from the collection's agency, she asked Adi to pay for it. Adi was 17 years old.*

THURSDAY, FEBRUARY 7, 2013:

WELL, IT'S 6:00 A.M. FRIDAY MORNING AND I HAVE NOT SLEPT ALL NIGHT. I AM GOING TO BE ONE TIRED GIRL TOMORROW. IT'S TOTALLY MY FAULT, THOUGH. I CANNOT SLEEP WITHOUT PAUL NEXT TO ME, AND HE IS IN THE KIDS' ROOM AGAIN 'CAUSE OF ME! I HAVE GOT TO STOP LEAVING IN THE MIDDLE OF THE NIGHT AND COMING HOME AT 3:30 OR 4:00 A.M. AFTER BEING GONE FOR A COUPLE OF HOURS OR MORE. IF I WOKE UP AND PAUL WAS GONE AND I HAD NO IDEA WHERE HE WAS AND HE DID IT EVERY SINGLE NIGHT, I WOULD FREAK THE FUCK OUT! I HAVE BEEN VERY SELFISH, AND I NEED TO START THINKING ABOUT PEOPLE THAT I LOVE AND CARE ABOUT MORE, INSTEAD OF ALWAYS THINKING ABOUT MYSELF. SO, I'M SITTING OUTSIDE ON OUR FRONT PORCH SMOKING AND IT'S COLD AS HELL. IT HAS BEEN THE WORST WINTER THAT I CAN REMEMBER. THIS IS ALMOST IMPOSSIBLE TO DRIVE IN. PAUL GETS UPSET WITH ME BECAUSE EVEN WHEN IT'S A BLIZZARD OUTSIDE, I STILL DRIVE, AND MY TIRES ARE NOT THE BEST IN THE WINTER! THERE I GO AGAIN, THINKING ONLY OF MYSELF WHEN PAUL PROBABLY JUST SITS HERE WORRIED TO DEATH UNTIL I GET HOME. HOW CRUEL CAN I BE? MY MOM HAS THE KIDS THIS WEEKEND SO I'M HOPING AND PRAYING THAT MY MOM AND DAD WILL LET ME SLEEP THERE AT LEAST ONE NIGHT SO I CAN BE WITH MY AWESOME KIDS. JALA IS SLEEPING OVER TOMORROW NIGHT WITH PAUL'S KIDS AND I GET TOTALLY SUPER EXCITED WHEN I GET MY LITTLE PRINCESS OVERNIGHT! I LOVE MY BABY GIRL MORE THAN ANYTHING IN THIS WORLD. ADI AND MAS ARE RIGHT THERE WITH HER!

SATURDAY, FEBRUARY 9, 2013:

ONCE AGAIN, IT'S REALLY LATE, I HONESTLY HAVE NO IDEA WHAT TIME IT IS AND I AM UP WRITING WHILE PAUL IS SOUND ASLEEP NEXT TO ME AND HAS BEEN FOR HOURS. LAST NIGHT WAS A HARD NIGHT. JALA SLEPT OVER AND I ALWAYS ABSOLUTELY LOVE THAT, BUT SHE IS A LITTLE SICK, SO I WAS UP WITH HER TILL 3:00 A.M. COUGHING. I GAVE HER MEDICINE AND LOTS OF LOVES, BUT SHE COULD NOT STOP COUGHING. SHE FINALLY WENT TO SLEEP AROUND 3:00 A.M. AFTER BEING UP FOR ABOUT THREE HOURS, SO I WENT RIGHT TO BED AND DIDN'T WAKE UP TILL 12:30, GOT UP, TOOK JALA TO JAY, CAME BACK HOME, SLEPT LONGER, THEN WENT WITH ANTHONY TO BRIAN'S *(to pick up drugs)*. ANTHONY HAD TO DRIVE 'CAUSE IT'S LITERALLY BLIZZARDING OUTSIDE AGAIN! THIS HAS BEEN A WINTER FROM HELL. CAME BACK, GOT INTO THE BATH, AND NOW WRITING AND FALLING ASLEEP. I CAN'T BELIEVE IT HAS BEEN ABOUT THE MOST LAZIEST SATURDAY I HAVE HAD IN A VERY, VERY LONG TIME. TOMORROW WILL BE BETTER!

SUNDAY, FEBRUARY 10, 2013:

ME AND MY BABY ARE GETTING READY TO GO TO A MOVIE. WE NEED IT, WE HAVE NOT BEEN OUT FOREVER! IT WAS REALLY FUN! WE WENT TO SUGARHOUSE TO THE DOLLAR MOVIES AND GOT A TCBY YOGURT. IT WAS REALLY NICE. THE MOVIE SUCKED, BUT TOGETHER WAS AWESOME! OK, SO NOW I'M FREAKING THE FUCK OUT! I JUST ATE SOME CEREAL AND ATE A LOT OF IT AND HALFWAY THROUGH THE BOWL, I SAW WORMS, WORMS! I THINK I ATE SOME AND I'M SHAKING SO BAD!!! I CAN'T STAND WORMS, BUGS, OR ANYTHING LIKE THAT, AND I ATE SOME!!! WHAT IN THE HELL DO I DO??? AND I LEFT AGAIN TONIGHT, SO PAUL IS REALLY MAD AT ME. I NEED HIM REALLY, REALLY BAD RIGHT NOW. I SHOULD

NOT HAVE LEFT TONIGHT BUT I DID, AND NOW I'M FUCKED. I HAVE TO SLEEP BY MYSELF AND I'M SCARED TO DEATH. I CAN'T BELIEVE THIS HAPPENED TO ME! KARMA'S A BITCH! I NEED TO START THINKING ABOUT THE ONES I LOVE AND NOT MYSELF ALL THE TIME. THIS IS THE REASON I AM WHERE I AM. WELL, HE CAME AND APOLOGIZED AT ABOUT 5:00 THIS MORNING AND HAS BEEN SO GOOD TO ME EVER SINCE. IT WAS MY FAULT, BUT SWEET HIM SAID HE DOESN'T WANT ME TO CHANGE WHO I AM AND ANYTHING THAT I DO THAT HE DOESN'T LIKE, HE WILL GET OVER IT AND USED TO IT. HE LOVES ME FOR WHO I AM! I GET JALA TOMORROW AND I AM SO STINKIN' EXCITED! I MISS THE CRAP OUT OF HER! SO, IT ENDED UP BEING A PRETTY GOOD DAY! I AM JUST HOPING THINGS WILL START LOOKING UP FOR ME, LIKE GETTING MY NAIL STUFF SO I CAN START EARNING MONEY AND TAKING CARE OF MYSELF. THAT WILL DEFINITELY HELP MY SELF-ESTEEM!

Nat's addiction kept her busy all day and night, every day. Between running around to get her drugs, selling, and the time she spent using, it was nonstop.

<u>THURSDAY, FEBRUARY 12, 2013</u>:

WELL, TODAY WAS AN ABSOLUTE HORRIBLE DAY. HAD A GREAT MORNING WITH PAUL, THOUGH, BUT AFTER THAT, IT WENT ALL DOWNHILL FROM ABOUT 9:00 A.M. TILL, WELL, IT'S NOT OVER. PAUL WOKE ME UP ABOUT 6:00 A.M., THEN I COULDN'T GET BACK TO SLEEP, SO I THOUGHT SINCE I WAS ALREADY UP TO GET READY FOR THE DAY AND GET AN EARLY START, SINCE I HAVE A *TON* OF IMPORTANT SHIT TO DO, AND I HAVEN'T EVEN STARTED ON ANY OF THEM! IT FRUSTRATES ME 'CAUSE I HAVE SO MANY WAY IMPORTANT THINGS THAT I *NEED* TO GET DONE *ASAP* AND I JUST DON'T KNOW WHERE THE HELL TO START, 'CAUSE IT'S ALL SO VERY CRUCIAL

THAT I GET THESE THINGS DONE! *(When she talks about her "errands" or important things she needs to do, she is talking about chasing her drugs, using drugs, supplying people with drugs, or other activities associated with her addiction.)* SO, PAUL LEFT TO WORK AROUND 8:30 AND THE BEGINNING OF MY HORRIBLE DAY STARTS. CAN'T FIND MY STINKIN' PHONE ANYWHERE. I LOOKED EVERYWHERE (I THOUGHT) AND NOWHERE TO BE FOUND, SO GOT READY BUT IT TOOK LIKE 2 1/2 HOURS 'CAUSE I COULD NOT HIT *(get a needle in a vein to shoot up)* AT ALL, THEN WENT TO PICK UP ANTHONY AND WE WENT TO SALT LAKE TO A PAWN SHOP TO TRY AND GET MONEY & NO LUCK, THEN WENT TO BRIAN'S TO TRY AND NEGOTIATE WITH HIM, NO LUCK AGAIN. SO, CAME BACK HOME AND LOOKED FOR MY FUCKING PHONE AND FINALLY FOUND IT...INSIDE MY STINKIN' PILLOWCASE! STILL HAD NO MONEY, SO AT THIS POINT, I WAS STARTING TO GET REALLY, REALLY SICK, SO I TALKED TO PAUL AFTER HE HAD BEEN CALLING ME ALL DAMN DAY, BUT COULDN'T GET AHOLD OF ME. I ASKED HIM IF HE COULD HELP ME WITH MY OTHER HALF OF MY SCRIPT. *(Her "script" is her Suboxone. She used this excuse to get money quite a bit with the family too.)* I KNEW I SHOULD NOT HAVE. ABOUT TWENTY MINUTES LATER, HE CAME HOME AND SHIT HIT THE FAN! HE FREAKED THE FUCK OUT ON ME, TOLD ME I WAS LYING TO HIM, BUT GAVE ME $100 (HE WAS NOT HAPPY ABOUT THAT). WELL, HE ENDED IT WITH ME, SO I LEFT 'CAUSE HE YELLED AT ME AND JALA (NOT OKAY WITH ME), AND I HAVE NO IDEA WHETHER WE ARE STAYING TOGETHER OR NOT!

The next day...

<u>WEDNESDAY, FEBRUARY 13, 2013</u>:

TODAY IS GOING TO BE A MUCH BETTER DAY THAN YESTERDAY. I HAVE THREE REASONS WHY...JALA, ADI, AND MAS! AND IT DEFINITELY HAS BEEN! WE HAD SUCH A GOOD DAY.

JALA AND MASON WERE BEING AWESOME TOGETHER. JALA AND MASON WERE BEING SO STINKIN' SWEET TODAY. JALA WAS FOLLOWING MASON ABSOLUTELY EVERYWHERE AND HE LOVED IT! PAUL AND I WENT TO TROLLY SQUARE AND SAT AT THE BAR AND PLAYED SHUFFLEBOARD AND HAD A GOOD TALK. IT WAS AWESOME, AND TOMORROW IS VALENTINE'S DAY AND IT'S GOING TO BE SO FUN! I'M EXCITED! WE ARE GOING TO DO GREAT, I KNOW IT! WE WERE MEANT TO BE TOGETHER. I AM SO GLAD WE WORKED THINGS OUT. SO, I TALKED TO SAMUEL TODAY. I GUESS HE IS ALRIGHT AFTER BEING SHOT. I WAS WORRIED ABOUT HIM, HE IS MY FRIEND. HE GOT SHOT FOUR TIMES IN THE ARM AND GOT THROUGH IT OKAY. I'M SO GLAD AND WOULDN'T WANT OR WISH WHAT HE WENT THROUGH ON ANYONE. THEY PUT THE GUN TO HIS HEAD AND PULLED THE TRIGGER AND IT DIDN'T GO OFF. ISN'T THAT CRAZY, HE ISN'T EVEN SCARED, I WOULD BE TERRIFIED.

THURSDAY, FEBRUARY 14, 2013:

VALENTINE'S DAY!! TODAY WAS AN AWESOME DAY! IT WAS MY FIRST VALENTINE'S DAY WITH PAUL AND IT WAS AMAZING! GOT JALA FROM SCHOOL AND WENT TO MY MOM'S, AND ME AND MY MOM MADE DINNER FOR MY DAD AND PAUL. THEN JALA AND I WATCHED TV TOGETHER FOR A COUPLE HOURS AND CUDDLED. THEN TOOK JALA TO JAY AND WENT HOME. WHEN I WALKED IN, PAUL HAD A PRESENT, A CARD, AND WHITE TULIPS ON THE LIVING ROOM COFFEE TABLE FOR ME. THE SWEETEST CARD EVER AND THE MOST BEAUTIFUL TULIPS. WE ATE DINNER, THEN WATCHED A MOVIE THAT HE BOUGHT ME, AND THEN WENT TO BED.

SO, JALA HAS BEEN HAVING A HARD TIME LATELY AND I HAVE NO IDEA WHAT TO DO ABOUT IT. SO, ALL I HAVE BEEN DOING IS GIVING HER LOTS AND LOTS OF LOVES AND LETTING HER KNOW JUST HOW MUCH SHE IS LOVED. I HATE THAT SHE HAS TO LIVE WITH SPLIT PARENTS. I LOVE PAUL,

BUT SHE IS NOT TOO FOND OF HIM, AND I TOLD MY KIDS IF THEY DON'T LIKE THE MAN I AM WITH, THEN I WOULD DROP HIM IN A HEARTBEAT, BUT I CAN'T, I AM FINALLY IN LOVE, REALLY IN LOVE!

SATURDAY, FEBRUARY 16, 2013:

TODAY HAS BEEN AN INTERESTING DAY. GOT UP TO GET JALA AND JUST HANG OUT THIS MORNING WITH HER, AND THEN I WAS TAKING HER BACK TO DROP HER OFF WITH JAY, JUST DOWN THE STREET, AND WE WERE GOING THROUGH THE LIGHT (IT WAS GREEN) AND SOME 25-YEAR-OLD KID PULLED OUT RIGHT IN FRONT OF ME AND I SLAMMED ON MY BREAKS, BUT I STILL HIT HIM. MY CAR IS MANGLED. THE WHOLE PASSENGER FRONT SIDE IS COMPLETELY OFF, SMASHED IN! LUCKILY, JALA NOR I GOT HURT AT ALL. JALA ACTUALLY SAID, "WHAT JUST HAPPENED?" I CAN'T BELIEVE NEITHER ONE OF US GOT HURT, THOUGH. WE HIT HARD! I WAS GOING ABOUT 45 MPH. IF WE DIDN'T HAVE OUR SEAT BELTS ON, WE BOTH WOULD HAVE WENT THROUGH THE WINDSHIELD! I AM SO GLAD MY BABY GIRL WAS OKAY! I WAS FREAKING 'CAUSE JALA WAS IN THE CAR. IF ANYTHING WOULD HAVE HAPPENED TO HER, I WOULD HAVE KILLED SOMEBODY! I'M SO MAD ABOUT MY CAR, THOUGH! THAT CAR WAS ALL I HAD. I'M GETTING A RENTAL CAR, THOUGH. I HOPE IT'S SOMETHING OKAY. THE KID WAS REALLY APOLOGETIC. I FREAKED OUT ON HIM AND FELT BAD, HE WAS DRIVING AN OLD HONDA CRV, SO IT DIDN'T MATTER TO HIM ABOUT HIS CAR BECAUSE IT WAS A PIECE OF SHIT. NOW, I'M JUST SITTING HERE WITH PAUL'S DAUGHTER WRITING. WE JUST GOT DONE WITH DINNER THAT PAUL MADE US. IT'S ABOUT 8:00 P.M. IT'S BEEN A VERY LONG DAY!

SUNDAY, FEBRUARY 17, 2013:

WELL, TODAY HAS BEEN A PRETTY GOOD DAY. PAUL HAS BEEN ABSOLUTELY INCREDIBLE TONIGHT AND THE PAST COUPLE DAYS. WHEN I GOT IN MY ACCIDENT YESTERDAY, HE CAME RIGHT OVER AND JUST HELD ME AND COMFORTED ME. EVERYTHING I NEEDED, HE TOOK CARE OF. HE IS GOING TO TAKE CARE OF ABSOLUTELY EVERYTHING, SO I DON'T HAVE TO DO A THING! HE SAID MY CAR WILL LOOK BETTER THAN IT DID BEFORE THE ACCIDENT. I HOPE THAT'S TRUE. I DEFINITELY TRUST HIM WITH IT MORE THAN ANYONE ELSE IN THIS WORLD. WELL, IT'S ABOUT 10:30 P.M. AND WE ARE WATCHING A MOVIE WHILE PAUL TICKLED MY BACK AND MASSAGED ME FOR OVER AN HOUR. NOW HE'S ASLEEP AND I'M GONNA GO TO BRIAN'S AGAIN *(to get drugs)*. I HATE IT, BUT I CAN'T GO OUT DURING THE DAY! GOODNIGHT!

MONDAY, FEBRUARY 18, 2013:

WELL, I SURE HOPE AND PRAY THAT TODAY TURNS OUT TO BE A BETTER DAY THAN YESTERDAY! ACTUALLY, YESTERDAY WAS JUST GREAT! ADI IS REALLY STRUGGLING AND IT'S TIMES LIKE THIS WHEN I DIDN'T KNOW WHAT TO DO AND NEEDED ADVICE FROM SOMEONE, ESPECIALLY WHEN IT WAS SOMETHING THIS IMPORTANT, I WOULD CALL SHALL, SHE WOULD ALWAYS HAVE JUST THE RIGHT THINGS TO SAY TO ME TO COMFORT ME AND HEAD ME IN THE RIGHT DIRECTION WITH ALL THE RIGHT THINGS TO DO. IN THIS CASE, I CAN'T. SHE WOULD TELL EVERYONE IN THE FAMILY, AND SHE WOULD JUDGE ADI. SHE IS NOT THE SAME SISTER I HAVE ALWAYS LOOKED UP TO. SHE HAS TOTALLY CHANGED! MY BABY IS SICK TODAY. JAY CALLED THIS MORNING AND SAID THAT JALA HAD BEEN UP ALL NIGHT LONG WITH A BAD EARACHE. SO NOW I HAVE HER AND I GAVE HER SOME MEDICINE AND WE ARE LAYING ON MY BED WATCHING A MOVIE JUST RELAXIN' TODAY, CLEANED

THE HOUSE AND CUDDLING WITH MY BABY GIRL, HOPEFULLY SHE GETS BETTER REALLY SOON.

SO, PAUL AND I HAVE BEEN BETTER THAN WE EVER HAVE BEEN. HE HAS BEEN SO INCREDIBLY GOOD TO ME. I HAVE BEEN IN COMPLETE HEAVEN. THIS TIME IT WILL LAST, I HAVE NO DOUBT IN MY MIND. OUR LOVE IS WAY TOO STRONG TO EVER LET ANYTHING COME BETWEEN US. I AM GOING TO MARRY THIS MAN, AND THIS TIME BE SO EXTREMELY HAPPY! SO, JALA DID SOMETHING VERY CRAZY YESTERDAY. I CAME IN FROM SMOKING AND SHE CAME TO ME AND SAID, "YOU'RE GOING TO BE MAD AT ME," AND I ASKED HER WHAT SHE DID AND SHE SAID SHE CHOKED THE KITTY. SHE SAID IT WAS BECAUSE THE KITTY WAS MEAN TO HER A LOT 'CAUSE SHE WON'T LEAVE HER ALONE. SHE FELT REALLY, REALLY BAD AFTER, STARTED CRYING AND WANTED TO SAY A PRAYER. SHE SAID THE SWEETEST PRAYER SAYING THAT SHE FORGIVES THE KITTY AND THAT SHE WAS SORRY AND SHE WOULD NEVER DO THAT AGAIN. I REALLY HOPE SHE DOESN'T BREAK HER PROMISE TO THAT! I LOVE THAT LITTLE GIRL MORE THAN ANYTHING IN THIS WORLD, AND THE OTHER TWO. MASON IS JUST AWESOME, NEVER EVER HAVE HAD ANY PROBLEMS WITH HIM, EVER! HE IS ALWAYS SO PROTECTIVE OVER ME AND THE SWEETEST LITTLE BOY IN THE ENTIRE WORLD. I AM AT JAY'S RIGHT NOW DROPPING OFF PRINCESS JALA AND JAY IS DANCING FOR ME! *(Jala never had another incident like this. She is very loving and adores all animals. She did not feel comfortable with Paul or like him at all. To this day, she does not have good memories of him and does not like him.)*

THURSDAY, FEBRUARY 19, 2013:

SITTIN' HERE WITH MY BOY AND JALA RIGHT NOW AT MY MOM'S. ADI DIDN'T COME OVER. SHE ISN'T ANSWERING ANY OF MY PHONE CALLS OR ANYTHING. THIS IS NOT GOOD AT ALL. ME AND ADI WERE GETTING SO CLOSE. THIS IS PROBABLY

THE CLOSEST WE HAVE EVER BEEN 'CAUSE SHE IS OLDER AND UNDERSTANDS ME A LOT MORE. I JUST PRAY TO GOD THAT SHE DOES NOT GO DOWN THE SAME ROAD I DID. SHE IS MUCH, MUCH SMARTER THAN I EVER WAS AND EVER WILL BE. SO, I KNOW IN MY HEART THAT SHE WON'T, BUT IT STILL ABSOLUTELY TERRIFIES ME! I HAVE DEFINITELY PUT THAT LITTLE GIRL THROUGH MORE THAN ANY KID EVER DESERVES, ESPECIALLY AN ANGEL LIKE HER. SHE IS A MUCH BETTER PERSON THAN ALL THIS AND I HAVE NOT BEEN THE MOM THAT I SHOULD FOR HER AT ALL OR ANY OF MY OTHER KIDS. WHY DID I DO THIS? WAS IT WORTH IT AT ALL? ABSOLUTELY NOT! I WISH EVERY DAY OF MY LIFE THAT I COULD TURN BACK TIME AND START ALL OVER, BE THE MOM THAT I KNOW I CAN BE (WHICH IS AN AWESOME ONE) AND THE MOM THAT MY THREE BEAUTIFUL CHILDREN ALL DESERVE! I DID NOT WANT THIS LIFE FOR ANY OF THEM. IT'S TOO LATE NOW TO BE A GREAT MOM AGAIN. JALA IS ONLY 7, MASON ONLY 13, AND ADI 16, BUT I HAVE TIME TO BE THEIR MOM AGAIN AND BE THERE FOR THEM AS THEY DESERVE!

Two days later...

THURSDAY, FEBRUARY 21, 2013:

SO, TODAY HAS BEEN QUITE A SHITTY DAY. THIS MORNING WAS AWESOME, BUT AFTER THAT AFTER PAUL LEFT, THE WHOLE DAY WENT TO COMPLETE SHIT! I HAD ANTHONY COME TO GET ME 'CAUSE I HAVE NO VEHICLE YET AND I NEEDED TO GET MY LAUNDRY DONE, WENT OVER THERE FOR A COUPLE HOURS, THEN MET UP WITH SAMUEL AND THEN CAME BACK HOME. WHEN I GOT HOME, I ATTEMPTED TO GET IN THE SHOWER BUT COULDN'T DO IT, I GOT SO EXTREMELY SICK I COULDN'T EVEN GET OUT OF BED. I WAS IN BED LITERALLY ALL AFTERNOON, IT SUCKED! PAUL GOT JALA FROM SCHOOL AND HER AND HIS DAUGHTER PLAYED UNTIL ABOUT

6:00 P.M., THEN I TOOK JALA TO JAY. I DROPPED HER OFF A LITTLE EARLY TONIGHT 'CAUSE I AM JUST NOT DOING SO GREAT. PAUL AND I HAVE BEEN GETTING ALONG SO GREAT LATELY, SO I THOUGHT WE WERE GOING TO HAVE A GOOD NIGHT TOGETHER BUT I HAD TO BE STUPID AND OPEN MY MOUTH ABOUT JANET *(Paul's friend),* AND NOW HE WON'T TALK TO ME AT ALL. HE HAS BEEN COMPLETELY IGNORING ME FOR ABOUT TWO AND A HALF HOURS NOW. YA, TOTALLY CHILDISH, BUT MY JEALOUSLY WAS ALSO VERY CHILDISH. I CAN'T HANDLE TENSION BETWEEN US, IT'S AWFUL. I WROTE HIM A LETTER, BUT HE WON'T READ IT OR HE'S ASLEEP. I AM IN OUR BED AND HE IS OUT IN THE LIVING ROOM ON THE COUCH. I HOPE HE COMES IN TO BED WITH ME TONIGHT, OR I WILL NOT BE SLEEPING. I CAN'T SLEEP WITHOUT HIM AND HE KNOWS THAT, SO I REALLY HOPE HE CAN STOP BEING SO SENSITIVE AND HE WILL COME INTO BED WITH ME TONIGHT 'CAUSE I REALLY, REALLY NEED SOME GOOD REST TONIGHT.

FRIDAY, FEBRUARY 22, 2013:

TODAY IS GOING TO BE A MUCH BETTER DAY THAN YESTERDAY, THAT'S FOR SURE. IT'S MY BIRTHDAY TOMORROW AND PAUL HAS SOMETHING PLANNED, BUT I HAVE NO IDEA WHAT AND I AM SO SUPER EXCITED! WHATEVER HE HAS PLANNED, I KNOW WE ARE GOING TO HAVE A BLAST! WE ALWAYS DO WHEN WE ARE TOGETHER! BESIDES, HE IS DEFINITELY NOT A BORING GUY AT ALL, SO HE ALWAYS FINDS WAY FUN THINGS FOR US TO DO! THAT'S ONE OF THE MANY REASONS I AM MADLY IN LOVE WITH HIM. BUT HE CAN DEFINITELY PISS ME OFF TOO AT TIMES, BUT THE MAJORITY OF THE TIME WE HAVE A TOTAL BLAST TOGETHER. I COULDN'T FIND A BETTER MAN TO SPEND THE REST OF MY LIFE WITH THAN PAUL!

WELL, I WAS REALLY HOPING THAT TODAY WOULD BE A MUCH BETTER DAY THAN YESTERDAY, 'CAUSE YESTERDAY SUCKED! WELL, TODAY IS EVEN WORSE. JUST GOT OFF

THE PHONE WITH DAVID. HE IS OUT OF JAIL FINALLY AND IS CALLING ME 24/7! HE LITERALLY WILL NOT LEAVE ME ALONE! I DON'T KNOW WHAT TO THINK ABOUT ALL THIS. HE IS A GOOD FRIEND AND WE HAVE BEEN THROUGH SO MUCH TOGETHER, BUT IF I START TALKING TO HIM, MARY WILL FREAK OUT ON ME AND THINGS WILL NOT BE TOO GOOD IN MY LIFE! I DON'T WANT TO BE RUDE TO HIM 'CAUSE HE HAS DONE A LOT FOR ME, BUT HE IS ALSO THE REASON I AM WHERE I AM RIGHT NOW! PAUL AND I ARE STILL FIGHTING, AND I TRIED TO MAKE IT UP TO HIM, BUT HE WON'T HAVE IT RIGHT NOW! HE TOLD ME TO GO FAR, FAR AWAY! I HATE IT WHEN HE SAYS THINGS LIKE THAT TO ME. ONE OF THESE NEXT TIMES, I AM GOING TO LEAVE...AND I REALLY DO NOT WANT TO BE WITHOUT HIM AT ALL, BUT I REALLY CAN ONLY TAKE SO MUCH! WHY CAN'T WE JUST GET ALONG? WHY IS IT SO DAMN HARD FOR US?

SATURDAY, FEBRUARY 23, 2013:

YEP, TODAY IS MY 34TH BIRTHDAY AND I DON'T EVEN CARE. THIS IS BY FAR THE ABSOLUTE *WORST* B-DAY I HAVE EVER, EVER HAD! PAUL BROKE UP WITH ME LAST NIGHT AND I HAVE TO FIND SOMEWHERE TO LIVE, FIGURE OUT WHAT TO DO WITH MY WRECKED CAR, AND TRY TO GET OVER THE HURT AND PAIN OF LOSING MY BABY! I CAN'T BELIEVE THIS HAPPENED! IT'S TOTALLY MY FAULT, IT ALWAYS IS! I CAN NEVER SEEM TO KEEP THE ONES I LOVE IN MY LIFE. I LOST MY KIDS, AND NOW THE ONE MAN I AM TRULY IN LOVE WITH. WHAT A BIRTHDAY! I AM PHYSICALLY SICK OVER THIS, I THOUGHT I WAS GOING TO SPEND THE REST OF MY LIFE WITH THIS MAN, AND NOW IT'S OVER! I WON'T BE ABLE TO GET OVER THIS ONE. I LOVE HIM MORE THAN ANYTHING.

IT'S ABOUT 3:30 P.M. AND NOW PAUL IS BEING ALL NICE, HE IS STUTTERING AND EVERYTHING. WHAT IN THE *HELL* AM I SUPPOSED TO DO? ALL I KNOW IS THAT I CAN'T GO

ON LIKE THIS ANY LONGER! I REALLY DON'T DESERVE ANY OF THIS. YEP, BACK FIGHTING AGAIN 'CAUSE I MENTIONED GOING WITH ANGIE AND RANDY TO A MOVIE TONIGHT. I CANNOT FIGHT WITH HIM ANYMORE. THIS BIRTHDAY HAS BEEN COMPLETELY AWFUL! I JUST WANTED TO HAVE ONE GOOD DAY! THAT'S JUST WAY TOO MUCH TO ASK! SHOULD I TRY WITH THIS MAN ANYMORE? I JUST DON'T KNOW WHAT IN THE HELL TO DO. I AM AT A LOSS WITH HIM. I TRY AND TRY AND TRY AND I AM GETTING ABSOLUTELY NOWHERE WITH HIM! I DON'T KNOW WHAT TO DO, I NEED ADVICE!!!

Same day, different journal:

I HAVE A LOT OF JOURNALS THAT I HAVE WRITTEN BUT THIS ONE IS GOING TO BE A LITTLE DIFFERENT! I AM ONLY GOING TO WRITE POSITIVE THINGS IN THIS JOURNAL. AND WHAT A BETTER DAY THAN THIS DAY TO START? MY BIRTHDAY. I TURNED 34 YEARS OLD TODAY AND I AM HAPPY ABOUT IT! A LOT OF PEOPLE HAVE TOLD ME THAT I AM A NEGATIVE PERSON AND THAT I CUT MYSELF DOWN ALL THE TIME. WELL, IT'S TRUE, BUT NOT FOR LONG. I AM DONE WITH ALL THE NEGATIVITY AND MY LIFE IS GOING TO BE MUCH DIFFERENT NOW 'CAUSE I AM GOING TO BE A POSITIVE AND HAPPY PERSON, THAT'S WHO I AM, NOT THE NEGATIVE NAT!

<u>SUNDAY, FEBRUARY 24, 2013</u>:

IT'S ABOUT 5:45 A.M. RIGHT NOW AND I AM HAVING A FABULOUS DAY SO FAR! I AM GOING TO SEE ALL MY KIDS TODAY, HOW MUCH BETTER CAN IT GET? IT REALLY MAKES ALL THE DIFFERENCE IN THE WORLD WHEN YOU THINK POSITIVE INSTEAD OF NEGATIVE. I ALWAYS KNEW THAT, BUT NEVER APPLIED IT TO MY LIFE. WELL, NOW I AM, LET'S SEE HOW MUCH DIFFERENT MY LIFE WILL BE. I AM SO EXCITED FOR THE REST OF THIS DAY! WE ARE HAVING MY BIRTHDAY DINNER

AT 4:30 AT MY MOM'S AND I WILL GET TO BE WITH ALL MY *WONDERFUL* KIDS! I LOVE THEM ALL SO VERY, VERY MUCH! THE ONLY DOWNFALL IS SHALL AND THE KIDS ARE NOT GOING TO BE THERE. THAT'S NOT BEING NEGATIVE, 'CAUSE THEY ARE HAPPY IN SAINT GEORGE. I JUST MISS THEM ALL SO MUCH EVERY SINGLE DAY.

SO, PAUL IS SOUND ASLEEP RIGHT NOW, POOR GUY! PAUL AND I ARE GOING TO SAN DIEGO NEXT WEEK, AND I AM SO SUPER EXCITED TO GET AWAY. WE REALLY NEED A VACATION, WITHOUT ANY KIDS, JUST THE TWO OF US. WE ARE GOING DOWN TO SEE HIS LITTLE BROTHER, THAT I HAVE NEVER MET. PAUL RARELY TALKS TO HIM, SO HE IS VERY EXCITED TO SEE HIM. I'M SCARED BUT EXCITED ALL AT THE SAME TIME. PAUL'S DAD IS DRIVING DOWN WITH US, THEN WE ARE STAYING FOR A WHOLE WEEK, THEN HIS DAD WILL FLY BACK TO WASHINGTON, WHILE PAUL AND I DRIVE BACK. WE WILL BE TAKING OUR TIME DRIVING OUT AND BACK. WE ARE GOING TO STAY WITH SHALL ONE NIGHT ON THE WAY THERE, AND ONE NIGHT ON THE WAY BACK. SO, I GET TO SEE MY FAVORITE SIS IN A COUPLE DAYS. WELL, ABOUT FIVE OR SIX, BUT IT WILL GET HERE FAST. WE ARE GOING TO HAVE A BLAST, I CAN'T WAIT!

MONDAY, FEBRUARY 25, 2013:

TODAY HAS BEEN A PRETTY GREAT DAY! SLEPT IN TILL LIKE 11:00 A.M., GOT UP, GOT READY, WENT SHOPPING TO TARGET WITH MY MOM. MY DAD GAVE ME A $100 GIFT CARD TO TARGET, SO ME AND MY MOM SPENT ABOUT AN HOUR AND A HALF THERE SHOPPING TOGETHER. WE HAD A LOT OF FUN! GOT SOME REALLY COOL THINGS AND SOME CUTE CLOTHES. THEN CAME HOME, CLEANED THE HOUSE TILL THE GIRLS GOT THERE, THEN HUNG OUT WITH THEM, MADE THEM DINNER, THEN TOOK JALA TO JAY. NOW, IT'S ABOUT 8:50 P.M. AND PAUL AND I HAVE BEEN PLAYING WITH MISS MACI *(her kitty)* AND

NOW GETTING READY TO WATCH A MOVIE. I AM SO EXCITED. WE ARE LEAVING THIS COMING SATURDAY TO SAN DIEGO FOR SEVEN DAYS, STAYING WITH SHALL AND TYE SATURDAY AND SUNDAY NIGHT, THEN STAYING THE REST OF THE TIME IN SAN DIEGO! PAUL'S DAD IS COMING IN ON THURSDAY AND DRIVING THERE WITH US, THEN HE WILL FLY HOME FROM SAN DIEGO WHILE PAUL AND I DRIVE BACK! I AM SO SUPER EXCITED! GOT SOME NEW CLOTHES TO GO DOWN THERE WITH AND I GET TO BE WITH MY MAN FOR EIGHT SOLID DAYS, NEVER LEAVING HIS SIDE. HOW MUCH BETTER CAN IT GET! WHEN I GET BACK, I AM GOING TO KICK ASS GETTING ALL MY NAIL STUFF AND STARTING A NEW SOON TO BE HUGE CLIENTELE AND NAIL BUSINESS! I DO REALLY GOOD WORK, SO IT WILL TRAVEL FAST. GOOD NEWS ALWAYS GETS AROUND FAST, ESPECIALLY IN THIS CITY! WE HAD MY BIRTHDAY DINNER AT MY MOM'S YESTERDAY, AND IT WAS AWESOME. ANGIE AND RANDY, OMI AND OPA *(our grandparents),* MY KIDS AND MY MOM AND DAD WERE ALL THERE AND IT WAS JUST A NICE, RELAXING, GREAT TIME TOGETHER. PAUL, MASON, AND DILLON WERE PLAYING BASKETBALL DOWNSTAIRS FOR HOURS, THEY WERE LOVING LIFE!

This is the happiest she seems in all of her journal entries.

TUESDAY, FEBRUARY 26, 2013:

TODAY IS GOING TO BE A FABULOUS DAY! LIVE EACH DAY LIKE IT'S YOUR LAST! (IN A GOOD WAY.) DON'T TAKE THINGS OR IMPORTANT PEOPLE IN YOUR LIFE FOR GRANTED. IF THE PEOPLE YOU HANG AROUND DON'T LIFT YOUR SPIRITS AND ARE NOT POSITIVE PEOPLE IN YOUR LIFE, *DROP* THEM AND FAST! I AM DOING THAT SLOWLY BUT SURELY. CAN'T WAIT FOR TOMORROW, GET TO BE WITH THE THREE MOST IMPORTANT PEOPLE IN MY LIFE! MY THREE WONDERFUL, MOST AMAZING, BEAUTIFUL KIDS, WEDNESDAYS ARE THE *BEST* DAYS! SO, FOUND

OUT TODAY THAT MY DAD HAS DIABETES. THIS MORNING, HE WENT TO THE DOCTOR AND FOUND OUT FOR SURE THAT HE HAS TYPE 2 DIABETES. I KNOW IT'S GOING TO BE REALLY HARD FOR HIM AND THAT BREAKS MY HEART, BUT HE NEEDS TO DO IT! HE WILL, I HAVE LOTS OF FAITH IN HIM, HE'S MY DAD, HE IS THE STRONGEST MAN I KNOW! I AM STAYING POSITIVE AND IT'S BEEN GREAT! EVERYTHING WORKS OUT WHEN YOU ARE THINKING POSITIVE. MY LIFE IS GETTING BETTER EVERY SINGLE DAY 'CAUSE MY ATTITUDE HAS CHANGED COMPLETELY. I AM SO STOKED, I LEAVE FOR SAN DIEGO IN TWO DAYS. EIGHT DAYS WITH MY MAN! HOW EXCITING IS THAT GOING TO BE? I CAN'T WAIT! WE DEFINITELY NEED THIS VACATION. WE ARE HARDLY EVER ALONE, AND WE WILL BE FOR EIGHT DAYS OR LONGER. YAY! YAY! YAY! IT WILL DEFINITELY BE LIKE HEAVEN FOR ME! I AM REALLY GOING TO MISS MY KIDS, BUT I WILL HAVE SO MUCH FUN! I GOT MY RENTAL CAR TODAY AND IT ROCKS!

WEDNESDAY, FEBRUARY 27, 2013:

TODAY, OF COURSE, IS GOING TO BE THE BEST DAY OF THIS WEEK, I GET TO BE WITH ALL THREE OF MY WONDERFUL KIDS! SITTIN' OUTSIDE JALA'S SCHOOL WAITING FOR MY LITTLE PRINCESS TO COME OUT, CAN'T WAIT TO SEE MY BEAUTIFUL BABY GIRL!

AT MY MOM'S NOW WITH PAUL'S DAUGHTER, ADI, MAS, JALA, ANGIE, DILLON, BROCK, AND MY MOM. MY MOM IS MAKING US ALL DINNER RIGHT NOW AND WE ARE HAVING A GREAT TIME HANGING OUT TOGETHER! IT'S ALWAYS A GREAT TIME OVER HERE AT MY MOM'S AND DAD'S. NEVER, EVER A DULL MOMENT, THAT'S FOR SURE! I GOT MY RENTAL CAR, IT'S A CHARCOAL COLORED CHRYSLER 200, THEY TOTALLY KICK ASS! I AM SO EXCITED! I DON'T WANT TO GIVE IT BACK, IT'S SO SWEET! THAT'S WHAT WE ARE DRIVING DOWN

TO SAN DIEGO AND IT'S GONNA BE AWESOME! I FEEL SO DANG COOL DRIVING THIS CAR!

THURSDAY, FEBRUARY 28, 2013:

GETTIN' READY TO GO ON OUR TRIP! ONLY TWO DAYS UNTIL WE GO. I AM SO STINKIN' EXCITED! EVERYTHING IS GOING PERFECT AND I KNOW IT WILL ALL WEEK LONG WHILE WE ARE HAVING A BLAST! IT'S GOING TO BE SO NICE TO BE IN WARM WEATHER. IT'S BEEN SO COLD HERE THAT I DEFINITELY NEED SOME WARM WEATHER AND SOME SUNLIGHT ON MY SKIN. MACI *(her kitty)* IS GOING TO HAVE SUCH A HARD TIME WITH US GONE, BUT PAUL'S SON WILL BE HERE TAKING CARE OF HER AND I TRUST HIM! JALA IS SITTING NEXT TO ME RIGHT NOW PLAYING WITH MY EARRINGS. I ABSOLUTELY LOVE HER! IT'S THE SWEETEST THING EVER! NOW, JALA AND PAUL'S DAUGHTER ARE PUTTING THE BLANKETS OUTSIDE ON THE LAWN IN THE FRONT YARD LAUGHING, COLORING, AND READING. THEY ARE SO SUPER CUTE TOGETHER. THEY ACT LIKE THEY ARE SISTERS ALREADY AND I LOVE IT! ALL THE KIDS GET ALONG SUPER WELL! PAUL AND I WERE DEFINITELY MEANT TO BE, EVERYTHING IS GOING JUST PERFECT AND OUR LITTLE FAMILIES GO TOGETHER JUST LIKE WE WERE ALL MEANT TO BE TOGETHER. WE ALL WILL BE TOGETHER FOREVER! PAUL'S DAD JUST GOT HERE AND IT'S SO GOOD TO SEE HIM. I LOVE THAT MAN SO MUCH! HE IS SO SUPER GOOD TO ME AND JALA. HE IS SO FUN TO BE AROUND, AND HE LOVES ME TOO. IT COULDN'T HAVE BEEN ANY BETTER, THIS DAY. PAUL WILL BE HOME ANY MINUTE AND IT'S SO CUTE TO SEE HIM WITH HIS DAD 'CAUSE THEY ARE SO CLOSE! HE HAS ALREADY STARTED ON MY CAR AND I COMPLETELY 100% TRUST HIM WITH MY CAR, NOBODY ELSE I WOULD EVER LET WORK ON MY CAR, BUT HIM. HE IS VERY GOOD AT WHAT HE DOES, ACTUALLY EXTREMELY GOOD. NOW, JUST WAITING FOR ANGIE TO CALL ME BACK 'CAUSE I NEED TO GO UP THERE

AND GRAB HER SUITCASE FOR ME TO USE ON MY VACATION! SAN DIEGO, BABY!!

FRIDAY, MARCH 1, 2013:

SITTIN' HERE IN MY BED WITH JALA AND PAUL'S DAUGHTER WHILE THEY ARE FALLING ASLEEP. CUTEST THING EVER! WE ARE WATCHING *GLEE*. YEP, SO INTO IT, HOW FUNNY IS THAT? NEVER IN A MILLION YEARS DID I EVER THINK I WOULD EVER LIKE THE SERIES *GLEE*, BUT IT'S REALLY FUNNY WATCHING IT WITH THE GIRLS. PAUL KNEW EXACTLY WHAT HE WAS DOING WHEN HE BOUGHT *GLEE* FOR US. WAITING FOR MISS JALA TO FALL ASLEEP, THEN I AM GOING TO WALMART TO GET TOILET PAPER. LEAVING IN THE MORNING! I AM SO SUPER EXCITED. IT'S GOING TO BE SO MUCH FUN! I CAN'T WAIT! ME AND PAUL NEED THIS VACATION MORE THAN ANYTHING. NO KIDS, JUST ME, HIM AND HIS DAD AND HIS BROTHER. HOW MUCH FUN DOES THAT SOUND? SO, I AM NOT GOING TO BE NEGATIVE AT ALL, 'CAUSE ONLY POSITIVE THINGS ARE GOING IN THIS JOURNAL, BUT SHALL MADE ME REALLY SAD AND HURT. WE TOLD HER ABOUT THIS TRIP A MONTH AGO AND I REMINDED HER ABOUT IT A WEEK AND A HALF AGO, SHE SAID EVERYTHING WAS OKAY AND I WAS SO EXCITED TO SEE HER AND THE KIDS, AND THEN AT THE VERY LAST MINUTE, TWENTY-FOUR HOURS BEFORE WE WERE SUPPOSED TO LEAVE, SHE BAILED ON US. WHICH MEANS, WE CAN'T STAY OVER THERE, SHE SAID SHE WAS WAY TOO BUSY, BUT I AM NOT ABOUT TO LET HER GET ME DOWN OR MAKE ME THINK NEGATIVE AND STAY THERE. I LOVE IT THERE ANYWAYS. THAT WON'T EVEN MAKE A DENT IN OUR FUN PLANS. WE ARE GOING TO HAVE THE TIME OF OUR LIVES AND I AM STILL SO SUPER EXCITED! ALMOST HERE!

I was very concerned about Paul and his father staying at my house. I had only met Paul once and had never met his father. I never knew who Nat was hanging around and I tried very hard to keep my home a safe place. I was not angry at Nat, but I did not feel comfortable letting strangers stay at my home. I had to constantly make decisions to keep my family safe, even though it hurt her feelings. I never saw her when she was in Saint George that time, but we did talk on the phone.

SATURDAY, MARCH 2, 2013:

WE LEFT FOR OUR VACATION AND WE ARE NOW IN ST. GEORGE AT A HOTEL. WE ARE ALREADY HAVING A GREAT TIME. THIS IS GOING TO BE AN AWESOME VACATION. I'M NOT GOING TO WANT TO COME HOME. WELL, I WILL WANT TO SEE THE KIDS, MY KIDS, AND MY PRECIOUS KITTY! IT'S ABOUT 12:30 AND WE ARE IN SAINT GEORGE AT QUALITY INN HOTEL. JUST GOT DONE EATING PIZZA AND THE BOYS ARE PASSED OUT FROM DRIVING 'CAUSE RIGHT WHEN WE GOT HERE AND CHECKED INTO OUR HOTEL, THE BOYS WENT STRAIGHT TO THE LIQUOR STORE. THEY WASTED NO TIME GETTING THEIR DRINK ON! THEY DESERVE IT, THOUGH, WE ALL DESERVE THIS TRIP, ESPECIALLY MY BABY PAUL. HE WORKS HIS ASS OFF ALL THE TIME EVERY DAY FOR THIS FAMILY, HE DEFINITELY DESERVES TO RELAX AND HAVE A FUN VACATION! CAN'T WAIT FOR THE REST OF THE WEEK! PAUL'S DAD IS HILARIOUS AND SO MUCH FUN TO BE AROUND. I AM COUNTING DOWN THE DAYS TILL PAUL ASKS ME TO MARRY HIM! I WILL SAY YES SO DAMN FAST!

SUNDAY, MARCH 3, 2013:

SITTIN' HERE ON THE STEPS OF MY HOTEL ROOM AT THE VIRGIN RIVER IN MESQUITE, NEVADA. HAVING THE VACATION, THE *BEST* VACATION OF MY LIFE! I AM HERE WITH PAUL AND HIS DAD, AND WE ARE HAVING THE TIME OF OUR LIVES. IT COULDN'T BE BETTER! WELL, THE ONLY THING THAT WOULD MAKE THIS TRIP BETTER IS IF WE HAD THE KIDS HERE WITH US! *ALL* OF OUR WONDERFUL KIDS!!

WEDNESDAY, MARCH 6, 2013:

WELL, FINALLY MADE IT TO SAN DIEGO! IT HAS BEEN A TON OF FUN BEING THE ONLY GIRL FOR A SOLID WEEK. THEY HAVE BEEN TAKING SUCH GREAT CARE OF ME! PAUL'S DAD ABSOLUTELY LOVES ME, SO HE IS ALWAYS ON MY SIDE RATHER THAN PAUL'S AND HE TREATS ME SO GOOD! PAUL AND I HAVE BEEN ABSOLUTELY AWESOME THIS TRIP! I WAS A LITTLE SCARED THAT WE MIGHT GET A BIT SICK OF EACH OTHER, AND POSSIBLY FIGHT, BUT NOPE, NOT EVEN ONCE. WE HAVE BEEN TOGETHER NON-STOP SINCE FRIDAY NIGHT AND IT HAS BEEN SO NICE! WE CAN'T GET ENOUGH OF EACH OTHER LATELY, I LOVE IT!

Four days later…

SUNDAY, MARCH 10, 2013:

I AM SO STINKIN' EXCITED TO SEE MY THREE BEAUTIFUL KIDS! THEY ARE THE CENTER OF MY WORLD AND MY WHOLE HEART! I CAN'T PICTURE EVER, WHAT MY LIFE WOULD BE LIKE WITHOUT THEM! I HONESTLY DON'T HAVE ANY IDEA WHY I WAS EVER UNHAPPY. I HAVE THREE WONDERFUL KIDS AND TWO SOON TO BE STEP-KIDS AND ONE ABSOLUTELY AMAZING FIANCÉ. WHAT MORE COULD I EVER ASK FOR? I REALLY WANT TO BE A SPIRITUAL PERSON, AND RIGHT NOW, I HAVE NONE OF THAT IN MY LIFE, SO THAT IS ANOTHER GOAL I WOULD REALLY LIKE TO WORK ON. ALONG WITH…BECOMING A BETTER MOM, A MUCH BETTER ONE, A BETTER FIANCÉ, AND A MUCH BETTER PERSON. I KNOW I HAVE A LONG, LONG WAY TO GO, BUT I WILL TRY MY VERY, VERY HARDEST EVERY DAY FROM HERE ON OUT! YOU GOT THIS, NAT!

MONDAY, MARCH 11, 2013:

IT'S ABOUT 3:00 A.M. MONDAY MORNING, AND OF COURSE, I AM UP WRITING AGAIN! WE WERE AT MY MOM'S PRETTY LATE TONIGHT 'CAUSE WE HAD ANGIE'S BIRTHDAY DINNER AND I STILL HADN'T UNPACKED COMPLETELY, SO HERE I AM! IT'S ANGIE'S BIRTHDAY TODAY, SO WE ARE ALL GOING TO LUNCH AT ROBINTINO'S. I WISH SHALL WAS HERE WITH US, BUT I DON'T FEEL BAD AT ALL, THOUGH, 'CAUSE SHE IS IN SUNNY FLORIDA WITH HER HUSBAND AND KIDS. SHE DESERVES EVERY FUN VACATION THAT SHE GETS! I LOVE HER AND MISS HER SO VERY, VERY MUCH. I REALLY NEED TO SEE HER MORE, THOUGH. SHE COMES OUT HERE QUITE OFTEN, SO I NEED TO TRY AND SEE HER EACH TIME SHE IS HERE, SHE REALLY NEEDS ME RIGHT NOW, BAD! I NEED TO BE HERE FOR HER, AS SHE HAS *ALWAYS* BEEN THERE FOR ME THROUGHOUT MY LIFE. SHE SENT US PICTURES TODAY OF THEM ON THE BEACH, SUNNY AS CAN BE, HAVING A BLAST. THEY DESERVE IT, DEFINITELY. I WANT TO GO TO FLORIDA SO BAD, SOMETIME SOON. MARRY MY BABY FIRST, THEN VACATION TIME! HOW STINKIN' FUN DOES THAT SOUND? WHAT MORE COULD I POSSIBLY WANT? I REALLY DO HAVE AN AWESOME LIFE! I CAN'T COMPLAIN, WE HAD A LOT OF FUN TODAY! ANGIE, MOM, OMI, ME, AND ADI ALL WENT TO ROBINTINO'S FOR LUNCH, THEN ADI, ME, AND ANGIE WENT TO LIZ'S NAILS AND ALL GOT OUR NAILS DONE! I THINK ANGIE HAD A GREAT BIRTHDAY. I GOT HER A BUNCH OF JEWELRY THAT SHE ABSOLUTELY LOVED AND AN AWESOME SILVER JEWELRY BOX, SHE LOVED IT! I WAS HAPPY!

TUESDAY, MARCH 12, 2013:

IT'S ABOUT 9:30 P.M. RIGHT NOW AND PAUL AND I ARE AT 'BOUT TIME WAITING TO GO TO A CONCERT AT THE VENUE. SOME HARDCORE CHIC, I AM ACTUALLY REALLY EXCITED 'CAUSE I HAVE NEVER SEEN OR HEARD ANYTHING LIKE HER!

OKAY, IT'S 3:00 A.M. NOW AND WE JUST GOT HOME A COUPLE HOURS AGO. IT WAS FUN, VERY, VERY DIFFERENT, NOT AT ALL WHAT I AM USED TO, DEFINITELY NOT NATALIE'S TYPE OF CROWD. PEOPLE WERE STARING AT ME ALL NIGHT 'CAUSE I STUCK OUT LIKE A SORE THUMB. I WALK INTO A CROWD OF PEOPLE WITH STUDS AROUND THEIR NECKS, COVERED IN TATTOOS, PRETTY MUCH VERY *HARD CORE* GOTHIC PEOPLE WITH A WHITE BOW IN MY HAIR, DESIGNER JEANS, AEROPOSTALE SHIRT AND JACKET AND THE KILLER WAS MY HIGH HEELS! I AM A PRISSY GIRL WALKING INTO THE DEVIL'S HOUSE! YA, I DEFINITELY DID NOT FIT IN AND USUALLY I WOULD CARE, I COULD CARE LESS TONIGHT! IT WAS GREAT! WE HAD AN AWESOME NIGHT AND PAUL PROTECTED ME LIKE I HAVE NEVER SEEN A MAN PROTECT HIS WIFE BEFORE. *(It really sounds like she believed she was his wife, even though they were not married.)* WE WERE IN THE MIDDLE OF A HUGE MOSH PIT AND PAUL DID NOT LET ONE PERSON GET NEAR ME OR BUMP ME IN ANY WAY. HE WAS TAKING THE HARDEST HITS IN HIS BACK FROM PEOPLE GETTING PUSHED INTO HIM AND HE DIDN'T EVEN FLINCH, HE WAS SO CONCERNED ABOUT ME AND MAKING SURE I WAS OKAY. IT WAS DEFINITELY AN EXPERIENCE I HAVE NEVER HAD BEFORE.

3-15-2013: Dr. Note–119 lbs. No relapse. DOPL *(Department of Occupational and Professional Licensing)* report ran consistent with treatment. *(This doctor was under investigation by DOPL. Someone reported him to the licensing committee and now he had to follow certain protocols.)* Natalie was in ER December 2012 for abscess in hip but no prescriptions. Prescribed Suboxone.

WEDNESDAY, MARCH 13, 2013:

TODAY WAS ANOTHER FANTASTIC DAY! PAUL AND I WOKE UP AT 2:00 IN THE AFTERNOON AND IT WAS GREAT! WE BOTH HAVE NOT SLEPT IN LIKE THAT IN A VERY, VERY LONG TIME. WE

BOTH REALLY NEEDED THE SLEEP! AFTER WE FINALLY WOKE UP, I WENT TO PICK UP LITTLE MISS JALA AND WENT OVER TO MY MOM'S, WHERE MY OTHER TWO AMAZING KIDS WERE AT. SPENT THE AFTERNOON WITH ALL THREE OF THOSE PERFECT LITTLE PEOPLE. JALA WAS BEING EXTRA, EXTRA GOOD THIS DAY. SHE WAS HELPING EVERYBODY OUT, IF ANYBODY NEEDED ANYTHING AT ALL, JALA WAS ON IT! HOW ABSOLUTELY SWEET IS THAT? SO, I AM REALLY LIKING THIS POSITIVE JOURNAL THING. WHEN I LOOK BACK AND READ WHAT I HAVE ALREADY WROTE, IT'S INCREDIBLE AND GIVES ME THE HIGHEST HOPES, MORE THAN I ALREADY HAVE! IT MAKES ME REALIZE ALSO JUST HOW GREAT MY LIFE IS! SUCH AN AWESOME FEELING, I AM SO SUPER HAPPY!

SATURDAY, MARCH 16, 2013:

IT HAS BEEN A WONDERFUL DAY SO FAR! JALA SLEPT OVER WITH ME LAST NIGHT AND IT FELT LIKE I HAD PART OF MY WHOLE FAMILY BACK! I FEEL COMPLETE WHEN MY BEAUTIFUL KIDS ARE WITH ME WHERE THEY SHOULD BE. I WOKE UP, WENT TO THE GROCERY STORE TO GET WAFFLES FOR JALA, THEN CAME BACK HOME, GOT JALA READY FOR THE DAY, WENT AND RAN A COUPLE ERRANDS WITH PAUL'S KIDS AND MY PRECIOUS JALA, THEN TOOK THEM TO GET SOME FOOD, THEN WE HAD A PICNIC AT THE PARK UNTIL PAUL GOT HOME. PAUL GOT HOME AND WE WENT TO ALL-A-DOLLAR AND GRABBED A COUPLE THINGS, NOW WE JUST PICKED UP PAPA MURPHY'S PIZZA AND GOT SOME MOVIES AND I'M THINKIN' WE AREN'T GOING OUT ANYMORE TONIGHT AND I AM TOTALLY, TOTALLY FINE WITH THAT. JUST RELAXIN' WITH THE FAMILY, WHAT COULD POSSIBLY BE ANY BETTER? JUST A FEW MORE PEOPLE HERE WITH US, ADI, MAS, & JALA, AND THE NIGHT WOULD BE ABSOLUTELY PERFECT! SOON, I KNOW IT, SOON! I HAVE

SO MUCH ON MY PLATE, BUT I ALWAYS DO AND SO DOES EVERYBODY ELSE, BUT I AM SO SUPER HAPPY! I HAVEN'T BEEN THIS HAPPY IN A VERY, VERY LONG TIME. IT'S SO NICE TO HAVE SO MUCH GOING ON IN MY LIFE AND I CAN HANDLE IT. I CAN HANDLE MY STRESS, NEVER BEEN ABLE TO DO THAT BEFORE, NEVER. HAVE REALLY LEARNED A LOT THE PAST YEAR AND I GIVE SOME OF THE CREDIT TO PAUL 'CAUSE HE HAS TAUGHT ME A WHOLE LOT. THE BEST IS, HE HAS MADE ME GRATEFUL FOR EACH AND EVERY DAY AND THAT I CAN SEE THE SUN RISE EACH DAY!

She seems to be handling stress well and was so happy.

SUNDAY, MARCH 17, 2013:

TODAY IS GOING TO BE A RELAXING, LAZY DAY AND I AM SO LOOKING FORWARD TO IT. SO, EVERYDAY JUST KEEPS GETTING BETTER AND BETTER. I THINK IT'S BECAUSE I HAVE COMPLETELY CHANGED MY ATTITUDE TOWARDS LIFE AND ME IN GENERAL. STAY POSITIVE AND TRY NOT TO COMPLAIN, 'CAUSE APPARENTLY, I DID A WHOLE LOT! AND IT'S BEEN SO MUCH NICER. I DID NOT LIKE BEING A NEGATIVE PERSON, IT GETS YOU ABSOLUTELY NOWHERE! I DON'T KNOW WHAT WE ARE GOING TO DO TODAY, BUT I KNOW WE WILL HAVE AN AWESOME DAY. IT WOULD BE EVEN BETTER, ACTUALLY *PERFECT,* IF I HAD THE THREE MOST IMPORTANT PEOPLE IN MY LIFE HERE WITH US. MY KITTY, THE MOST CUTEST KITTY IN THIS WORLD, IS CUDDLING WITH ME RIGHT NOW WHILE I WRITE. SHE BRIGHTENS UP MY DAY EVERY TIME I WALK IN THE DOOR AFTER BEING GONE. SHE RUNS TO GREET ME AND WON'T LEAVE MY SIDE PRETTY MUCH THE REST OF THE DAY. SHE IS *BY FAR* THE *BEST* ANIMAL I HAVE EVER HAD! I LOVE HER TO PIECES!

MONDAY, MARCH 18, 2013:

SO, PAUL AND I HAD HIS KIDS WITH US ALL WEEKEND, SO WE DIDN'T GET TO SEE MUCH OF EACH OTHER, SO HE TOOK ME OUT TONIGHT TO THE GARAGE, A COOL, COOL BAR AND WE HAD A BLAST! NO SURPRISE THOUGH, WE ALWAYS DO WHEN WE GO OUT! THIS PLACE IS AWESOME, THOUGH, WE ARE ACTUALLY THINKING ABOUT HAVING OUR WEDDING THERE. VERY, VERY STRONGLY THINKING ABOUT IT. IT'S JUST RIGHT BY MY DAD'S WORK ON BECK STREET. IT DOESN'T LOOK THE GREATEST ON THE OUTSIDE, BUT ON THE INSIDE, IT *ROCKS!* AND THEY HAVE A NEW PATIO OUT BACK THAT KICKS ASS! I'M NOT EVEN KIDDING, IT WOULD BE ABSOLUTELY *FABULOUS* TO GET MARRIED TO THE COOLEST GUY ON THE EARTH AT THE "GARAGE" IN SALT LAKE CITY. OH, AND IT'S SO OUR NEW HANG OUT! IT'S MINE AND MY MAN'S PLACE NOW! JUST "OURS"! IT WAS DEFINITELY A NIGHT TO REMEMBER. WE ATE DINNER AND THE FOOD ROCKED, WHICH IS WEIRD AT A BAR, AND WE PLAYED THIS TRIVIA GAME FOR AT LEAST TWO HOURS OR MORE, WE ENTERTAIN EACH OTHER VERY EASY, WE JUST HAVE SO MUCH STINKIN' FUN TOGETHER! REALLY, PAUL AND I ARE DEFINITELY A KICK ASS PAIR! GOT HOME, STARTED TO WATCH A MOVIE BUT WE TALKED INSTEAD, WHICH ACTUALLY HAPPENS QUITE OFTEN, GOT SLEEPY, LAID DOWN FOR A COUPLE MINUTES, AND OF COURSE, IT WAS PAST 10:00 P.M. SO MY BABY WAS OUT COLD! SO, I GOT IN THE BATH, CLEANED UP, GOT ALL READY FOR BED, NOW I AM GOING TO CURL UP NEXT TO MY SLEEPY MAN AND HAVE A GOOD NIGHT'S SLEEP. I AM A HAPPY WOMAN!

TUESDAY, MARCH 19, 2013:

VERY, VERY TIRED TODAY 'CAUSE I GOT ZERO SLEEP LAST NIGHT, AND I'M TOTALLY OK WITH IT! WE HAD A VERY GOOD NIGHT! WE HAVE BEEN HAVING A LOT OF THAT LATELY! WE

ARE JUST GREAT TOGETHER! I AM REALLY EXCITED TO DO NAILS AGAIN! I THINK WE ARE GOING TO GET MY STUFF VERY, VERY SOON. THEN, MONEY MAKING TIME! IT'S REALLY HARD TAKING MONEY FROM PAUL ALL THE TIME. HE IS SO GOOD TO ME AND NEVER, EVER COMPLAINS, BUT HE WORKS HIS ASS OFF EVERY DAY AND HAS TO KEEP HANDING ME OVER MONEY EVERY DAY! I GET TO BE WITH ALL MY KIDS TOMORROW AND I'M SUPER EXCITED! I AM GOING TO MAKE DINNER FOR EVERYONE (HOPE I DON'T BURN ANYTHING) AND JUST HANG OUT. MAYBE TAKE MY THREE SWEET BABIES TO GET AN ICE CREAM OR SOMETHING AFTER SCHOOL. WHATEVER IT IS, I AM JUST SUPER EXCITED TO SEE MY BABIES!

A few days later...

FRIDAY, MARCH 22, 2013:

RUNNIN', RUNNIN' LIKE CRAZY TODAY! BUT THAT'S WHAT I LIKE. I AM NOT THE KIND OF PERSON THAT JUST SITS AT HOME ALL DAY. I ALWAYS HAVE TO BE DOING SOMETHING. MY PRECIOUS LITTLE JALA IS SLEEPING OVER WITH ME TONIGHT. I LOVE IT WHEN MY PRINCESS IS HERE WITH ME. I THINK I GET TO SPEND SOME TIME WITH MY OTHER TWO FAVORITE PEOPLE IN THIS WORLD THIS WEEKEND (ADI AND MAS, OF COURSE)! WELL, GOOD NEWS, SHALL HAS BEEN IN THE HOSPITAL THIS WHOLE WEEK WITH HEART PROBLEMS, APPARENTLY LAST WEEK SHE FELL IN SHOWER (BLACKED OUT), FELL, AND BROKE HER NOSE. SHE DIDN'T GO STRAIGHT TO THE HOSPITAL, BUT WHEN SHE DID, A COUPLE DAYS LATER, THEY FOUND OUT THINGS WEREN'T GOING WELL WITH HER HEART. WE WERE ALL FREAKED OUT, *BAD!* MY MOM FLEW RIGHT OUT THERE AND STAYED WITH HER AND WHEN TYE WAS WITH HER, SHE WENT HOME WITH THE KIDS. WELL, SHE HAD A COUPLE SURGERIES AND SHE IS HOME NOW DOING A LOT BETTER. SHE CAN MAKE IT THROUGH ANYTHING, THOUGH. SHE IS MY

IDOL, ALWAYS HAS BEEN, ALWAYS WILL. PLUS, GOD WOULD NEVER DO THAT TO ME, LET ANYTHING HAPPEN TO MICHELLE, 'CAUSE GOD KNOWS I COULDN'T MAKE IT THROUGH THAT! BUT A COUPLE GOOD THINGS CAME OUT OF IT…SHE IS GOING TO SLOW DOWN A BIT, SHE GOES NON-STOP, JUST LIKE MY MOM DOES. THEY ARE A LOT ALIKE, SHALL FINALLY ADMITS TO THAT! GONNA GET SOME SLEEP NOW, PAUL AND I HAVE A LONG FUN DAY AHEAD OF US TOMORROW!

SATURDAY, MARCH 23, 2013:

TODAY WAS AN AWESOME DAY. WENT TO THE CANYONS WITH PAUL AND MET SOME MORE OF HIS FRIENDS AND WENT TO A CONCERT. IT WAS OUTSIDE AND IT WAS SNOWING, ACTUALLY BLIZZARDING, THE WHOLE TIME, BUT IT WAS OKAY, IT WAS FREEZING COLD BUT PAUL HELD ME THE ENTIRE TIME TRYING TO KEEP ME WARM, SO IT WAS OKAY. HIS FRIEND WAS THE ONE WHO GOT US UP THERE, HE'S A BIT DIFFERENT, BUT NICE. I AM SO EXCITED FOR TOMORROW 'CAUSE I GET TO SPEND THE DAY WITH MY BOY! I LOVE THAT KID WITH ALL MY HEART AND SOUL, HE IS MY HEART! HE IS HONESTLY THE *BEST* LITTLE BOY A MOTHER COULD EVER ASK FOR! PAUL IS LAYING RIGHT NEXT TO ME OUT COLD AND HE IS SO STINKIN' CUTE! YESTERDAY, HE BROUGHT HOME FOR ME A NEW COUCH, A REALLY NICE SECTIONAL AND A KITCHEN TABLE. NOW IT FINALLY FEELS LIKE A HOME. IT DID BEFORE, BUT NOW EVEN MORE. I AM SO HAPPY! SO, WE ARE ON THE NEW COUCH, WHICH HAS A RECLINER AND A BED, JALA AND HIS DAUGHTER SLEPT ON THE COUCH BED LAST NIGHT AND THEY BOTH SAID HOW COMFY IT WAS. I AM SO EXCITED, IT ACTUALLY MAKES OUR LIVING ROOM BIGGER. I BETTER TRY AND GET HIM UP NOW TO GO TO BED, EVEN THOUGH IT'S VERY CHALLENGING TO DO THAT! GOOD LUCK, NAT!

SUNDAY, MARCH 24, 2013:

HEADING OVER TO MY MOM'S RIGHT NOW FOR DINNER AND TO HANG OUT WITH THE TWO COOLEST KIDS IN THIS WORLD! THE CUTEST THING EVER...WE JUST GOT DONE EATING AND PAUL IS OUTSIDE PLAYING WITH JUSTIN AND MASON AND DILLON. HE IS SO STINKIN' CUTE WITH MY KIDS. IT LITERALLY MELTS ME! ADI, KAILEE, AND I WATCHED A REALLY GOOD MOVIE TOGETHER, IT WAS CALLED SPARKLE AND ADI LAID ON MY LAP THE ENTIRE TIME, IT WAS AWESOME! THAT IS MY FAVORITE THING IN THIS WORLD TO SPEND TIME WITH MY KIDS! JUST GOT HOME, IT'S ABOUT 7:00 AND PAUL AND I ARE SITTING DOWN WATCHING A MOVIE. EVEN THOUGH WE REALLY DON'T NEED ANYTHING TO ENTERTAIN US, WE DO JUST GREAT ALONE WITH EACH OTHER. EMILY WAS OVER AT MY MOM'S AND SHE WAS ACTUALLY TALKING TO ME! IT HAS BEEN YEARS THAT I HAVE BEEN TRYING TO GET MY LITTLE SISTER TO TALK TO ME, AND SHE FINALLY IS! I KNOW SHE'S STILL NOT OKAY WITH ME, BUT AT LEAST THIS IS A START! I WOULD GIVE ANYTHING TO HAVE A RELATIONSHIP WITH MY LITTLE SISTER AGAIN. IT WILL HAPPEN. I HAVE FAITH ON THIS ONE. SO, OMI WROTE ME A LETTER TODAY AND GAVE IT TO ME AT MY MOM'S. I AM VERY INTERESTED TO SEE WHAT IT SAYS. IT'S THREE PAGES LONG, LOOKS PRETTY INTENSE! GOTTA GET SOME SLEEP, BIG DAY TOMORROW! SMILE AND BE POSITIVE AND EVERYTHING WILL WORK OUT FOR THE BETTER!

Omi, our grandmother, would often write letters to us when we were struggling in life. She would offer advice, and on many occasions, helped me make different choices that were better for me. She lived very close to us, and we saw her all the time.

MONDAY, MARCH 25, 2013:

SITTIN' OUTSIDE ON THE LAWN CHAIR AT MY MOM'S WATCHING JALA DRAW WITH OUTSIDE CHALK. PAUL PICKED HER UP FROM SCHOOL AND BROUGHT US BOTH DOWN HERE SO HE COULD GO BACK TO THE AIRPORT FOR A COUPLE HOURS. I HAD TO TAKE THE RENTAL CAR BACK, SO I AM STUCK WITHOUT A CAR. IT'S FINE, THOUGH, I GET MY CAR BACK IN ABOUT A WEEK, I CAN HANDLE IT TILL THEN. I AM SO EXCITED TO GET MY CAR BACK, I CAN HARDLY STAND IT! PAUL AND I ARE GOING TO SEE A MOVIE TONIGHT, I'M EXCITED AS ALWAYS, WE HAVE SO MUCH FUN TOGETHER! IT'S STILL PRETTY COLD OUTSIDE, IT SNOWED A COUPLE DAYS AGO, SO WE ARE GOING INSIDE TO HANG OUT NOW.

TUESDAY, MARCH 26, 2013:

WASN'T FEELING ALL THAT GREAT TODAY, SO I LITERALLY SLEPT ALL DAY. WHEN PAUL GOT HOME, HE TOTALLY TOOK CARE OF ME AND WHEN JALA GOT HERE, WE JUST RESTED AND WATCHED A MOVIE TOGETHER. IT ALWAYS MAKES ME HAPPY, THOUGH, WHENEVER I AM WITH ANY OF MY KIDS. WHETHER I AM SICK OR DOING NOTHING AT ALL, IF I HAVE MY CUTE KIDS, ANY OF THEM, I AM *GREAT!* STILL REALLY SLEEPY 'CAUSE I HAVEN'T BEEN FEELING SO GOOD, SO TONIGHT IS GOING TO BE AN EARLY NIGHT. GOODNIGHT, SWEET DREAMS!

WEDNESDAY, MARCH 27, 2013:

TODAY WAS ANOTHER DAY BEING LAZY. HAVEN'T BEEN FEELING ALL THAT GOOD SO I HAVE JUST BEEN RESTING. PAUL IS TAKING ME OUT TONIGHT TO SEE BOONDOCK SAINTS AT BREWVIE'S. EVERY WEEK THERE, THEY HAVE A FREE MOVIE NIGHT AND WE ALWAYS TRY AND GO TO THEM IF THEY ARE DECENT MOVIES. WELL, THIS ONE DEFINITELY IS. I HAVEN'T

SEEN IT FOR A LONG TIME, SO IT WILL BE EVEN BETTER. MASON JUST CALLED ME AND TOLD ME THAT I HAVE HIM HIS WHOLE BIRTHDAY!!! IT'S A FRIDAY NIGHT SO WE ARE GOING TO HAVE A BIG BIRTHDAY PARTY AT MY MOM'S HOUSE, THEN I AM GOING TO SPEND THE NIGHT AT MY MOM'S WITH HIM. I GET HIM THE ENTIRE DAY!! I AM SO EXCITED, ESPECIALLY SINCE I DON'T GET TO SEE HIM THIS WEEK 'CAUSE I HAVEN'T BEEN FEELING SO HOT, IT WILL GO AWAY FAST, I KNOW IT! SEE, I AM ALREADY STARTING TO FEEL A LITTLE BETTER WHEN I KNOW I GET TO SEE MY KIDS SOON, IT ALWAYS MAKES ME BETTER, NO MATTER WHAT I AM GOING THROUGH! ADI'S SO SWEET, SHE HAS BEEN CALLING ME ALL DAY LONG TO CHECK ON ME. I DIDN'T ANSWER HER CALLS 'CAUSE I WAS SLEEPING, SO SHE CALLED PAUL TO SEE IF I WAS OKAY. HOW SWEET IS THAT? SHE IS SO DARLING! WELL, SHE IS CALLING ME RIGHT NOW, SO I NEED TO TALK TO MY BABY FOR A MINUTE. SHE FOUND HER PROM DRESS, $300, PAUL IS TAKING HER, HOW STINKIN' CUTE IS THAT? IT MELTS MY HEART! HE IS SO WONDERFUL WITH MY KIDS, "OUR KIDS"!

THURSDAY, MARCH 28, 2013:

SO, EVEN THOUGH I WAS A LITTLE SICK, WE HAD A LOT OF FUN LAST NIGHT! WE WENT TO BREWVIE'S (A CHILL MOVIE THEATRE THAT YOU CAN EAT AND DRINK IN) AND WATCHED BOONDOCK SAINTS. I ABSOLUTELY LOVE THAT SHOW AND HAVEN'T SEEN IT FOR A VERY LONG TIME. IT WAS NICE AND RELAXING. WE ARE GOING TO TRY AND GO TO THE FREE MOVIE NIGHT EVERY WEEK, WE NEED IT! WE ARE GOING RIGHT NOW TO GRAB ME THE BROWNIE SUNDAE THAT I AM ALWAYS CRAVING AT CHILI'S, HOW PATHETIC IS THAT? IT'S ABOUT 8:00 P.M. AND WE ARE JUST SITTING DOWN GETTING READY TO WATCH A MOVIE. I KNOW NEITHER ONE OF US ARE GOING TO MAKE IT THROUGH THE WHOLE MOVIE BECAUSE WE ARE BOTH SO STINKIN' TIRED! WE HAVE ALL THE KIDS THIS WEEKEND

AND JALA OVERNIGHT ON FRIDAY. I AM WAY EXCITED! I LOVE IT WHEN SHE SLEEPS OVER! SO, IT'S JUST STARTING TO GET WARM OUTSIDE! YAY! SUNDRESS WEATHER, I LOVE IT! WELL, WE ARE GETTING READY TO WATCH OUR MOVIE, THAT WE MOST LIKELY WON'T GET THROUGH!

FRIDAY, MARCH 29, 2013:

SITTING OUTSIDE WATCHING JALA AND PAUL'S DAUGHTER PLAY. IT'S ABOUT 3:30 AND WE ARE JUST PLAYIN' OUTSIDE TILL I GET DINNER STARTED. I HAVEN'T TALKED TO SHALL IN A WHILE, BUT I THINK SHE IS DOING A LOT BETTER AFTER HER SURGERY.

IT'S ABOUT 11:30 P.M. AND WE HAD A FUN NIGHT. TOOK PAUL TO THE GOLF COURSE, THEN CAME BACK, GOT HIS KIDS AND PRINCESS JALA AND TOOK THEM TO ALL-A-DOLLAR TO GET EGG DYE STUFF. MASON CALLED WHILE WE WERE SHOPPING WONDERING WHAT WE WERE DOING SO I TOOK THEM ALL TO MY MOM'S, WE COLORED EGGS AND HUNG OUT. PAUL'S SON SLEPT OVER WITH MAS, AND PAUL GOT DROPPED OFF AT MY MOM'S. WE CAME BACK HOME, GOT JALA IN THE BATH, WATCHED A MOVIE, PAINTED THE GIRLS' FINGERNAILS, AND NOW PAUL AND I ARE JUST GETTING INTO BED. WE HAVE A LONG DAY TOMORROW, SO WE BETTER GET SOME SLEEP! GOODNIGHT!

SATURDAY, MARCH 30, 2013:

SO, OF COURSE, EVERYONE IS ASLEEP RIGHT NOW, BUT ME! I AM SUCH A NIGHT PERSON. I HATE MORNINGS WITH A PASSION, BUT I LOVE NIGHTTIME! I HAVE ALWAYS BEEN LIKE THIS. WE ARE GOING TO OMI'S TODAY FOR AN EASTER DINNER AT 1:00. ALL THE KIDS ARE COMING WITH US! IT WILL BE SO GREAT! I WAIT DAY AFTER DAY FOR DAYS LIKE THIS! I KNOW WE WILL GET MORE VERY, VERY SOON. IT'S EASTER TOMORROW, SO TOMORROW WE WILL BE WITH ALL OF

THEM AGAIN TOO! HOW LUCKY AM I? I COULDN'T ASK FOR ANYTHING MORE. MY MAN AND ALL MY BEAUTIFUL, ABSOLUTELY WONDERFUL KIDS ALL TOGETHER WITH ME, I AM ONE *HAPPY* WOMAN! JUST WOKE UP AND PAUL JUST WENT TO GET THE KIDS SOME PLASTIC EGGS SO WE CAN HIDE THEM AND THEY CAN HAVE AN EASTER EGG HUNT! HE TOLD JALA THAT HE IS THE EASTER BUNNY'S HELPER. SO JALA AND I ARE JUST HANGING OUT TOGETHER RIGHT NOW. IT'S ONLY ABOUT 9:00 A.M., I NEVER WAKE UP THIS EARLY, EVER! BUT MY BABY GIRL IS HERE AND I WANT TO SPEND AS MUCH TIME WITH HER AS I CAN!

IT'S ABOUT 2:40 NOW AND I JUST TOOK JALA TO JAY 'CAUSE I GET HER ALL DAY TOMORROW, SO NOW, I'M JUST SITTIN' OUTSIDE SMOKING AND ENJOYING THE SUN! TOMORROW SHOULD BE A REALLY FUN DAY! I GET TO BE WITH ALL MY KIDS AND MY HONEY, WHAT MORE COULD I POSSIBLY ASK FOR? ABSOLUTELY NOTHING! GIVE ME MY KIDS AND MY MAN AND I AM VERY HAPPY!

SUNDAY, MARCH 31, 2013:

IT'S *EASTER* SUNDAY TODAY AND IT WAS A *FABULOUS* DAY! WOKE UP, DID AN EASTER EGG HUNT WITH THE KIDS, THEN GOT READY AND WENT TO LUNCH AT OMI'S. WE WERE ONLY THERE ENOUGH TIME TO EAT, VISIT WITH OMI FOR A MINUTE, THEN WENT TO MY MOM'S. PAUL WAS HELPING ADI LEARN HOW TO PLAY THE GUITAR, SHE IS GETTING REALLY GOOD AT IT. ADI SINGS ABSOLUTELY BEAUTIFULLY, NOW PLAYS THE GUITAR AND WRITES MUSIC. SHE HAS A WHOLE LOT OF MUSIC THAT SHE HAS WRITTEN. SHE NEEDS TO DO MORE WITH HER TALENT. SHE IS INCREDIBLY TALENTED, I KNEW IT EVER SINCE SHE WAS A REALLY LITTLE GIRL! TALKING ABOUT SINGING, WE JUST GOT DONE WATCHING *PITCH PERFECT*! IT WAS SUCH A CUTE SHOW! IT WAS ABOUT SINGING AND IT WAS ABSOLUTELY DARLING! I WOULD DEFINITELY WATCH THAT SHOW AGAIN AND

AGAIN. I LOVE SHOWS THAT PUT A SMILE ON MY FACE AND MAKE ME LAUGH! IT JUST PUTS YA IN A GOOD MOOD!

WELL, IT'S ABOUT 11:30 P.M. AND I'M NOT EVEN TIRED, ONE SINGLE BIT! THINK I AM GOING TO WRITE IN MY KIDS' JOURNALS FOR A MINUTE. I HAVE A JOURNAL FOR EACH OF MY KIDS THAT I TRY TO WRITE IN EVERY DAY. IT DOESN'T ALWAYS HAPPEN EVERY DAY, BUT I TRY, I WRITE TO THEM WHAT WE DID THAT DAY AND HOW I AM FEELING AND HOW AND WHAT I THINK ABOUT THEM. WHICH I AM ALWAYS VERY, VERY PROUD OF EACH AND EVERY ONE OF THEM. TALKED TO SHALL TODAY, YAY, 'CAUSE WE HAVE BEEN PLAYING PHONE TAG FOR A WEEK NOW. SHE IS OUT OF THE HOSPITAL AND DOING GREAT! HER HEART IS IN GREAT CONDITION RIGHT NOW AND IF SHE DOES WHAT HER DOCTOR SAYS, SHE WILL BE JUST FINE. WHAT A HUGE RELIEF!

After Nat passed away, we found multiple journals for each of her children that we were able to give them.

MONDAY, APRIL 1, 2013:

JUST ANOTHER RELAXING DAY! NOT DOING MUCH OF ANYTHING TODAY. IT'S SPRING BREAK AND WE DON'T HAVE ANY PLANS REALLY. PAUL AND ADI JUST WENT PROM DRESS SHOPPING. THEY WERE GONE ALL DAY. THEY WENT TO LIKE FOUR STORES, WENT TO LUNCH AND HAD A GREAT TIME. SHE FOUND A BRIGHT PINK DRESS THAT'S REALLY, REALLY PRETTY! SHE IS SUCH A PRETTY GIRL! SO, HE JUST GOT BACK AND HE SAID THEY HAD SO MUCH FUN TOGETHER! HE SAID ADI WAS MAKING HIM LAUGH SO HARD! SHE DEFINITELY HAS A GOOD SENSE OF HUMOR! I LOVE MY KIDS! THEY ARE ALL SO STINKIN' AWESOME! IT'S REALLY, REALLY RAINY TODAY SO PAUL AND I ARE JUST GOING TO GO TO THE GARAGE, A LITTLE BAR ON BECK STREET, AND JUST CHILL AND HAVE SOMETHING TO EAT.

SO, PAUL AND I GOT INTO A HUGE FIGHT AND I TOLD HIM I WAS DONE. I HAVE *NEVER* SAID THAT TO HIM BEFORE, BUT I REALLY WAS, I WAS DONE! WELL, SOMETIMES BAD THINGS NEED TO HAPPEN TO HAVE SOMETHING REALLY GOOD COME OUT OF IT. AND IT DID, I LEARNED SOME THINGS ABOUT HIM THAT I NEVER KNEW AND THAT I NEEDED TO HEAR, AND I STOOD UP TO HIM AND NEEDED THAT *BAD!* I DON'T THINK WE WILL EVER FIGHT THAT BAD AGAIN. WE ARE BETTER THAN WE EVER HAVE BEEN NOW! WE JUST STARTED DATING AGAIN AND WE CAN'T STAY AWAY FROM EACH OTHER! I LOVE THIS MAN MORE THAN ANY MAN I HAVE EVER LOVED IN MY ENTIRE LIFE. I AM GOING TO MARRY HIM!

TUESDAY, APRIL 2, 2013:

TODAY WAS A *FANTASTIC* DAY! DID NOTHING SPECIAL. IT WAS JUST A GREAT DAY. I GOT READY, PICKED UP THE HOUSE A LITTLE BIT, THEN MY MOM CAME AND GOT ME TO HANG OUT AT HER HOUSE FOR A WHILE. ADI CAME OVER AND MY MOM AND HER WENT SHOPPING, THEY WANTED ME TO GO BUT MY TUMMY WAS A LITTLE QUEASY SO I STAYED AT MY MOM'S AND RESTED A BIT. *(She missed out on so many things with her kids and family because she was always sick.)* AFTER A WHILE, AMY CAME AND GOT ME AT MY MOM'S AND WE WENT TO SEE BRIAN REALLY QUICK AND IT WAS SURPRISINGLY QUICK, THEN SHE DROPPED ME OFF AT HOME. PAUL GOT HOME ABOUT THIRTY MINUTES AFTER I DID, WHICH COULDN'T HAVE BEEN MORE PERFECT. WE TALKED FOR A WHILE, I CLEANED THE HOUSE WHILE HE DID SOME INVOICES FOR WORK, THEN HE GOT IN THE SHOWER AND THEN WENT TO THE GARAGE, OUR NEW FAVORITE LITTLE BAR, AND ATE $1 TACOS! WE PLAYED BEAN BAG TOSS, WHICH WAS REALLY, REALLY STUPID BUT WE HAD FUN 'CAUSE IT WAS SOMETHING WE WERE DOING TOGETHER. STAYED THERE FOR A COUPLE HOURS, CAME HOME, THEN SETTLED INTO A MOVIE. OF COURSE, MY BABY FELL

ASLEEP AFTER ONLY ABOUT 25 MINUTES INTO THE MOVIE, BUT I WATCHED THE WHOLE THING AND IT WAS A REALLY GOOD SHOW. WE BOTH JUST GOT INTO OUR BED, HE IS STILL OUT COLD. I'M ACTUALLY REALLY SHOCKED I GOT HIM IN HERE SO QUICK BEING ASLEEP ON THE COUCH. THAT IS USUALLY SO DIFFICULT TO DO! AND I AM, OF COURSE, WRITING, BUT GETTING VERY, VERY SLEEPY, GOOD NIGHT!

WEDNESDAY, APRIL 3, 2013:

JUST SITTING OUTSIDE WITH JALA WAITING FOR PAUL TO GET HOME SO I CAN TAKE HER TO JAY. SHE WAS AWESOME TODAY. SHE IS ALWAYS AWESOME, BUT TODAY SHE WENT OUT OF HER WAY TO BE ABSOLUTELY AMAZING! I HAD AN AWESOME DAY TODAY. SPENT THE ENTIRE DAY WITH ADI AND JALA, WE HAD A BLAST. ADI CAME AND GOT ME AROUND 10:30 THIS MORNING, WE WENT TO CAROLYN'S TO TRY ON HER DRESS WITH HER SHOES. SHE LOOKED ABSOLUTELY FABULOUS! I LEARN THINGS FROM HER EVERY DAY! ALL THREE OF MY KIDS TEACH ME SO MUCH EVERY SINGLE DAY! THEY MAKE ME WANT TO BE A BETTER PERSON. I AM ALWAYS PUTTING MYSELF DOWN AS A MOTHER 'CAUSE OF THE PAST, BUT I COULDN'T HAVE DONE THAT TERRIBLE OF A JOB BECAUSE I HAVE AWESOME, WELL MANNERED, POLITE, SMART, SWEET, AND CARING KIDS. THAT MAKES MY LIFE 100% BETTER! THEY ARE MY HEART AND SOUL!

THURSDAY, APRIL 4, 2013:

SO, I'M SUPER EXCITED! IT'S MY BOY'S BIRTHDAY TOMORROW. WE ARE JUST GOING TO HANG OUT AND BE TOGETHER ALL DAY AT MY MOM'S HOUSE. I AM SO EXCITED! HE IS SUCH AN AMAZING BOY! I COULDN'T BE MORE PROUD THAN I ALREADY AM OF HIM. HIS DREAM IS TO BE A PROFESSIONAL FOOTBALL PLAYER, AND HE IS SO SERIOUS ABOUT IT! I REALLY DO THINK HE WILL ACHIEVE HIS GOALS AND BE IN

THE NFL. HOW AWESOME WILL THAT BE...TO GO TO THE NFL TO WATCH MY SON PLAY FOOTBALL? SO AWESOME! SO, I KNOW I SAID THIS JOURNAL WAS GOING TO BE NOTHING BUT POSITIVE, 'CAUSE EVERYONE IS ALWAYS SAYING HOW NEGATIVE I AM, BUT THERE IS ALWAYS GOING TO BE SOME NEGATIVE EVEN THOUGH WE STAY POSITIVE. I JUST LIKE TO WRITE EVERYTHING THAT IS GOING ON...WHAT I DID THAT DAY, HOW I FELT ABOUT IT, AND JUST HOW I AM FEELING. WELL, LATELY I HAVE BEEN GREAT, I SEE MY KIDS A LOT, ESPECIALLY RIGHT NOW 'CAUSE IT'S SPRING BREAK AND I HAVE MY PRINCESS JALA EVERY SINGLE DAY. WHAT MORE COULD I POSSIBLY ASK FOR? I AM SO HAPPY! PAUL DOESN'T ALWAYS THINK I AM, BUT I AM. HE DOES ABSOLUTELY EVERYTHING FOR ME. HE COMPLETELY TAKES CARE OF ME, EVERYTHING I EVER WANT OR NEED, HE TAKES CARE OF! HE IS SUCH AN AMAZING GUY, I WANT TO DO SOMETHING REALLY SPECIAL FOR HIM, BUT I DON'T KNOW WHAT. I REALLY NEED TO SIT AND THINK ABOUT IT. REALLY, REALLY THINK!

FRIDAY, APRIL 5, 2013:

SO, IT WAS MASON'S BIRTHDAY TODAY! WE HAD AN AWESOME DAY TOGETHER! WE JUST HUNG OUT AT MY MOM'S ALL DAY LONG, GOT LUNCH FROM APOLLO BURGER, GOT DINNER AT LITTLE CAESARS, AND JUST HUNG OUT ALL DAY. IT WAS A LOT OF FUN! I WENT OVER THERE AT 11:00 A.M. AND PAUL AND HIS SON CAME AND BROUGHT MASON A WHOLE BUNCH OF PRESENTS. HE EVEN GOT HIM A CARD WITH $20.00 IN IT. HOW STINKIN' SWEET IS THAT? HE IS SUCH A GREAT GUY! WE HUNG OUT TILL ABOUT 7:30 P.M., THEN CAME HOME AND CLEANED. THE HOUSE WAS KIND OF A DISASTER, SO I CLEANED AND DID LAUNDRY. IT'S REALLY HARD NOT HAVING A WASHER OR DRYER HERE, SO I HAVE TO DO IT AT MY MOM'S ALL THE TIME AND IT REALLY SUCKS. IT'S JUST A BIG PAIN TO LOAD ALL THE DIRTY LAUNDRY AROUND, THEN ONCE IT'S

CLEAN TO FOLD IT AND BRING IT ALL BACK. I ACTUALLY DON'T MIND DOING LAUNDRY AT ALL, IT'S THE TAKING IT BACK AND FORTH THAT REALLY BUGS. SO, IT'S ABOUT 11:45 P.M. AND PAUL JUST WENT TO SLEEP, SO I GOT OUT OF THE BATH ABOUT TWENTY MINUTES AGO, SO I AM A LITTLE MORE RELAXED, I THINK I MIGHT HOP INTO BED WITH MY MAN! MY BABY BOY TURNED 14 TODAY! HE IS GETTING SO OLD, THEY ALL ARE, AND IT IS REALLY, REALLY HARD! IT'S AWESOME WATCHING THEM GROW UP INTO TEENAGERS BUT ALSO REALLY SAD, 'CAUSE THEY ARE NOT MY BABIES ANYMORE AND I WILL NEVER HAVE A BABY AGAIN. OH WELL, ENJOY THEM WHILE THEY ARE ALL THIS AGE, 'CAUSE TIME GOES BY SO FAST!

SATURDAY, APRIL 6, 2013:

JUST RELAXIN' RIGHT NOW, IT'S ABOUT 3:00 P.M. AND I HAVE BEEN CLEANING ALL MORNING AND AFTERNOON. PAUL AND HIS SON JUST GOT HOME FROM WORKING AND THEY ARE SHOWERING AND THEN WE ARE GOING TO DO SOMETHING FUN, I DON'T KNOW WHAT, BUT SOMETHING FUN! SO, IT'S JUST ME, PAUL, AND HIS SON TODAY AND WE ARE GOING TO A NEW STORE OUT IN DRAPER TO CHECK IT OUT. I GUESS IT HAS A FERRIS WHEEL INSIDE AND IT HAS ABSOLUTELY EVERYTHING! SO, I'M SITTING OUTSIDE ACTING READY TO GO AND SOMEONE IS WATCHING CONFERENCE AND IT IS SO STINKIN' LOUD! *(Conference is held twice a year in our church and is broadcast on TV.)* GET ME THE HELL OUT OF HERE! I DON'T MIND PEOPLE WATCHING IT, BUT WHEN THE WHOLE DAMN NEIGHBORHOOD CAN HEAR IT, THEN I GET A LITTLE BUGGED! MY MOM LEFT TO SAINT GEORGE THIS MORNING TO WATCH SHALL'S KIDS WHILE THEY GO ON A CRUISE FOR 12 DAYS. I WISH I COULD HAVE GONE UP THERE WITH HER. PAUL AND I JUST GOT DONE HAVING AN AWESOME CONVERSATION. HE REALLY IS TRYING HARD TO KEEP HIS TEMPER UNDER CONTROL. HE HAS BEEN DOING AWESOME, BUT EVERY ONCE IN A WHILE, HE HAS HIS

MOMENTS. BUT NOW THAT WE TALKED, I UNDERSTAND HIM A LOT MORE AND IT HAS ABSOLUTELY NOTHING TO DO WITH ME!

SUNDAY, APRIL 7, 2013:

IT'S ABOUT 1:00 A.M. SUNDAY MORNING. WE HAD A WAY FUN NIGHT. IT WAS JUST ME, PAUL, AND HIS SON. WE HAD A WATER FIGHT INSIDE THE HOUSE. PAUL AND I WERE AFTER HIS SON AND IT WAS ABSOLUTELY HILARIOUS. HIS SON TRIED TO BARRICADE HIMSELF INSIDE HIS ROOM. HE HAD NO LUCK! PAUL GOT IT OPEN AFTER ALMOST BUSTING THE DOOR, IT WAS A REALLY FUN NIGHT! TODAY, WE WOKE UP AROUND 10:00 A.M., RELAXED ALL MORNING, THEN WENT TO TARGET TO LOOK AROUND, THEN CAME HOME FOR A BIT. I TOOK THE BOYS TO A CHURCH A COUPLE BLOCKS AWAY TO RIDE THEIR LONGBOARDS WHILE I GOT READY. WHEN I WENT TO PICK THEM UP, I TOOK MACI WITH ME AND SHE FREAKED ON THE WAY THERE, BUT NOT ON THE WAY BACK 'CAUSE HER DADDY WAS HOLDING HER. I ABSOLUTELY LOVE MY KITTY! WE GOT HER A TAG—FINALLY—SATURDAY, IT LOOKS SO CUTE ON HER, MAKES ME AND PAUL FEEL A LOT BETTER TOO. TOOK PAUL'S SON HOME AROUND 4:30 P.M., THEN WENT BACK TO SEE SAMUEL FOR ABOUT 20 MINUTES, GOT BACK AND PAUL AND I HAD A DEEP, AWESOME TALK THAT HELPED US BOTH A LOT. AFTER OUR TALK, WE WENT TO A BAR ON 17TH SOUTH IN SALT LAKE CALLED BATTER'S UP. IT WAS A REALLY COOL LITTLE PLACE. WE HAD CHEESE FRIES AND PLAYED POOL. IT WAS NICE. WELL, I'M EXHAUSTED! GOODNIGHT, TILL TOMORROW!

MONDAY, APRIL 8, 2013:

IT'S ABOUT 2:00 A.M. MONDAY MORNING AND MY BABY IS SOUND ASLEEP WHILE I WRITE IN MY JOURNAL AND TEXT SAMUEL AND MARIA. I THINK THEY ARE BOTH COMING OVER IN THE MORNING TO HANG OUT WITH ME. THAT WOULD BE

FANTASTIC IF SAMUEL CAME BY 'CAUSE I HAVE NO VEHICLE AND I DON'T WANT TO LEAVE AT NIGHT WHEN PAUL IS HOME! WELL, IT'S ABOUT 5:00 A.M. AND I AM STILL STINKIN' AWAKE! I BETTER GET SOME SLEEP OR PAUL IS DEFINITELY GONNA THINK SOMETHING IS UP! DON'T WANT THAT AT ALL!! I WROTE A NOTE TO ANTHONY TONIGHT TELLING HIM THAT IS IT WITH OUR FRIENDSHIP. HE WENT WAY OVER THE LINE THIS TIME AND I AM SO *DONE* WITH HIM! HE WAS MADLY IN LOVE WITH ME ANYWAYS, AND EVEN THOUGH I THOUGHT HE WAS THE MOST DISGUSTING MAN ON EARTH AND I REALLY DID DISLIKE HIM A LOT, IT'S NOT FAIR TO EVEN COMMUNICATE WITH ANYONE THAT HAS FEELINGS LIKE THAT FOR ME. HE WAS *NEVER* GOING TO GET OVER ME, EITHER! HE TOLD ME HE HAS NEVER LOVED ANYONE LIKE HE DOES ME AND THAT HE CARES MORE ABOUT ME THAN HIS OWN TWO KIDS! HOW FUCKED UP IS THAT? WELL, I TOOK HIM HIS LETTER AND SAW HIM WALKING UP THE STREET AS I WAS PULLING OUT AND HE THREW HIS HANDS UP IN THE AIR LIKE, "WHAT THE FUCK," OH WELL, GOOD RIDDANCE, DUDE!!! I'M GOING TO WATCH A MOVIE WITH MY BABY NOW, I DON'T HAVE ANY IDEA WHAT IT IS, I'M JUST HAPPY TO BE WITH HIM!!

TUESDAY, APRIL 9, 2013:

TODAY REALLY WASN'T TOO EXCITING OF A DAY. I WAS IN A REALLY BAD MOOD ALL DAY AND I REALLY DIDN'T KNOW WHY. JAY LET ME BORROW HIS CAR TODAY, BUT I WAS SO STRESSED ALL DAY HAVING IT 'CAUSE IF PAUL WAS TO FIND OUT THAT I WAS DRIVING HIS CAR, HE WOULD FLIP! I GOT IT BACK TO HIM BEFORE PAUL GOT HOME AT 3:00. JALA AND HIS DAUGHTER WERE OVER TODAY AND I'M JUST GETTING REALLY IRRITATED WITH HIS DAUGHTER LATELY, LIKE REALLY, REALLY BAD! I LOVE THAT LITTLE GIRL TO DEATH, BUT THE WAY PAUL TREATS HER, IT'S REALLY NOT RIGHT! HE ACTS LIKE SHE IS HIS GIRLFRIEND! A LOT OF

PEOPLE HAVE POINTED THAT OUT TO ME ALSO! I CAN'T SAY ANYTHING TO HIM, THAT WOULD TOTALLY BE OUT OF LINE! SO, I JUST HAVE TO SIT HERE AND WATCH IT. HIS DAUGHTER COULD *NEVER* DO WRONG IN PAUL'S EYES, *EVER!* SHE IS GETTING AN ATTITUDE WITH ME LATELY AND WITH JALA. I DON'T CARE IF SHE GETS ONE WITH ME, I CAN HANDLE IT, I HAVE FROM DAY ONE, BUT GETTING AN ATTITUDE WITH MY BABY GIRL, *OH HELL NO!* WELL, I JUST HAVE TO BITE MY TONGUE ON THIS ONE 'CAUSE IF I EVER SAID ANYTHING, EVEN HALFWAY WRONG ABOUT "HIS LITTLE PRINCESS," WE WOULD DEFINITELY BE OVER!

WEDNESDAY, APRIL 10, 2013:

TODAY WAS SUCH A FUN DAY! THERE WAS ONLY ONE BAD THING AND THAT WAS THAT I DIDN'T HAVE JALA TODAY. SHE WENT WITH ONE OF JAY'S FRIENDS 'CAUSE HE HAD A CONCERT TO GO TO AND JALA GOT A PLAY DATE. IT ACTUALLY TURNED OUT OKAY. I GOT SOME ONE ON ONE TIME WITH MY BABY BOY, I CAN'T REMEMBER THE LAST TIME I GOT TO SPEND TIME WITH HIM ALONE. SO, WOKE UP AROUND 11:45 A.M., HOW STINKIN' LAZY AM I? AMY CAME OVER, WE TOOK A RIDE OUT TO 17TH SOUTH *(Nat had suppliers there)* AND THEN BACK HOME. GOT IN THE BATH, THEN HAD MARIA COME GET ME TO TAKE ME TO MY MOM'S SO I COULD START DINNER FOR MY DAD, PAUL, MASON, ADI, AND ME. I STARTED ABOUT 4:00, THEN MY BABY BOY CAME THROUGH THE DOOR AND THE REST OF MY DAY JUST TURNED FROM GOOD TO ABSOLUTELY *FANTASTIC!* MAS HELPED ME COOK DINNER AND IT WAS AWESOME! ADI HAD TO TRY OUT FOR CONCERT CHOIR, WHICH OF COURSE, SHE MADE IT! SO SHE GOT THERE A LITTLE LATER, BUT WAS STILL ABOUT 5:15 P.M. COOKED DINNER AND HUNG OUT WITH ADI AND MAS FOR A WHILE, WHICH WAS SO EXTREMELY WONDERFUL FOR ME! THEN MY DAD AND PAUL GOT THERE, DINNER GOT DONE RIGHT WHEN THE MEN WALKED

IN, IT COULDN'T HAVE GONE BETTER. WE ALL ATE, THEN ADI BAKED SOME BROWNIES WHILE MY DAD AND I WATCHED TV AND PAUL WAS OUTSIDE PLAYING FOOTBALL WITH MAS AND HIS FRIENDS. WE LEFT AROUND 7:00, CAME HOME AND WATCHED THOR, WHICH WAS A GREAT MOVIE, NOW GOING TO BED. IT WAS A *GREAT DAY TODAY!*

THURSDAY, APRIL 11, 2013:

SITTING HERE WITH JALA AND PAUL'S DAUGHTER WATCHING MOVIES. PAUL IS WORKING AND JAY WILL BE HERE IN ABOUT AN HOUR TO PICK JALA UP AND PAUL'S EX WILL BE HERE ANY MINUTE TO PICK HIS DAUGHTER UP. THESE TWO GIRLS ARE REALLY GOOD TOGETHER AT FIRST, THEN THEY START FIGHTING REALLY BAD! PAUL IS GOING TO BE GONE ALL NIGHT WORKING, WON'T BE HOME UNTIL LIKE 11:00 P.M. TONIGHT! HOW SAD IS THAT? HE IS WORKING HIS ASS OFF. I FEEL REALLY, REALLY BAD! HE TOTALLY TAKES CARE OF ME AND MY KIDS! I'M GOING INTO WORK TOMORROW WITH PAUL UNTIL ABOUT 1:30, WHEN THE KIDS GET OUT OF SCHOOL. HE NEEDS ALL THE HELP HE CAN GET RIGHT NOW, 'CAUSE HE IS OVERLOADED WITH CARS AT THE AIRPORT. GOT TO GET TO BED EARLY TONIGHT 'CAUSE HE IS WANTING TO GET UP EARLY AND GO. ADI TOOK OFF TO SAINT GEORGE TODAY WITH ANGIE TILL TUESDAY. RANDY COULDN'T GO DOWN THERE WITH THEM AND KAILEE HAS TO PERFORM, SO ADI WENT WITH HER SO SHE DIDN'T HAVE TO GO ALONE. I MISS MY ADI, I HAVEN'T REALLY SEEN HER ALL THIS WEEK EXCEPT FOR A COUPLE HOURS YESTERDAY. ME AND MAS HAD A REALLY GOOD DAY TOGETHER, THOUGH. YESTERDAY WAS AN AWESOME DAY. TODAY, *BLAH!*

FRIDAY, APRIL 12, 2013:

SITTING HERE ON THE COUCH RIGHT NEXT TO MY BABY GIRL WHILE SHE IS WATCHING FAMILY GUY 'CAUSE I JUST GOT HER OUT OF THE BATH. IT'S ABOUT 9:00 P.M. AND IT WAS AN OKAY DAY. GOT UP REALLY EARLY, A LOT EARLIER THAN I AM USED TO AND THAT I LIKE, 'CAUSE WE HAD TO GO TO THE AIRPORT AND WORK. PAUL REALLY NEEDED MY HELP 'CAUSE HE WAS REALLY OVERLOADED WITH CARS. GOT DONE ABOUT 12:45 AND I WENT TO SEE BRIAN FOR JUST A SECOND, THEN CAME BACK HOME, GOT READY, TOOK THE GIRLS TO GET A TREAT AND SLURPEE, THEN WENT TO THE PARK TILL I HAD TO PICK UP PAUL'S SON FROM HIS SCHOOL DANCE, THEN PICK UP PAUL FROM THE AIRPORT. WE RAN A COUPLE ERRANDS, THEN CAME BACK HOME, MADE DINNER, THEN HUNG OUT FOR A LITTLE BIT. NOW, WE ARE ALL JUST CHILLIN' AND PAUL AND HIS SON WENT TO GET SOME TREATS AND WE ARE GOING TO WATCH MOVIES. WE ARE GOING TO DO SOMETHING FUN TOMORROW, SO WE ARE JUST RELAXIN' TONIGHT. JALA WAS ABSOLUTELY AWESOME THIS WEEKEND WITH US. SHE HAS HAD A REALLY HARD TIME LATELY 'CAUSE SHE GETS JEALOUS OF PAUL'S DAUGHTER AND THAT I AM AROUND HER A LOT. SO, EVERY TIME SHE COMES OVER, SHE ACTS OUT. IT'S BEEN VERY HARD WITH HER, BUT I COMPLETELY UNDERSTAND WHY SHE ACTS OUT. I AM WITH HIS DAUGHTER A LOT MORE THAN HER, WAY MORE, WAY MORE THAN ADI AND MAS. I HATE IT!! BUT THE LAST COUPLE DAYS, SHE HAS BEEN AWESOME. I AM TOTALLY FOCUSING ON HER AND THAT HELPS A LOT!!! *I LOVE MY BABY GIRL!!*

SATURDAY, APRIL 13, 2013:

SO, TODAY STARTED OUT AS AN AWESOME DAY UNTIL NOW. IT'S ABOUT 5:00 P.M. AND I HAD JALA LAST NIGHT AND THIS MORNING AND SHE WAS ABSOLUTELY INCREDIBLE! IT

WAS WAY FUN WITH HER. SHE DID REALLY GOOD WITH US! TOOK HER TO JAY AROUND 1:00 P.M., THEN RAN A BUNCH OF ERRANDS. PAUL WAS GOING TO GO INTO WORK BUT INSTEAD HE WANTED TO STAY WITH US, EXCEPT HE LEFT FOR TWO HOURS WITH THE KIDS, SHOPPING FOR THEIR MOM'S BIRTHDAY PRESENT. HOW FUCKED UP IS THAT? HE LEFT ME AT HOME WHILE HE WAS SHOPPING FOR HIS EX WITH HIS KIDS! HOW FUCKED UP IS THAT? I SHOULDN'T CARE, BUT WHENEVER ANYONE EVEN MENTIONS JAY'S NAME, HE LITERALLY FLIPS! ON A POSITIVE NOTE, JAY WENT AND PAID MY PHONE BILL AND I DIDN'T EVEN ASK HIM TO! HOW FREAKING SWEET IS THAT? IT'S BEEN TURNED OFF FOR OVER A MONTH NOW AND NOW IT'S ON, THANKS TO JAY! YAY! WELL, I'M NOT GOING TO LET THAT RUIN MY NIGHT. PAUL JUST MADE US ALL DINNER, PORK CHOPS, CORN, AND RICE. IT WAS ABSOLUTELY AWESOME! WE ARE WATCHING ROCKY 3 NOW AND RELAXING FOR THE NIGHT.

OH MY STINKIN' HELL! SO, IT WAS ABOUT 11:00 P.M., I LEFT FOR A MINUTE AND WAS ON BECK STREET IN SALT LAKE AND THE FUCKING VAN WOULD NOT START! DAVID HAD TO GET JUMPER CABLES AND JUMP IT, BUT WHILE WE WERE TRYING TO FIGURE IT OUT, I WAS IN HYSTERICS!! I AM NEVER TAKING THAT STINKIN' VAN ALONE AGAIN!!!

SUNDAY, APRIL 14, 2013:

TODAY STARTED OFF VERY, VERY SHITTY, THEN TURNED INTO *FANTASTIC!* MASON GOT ORDAINED *(an ordinance in our church)* TODAY IN CHURCH TO BECOME A TEACHER AT 12:00. HE TOLD ME ABOUT IT WEDNESDAY WHEN I WAS WITH HIM, BUT I'M RETARDED AND TOTALLY SPACED IT. I HAD PROMISED HIM THAT I WOULD BE THERE TOO, AND I DIDN'T MAKE IT! HOW HORRIBLE AM I? BY THE TIME I FINALLY FOUND A RIDE, 'CAUSE PAUL WAS OUT AT THE AIRPORT, I GOT TO THE CHURCH AT 12:15. I BARELY MISSED IT, I WAS SO

UPSET! MASON WALKED OUT OF THE BISHOP'S OFFICE AND CAME RIGHT UP AND HUGGED ME. I TOLD HIM HOW VERY, VERY SORRY I WAS AND TOLD HIM THE STORY. WELL, THE ABSOLUTELY INCREDIBLE BOY THAT MASON IS...(AND THAT'S AN UNDERSTATEMENT) HE LOOKED AT ME WITH A BIG GRIN AND SAID, "MOM, AT LEAST YOU'RE HERE. I KNOW YOU DID YOUR BEST AND THAT'S ALL THAT MATTERS!" I WAS CRYING AND HE JUST HUGGED ME AND KEPT TELLING ME IT WAS NO BIG DEAL AND AT LEAST I DID MAKE IT THERE...EVEN THOUGH I WAS LATE. I WENT HOME, CHANGED, WENT BACK TO MY MOM'S TO SPEND THE DAY WITH MAS, AND THAT'S EXACTLY WHAT I DID. GOT TO MY MOM'S AND MY DAD TOOK MAS AND I OUT TO LUNCH (COSTA VIDA), THEN WENT BACK TO MY MOM'S AND JUST MAS AND ME HUNG OUT, WATCHED X-FACTOR ON HIS NEW IPAD, AND MADE BROWNIES. IT WAS JUST ME AND MASON ALL DAY LONG AND RIGHT UNTIL ABOUT 7:45 P.M. IT WAS AWESOME, I COULDN'T HAVE ASKED FOR A BETTER DAY. THEN, WHEN I WAS LEAVING, ADI POPPED IN TO SAY HI. I HAVEN'T SEEN HER IN A WEEK 'CAUSE SHE WAS IN SAINT GEORGE. SHE TOOK ME HOME. I LOVE MY BEAUTIFUL KIDS!!!

<u>MONDAY, APRIL 15, 2013</u>:

IT'S ABOUT 6:30 P.M. RIGHT NOW AND I'M SITTIN' HERE WATCHING A MOVIE WITH JALA AND PAUL'S DAUGHTER. ADI, JALA, AND I ARE GOING TO GET AN ICE CREAM HERE IN A LITTLE BIT.

GETTING READY TO GO OUT WITH MY MAN! YAY! WE HAVEN'T DONE ANYTHING ALONE IN A LONG TIME! PAUL AND I JUST HUNG OUT TONIGHT AND JUST RELAXED 'CAUSE PAUL WAS IN THE COLD WORKING ALL DAY LONG. HE NEEDS A BREAK IN A REALLY BAD WAY. I KEEP TELLING HIM THAT, BUT HE WON'T STOP. HE IS LIKE AN ENERGIZER BUNNY, HE KEEPS GOING AND GOING AND GOING AND GOING. ONE OF THESE DAYS SOON, HE IS GOING TO CRASH AND FALL. I REALLY HOPE NOT,

BUT IT'S REALITY, YOU CAN ONLY GO FOR SO LONG UNTIL YOU REALLY NEED A BREAK. I CLEAN THE HOUSE SPOTLESS EVERY SINGLE DAY AND I DON'T KNOW WHY BECAUSE WHEN THE GIRLS GET HERE, THEY LITERALLY TRASH IT! I LOVE HAVING THE GIRLS WITH ME EVERY DAY, BUT THEY ARE STARTING TO FIGHT AND ARGUE OVER EVERYTHING. I KNEW THIS DAY WAS COMING, JUST DIDN'T KNOW IT WOULD COME THIS SOON. MY MOM IS COMING HOME TOMORROW AFTER BEING GONE FOR 12 DAYS IN ST. GEORGE. WHENEVER MY MOM IS GONE, IT MAKES ME REALIZE JUST HOW MUCH I REALLY NEED HER. I REALLY TAKE HER FOR GRANTED, THAT SHE LIVES RIGHT AROUND THE CORNER FROM ME AND SHE IS THERE WHENEVER I NEED HER, NO QUESTIONS ASKED. I REALLY NEED TO DO SOMETHING FOR HER, SHE'S AWESOME!!

TUESDAY, APRIL 16, 2013:

IT WAS A FAIRLY GOOD DAY. I DROPPED PAUL OFF AT THE AIRPORT AROUND 10 THIS MORNING AFTER GOING TO A DRIVE THROUGH FOR BREAKFAST (WHICH WAS TOTALLY FINE WITH ME BECAUSE I DON'T LIKE BREAKFAST USUALLY AND PAUL WAS IN A HUGE HURRY). CAME HOME, GOT READY FOR THE DAY, THEN MET MY SWEET ADI AND HER BEST FRIEND AT ROBINTINO'S FOR LUNCH. THOSE GIRLS CAN EAT! OUR BILL FOR THE THREE OF US AT ROBINTINO'S WAS $30.00, ISN'T THAT CRAZY? I DIDN'T EVEN EAT, I JUST MUNCHED ON BREADSTICKS. IT KIND A MADE ME MAD 'CAUSE I DON'T HAVE THE $ RIGHT NOW TO SPEND $30.00 ON LUNCH! I DIDN'T LET ADI KNOW I WAS BUGGED, 'CAUSE SHE WAS HAPPY AND SEEING THAT BEAUTIFUL SMILE ON ADI'S FACE MADE IT ALL WORTH IT! I WOULD SPEND MY VERY LAST DIME ON ANY OF MY KIDS IF I COULD SEE A SMILE ON THEIR FACE. THAT'S WHAT LIFE IS ALL ABOUT...BEING TOGETHER, HAVING FUN AND WATCHING OUR BEAUTIFUL, AMAZING KIDS GROW UP AND BE HAPPY! TIME GOES BY WAY TOO FAST, THOUGH! I CAN'T TAKE ANY

MORE MINUTES WITH MY KIDS FOR GRANTED. I NEED (WANT) TO SPEND EVERY SECOND THAT I CAN WITH ALL 3 OF MY WONDERFUL KIDS. WELL, WE WATCHED A MOVIE, GOT ICE CREAM, AND I HAD A FEVER ALL DAMN NIGHT, SO DIDN'T FINISH THE MOVIE, GOT IN THE BATH 'CAUSE I WAS FREEZING FROM MY FEVER, THEN JUST GOT REALLY, REALLY SICK, REALLY, REALLY FAST AND I HAVE NO IDEA WHY. WHAT A BUMMER! PAUL GAVE ME SOME NYQUIL, PUT ME TO BED WITH A BOWL ON THE SIDE OF ME 'CAUSE I WAS SO NAUSEOUS, FELL ASLEEP PRETTY DAMN FAST, GOODNIGHT!

4-17-2013: Dr. Note–119 lbs. Prescribed Suboxone. Denies relapse, denies medications from other doctors. She feels stable.

THURSDAY, APRIL 18, 2013:

TODAY WAS ANOTHER GREAT DAY! GOT TO BE WITH ALL OF MY WONDERFUL KIDS AND PAUL'S DAUGHTER CAME OVER TO MY MOM'S WITH ME TOO. JAY WENT ON A DATE TONIGHT, SO JALA GOT TO SLEEP OVER HERE WITH US. SHE DID ABSOLUTELY AWESOME! GOT HER IN THE BATH WHEN WE GOT HOME, THEN THE GIRLS PLAYED FOR A LITTLE BIT, THEN I PUT THEM TO BED AROUND 9:30 P.M., JALA WENT RIGHT TO SLEEP SO GOOD! SHE HAS BEEN SUCH AN AMAZING LITTLE GIRL LATELY. I LOVE HER! I WAS CLIPPING HER TOENAILS TONIGHT BEFORE, ACTUALLY AFTER I GOT HER IN THE BATH AND SHE WAS SITTING ON THE TOILET AS STILL AS COULD BE AND SHE WAS SAYING HOW BEAUTIFUL I WAS AND THAT I WAS THE PRETTIEST WOMAN IN THE WORLD! SHE ALSO SAID THAT JESUS MADE ME TO BE THE MOST BEAUTIFUL WOMAN AND MOTHER IN THE WORLD. SHE KEPT GOING OFF ABOUT IT, SAYING, "I'M NOT LYING, MOM, YOU ARE SO BEAUTIFUL." HOW FREAKING CUTE IS THAT? SHE MADE MY ENTIRE NIGHT! I CAN'T GET ENOUGH OF THIS LITTLE GIRL! SHE MAKES MY LIFE 100% BETTER! SO DO MY OTHER 2, I DON'T

KNOW WHAT I WOULD DO WITHOUT ANY OF THEM. THEY ARE THE 3 BIGGEST BLESSINGS IN MY ENTIRE LIFE. I TRY AND LET THEM KNOW, BUT I REALLY DO HOPE THEY KNOW JUST HOW MUCH I LOVE AND ADORE THEM. I HAVE NOT BEEN THE GREATEST MOM, ACTUALLY, I HAVE BEEN A TERRIBLY SHITTY MOM AND IT BREAKS MY HEART TO PIECES 'CAUSE THEY ARE MY WHOLE LIFE. I'M TRYING TO TURN IT ALL AROUND AND DOING MY BEST AS A MOTHER, BUT I HAVE A WHOLE HELL OF A LOT OF MAKING UP TO DO!!!

SATURDAY, APRIL 20, 2013:

I WAS IN KIND OF A BAD MOOD TODAY AND I HAVE NO IDEA WHY! I HAVEN'T SEEN MUCH OF MY MAN LATELY 'CAUSE HE HAS BEEN WORKING HIS ASS OFF. I MISS HIM SO MUCH! MY CAR IS STILL NOT DONE. IT'S BEEN ALMOST 2 MONTHS AND I AM FREAKING OUT! I MISS IT SO BAD! I HAVE TO DRIVE THAT STUPID UGLY AS SHIT VAN AND IT EMBARRASSES THE CRAP OUT OF ME! NOT TO MENTION THAT IT'S GOING TO BREAK DOWN ANY DAY NOW, IT ALREADY HAS ON ME ONCE BEFORE. LAST WEEK, I WENT TO MEET DAVID IN SALT LAKE AT 1:00 A.M. AND THE STUPID VAN BROKE DOWN. I WAS STUCK OUT THERE FOR ABOUT AN HOUR. THEY FINALLY JUMPED IT AND IT STARTED. I HAVE NEVER BEEN SO FREAKED OUT IN MY ENTIRE LIFE, 'CAUSE WHAT IN THE HELL WOULD I HAVE TOLD PAUL? WELL, I'M SO SUPER LUCKY I MADE IT HOME. I JUST WANT MY STINKIN' CAR BACK. I'M GLAD PAUL IS FIXING IT BUT IT IS TAKING HIM WAY TOO DAMN LONG. I AM HOPING HE WILL WORK ON IT IN THE NEXT COUPLE DAYS 'CAUSE IT'S ALMOST DONE. WISH ME LUCK THAT I GET MY CUTE CAR BACK SOON!!

A few days later...

TUESDAY, APRIL 23, 2013:

SO, PAUL'S DAUGHTER HAS BEEN TELLING ME ABOUT HER SCHOOL PERFORMANCE FOR THE PAST MONTH NOW AND I FORGOT! I WAS OUT AT BRIAN'S *(one of her dealers)* WHEN I GOT A TEXT FROM PAUL SAYING, "YOU GONNA BE HERE ANYTIME SOON?" I ASKED WHY AND HE TOLD ME HE WAS AT HIS DAUGHTER'S PROGRAM THAT HAD JUST STARTED!! THERE WAS NO WAY I COULD MAKE IT. I WASN'T EVEN READY, AND IT TAKES AT LEAST 15/20 MINUTES TO GET HOME FROM HIS PLACE. I FEEL BAD, SOMEWHAT. JUST KIND OF A CHILL DAY TODAY. JAY LET ME BORROW HIS CAR THIS MORNING, THAT'S HOW I MADE IT OUT, THEN ADI CAME TO GET ME AT THE GYM AFTER I DROPPED HIS CAR BACK OFF TO HIM AND TOOK ME HOME. IT WAS GREAT TO SEE HER FOR AT LEAST A MIN. WE WENT TO LUNCH YESTERDAY, JUST ME AND HER, AND IT WAS WONDERFUL! SHE TOLD ME ABOUT PROM AND HOW MUCH FUN IT WAS! ANYWAYS, AFTER ADI DROPPED ME OFF AT HOME, I HURRIED AND JUMPED IN THE BATH, THEN PAUL CAME HOME AND I TOOK HIM TO LAKESIDE WHILE I PICKED UP JALA. JALA AND I CAME HOME AND MARIA CAME OVER AND HUNG OUT WITH US FOR A COUPLE HOURS. WE GOT PIZZA AND JUST HUNG OUT. PAUL CAME HOME ABOUT 20 MIN. AFTER MARIA LEFT AND I TOOK JALA BACK TO JAY. PAUL AND I WENT TO WALMART TO GET A NEW MIRROR (STANDING ONE) 'CAUSE MACI BROKE MY OTHER ONE, AND SOME BEER. I COULDN'T BELIEVE I GOT HIM INTO WALMART, I'M GOOD! THEN CAME HOME AND CHILLED!

WEDNESDAY, APRIL 24, 2013:

SITTIN' HERE WITH MY 3 AWESOME KIDS! SO, ME, ADI, MAS, AND JALA ARE HANGING OUT AT MY MOM'S FOR THE DAY AND NIGHT. THIS IS THE BEST OF TIMES OF MY LIFE BEING WITH MY KIDS. I RARELY GET TO BE WITH ALL OF THEM BY MYSELF WITHOUT ANYBODY ELSE AROUND. JALA HAS SO MUCH FUN BEING WITH HER SISTER AND BROTHER, BUT SHE GETS REALLY, REALLY CLINGY AND JEALOUS TOO. IT'S SAD 'CAUSE I TRY TO EXPLAIN TO HER THAT THEY ARE MY KIDS TOO, BUT SHE DOESN'T QUITE GET IT YET. SHE NEEDS A LOT OF ATTENTION RIGHT NOW, SO I AM TRYING TO GIVE IT TO HER.

A week later...

WEDNESDAY, MAY 1, 2013:

WELL, TODAY HAS NOT BEEN A VERY GOOD DAY AT ALL! I WAS SO STINKIN' EXCITED TO SEE MASON AND ADI 'CAUSE IT'S WEDNESDAY, AND AS SOON AS THEY GOT THERE, OF COURSE, MAS RAN UP AND GAVE ME A *BIG* HUG, THEN I WENT UP TO ADI AND TRIED TO GIVE HER A HUG AND SHE SAID, "DON'T TOUCH ME, DON'T TALK TO ME, I WISH YOU WEREN'T EVEN HERE." USUALLY, WHEN YOUR KIDS SAY THINGS LIKE THAT TO US, WE USUALLY BLOW IT OFF AND DON'T CARE, BUT NOT ME, NOT WHEN I RARELY GET TO SEE MY KIDS... ANYWAYS! WHEN ANY OF MY KIDS ARE EVEN SLIGHTLY MAD AT ME, I FREAK! IT'S COMPLETE TORTURE FOR ME! I HATE IT WHEN ADI IS MAD AT ME, IT ABSOLUTELY KILLS ME AND ALL I DO IS CRY, CRY, CRY! I KNOW SHE WILL GET OVER IT EVENTUALLY, BUT I HAVE ALREADY LOST SO MUCH PRECIOUS TIME WITH ADI THAT I CANNOT LOSE ANY MORE WITH HER. I HONESTLY DO NOT KNOW WHAT TO DO, SHE WON'T EVEN LET ME APOLOGIZE TO HER. IS SHE EVER REALLY GOING TO GET

OVER ALL THIS ANGER SHE HOLDS ONTO FOR ME ANYTIME SOON? I DON'T BLAME HER FOR HER ANGER AND I CAN'T TURN BACK TIME, ALL I CAN DO IS TRY EVEN HARDER WITH HER AND BE PATIENT AND GIVE HER SPACE AND LOTS AND LOTS OF LOVE. HOPEFULLY ONE DAY SOON, ADI CAN TRULY FORGIVE ME AND WE CAN START A RELATIONSHIP TOGETHER (A MOTHER/DAUGHTER RELATIONSHIP). THAT WOULD BE A DREAM COME TRUE FOR ME, GOD, I PRAY!

<u>THURSDAY, MAY 2, 2013</u>:

WELL, DON'T KNOW QUITE YET JUST HOW TODAY IS GOING TO TURN OUT. IT'S ABOUT 2:15 A.M. AND I CAN'T SLEEP 'CAUSE EVERY TIME I START FALLING ASLEEP, I WAKE UP SOBBING THINKING ABOUT ADI. SHE IS JUST 1 PERSON I JUST CANNOT FIGHT WITH WITHOUT GETTING TOTALLY EMOTIONAL AND A COMPLETE WRECK! THE REASON WHY IT UPSETS ME SO MUCH IS BECAUSE I KNOW WHAT I HAVE PUT THAT LITTLE GIRL THROUGH, AND SHE JUST DOESN'T NEED ANY MORE NEGATIVE AT ALL WHEN IT COMES TO ME. SHE JUST NEEDS HER MOTHER, A *REAL MOM!* I AM TRYING SO STINKIN' HARD TO BE A GOOD, SOLID, STRONG MOTHER FOR HER. A WOMAN SHE CAN FINALLY LOOK UP TO AND I JUST KEEP GOING COMPLETELY *WRONG* SOMEWHERE. I JUST REALLY HOPE THAT GOD CAN SOFTEN THAT LITTLE GIRL'S HEART SOMETIME SOON AND SHE CAN COMPLETELY FORGIVE ME AND START BUILDING A REAL MOTHER/DAUGHTER RELATIONSHIP WITH ME. WHAT I WOULD GIVE FOR THAT!! ABSOLUTELY ANYTHING AND EVERYTHING!!

IT'S ABOUT 8:45 THURSDAY MORNING, PAUL IS STILL ASLEEP WHILE I AM UP AND READY TO START THE DAY! J/K, I'M UP, BUT JUST BARELY, I NEED TO GO GRAB *(get her drugs)*, OR I OR ANYBODY AROUND ME TODAY WILL NOT BE HAVING A GOOD DAY. I REALLY DO *HATE* THIS MORE THAN I COULD EVER TRY AND EXPLAIN. WELL, I'M BOUND AND DETERMINED

TO HAVE A WONDERFUL/AWESOME DAY TODAY, SO I WILL!! GOING TO GET A COFFEE RIGHT NOW.

SATURDAY, MAY 4, 2013:

SO, PAUL JUST TOOK ME TO MY VERY 1ST BLAZE GAME! IT WAS ACTUALLY REALLY, REALLY FUN. IT WAS AT THE ENERGY SOLUTIONS ARENA AND IT'S FOOTBALL PLAYED INSIDE, WITH JUST A BIT DIFFERENT RULES. BLAZE KICKED ASS AND WON! THEY WERE REALLY GOOD, I HAVEN'T SEEN FOOTBALL PLAYERS PLAY THAT GOOD IN A LONG TIME OR *EVER!* (NOT EVEN IN THE NFL.) IT WAS WAY FUN. PAUL GETS *SO* INTO IT AND SCREAMS AND YELLS THE ENTIRE GAME THAT EVERYONE IS LOOKING AT HIM. KIND OF EMBARRASSING AT TIMES, BUT AT LEAST HE IS HAVING A GOOD TIME! SO, ADI STILL WON'T TALK TO ME. IT'S REALLY KILLING ME. SHE IS MY BABY GIRL AND I HAVE ALREADY LOST SO MUCH TIME WITH HER, I CAN'T LOSE ANYMORE! I HONESTLY DON'T KNOW WHAT TO DO! I WANT TO CALL HER, BUT PAUL SAYS TO GIVE HER TIME, LET HER COOL OFF FOR A WHILE. I HONESTLY DON'T EVEN KNOW WHAT THE *HELL* I DID. I DIDN'T DO ANYTHING TO HER! I TRY SO DAMN HARD WITH HER. I WOULD GIVE THAT GIRL ANYTHING AND MY LAST DIME IF SHE NEEDED IT! I LOVE HER SO MUCH! AMY CAME OVER TODAY FOR A COUPLE HOURS, IT WAS KIND OF NICE HAVING ONE OF MY FRIENDS OVER FOR A CHANGE. SHE IS LITERALLY COMING OVER EVERY SINGLE DAY NOW! I LIKE IT AND I DON'T! I NEED MY SPACE FROM FRIENDS AT TIMES. I KNOW PAUL DOESN'T THINK TOO HIGHLY OF HER, BUT HE'S NICE TO HER!

IT'S LIKE 3:00 A.M. RIGHT NOW AND PAUL IS SOUND ASLEEP WHILE I AM WIDE AWAKE! I WISH I COULD FALL ASLEEP WITH HIM, BUT I CAN'T. HE ALWAYS GOES TO BED SO *DAMN* EARLY. AND I AM OUT OF BLK *(heroin)* RIGHT NOW AND I CANNOT SLEEP AT ALL WITHOUT IT. I START GETTING SO DAMN RESTLESS AND IT REALLY SUCKS. I WISH SAMUEL

WAS OUT OF JAIL, I HATE GOING ALL THE WAY TO SALT LAKE EVERY STINKIN' DAY! I JUST HATE ALL THIS, PERIOD!!!

SUNDAY, MAY 5, 2013:

IT'S ABOUT 3:00 P.M. AND I AM SITTIN' AT MY MOM'S RIGHT NOW WHILE PAUL IS AT THE AIRPORT. MY MOM'S GOT ANGIE'S KIDS TODAY, TOMORROW, AND WEDNESDAY 'CAUSE THEY WENT TO VEGAS FOR THEIR ANNIVERSARY. SO, ME, MAS, KAILEE, BROCK, DILLON, MY MOM, AND ADI (THAT YEP, IS STILL IGNORING ME) ARE ALL JUST HANGING OUT IN THE LIVING ROOM, JUST RELAXIN'. I LOVE SUNDAYS 'CAUSE IT'S A DAY OF RELAXIN'. KAILEE IS TAKIN' A PICTURE OF 2 PEOPLE ON HER PHONE AND FUSING THEM TOGETHER TO SEE WHAT THEY WOULD LOOK LIKE TOGETHER. HOW FREAKY IS THAT? THE THINGS WE CAN DO WITH OUR PHONES NOW-A-DAYS! KAILEE AND I JUST GOT DONE PLAYING CARDS, WE PLAYED A GAME, I DON'T REMEMBER THE NAME, THEN JUST PLAYED BS. BROCK WAS PLAYING WITH US AND HE WON, SO IT WAS KAILEE AND I FOR ABOUT AN HOUR BACK AND FORTH. IT WAS WAY FUN! PAUL IS GOING TO BE BACK IN ABOUT AN HOUR AND A HALF, BUT IN THE MEANTIME, WE ARE HEADING UP TO ANGIE'S TO HANG OUT. I HAVEN'T BEEN THERE FOR SO LONG. PAUL AND I HAVE BEEN TOGETHER FOR OVER A YEAR AND HE HASN'T BEEN TO ANGIE'S HOUSE. I'M EXCITED FOR HIM TO SEE HER BEAUTIFUL HOUSE. I TRIED TALKING TO ADI AND SHE COMPLETELY IGNORED ME. THIS SUCKS! I WANT MY BABY GIRL TO TALK TO ME! I DON'T KNOW WHAT TO DO! I GUESS JUST GIVE IT A LITTLE MORE TIME. IN THE MEANTIME, I AM COMPLETELY HEARTBROKEN!

SO, WE WENT TO ANGIE'S AND ME, KAILEE, AND ADI ALL WENT TO KAILEE'S ROOM TO LOOK AT HER CLOTHES AND SHE *FINALLY* TALKED TO ME! IT WAS ABOUT CLOTHES SHOPPING, BUT SO WHAT, WE HAD TO START SOMEWHERE, RIGHT? IT MADE ME LITERALLY WANT TO CRY! I HOPE SHE KEEPS

TALKING TO ME AND WE CAN FORGET ALL ABOUT HER BEING MAD AT ME! THAT WOULD BE FANTASTIC!!

Adi does not recall why she was mad at Nat. Nat literally carried a journal with her in her purse at all times and pulled it out to write often. I have vivid memories of her at my mom's house, sitting on the couch with her turntable of gel pens, writing in her journal and sucking on suckers. When she used meth or other uppers, she would suck on candy all the time and always had to be doing something with her hands, so she would write.

MONDAY, MAY 6, 2013:

MY MOM IS PICKING ME UP AT 9:00 A.M. TO RUN SOME ERRANDS AND SO I CAN DO MY WASH. I AM GOING TO HAVE AN AWESOME DAY TODAY, I WILL MAKE DAMN SURE OF THAT! WELL, MY MOTHER FORGOT TO PICK ME UP! IT'S 10:30 A.M. AND I'M ALL READY TO GO, BUT NO MOM! I DON'T HAVE A CAR AND MY PHONE TOTALLY BROKE ON ME THIS WEEKEND, I HAVE NO CAR, NO PHONE, AND I'M FREAKING OUT! I'M HERE ALONE 'CAUSE PAUL GOT UP EARLY TO GO TO THE AIRPORT, SO I AM JUST WAITING. I HAVE TO PICK UP JALA AT 3:25, SO I REALLY HOPE SOMEBODY SHOWS UP HERE TODAY! THE FUNNY THING IS, WHEN I WAS LEAVING ANGIE'S HOUSE LAST NIGHT, I TOLD MY MOM NOT TO FORGET ME, SHE SAID, "I WON'T," I HAD A FEELING. IT'S NOT VERY WARM TODAY. IT'S GLOOMY, BUT HOT OUTSIDE, THE SUN IS NOT SHINING. IT HAS BEEN A VERY COLD YEAR THIS YEAR. I'M SITTING OUTSIDE RIGHT NOW JUST HOPING SOMEBODY WILL SHOW UP... OH, AND SMOKING. (NASTY, NASTY HABIT!) WHEN I WAS AT MY MOM'S ON WEDNESDAY WITH MASON, I WAS SMOKING AND HE TOOK IT OUT OF MY HAND AND SMASHED IT ON THE GROUND AND SAID, "MOM, PLEASE STOP SMOKING, I DON'T WANT YOU TO DIE." HOW STINKIN' SAD IS THAT? ONE THING AT A TIME, AND WE KNOW WHAT NEEDS TO COME TO AN END 1ST!

TUESDAY, MAY 7, 2013:

TODAY WAS NOT A GOOD DAY AT ALL. AMY AND MARIA WERE OVER WITH ME MOST OF THE DAY, BUT I CAN'T REALLY DO ANYTHING 'CAUSE MY BACK WAS HURTING SO STINKIN' BAD. I HAVE NO IDEA WHAT IN THE HELL I DID TO IT, BUT I COULD HARDLY MOVE ALL DAY LONG! THEN I GOT REALLY, REALLY NAUSEATED AND FELT LIKE I WAS GOING TO THROW UP. MARIA FELT THE EXACT SAME WAY, SO I WENT AND GOT US QUIZNO'S SOUP AND WE JUST LAID ON MY BED. AMY IS DRIVING ME ABSOLUTELY CRAZY. IT REALLY FEELS LIKE ALL SHE IS DOING IS USING ME. SHE COMES OVER EVERY SINGLE DAY AND SHE NEVER HAS MONEY AND ALWAYS EXPECTS SOMETHING FROM ME. I REALLY AM SICK OF IT, I CAN'T SUPPORT BOTH OF US! I DON'T HAVE A JOB AND SHE HAS 2. IT'S PAUL'S DAUGHTER'S BIRTHDAY TODAY, BUT SHE WILL BE AT HER MOM'S, SO WE ARE CELEBRATING IT TOMORROW. PAUL'S IS SATURDAY AND I AM SO STRESSED 'CAUSE I HAVE NO IDEA WHAT TO DO FOR HIM AND I HAVE NO STINKIN' MONEY! HOW IN THE HELL AM I GOING TO SWING THIS? MY PHONE BROKE, I HAVE NO CAR YET, AND I AM REALLY GETTING PISSED! I CAN'T EVEN SEE MY KIDS TOMORROW 'CAUSE WE ARE CELEBRATING HIS DAUGHTER'S BIRTHDAY! HOW MESSED UP IS THAT? HOW MANY TIMES HAVE HIS KIDS CAME BEFORE MINE? *A LOT!*

WEDNESDAY, MAY 8, 2013:

WELL, I REALLY WAS TRYING TO MAKE THIS JOURNAL A POSITIVE ONE AND IT WAS FOR THE 1ST LITTLE BIT, BUT LET'S FACE IT…MY LIFE IS WAY TOO FUCKED UP TO WRITE ONLY POSITIVE THINGS. IF I DID THAT, I WOULD BE LEAVING OUT THE MAJORITY OF MY LIFE! TODAY WAS *ANOTHER* FUCKED UP DAY. ALL I KNOW IS THAT I REALLY NEED TO FOCUS ON MY KIDS, *NOT ON* PAUL, HIS KIDS, OR ANYTHING

ELSE! MY KIDS ARE MY ENTIRE LIFE! THEY ARE EVERYTHING I HAVE, THE ONLY PEOPLE THAT WILL NEVER GO AGAINST ME, ALWAYS FORGIVE ME, AND THAT WILL ALWAYS BE BY MY SIDE! THEY ARE MY WORLD AND I REALLY NEED TO START SHOWING THEM THAT THEY ARE! I'M SO SICK OF FOCUSING ON THE NOT IMPORTANT STUFF IN MY LIFE AND NOT MY OWN CHILDREN! WHAT KIND OF MOTHER AM I?!? AN AWFUL ONE, I DO KNOW THAT! I REALLY NEED TO CHANGE THAT AND FAST, REALLY FAST! RAN SOME ERRANDS WITH DAVID MOST OF THE DAY, THEN WENT TO MY MOM'S FOR A MINUTE, SAW MAS AND GOT JALA, THEN ADI TOOK ME TO GET A PRESENT FOR PAUL'S DAUGHTER, THEN DROPPED JALA AND I OFF AT HOME. CAME HOME, GOT THE PRESENT ORGANIZED, AND WAITED FOR PAUL AND HER TILL 6:45 P.M. THEN TOOK JALA TO JAY, CAME HOME, THEN WENT BACK TO MY MOM'S FOR A SPLIT SECOND, NOW AT HOME, FIGHTING WITH PAUL. HOW ODD! HE TOLD ME TONIGHT HOW SELF-CENTERED I WAS!!

THURSDAY, MAY 9, 2013:

IT'S A BRAND NEW DAY TODAY AND IT'S GOING TO BE A *GREAT* ONE! LEAVE YESTERDAY BEHIND AND MAKE TODAY AN *AWESOME* ONE! WELL, PAUL AND I HAVE BEEN COMPLETELY AWFUL LATELY, I DON'T KNOW WHAT IS GOING TO HAPPEN WITH US, BUT I AM REALLY, REALLY SCARED! I DO LOVE THIS MAN MORE THAN ANYTHING IN THIS WORLD AND IT'S REALLY HARD BECAUSE HE HAS SO MANY PROBLEMS, WELL, NOT REALLY, JUST VERY, VERY *BI-POLAR* AND HAS A VERY, VERY *BAD* TEMPER! HE CAN BE THE CRUELEST MAN I HAVE EVER BEEN AROUND IN MY ENTIRE LIFE! BUT, I MADLY LOVE HIM WITH ALL MY HEART. I PRAY TO GOD EVERYTHING WORKS OUT BETWEEN US, BECAUSE HE IS IT FOR ME! IT'S HIS BIRTHDAY SATURDAY AND I WANT TO DO SOMETHING *GREAT* FOR HIM, BUT DON'T KNOW WHAT 'CAUSE I HAVE NO $ TO WORK WITH.

Two days later...

SATURDAY, MAY 11, 2013:

WELL, THIS HAS DEFINITELY BEEN THE WORST WEEKEND OF MY ENTIRE LIFE! AND IT'S EVEN MOTHER'S DAY TOMORROW. BUT, I'M A SHITTY MOM ANYWAYS, SO I GUESS THAT DAY DOESN'T APPLY TO ME! SO, PAUL AND I HAVE BEEN FIGHTING PRETTY DAMN BAD, ACTUALLY WORSE THAN EVER! YESTERDAY, I LEFT EARLY IN THE MORNING WITH MY MOM TO RUN ERRANDS AND FORGOT TO LEAVE THE DOOR UNLOCKED FOR HIS DAUGHTER. COMPLETELY FORGOT! WELL, HE THINKS I DID IT ON PURPOSE, SO HE KICKED ME OUT OF HIS HOUSE AND WILL NOT EVEN LET ME GET SOME THINGS FOR THE NEXT COUPLE DAYS. HOW EXTREMELY RIDICULOUS IS THAT? AND OF ALL THINGS, IT'S PAUL'S FREAKING BIRTHDAY TODAY! I SLEPT AT MY MOM'S LAST NIGHT WITH MASON AND JALA, AND MY DAD CAME AND WOKE ME UP AT 7:00 A.M. AND SAID, "I'M TAKING YOU HOME." HE KNEW IT WAS PAUL'S BIRTHDAY, SO HE WANTED ME HOME WITH HIM. *(None of us had any idea how Paul treated her. My dad is very protective of his girls and would NOT have been okay with Paul if he had known how he treated Nat.)* WELL, I GOT HIM A BIRTHDAY CAKE AND WHEN I WALKED IN, HE SAID, "WHAT ARE YOU DOING HERE?" THEN HE SAID, "WHY IN THE HELL DID YOU BRING ME A CAKE, YOU KNOW I DON'T LIKE CAKE." THEN HE PRETTY MUCH KICKED ME OUT! HE LITERALLY KICKED ME OUT AND TOLD ME HE NEVER WANTED TO SEE ME AGAIN, *EVER!* IT BROKE MY HEART IN TWO. I LOVE THAT MAN MORE THAN ANYTHING IN THIS WORLD! WHAT DO I DO? I CAN'T BE TREATED LIKE THAT, BUT I DON'T WANT TO LIVE WITHOUT HIM EITHER! I AM A *MESS!* I BEGGED HIM TO COME HOME TONIGHT AND HE TOLD ME TO STAY AWAY FROM HIM AND TO STAY AWAY FROM HIS KIDS, TO JUST *STAY AWAY!* I HAVE TO RESPECT HIS WISHES AND I DIDN'T HAVE ANYWHERE TO GO, SO I HAD TO

STAY AT MOTEL 6 TONIGHT AND I AM LITERALLY WANTING TO DIE. TOMORROW IS MOTHER'S DAY AND IT'S GOING TO BE THE WORST DAY EVER!! I AM SO *SAD!*

SUNDAY, MAY 12, 2013:

TODAY WAS MOTHER'S DAY AND I WAS LITERALLY IN TEARS ALL DAY! PAUL COMPLETELY ENDED IT WITH ME AND HAS BASICALLY TOLD ME THAT, THE PAST FEW DAYS THAT I HAVE BEEN GONE, HE HAS BEEN SO HAPPY. WHETHER HE IS LYING OR NOT, THAT IS THE CRUELEST THING ANYONE HAS EVER SAID TO ME! THAT IS GOING TO HURT FOR A LONG, LONG TIME! I REALLY DID LOVE HIM, BUT I NEED TO GET OVER HIM NOW, QUICK! I CAN'T PUT ANOTHER THOUGHT INTO THIS MAN! HE SAID THAT THE PAST YEAR WE WERE TOGETHER HAS BEEN THE MOST HORRIBLE TIME OF HIS LIFE! THE THINGS HE HAS SAID TO ME THE PAST FEW DAYS, I WILL *NEVER* FORGET! HE HONESTLY IS THE MOST *EVIL* MAN I HAVE EVER KNOWN. WHAT DID I DO TO MYSELF, GETTING INVOLVED WITH SUCH AN *EVIL PERSON* AND DIDN'T EVEN KNOW IT! ALL I KNOW IS, I AM NOT DATING FOR AT LEAST 2 YEARS! I AM DONE WITH MEN FOR A WHILE, FOR A LONG, LONG TIME 'CAUSE I HAVE NEVER BEEN THIS HURT BY ANYONE IN MY LIFE! WHAT A DICK! HE'S NOT EVEN VERY CUTE AT ALL, HE HAS A BEER BELLY FROM *HELL* AND IS THE HAIRIEST MAN I HAVE EVER SEEN! YUCK! AT LEAST, I AM TRYING TO TELL MYSELF THAT! SO, ADI CAME OVER TODAY AND BROUGHT ME FLOWERS AND A HUGE COOKIE THAT SAID, "LOVE YOU, MOM." SHE APOLOGIZED FOR WHAT SHE HAD SAID TO ME A COUPLE DAYS AGO THAT HURT ME SO MUCH! WE SPENT THE ENTIRE DAY TOGETHER AND IT WAS GREAT, EVEN THOUGH I WAS UPSET ALL DAY 'CAUSE OF FUCK FACE! ADI AND MAS MADE MY DAY AT LEAST BRIGHT AND NICE. I LOVE MY STINKIN' KIDS! JALA IS LAYING RIGHT NEXT TO ME WHILE JAY AND I ARE ON

EACH SIDE OF HER WATCHING A SHOW. THANK GOD, JAY HAS THE HEART TO HELP ME OUT AND GIVE ME A PLACE TO STAY!

MONDAY, MAY 13, 2013:

SLEPT AT JAY'S LAST NIGHT AND IT WAS ACTUALLY OKAY. WE PUT JALA TO SLEEP AND JUST WATCHED A MOVIE TOGETHER AND WROTE. IT WAS ACTUALLY PRETTY NICE, SINCE PAUL PUT ME THROUGH *HELL* AND BACK THE PAST FOUR DAYS. I CAN'T TAKE IT ANYMORE. I'M HURTING SO MUCH AND JUST NEED TO TRY AND GET PAUL OUT OF MY HEAD AS MUCH AND AS BEST AS I CAN!

WELL, PLANS OF MINE CHANGED, IT'S ABOUT 10:30 P.M. AND I AM AT HOME (PAUL'S HOUSE) 'CAUSE WE TALKED TODAY AND WE ARE GOING TO TRY AND WORK THINGS OUT. WELL, WE ARE GOING TO GIVE IT A COUPLE WEEKS, JUST SEE HOW WE DO TOGETHER. I DON'T LIKE SAYING THIS AT ALL, BUT I REALLY DON'T THINK WE ARE GOING TO MAKE IT AT ALL! I HAD ALL THE HOPES IN THE WORLD FOR US, BUT AFTER THE PAST 4/5 DAYS, IF WE DO GET PAST ALL OF THIS, IT WILL BE A *MIRACLE*, A COMPLETE *MIRACLE*. I HOPE WE CAN GET THROUGH THIS, BUT IT'S A LONG SHOT, LIKE I SAID. EVERY TIME I HEAR HIM ON THE PHONE WITH HIS PRECIOUS DAUGHTER, I WANT TO STRANGLE SOMEONE! I DON'T KNOW WHY, BUT THEY DRIVE ME *COMPLETELY CRAZY* WHEN THEY ARE TOGETHER! THAT'S ALL THIS MAN CARES ABOUT. AND IT'S GOOD THAT HE IS LIKE THIS WITH HIS KIDS, BUT HE HAS NO TIME IN HIS LIFE FOR LOVE WITH A WOMAN! HE HAS NO MORE ROOM IN HIS HEART AT ALL! I REALLY THOUGHT I COULD HANDLE IT, BUT I CAN'T!!! I WANT AND NEED SOMEBODY THAT GIVES ME THE RESPECT THAT I DESERVE. HE GIVES ME NO RESPECT AT ALL RIGHT NOW AND I AM HEAD OVER HEELS IN LOVE WITH HIM! WHAT IN THE HELL IS WRONG WITH ME, WHY DO I LOVE HIM SO MUCH? HE IS NOT EVEN VERY ATTRACTIVE TO OTHER PEOPLE,

BUT TO ME, HE IS BY FAR THE SEXIEST MAN I HAVE EVER BEEN WITH OR EVEN CAME ACROSS IN MY LIFE!

Nat would get into this vicious cycle of taking drugs to numb her feelings and then get angry at herself for using which would only perpetuate the drug abuse. She would get so numb that she could be in an unthinkable situation and not be too fazed by it. For instance, being at Paul's when she knew he didn't want her there or after he said such horrible things and treated her terribly.

TUESDAY, MAY 14, 2013:

TODAY HAS BEEN BETTER THAN THE LAST 5 DAYS, FOR SURE! I'M SITTING HERE WITH JALA RIGHT NOW AT MY MOM'S, DOING LAUNDRY AND WAITING TO PICK UP PAUL. HE LET ME TAKE THE VAN TODAY, SO I HAVE TO PICK HIM UP IN A COUPLE HOURS AT THE SHOP WHERE HE IS WORKING ON MY CAR. HE IS LEAVING SATURDAY WITH HIS KIDS UP TO SNOWBIRD, HE ASKED ME TODAY IF I WANTED TO GO, BUT I TOLD HIM NO. HE SAID MY CAR WOULD BE DONE BY FRIDAY, THE LATEST! HE BETTER FOLLOW THROUGH THIS TIME OR I WILL COMPLETELY LOSE IT! JALA AND I ARE WATCHING CAT IN THE HAT! I LOVE JUST RELAXIN' WITH MY BABY GIRL. NO DRAMA, NO FIGHTING, AND NO NEGATIVITY! GOSH, THIS IS NICE AFTER HAVING THE HORRIBLE WEEKEND THAT I DID! I'M LITERALLY GOING TO PRAY TO GOD THAT ME AND THIS MAN WORK! HE IS EVERYTHING TO ME, I DON'T KNOW WHY HE IS DIFFERENT THAN ANYBODY ELSE AND THAT I LOVE HIM AS MUCH AS I DO BUT I DO, A WHOLE, WHOLE LOT! I PRAY TO GOD THAT WE CAN WORK THIS OUT AND BE BETTER THAN *EVER* AND BE BEST FRIENDS AGAIN.

WE HAD A GREAT NIGHT TOGETHER TONIGHT. HE MADE ME DINNER, WE LISTENED TO MUSIC, WE TALKED POSITIVELY AND WENT TO GET MOVIES TOGETHER. WE DID AWESOME TONIGHT. IT'S GOING TO STAY THAT WAY, NO MATTER WHAT! ANOTHER

REASON I LOVE IT WHEN WE ARE GETTING ALONG IS BECAUSE I CAN FOCUS ON MY KIDS AND NOT OUR RELATIONSHIP SO MUCH! TOMORROW IS MY DAY WITH THE KIDS, AND NOW THAT ME AND PAUL ARE GETTING ALONG SO WELL, I WON'T HAVE TO STRESS ABOUT US AND I CAN BE WITH MY 3 FAVORITE PEOPLE IN THE WORLD AND HAVE FUN WITH THEM. I GET SO SUPER EXCITED TO SEE MY KIDS! I LOVE THEM!

WEDNESDAY, MAY 15, 2013:

K, SO I AM SUPER EXCITED! MAS JUST TEXTED ME AND SAID THAT THE SCOUTS ARE HAVING A MOTHER/SON BARBECUE TONIGHT AND HE NEEDS ME TO BE THERE. I HAVE NOT DONE SOMETHING LIKE THAT WITH MASON FOR WHO KNOWS HOW LONG. I'M SO EXCITED!! SPENDING TIME WITH MY BOY, WHAT MORE COULD I POSSIBLY ASK FOR? MY LITTLE BOY IS MY FAVORITE PERSON IN THIS WORLD! LIKE ALWAYS, HE HAS ABOUT 5 FRIENDS OVER HERE AT MY MOM'S WITH HIM. HE IS SUCH A LITTLE STUD! I DON'T KNOW HOW IN THE HELL HE TURNED OUT THE WAY HE DID, BUT HE IS A *PERFECT* LITTLE BOY! ADI IS ON THE COUCH WATCHING HER IPOD AND JALA IS IN THE KITCHEN WITH MY MOM HELPING HER MAKE COOKIES. I'M SURE SHE IS IN THERE EATING ALL THE COOKIE DOUGH! ADI AND I JUST GOT BACK FROM RUNNING TO ROBINTINO'S 'CAUSE SHE WANTED SOME BREADSTICKS. MAS AND I ARE LEAVING IN ABOUT A HALF HOUR. PAUL IS AT HOME HELPING HIS SON WITH HIS HOMEWORK 'CAUSE HE IS TAKING A COUPLE OF CLASSES. HE JUST TEXTED ME AND SAID HE WAS SO SORRY FOR EVERYTHING AND WE ARE GREAT TOGETHER AND THAT HE LOVES ME. I NEEDED TO HEAR THAT. IT'S GOING TO BE AN INCREDIBLY GREAT NIGHT!

WELL, IT WAS! IT WAS AN AWESOME NIGHT. MASON AND I HAD A GREAT TIME. I TALKED TO A FAMILY FRIEND THE WHOLE TIME WHILE, OF COURSE, MAS AND HER SON WERE INSEPARABLE. THEN CAME HOME, WENT TO MAVERICK AND GOT

PAUL AND I SOME TREATS, THEN CAME HOME AND WATCHED A MOVIE *(GRUDGE 2)*. IT WAS NICE WATCHING A MOVIE WITH MY LOVE.

Spanning years, the memories I have of Nat at my house, my mom's, or Angie's are of her lying on the couch, not feeling well. Even if her kids were around, most of the time, she was lying around sick.

THURSDAY, MAY 16, 2013:

YA, IT'S 1:30 A.M. THURSDAY MORNING, I BEST BE GOING INTO BED ABOUT NOW. PAUL HAS BEEN ASLEEP FOR AT LEAST 3 HOURS NOW AND HE WAS WAITING FOR ME, HOW STINKIN' SAD IS THAT? HE FALLS ASLEEP SO EARLY AND I AM SO A NIGHT PERSON, NOT AT ALL A MORNING PERSON! GOODNIGHT!

NOW, I AM AT MY MOM'S AND IT'S ABOUT 3:10, JUST WAITING TO PICK UP JALA IN A FEW MINUTES. DROPPED PAUL OFF AT MY CAR, HOPEFULLY IT'S DONE EITHER TOMORROW OR SUNDAY. I'M GROWING VERY, VERY IMPATIENT WITH THIS SITUATION. IT'S BEEN ABOUT 3 MONTHS, WHEN IT SHOULD HAVE BEEN DONE IN A WEEK!

IT'S ABOUT 9:40 P.M. AND PAUL AND I ARE JUST SITTING DOWN TO WATCH A MOVIE. HE'S BEEN WORKING ON MY CAR ALL DAY AND I HAVE HAD MY PRECIOUS JALA. HE GOT HOME ABOUT 8:30, I GOT HOME ABOUT 9. I HAD TO GO UP TO BRIAN'S TO HELP THIS GIRL BECAUSE SHE HAS THIS *HUGE* ABSCESS ON HER LOWER ARM. IT'S SO BAD THAT IT'S CLOSE TO KILLING HER. I WENT OVER THERE AND GAVE HER SOME ANTIBIOTICS AND DRAINED THE ABSCESS WITH A NEEDLE. *(I am curious why she was called to do this, and if she had done stuff like this often).*

DIDN'T DO TOO MUCH 'CAUSE I DIDN'T WANT TO MESS WITH IT MUCH. I'M GLAD TO BE HOME, THOUGH. I LOVE JUST SITTIN' DOWN RELAXIN' WITH MY BABY! WE HAVE BEEN DOING REALLY, REALLY GOOD THE LAST FEW DAYS, I'M SO,

SO GLAD! I AM GOING TO GO TO BED EARLY TONIGHT 'CAUSE LAST NIGHT I WAS REALLY LATE (LIKE 3:00 A.M. LATE) AND PAUL WOKE ME UP AROUND 7:00, NEVER WENT BACK TO SLEEP, AND I'M STILL NOT TIRED RIGHT NOW!

FRIDAY, MAY 17, 2013:

HUNG OUT WITH AMY ALL DAY, IT WAS OKAY, SHE JUST REALLY, REALLY BUGS AFTER A COUPLE HOURS! WENT TO GET JALA AT 1:25, THEN CAME HOME AND PAUL'S DAUGHTER WAS HERE. THEY WERE SO SUPER EXCITED TO SEE EACH OTHER, IT WAS THE CUTEST THING EVER. SO, I WAS IN THE BATHROOM AND THE GIRLS CAME RUNNING IN FREAKING OUT! THEY WERE SCREAMING, SAYING MACI WAS ON OUR ROOF! HOW FUNNY IS THAT? I WAS LAUGHING SO HARD. WE HAVE A LITTLE DOG/CAT DOOR IN OUR KITCHEN THAT SHE FIGURED OUT, SO UNLESS WE LOCK IT, SHE KNOWS HOW TO GO IN/OUT. SHE THINKS SHE IS THE *SHIT* NOW!! SHE IS THE PRINCESS OF THE HOUSE, THOUGH. SHE ABSOLUTELY RUNS THIS HOUSE AND EVERYONE IN IT!

IT'S SHALL'S BIRTHDAY TODAY AND TYE TOOK HER TO VEGAS FOR THE NIGHT AND THEY WENT TO SEE BOYS II MEN IN CONCERT. HOW SILLY IS THAT? I HAVEN'T HEARD ABOUT BOYS II MEN FOR YEARS, LIKE 10 YEARS! BUT HOW STINKIN' FUN! IT'S HER 40TH BIRTHDAY TODAY AND SHE IS HAVING A COMPLETE MELTDOWN. I'M GLAD TYE DID SOMETHING BIG FOR HER, I THINK SHE WOULD HAVE HAD A PANIC ATTACK OR SOMETHING 'CAUSE NOW SHE'S 40!!!

SATURDAY, MAY 18, 2013:

IT'S ABOUT 3:00 P.M. RIGHT NOW AND I AM WITH PAUL'S SON RIGHT AT THIS SECOND PICKING UP PAUL FROM THE SHOP AND THEN WE ARE HEADING HOME, THEN GOING UP TO SNOWBIRD. WE HAVE A CONDO UP THERE FOR A WEEK. IT'S

WAY STINKIN' FUN! WE DEFINITELY NEED IT, TOO! THE KIDS ARE COMING WITH US TONIGHT, BUT WE WILL HAVE SOME TIME UP THERE ALONE TOO THIS WEEK. I NEED TO GET AWAY ANYWAYS, *BAD!* AMY CAME OVER AGAIN THIS MORNING AND SPENT THE ENTIRE DAY WITH ME AGAIN, WELL, AT LEAST TILL NOW. IT DOESN'T REALLY BOTHER ME OTHER THAN WHEN SHE SHOWS UP WITHOUT CALLING FIRST.

GETTING READY TO GO UP TO SNOWBIRD NOW. HAVE NO IDEA HOW LONG WE WILL BE UP THERE, WE HAVE A WEEK, BUT I USUALLY COME BACK AND FORTH. PLUS, WE ARE FIGHTING *AGAIN*, SO I DON'T KNOW WHAT'S GOING TO HAPPEN. HE MIGHT JUST BE TAKING ME HOME, HE IS PISSED AND IT'S SO SUPER HARD TO CALM HIM DOWN! I TRY AND TRY AND TRY AND I GET ABSOLUTELY NOWHERE WHEN HE IS ANGRY! WHY DOES THIS HAVE TO BE SO HARD? WHY CAN'T WE JUST GET ALONG, SINCE HE IS THE MAN I WANT TO SPEND THE REST OF MY LIFE WITH? I FEEL LIKE I KISS HIS ASS ALL THE DAMN TIME, AND IT MAKES ME FEEL SO DAMN STUPID! I FEEL DUMB AROUND HIS KIDS NOW ALL THE TIME 'CAUSE THEY SEE US FIGHT ALL THE TIME AND THEY SEE ME KISSING HIS ASS ALL THE TIME. I LOVE HIM AND I HATE HIM, HOW IN THE HELL DOES THAT WORK? I WISH I KNEW WHAT TO DO...WHAT I WANT IS JUST NOT HAPPENING FOR US, TO GET ALONG AND BE IN LOVE!

SUNDAY, MAY 19, 2013:

BEEN UP AT SNOWBIRD ALL DAMN DAY WITH PAUL AND HIS KIDS AND I'M REALLY MAD! WHY CAN'T IT BE MY KIDS WE WERE WITH? WHY DOES IT ALWAYS HAVE TO BE HIS KIDS? IT MAKES ME LITERALLY SICK TO MY STOMACH THAT I AM WITH HIS KIDS A HELL OF A LOT MORE THAN MY OWN KIDS. I WANT TO BE WITH MY OWN KIDS, NOT SOMEONE ELSE'S. I KNOW IT'S NOT JUST SOMEBODY'S KIDS, IT'S THE MAN THAT I'M IN LOVE WITH'S KIDS AND IF WE GET MARRIED,

THEY WILL BE MY KIDS TOO, BUT WE CAN'T EVEN GET ALONG FOR A WHOLE DAY RIGHT NOW. I WISH WE COULD, AND I AM TRYING MY HARDEST, BUT IT DOESN'T GET ANYWHERE WITH ONLY ONE PERSON TRYING. BOTH NEED TO PUT IN AN EFFORT! MASON AND ADI WERE AT MY MOM'S ALL DAY TODAY, I TRIED LIKE HELL TO GET BACK DOWN TO THE CITY, BUT OF COURSE, DIDN'T MAKE IT! I AM SO UPSET. I DON'T EVEN WANT TO KNOW WHAT IS GOING THROUGH POOR MASON'S HEAD…THAT HIS MOMMY IS WITH SOMEONE ELSE'S KIDS WHEN I COULD HAVE BEEN WITH HIM. THAT TOTALLY BREAKS MY HEART IN TWO! I KNOW I SUCK AT THIS MOTHER THING AND I DON'T SHOW IT AT ALL, BUT MY 3 KIDS ARE THE *MOST IMPORTANT* THING IN MY LIFE. EVERYONE ALWAYS TELLS ME HOW SELFISH I AM, AND I WOULD ALWAYS ARGUE BACK SAYING I WASN'T, BUT WHEN I REALLY THINK ABOUT IT, I TOTALLY AM. I COULDN'T BE ANY MORE SELFISH! I HAVE A GOOD HEART AND I DO WHAT I CAN FOR PEOPLE, BUT NOT THE RIGHT PEOPLE! I NEED TO TAKE A STEP BACK A LITTLE MORE OFTEN AND LOOK AT WHAT I AM DOING TO MYSELF, TO MY KIDS AND THE PEOPLE I LOVE. IT'S REALLY, REALLY HARD NOT TO BE SELFISH, BUT I NEED TO GET CLEAN, NOT TRY, JUST DO IT! AT LEAST FOR MY 3 KIDS!!

<u>MONDAY, MAY 20, 2013</u>:

SO, MY CAR IS STILL NOT DONE, AND THE VAN IS COMPLETELY BREAKING DOWN. IT OVERHEATED ON US ON THE WAY TO SNOWBIRD, AND ON THE WAY BACK DOWN, WE HAD TO PULL OVER A COUPLE TIMES 'CAUSE IT WON'T SHIFT AT ALL! YEP, WE ARE GOING TO BE STUCK WITH NO VEHICLE! I AM SERIOUSLY LIVID! WELL, IT'S ABOUT 1:00 A.M. MONDAY MORNING AND I'M FINALLY GOING TO BED…DEPRESSED AS FUCK 'CAUSE I DIDN'T SEE MY KIDS TODAY, I HAVE NO IDEA WHAT'S GOING ON WITH MY RELATIONSHIP WITH PAUL AND ABSOLUTELY NO MONEY TO MY NAME AND NO VEHICLE YET! WHAT MORE COULD

I ASK FOR? JUST WANT TO BE HAPPY WITH MY KIDS AND PAUL, IS THAT TOO MUCH TO ASK? PAUL IS ACTING REALLY SICK RIGHT NOW, WHEN WE WERE UP AT SNOWBIRD, HE WAS BURNING UP WITH A HIGH FEVER! I MEAN REALLY, REALLY HOT! I HAVE BEEN TRYING TO TAKE CARE OF HIM, BUT HE WILL *NOT* LET ME. KEEPS SAYIN', "I'M FINE, I'M FINE," WHICH I KNOW HE IS NOT, HE IS SHIVERING AND BURNING UP *BAD!* BUT HE WON'T LET ME HELP HIM, SO I HOPE HE GETS BETTER SOON.

Same day, different journal:

WELL, TODAY HAS ACTUALLY BEEN PRETTY DAMN GOOD. MY MOM PICKED ME UP AROUND 10:00 A.M. AND WE WENT TO HER FRIEND'S HOUSE 'CAUSE SHE DIED AND I GOT LOTS OF CUTE STUFF, CUTE CLOTHES, SILVERWARE, CANDLES, ETC. THEN PAUL PICKED ME UP AND WE WENT TO NORTH OGDEN TO LOOK AT SUBURBANS 'CAUSE THE VAN BROKE DOWN, AND NOW BACK AT MY MOM'S GETTING READY TO PICK UP JALA. PAUL AND I ARE DOING FANTASTIC TODAY! I'M SO HAPPY!!!

These last two entries were written on the same day, but they're quite different.

<u>TUESDAY, MAY 21, 2013</u>:

IT'S ABOUT 1:00 A.M. TUESDAY MORNING, AND ONCE AGAIN, I AM UP AND PAUL IS SOUND ASLEEP. I'M ACTUALLY WAITING FOR DAVID TO MEET ME 'CAUSE I AM OUT *(of drugs)* AND HE IS NOT CALLING BACK. THAT'S NOT LIKE HIM AT ALL! I'M REALLY SCARED HE MIGHT HAVE GOT PULLED OVER. THAT WOULD BE SO SAD IF HE WENT BACK TO JAIL 'CAUSE HE WAS ON HIS WAY TO TAKE CARE OF ME…I AM GOING TO THINK POSITIVELY! WELL, EVERYTHING WAS FINE, HE JUST WASN'T ANSWERING HIS PHONE.

WOKE UP THIS MORNING TO PAUL KISSING MY NECK. IT WAS SO SWEET! HE WENT TO WORK ON MY CAR AND I SLEPT TILL LIKE 11:00 A.M. IT WAS NICE! NOW, I'M AT MY MOM'S, ABOUT 7:00 P.M., AND I AM JUST RELAXIN' TALKIN' TO MY MOM, DOING OUR LAUNDRY WHILE I WAIT FOR PAUL TO GET HOME. HE IS FIXING THE RADIATOR IN THE VAN AND FIXING MY CAR AT THE SAME TIME. HE DEFINITELY HAS A TON GOING ON RIGHT NOW. IT'S WEDNESDAY TOMORROW AND WE HAVE NOT BEEN UP AT SNOWBIRD AT ALL OTHER THAN SATURDAY NIGHT. PAUL IS REALLY UPSET BY THAT. BUT WE DON'T HAVE ANY VEHICLE TO DRIVE UP THERE RIGHT NOW. WHEN IT RAINS, IT POURS! BUT WE WILL GET BY, WE ALWAYS DO!

I'M NOW HOME BY MYSELF, SITTING IN BED, WRITING, WAITING FOR PAUL TO GET HOME AND I HAVE NO IDEA WHEN THAT'S GOING TO BE. IT'S 10:00 P.M. NOW AND IT'S SO PAST PAUL'S BEDTIME, SO I'M REALLY HOPING HE'LL POP IN HERE SHORTLY. I AM LITERALLY FALLING ASLEEP AS I WRITE! GOODNIGHT TILL TOMORROW!

5-22-2013: Dr. Note–120 lbs. Prescribed Suboxone. Denies relapse, feels stable.

WEDNESDAY, MAY 22, 2013:

HAD AN OKAY DAY TODAY OTHER THAN FIGHTING WITH PAUL AGAIN! GOT UP, WENT TO THE DR., THEN WENT TO RITE AID AND THEN PICKED UP PAUL FROM THE SHOP, WENT HOME AND TALKED FOR A BIT, THEN ADI CAME AND GOT ME AND WE WENT TO WALMART, THEN WENT AND GOT MASON AND JALA FROM SCHOOL, THEN WENT TO MY MOM'S. NOW JUST RELAXIN' HERE TILL I GET READY TO GO TO ADI'S CHOIR CONCERT TONIGHT. NEVER MIND, GOING TO ADI'S CONCERT TOMORROW INSTEAD. THE MISSIONARIES *(from our church)* JUST CAME OVER AND ATE DINNER WITH US AT MY MOM'S AND GAVE ME A LESSON ON QUITTING SMOKING. APPARENTLY, THEY HAVE A

NON-SMOKING PROGRAM THAT HELPS PEOPLE STOP SMOKING. I THINK I AM GOING TO START IT NEXT WEEK. THEY ARE MEETING WITH ME AGAIN NEXT WEDNESDAY AND I THINK I AM GOING TO COMMIT TO THE PROGRAM, AT LEAST FOR MY KIDS' SAKE. THEY KEEP ASKING ME TO STOP, THAT IS A BIG ENOUGH INCENTIVE FOR ME! JAY CAME AND GOT JALA AND I HAD HIM DROP ME OFF AT ANTHONY'S SO I COULD HANG AND TALK FOR A MINUTE, AND NOW I'M STUCK HERE! JUST CALLED MARIA AND SHE SAID SHE WOULD COME AND GET ME BUT YA NEVER KNOW, SHE IS FLAKY AT TIMES. THIS NOT HAVING A CAR THING IS REALLY PISSIN' ME OFF, ACTUALLY, I'M BEYOND PISSED, HE SHOULD HAVE MY CAR BACK!

SO, I GOT HOME TONIGHT AROUND 10:00 P.M. AND NO PAUL! I WENT INTO THE BEDROOM AND HALF OF HIS CLOTHES ARE GONE AND HIS SUITCASE. HE LEFT ME! I KNOW HE'S UP AT SNOWBIRD AND THAT HURTS EVEN MORE BECAUSE WE WERE SUPPOSED TO BE UP THERE TOGETHER! I AM LITERALLY FREAKING THE FUCK OUT!!! I CAN'T LOSE THIS MAN... BUT I THINK HE'S ALREADY GONE!

<u>THURSDAY, MAY 23, 2013</u>:

IT'S ABOUT 3:05 A.M. AND I'M SITTING ON MY BED FREAKING OUT! PAUL LEFT ME TODAY AND I AM HERE ALL ALONE AND I KEEP HEARING NOISES AND IT'S SCARING ME TO DEATH. ANTHONY CAME OVER AROUND MIDNIGHT AND WE WALKED TO WALMART AND THEN GOT A RIDE HOME FROM SOMEONE THAT WORKED THERE THAT WAS HEADING HOME. I CAN'T BELIEVE PAUL LEFT ME! I KNOW HE'S UP AT SNOWBIRD AND I HAVE A KEY, BUT I AM NOT ABOUT TO LOWER MYSELF AND CHASE HIM. WHAT AM I DOING SO WRONG? HE SAYS I'M HARD TO LIVE AND DEAL WITH...HOW?!? I DO ANYTHING AND EVERYTHING FOR THAT MAN! I AM ALWAYS EXTREMELY GOOD TO HIM, TREAT HIM WITH RESPECT, GIVE HIM WHATEVER HE NEEDS WHENEVER HE WANTS IT, TAKE CARE OF HIS KIDS, MORE THAN I DO MINE,

AND TREAT HIM LIKE GOLD AND LOVE HIM TO DEATH! WHAT ON EARTH AM I DOING SO WRONG? AM I TOO GOOD TO HIM? DO I NEED TO GIVE THIS MAN SOMEWHAT OF A CHALLENGE? I'M TOO SCARED TO DO THAT, WITH FEARS THAT I WILL LOSE HIM. BUT, WHAT HAVE I BEEN DOING, OBVIOUSLY IT'S NOT THE RIGHT WAY WITH HIM. I PRAY TO GOD THAT I DIDN'T LOSE PAUL! I PRAY HE COMES HOME IN THE MORNING AND WE TALK AND WORK THINGS OUT, I WOULD GIVE ABSOLUTELY ANYTHING! DAVID WAS SUPPOSED TO BE COMING OUT 'CAUSE I AM FREAKING OUT SO BAD, BUT OF COURSE, BEEN WAITING ON HIM FOR THE PAST 2 HOURS NOW. JUST CALLED ANTHONY BACK OVER, BUT THAT'S GOING TO TAKE A WHILE 'CAUSE HE LIVES QUITE A WAYS AWAY AND HE IS WALKING (NO CAR). I JUST HOPE ONE OF THEM HURRIES!

It must have been so terrifying and exhausting for her to have been that dependent on something to stay well.

FRIDAY, MAY 24, 2013:

I DON'T CARE WHAT IS GOING ON IN MY LIFE RIGHT NOW, I AM GOING TO HAVE A *FANTASTIC* DAY! ESPECIALLY WITH THE WEEK I HAVE HAD THIS WEEK, I DESERVE AT LEAST ONE GOOD DAY THIS WEEK! I'M NOT THAT *BAD* OF A PERSON, MY INTENTIONS ARE USUALLY ALWAYS GOOD! SO WHY IN THE HELL DO I HAVE SO MUCH BAD LUCK? I KNOW ONE REASON, BUT I'M NOT READY YET, I KNOW THERE WILL *NEVER* BE A PERFECT TIME, BUT WITH ALL THIS GOING ON, IF I CHANGE AND QUIT NOW, I JUST MIGHT GET SUICIDAL. ACTUALLY, I ALMOST GUARANTEE THAT I WOULD WANT AND THINK ABOUT KILLING MYSELF IF I TRIED TO QUIT THAT RIGHT NOW. IT'S JUST NOT A GOOD TIME. I AM LOSING THE ONE MAN I TRULY LOVED WITH ALL MY HEART AND THOUGHT I WAS GOING TO SHARE THE REST OF MY LIFE WITH HIM. I AM COMPLETELY HEARTBROKEN!!

This letter was in her journal, she never gave it to Paul.

LETTER FROM NAT TO PAUL, SATURDAY, MAY 25, 2013:

I'M WRITING THIS LETTER, BUT I AM NOT GIVING IT TO YOU. THERE ARE SO MANY THINGS I WANT TO SAY TO YOU, PAUL, BUT CAN'T BECAUSE OF YOUR TEMPER AND HOW YOU REACT. YOU DON'T *EVER* LISTEN TO ME AND WHAT I HAVE TO SAY, YOU JUST HEAR WHAT YOU WANT AND USUALLY IT'S NOT AT ALL WHAT I'M EVEN TRYING TO SAY! HONEY, I KNOW YOU THINK A LOT OF OUR FIGHTING IS BECAUSE OF ME, BUT PAUL, IT'S NOT AT ALL. I KNOW WHEN I AM IN THE WRONG OR DISRESPECTFUL AND IF I AM, I IMMEDIATELY NOTICE IT AND TRY TO FIX IT, BUT IT'S NOT VERY OFTEN. PAUL, I KNOW YOU'RE BIPOLAR, BUT YOU ARE VERY, VERY SICK MENTALLY. I WISH I COULD GET THROUGH TO YOU, OR SOMEBODY, BUT IT'S ABSOLUTELY IMPOSSIBLE WITH YOU. I NEVER HAVE WALKED ON EGGSHELLS WITH ANYONE BEFORE OR TIP TOED AROUND ANYONE LIKE I DO YOU. I KNOW NOW EXACTLY WHAT YOUR KIDS ARE TALKING ABOUT. I AM ABSOLUTELY TERRIFIED OF YOU NOW. YOU LOOK AT ME WRONG AND I WANT TO PEE MY PANTS. NOBODY IN MY ENTIRE LIFE HAS EVER SCARED ME, BUT I HAVE *NEVER* EVEN CAME CLOSE TO BEING HIT, CHOKED, OR MENTALLY ABUSED LIKE I HAVE BY YOU. WHAT HAPPENED THE OTHER NIGHT, WOULD TERRIFY ABSOLUTELY ANYONE! YOU DEFINITELY DIDN'T DESERVE TO BE HIT EITHER, BUT PAUL, TO SAY YOU'RE DEFENDING YOURSELF AGAINST ME IS RIDICULOUS! I DIDN'T HURT YOU! LOOK AT ME, LOOK AT YOU! YOU FULL FISTED HIT ME. YOU ALMOST KNOCKED ME OUT! WHY AM I STILL HERE, I HAVE NO IDEA WHY I EVEN TALK TO YOU STILL, LET ALONE TRY AND WORK THINGS OUT WITH YOU, I MUST BE ABSOLUTELY CRAZY!! BUT, I LOVE YOU STILL, WHY? WHY DID I FALL IN LOVE WITH A COMPLETE PSYCHO?

SUNDAY, MAY 26, 2013:

ANOTHER *FANTASTIC* DAY! I'M SAYING THAT VERY SARCASTICALLY. WOKE UP AND RIGHT OFF THE BAT, PAUL STARTED FIGHTING WITH ME SO BAD. HE LEFT, BUT BEFORE HE DID, HE SAID I HAVE TILL MY CAR IS DONE, THEN I NEED TO GET OUT. DAVID CAME AND GOT ME, AND WE WENT TO HIS DAD'S GRAVESITE FOR ABOUT A HALF HOUR, THEN DELIVERED SOME BAGS *(drugs)*, THEN WENT AND MET UP WITH A NEW CRYS DEALER. IT WAS AWESOME STUFF. BUT IT TOOK ALL DAMN DAY RUNNING HERE AND THERE! MY PARENTS WEREN'T HOME AND I NEEDED TO LEAVE PAUL'S HOUSE, SO I HAD NO CHOICE THAN TO HANG WITH DAVID FOR THE DAY. HE DROPPED ME OFF AROUND 5:30 P.M. AND I GOT IN THE SHOWER, GOT READY AND HAD JAY COME AND GET ME BEFORE PAUL GOT HOME. I LUCKILY MADE IT OUT BEFORE HE GOT HOME. WENT TO JAY'S, HE MADE JALA AND I SOME AWESOME DINNER AND JALA AND I WORKED ON HER POSTER FOR SCHOOL 'CAUSE SHE IS THE STAR STUDENT THIS WEEK! HUNG OUT AFTER DINNER FOR A BIT, THEN JAY TOOK ME HOME AROUND 10:30. I WENT IN AND IMMEDIATELY, PAUL STARTED OFF ON ME. HE KEPT SAYING, "WHY DIDN'T YOU JUST STAY WITH WHOEVER YOU WERE WITH?" I JUST IGNORED HIM TILL IT STARTED GETTING MUCH WORSE! I CALLED JAY AND HAD HIM TURN AROUND AND COME BACK AND GET ME! PAUL WOULDN'T EVEN LET ME GET MY JAMMIES OR ANYTHING I NEEDED. THIS MAN IS ABSOLUTELY CRAZY AND VERY, VERY MENTALLY SICK. AND I LOVE HIM STILL, WHY?!?! I DON'T KNOW WHAT I AM GOING TO DO!

MONDAY, MAY 27, 2013:

WELL, MY SELF-ESTEEM HAS COMPLETELY 100% DISAPPEARED! AFTER PAUL AND ANTHONY, I FEEL LIKE THE BIGGEST PIECE OF SHIT IN THE WORLD! AM I THAT BAD OF A PERSON? I

DIDN'T THINK SO, BUT I NEED TO LOOK IN THE MIRROR A LITTLE HARDER AT MYSELF! ANTHONY TOLD ME I WAS A WASTED PIECE OF FLESH! I REALLY DON'T CARE AT ALL WHAT HE THINKS, BUT WHEN HE SAYS SOMETHING LIKE THAT AND PAUL SAYS HORRIBLE THINGS ALSO, IT DOES END UP GETTING TO ME. SLEPT AT JAY'S LAST NIGHT, AND MARIA CAME AND GOT ME THIS MORNING, THEN I CAME HOME, GOT IN MY SWIMMING SUIT, THEN ME, JAY, AND JALA WENT TO THE REC CENTER TO SWIM. THEN CAME HOME, CLEANED THE HOUSE, NOW GOING TO DINNER WITH PAUL! HE CAME WITH ME TO DINNER SO WE COULD TALK AND IT'S BEEN REALLY, REALLY NICE! IT WAS LIKE WE HAD JUST MET AGAIN. HE SAID HE HAS MISSED ME, I WISH I REALLY BELIEVED HIM. HE IS THE HARDEST MAN TO READ! SO, ABOUT 6:00 P.M., WE WENT TO THE BOWLING ALLEY TO HAVE A COUPLE BEERS (HE DID), I HAD WATER. WE PLAYED GOLF ON THIS ARCADE GAME, I KICKED BUTT, THEN WENT TO EMPIRE BUFFET IN NORTH SALT LAKE. I JUST DON'T KNOW WHAT TO DO! I'M NOT BEGGING HIM ANYMORE, BUT I'M NOT LETTING HIM GO EITHER! WHAT IS THE RIGHT THING TO DO? WHAT WILL MAKE ME AND MY KIDS THE HAPPIEST? I REALLY NEED TO SIT DOWN WITH MYSELF FOR A COUPLE MIN/HRS EVERY DAY AND REALLY DIG DEEP AND FIGURE OUT JUST WHAT I WANT, WEIGH OUT ALL MY OPTIONS, ETC. *GOOD LUCK!*

TUESDAY, MAY 28, 2013:

TODAY HAS NOT BEEN BAD AT ALL! I ABSOLUTELY LOVE BEING WITH MY MAN! FELL BACK TO SLEEP AFTER PAUL WENT TO WORK, WOKE UP AROUND 1, GOT IN THE SHOWER, THEN TOOK PAUL TO THE SHOP TO WORK ON MY CAR, THEN WENT AND PICKED MY BABY GIRL UP! NOW JALA AND I ARE WATCHING TV AT MY MOM'S RIGHT NOW. PAUL AND I ARE PLANNING TO GO OUT TONIGHT. I'M EXCITED. I JUST HOPE NOTHING GOES WRONG, WE HAVE BEEN DOING AWESOME THE LAST FEW DAYS!

WENT AND PICKED HIM UP AROUND 6:00 P.M., THEN WENT TO THE STORE TOGETHER AND GOT STUFF TO MAKE DINNER, THEN CAME HOME AND HE COOKED AN AWESOME DINNER FOR US, THEN WE WATCHED A MOVIE. HE FELL ASLEEP RIGHT BEFORE THE MOVIE ENDED, SO I WENT TO MEET DAVID. I KNOW WHAT HE HAS DONE AND WHAT HE DOES, BUT HE IS A VERY NICE GUY. IT'S REALLY HARD TO HATE HIM. NOW, MARY ON THE OTHER HAND, NOT SO MUCH! SHE IS VERY, VERY EASILY HATED! WAS WITH JALA FOR ABOUT 4 HOURS TODAY AND SHE WAS FANTASTIC! SHE'S BEEN SO STINKIN' GOOD LATELY! I JUST WANT TO EAT HER UP! SHE IS THE STAR STUDENT THIS WEEK IN HER CLASS AND WE HAD TO DO A POSTER FOR HER CLASS WITH PICTURES, ETC. IT TURNED OUT SUPER, SUPER CUTE. I FOUND OUT A FEW THINGS ABOUT MY BABY GIRL, THOUGH, LIKE I HAD NO IDEA THAT HER FAVORITE FOOD WAS SALMON! DEFINITELY DOESN'T TAKE AFTER ME ON HER FOOD HABITS! SHE DOESN'T EVEN REALLY LIKE CANDY, HOW WEIRD IS THAT? AWESOME, BUT WEIRD! AND SHE'S *MY* DAUGHTER!!

WEDNESDAY, MAY 29, 2013:

MY DAY WITH MY AWESOME KIDS!! YAY! I AM GOING TO BE AT MY MOM'S FOR THE MAJORITY OF THE DAY TODAY AND EMILY IS HERE, WE'LL SEE HOW THAT TURNS OUT!

WELL, SITTIN' HERE AT MY MOM'S WITH MY KIDS, EMILY, JASA, AND JUSTIN. EMILY IS ACTUALLY TALKING TO ME, SHOCK, SHOCK, AND IT'S SO STINKIN' NICE! I WISH WE WERE THE WAY WE USED TO BE. I'M SUPPOSED TO JUST KEEP TRYING WITH HER, BUT IT'S BEEN OVER SEVERAL, SEVERAL YEARS AND NOTHING CHANGES AT ALL. I HONESTLY THINK EMILY WILL HATE ME FOREVER! SHE HOLDS GRUDGES LIKE NO OTHER PERSON THAT I KNOW. BUT, I WILL KEEP TRYING TILL THE DAY I DIE, SHE IS MY LITTLE SISTER. I MET WITH THE MISSIONARIES TODAY AT MY MOM'S AND THEY ARE CHALLENGING ME TO MAKE A COMMITMENT TO STOP SMOKING.

I TOLD THEM THAT I WILL DEFINITELY TRY, BUT I CANNOT MAKE ANY PROMISES. SO, THEY ARE GOING TO COME MEET WITH ME AGAIN NEXT WEDNESDAY TO SEE IF I'M ANY CLOSER TO MAKING THAT COMMITMENT. TO BE COMPLETELY HONEST, I DON'T THINK I WILL BE READY TO MAKE THAT PROMISE FOR A LONG TIME. I WISH I COULD 'CAUSE I THINK IT'S A DISGUSTING HABIT, BUT I KNOW I CAN'T RIGHT NOW!

IT'S ABOUT 11:00 P.M. AND I'M SITTIN' AT HOME WITH PAUL WATCHING *STAR TREK*, IT'S ACTUALLY AN AWESOME SHOW! I HATE *STAR TREK*, BUT I REALLY LIKE THE MOVIE. OF COURSE, MACI IS ON TOP OF PAUL 'CAUSE SHE NEVER LEAVES HIS SIDE! I THINK IT'S STINKIN' CUTE BUT I THINK IT GETS TO PAUL A BIT! ALL IN ALL, IT WAS A GOOD DAY. ADI, ME, AND MARIA WENT SHOPPING FOR A COUPLE HOURS TODAY AND IT WAS REALLY FUN. I LOVE MY PRETTY LITTLE GIRL!

THURSDAY, MAY 30, 2013:

GOING TO JALA'S SCHOOL TODAY BECAUSE SHE IS THE SPOTLIGHT STUDENT THIS WEEK AND I HAVE TO GO TALK TO HER CLASS ABOUT HER AND THE POSTER WE DID TOGETHER!

JUST GOT BACK FROM JALA'S SCHOOL, IT WENT REALLY WELL. ALL THE KIDS HAVE LOTS OF QUESTIONS AND JALA ANSWERED THEM REALLY GOOD. JUST WENT AND GOT PAUL'S DAUGHTER AND SHE HAD A WHOLE HECK OF A LOT TO TELL ME. SHE TOLD ME THAT PAUL TOLD THEM I WAS CRAZY AND WAS ON DRUGS. HOW COULD HE POSSIBLY DO THAT? SO, I TOLD HIS DAUGHTER HE WAS ON WEED. IF HE IS GOING TO TALK ABOUT ME, I WILL FOR SURE TALK ABOUT HIM. WHAT AN ASSHOLE! WELL, I'M NOT GOING TO SAY A WORD! I'M GOING TO ACT LIKE EVERYTHING IS OKAY AND FINE UNTIL I GET MY CAR BACK, THEN I CAN DO WHATEVER AND WHENEVER. HE'S GOING TO BE SO SORRY HE EVER BEAT ME OR TOLD HIS KIDS THE THINGS HE DID! I'M SITTING OUTSIDE

WITH HIS DAUGHTER, JALA, JASA, AND JUSTIN, WATCHING THEM PLAY. THEY ARE ALL BEING SUPER, SUPER CUTE. I AM JUST REALLY LIVID RIGHT NOW. HOW IN THE HELL COULD THE MAN I REALLY FELL IN LOVE WITH TURN OUT TO BE A COMPLETE PSYCHOPATH? AND, I STILL LOVE HIM. WHAT IN THE HELL AM I GOING TO DO? HOW CAN I POSSIBLY LOVE SOMEBODY LIKE THIS? WELL, I REALLY HAVE TO PROMISE MYSELF THAT IF IT GETS BAD LIKE THAT AGAIN, I LEAVE, NO QUESTIONS ASKED, JUST LEAVE AND REALLY FAST, 'CAUSE IF I DON'T, HE WILL PROBABLY END UP KILLING ME! HOW IN THE HELL DOES MY LIFE KEEP GETTING THIS BAD? IT SHOULD BE GETTING BETTER, NOT WORSE! HOW DO I TURN IT AROUND? I REALLY NEED TO 'CAUSE I WANT A GOOD LIFE FOR ME AND MY KIDS.

FRIDAY, MAY 31, 2013:

TODAY IS GOING TO BE A *FABULOUS* DAY. I AM GOING TO MAKE SURE OF IT. SO, SHOCKINGLY, PAUL AND I HAD AN AWESOME NIGHT TOGETHER LAST NIGHT. WE LAUGHED AT EACH OTHER WHILE DOING STUPID THINGS AND LISTENING TO MUSIC. I ALSO PLUCKED ALL THE HAIR OFF HIS EARS 'CAUSE HE IS SO EXTREMELY HAIRY. I HAVE ALWAYS HATED HAIR SO STINKIN' BAD, BUT FOR SOME ODD REASON, I ABSOLUTELY LOVE PAUL'S HAIR! AND I'M GLAD I DO 'CAUSE HE IS LITERALLY COVERED IN HAIR. HE CALLS HIMSELF A GORILLA. HE TOLD ME ALL WEEK I WAS GETTING MY CAR BACK TODAY, I PRAY IT REALLY HAPPENS TODAY 'CAUSE I HAVE BEEN WAITING LONG ENOUGH AND I AM SO FAR PAST THE POINT OF IMPATIENT! BETTER BE TODAY!

IT'S ABOUT 12:15 FRIDAY MORNING, AND OF COURSE, PAUL IS SOUND ASLEEP AND I AM WIDE AWAKE. PROBABLY GOING TO MEET WALTER AT WALMART HERE IN A MIN. I KNOW IT'S REALLY MEAN, BUT HE LIKES BUYING ME THINGS AT WALMART, SO, OF COURSE, I LET HIM. WHY NOT? NOBODY

ELSE BUYS ME ANYTHING, EVEN PAUL DOESN'T ANYMORE. I DON'T KNOW WHEN THE LAST TIME PAUL HAS BOUGHT ME ANYTHING. IT USED TO BE ALL THE TIME, FOR A WHILE ALMOST EVERY TIME HE CAME HOME FROM WORK, HE WOULD HAVE ME SOMETHING JUST FOR THE HECK OF IT. THOSE DAYS ARE SO LONG GONE! I'M OVER IT, I'M JUST GOING TO FOCUS ON ME AND MY WONDERFUL KIDS! MY MOM IS COOKING HOT DOGS AND DOING S'MORES AND MAS IS THERE, SO ME AND JALA ARE ON OUR WAY TO GRANDMA'S!

SATURDAY, JUNE 1, 2013:

HAD AN AWESOME DAY YESTERDAY WITH MY BABY GIRL. JALA WAS ABSOLUTELY WONDERFUL! I LOVE THAT LITTLE GIRL! SO, IT'S ABOUT 2:30 A.M. SATURDAY MORNING AND WE HAD A LOT OF FUN LAST NIGHT! ME, PAUL, AND HIS KIDS PLAYED GAMES, ATE DINNER, AND JUST HUNG OUT AND WE HAD A *BLAST!* I HAVE NOT HAD THAT MUCH FUN WITH ALL THEM IN A VERY, VERY LONG TIME. IT WAS GREAT!

WENT TO SEE DAVID ABOUT 11:30 P.M., THEN WENT AND SAW BRIAN. GOT UP AND AMY CAME AND GOT ME AND WE WENT DOWN TO SEE DAVID, THEN CAME HOME TO GET READY AND NOW WE ARE GOING TO AMY'S HOUSE FOR A BIT, THEN GOING TO JUDITH'S TO GRAB *(drugs).* TODAY IS NOT A BAD DAY AT ALL AND ME AND PAUL ARE GETTING ALONG GREAT.

SUNDAY, JUNE 2, 2013:

WHAT A DAY TO BE ALIVE! AND, IT'S GOING TO BE A PERFECT DAY, 'CAUSE I WILL HAVE MY KIDS WITH ME AND THEY ARE MY ENTIRE WORLD, MY ENTIRE HEART! SO, YESTERDAY WAS ACTUALLY A REALLY GOOD DAY. SPENT THE DAY WITH AMY, THEN PAUL TOOK ME TO BREWVIE'S TO SEE *HANGOVER* AND IT WAS WAY FUNNY! IT WAS SO GREAT TO FEEL THAT PAUL LOVES ME AGAIN! IT'S BEEN A GOOD DAY SO FAR. I WENT TO

WALMART TO GET SOME CEREAL AND MILK, CAME BACK HOME, FELL ASLEEP WITH PAUL UNTIL ABOUT 10:30 A.M., GOT UP, GOT READY, AND NOW WE ARE SHOPPING AT GORDMAN'S. WE ARE GETTING ALONG ABSOLUTELY GREAT, BUT MY CAR IS *STILL* NOT DONE. THIS IS COMPLETELY RIDICULOUS AND I CAN'T SAY ANYTHING OR IT WOULD CAUSE A HUGE, HUGE FIGHT. SO, I JUST HAVE TO KEEP WAITING.

WELL, I SPOKE TOO SOON, PAUL AND I WERE DOING AWESOME, WE WENT TO GORDMAN'S AND LOOKED AROUND, AND ON THE WAY HOME, HE BECAME COMPLETELY SILENT. I ASKED HIM WHAT WAS WRONG AND ALL HE SAID WAS, "IT DOESN'T MATTER, DOES IT." CAME HOME, PACKED A BAG, THEN WENT INTO THE KIDS' ROOM AND SHUT THE DOOR. I HAVE NO IDEA WHAT IN THE HELL I DID, AND NOW WE AREN'T EVEN TALKING. I'M FED UP WITH THESE STUPID GAMES! HE WON'T EVEN TELL ME WHAT THE HELL I DID, AM I SUPPOSED TO READ HIS MIND? WHAT AM I DOING WRONG, OR WHAT AM I NOT DOING? I'M JUST NOT GOOD ENOUGH FOR HIM?

MONDAY, JUNE 3, 2013:

WOW, HAS IT BEEN A WEEKEND! AND I CAN'T REALLY SAY FOR THE BEST! MY FRIEND AMY THAT IS LITERALLY WITH ME *EVERY SINGLE DAY* (AT LEAST HAS BEEN FOR THE PAST 3/4 MONTHS) WENT TO WENDOVER WITH DAVID AND A COUPLE OF HIS BUDDIES AND SHE OVERDOSED AND DIED FOR 15/20 MINUTES AND THEY REVIVED HER! THEY FLEW HER ON LIFE FLIGHT TO THE UNIVERSITY OF UTAH AND SHE WAS IN A COMA FOR A FEW DAYS AND NOW SHE'S AWAKE, BUT NOT THE SAME PERSON AT ALL. CAN'T REMEMBER ANYTHING FROM THE PAST 5 MONTHS TO TODAY. DON'T KNOW IF HER MEMORY EVEN COMES BACK AT ALL! I WAS A MESS, BUT AT THE SAME TIME, SUPER DUPER PISSED 'CAUSE SHE COMPLETELY LIED TO ME ABOUT THE WHOLE WENDOVER TRIP. IT WAS ORIGINALLY SUPPOSED TO BE AMY AND I AND WHOEVER ELSE WANTED TO GO.

WELL, I WANTED TO STAY WITH PAUL, AND I DIDN'T FEEL GOOD ABOUT GOING. WELL, AMY AND DAVID HAD ONLY MET A COUPLE TIMES IN THE PAST FEW DAYS. THEY DIDN'T KNOW EACH OTHER AT ALL! THEY WENT TO WENDOVER TOGETHER, AND AMY KEPT TELLING ME I PROMISE I DIDN'T COME WITH DAVID, I CAME WITH KYLE. SHE KEPT TELLING ME SHE WOULD NEVER DO THAT TO ME, STEP ON MY TOES WITH *MY* FRIENDS, BUT OF COURSE, SHE DID! AND THEN DENIED IT AGAIN OVER AND OVER TO MY FACE! (WELL, ON THE PHONE.) WHY DID SHE NEED TO LIE TO ME? I WOULD HAVE BEEN FINE WITH DAVID GOING DOWN THERE WITH HER, SO SHE COULD GET AWAY, BUT INSTEAD SHE LIED TO ME AND IS TRYING TO FUCK WITH ME NOW. JEREMY, HER HUSBAND, ACTUALLY CAME OVER TONIGHT AND WE TALKED FOR A GOOD HOUR. HE IS DEFINITELY AN AWESOME GUY! SHE *DOES NOT* DESERVE HIM AT ALL. AMY HAD KARMA THROWN IN HER FACE JUST A BIT THIS WEEKEND, DIDN'T SHE? ANOTHER GIRLFRIEND, BYE, BYE! I DON'T GET IT, EVERY STINKIN' GIRL IN MY LIFE THAT I BECOME GOOD FRIENDS WITH, SLOWLY DISAPPEARS BECAUSE THEY END UP FUCKING WITH ME, FUCKING ME OVER! I *WON'T* TAKE IT ANY LONGER AND I AM GOING TO BE SUPER CAREFUL PICKING MY FRIENDS FROM THIS POINT ON!!

Her days and timing of events are all mixed up...

I AM HOPING AND PRAYING THAT I GET MY CAR BACK TODAY! I MEAN HELL, IT'S ONLY BEEN LIKE 4 MONTHS! I JUST DON'T WANT TO KEEP PESTERING HIM ABOUT IT 'CAUSE IT IS REALLY HARD WORK AND HARD WORK FOR FREE. I KNOW HE HAS BEEN WORKING HARD ON IT THE PAST WEEK, SO I AM JUST PATIENTLY WAITING, BUT ABOUT READY TO LOSE MY MIND!! WELL, JUST FOUND OUT THAT DAVID DID GO TO WENDOVER WITH AMY AND SHE WAS COMPLETELY LYING TO ME. LAST NIGHT, SHE OVERDOSED ON BLK *(heroin)* AND GOT LIFE FLIGHTED TO THE U OF U. SHE WAS DEAD BUT

THEY REVIVED HER AND NOW SHE IS IN A COMA AT THE U OF U. I HONESTLY DON'T THINK SHE IS GOING TO MAKE IT THROUGH THIS ONE. SHE WAS ONE OF MY ONLY FRIENDS. I WAS SUPPOSED TO GO TO WENDOVER WITH THEM, BUT DIDN'T. I CAN'T BELIEVE SHE DID THIS! WHAT IN THE HELL WAS SHE THINKING? SHE DOESN'T EVEN DO BLK! PAUL IS NOW BEING WAY GOOD TO ME 'CAUSE OF AMY AND HE FEELS BAD FOR ME, BUT FOR HOW LONG? MAYBE A COUPLE DAYS, IF I'M LUCKY A WEEK, BUT THAT'S PUSHIN' IT! I MISS HER ALREADY. SHE WAS WITH ME EVERY SINGLE DAY AND NOW, I'M PROBABLY NEVER GOING TO SEE HER AGAIN? THIS SUCKS! IT SCARES ME REALLY, REALLY BAD! I BETTER QUIT ALL THIS SHIT OR I WILL BE NEXT TO OVERDOSE OR SOMETHING ELSE. THIS WAS A REALLY BIG EYE OPENER, BUT CAN I DO IT? I KNOW I CAN, I'M MUCH STRONGER THAN I GIVE MYSELF CREDIT FOR. SITTIN' HERE WITH MY BABY GIRL RIGHT NOW AT MY MOM'S. SHE ALWAYS MAKES ME FEEL SO MUCH BETTER! SHE IS MY LIFE AND MY HEARTBEAT, ALL MY KIDS ARE!

TUESDAY, JUNE 4, 2013:

PAUL JUST WROTE ME A LETTER TELLING ME HOW SORRY HE WAS FOR US TO HAVE GOTTEN THIS BAD AND HOW MUCH HE LOVES ME AND LOVES THE PERSON THAT I AM. I REALLY NEEDED THAT BECAUSE RIGHT BEFORE THAT, HE WAS CALLING ME NAMES AND TELLING ME HOW BIG OF A PIECE OF SHIT I AM. THIS IS ONLY HIS 2ND LETTER THAT HE HAS EVER WRITTEN ME. IT MADE ME FEEL SO DAMN GOOD. THEN, I CAME INTO THE LIVING ROOM TO WRITE AND I TURNED ON WILLY NELSON (SCIENCE) TO LISTEN TO AND HE CAME IN AND TOOK THE PEN OUT OF MY HAND AND PUT IT DOWN AND PICKED ME UP AND SLOW DANCED WITH ME FOR THE WHOLE SONG. IT WAS SO STINKIN' SWEET! SO, TODAY HAS BEEN A GOOD DAY SO FAR.

IT'S ABOUT 12:00 AND I'M AT LIZ'S NAILS GETTING MY NAILS DONE. PAUL HAS BEEN SO STINKIN' SWEET THIS MORNING, BROKE DOWN IN TEARS AND TELLING ME HOW SORRY HE WAS FOR EVERYTHING AND HOW MUCH HE LOVES ME. IT WAS SO NICE SEEING HIM CRY FOR A CHANGE, INSTEAD OF ME! I CAN'T FIND MY PHONE, THOUGH. I HAVE NO IDEA WHERE IN THE HELL IT IS; HOPEFULLY I'LL FIND IT SOON, I'M DYING WITHOUT MY PHONE! JALA WAS SO ABSOLUTELY INCREDIBLE TODAY! SHE WAS SO GOOD FOR ME TODAY AND WE HAD A BLAST TOGETHER! SO, I HATE AMY WITH A PASSION, SHE HAS BEEN LYING TO ME FOR MONTHS! I KNEW IT!

WEDNESDAY, JUNE 5, 2013:

WELL, IT'S ABOUT 1:00 A.M. AND I DEFINITELY DID NOT START THIS MORNING OUT GOOD. JUST WENT TO GRAB *(drugs)* WITH ANTHONY FROM DAVID (OF ALL PEOPLE, THE ONE PERSON THAT I THOUGHT I COULD SOMEWHAT TRUST) AND HE FUCKS US OVER! MADE US WAIT AT A GAS STATION IN SALT LAKE ON 1300 SOUTH FOR ALMOST 2 FUCKING HOURS! IT JUST KEEPS GETTING BETTER AND BETTER! EVERYBODY THAT I THOUGHT WERE MY FRIENDS ARE SLOWLY SHOWING THEIR TRUE COLORS AND FUCKING WITH ME! REALLY? DO I DESERVE THIS? I DON'T THINK SO, BUT MAYBE I NEED TO TAKE ANOTHER LOOK AT MYSELF AND WHAT I DO TO PEOPLE, OR MY SO-CALLED FRIENDS! I REALLY NEED TO STRAIGHTEN MY LIFE OUT, THIS IS NOT WHO I AM. I AM A GOOD PERSON THAT HAS A HEART AND CARES ABOUT PEOPLE, AND I AM NOT PROVING THAT TO ANYONE RIGHT NOW! I NEED TO START BY BEING HONEST WITH THE PEOPLE I TRULY CARE ABOUT AND LOVE. HOPEFULLY, I PRAY THAT THEY WILL STAY BY MY SIDE, 'CAUSE GOD KNOWS I COULD USE ALL THE SUPPORT I CAN GET RIGHT NOW! PRAY, PRAY, PRAY, NAT. KEEP PRAYING THINGS WILL ALL WORK OUT FOR THE BETTER.

THURSDAY, JUNE 6, 2013:

I AM SO DISAPPOINTED IN MYSELF FOR GETTING FUCKED OVER BY *ANOTHER* GIRLFRIEND! DO I HAVE A SIGN ON MY FOREHEAD THAT SAYS...COME BE MY FRIEND, THEN YOU CAN FUCK ME OVER AND RUIN MY LIFE! EVERY SINGLE GIRL IN MY ENTIRE LIFE HAS DONE SOMETHING HORRIBLE TO ME! AND *NO,* I HONESTLY DID NOT DESERVE IT, *EVER!* EVERY TIME I MAKE A FRIEND, I TRY AND MAKE SURE THAT I PICK THE RIGHT PEOPLE AND THAT THEY ARE PEOPLE I WOULD BRING AROUND MY KIDS AND SOMEONE THAT IS POSSIBLY SOMEONE I COULD EVENTUALLY TRUST. BUT I PICK THE WRONG PEOPLE EVERY TIME! MARIA AND DEBORAH ARE LITERALLY MY ONLY GIRLFRIENDS RIGHT NOW, AND ANTHONY IS GOING TO BE OUT OF MY LIFE VERY SOON. AMY REALLY DID A NUMBER ON ME. SO MANY PEOPLE WARNED ME ABOUT HER, AND OF COURSE, AS ALWAYS, I DIDN'T LISTEN AND THOUGHT SHE WAS A GOOD FRIEND. WHY DON'T I SEE IT? OR AT LEAST SEE IT COMING! I ASKED MARIA WHAT IT WAS I WAS DOING WRONG WITH MY FRIENDS, AND SHE SAID I GIVE PEOPLE *WAY* TOO MANY CHANCES. WELL, EVERYBODY MAKES MISTAKES. I HAVE MADE PLENTY OF THEM, SO I GIVE MY FRIENDS CHANCES WHEN THEY FUCK UP, THINKING THAT THEY MADE THE MISTAKE ONCE, THEY WON'T DO IT AGAIN, AND THEY DO, AND I KEEP FORGIVING! WELL, *NO MORE!* I AM NOT GOING TO BE WALKED ALL OVER BY ANYONE ANYMORE! AND THIS TIME, WHEN I MAKE A NEW FRIEND, I AM GOING TO MAKE DAMN SURE THAT THEY ARE NOT AT ALL LIKE THE PEOPLE THAT I HAVE LET INTO MY LIFE BEFORE. THAT'S GOING TO BE VERY HARD TO FIND, BUT THAT'S OKAY, ALL I NEED IS MY FAMILY, THEY *NEVER* FUCK ME OVER AND I KNOW THEY CARE AND LOVE ME!!!

WELL, THE DODGE (POO POO) CARAVAN *FINALLY* TOOK A FALL! IT'S DONE! IT BROKE DOWN TODAY AT THE AIRPORT WHEN I WAS PICKING UP PAUL, SO PAUL HAS TO WORK ALL

NIGHT ON MY CAR TILL IT IS DONE 'CAUSE WE HAVE NO VEHICLE RIGHT NOW!

SITTIN' HERE WITH JALA RIGHT NOW AT MY MOM'S WATCHING THE *MONSTER HIGH* DVD. JALA'S ABOUT TO FALL ASLEEP! PAUL AND I ARE HARDLY TALKING AT ALL RIGHT NOW 'CAUSE APPARENTLY SOMEBODY CALLED HIM LAST NIGHT AND TOLD HIM THERE WAS A MAN AT THE HOUSE WITH ME FOR A VERY LONG TIME. I'M THINKIN' IT WAS ONE OF THE KIDS (HIS KIDS) OR HIS EX! BUT IT DOESN'T MATTER ANYWAYS, IT WAS JEREMY, AMY'S HUSBAND, WANTING TO GET HER HOT TOPIC DRESS BACK AND TO FIND OUT INFO! WELL, I GLADLY GAVE HIM ALL THE INFO I KNEW! I NORMALLY WOULD NOT DO THAT, 'CAUSE NO MATTER HOW MUCH I HATE SOMEONE, I NEVER TRY TO INTERFERE OR MESS WITH THEIR LIFE. I JUST SIMPLY FORGET ABOUT THEM. I WISH GIRLS TOOK THAT APPROACH WITH ME, BUT THEY DON'T, THEY DO EVERYTHING THEY POSSIBLY CAN TO HURT ME!

SO, PAUL *STILL* IS NOT TALKING TO ME AT ALL. HE JUST GOT HOME A LITTLE BIT AGO AND HE DIDN'T SAY A STINKIN' WORD TO ME AND THEN TOOK OFF WALKING. I WONDER WHERE HE WENT? HE WENT TO SEE HIS 2 KIDS THAT LITERALLY LIVE A COUPLE BLOCKS FROM OUR HOUSE. HOW GAY IS THAT? I STILL REALLY, REALLY WANT TO KNOW WHO TOLD HIM THAT A GUY CAME OVER LAST NIGHT, I MEAN THE NIGHT BEFORE. I KNOW FOR A FACT THAT IT'S EITHER HIS KIDS, OR HIS UGLY EX! ANY OF THEM WILL PISS ME THE FUCK OFF! IT'S NONE OF THEIR DAMN BUSINESS WHO COMES TO MY HOUSE TO SEE ME! AND SERIOUSLY, IT WAS JEREMY, TELLING ME ABOUT AMY AND GETTING HER CLOTHES BACK. HOW COULD PAUL POSSIBLY BE MAD AT ME? I DIDN'T TELL HIM OR INVITE HIM OVER THAT NIGHT. I CAME HOME FROM MY MOM'S AND HE WAS SITTING IN FRONT OF OUR HOUSE! I WAS IN SHOCK!! IT TURNED OUT GOOD, THOUGH, REALLY GOOD!

FRIDAY, JUNE 7, 2013:

IT'S 1:30 A.M. FRIDAY MORNING AND I JUST GOT BACK FROM RUNNING OUT TO BRIAN'S WITH MARIA. WE WENT SO LATE 'CAUSE I HAVE NO VEHICLE AND I HAD TO WAIT FOR PAUL TO GET DONE AT WORK. SOMETIMES, I REALLY DO MISS IT THERE *(Iggy's)*. BUT, I WILL *NEVER, EVER* GO BACK, ESPECIALLY 'CAUSE KENNETH IS STILL ONE OF THE MANAGERS OVER THERE. HE REALLY NEEDS TO GET THE SHIT KICKED OUT OF HIM AT LEAST ONCE, THEN MAYBE IT WILL BRING HIS EGO DOWN A COUPLE NOTCHES WHERE IT SHOULD BE! PAUL IS *STILL* NOT TALKING TO ME AT ALL! HE CAME HOME TONIGHT, DIDN'T SAY A SINGLE WORD TO ME, THEN WALKED (I THINK TO SEE THE KIDS), AND NOTHING AFTER THAT! I HAVE ABSOLUTELY *NO IDEA* WHAT'S GOING ON, BUT I'M SCARED 'CAUSE I DON'T KNOW WHAT HE'S THINKING OR WHAT HE HAS PLANNED, WHICH I HOPE HE DOESN'T. HE HAS BEEN SO EXTREMELY SHADY THE PAST FEW DAYS. EVER SINCE JEREMY CAME OVER, PAUL HAS ACTED LIKE HE DOESN'T EVEN KNOW ME! WHAT IS GOING ON? I HOPE HE STILL LOVES ME, 'CAUSE I LOVE HIM SO MUCH! TOO MUCH THAT IT MAKES ME MAD. MY SELF-ESTEEM NEEDS TO GET *A LOT* BETTER! I HAVE ABSOLUTELY NO CONFIDENCE ANYMORE AND I FEEL LIKE I AM TRAILER TRASH ALL THE DAMN TIME! I NEED TO FIX THOSE ISSUES, AND QUICK 'CAUSE THAT'S NOT ATTRACTIVE TO ANYBODY! MARIA AND I WERE TALKING ON OUR WAY BACK FROM BRIAN'S AND WE WERE SAYING HOW SAD IT WAS THAT AMY LET DRUGS TAKE OVER HER. SHE DIDN'T USED TO BE LIKE THIS (NOW SHE IS A COMPULSIVE LIAR) AND SHE IS PURE EVIL AND SO EXTREMELY SELFISH! THAT IS DEFINITELY DRUGS! SHE WASN'T THE SAME ANYMORE, AND I HONESTLY DON'T THINK SHE IS EVER COMING BACK. IT'S KIND OF CREEPY 'CAUSE I LOOK BACK AND ALL THE TIMES THAT WE WERE TOGETHER, WHICH WAS LITERALLY ALMOST EVERY SINGLE DAY FOR THE PAST 5 MONTHS, I NEVER REALLY KNEW HER!

SHE WASN'T THE AMY I MET 2 1/2 YEARS AGO. AFTER SHE GOT FIRED FROM IGGY'S, HER WHOLE LIFE STARTED GETTING OUT OF CONTROL, AND THEN SHE MADE IT ALL THE WAY TO OVERDOSING IN WENDOVER!

SATURDAY, JUNE 8, 2013:

TODAY BETTER BE A BETTER DAY THAN YESTERDAY! PAUL HAS NOT TALKED TO ME AT ALL FOR 3 DAYS NOW. I STILL HAVE NO IDEA WHAT HE IS MAD ABOUT. HE WON'T TELL ME, I HAVE ASKED HIM A COUPLE TIMES TO GIVE ME AN EXPLANATION BUT HE WON'T. HE DIDN'T EVEN SLEEP IN THE SAME BED AS ME LAST NIGHT. HE PROMISED ME MY CAR WOULD BE DONE THIS WEEK, FOR SURE…WELL, ONCE AGAIN, IT'S NOT! NOW HE'S SAYING TUESDAY. I HONESTLY DON'T KNOW IF I AM EVER GOING TO SEE MY CAR AGAIN! HE'S SAYING IT'S MY FAULT TOO. HOW IN THE *HELL* IS THIS MY FAULT? I'M THE ONE WHO GOT HIT, AND HE IS THE ONE THAT OFFERED TO FIX IT, AND HE IS THE ONE TAKING FOREVER TO GET IT DONE. HE TELLS ME THINGS ALL THE DAMN TIME AND *NEVER* FOLLOWS THROUGH WITH THEM! SINCE DAY 1! HE HAS NOT KEPT HIS WORD ON ANYTHING THAT HE HAS SAID TO ME, NOT EVEN 1! DON'T SAY THINGS THAT YOU CAN'T DO! HE NEVER GETS THINGS DONE, EITHER! I AM SITTING HERE IN A HOUSE THAT IS 92 DEGREES, I AM DRIPPING SWEAT, ALL HE HAS TO DO IS CLEAN THE SWAMP COOLER, THEN IT SHOULD WORK, BUT HE WON'T SO I HAVE TO SIT HERE AND DRIP SWEAT EVERY DAY. HOW AWFUL IS THAT? TODAY IS GOING TO BE A MUCH BETTER DAY!

OKAY, SO I AM COMPLETELY OUT OF MY MIND. PAUL AND I ARE NOT GETTING ALONG AT ALL RIGHT NOW. HE IS IN THE KIDS' ROOM AND I AM IN OUR ROOM. IT'S 3:00 A.M. AND I JUST TEXTED HIM. MY SELF-ESTEEM IS COMPLETELY GONE, IT'S HANGING ON TO ME LIKE A THREAD RIGHT NOW. I AM REALLY THE STUPIDEST GIRL ALIVE RIGHT NOW. I

LOOK LIKE A COMPLETE IDIOT. I AM SITTING HERE WANTING TO CRY AND I FEEL LIKE A TOTAL JACKASS! MY LIFE JUST KEEPS GETTING BETTER AND BETTER. IF PAUL AND I DON'T MAKE IT THROUGH THIS ONE, WHICH I KNOW WE WILL, WE ALWAYS DO…I WILL BE A MESS AND DON'T KNOW IF I WILL BE ABLE TO GO ON MUCH LONGER. I AM A COMPLETE FUCK UP!

SUNDAY, JUNE 9, 2013:

YESTERDAY AND LAST NIGHT WAS ONE OF THE WORST DAYS I HAVE EVER HAD IN MY LIFE. CHASED *(ran around trying to get drugs)* ALL DAY IN A CAR WITH NO AIR CONDITIONING AND IT WAS AT LEAST 100 DEGREES. FINALLY GOT HOME ABOUT 11:30 P.M. AND PAUL RIPPED INTO ME AND TOLD ME HOW BIG OF A SHIT HOLE AND PIECE OF SHIT THAT I AM. HE SAID HE WANTS ME TO REMEMBER THAT. WHY DOES HE LIKE TO TREAT PEOPLE LIKE THIS? I HAVE REALLY TRIED HARD WITH HIM BUT I AM OLDER NOW, AND IT'S GOING TO BE SO HARD TO FIND SOMEBODY AGAIN! I DON'T WANT EVER TO FALL AGAIN, IT HURTS WAY TOO MUCH. I REALLY THOUGHT HE LOVED ME, I REALLY DID!!! HOW COULD I HAVE BEEN SO BLIND AND STUPID? WHY IN THE *HELL* DID HE GET ME TO FALL IN LOVE WITH HIM IN THE FIRST PLACE? I HAVE DEFINITELY COME TO THE CONCLUSION THAT HE IS A VERY EVIL PERSON. I AM ON THE COUCH RIGHT NOW WHILE HE IS IN THE BED. HOW ABSOLUTELY CRUEL IS THAT? I DON'T THINK THIS MAN HAS A HEART AT ALL. DO I REALLY DESERVE ALL THIS? I AM NOT THAT BAD OF A PERSON, I HAVE A HEART AND CARE ABOUT EVERYBODY THAT COMES INTO MY LIFE.

IT'S ABOUT 1:00 A.M. AND I AM STILL ON THE STINKIN' COUCH. I WANTED MY LIFE TO GET BETTER, NOT WORSE. AND IT'S THE WORST IT'S EVER BEEN WITHOUT A DOUBT. WHY CAN'T I CATCH A BREAK? WHY? I NEED SOMEBODY THAT CARES ABOUT ME TO HELP ME. THE PROBLEM IS, I REALLY

DON'T KNOW ANYONE RIGHT NOW THAT ACTUALLY CARES ABOUT ME. HOW SAD IS THAT? EVEN MY FAMILY WANTS NOTHING TO DO WITH ME AND PAUL KEEPS REMINDING ME OF THAT EVERY DAY!! I PRAY THINGS GET BETTER SOON, AND I CAN ACTUALLY LIKE LIFE.

MONDAY, JUNE 10, 2013:

SO, YESTERDAY WAS A MUCH BETTER DAY THAN SATURDAY. HAD MARIA'S CAR ALL DAY SO I WASN'T STUCK HOME. WENT TO SEE MY CAR AND IT LOOKS BETTER THAN IT DID WHEN I BOUGHT IT, IT WAS LIKE BRAND STINKIN' NEW. THEN WENT TO MY MOM'S AND HUNG OUT WITH EVERYONE. SHALL IS HERE FOR A WEEK, SO HOPEFULLY I CAN GET SOME TIME WITH HER. I MISS HER SO MUCH! I HATE IT, THOUGH, 'CAUSE EVERY TIME I AM AT MY MOM'S HOUSE AND EVERYONE IS THERE, THEY ALL TREAT ME SO MUCH DIFFERENTLY THAN THEY USED TO, I HATE IT! I AM NOT JUST BEING PARANOID, THEY ALL TREAT ME LIKE I AM A PIECE OF TRASH. AND NO, I AM NOT, OR AM I JUST TRYING TO CONVINCE MYSELF? I AM LITERALLY A COMPLETE MESS RIGHT NOW. PAUL WILL NOT TALK TO ME AT ALL AND I KNOW I WON'T HAVE A HOUSE TO LIVE IN AS SOON AS MY CAR IS DONE. WHAT IN THE *HELL* AM I GOING TO DO? I'M SO SCARED AND FEEL SO LOST. PAUL IS MY HOME AND MY FAMILY, AND I WILL NOT BE COMPLETE WITHOUT HIM! I REALLY NEED TO FIGURE OUT WHAT I AM GOING TO DO AND QUICK. I KEEP TRYING TO TELL MYSELF THAT I DON'T NEED A MAN OR PAUL TO KEEP ME HAPPY, BUT I DO, I NEED PAUL. I NEED HIM 'CAUSE HE DOES MAKE ME HAPPY THE MAJORITY OF THE TIME (EXCEPT FOR LATELY) AND I AM MADLY IN LOVE WITH HIM. HOW DID I FALL IN LOVE WITH SUCH A PSYCHO CREEP? AND I ABSOLUTELY LOVED HIS KIDS AT FIRST, BUT AFTER BEING WITH ALL OF THEM TOGETHER AND HOW PAUL TREATS THEM, I WANT TO PUNCH

THEM IN THE FACE! IT'S PATHETIC. HE IS SO SUPER WEIRD WITH HIS KIDS.

TUESDAY, JUNE 11, 2013:

MY LIFE HAS DEFINITELY BEEN BETTER THAN IT IS RIGHT NOW. GOT IN A HUGE FIGHT WITH MY MOM AND MICHELLE YESTERDAY. *(Adi told me that her mom was dealing to kids in her school.)* MICHELLE TOLD EVERYONE THAT I WAS MEETING A DEALER THE NIGHT BEFORE AND THAT SET MY MOM OFF AND MY MOM TOLD ME THAT I AM NOT ALLOWED AT HER HOUSE WHEN SHE IS NOT THERE. HOW COMPLETELY FUCKED UP IS THAT? IT'S ALL BECAUSE OF MICHELLE, SHE STARTS AND CREATES SO MUCH FREAKING DRAMA. IT'S SO PATHETIC. THERE IS ABSOLUTELY NO REASON FOR ALL THIS. I CAN'T GO TO MY MOM'S RIGHT NOW. MASON WAS SO UPSET, IT BROKE MY STINKIN' HEART. HOW IN THE *HELL* AM I EVER GOING TO SEE MY SON? THIS IS GOING TO BE A VERY HARD SUMMER. WENT HOME LAST NIGHT AROUND 10:00 P.M. TO GET SOME STUFF 'CAUSE JALA WANTED ME TO SLEEP OVER. WELL, I DECIDED TO STAY WITH JALA 'CAUSE PAUL HASN'T TALKED TO ME ALL WEEKEND! WENT HOME AND HE LOCKED THE DOORS, HE YELLED THROUGH THE WINDOW, WHAT DO YOU WANT, LEAVE STUPID BITCH, I DON'T WANT YOU HERE! I HAVE NO IDEA WHAT IN THE HELL I EVER DID TO DESERVE ANY OF THAT. WHAT IS WRONG WITH HIM? AND WHY AM I STILL IN LOVE WITH HIM? I MUST BE FUCKED UP BAD. I AM SO EXTREMELY LOST AND SCARED RIGHT NOW AND I HAVE NO IDEA WHAT I AM GOING TO DO. TALKED TO HIM THIS MORNING AND HE TOLD ME HE WOULDN'T CALL ME ANYMORE NAMES, BUT WE NEED TO GET THIS RELATIONSHIP DONE BEFORE IT LITERALLY RIPS MY HEART APART. I DO NOT WANT TO BE WITHOUT HIM, *EVER!* JALA IS GOING TO LAGOON TODAY WITH MY MOM AND SHALL AND KIDS. WISH I WAS THERE.

WEDNESDAY, JUNE 12, 2013:

I WAS HOPING THAT TODAY WOULD BE MUCH BETTER THAN YESTERDAY, BUT I DON'T THINK IT IS! THE WHOLE FAMILY IS GOING TO CHERRY HILL, AND OF COURSE, I WAS NOT INVITED! IT BREAKS MY HEART FOR MY KIDS 'CAUSE I CAN'T BE WITH THEM AT ALL. HOW DOES THAT MAKE THEM FEEL? MASON WAS ON THE VERGE OF TEARS 'CAUSE HE ASKED ME IF I WAS GOING AND I SAID NO, FIRST OFF BECAUSE I DIDN'T KNOW ABOUT IT, AND SECOND, NOBODY BUT MASON AND JALA WANTS ME TO GO AND I AM NOT ABOUT TO BE AROUND MICHELLE. I HATE THIS SO BAD! I WANT TO BE AROUND MY FAMILY SO BAD, AND THEY ALL LITERALLY HATE ME *(her perception)*. WHAT AM I GOING TO DO? I KNOW THE FIRST THING THAT I NEED TO DO BUT CAN'T AFFORD IT, AND I AM SO TERRIFIED! I NEED TO DO IT, THOUGH, AND I NEED TO DO IT SOON OR I AM GOING TO END UP DEAD. THEN, HOW WOULD MY POOR KIDS FEEL? I DON'T EVEN WANT TO THINK ABOUT IT. I JUST NEED TO STOP BEING SO DAMN SELFISH AND GET OVER MY FEARS AND BE STRONG AND JUST DO IT! I KNOW I CAN, I AM MUCH STRONGER THAN I GIVE MYSELF CREDIT FOR.

THURSDAY, JUNE 13, 2013:

WELL, MY LIFE HAS GONE FROM NOT VERY GOOD TO ABSOLUTELY SHITTY! I HAVE NO PLACE TO LIVE RIGHT NOW, NO CAR YET (STILL), AND NOT ANY FRIENDS ON MY SIDE AT ALL. I STAYED AT JAY'S LAST NIGHT AND AM GOING TO TONIGHT TOO, BUT AFTER TONIGHT, I CAN'T ANYMORE AND I HAVE ABSOLUTELY NO IDEA WHAT IN THE *HELL* I AM GOING TO DO! SHALL CAME INTO TOWN ALMOST A WEEK AGO, AND EVER SINCE THE DAY SHE GOT HERE, SHE HAS COMPLETELY TURNED MY LIFE UPSIDE DOWN. SHE RUINED MY LIFE AGAIN! SERIOUSLY, SHE IS MY SISTER, THE SISTER I HAVE ALWAYS

BEEN THE CLOSEST TO! WHY IS SHE DOING THIS? SO, MY MOM IS NOW AGAINST ME AND SO IS EVERYBODY ELSE! I WAS OVER AT MY MOM'S WEDNESDAY AND NOW I CAN'T EVEN GO OVER THERE! MASON WAS IN TEARS LAST NIGHT 'CAUSE HE MISSES ME SO MUCH! THAT BREAKS MY HEART! SHE HAS EVEN TAKEN MY KIDS AWAY FROM ME. ADI WANTS NOTHING TO DO WITH ME RIGHT NOW EITHER. MY WORLD HAS FALLEN APART! PAUL AND I ARE PRETTY MUCH OVER! I HAVEN'T TALKED TO HIM FOR A COUPLE DAYS. HE CALLED LAST NIGHT AND THIS MORNING OVER AND OVER AGAIN, BUT I AM NOT ABOUT TO TALK TO HIM AGAIN AFTER WHAT HE PUT ME THROUGH THE OTHER NIGHT. I WAS IN TEARS ALL NIGHT WITH HIM SCREAMING AT ME, CALLING ME NAMES, FOLLOWING ME AROUND THE HOUSE TELLING ME HOW BIG OF A PIECE OF SHIT I AM!! I AM SO MUCH BETTER THAN THIS, I AM NOT GOING TO PUT MYSELF THROUGH THIS ANY LONGER. I AM TRYING TO SPEND AS MUCH TIME WITH JALA AS I POSSIBLY CAN, SO HOPEFULLY I HAVE HER TOMORROW TOO!

Everything I did was done out of love and protection for Nat's kids and the rest of the family. I was always honest with them and would tell them the things I knew, and that, more often than not, resulted in her lashing out at me.

FRIDAY, JUNE 14, 2013:

STAYED AT JAY'S AGAIN LAST NIGHT 'CAUSE I LITERALLY HAVE NOWHERE TO GO. HOUSE JUMPING AGAIN, HOW MANY TIMES DO I REALLY HAVE TO DO THIS IN MY LIFE? THIS IS RIDICULOUS! I THOUGHT I FINALLY FOUND THE MAN OF MY DREAMS THAT I LOVE SO MUCH, AND HE TURNS OUT TO BE THE MOST PSYCHOTIC MAN I HAVE EVER BEEN WITH OR EVEN KNOWN!! IT'S ABOUT 9:00 P.M. AND I AM LIVID! PAUL SAID HE WAS GOING TO MEET ME AT THE HOUSE TONIGHT TO GET SOME OF MY THINGS AND HE WON'T ANSWER ANY OF MY CALLS

OR TALK TO ME NOW. I NEED MY THINGS AND MY KITTY! BUT ON A GOOD NOTE, I FINALLY GOT MY CAR BACK. IT DOES LOOK ABSOLUTELY INCREDIBLE, BUT HE JUST KEEPS REMINDING ME HOW MUCH TIME AND MONEY HE PUT INTO IT. HE IS THE ONE THAT OFFERED, SO THIS IS ON HIM. I TEXTED MY MOM TODAY TO SEE IF I COULD COME OVER AND CLEAN MY CAR AND SHE SAID NOPE, TOO MUCH DRAMA, I NEED SPACE. I AM NOT ALLOWED OVER THERE RIGHT NOW AND THERE IS ABSOLUTELY NO REASON WHY! IT'S JUST 'CAUSE MICHELLE IS STILL HERE. WHY IS SHE BEING SUCH A BITCH? WHAT DID I DO TO HER? IT'S 'CAUSE SHE NEEDED TO SWITCH THE FOCUS OFF HER AND BACK ON ME. WHAT A SISTER, OR IS SHE EVEN MY SISTER? ANGIE IS THE ONLY ONE OUT OF OUR FAMILY THAT IS TALKING TO ME!

SATURDAY, JUNE 15, 2013:

THINGS JUST KEEP GETTING WORSE AND WORSE. IT'S SO TRUE WHEN THEY SAY…WHEN IT RAINS, IT POURS! WELL, IT'S LITERALLY POURING IN MY LIFE RIGHT NOW! WHY CAN'T ANYTHING GO RIGHT FOR ME? IT'S BEEN SO STINKIN' LONG SINCE THINGS WENT REALLY WELL IN MY LIFE. IT'S TIME THINGS START LOOKING UP FOR ME. MASON WAS IN TEARS LAST NIGHT AGAIN 'CAUSE HE MISSED ME SO MUCH AND MY MOTHER WILL NOT ALLOW ME AROUND RIGHT NOW, AND HONESTLY, I HAVE NO IDEA WHAT I DID TO DESERVE ALL THIS. THINGS ARE GONNA BE GOOD TODAY, I AM GOING TO MAKE SURE OF IT. I AM THE ONLY ONE THAT DETERMINES MY HAPPINESS. I CAN'T KEEP LETTING PEOPLE HAVE POWER OVER ME AND CONTROL ANY PART OF MY LIFE. I AM IN CHARGE OF MY LIFE AND MY HAPPINESS, *ME!!* PAUL GOT EVICTED FROM OUR HOUSE LAST NIGHT. THE LANDLORD TOLD PAUL WE HAD 24 HOURS TO GET ALL OUR STUFF OUT. HE SAID THERE WAS NO POSSIBLE WAY SHE WAS GIVING US 48 HOURS. SO, BY TOMORROW NIGHT, I HAVE TO HAVE ALL MY SHIT OUT OF MINE

AND PAUL'S HOUSE, THEN NO MORE TIES AT ALL TO PAUL. HE IS SERIOUSLY TALKING ABOUT LEAVING THE STATE. I LITERALLY FREAKED WHEN HE TOLD ME THAT! I CRY ALMOST ALL DAY LONG EVERY STINKIN' DAY 'CAUSE I DON'T WANT TO BE AWAY FROM PAUL FOR EVEN ONE DAY. HOW IN THE *HELL* AM I GOING TO GET THROUGH THIS ONE? ESPECIALLY SINCE I DON'T HAVE MY FAMILY BY MY SIDE EITHER? THE ONLY PEOPLE THAT ARE HERE WHICH PUT A *BIG* SMILE ON MY FACE EVERY DAY ARE MASON, JALA, AND JAY. I CAN AND WILL GET THROUGH THIS!

Nat moved in with Jay during this time.

SUNDAY, JUNE 16, 2013:

IT'S FATHER'S DAY TODAY AND GUESS WHO DOESN'T GET TO SEE THEIR DAD? YEP, ME! MY ENTIRE FAMILY APPARENTLY HAS TURNED AGAINST ME…AGAIN! BUT THIS TIME I REALLY DIDN'T DO ANYTHING TO BE TREATED THIS WAY. A COUPLE DAYS AGO, I ASKED MY MOM IF I COULD COME OVER AND USE THEIR SHOP VAC ON MY CAR TO CLEAN IT AND SHE SAID NO, SHE NEEDED SPACE FOR A WHILE. STILL, NO IDEA WHY. SO, I TEXTED MY DAD THIS MORNING AND ASKED HIM AND HE SAID YES, COME NOW, SO I DROPPED JALA OFF AT JAY'S WORK AND I WENT OVER TO CLEAN MY CAR. MY DAD WAS BEING AWESOME TO ME AT FIRST, AND THEN WHEN I WAS ABOUT TO LEAVE, HE ASKED ME TO COME TALK TO HIM. THE FIRST THING HE SAID TO ME WAS, YOU HAVE BEEN LYING TO ME SINCE YOU WERE FIFTEEN YEARS OLD, SO I DON'T SEE ME EVER GETTING AN HONEST ANSWER OUT OF YOU, BUT WE ALL THINK YOU ARE SELLING DRUGS. THERE'S JUST NO WAY FOR YOU TO BE PAYING FOR THINGS IF YOU WEREN'T. AND, WE THINK IT'S A GOOD IDEA IF YOU STAY AWAY FROM YOUR KIDS RIGHT NOW. I WAS IN COMPLETE SHOCK! I HONESTLY HAD NO IDEA WHAT TO SAY, THAT WAS THE LAST THING I

WAS EXPECTING! SAD THING IS, THERE IS ABSOLUTELY NO WAY OF CHANGING ANY OF THEIR MINDS. MICHELLE GOT TO THEM AND THAT'S WHAT'S HAPPENING, APPARENTLY. I GUESS I AM NOT GOING TO BE SEEING MY FAMILY FOR A WHILE!

MONDAY, JUNE 17, 2013:

WELL, I HAVE NOT BEEN THIS LOST OR DEPRESSED IN A VERY, VERY LONG TIME. I AM IN TEARS EVERY SINGLE DAY. I CAN'T GET OVER THIS! I AM HURTING SO MUCH, IT'S WORSE THAN PHYSICAL PAIN. I WOULD RATHER BE BEATEN AND BEATEN AND BEATEN THAN FEEL THIS PAIN ANYMORE! WHY COULDN'T HE JUST LOVE ME THE WAY I LOVED HIM? I HATE THE WAY I FEEL RIGHT NOW! I HAVE NO SELF-ESTEEM AT ALL. THIS HAS MADE ME FEEL LIKE SHIT! I REALLY NEED TO COME OUT OF THIS PAIN AND DEPRESSION OR I THINK SOMETHING TERRIBLE IS GOING TO HAPPEN. I AM REALLY NOT DOING GOOD. IT'S SCARING ME. I DO NOT WANT TO LIVE WITHOUT PAUL. I LOVE HIM! I CAN'T GO ON LIKE THIS ANYMORE. MY LIFE JUST KEEPS GETTING WORSE AND WORSE. I THOUGHT THE OLDER I GOT, THE BETTER MY LIFE WOULD BE 'CAUSE I WOULD BE WHERE I WANT TO BE AND BE WITH WHO I WANT TO BE WITH. I PRAY TO GOD PAUL COMES BACK TO ME AND WE GET MARRIED AND WE STAY TOGETHER FOREVER, THEN I WOULD BE HAPPY! I CAN'T HAVE MY OWN KIDS, SO WHY CAN'T I HAVE PAUL? WE WERE MEANT FOR EACH OTHER! PLEASE HELP ME, EITHER WAY, IF THERE IS A GOD OUT THERE, I NEED YOU TO BRING ME PEACE, CALM ME DOWN, AND HELP ME LOVE MYSELF AND LIFE. I HATE MYSELF AND I DON'T HAVE ANY IDEA HOW TO CHANGE THAT! I NEED ALL THE HELP I CAN GET AND GET THE LOVE THAT I CAN GET. PLEASE HELP ME FEEL LOVED BY THOSE THAT MEAN SOMETHING TO ME. I NEED *SOMEBODY!*

It seems that, in her mind, all her unhappiness was because of Paul and our family and everyone else. She was so lost and hurt here, and it is so sad that she didn't know what to do at that moment to find any peace or happiness.

WEDNESDAY, JUNE 19, 2013:

TODAY WAS JALA'S DAY! SHE WENT WITH HER BABYSITTER MONDAY AND TUESDAY LIKE SHE ALWAYS DOES EVERY SUMMER, THEN I HAVE HER EVERY DAY. WE HAD A GOOD TIME TOGETHER OTHER THAN I HAVE *NEVER* IN MY LIFE BEEN THIS DEPRESSED! I MISS PAUL SO DAMN MUCH! I WAS TEXTING HIM A LOT, AND THE LAST TIME I TALKED TO HIM, HE SAID I WAS ACTING LIKE A STALKER. WHAT HAVE I MADE MYSELF LOOK LIKE? I LOOK LIKE A DESPERATE WOMAN THAT IS A PIECE OF SHIT! I FEEL LIKE SUCH AN IDIOT. I AM NO STALKER! I WAS JUST REALLY TRYING HARD TO LET HIM KNOW HOW I FELT AND POSSIBLY TALKING HIM INTO GIVING US ANOTHER CHANCE, BUT HE ALREADY KNOWS HOW I FEEL. SO, I'M DONE CALLING, DONE TEXTING. I WILL NOT MAKE MYSELF LOOK LIKE THIS ANYMORE! NOT ONLY LOSING HIM, I LET HIM KEEP MACI *(her kitty)* AND NOW I AM FREAKED THE FUCK OUT. HE SAID I COULD COME SEE HER WHENEVER I WANT, BUT THAT DOESN'T HELP AT ALL. I MISS HER SO MUCH. I MISS SLEEPING WITH HER AT NIGHT AND COMING HOME TO HER AND HEARING HER BELL JINGLE EVERY TIME WE CAME HOME. I AM NOT DOING GOOD AT ALL. I WANT TO GO BACK HOME. SO, JAY WAS THE ONLY ONE THAT WOULD TAKE ME IN. I AM VERY GRATEFUL. IT'S SO NICE TO BE WITH JALA! SHE IS THE REASON I HAVE A SMILE ON MY FACE WHEN I WAKE UP IN THE MORNINGS, 'CAUSE IF I WASN'T WITH HER RIGHT NOW, I REALLY DON'T THINK I WOULD EVEN WAKE UP. I WOULD COMPLETELY GIVE UP. SHE HAS SAVED MY LIFE!!

THURSDAY, JUNE 20, 2013:

TODAY HAS BEEN A VERY INTERESTING DAY. HAD A GREAT MORNING WITH JALA, THEN CALLED ANGIE TO SEE WHAT SHE WAS DOING, SEEMS SHE IS THE ONLY ONE IN MY FAMILY THAT IS TALKING TO ME AND SHE SAID IT WAS BROCK'S BIRTHDAY AND TO COME OVER, THEN GO TO KAILEE'S DANCE RECITAL AT 4:00. SO, JALA AND I GOT READY AND WENT UP TO ANGIE'S HOUSE. WHEN WE PULLED UP, I NOTICED THAT MY MOM'S CAR WAS THERE, DIDN'T WANT TO CAUSE ANY DRAMA SO I STAYED AND WAS JUST GOING TO STAY OUT OF HER WAY, BUT RIGHT WHEN WE PULLED UP, ANGIE CAME RUNNING OUT AND SHE SAID THAT ADI AND KIERRA WERE UNCOMFORTABLE WITH ME COMING OVER. *(They were still upset about the last episode when they learned that Nat was selling to High School kids at Adi's school.)* ANGIE SAID SHE WAS SO SORRY, SHE HAD NO IDEA WHAT WAS GOING ON, BUT SHE DIDN'T WANT ANY TENSION AT HER HOUSE, ESPECIALLY ON BROCK'S BIRTHDAY. I IMMEDIATELY STARTED CRYING AND DIDN'T SAY ANYTHING, LEFT JALA THERE AND LEFT. I WAS IN TEARS FOR HOURS. ADI, MY MOM, AND MASON DROPPED JALA OFF A COUPLE HOURS LATER AT JAY'S WORK, AND JAY TALKED TO ADI AND MAS AND MY MOM AND TOTALLY HAD MY BACK. TOLD THEM HOW GOOD I WAS DOING. *(Nat was very good at convincing people she was clean, and Jay believed she was clean at this time.)* OF COURSE, ADI DIDN'T LISTEN, NEITHER DID MY MOM. MASON IS HAVING SUCH A HARD TIME, HE JUST WANTS TO BE WITH ME SO BAD AND HE CAN'T, IT'S SO NOT FAIR, HE DOESN'T DESERVE ANY OF THIS, HE NEEDS HIS MOM! I NEED TO CHANGE THINGS *NOW!!*

SUNDAY, JUNE 23, 2013:

OKAY, I HAVE REALLY HAD ENOUGH OF THIS SHIT! I MISS PAUL SO MUCH THAT IT PHYSICALLY HURTS. I NEVER THOUGHT

THAT PAUL AND I WOULD *EVER* BE APART, AND WE ARE. DON'T GET ME WRONG, I AM VERY, VERY GRATEFUL FOR JAY FOR HELPING ME AND GIVING ME A PLACE TO STAY AND I GET TO BE WITH MY BABY GIRL, BUT I JUST CAN'T HANDLE BEING AWAY FROM PAUL ANYMORE! IT'S MY MOM'S BIRTHDAY TOMORROW AND I CAN'T EVEN GO SEE HER ON HER BIRTHDAY. IT'S SO ABSOLUTELY FUCKED UP! I AM REALLY NOT IN A GOOD PLACE RIGHT NOW! I HAVE NOT BEEN THIS BAD IN A VERY LONG TIME. I THINK I AM GOING TO PICK UP MY KITTY TOMORROW. I MISS HER SO MUCH, I CAN'T STAND IT ANYMORE. I JUST WANT MY LIFE WITH PAUL BACK, WHY DID I EVER COMPLAIN WITH HIM? I HAD EVERYTHING I WANTED AND MORE AND I WASN'T HAPPY, NOW I'M IN PURE HELL AND AT THE BOTTOM OF MY LIFE, WHY COULDN'T I HAVE JUST KEPT MY MOUTH SHUT?!? I WANT PAUL BACK!

6-24-2013: Dr. Note–119 lbs. Denies relapse. Prescribed Suboxone.

WEDNESDAY, JUNE 26, 2013:

WENT OVER TO PAUL'S TONIGHT, LIKE A PATHETIC, DESPERATE LOSER! OF COURSE, HE WASN'T HOME. I HAVE NO IDEA WHERE THE *HELL* HE COULD BE. I WENT OVER AROUND 7:00 P.M. AND PICKED MACI *(her kitty)* UP, BROUGHT HER TO JAY'S APARTMENT FOR A COUPLE HOURS, THEN TOOK HER BACK HOME ABOUT 9:45 P.M. HE STILL WASN'T HOME! I GOT ALL DRESSED UP, LIKE A PATHETIC LOSER, AND HE WASN'T EVEN HOME! I AM REALLY LOSIN' IT!!! I MISS HIM SO MUCH, I CAN'T BE HAPPY IF I TRIED. I HAVEN'T ACTUALLY SPOKE TO PAUL FOR A COUPLE WEEKS NOW AND I AM LITERALLY GOING CRAZY!!! I HONESTLY HAVE NEVER IN MY ENTIRE LIFE BEEN LIKE THIS! I AM REALLY SCARING MYSELF. MY FAMILY STILL WON'T TALK TO ME, MY DAUGHTER ADI WANTS ABSOLUTELY NOTHING TO DO WITH ME, AND MY FAVORITE NIECE KIERRA WANTS NO CONTACT WHATSOEVER WITH ME EITHER!

WHAT IN THE *HELL* DID I REALLY DO? THEY ALL SAY I HAVE BEEN ACTING WEIRD. IT'S BECAUSE PAUL AND I WERE SO BAD, AND I DON'T HAVE ANY TRACK MARKS ANYWHERE THAT ARE NEW. THEY ARE JUST LISTENING TO MICHELLE AND HER PATHETIC LITTLE STORIES THAT SHE MAKES UP ABOUT ME... THE SAD THING IS THE *ENTIRE* FAMILY WILL LISTEN TO HER AND BELIEVE EVERYTHING SHE IS SAYING. I NEED TO LET MY FAMILY GO. IF THEY WANT TO BE PART OF MY LIFE, THEY WILL COME BACK AROUND, BUT I AM NOT ABOUT TO CHASE MY FAMILY LIKE I AM PAUL. I ALREADY FEEL LIKE THE BIGGEST LOSER IN THE WORLD, I HAVE NO SELF-ESTEEM ANYMORE. I HAVE LOST MYSELF ALL TOGETHER!!

THURSDAY, JUNE 27, 2013:

JUST ANOTHER DAY IN PARADISE! I AM STILL AT JAY'S HOUSE AND I AM LITERALLY GOING CRAZY! IT'S ABOUT 12:45 AT NIGHT AND I AM SITTING HERE WITH JAY, AND YEP, STILL GOING CRAZY! I MISS PAUL SO MUCH! I CAN'T EVEN PUT IT INTO WORDS. I HAVE *NEVER* FELT LIKE THIS BEFORE! I DON'T EVEN KNOW WHAT TO DO ANYMORE. ALL I THINK ABOUT IS HIM, ALL DAY AND ALL NIGHT. I AM SERIOUSLY TURNING INTO A STALKER (HOW PATHETIC IS THAT?). I NEED HELP, BAD, *SUPER BAD!* MY WHOLE FOCUS EVERY SINGLE DAY NOW IS TO TRY AND THINK OF A GOOD WAY TO GET HIM TO TALK TO ME OR IF I SHOULD SHOW UP AT THE AIRPORT OR AT HIS WORK ONE DAY. I CAN'T DO THAT, I KNOW THAT, BUT I NEED HIM TO TALK TO ME!!!

I REALLY CAN'T DO THIS LIFE WITHOUT THE MAN THAT I TRULY LOVED. WHY? WHY DID IT END UP LIKE THIS? I LOVE HIM WITH ALL MY HEART AND WANT TO FOCUS ON OTHER THINGS LIKE MY KIDS, NOT A MAN! I AM HURTING SO MUCH! I CAN NEVER SMILE ANYMORE OR EVEN LAUGH, I AM TOTALLY AND COMPLETELY MISERABLE! I FEEL SO BAD THAT JALA, ADI, AND MAS HAVE ME AS THEIR MOTHER! I AM A HORRIBLE

MOTHER, A HORRIBLE GIRLFRIEND, AND A HORRIBLE FRIEND! HOW DO I TURN THINGS AROUND? OR IS IT TOO LATE? THIS IS HOW BAD MY LIFE IS…I'M AT THE LAUNDROMAT ON 2ND WEST IN BOUNTIFUL DOING MY LAUNDRY 'CAUSE NOBODY WILL LET ME COME OVER TO DO MY LAUNDRY! MY LIFE IS AT ITS DEFINITE WORST! I REALLY NEED TO PICK MYSELF UP AND MAKE A CHANGE. I DON'T WANT TO LIVE WITHOUT PAUL. I LOVE HIM AND I AM SERIOUSLY GOING CRAZY, PLEASE GOD, BRING MY BABY BACK TO ME!!!

FRIDAY, JUNE 28, 2013:

JALA AND I ARE GOING SWIMMING AT THE POOL AT OUR *(Jay's)* APARTMENT TODAY. IT'S ABOUT 105 DEGREES SO WE WON'T BE ABLE TO STAY OUT IN THE SUN FOR VERY LONG. I ABSOLUTELY LOVE BEING WITH MY BABY GIRL, THOUGH, EVEN THOUGH I AM SO DEPRESSED AND SO SAD, JALA MAKES MY DAYS SO MUCH BRIGHTER! SHE IS MY LIGHT RIGHT NOW, MY ONLY LIGHT. I REALLY NEED TO GET OUT OF THIS FUNK, STOP THINKING ABOUT PAUL ALL THE DAMN TIME!

DIDN'T DO MUCH TONIGHT. WENT TO THE LAUNDROMAT FOR ABOUT AN HOUR AND A HALF AND ONLY GOT ONE LOAD OF LAUNDRY DONE AND THEN WENT HOME AND DID NOT MUCH OF ANYTHING. AND MY LIFE SERIOUSLY, SERIOUSLY SUCKS! TALKED TO MAS TONIGHT AND HE IS HAVING SUCH A HARD TIME NOT BEING ABLE TO SEE ME. IT BREAKS MY HEART! THAT LITTLE BOY DOES NOT DESERVE ANY OF THIS HEARTACHE! IT KILLS ME KNOWING THAT HE IS HAVING SUCH A DIFFICULT TIME. HE IS HONESTLY THE *BEST* LITTLE BOY IN THIS ENTIRE WORLD! I WOULDN'T TRADE THAT KID FOR ANYTHING IN THIS WORLD! I REALLY WISH ADI WOULD TALK TO ME. I MISS HER SO MUCH! I WISH SHE DIDN'T JUST ASSUME EVERYTHING AND SHE WOULD FIND OUT WHAT'S REAL AND WHAT'S NOT. HER AND PAUL, THE TWO MOST IMPORTANT PEOPLE IN MY LIFE, AND THEY WON'T EVEN TALK TO ME ON

THE PHONE! THEY ACT LIKE I AM THE DEVIL! I HAVE A *BIG* HEART AND THEY ARE LITERALLY KILLING ME RIGHT NOW! I NEED TO FIND A WAY TO GET BOTH OF THEM TO TALK TO ME, JUST FOR A MINUTE. WHY DID *EVERYONE* TURN ON ME ALL AT THE SAME TIME? IT'S JUST NOT FAIR AT ALL AND IT'S SERIOUSLY *KILLING* ME!!!

Adi was old enough to understand what was really going on. Mas was more protected by everyone and he didn't ask questions or really want to know what was going on; he was able to be a kid. He just wanted to be with his mom. He did find out the extent of Nat's addiction when he was a little older, and he had a hard time understanding why he didn't know details before. It was really hard watching him face the reality, but it never changed his love for her. He adored his mom.

SATURDAY, JUNE 29, 2013:

JUST ANOTHER UNEVENTFUL DAY IN MY PATHETIC LIFE! IT'S SERIOUSLY SO HARD TO EVEN CRACK A SMILE LATELY. I TRY NOT TO ACT SAD OR DEPRESSED FOR JALA'S SAKE BUT I KNOW THAT LITTLE GIRL CAN SEE RIGHT THROUGH ME. SHE SEES ME MORE THAN ANYBODY, KNOWS ME MORE THAN ANYBODY, AND LOVES ME MORE THAN ANYBODY! I CANNOT LET HER DOWN ANYMORE! IT'S MY JOB TO GIVE MY KIDS A FANTASTIC CHILDHOOD AND I HAVE ALREADY DESTROYED ADI'S, MASON STILL HAS HOPE, JALA HAS HER LIFE STILL, AND IF I GET MY HEAD OUT OF MY ASS SOMETIME SOON, THEN JALA STILL HAS A CHANCE TO HAVE A WONDERFUL CHILDHOOD. I WANT HER TO HAVE A CHILDHOOD THAT SHE WILL ALWAYS REMEMBER AND WHEN SHE LOOKS BACK ON IT, SHE CAN HAVE A BIG SMILE ON HER FACE!

WE WOKE UP ABOUT 11:30 A.M. 'CAUSE, OF COURSE, IT'S SUMMER! WE LIKE TO STAY UP LATE, SO WE ENJOYED SLEEPING IN THIS MORNING. JAY GOT HOME ABOUT 12:30. I GOT THE REST OF MY LAUNDRY DONE, YAY, WHILE JAY AND

JALA HUNG OUT AT THE APARTMENT, THEN I GOT READY. I FOUND THE PAINT CHIPPING OFF THE HOOD OF MY CAR, SO I CALLED AND TEXTED PAUL, AND OF COURSE, NO RESPONSE AND NO ANSWER WHATSOEVER! IT'S GETTING REALLY RIDICULOUS! THEN CAME BACK, TOOK JALA SWIMMING FOR A BIT, THEN CAME HOME AND JAY MADE US SOME REALLY NUMMY CHICKEN. TOMORROW, I AM GOING TO PAUL'S HOUSE SO HE CAN LOOK AT MY CAR! I REALLY HOPE I CAN CATCH HIM SOMEWHERE TOMORROW. I NEED TO SEE MY MAN. I LOVE HIM AND I PRAY TO GOD I GET A CHANCE TO BE WITH HIM AGAIN.

<u>SUNDAY, JUNE 30, 2013</u>:

TODAY WAS FAR WORSE THAN HORRIBLE. TRIED TO GO TO PAUL'S EARLIER TODAY AND NOBODY WAS HOME. THEN WENT TO PAYNE'S AND CLEANED HIS HOUSE FOR SOME MONEY AND GOT REALLY IRRITATED BECAUSE I WAS HIS LITTLE BITCH FOR ABOUT TWO AND A HALF HOURS. I LEFT SO PISSED OFF! WENT BACK TO PAUL'S AT ABOUT 10:45 P.M. AND HE WAS THERE, BUT I WAS TOO FRUSTRATED AND SCARED AT THAT POINT TO TALK TO HIM. NOW SITTING HERE WATCHING DEXTER WITH JAY, I WISH I WAS WITH PAUL. I HAVE NEVER IN MY ENTIRE LIFE NOT WANTED TO LIVE OVER A GUY. I'M OLDER NOW, A DRUG ADDICT THAT IS A WORTHLESS PIECE OF SHIT! I WON'T FIND ANYONE AGAIN, IT'S TOO LATE! I WILL NEVER FEEL LOVE AGAIN, PAUL WAS THE MAN FOR ME, AND I NEED TO TAKE THE BRUTAL TRUTH THAT HE IS GONE. KARMA IS DEFINITELY A BITCH! I KNOW THIS IS MY KARMA BECAUSE OF ALL THE HORRIBLE THINGS I HAVE DONE TO MY EX-HUSBANDS AND TO MY CHILDREN. I AM IN THE WORST PAIN EVER AND DON'T THINK I AM EVER GOING TO COME OUT OF IT! I SHOULD HAVE BEEN HONEST WITH EVERYONE, ESPECIALLY THE ONES I LOVE. NOW, MY LIFE CONSISTS OF NOTHING. JALA AND MASON ARE ALL THAT I HAVE. HOW DID I GET THIS WAY?

I often wonder, if she had been honest with us, if it would have helped take some of her pain away...she spent so much time and energy trying to live two separate lives. Her lying contributed to so much hurt and anger within her and with all of us. There were so many times we would ask ourselves, "Why can't she just be honest?" We knew she was using, and it frustrated us that she thought we didn't know.

MONDAY, JULY 1, 2013:

IT'S ABOUT 2:00 A.M. MONDAY MORNING AND HERE I SIT TRYING TO FIGURE OUT A WAY TO GET PAUL TO TALK TO ME. I AM SO MISERABLE, THAT'S ACTUALLY A HUGE UNDERSTATEMENT! I AM LITERALLY SUICIDAL. IT'S REALLY HARD FOR ME TO WANT TO LIVE ANYMORE. I LOST THE MAN I TRULY LOVE, I LOST ADI, NEVER GET TO SEE MAS, AND I AM SO NOT HAPPY WITH MYSELF AND DON'T REALLY THINK I EVER WILL BE!

PAUL CALLED ME! I WAS DRIVING DOWN TO PAUL'S SHOP AND HE CALLED ME. HE ASKED IF I WAS TRYING TO GET AHOLD OF HIM. WELL, HE AGREED TO MEET UP WITH ME TONIGHT AND IT DIDN'T GO AT ALL AS I PLANNED OR HOW I WANTED IT TO GO. HE GOT ME TO TELL HIM THE TRUTH. I TOLD HIM FINALLY THAT I WAS USING. HE CALLED ME A JUNKIE AND ASKED ME TO STAY OUT OF HIS LIFE! IT KILLED ME, I FINALLY OPENED UP TO HIM, TOLD HIM THE TRUTH, AND LOOK WHERE THAT GOT ME! STILL ALONE AND AWAY FROM THE MAN THAT I LOVED! HE ASKED ME IF I HAD HEPATITIS! ARE YOU KIDDING ME?! WHEN IT CAME TO CHEATING, HE HAD NOTHING TO WORRY ABOUT. I MIGHT BE A STUPID JUNKIE, BUT I AM IN LOVE WITH ONE MAN AND I WILL STAY FAITHFUL TO HIM NO MATTER HOW LONG IT TAKES. THIS MAN HAS A HOLD OF MY HEART LIKE NO OTHER MAN EVER HAS. HOW DO I LET HIM GO AND TRY TO MOVE ON? HOW?

IT'S ABOUT 1:00 A.M. AND JALA AND I WENT TO THE STORE AND GOT SOME ICE CREAM, THEN WE CAME HOME,

RELAXED A LITTLE, WATCHED A MOVIE, NOW WE JUST GOT INTO BED. GOODNIGHT. TOMORROW WILL BE A BETTER DAY!

THURSDAY, JULY 2, 2013:

IT'S ABOUT 1:15 A.M. TUESDAY MORNING. JUST GOT INTO BED WITH MY FAVORITE LITTLE GIRL IN THE WHOLE WORLD! I KNOW I MENTIONED THIS ONCE BEFORE, BUT I CAN'T SAY IT ENOUGH, JALA BRIGHTENS MY DAYS. WHEN I THOUGHT FOR SURE THERE WAS NO MORE LIGHT LEFT IN MY LIFE, I LOOK AT HER AND EVERYTHING CHANGES FOR THE BETTER! I COULDN'T ASK FOR A MORE BEAUTIFUL LITTLE GIRL THAN HER. SHE MAKES ME HAPPY. MASON CALLED TONIGHT, AS HE DOES EVERY NIGHT, AND IT BREAKS MY STINKIN' HEART! I MISS HIM SO MUCH IT HURTS! I NEED MY SON IN MY LIFE JUST AS MUCH AS HE NEEDS ME! I CAN'T DO THIS LIFE WITHOUT MY BABIES. ALL MY BABIES. I AM PRAYING THAT ADI COMES AROUND SOONER THAN LATER. I MISS MY LITTLE GIRL!

IT'S ABOUT 4:30 P.M. AND JALA AND I JUST GOT BACK FROM MCDONALD'S SO SHE COULD EAT AND PLAY, AND NOW WE ARE CHILLIN' ON JALA'S BED WATCHING MONSTER HIGH, SHE IS ABSOLUTELY OBSESSED WITH IT! TODAY ACTUALLY HASN'T BEEN TOO TERRIBLE. WOKE UP, GOT READY, TOOK JALA TO MCDONALD'S, NOW WE ARE GETTING READY TO GO TO THE STORE AFTER THE MONSTER HIGH MOVIE IS OVER! CARL *(a boy Nat met at her last rehab)* JUST STOPPED BY, AND WHILE HE WAS HERE, JALA SAID, "WHY DOES THAT BOY HAVE SO MANY TATTOOS?" I JUST REPLIED SAYING, "'CAUSE HE LIKES THEM," WHAT ELSE COULD I SAY?

FRIDAY, JULY 3, 2013:

TAKING JALA DOWN TO MY MOM'S AT 1:00 'CAUSE THEY WANT HER TO BE WITH HER SISTER AND BROTHER, BUT I CAN'T GO.

I HAVE TO JUST DROP HER OFF! HOW COMPLETELY FUCKED UP IS THAT? MY MOM TEXTED ME AND SAID, "WE LOVE YOU, HOPE YOU'RE DOING GOOD." MAS CALLED ME LAST NIGHT AND IT BROKE MY HEART. HE WAS CRYING AND CRYING, TELLING ME HOW MUCH HE MISSED ME AND LOVES ME AND TOLD ME THE HOLY GHOST WAS ALWAYS WITH ME. I WISH I BELIEVED THAT. IT WOULD MAKE LIFE A LOT EASIER. THAT BOY OF MINE IS ABSOLUTELY AMAZING! HE ALWAYS KNOWS WHEN THERE IS SOMETHING WRONG AND HE IS ALWAYS THERE FOR ME! ALWAYS! I LOVE THAT KID MORE THAN ANYTHING IN THIS WORLD! WENT AND TALKED TO PAUL AGAIN LAST NIGHT AND IT'S CONFIRMED HE HAD TALKED TO AMY. THAT BITCH IS THE REASON PAUL LEFT ME! HE DOESN'T HAVE ANY TIME WITH HIS KIDS NOW 'CAUSE HIS EX TOOK THEM AWAY AGAIN 'CAUSE I TOLD HIS DAUGHTER HE WAS SMOKING POT! SO NOW HE BLAMES ME FOR NOT BEING ABLE TO BE WITH HIS KIDS. THAT'S THE BIG REASON HE LEFT ME AND PUT A GPS ON MY CAR AND GOT INTO ALL MY TEXT MESSAGES! I DON'T KNOW EXACTLY HOW HE DID IT, BUT HE DID, AND NOW I'M TERRIFIED OF WHO HAS SEEN ALL MY TEXTS. I COULD BE IN A LOT OF TROUBLE IF ANYONE ELSE SAW ANY OF MY TEXTS!! SO, MASON TOLD ME LAST NIGHT THAT MY MOM TOLD HIM THAT SHE DIDN'T FEEL SAFE WITH ME AROUND AND THAT IF I EVER WANTED TO COME OVER AGAIN, THEN I NEED TO BRING THEM A DRUG TEST. SHE CAN KISS MY ASS FOR ALL I CARE RIGHT NOW! I AM NOT ABOUT TO BEG FOR MY FAMILY BACK OR ASK TO GO OVER THERE ANYMORE!!

SATURDAY, JULY 4, 2013:

NO DRAMA TODAY AND NO HURT. IT'S GOING TO BE A FANTASTIC DAY! I REALLY WANT TO WRITE PAUL A LETTER AND LET HIM KNOW JUST HOW I REALLY FEEL, BUT MY EMOTIONS ARE WAY TOO OUT OF CONTROL TO EVER PUT INTO WORDS. ALL I REALLY WANT HIM TO KNOW IS HOW VERY SORRY I AM

AND THAT I LOVE HIM WITH ALL MY HEART AND SOUL! MY LIFE WILL DEFINITELY NOT BE THE SAME. AMY CAME OVER LOOKING FOR ME YESTERDAY, WENT TO MY MOM'S AND THEN JAY'S WORK, THEN TO JAY'S HOUSE. SHE FINALLY FOUND ME 'CAUSE SHE GAVE JAY HER NUMBER AND I CALLED HER. I FOUND OUT THAT EVERYTHING THAT PAUL KNOWS ABOUT ME CAME ALL FROM JEREMY. I THINK I MIGHT HAVE SOMEONE PAY THAT MAN A NOT SO FRIENDLY VISIT. *(I remember Nat telling me that there were these guys in the drug world, each simply called "The Tax Man," and they would go after and hurt or kill the people that didn't pay up for their drugs. She said she would go on runs with them, and she saw one Tax Man pick someone up by the neck and throw them across a yard, and it killed the man.)* HE RUINED MY ENTIRE LIFE! PAUL LEFT ME BECAUSE ALL THAT HE SAID. PAUL THINKS I CHEATED ON HIM WHEN I NEVER DID, AND WHO KNOWS WHAT ELSE HE THINKS. WHY DO PEOPLE GO TO SUCH LENGTHS TO RUIN OTHERS' LIVES? I DIDN'T EVEN DO ANYTHING TO THIS MAN. I FEEL A LOT BETTER KNOWING IT WASN'T AMY, THOUGH. BUT WHO KNOWS WHAT ELSE JEREMY HAS UP HIS SLEEVE! I REALLY NEED TO LAY LOW FOR A WHILE! I NEED TO KEEP AMY AT A DISTANCE, FOR SURE. I'M PRAYING THAT HER FINDING ME TODAY DOESN'T CAUSE ME ANY GRIEF IN MY LIFE AT ALL! JAY HAS BEEN SO INCREDIBLY WONDERFUL TO ME LATELY. I DON'T KNOW WHY, BUT IT'S NICE TO ACTUALLY HAVE SOMEONE IN THIS WORLD THAT IS ON MY SIDE AND NOT TRYING TO RUIN MY LIFE. HE ACTUALLY WANTS TO BETTER MY LIFE AND HELP ME ALL THAT HE CAN. I DID PICK TWO GREAT GUYS TO MARRY, THAT'S FOR SURE!

SUNDAY, JULY 5, 2013:

SO, LAST NIGHT WAS THE FIRST YEAR THAT I DID ABSOLUTELY NOTHING ON THE FOURTH OF JULY. I WAS COMPLETELY ALONE! JAY TOOK JALA TO OGDEN TO HAVE A BARBECUE WITH

HIS FAMILY AND TO WATCH FIREWORKS. JALA HAD A LOT OF FUN! I JUST WENT TO THE STORE, GOT SOME CHICKEN SOFT TACOS FROM DEL TACO, WENT BY ANTHONY'S FOR A MINUTE, THEN CAME HOME, GOT IN THE BATH, AND JUST HUNG OUT ALL BY MYSELF. IT REALLY WASN'T ALL THAT BAD. I TEXTED ADI AGAIN TODAY TELLING HER I LOVED HER SO MUCH AND WAS DYING WITHOUT HER, AND NO RESPONSE WHATSOEVER. IT'S KILLING ME MORE AND MORE EACH DAY THAT GOES BY, AND IT'S ANOTHER DAY I HAVE LOST WITH ADISON. I CAN'T AFFORD TO LOSE ANY MORE DAYS WITHOUT MY BABY GIRL! I KNOW I HAVE BEEN A TERRIBLE MOTHER, OKAY THAT'S AN UNDERSTATEMENT. I HAVE THE POTENTIAL TO BE A WONDERFUL MOTHER AND BE AN EXAMPLE TO ADI AND GIVE HER SOMEONE TO LOOK UP TO, NOT HER JUNKIE MOTHER THAT CAN'T KEEP HER KIDS, FAMILY, AND NOW EVEN HER MAN IN HER LIFE! COME ON, *NAT*...IS THIS HOW YOU DREAMED YOUR LIFE WAS GOING TO BE LIKE?!?

CALL MASON ON WEDNESDAY IF HE IS NOT AT GRANDMA'S OR IF HE IS WITH FRIENDS, BECAUSE HE WOULD RATHER SPEND MORE TIME WITH YOU THAN HIS FRIENDS. *(This was written on this entry.)*

ALMOST DONE WITH THIS JOURNAL, AND TIME TO MOVE ON TO A NEW ONE. MY NEXT JOURNAL IS GOING TO BE A LOT MORE UPLIFTING. NO MORE OF THIS DEPRESSING SHIT! I AM GOING TO MAKE SURE MY LIFE GETS BETTER THAN IT IS RIGHT NOW, AND I WILL HAVE ALL THREE OF MY KIDS IN MY LIFE AND A MAN THAT I LOVE MORE THAN ANY MAN I HAVE HAD IN MY LIFE, AND HE WILL LOVE ME EVEN MORE! IT'S GOING TO HAPPEN!! WELL, I'M AT THE END OF MY BOOK! TIME FOR A NEW ONE, AND YOU BETTER BELIEVE THAT I WILL HAVE LOTS OF GOOD STUFF TO WRITE INSTEAD OF SHITTY DEPRESSING STUFF. I KNOW I NEED TO CHANGE MY LIFE AND QUICK! IT'S JUST GOING TO BE REALLY, REALLY HARD

WITHOUT PAUL BY MY SIDE. I WANT HIM WITH ME, BUT I DON'T THINK THAT'S GOING TO HAPPEN, BUT I AM WISHING MYSELF LUCK AND PRAYING EVERY DAY THAT HE WILL COME BACK TO ME! I KNOW HE LOVED ME, SO IT'S NOT A LONG SHOT, BUT I HOPE IT'S SOON. I NEED HIM! HE GIVES ME LIGHT AT THE END OF MY TUNNEL, JUST AS MY KIDS DO! I DEFINITELY LOVE THIS MAN WITH ALL MY HEART, AND I HOPE HE STILL LOVES ME!

Five days later…

WEDNESDAY, JULY 10, 2013:

WELL, TODAY WAS PRETTY MUCH ANOTHER WORTHLESS DAY. I MISS MY TWO OLDER KIDS MORE THAN ANYTHING IN THIS WORLD. MASON JUST TOLD ME THAT ADI IS TRYING OUT FOR AMERICAN IDOL TOMORROW. I HAD NO IDEA, ADI HAS NOT SPOKEN TO ME IN OVER TWO MONTHS. IT'S ABSOLUTELY KILLING ME! IT'S AT THE ENERGY SOLUTIONS ARENA, SO I THINK I AM JUST GOING TO SHOW UP THERE! I NEED TO BE THERE FOR HER, THIS IS GOING TO BE ONE OF THE MOST IMPORTANT DAYS IN HER LIFE. YA, I REALLY NEED TO GO. SO, I DID SAY THAT THE NEXT JOURNAL I AM GOING TO FINISH, IT'S GOING TO BE FULL OF HAPPY THINGS. NOT THESE DEPRESSING MISERABLE THINGS I KEEP WRITING 'CAUSE MY LIFE COULDN'T BE MORE MISERABLE! I DON'T KNOW HOW TO START OVER AND MAKE MY LIFE BETTER. THE ONE GOOD THING IN MY LIFE RIGHT NOW IS MY SWEET PRECIOUS JALA! I HAVE HER WITH ME AND SHE IS THE ONE THING THAT KEEPS ME GOING EVERY DAY! IF IT WASN'T FOR HER, I DON'T THINK I WOULD BE ALIVE! THANK GOD FOR MY BABY GIRL! STILL LIVING AT JAY'S HOUSE, HAVE BEEN HERE FOR ABOUT A MONTH NOW. HE IS THE ONLY ONE IN MY LIFE THAT IS HELPING ME AND MAKING SURE I AM OKAY!

FRIDAY, JULY 12, 2013:

IT'S ABOUT 1:30 A.M. AND JAY AND I ARE SITTIN' HERE WATCHIN' SONS OF ANARCHY! I AM VERY THANKFUL THAT HE IS JALA'S FATHER 'CAUSE HE IS AN AWESOME DAD!

JALA AND I ARE NOW AT THE POOL AT THEIR APARTMENTS. SHE LOVES IT 'CAUSE EVERY TIME SHE COMES, SHE HAS A FRIEND TO PLAY WITH. SHE HAS THE CUTEST LITTLE BODY I HAVE EVER SEEN IN MY LIFE! SHE LOVES TO SWIM, THAT IS PROBABLY HER FAVORITE THING TO DO IN THE SUMMER. I GOT HER LOTS OF HELLO KITTY FLOATIES AND A LITTLE BOARD SHE CAN FLOAT ON. SHE IS LOVING LIFE THIS SUMMER! I AM SO GLAD!

I'M PRAYING THIS JOURNAL WILL BE A LOT MORE POSITIVE AND A LOT LESS DEPRESSING TO LOOK BACK ON, OTHER THAN MY PAST FEW JOURNALS! THAT REALLY DOES TELL ME A WHOLE LOT! IT MEANS *CHANGE YOUR FREAKING LIFE, NAT!* IT'S BEEN THIS *BAD* FOR WAY TOO FUCKING LONG NOW! WE ONLY HAVE ONE LIFE…AND THIS IS *SO NOT* HOW MY LIFE IS GOING TO STAY! I AM SO MUCH BETTER THAN THIS, I KNOW THAT, BUT I AM WAY TOO SCARED TO CHANGE ANYTHING. THAT'S WHAT GETS ME IN TROUBLE. I DON'T LIKE CHANGE AND I AM TOO BIG OF A COWARD TO MAKE ANY KIND OF CHANGE, EVEN IF IT'S GOING TO BETTER MY LIFE. WELL, I WOKE UP…*FINALLY!!* I DON'T WANT TO BE PORTRAYED AS I AM NOW AND HAVE BEEN FOR A WHILE NOW! JUST TO CATCH THINGS UP TO SPEED…PAUL KICKED ME OUT OF OUR HOUSE ABOUT A MONTH AGO, OR EVEN A LITTLE LONGER. I HAD NOWHERE ELSE TO GO, SO JAY LET ME COME STAY WITH HIM AND JALA. MY FAMILY WANTS NOTHING AT ALL TO DO WITH ME AGAIN, BUT THIS TIME IT'S *BAD!* EVEN THE KIDS ARE NOT SPEAKING TO ME NOW, LIKE KIERRA, AUSTIN, AND MOST DEVASTATING, ADISON! SHE WANTS NOTHING TO DO WITH ME AND TOLD ME OVER A MONTH AND A HALF AGO TO LEAVE HER AND THE REST OF THE FAMILY ALONE! PAUL KEPT MY

MACI, AND I AM LITERALLY MORE MISERABLE THAN I EVER HAVE BEEN IN MY ENTIRE LIFE. I KNOW I HAVE SAID THIS BEFORE, BUT BELIEVE ME, THIS TIME IS *VERY BAD!* THERE IS *ABSOLUTELY* NO LIGHT AT THE END OF THE TUNNEL! I HAVE NO FRIENDS AT ALL TO LEAN ON OR VENT TO, SO I AM DOING THIS ALL ON MY OWN. I ACTUALLY CALLED IGGY'S YESTERDAY TO SEE IF I COULD GET MY JOB BACK THERE AND PAYNE TOLD ME THERE WAS NO WAY! I DEFINITELY DID A GREAT JOB ON BURNING A LOT OF BRIDGES! ADI TRIED OUT FOR AMERICAN IDOL YESTERDAY AND SHE DIDN'T EVEN WANT ME TO BE THERE, SHE DIDN'T EVEN TELL ME ABOUT IT, I HEARD IT FROM MASON. HER DAD TOOK HER, AND I WANTED TO BE THERE FOR HER SO BAD 'CAUSE THIS WAS A VERY IMPORTANT DAY FOR HER, AND I COULDN'T EVEN SHARE IT WITH HER. THANK GOD FOR JALA AND MASON OR I SERIOUSLY DON'T THINK I WOULD BE ALIVE TODAY. IF IT WASN'T FOR THOSE 2 BEAUTIFUL, AMAZING KIDS OF MINE! I AM STILL COMPLETELY, MADLY IN LOVE WITH PAUL AND I DON'T THINK HE WILL EVER SPEAK TO ME AGAIN. HE FOUND OUT EVERYTHING AND HE ALWAYS SAID TO ME, PLEASE DON'T EVER LIE TO ME…WE CAN ALWAYS WORK THROUGH THINGS JUST AS LONG AS WE ARE HONEST WITH EACH OTHER. WELL, I DEFINITELY BROKE THAT TRUST. WHY, NAT, WHY? I HAVE RUINED MY LIFE IN MORE WAYS THAN ONE, IS IT GOING TO GET ANY BETTER? WHY DOES IT TAKE LOSING *EVERYTHING* TO OPEN MY EYES? WELL, BE STRONG AND FIGHT FOR YOUR KIDS AND FIGHT FOR YOURSELF, FIGHT TO GET THAT LIFE BACK THAT I KNOW I DESERVE!

<u>SATURDAY, JULY 13, 2013</u>:

WELL, FINALLY GOT MY TWO CAR PAYMENTS MADE, SINCE THEY WERE BOTH LATE! DEBORAH AND EDWARD HELPED ME. THEY WEREN'T TOO HAPPY ABOUT IT, THAT'S FOR SURE! I'M NOT REALLY FOND OF THEM ANYWAYS, EVERYTHING I

TELL DEBORAH GOES STRAIGHT TO MARY! YA, MARY AND I ARE TOTALLY PAST OUR BEST-FRIENDSHIP, WE CAN'T EVEN STAND EACH OTHER ANYMORE. I AM WAY CLOSER TO DAVID THAN HER, BY FAR. I GO SEE DAVID AT LEAST ONCE A WEEK AT DAVIS COUNTY JAIL. HE REALLY IS SUCH A GREAT MAN. SO GOOD AND FAITHFUL TO MARY (WHICH SHE DEFINITELY DOESN'T DESERVE). ME AND HIM GET ALONG GREAT, BUT THAT WOULD NEVER, EVER FLY! HE IS LIKE MY BEST FRIEND RIGHT NOW! I TOLD HIM THAT ROBERT CONTACTED ME THE OTHER DAY AND WAS TRACKING ME DOWN, AND HE FLIPPED OUT! I KNOW WHAT I NEED TO DO, THOUGH, AND I NEED TO GET AWAY FROM THIS WHOLE CROWD. LOVE DAVID TO DEATH, BUT IT'S JUST NOT WORTH IT TO ME ANYMORE. I NEED TO FOCUS ON GETTING MY LIFE BACK TOGETHER! I KNOW I KEEP SAYING THIS, BUT LET'S FACE IT, NAT, IT'S BEEN LONG ENOUGH! TIME TO GET MY LIFE BACK, MY KIDS BACK, MYSELF BACK!!! I DON'T HAVE ANY IDEA WHO I AM ANYMORE. IT'S BEEN THAT WAY FOR A WHILE NOW. *MY ENTIRE LIFE IS ONE BIG LIE!* IT'S NOT FAIR TO ME OR THE PEOPLE THAT LOVE ME, ESPECIALLY MY SWEET, INNOCENT KIDS, THEY ARE THE ONES THAT ARE SUFFERING THE MOST! PULL YOUR HEAD OUT, NAT...YOU REALLY NEED TO BUCK UP AND GET THINGS RIGHT IN YOUR LIFE AGAIN, YOU ARE STRONG ENOUGH, WE ALL KNOW THAT!!!

<u>SUNDAY, JULY 14, 2013</u>:

WELL, IT'S BEEN A VERY INTERESTING WEEKEND! LAST NIGHT I HAD ABOUT 30 TEXT MESSAGES OR MORE FROM ANTHONY HARASSING ME! HE SAID THINGS TO ME I HAVE NEVER BEEN TOLD IN MY ENTIRE LIFE! I HONESTLY DON'T GIVE 2 SHITS WHAT THAT MAN THINKS OF ME, BUT I AM AFRAID OF WHAT HE IS CAPABLE OF! HE WOULD DO ANYTHING 'CAUSE HE IS NOT SCARED OF ANYONE AND DOESN'T CARE IF HE LIVES OR DIES, OR WHAT PEOPLE MIGHT THINK OF HIM! THE MAN IS

COMPLETELY PSYCHO! JEREMY TOLD ME NOT TO WORRY BECAUSE HE IS GETTING HIM TAKEN CARE OF. I DON'T REALLY KNOW EXACTLY WHAT THAT MEANS, AND DON'T WANT TO KNOW! I JUST WANT TO BE SAFE AND NOT HAVE ANY TYPE OF DANGER OR DANGEROUS PEOPLE AROUND ME AND MY BABY GIRL. THE LESS I KNOW, THE BETTER! I HAD AN AWESOME DAY TODAY, THOUGH! I HAVEN'T BEEN ABLE TO SAY THAT IN SUCH A LONG TIME NOW! GOT TO HANG OUT WITH MY BOY FOR A COUPLE HOURS AT MY MOM'S, JUST ME AND HIM! I HAVEN'T SEEN HIM IN OVER A MONTH 'CAUSE MY FAMILY IS ACTING CRAZY AGAIN, SO I HAVEN'T BEEN ABLE TO GO TO MY MOM'S AT ALL TILL TODAY! I GUESS MASON ASKED MY MOM AND DAD IF I COULD COME OVER AND THEY BOTH SAID YES, EVEN THOUGH LAST WEEK I WASN'T ALLOWED ANYWHERE NEAR THE HOUSE! I CAN'T BELIEVE MY FAMILY IS HOW THEY ARE! I THOUGHT THEY WOULD ALWAYS HAVE MY BACK, NO MATTER WHAT HAPPENED, BUT THEY DON'T AT ALL! THEY TOTALLY TURNED THEIR BACKS ON ME AND BASICALLY SAID GOODBYE TO ME!!! WHAT KIND OF FAMILY DOES THAT??

Throughout her years of using, there was always someone in the family that would still be there for her. One family member would burn out and another would step in. During this time, everyone in the family was hurt and burned out at the same time, and this was the first time everyone backed away all at once.

MONDAY, JULY 15, 2013:

I GUESS EVERY DAY IS GETTING A LITTLE BETTER AND SOMEWHAT EASIER. I GOT TO GO OVER TO MY MOM'S TODAY AND SEE MAS FOR A COUPLE MIN AND DO A COUPLE LOADS OF LAUNDRY (WOW). THE ONE PERSON THAT SAYS MORE THAN ANYONE I KNOW "GET OVER IT" IS HOLDING A GRUDGE WITH ME BAD THIS TIME! *(She's talking about our mother.)* I KNOW THIS TIME IS PROBABLY WORSE THAN OTHER TIMES 'CAUSE

THEY HAD BELIEVED I HAD CHANGED AND WAS A DIFFERENT PERSON, BUT THEY DIDN'T CATCH ME IN ANYTHING! THEY ARE ABSOLUTELY *NOT* STUPID, THOUGH! I JUST HOPE THAT SOMEDAY REALLY, REALLY SOON MY WHOLE ENTIRE FAMILY WILL BE BACK TO NORMAL THE WAY IT ALWAYS USED TO BE. I DON'T KNOW THIS FAMILY RIGHT NOW! THIS STAYING AT JAY'S PLACE IS REALLY TAKING A TOLL ON ME. DON'T GET ME WRONG, I AM VERY, VERY GRATEFUL. WE GOT IN A HUGE FIGHT TONIGHT. HE GOT REALLY MAD AT ME 'CAUSE I TOLD HIM HIS NEW GIRLFRIEND LOOKED LIKE A STRIPPER AND THAT ALL HE SEES WHEN HE LOOKS FOR A PARTNER IS THEIR BODY. I ALSO TOLD HIM HOW SHALLOW THAT WAS AND THAT HE IS TOO. WHOOPS! THAT DIDN'T GO OVER VERY WELL AT ALL!

TUESDAY, JULY 16, 2013:

IT'S ABOUT 11:45 P.M. TUESDAY NIGHT AND I AM SITTING HERE ALL ALONE WRITING IN MY JOURNAL. I DON'T KNOW IF I AM BUGGED OR NOT! I'M TOO TIRED TO EVEN CARE ABOUT A THING RIGHT NOW! I HAVE BEEN AWAKE FOR 2 SOLID DAYS STRAIGHT NOW! DOESN'T SOUND VERY LONG, BUT I HAVE NOT DONE THIS TWEEKIN' (STAYIN' AWAKE) THING IN SUCH A LONG TIME, I DON'T LIKE IT, NOT ONE BIT! *(Meth and Bath Salts kept Nat awake; they are uppers and made her fidgety and not want to eat. She preferred Heroin because it is a depressant and it calmed her. Anytime she mentions being up for days, she has used an upper like Meth, Bath Salts, or Cocaine.)* JAY HAS JALA WITH HIM IN SANDY AT HIS NEW GIRLFRIEND'S HOUSE. I DON'T KNOW IF I AM HAVING ANY FEELINGS ABOUT IT WHATSOEVER! I JUST PRAY THAT WHOEVER JAY ENDS UP WITH, SHE WILL TREAT MY JALA LIKE HER OWN, TREAT HER WITH THE RESPECT THAT MY LITTLE GIRL DESERVES. SHE DESERVES THE WHOLE WORLD AND I'M NOT ABOUT TO LET

ANYONE TREAT MY SWEET GIRL LIKE SHE IS 2ND OR MAKE HER FEEL BAD IN ANY WAY AT ALL!! I FELT SO BAD FIGHTING IN FRONT OF HER LAST NIGHT. *I DO NOT* AND *WILL NOT* LET THIS PRECIOUS LITTLE GIRL OF MINE GO THROUGH ANY KIND OF MISERY OR UNHAPPINESS LIKE SHE DID A COUPLE TIMES. SHE HAS LITERALLY SAVED MY LIFE SO MANY, SO MANY, SO MANY TIMES! SHE IS MY SWEET LITTLE ANGEL! MY ENTIRE HEART, SHE IS THE BEST AND MAKES MY HEART SMILE! I AM TRULY BLESSED IN MORE WAYS THAN ONE! I HAVE THE 3 MOST AMAZING CHILDREN ON THIS PLANET!

THURSDAY, JULY 18, 2013:

WELL, EVERY DAY IS JUST GETTING WORSE AND WORSE FOR ME! I HONESTLY DON'T EVER THINK I AM GOING TO GET OVER THIS MAN! PAUL HAS MY HEART AND I AM NOT OKAY BEING WITHOUT HIM. I LOVE HIM WITH ALL MY HEART AND SOUL! I WANT HIM BACK! RIGHT NOW, HE THINKS I AM A STALKER, THOUGH, SO I NEED TO WATCH MYSELF AND MAKE SURE THAT I DON'T MAKE MYSELF LOOK LIKE THAT! I WANT MY KITTY TOO! JAY IS GIVING ME THE 3RD DEGREE RIGHT NOW! ASKING ME WHERE I JUST WAS AND WHERE I GO AT NIGHT. I DON'T EVER ASK HIM WHENEVER HE LEAVES! THIS WHOLE LIVING TOGETHER WITH JAY THING IS JUST NOT GOING TO WORK! HE IS THE ONLY ONE THAT HAS OPENED HIS ARMS TO ME AND GAVE ME A SAFE PLACE TO STAY. HOW DID I GET THIS *BAD?* I HAVE RUINED MY WHOLE LIFE! I HAD A WONDERFUL MAN BY MY SIDE AND I FUCKED IT UP, JUST LIKE I ALWAYS DO! I DON'T KNOW IF I CAN *EVER* GET PAST THIS ONE EITHER. I REALLY DO NOT WANT TO GO ON WITHOUT HIM. I AM SO UNHAPPY EVERY SINGLE DAY AND I CAN'T GET HIM OFF MY MIND. I JUST CAN'T. ADI STILL HASN'T TALKED TO ME, EITHER. I MISS HER SO MUCH! IT'S BEEN OVER 2 MONTHS, I AM FREAKING HATING MY LIFE RIGHT NOW!!

FRIDAY, JULY 19, 2013:

IT'S ABOUT 1:30 A.M. AND I JUST GOT HOME FROM PAYNES. HE LIKES ME AND THAT MAKES ME SERIOUSLY ILL! I ONLY WANT PAUL! EVERY OTHER MAN IN THIS WORLD MAKES ME SICK! IF I HAD ALL OF MY KIDS WITH ME, MY LIFE WOULD BE A WHOLE LOT HAPPIER AND I WOULDN'T CARE, WELL AT LEAST AS MUCH AS I DO NOW ABOUT PAUL OR NOT HAVING HIM. ADI IS LITERALLY KILLING ME! I KNOW I AM AT FAULT AND I KNOW WHY SHE WANTS NOTHING TO DO WITH ME, BUT I AM HER MOM! SHE HAS TO FORGIVE ME SOMETIME, DOESN'T SHE? I HONESTLY DON'T KNOW HOW MUCH LONGER I WILL BE ALIVE OR HOW MUCH LONGER I CAN GO ON WITHOUT ADI AND PAUL! I KNOW I STILL HAVE MASON AND JALA AND THAT DEFINITELY IS ENOUGH TO KEEP ME GOIN' AND FIGHTIN', BUT NOT HAVING THOSE 2 IS TAKING OVER A GREAT DEAL OF ME LATELY! I DON'T WANT MAS OR JALA TO SEE ME THIS WAY, DEPRESSED, UNHAPPY, SICK, HORRIBLE! IT'S NOT FAIR TO ANY OF MY KIDS WHAT I HAVE DONE TO THEM. I AM DONE WITH THIS SHIT! I AM SO SICK OF THIS DRUG LIFE! I HAVE BEEN IN IT WAY TOO LONG NOW AND I WANT OUT! I JUST DON'T WANT TO DO IT! I DEFINITELY CANNOT GO BACK TO JAIL, I WOULD KILL MYSELF 1ST, FOR SURE. I AM SO READY TO START MY WHOLE LIFE OVER WITH MY KIDS AND BEING THEIR MOTHER, THE MOTHER THEY DESERVE FOR A CHANGE. THEY ALL DESERVE THE BEST AND I NEED TO GIVE THAT TO THEM. GET STRONG AND *FIGHT THIS BATTLE TO THE END, NAT!* YOU CAN DO IT!!!

SATURDAY, JULY 20, 2013:

WELL, I DID IT! I WENT AND GOT MY KITTY! I WENT TO HIS HOUSE, KNOCKED ON HIS DOOR, AND HIS SON WAS SITTING ON THE COUCH WHEN PAUL ANSWERED THE DOOR. HE LOOKED AT ME, MACI RAN OUT, THEN HE SHUT THE DOOR IN MY FACE. I

GRABBED MACI AND WE GOT IN THE CAR. PAUL CAME OUT AND WATCHED ME LEAVE. HE HASN'T CALLED, NOTHIN'! SO NOT WHAT I EXPECTED! MACI IS SITTING UNDER THE BED RIGHT NOW AND I FEEL REALLY BAD BECAUSE I AM SURE SHE IS REALLY SCARED. I LOVE THIS KITTY MORE THAN ANYTHING. I WANT TO KEEP HER, BUT I THINK THAT WOULD BE SELF-ISH! PAUL IS MOVING OUT OF THAT HOUSE SOON ANYWAYS. I COULD BE GETTING MY UNEMPLOYMENT ON MONDAY AND I PRAY THAT I DO GET IT 'CAUSE I AM LIVING ON ABSOLUTELY NOTHING RIGHT NOW AND IT'S MAKING ME CRAZY! I HAVE JALA EVERY SINGLE DAY AND I ABSOLUTELY LOVE IT, BUT I NEED PAUL BACK. MY LIFE IS NOT COMPLETE WITHOUT HIM. I DIDN'T THINK HE WOULD LET MACI GO LIKE THIS. HE HASN'T CALLED OR ANYTHING. I GUESS HE REALLY DOESN'T CARE OR HE REALLY, REALLY WANTS ME OUT OF HIS LIFE. I MESSED UP BAD WITH THIS ONE!!

SUNDAY, JULY 21, 2013:

TODAY IS GOING TO BE AN AWESOME DAY AND I AM NOT GOING TO BE DEPRESSED AT ALL TODAY! IT'S ABOUT 3:00 A.M. SUNDAY MORNING, AND YES, I AM STILL UP. JAY'S FRIEND STOPPED BY WITH HIS WIFE AND TALKED TO US FOR A COUPLE HOURS. THEY ARE NICE PEOPLE. I TOOK MACI BACK YESTERDAY TO PAUL AND ALL HE SAID WAS THANK YOU! NOTHIN' ELSE! I MISS HIM! I TEXTED ADI YESTERDAY AND TOLD HER I MISSED HER AND LOVED HER SO MUCH AND COULDN'T GO ON MUCH LONGER WITHOUT HER IN MY LIFE. I BEGGED HER TO TALK TO ME, AND ABSOLUTELY NOTHIN'. IT'S BREAKING MY HEART INTO A MILLION LITTLE PIECES WITHOUT MY BABY GIRL AND PAUL! I LITERALLY HATE/DESPISE MY LIFE RIGHT NOW! I PRAY IT GETS BETTER SOON WITHOUT SOMETHING TRAUMATIC HAPPENING TO ME. SERIOUSLY, WHAT AM I GOING TO DO? I HAVE NEVER IN MY LIFE BEEN AS SCARED AS I AM NOW! I'M TOO OLD TO START OVER AND MAKE A NEW LIFE FOR MYSELF.

I HAVE NO MONEY, NOWHERE TO LIVE, NO FAMILY TO HELP ME AND STAND BY MY SIDE, NO FRIENDS TO SUPPORT ME, AND ABSOLUTELY NO SELF-ESTEEM TO KEEP ME GOING. THIS IS DEFINITELY THE LOWEST I HAVE EVER BEEN. I KNOW I HAVE SAID THAT BEFORE, BUT THIS TOPS IT ALL! MY LIFE OFFICIALLY SUCKS! I THINK MY FAMILY AND THE PEOPLE THAT DID LOVE ME THINK I WOULD BE BETTER OFF DEAD. SO THAT'S WHAT THEY ARE ALL WAITING FOR. HOW SAD IS THAT? WELL, I'M NOT DEAD, I'M ALIVE AND NEED MORE IN MY LIFE THAN THIS. I NEED ALL THREE OF MY BEAUTIFUL CHILDREN, PAUL, MACI, AND MY FAMILY, THEN I WOULD BE THE HAPPIEST WOMAN ON EARTH!

7-22-2013: Dr. Note–121 lbs. Tried to wean herself off Suboxone, had a hard time. Prescribed Suboxone.

MONDAY, JULY 22, 2013:

I AM TRYING LIKE HELL TO BETTER MY LIFE AND IT JUST AIN'T WORKIN'! GOD, GIVE ME A BREAK, PLEASE! I CAN'T TAKE MUCH MORE AT ALL. I'M AT THE END OF MY WORLD. I'M AT THE VERY, VERY BOTTOM OF MY HOLE, CAN'T GET ANY FARTHER DOWN THAN I AM NOW. SO, PLEASE, LIFE, GET BETTER, GET MUCH, MUCH BETTER. I PRETTY MUCH NEED A MIRACLE TO HAPPEN TO TURN MY LIFE AROUND. I WILL JUST HOPE AND WISH AND PRAY FOR A MIRACLE TO HAPPEN IN MY LIFE. WELL, I WAS DRIVING YESTERDAY AND DECIDED TO PICK UP MY PHONE TO CALL PAUL. I WAS NOT AT ALL EXPECTING HIM TO ANSWER HIS PHONE, AND HE DID! I WAS IN SHOCK! I ASKED HIM IF HE WOULD BE WILLING TO FIX MY CAR AND HE SAID HE WOULD, SURPRISINGLY, BUT IT MIGHT BE A LITTLE BIT 'CAUSE HE WAS REALLY, REALLY BUSY! WELL, I ASKED HOW THE KIDS WERE AND HE SAID THEY WERE STILL HAVING A VERY HARD TIME, BUT THEY WOULD MAKE IT THROUGH IT! A LITTLE WHILE AFTER THAT,

ABOUT A COUPLE HOURS LATER, I GOT A TEXT FROM HIM SAYING THAT WE COULD HAVE HAD SOMETHING BEAUTIFUL. I WROTE BACK AND SAID THAT WE STILL COULD, AND I ASKED HIM IF HE WOULD SIT DOWN AND TALK WITH ME. HE WROTE BACK AND SAID MAYBE, BUT NOT RIGHT NOW 'CAUSE HE HAD HIS KIDS AND HE DIDN'T KNOW IF HE WAS READY YET OR NOT AND IT WAS VERY, VERY HARD TO SEE ME. YOU HAVE NO IDEA HOW HAPPY I WAS THAT HE WAS EVEN THINKING ABOUT SITTING DOWN AND TALKING WITH ME. IF HE DOES, I NEED TO BE CAREFUL ON WHAT I SAY, 'CAUSE I WILL NOT LOSE HIM ALL OVER AGAIN…I KNOW I CAN GET PAUL BACK WITH ME, I KNOW HE STILL LOVES ME, I KNOW IT!

TUESDAY, JULY 23, 2013:

IF I HAVEN'T HEARD FROM PAUL TOMORROW, I AM GOING TO CALL HIM. I AM NOT LETTING THIS (MY) MAN GET AWAY ANY LONGER. OKAY, NAT, TAKE A LOOK BACK THROUGH THIS BOOK!…I NEED TO PICK MYSELF UP, GET MY SELF-ESTEEM BACK, STAND ON MY OWN 2 FEET, AND KICK SOME ASS ON GETTING MY LIFE BACK ON TRACK OR AT LEAST GET OUT OF THIS JUNKY LIFE AND TAKE CONTROL OF MYSELF AND LIVE… LIVE FOR ME AND MY 3 BEAUTIFUL KIDS THAT DESERVE A HELL OF A LOT MORE THAN WHAT I HAVE BEEN GIVING THEM. I'M BETTER THAN THIS, WAY, WAY, BETTER THAN THIS AND I KNOW IT…SO, WHAT AM I SO AFRAID OF? TIME GOES BY WAY TOO FAST, SO CHANGE YOUR LIFE, NAT, *CHANGE!* I KNOW YOU CAN DO IT, SO TAKE CHARGE AND TAKE YOUR LIFE BACK!! SO, I TALKED TO PAUL LAST NIGHT, WELL, TEXTING, AND WE ARE MEETING TOMORROW NIGHT AT THE GREEN PIG AT 7:30. I'M SO EXCITED, BUT AT THE SAME TIME, SO SUPER NERVOUS! I CAN'T WAIT TO SEE HIM, BUT I DON'T WANT A THING TO GO WRONG. IT WON'T, THIS IS MY CHANCE TO GET HIM BACK AND IF I DO, I AM CHANGING FOR THE GOOD, NO QUESTIONS ASKED, IT'S DONE!!! I PRAY, PRAY, PRAY

TOMORROW NIGHT TURNS OUT INCREDIBLE AND PAUL AND I START OVER WITH A FRESH START AND GET BACK TOGETHER. PLEASE, BE WITH ME TOMORROW NIGHT THAT I SAY EVERYTHING RIGHT, AND HE REALIZES HOW MUCH HE REALLY DOES LOVE ME! I NEED THIS NIGHT TO GO WELL, VERY WELL. I CANNOT LOSE HIM ALL OVER AGAIN. I CAN'T! SOMETHING NEEDS TO TURN FOR THE GOOD IN MY LIFE, AND IT NEEDS TO BE THIS, OR I DON'T KNOW HOW MUCH MORE I CAN TAKE! THIS IS IT, PLEASE TURN OUT MY WAY FOR A CHANGE!

IT'S ABOUT 5:00 A.M. AND I CANNOT SLEEP FOR THE LIFE OF ME! I AM MEETING UP WITH PAUL TONIGHT AND I AM ABSOLUTELY TERRIFIED! I WANT AND NEED EVERYTHING TO GO ABSOLUTELY *PERFECT!* THIS IS MY CHANCE TO GET MY LIFE BACK AND I CANNOT *FUCK* THIS ONE UP! I JUST CAN'T! I REALLY, REALLY HOPE THAT GOD SOFTENS HIS HEART BEFORE HE SEES ME THIS NIGHT...AND THE WHOLE TIME WE ARE TOGETHER. THIS COULD POSSIBLY BE RIDING ON MY ENTIRE FUTURE! I HAVE A LITTLE BIT OF CONFIDENCE. WELL, I NEED TO TAKE *ALL* THE STRENGTH, SELF-ESTEEM (GOOD), AND CONFIDENCE THAT I HAVE AND STAND TALL AND GET BACK WHAT'S MINE!! I'M GETTING MY MAN BACK TONIGHT AND I WILL MOW OVER ANYONE THAT TRIES TO GET IN MY WAY! THIS IS MY BABY AND MY FUTURE, AND I NEED THIS TO MOVE FORWARD IN MY LIFE AND GET BACK ON TRACK 'CAUSE IF IT DOESN'T HAPPEN, I DON'T KNOW HOW MUCH LONGER I CAN REALLY TRULY GO ON! I REALLY HATE AND THINK IT'S COMPLETELY *PATHETIC* TO LET SOMEONE DICTATE MY LIFE LIKE I HAVE ALLOWED HIM TO, BUT THIS IS HONESTLY THE FIRST TIME I HAVE TRULY, WITH ALL MY HEART AND SOUL AND EVERYTHING THAT I AM, BEEN IN LOVE WITH SOMEONE. I CAN'T LET HIM OUT OF MY LIFE WHEN I KNOW WITHOUT A SHADOW OF A DOUBT THAT WE ARE MEANT FOR EACH OTHER AND MY LITTLE FAMILY CAME TOGETHER FOR A VERY SPECIAL, IMPORTANT REASON. I AM GETTING MY FAMILY BACK!

WEDNESDAY, JULY 24, 2013:

WHAT A *WONDERFUL* DAY TO BE ALIVE! LIVE TODAY LIKE IT WAS MY LAST! BE *HAPPY, HAPPY, HAPPY!!*

WELL, LAST NIGHT WENT REALLY BAD TO PRETTY DAMN GOOD. WELL, TO THE POINT THAT I WOKE UP THIS MORNING IN HIS BED! NOTHING HAPPENED (EVEN THOUGH I REALLY WANTED IT TO), HE JUST HELD ME THE WHOLE NIGHT! I WAS IN HEAVEN, PURE HEAVEN! BUT NOW, TODAY, IT TURNED COMPLETELY AROUND. I ASKED HIM IF I COULD TAKE HIM TO DINNER TONIGHT, AND HE BASICALLY TOLD ME GOODBYE AND ASKED ME TO RESPECTFULLY LEAVE HIM ALONE AND NEVER, EVER COME AROUND HIM AGAIN. I HAD NO IDEA WHAT IN THE *HELL* HAPPENED. SO, I WENT OVER THERE, HE IMMEDIATELY CAME OUT AND SAID HE COULDN'T BELIEVE THAT I WOULD HAVE HIM THREATENED! I DON'T KNOW WHAT THE FUCK HE IS TALKING ABOUT! HE SAID HE HAS HAD PEOPLE ALL DAY THREATENING HIM. THEN HE TOLD ME TO GO HOME AND GET IN MY CAR AND LEAVE, AND IF ANYTHING HAPPENED TO HIM OR HIS KIDS, THEY ARE COMING AFTER ME. WHO IS THEY? AND I HONESTLY HAVE NO CLUE AT ALL WHAT HE IS TALKING ABOUT! I WAS SO HAPPY 'CAUSE I THOUGHT WE GOT SOMEWHERE LAST NIGHT AND THAT I MIGHT HAVE A CHANCE WITH MY MAN AGAIN. HELL, NOW IT'S WORSE THAN EVER, AND I DON'T KNOW WHAT TO DO FROM HERE ON OUT. I CANNOT LET THIS ONE GO. I WILL NOT BE OKAY WITH PAUL THINKING THAT I WANT HIM KILLED! (I AM MADLY IN LOVE WITH HIM AND I WOULD ABSOLUTELY DIE IF ANYTHING HAPPENED TO HIM!) HOW DID IT GET THIS FAR AND WHO IS THREATENING PAUL? I AM WRACKING MY BRAIN TRYING TO FIGURE OUT WHO WOULD DO THAT, I CAN'T THINK OF ANYONE. WHAT SHOULD I DO? THIS IS CONSUMING ME, MY MIND, I CAN'T THINK OF ANYTHING EVER, BUT A WAY TO GET MY MAN BACK! I AM SO AFRAID, ACTUALLY TERRIFIED TO WAKE UP TOMORROW MORNING AND TRY AND HAVE A GOOD DAY, WHEN I AM SO

EXTREMELY UNHAPPY! THIS HONESTLY IS THE WORST I HAVE EVER FELT, EVER. I KNOW I HAVE SAID THIS BEFORE, BUT THIS DEFINITELY TOPS IT!

THURSDAY, JULY 25, 2013:

SO, I THINK I MIGHT HAVE AN IDEA WHO IS THREATENING PAUL. I THINK IT'S DAVID. HE IS IN JAIL, AND I BET HE HAD SOMEBODY IN THERE CONTACT SOMEONE FROM THE OUTSIDE TO PUT A HIT ON PAUL. I AM DEFINITELY PAYING MY LITTLE FRIEND A VISIT TODAY. HE BETTER NOT HAVE DONE ANYTHING LIKE THAT, OR I WILL HAVE HIM KILLED! TUESDAY, ADI TEXTED JAY AND ASKED HIM IF SHE COULD COME PICK UP JALA FOR THE DAY AND TAKE HER SHOPPING AND TO LUNCH. OF COURSE, HE SAID YES, BUT WHEN SHE GOT HERE, I WAS GOING TO GO OUT AND TALK TO HER, BUT I DIDN'T, I WILL NOT PUSH HER ANYMORE! SHE WILL COME TO ME WHEN SHE'S READY. MASON WAS WITH HER, THOUGH, AND IF I WOULD HAVE KNOWN THAT, I WOULD HAVE DEFINITELY WENT OUT AT LEAST TO SAY HI TO MY BABY BOY! JAY SAID ADI LOOKED ABSOLUTELY BEAUTIFUL, THAT DOESN'T SURPRISE ME ONE BIT, MY DAUGHTER IS DROP DEAD GORGEOUS! I MISS HER! I PRAY SHE COMES BACK TO ME REALLY, REALLY SOON! BEEN HANGING OUT WITH JENNIFER AND JALA ALL DAY AND IT'S ACTUALLY BEEN NICE. I DON'T WANT TO GET TOO CLOSE TO HER, THOUGH, BUT TODAY WAS A GOOD DAY. JALA AND I ORDERED PIZZA WHEN WE WOKE UP, THEN JENNIFER CAME OVER A COUPLE HOURS LATER AND WE ALL WENT TO YOGURTLAND AND GOT A YOGURT, THEN WENT TO TJ MAXX AND GOT JALA A CUTE MONSTER HIGH GUITAR, THEN WENT HOME AND HUNG OUT TILL JAY GOT HOME. I HAVE NOT TEXTED PAUL YET TODAY, BUT I'M PLANNING ON IT, AND I HAVE NOT HEARD FROM HIM AT ALL BUT THAT DOESN'T SURPRISE ME. I WAS SO STINKIN' EXCITED YESTERDAY AFTER I SPENT THE NIGHT WITH PAUL, THEN LAST NIGHT HAPPENED! HE SENT

ME TEXTS TELLING ME TO LEAVE HIM THE FUCK ALONE AND THAT I WAS A STALKER! I AM NO STALKER, BUT I'M DONE, I'M DONE WITH THAT MAN...MOVE ON, NAT!!

A week later...

FRIDAY, AUGUST 2, 2013:

GETTING READY TO GO TO DINNER WITH MY BABY! I'M SO STINKIN' EXCITED! SO, I HAVEN'T WRITTEN IN A WHILE 'CAUSE I HAVE BEEN *SO SICK!* JAY GOT THE FLU, A BAD FLU, GAVE IT TO JALA, THEN GAVE IT TO ME, AND OF COURSE, FOR EVERYONE ELSE, IT ONLY LASTED 24 HOURS, FOR ME, 3 FUCKING DAYS! I HAVE NOT BEEN THAT SICK IN SO, SO LONG! SO, TONIGHT, I DID SOMETHING I THOUGHT I'D NEVER, EVER DO! SOME GUY NAMED RONALD THAT I MET WANTED ME TO DANCE FOR HIS LITTLE BROTHER'S BACHELOR PARTY! IT ACTUALLY WENT REALLY, REALLY GOOD! THEY WERE VERY RESPECTABLE, AND RONALD WAS MY BODY GUARD THE WHOLE TIME! THEY GAVE ME $500 TO DO IT. I THINK I WOULD DEFINITELY DO IT AGAIN!

Almost two weeks later...

THURSDAY, AUGUST 15, 2013:

WELL, SITTING BACK UP AT LDS HOSPITAL IN THE WAITING ROOM FROM ANOTHER STINKIN' ABSCESS! THIS ONE IS ABSOLUTELY HORRIBLE, IT'S IN MY GROIN AND HURTS LIKE A BITCH! I KNOW I SAY THAT EVERY TIME, BUT THIS ONE IS AWFUL! THE FIRST TIME I CAME IN, THE DR. CUT ME OPEN AND DUG FOR LITERALLY 2 1/2 HOURS FOR A BUNCH OF LITTLE ABSCESS POCKETS THAT WERE IN THERE. COULDN'T QUITE GET THE ONE HE WANTED TO REALLY HAVE PUNCTURED, SO HE CALLED A SURGEON DOWN, HE TOOK HIS THREE FINGERS,

CAME OVER TO WHERE HE HAD ME CUT OPEN, AND OPENED IT WAY BIGGER WITH HIS STINKIN' FINGERS! OH, MY HEAVEN SAKES, IT HURT SO BAD! I WAS EVEN NUMB DOWN THERE, THE OTHER DR. SHOT ME AT LEAST 16 TIMES WITH NUMBING MEDICATION BEFORE HE STARTED CUTTING. THE PAIN WAS SO INTENSE THAT I COULD FEEL EVERYTHING! NOT AS BAD AS IT WOULD HAVE WITHOUT THE NUMBNESS, BUT I COULD STILL FEEL IT! AFTER ABOUT 4 HOURS AT LDS HOSPITAL, AND MARY WAS THE ONLY ONE THERE WITH ME, COMPLETELY HIGH AND FADING OUT, THEY PACKED IT AND SENT ME ON MY WAY. WELL, THE NEXT DAY, IT GOT A LOT WORSE. MY WHOLE ENTIRE STOMACH WAS SWOLLEN, IT LOOKED LIKE I WAS PREGNANT. IT WAS GETTING WORSE, WAY WORSE! MARY TOOK ME BACK UP THERE, THEY LOOKED AT ME AND RUSHED ME TO THE 6TH FLOOR TO HAVE EMERGENCY SURGERY 'CAUSE IT WAS MORE INFECTED THAN EVER AND GOING STRAIGHT TO MY HEART! I WAS THERE FOR THREE SOLID DAYS! THEY COULDN'T GET THE INFECTION UNDER CONTROL, AND IT WAS SLOWLY KILLING ME. SO, NOW, AFTER HOSPITAL STAYS AND VISITS ALL WEEK LONG, I HAVE A *HUGE* OPEN WOUND IN MY RIGHT GROIN AREA. MARY HAS TO REPACK IT EVERY MORNING AND NIGHT, NO MATTER WHAT! ON TOP OF ALL THAT'S GOING ON, I GET A FUCKING ABSCESS THAT ALMOST KILLED ME! I NEED TO CHANGE THINGS, AND I KNOW THAT AND HAVE FOR A LONG TIME NOW, BUT THE PAST FEW WEEKS, REALITY HAS FINALLY HIT! I'M AT ROCK FUCKING BOTTOM!

She is now living with Mary.

Five days later...

8-20-2013: Dr. Note–120 lbs. Prescribed Suboxone.

TUESDAY, AUGUST 20, 2013:

IT'S ABOUT A LITTLE AFTER MIDNIGHT TUESDAY MORNING. I AM SITTING HERE AT MY BABY'S HOUSE (PAUL'S) ON HIS BED 'CAUSE WE WENT TO DINNER AT THE GATEWAY AND NOW HE PASSED OUT! I LOVE BEING HERE! I FEEL LIKE I AM HOME AGAIN! *(I don't know how they ended up back together.)* I CAN'T BE AWAY FROM HIM ANY LONGER! HE IS MY LIFE! TONIGHT COULD HAVE BEEN A BAD NIGHT 'CAUSE WE STARTED ARGUING ON THE WAY TO DINNER, BUT WE GOT THROUGH IT AND HAD AN INCREDIBLE NIGHT. I AM GOING TO BE ONE TIRED MAMMA TODAY. SO, JAY KICKED ME OUT OF HIS HOUSE 'CAUSE HE THOUGHT I WAS HANGING OUT WITH MY COUSIN, WHICH I WAS, BUT I AM SURE AS *HELL* NOT NOW, SO I HAD NOWHERE TO STAY OTHER THAN THE HOSPITAL AND PAUL'S HOUSE EVERY SO OFTEN. MY DAD LET ME COME AND STAY WITH HIM AFTER I GOT OUT OF THE HOSPITAL WHILE MY MOM WAS GONE, BUT THE SECOND SHE GOT HOME, I HAD TO LEAVE. I HAD TO GET ALL MY STUFF OUT AND NOWHERE TO STAY. AFTER I GOT ALL MY STUFF, I GOT A TEXT FROM HER SAYING, "GOOGLE WOMEN'S SHELTER, THEY HAVE SOME NICE ONES IN SLC, LOVE YOU!" I ABOUT DIED! I COMPLETELY LOST IT! MY CAR IS FULL OF ALL MY SHIT AND I HAVE ABSOLUTELY NOWHERE TO GO! JAY WILL NOT LET ME STAY THERE, PAUL CAN'T LET ME OR HIS KIDS WILL BE TAKEN, AND I LITERALLY HAVE ZERO FRIENDS! SO, I HAD TO COME STAY WITH MARY. MY LAST RESORT, AND IF ANYONE FINDS OUT, I AM COMPLETELY FUCKED! I AM LITERALLY AT ROCK FUCKIN' BOTTOM! WHEN IT RAINS, IT FUCKIN' POURS, ESPECIALLY FOR ME! WHY? WHY? I DON'T AND *CAN'T* DO THIS ANY LONGER! MARY LIVES IN A DISGUSTING HOUSE WITH A BUNCH OF DOGS THAT MAKE IT STINK! I AM GOING TO HAVE A NERVOUS FUCKIN' BREAKDOWN. ON TOP OF IT ALL, ADI AND MAS JUST GOT HOME FROM SAN FRANCISCO AND I ONLY GOT TO SEE THEM FOR A MIN. I WANT TO DIE!

A couple of weeks later...

THURSDAY, SEPTEMBER 5, 2013:

WELL, MY LIFE HAS DEFINITELY GONE FROM BAD, TO *ABSOLUTELY HORRIBLE!* EVER SINCE I MOVED OUT OF PAUL'S, I HAVE HAD NO PLACE TO LIVE AT ALL. SO, I HAVE BEEN STAYING AT MARY'S HOUSE, WHICH IS A NIGHTMARE! WE ARE IN A TINY LITTLE ROOM WITH NOWHERE TO EVEN MOVE AND IT'S COMPLETELY FILTHY! I'M 34 YEARS OLD, HOMELESS, JUNKY THAT HAS NOTHIN' GOING FOR ME! I CAN'T CHANGE MY LIFE RIGHT NOW 'CAUSE I HAVE NO PLACE TO GO RIGHT NOW AND NOWHERE TO KICK *(get clean)* OR GET ANY HELP! WHAT IN THE *HELL* SHOULD I DO? I AM STILL MADLY IN LOVE WITH PAUL AND I CAN'T EVER GET HIM OFF MY MIND! IT SUCKS THAT I LOVE HIM SO MUCH CAUSE HE'S ALWAYS ON MY MIND, *ALWAYS!* HE IS PLAYING GAMES WITH ME RIGHT NOW, THOUGH. HE ASKED ME WHERE I WAS AND TOLD ME HE IS COMING OUT HERE 'CAUSE HE THINKS I AM WITH A MAN. I WOULD NEVER AND COULD NEVER BE WITH ANOTHER MAN, EVER! I WISH WITH ALL MY HEART AND SOUL THAT HE WOULD BELIEVE THAT AND SEE THAT. I NEVER MEANT TO HURT ANYONE WITH MY RIDICULOUS DRUG HABITS. I THOUGHT I WAS ONLY HURTING MYSELF, BUT IN REALITY, I WAS AND AM HURTING MY KIDS, PAUL, MY PARENTS, MY SISTERS, AND LOVED ONES TEN TIMES WORSE! I KNOW I CAN TURN THINGS AROUND, I JUST NEED TO DO IT, MAN UP AND *DO IT!* IT'S GOING TO SUCK SO EXTREMELY BAD, BUT IF I DON'T DO IT, AND KEEP GOING LIKE THIS, I WILL BE DEAD WITHIN MONTHS. I AM NOT IN A GOOD PLACE RIGHT NOW AND IT NEEDS TO CHANGE, QUICK! I HAVE ALL MY SHIT, SHOES, CLOTHES, ETC. AT JAY'S HOUSE. IT'S REALLY, REALLY NICE OF HIM TO LET ME DO THAT.

Six days later…

MONDAY, SEPTEMBER 9, 2013:

SO, I'VE BEEN SPENDING A LOT OF NIGHTS AT PAUL'S AND IT'S BEEN GREAT! WE HAVE OUR MOMENTS, BUT WE GET OVER THEM QUICKLY AND THEN HAVE A FANTASTIC NIGHT TOGETHER. I HAVE ALL MY STUFF AT JAY'S, WHICH I KNOW IS EXTREMELY WEIRD, BUT I HAVE NOWHERE ELSE TO TAKE IT, WHEN I NEED TO HAVE ACCESS TO IT ALL THE TIME. IT WORKS WITH JALA TOO. WHEN I PICK HER UP FROM SCHOOL, WHICH IS EVERY SINGLE DAY, I CAN BRING HER BACK TO JAY'S APARTMENT UNTIL HE GETS OFF WORK AT 7:00 P.M. IT'S BEEN WORKING OUT OKAY, I GUESS. MARY HAS BEEN LIVID WITH ME, THOUGH, 'CAUSE SHE WANTS ME THERE ALL THE DAMN TIME. SHE IS SUCH A BITCH TO ME, BUT I NEED HER, AND THE SAD THING IS THAT SHE KNOWS THAT, AND SHE COMPLETELY TAKES ADVANTAGE OF IT, BUT THE MAJORITY OF THE TIME, SHE IS SUCH A BITCH! I DON'T LIKE THIS WORLD I AM IN AT ALL! I WANT TO GET OUT OF IT SO BAD, BUT DON'T KNOW HOW AND DON'T KNOW IF I AM QUITE READY. I SAY I AM, BUT WHEN IT REALLY COMES DOWN TO IT, I DON'T KNOW THAT I AM. I CANNOT LOSE PAUL OR MY KIDS AGAIN, I KNOW THAT, AND THEY ARE ALL WAY MORE IMPORTANT THAN ANY STUPID DRUG! I HAVEN'T TALKED TO MY SISTERS IN MONTHS. I SAW ANGIE ON SUNDAY FOR A MINUTE, BUT OTHER THAN THAT, HAVEN'T TALKED OR SEEN HER IN MONTHS. I HAVE COMPLETELY GIVEN UP ON EMILY, SHE WILL NEVER COME AROUND AND BE OKAY WITH ME, I HAVE TO ACCEPT THAT!

Anytime Nat wrote about getting clean and what she needed to do to get clean, she consistently said she wasn't ready.

A few days later...

THURSDAY, SEPTEMBER 12, 2013:

WELL, I HAVE SPENT EVERY SINGLE NIGHT THIS WEEK OVER AT PAUL'S. IT'S BEEN SO NICE! I LOVE THAT LITTLE HOUSE, 'CAUSE I STILL FEEL LIKE IT'S MINE *(Paul never was evicted from that house, and to my knowledge, he still lives there today).* ALL MY APPLIANCES AND ETC. ARE STILL THERE, AND ALL THE FURNITURE THAT'S IN THERE PAUL BOUGHT FOR ME. I WANT US BACK TO THE WAY WE USED TO BE, I MISS "US" (HIM) SO STINKIN' BAD! I'M IN JAY'S BED RIGHT NOW SITTIN' NEXT TO MY LITTLE PRINCESS WHILE SHE FALLS ASLEEP. JAY IS AT A MOVIE WITH GOD KNOWS WHO. AFTER I PICKED JALA UP FROM SCHOOL, SHE BROUGHT A FRIEND HOME WITH HER (THE GIRL RIGHT ABOVE THEIR APARTMENT) AND THEY PLAYED SO GOOD UNTIL ABOUT AN HOUR AGO. THEY ARE REALLY CUTE TOGETHER. SHE IS A LITTLE MEXICAN GIRL THAT LOVES JALA AND JALA REALLY LIKES HER. I AM SO EXTREMELY GLAD THAT JALA HAS FINALLY FOUND A FRIEND TO PLAY WITH AND ASSOCIATE WITH. I WAS GETTIN A LITTLE WORRIED 'CAUSE ALL SHE EVER DID IS HANG OUT WITH ME OR JAY. I DIDN'T GET TO SEE PAUL TONIGHT 'CAUSE HE WAS WORKING GRAVEYARD DOING GOD KNOWS WHAT, SO HE IS GONE ALL DAMN NIGHT! IT SUCKS, I ALREADY MISS HIM. IT WAS REALLY GREAT, THOUGH, HANGING OUT WITH MY LITTLE SUNSHINE! I LOVE THIS LITTLE GIRL! SHE IS MY WORLD, MY LIGHT, WITHOUT HER, I COULD NEVER GO ON! I REALLY, REALLY NEED TO GET MY SHIT TOGETHER, FIGURE OUT A PLACE TO LIVE, A JOB TO WORK AT, AND STARTING A WHOLE NEW LIFE. A LIFE WITH MY KIDS AND PAUL. A LIFE WITHOUT MARY AND WITHOUT DRUGS. I AM SUPPOSED TO BE TAKING MARY TO THE HOSPITAL WHEN JAY GETS BACK 'CAUSE SHE HAS AN ABSCESS ON HER ARM THAT HAS SPREAD DOWN HER WHOLE ENTIRE ARM AND IS VERY BAD! BUT I DON'T

WANT TO LEAVE JALA TONIGHT, SO I DON'T THINK I WILL, SORRY MARY!

FRIDAY, SEPTEMBER 13, 2013:

WELL, LAST NIGHT I ENDED UP TAKING MARY TO THE HOSPITAL 'CAUSE SHE WAS IN HORRIBLE PAIN FROM THE ABSCESS ON HER ARM. IT WAS REALLY BAD! IT WAS AT THE TOP OF HER FOREARM AND IT SPREAD CLEAR DOWN TO HER ELBOW. I DON'T KNOW WHY I ALWAYS SAY THEY ARE *BAD* WHEN I REFER TO AN ABSCESS 'CAUSE NONE OF THEM ARE GOOD, THEY ARE ALL THE MOST HORRIFIC, PAINFUL OWIES ANYONE COULD GET! I HAVE DEFINITELY HAD MY SHARE OF THEM, YA THINK WE WOULD HAVE LEARNED BY NOW!

She is now living with Jay again.

Same day, different journal.

SO, WENT TO TAKE MARY TO THE HOSPITAL LAST NIGHT AND, OF COURSE, DIDN'T HAPPEN. SHE HAD MORE IMPORTANT THINGS GOING ON. SHE HAS THE MOST SHADY PEOPLE I HAVE EVER SEEN IN HER LIFE AND AROUND HER CONSTANTLY. I CAN'T HANDLE IT, EVEN FOR ONE MINUTE. SO, DIDN'T GET ANYTHING ACCOMPLISHED AT ALL LAST NIGHT, GOT HOME (BACK TO JAY'S) ABOUT 11:30 A.M., THEN PICKED UP JALA AT 1:25 (EARLY OUT). ME AND JALA HAVE JUST BEEN HANGING OUT AT HOME 'CAUSE SHE IS TIRED AND I FEEL LIKE SHIT TODAY. WE HAVE BEEN MAKING VIDEOS ON MY PHONE AND JUST HAVING A GREAT TIME TOGETHER! THIS LITTLE GIRL IS MY ENTIRE LIFE, THE MOST IMPORTANT PERSON IN MY WORLD! WE ARE EATING SOUR PATCH KIDS, EATING JUNK AND WATCHING MONSTER HIGH! JAY GETS HOME IN ABOUT AN HOUR AND I AM NOT GOING OUT TO MARY! I AM JUST GOING TO RELAX HERE AND BE WITH MY BABY GIRL. PAUL HAS HIS

KIDS TONIGHT AND HIS DAUGHTER IS REALLY SICK WITH A HIGH FEVER AND THROWING UP, SO I CAN'T SEE MY MAN EITHER, WHAT A BUMMER!

SATURDAY, SEPTEMBER 14, 2013:

TODAY HAS BEEN A VERY, VERY INTERESTING DAY. WOKE UP, WENT TO MASON'S GAME WITH JALA AND SAT WITH MY MOM AND DAD. THEY WERE BEING REALLY NICE, OF COURSE. THEY LOST AGAIN, WHICH SUCKS, THEY JUST AREN'T PLAYING GOOD THIS YEAR. THEY PLAYED INCREDIBLY AWESOME LAST YEAR AND THIS YEAR THEY REALLY DO SUCK. I ABSOLUTELY LOVE GOING TO HIS GAMES, THOUGH, THEY ARE MY FAVORITE THING TO DO IN THE FALL, WATCH MY SWEET LITTLE BOY PLAY HIS HEART AND GUTS OUT, HOPEFULLY, EVENTUALLY BECOMING AN NFL PLAYER. I HAVE COMPLETE FAITH IN HIM, THOUGH, AND HAVE ABSOLUTELY ZERO DOUBT THAT HE WILL BE AN NFL PLAYER WHEN HE GROWS UP. HE IS MY LITTLE FOOTBALL STAR. SO, PAUL AND I WERE DOING EXCELLENT AND THEN HE SPINS ON ME *AGAIN!* HE CALLED ME THIS MORNING, OF COURSE, RIGHT BEFORE MASON'S GAME AND SAID HE KNEW WHAT I WAS DOING LAST NIGHT AND KNEW THAT I HAD MEN AROUND ME AND WITH ME. I TRIED TO EXPLAIN THAT WASN'T TRUE, BUT HIS MIND IS DEFINITELY MADE UP, THERE IS NO CHANGING IT ANYWAY. HE KEPT SAYING HE DESERVES MUCH BETTER AND THAT I AM A JUNKIE! I DO NOT DESERVE TO BE TREATED LIKE THAT AT ALL, I LOVE HIM WITH ALL MY HEART AND SOUL, BUT HE DOESN'T TRUST ME AT ALL! JEREMY CAME OVER FOR A MINUTE WHEN JAY AND JALA WENT TO OGDEN AND HE MAKES ME PHYSICALLY ILL. HE WANTED TO HAVE SEX WITH ME, AND I PRETTY MUCH TOLD HIM, *"HELL NO."* THE ONE AND ONLY MAN I WILL EVER SLEEP WITH IS PAUL. I JUST HOPE AND PRAY THAT IT'S NOT TOO LATE! I WANT MY FAMILY BACK! ADI, MAS, JALA, PAUL'S KIDS, AND

PAUL! PLEASE BRING MY FAMILY BACK TO ME, PLEASE DON'T EVER LET THEM BE AWAY FROM ME AGAIN, EVER AGAIN! THEY ALL BELONG TO ME (WITH ME). JUST GOT BACK TO JAY'S AND FALLING ASLEEP WITH JALA, IT'S ABOUT 1:00 A.M. SUNDAY MORNING.

<u>SUNDAY, SEPTEMBER 15, 2013</u>:

HAVIN' A REALLY HARD DAY THIS MORNING ALREADY. WAKING UP KNOWING THAT PAUL ISN'T IN MY LIFE ANYMORE REALLY MAKES ME NOT EVEN WANT TO GET OUT OF BED. I KNOW I NEED TO PULL IT TOGETHER AND STOP BEING SO FUCKING PATHETIC, BUT I CANNOT FIND ANY HAPPINESS WITHOUT HIM. I ABSOLUTELY HATE THAT I GIVE HIM SO MUCH POWER, BUT I DON'T KNOW HOW ELSE TO FEEL! MAS TEXTED ME THIS MORNING TO GO TO CHURCH WITH HIM, BUT I DIDN'T GET THE TEXT TILL AFTER IT WAS ALREADY OVER. HOW SAD IS THAT? I THINK I WILL POSSIBLY GO OVER TO MY MOMS FOR A LITTLE BIT TODAY, BUT I'M NOT SURE! YEP, MASON CALLED ME THREE TIMES TO GO OVER THERE, SO OF COURSE, I DID. I WOULD DO ABSOLUTELY ANYTHING FOR THAT KID. WENT OVER THERE FOR A COUPLE HOURS AND HUNG OUT WITH MY BOY. THEN LEFT, WENT TO MARY'S AND FOUGHT WITH PAUL THE ENTIRE WAY THERE. WE WERE BEING HORRIBLE WITH EACH OTHER. I REALLY COULDN'T BELIEVE IT, HE TOLD ME I LOOKED LIKE I WAS 60 YEARS OLD! THAT'S NOT EVEN THE

Nat and Adi

HALF OF IT! WE WERE CRUEL TO EACH OTHER! SO, WHEN I GOT TO MARY'S I WAS IN TEARS. ABOUT 20 MINUTES LATER, HE CALLED OVER AND OVER AND OVER. I WOULDN'T ANSWER IT, BUT HE WOULDN'T STOP, SO I FINALLY ANSWERED, AND HE APOLOGIZED UP AND DOWN. THEN I WENT TO HIS HOUSE AND WE HAD THE BEST NIGHT WE HAVE EVER HAD IN A VERY LONG TIME. HE WAS SO SWEET, CARRIED ME INTO HIS ROOM.

9-16-2013: Dr. Note–118 lbs. Prescribed Suboxone.

Ten days later...
She is living with Mary.

THURSDAY, SEPTEMBER 26, 2013:

THE PAST FEW WEEKS HAVE BEEN ABSOLUTELY GREAT WITH PAUL. I STAYED AT HIS HOUSE EVERY NIGHT DURING THE WEEK, AND WE HAVE BEEN GETTING ALONG SO STINKIN' GOOD. BUT I DON'T KNOW IF IT'S GOING TO LAST 'CAUSE HE IS STILL SO ANGRY WITH ME AND HOLDS A LOT OF RESENTMENT. I HOPE IT STAYS LIKE THIS, THOUGH, I HOPE SO! I WAS WITH PAUL FOR ABOUT AN HOUR, AND JAY TOOK ALL MY THINGS AND PUT THEM IN MY CAR! I HAVE ABSOLUTELY NOWHERE TO GO, SO GUESS WHERE I AM? AT THE WORST PLACE IN THE WORLD, MARY'S HOUSE. IT'S SO STINKIN' MESSY HERE AND ABSOLUTELY DISGUSTING. BUT I HAVE NOWHERE TO GO! WHAT AM I GOING TO DO? I'M 2 1/2 MONTHS LATE ON MY CAR PAYMENT, LATE ON MY INSURANCE, AND MARY STILL HAS NOT PAID FOR THE TICKET THAT I GOT FOR HER WRECKING MY CAR! *(Mary wrecked her car, and Nat took the blame for it so Mary wouldn't end up back in jail.)* I'M LITERALLY FUCKED! I NEED A MIRACLE TO HAPPEN, OR I AM GOING TO LOSE MY CAR OR LOSE MY LIFE, 'CAUSE IF I HAVE NO STINKIN' CAR, I WON'T MAKE IT, I JUST WON'T! I'M SITTIN' HERE AT MARY'S WITH ANDREW CAUSE TIMOTHY

AND DENNIS JUST TOOK MARY TO THE HOSPITAL. SHE HAS BEEN HAVING CHEST PAINS AND HER ARM HAS BEEN GOING NUMB. THAT IS SIGNS OF A HEART ATTACK. SHE HAS HER BABY (HER GRANDBABY) THIS WEEKEND. SO ANDREW AND I ARE WATCHING HER WHILE SHE IS GONE. MY LIFE HAS BEEN ABSOLUTELY WRECKED. I HAVE GONE TO A VERY, VERY BAD PLACE! I CAN'T TAKE IT ANYMORE! I JUST CAN'T BELIEVE I HAVE GOT THIS FAR DOWN.

A few weeks later...

SATURDAY, OCTOBER 12, 2013:

ANOTHER VERY INTERESTING DAY SO FAR. STILL AT MARY'S HELPING HER WITH HER GRANDBABY 'CAUSE SHE WAS IN THE HOSPITAL WITH PAINS IN HER CHEST. SCARY, SCARY! SHE IS OKAY, THOUGH, THEY SAID SHE MOST LIKELY PULLED THE MUSCLE AROUND HER HEART AND TO TAKE IT EASY. THAT'S NOT GONNA BE VERY EASY TO GET THIS WOMAN TO TAKE IT EASY! SHE IS A BITCH TO ME THE MAJORITY OF THE TIME, BUT SHE IS STILL MY VERY BEST FRIEND. WE HAVE BEEN THROUGH SO MUCH TOGETHER AND SHE REALLY ALWAYS HAS BEEN THERE FOR ME. I HOPE SHE CAN SAY THE SAME ABOUT ME. DAVID IS STILL IN JAIL AND WILL BE FOR A LITTLE WHILE LONGER, DON'T KNOW WHAT'S GOING TO HAPPEN WHEN HE GETS OUT 'CAUSE MARY HAS FOUND SOMEONE THAT MAKES HER SUPER, SUPER HAPPY, AND IT'S NOT HER HUSBAND! IT'S A 24-YEAR-OLD, COCKY AS FUCK BOY THAT IS ONLY WITH HER FOR THE DOPE. HOW SAD IS THAT? 'CAUSE SHE IS MADLY IN LOVE WITH HIM AND HASN'T EVEN TOLD HER HUSBAND YET. THIS KID IS GOING TO DROP HER ON HER ASS HERE PRETTY SOON, AND IT'S NOT GONNA BE PRETTY. I WANT TO TELL HER, BUT THAT WOULD BREAK HER HEART AND SHE PROBABLY WOULDN'T BE ABLE TO GRASP IT OR BELIEVE ME AT ALL. WENT TO MASON'S FOOTBALL GAME THIS MORNING ON 1100

SOUTH IN SOUTH JORDAN. IT WAS FREEZING AND JALA HAD A REALLY HARD TIME. MASON'S TEAM IS JUST NOT DOING GREAT THIS YEAR AT ALL! LAST YEAR, THEY KICKED ASS AND ALMOST WON THE CHAMPIONSHIP, BUT THIS YEAR, THEY'RE ABSOLUTELY HORRIBLE! IT'S SAD 'CAUSE MAS PLAYS HIS LITTLE HEART OUT AND HIS TEAM JUST PLAIN OUT SUCKS! THAT KID IS SO GOING TO THE NFL, THAT HAS BEEN HIS DREAM AND GOAL SINCE THE FIRST YEAR HE STARTED PLAYING FOOTBALL. HE PLAYS LINEBACKER AND DEFENSE AND HE KILLS IT ON THE FOOTBALL FIELD. STILL THE SHORTEST, SMALLEST KID ON THE TEAM, BUT THAT DOESN'T STOP HIM ONE LITTLE BIT! HE KICKS ASS AND I KNOW WITHOUT A DOUBT HE WILL MAKE IT ALL THE WAY. I'M SO PROUD OF ALL MY KIDS, THEY ARE BY FAR THE BEST!

<u>SUNDAY, OCTOBER 13, 2013</u>:

SITTIN' HERE WITH ANDREW AND HIS COUSIN AT MOTEL 6 'CAUSE JAY TOOK ALL OF MY SHIT AND PUT IT IN MY CAR *(a few weeks prior).* I GET TO SEE MY MAN TONIGHT AND I GET SO SUPER EXCITED! I CAN'T WAIT! I KNOW I ALWAYS SAY THIS, BUT I LOVE THIS MAN! PAUL, ALONG WITH MY PRECIOUS KIDS, ARE MY ENTIRE LIFE. HE IS THE MAN FOR ME! I DON'T EVER WANT TO HURT OR LIE TO HIM AGAIN. I REALLY NEED TO START WATCHING AND NOTICING WHAT I AM DOING FROM NOW ON. I NEED TO BE A LOT LESS SELFISH AND REALLY NEED TO CHANGE MY LIFESTYLE OR I AM NOT GOING TO GET ANYWHERE. I PRAY TO GOD THAT PAUL WILL GIVE US AND OUR FAMILY ANOTHER SHOT 'CAUSE I *KNOW* I WILL NOT AT ALL FUCK IT UP AGAIN WITH HIM. IT HURTS SO STINKIN' BAD NOT BEING WITH HIM OR LIVING WITH HIM ANYMORE. I NEED HIM AROUND ALL DAY, EVERY DAY. I LOVE HIM!!!

<u>TUESDAY, OCTOBER 15, 2013</u>:

AT MY BABY'S HOUSE RIGHT NOW AND WE ARE GETTING READY TO WATCH A MOVIE. I STAY OVER HERE ALMOST EVERY NIGHT EXCEPT FOR THE WEEKENDS WHEN HIS KIDS ARE WITH HIM. PAUL HAS BEEN TREATING ME SO STINKIN' GOOD. HE TOOK ME TO A CONCERT 2 NIGHTS AGO AND WE HAD A BLAST! HE HELD ME THE ENTIRE TIME, IT WAS AT URBAN LOUNGE IN SLC AND I WILL NEVER FORGET IT. I GOT A VIDEO OF HIM AFTER THE CONCERT 'CAUSE HE WAS DRUNK OFF HIS ASS. IT WAS THE FUNNIEST THING I HAVE EVER SEEN, I REALLY HAVE NEVER LAUGHED SO HARD IN MY LIFE. HE KEPT TELLING ME HOW MUCH HE LOVED ME ALL NIGHT LONG. IT WAS NICE TO HEAR THAT. I REALLY HOPE WE CAN GET THINGS BACK ON TRACK, I LOVE THIS MAN! AT THE CONCERT, HE WHISPERED IN MY EAR HOW PROUD OF ME HE WAS AND HE SAID, "FIGHT, BITCH, FIGHT." I WILL, I WILL START FIGHTING! I NEED MY LIFE BACK. I DON'T NEED THIS LIFE THAT I HAVE BEEN LIVING FOR SO LONG. I KNOW I AM STRONG ENOUGH, I JUST NEED TO DO IT. I NEED TO FIND A PLACE TO LIVE FIRST, THEN I WILL KICK THIS SHIT! IT'S KILLING ME AND I AM NOT READY TO DIE YET! I NEED MY LIFE WITH PAUL AND MY KIDS. I KNOW I STILL HAVE A LONG TIME TO GO, SO I AM NOT ABOUT TO LET HEROIN KILL ME FIRST!! I AM A MUCH BETTER PERSON THAN ALL THIS! WELL, I'M *FINALLY* AWAY FROM MARY! SHE DISRESPECTED ME FOR THE VERY *LAST* TIME! THAT WOMAN IS LITERALLY THE *DEVIL!* EVEN HER OWN KIDS THINK THAT. HER SON HAS BEEN HANGING OUT WITH ME THE PAST FEW DAYS, AND IF MY KIDS EVER TALKED ABOUT ME THE WAY HE DOES ABOUT HER, I WOULD DIE. I REALLY NEED TO GET ANOTHER JOB OR GET ALL MY NAIL STUFF AND START DOING NAILS AGAIN. I CAN'T HANDLE LIVING OFF OTHER PEOPLE, ESPECIALLY WHEN I DON'T HAVE ANYONE IN MY LIFE. SERIOUSLY, MY WHOLE LIFE COULDN'T GET ANY

WORSE THAN IT IS NOW. BE STRONG, *NAT,* WE CAN FIGHT THIS *DEMON* AND WE CAN *WIN!!*

10-16-2013: Dr. Note–119 lbs. Prescribed Suboxone.

THURSDAY, OCTOBER 17, 2013:

ANOTHER ROUGH, ROUGH DAY FOR ME. I HONESTLY JUST DON'T KNOW HOW MUCH MORE I CAN HANDLE. IT'S ABOUT 6:30 A.M. AND I JUST GOT HOME FROM WEST VALLEY, WELL, I SHOULD SAY, JAY'S HOUSE. WHEN I WAS GONE THE OTHER DAY WITH SAMUEL, I GOT BACK TO JAY'S APARTMENT AND ALL MY SHIT WAS PACKED UP IN MY CAR. IT WAS LITERALLY FULL! I CAN'T EVEN LOOK OUT OF MY WINDOWS. I COULDN'T PUT EVEN ONE MORE THING IN MY CAR. WELL, HE'S THREATENING TO TAKE JALA AWAY FROM ME NOW AND GIVING ME A VERY, VERY HARD TIME. I HAVE BEEN STAYING WITH PAUL EVERY SINGLE NIGHT AND IT'S BEEN AWESOME. BUT WHEN THE WEEKENDS ROLL AROUND, I AM MISERABLE AND DEPRESSED 'CAUSE I CAN'T SEE MY MAN AT ALL! WELL, I HAVE ABSOLUTELY *NO PLACE* TO GO RIGHT NOW DURING THE DAY. I HAD TO TAKE ALL MY SHIT TO OMI'S HOUSE IN HER GARAGE, AND I AM TRYING TO FIGURE OUT WHERE TO SHOWER AND GET READY FOR THE DAY. I ASKED MY MOM AND SHE WON'T LET ME SHOWER THERE, GET READY THERE, OR DO ANY OF MY LAUNDRY THERE. SO, SINCE ALL OF MY STUFF WAS AT OMI'S, I ASKED HER IF I COULD SHOWER THERE, AND SHE TOLD ME NO. HOW PATHETIC IS THAT? MY FAMILY DEFINITELY HAS SOME SCREWS LOOSE! I REALLY DIDN'T THINK MY FAMILY WAS SO EVIL, BUT THEY ARE. AND THIS TIME, MY DAD IS ACTUALLY BEING REALLY COOL, IT'S MY MOM THAT ACTS LIKE I'M A CRIMINAL. WELL, I'M DEFINITELY *HIT* THIS TIME. MY LIFE COULDN'T GET ANY WORSE AND I COULDN'T BE A BIGGER LOSER THAN I AM NOW. TIME TO *FINALLY CHANGE, NAT!*

FRIDAY, OCTOBER 18, 2013:

WELL, PAUL IS DONE WITH ME AGAIN! AFTER HE HAS BEEN SO GOOD TO ME ALL WEEK LONG! THEN LAST NIGHT, HE FREAKED OUT ON ME AND LOCKED ME OUT OF HIS HOUSE. NOW TONIGHT, HE IS TEXTING ME SAYING THAT HE WAS DONE 'CAUSE HE THOUGHT I WAS A FIGHTER AND HE KNOWS I'M NOT! HE SAYS HE DESERVES BETTER THAN ME AND THAT I AM A JUNKIE AND ALWAYS WILL BE! I CAN'T TAKE THIS BACK AND FORTH SHIT ANYMORE! I AM GONNA FIGHT AND I AM GOING TO FIGHT *HARD,* BUT I NEED TO FIND A PLACE TO LIVE FIRST! I CAN'T JUST KICK *(get clean)* AT WHOEVER'S HOUSE I'M AT THAT NIGHT. I HATE CARRYING ALL MY THINGS IN SUITCASES, THIS IS THE *WORST!* JAY IS ACTUALLY BEING OKAY WITH ME TODAY AND TONIGHT! HE IS AT LEAST LETTING ME KEEP MY THINGS AT HIS HOUSE. JUST GOT OFF THE PHONE WITH PAUL AND I TOLD HIM TO TELL ME EVERYTHING HE NEEDED TO SAY, AND HE DID. HE SAID, "I DON'T HAVE TO, YOU'VE HEARD IT ALL BEFORE, YOU HAVE A TRACK RECORD, YOU HATE YOURSELF AND YOU WILL NEVER STOP." I WILL PROVE HIM WRONG, I WILL! I MISS MASON SO STINKIN' MUCH! I NEVER GET TO SEE HIM OTHER THAN HIS FOOTBALL GAMES, WHICH IS TOMORROW! JEFFREY IS GOING WITH ME, THAT WILL HELP ME A LITTLE, KEEPING ME COMPANY. HE IS NOT ANYONE I WOULD EVER SETTLE DOWN WITH, BUT HE IS FUN EVERY ONCE IN A WHILE.

SUNDAY, OCTOBER 20, 2013:

WELL, AFTER HE SAID HE WAS DONE, OF COURSE, PAUL CALLED ME AND ASKED ME TO COME OVER TONIGHT. IT MADE ME REALLY HAPPY 'CAUSE HE CALLED ME INSTEAD OF ME CALLING HIM. I REALLY THOUGHT MY LIFE COULD BE TURNED AROUND, BUT NOW I DON'T KNOW IF IT CAN. I HAVE GONE WAY TOO DEEP! I DON'T KNOW HOW TO GET OUT NOW! I WANT

OUT AND NEED HELP, BUT DON'T KNOW WHERE TO TURN TO ASK FOR IT! I NEED TO GET SMART, OPEN MY MIND AND MY HEART, GET AWAY FROM ALL THESE DRUG ADDICTS AND GET CLEAN. I NEED TO GET CLEAN! PAUL WANTS ME BACK IF I CAN GET CLEAN, MY KIDS WILL BE ABLE TO BE WITH ME IF I GET CLEAN, AND MY FAMILY WILL COME AROUND AND WANT ME BACK IN THEIR LIVES IF I GET CLEAN! WHY IN THE *HELL* CAN I NOT GET CLEAN? IS IT BECAUSE THERE IS SO MUCH RIDING ON MY GETTING CLEAN AND I'M JUST AFRAID OF FAILING AGAIN? WHATEVER IT IS, I BETTER FIGURE IT OUT, AND QUICK, 'CAUSE IF I DON'T AND I STAY LIKE THIS, I WILL DIE! IF YOU LIVE LIKE THIS LONG ENOUGH, YOU WILL DIE, BOTTOM LINE!

SO, PAUL AND I HAD THE BEST NIGHT TONIGHT! I WENT OVER THERE, AND WE FELL ASLEEP! IT WAS FANTASTIC! I COULDN'T ASK FOR A BETTER NIGHT, IT WAS LIKE HEAVEN! I REALLY HOPE I SHAPE MY ASS UP AND HE ASKS ME TO MARRY HIM, 'CAUSE I WOULD IN A HEARTBEAT! I WANT TO MARRY THIS GUY MORE THAN ANY MAN I HAVE EVER WANTED TO BE WITH! I LIKE HIS KIDS A LOT AND I ABSOLUTELY AM MADLY IN LOVE WITH HIM AND MY KIDS LIKE HIM TOO AND ALL OF OUR KIDS TOGETHER GET ALONG WONDERFULLY! WELL, BETTER GET SOME SLEEP, 'CAUSE I HAVE ANOTHER FANTASTIC DAY AHEAD OF ME IN NATALIE'S *SHIT HOLE* LITTLE LIFE!

MONDAY, OCTOBER 21, 2013:

TODAY HAS DEFINITELY BEEN ONE OF THE WORST DAYS OF MY LIFE! ANDREW AND I WERE IN MY CAR THIS MORNING WITH NO REGISTRATION ON IT AND WE GOT PULLED OVER. ANDREW HAD A LOT OF DOPE ON HIM AND I HAD SOME CRYS *(crystal meth)* IN MY PURSE AND A LOADED RIG *(needle)* IN MY SHIRT WITHOUT A BRA. WELL, THEY CALLED A WOMAN OFFICER TO SEARCH ME. I HAD A SPOON ON ME TOO. WELL, SHE CHECKED ME, BUT DIDN'T FIND A THING! THE ANGELS

WERE DEFINITELY WITH ME TODAY. BUT, NOT WITH ANDREW! THEY TOOK HIM RIGHT IN! I FEEL ABSOLUTELY HORRIBLE. THEY SEARCHED MY CAR AND FOUND A BAGGIE ON THE FLOOR, BUT THANK GOD, THEY DIDN'T CHARGE ME FOR IT! THAT WAS A BLESSING IN DISGUISE THIS MORNING, AND I NEED TO REMEMBER THAT NEXT TIME I THINK ABOUT PICKING UP! SO, THE REST OF MY DAY HAS BEEN COMPLETELY *SHOT!* I DO NOT EVEN DARE GET INTO MY CAR AT ALL UNTIL THE REGISTRATION IS TAKEN CARE OF. I AM *NOT* GOING TO JAIL!

SO, I AM AT PAUL'S RIGHT NOW AND WE AREN'T DOING GOOD AT ALL. PERFECT DAY FOR HIM TO BE UPSET WITH ME. I WALKED INTO HIS HOUSE AND HE LOOKED ME UP AND DOWN AND SAID, "WHAT'S WRONG WITH YOU?" I SAID, "I HAVE JUST HAD A *HORRIBLE* DAY," HE REPLIED, "YA, IT SHOWS." HOW FREAKING CRUEL IS THAT? I DID LOOK ALL TORE UP, THOUGH. I HAVEN'T SLEPT IN 3 DAYS STRAIGHT, THEN WHAT HAPPENED THIS MORNING PUSHED ME RIGHT OVER THE EDGE! I SAT HERE IN TEARS, *AGAIN,* LISTENING TO PAUL TELL ME HOW BIG OF A PIECE OF SHIT I AM! THAT WAS NOT EVEN THE WORST, HE ALSO SAID THAT EVERYTHING AND EVERYBODY THAT COMES AROUND ME, THEY DIE! HE SAYS I FIGHT WITH ABSOLUTELY EVERYONE IN MY LIFE AND THAT I THINK I'M ALWAYS RIGHT. HE SAID AT LEAST 4 TIMES, "YOU'RE GONNA BE DEAD WITHIN A YEAR." ALL THAT HURTS MUCH, MUCH WORSE THAN BEING PHYSICALLY BEATEN! BUT, I STILL LOVE HIM, GO FIGURE!!

TUESDAY, OCTOBER 22, 2013:

TODAY IS GOING TO BE A MUCH, MUCH BETTER DAY THAN YESTERDAY! I WILL MAKE SURE OF IT!

WELL, TODAY HAS DEFINITELY BEEN A MUCH BETTER DAY THAN YESTERDAY. PAUL RIPPED ME APART LAST NIGHT, AND THEN THIS MORNING HE WAS AWESOME! HE MADE ME BREAK-FAST, THEN WE LAID TOGETHER IN BED ALL MORNING. I

DON'T KNOW HOW MUCH LONGER I CAN HANDLE THE BACK AND FORTH SHIT, BUT, WHEN HE IS GOOD TO ME, HE IS ABSOLUTELY INCREDIBLE!

IT'S ABOUT 7:00 P.M. AND I HAVE JALA AND HER FRIEND AT THE PARK BEFORE I GO TO PAUL'S HOUSE. HOPEFULLY, WE HAVE A GOOD NIGHT TOGETHER.

IT WAS A *FANTASTIC* NIGHT! WE WATCHED A REALLY, REALLY GOOD MOVIE TOGETHER (SLUMDOG MILLIONAIRE) THEN FELL ASLEEP TOGETHER ON THE COUCH. DIDN'T REALLY GET TO SEE HIM THE NEXT MORNING 'CAUSE WHEN I WOKE UP, HE WAS LEAVING. HE JUST TOLD ME TO LEAVE THE DOOR UNLOCKED WHEN I LEFT AND TO HAVE A GOOD DAY. I HONESTLY DON'T HAVE ANY IDEA WHAT TO DO ABOUT THAT WHOLE SITUATION. I LOVE THE MAN WITH ALL MY HEART, BUT I HAVE HURT HIM SO BADLY, THAT I DON'T KNOW IF HE CAN EVER REALLY FORGIVE ME OR NOT. OH, BEFORE WE WATCHED OUR MOVIE, HE TOOK ME TO HIS FAVORITE RESTAURANT, WHICH IS THE MANDARIN. IT WAS AWESOME. I HOPE TOMORROW NIGHT WE HAVE A GOOD NIGHT TOGETHER TOO. I GET KIND OF SCARED BECAUSE HE IS SO STINKIN' BIPOLAR, AND WHEN HE IS MAD AND NOT HAPPY, IT'S NOT A PRETTY SIGHT! BUT WHEN HE IS HAPPY, I FEEL LIKE I'M IN HEAVEN! THAT'S HOW HE MAKES ME FEEL WHEN HE IS HAPPY AND LOVES ME. I'M SO SAD TODAY, I WAS SUPPOSED TO HAVE ALL MY KIDS TODAY, JUST LIKE I DO EVERY WEDNESDAY, BUT MY MOM IS IN SAINT GEORGE WATCHING MICHELLE AND TYE'S KIDS WHILE THEY ARE IN HAWAII. MASON WENT DEER HUNTING YESTERDAY AFTER SCHOOL, SO THIS WEEK, I DON'T EVEN GET TO SEE MY MOST FAVORITE LITTLE BOY IN THIS WORLD. I MISS THAT KID MORE THAN ANYTHING, MY HEART ACHES FOR HIM EVERY SINGLE DAY, FOR ADI TOO, BUT SHE COMES TO SEE ME A LOT 'CAUSE SHE HAS A CAR. I LOVE MY 3 KIDS SO STINKIN' MUCH!!

A couple of days later...

THURSDAY, OCTOBER 24, 2013:

WELL, TODAY WAS NOT A GOOD DAY AT ALL! I SAY THAT WAY TOO MUCH! WHY CAN'T I HAVE A FUCKING GOOD DAY *EVER?* PAUL ASKED ME TONIGHT THE ONE AND ONLY THING I *NEVER* WANTED HIM TO EVER ASK ME. HE ASKED ME TO LET HIM GO. WELL, I AM NOT GOING TO TRY AND BE WITH SOMEONE THAT DOESN'T WANT TO BE WITH ME. I WILL DO WHAT HE ASKED. THIS IS DEFINITELY GOING TO BE THE HARDEST THING I EVER HAD TO DO, BESIDES LOSING MY KIDS LIKE I DID. BUT, I DO LOVE HIM AND I DO WANT THE BEST FOR HIM. I HATE MY LIFE. ON TOP OF ALL THIS, JAY TOLD ME OUR DIVORCE PAPERS WILL BE READY TO BE SIGNED BY THE BEGINNING OF NEXT WEEK AND NOT TO GIVE HIM A HARD TIME WITH THEM. I ASKED HIM WHY HE THOUGHT I WOULD GIVE HIM A HARD TIME WITH THEM, 'CAUSE I HAVE WANTED OUR MARRIAGE OVER A LONG TIME AGO, AND THE REASON WHY IS BECAUSE HE IS GOING FOR FULL CUSTODY. *(They never divorced. They were very good friends and stayed in each other's lives until Nat passed. My mom paid twice for the parent divorce class they needed to go to in order to finalize their divorce, but they never attended.)* MY LIFE DEFINITELY COULD NOT GET ANY WORSE. I JUST STARTED CRYING. OF COURSE, I AM GOING TO FIGHT HIM ON THAT, I AM NOT ABOUT TO GIVE JAY FULL CUSTODY OF MY BABY GIRL! NO WAY IN *HELL!* HE SAID, "YOU DON'T HAVE A PLACE TO LIVE AND YOU CAN'T PROVIDE FOR HER." WELL, THAT'S *BULLSHIT!* JUST BECAUSE I HAVE MADE A LOT OF MISTAKES, I STILL CAN TURN THIS AROUND AND GIVE JALA A GOOD MOTHER! I JUST NEED A LITTLE HELP TO START OVER AND NOBODY WILL LEND A HAND TO ME OR BE THERE FOR ME. *(She never knew how much our entire family sacrificed to try to help her.)* SO, I JUST KEEP SINKING

AND SINKING. I WILL NEVER GET BACK ON TOP IF I DON'T GET A LITTLE HELP, OR AT LEAST A FRIENDLY SHOULDER TO CRY ON. I DON'T HAVE ONE SINGLE FRIEND THAT TRULY CARES ABOUT ME AND WANTS THE BEST FOR ME. IT HURTS! WHAT HURTS THE MOST IS PAUL IS IN HIS ROOM GOING TO SLEEP WHILE I AM OUT HERE CRYING AND BEGGING HIM TO HOLD ME JUST ONE LAST TIME. THIS MAN IS SO STINKIN' DIFFICULT TO UNDERSTAND, PLUS VERY, VERY BIPOLAR! I MIGHT BE A JUNKIE, AS HE CALLS ME, BUT AT LEAST I DON'T HAVE 2 DIFFERENT PERSONALITIES!

A couple of days later...

SATURDAY, OCTOBER 26, 2013:

ALRIGHT, *NAT,* IT'S ABOUT TIME TO *WAKE THE FUCK UP* AND CHANGE YOUR MISERABLE LIFE! I HAVE BEEN FUCKING AROUND FOR WAY TOO DAMN LONG NOW. I HAVE LOST ALMOST EVERYBODY THAT I LOVE THE MOST IN MY LIFE. WHAT MORE NEEDS TO HAPPEN BEFORE I FINALLY REALIZE THAT THIS IS ABSOLUTELY *NOT* THE LIFE I WANT TO LIVE? I WANT MY LIFE BACK WITH MY KIDS, MY PAUL AND THE ONES I LOVE. I KNOW I AM STRONG ENOUGH TO DO IT, SO WHY THE *HELL* HAVE I NOT DONE IT YET? YA, I AM TERRIFIED, I'M TERRIFIED TO CHANGE BECAUSE I HAVE BEEN DOING THIS FOR OVER A DECADE NOW (HOW FUCKING PATHETIC), BUT WHEN IS ENOUGH, ENOUGH? I DON'T WANT TO MISS OUT ON ANYMORE OF MY KIDS' LIVES, LIKE I ALREADY HAVE. I DON'T WANT TO HURT ANYMORE, AND I DON'T WANT TO BE THIS PERSON ANYMORE! I PROMISED HEAVENLY FATHER AND I PROMISED MYSELF THE OTHER DAY, WHEN ME AND ANDREW GOT PULLED OVER AND I ALMOST GOT ARRESTED, THAT I WOULD CHANGE, THAT I WOULD *NEVER* USE AGAIN IF THEY LET ME GO THAT DAY. WELL, THEY DID, AND I DIDN'T KEEP MY WORD. BUT, IT'S ONLY BEEN A COUPLE DAYS, I CAN STILL DO IT. I

DON'T WANT THIS FUCKED UP LIFE ANY LONGER. I AM PRAYING TO GOD THAT I WILL BE STRONG ENOUGH AND HAVE ENOUGH WILL POWER TO STOP ALL THIS AND NEVER GO BACK, *EVER!*

GET AWAY FROM ALL THESE SHADY PEOPLE THAT DON'T GIVE A FUCK ABOUT ME AND COMPLETELY CHANGE MY LIFE, AND WHO I'VE BEEN FOR THE PAST DECADE. IF I DO, I JUST MIGHT HAVE A CHANCE TO GIVE MY KIDS THE LIFE THEY DESERVE WITH A GOOD MOTHER, AND I MIGHT HAVE A CHANCE AGAIN WITH THE ONE MAN I LOVE MORE THAN ANY MAN I HAVE EVER LOVED BEFORE IN MY ENTIRE LIFE. I KNOW I CAN DO THIS! PROVE TO ALL THE PEOPLE IN MY LIFE THAT EVER DOUBTED ME THAT I CAN DO THIS ALL ON MY OWN AND MAKE MYSELF PROUD! LOVE YOURSELF AGAIN, *NAT,* YOU KNOW YOU CAN. DON'T KILL YOURSELF ANY LONGER, DON'T DO THAT TO YOUR INNOCENT KIDS THAT HAVE ALWAYS LOVED YOU, DON'T DO THAT TO YOURSELF, YOU ARE MUCH, MUCH BETTER THAN ALL THIS!

At this point, Nat still believed that getting clean meant having the willpower to do it on her own, but in reality, it has nothing to do with willpower. She needed professional help for her disease.

MONDAY, OCTOBER 28, 2013:

SITTIN' HERE AT MY BABY'S HOUSE. WE ARE GETTING READY TO GO TO DINNER, THEN WE ARE GOING TO COME BACK AND WATCH A MOVIE TOGETHER. WASN'T A VERY EXCITING DAY AT ALL! JUST HUSTLED *(chased drugs)* ALL DAY TILL I HAD TO GET JALA, THEN CAME HOME *(not sure what home means here)* GOT READY, AND MADE JALA DINNER. JUST DROPPED HER OFF AT JAY'S WORK AND NOW I AM AT MY MAN'S HOUSE! I TRIED TO TALK PAUL INTO GOING TO A HAUNTED HOUSE, BUT THAT DIDN'T FLY AT ALL, HE WILL HAVE NOTHING AT ALL TO DO WITH ANY HAUNTED HOUSE. I THINK IF I TOOK HIM TO ONE, HE WOULD LITERALLY KILL ONE OF THE WORKERS.

HE DOESN'T CARE IF SOMEONE GOT IN HIS FACE, WHOEVER IT IS, HE WOULD KILL THEM! HE DOESN'T DO WELL WITH PEOPLE GETTING IN HIS FACE. MARY AND RYAN HAVE BEEN BLOWING UP MY PHONE ALL DAMN DAY! *(Ryan is the man Nat ended up living with until she passed away, we are not sure how they met originally.)* IT'S DRIVING ME *NUTS!* THEY ARE BOTH DRIVING ME COMPLETELY CRAZY. SHE STILL HASN'T PAID MY TICKET YET. THE WRECK SHE GOT IN, AND I SAVED HER ASS BY TELLING THE POLICE IT WAS ME. NOW THE TICKET IS UP TO ALMOST $300 AND SHE HASN'T DONE A THING ABOUT IT, OR EVEN SAID A SINGLE WORD ABOUT IT! WHAT A GREAT FRIEND, HUH? I HAVE DEFINITELY COME TO THE CONCLUSION THAT SHE IS NOT A FRIEND AT ALL TO ME. SHE IS NOTHING. SHE IS THE DEVIL IN MY WORLD. SHE IS *TOXIC* TO ME AND I NEED AND WANT TO STAY AWAY FROM HER. SHE IS NOT GOOD TO HAVE IN MY LIFE. IT WILL BE BEST FOR ME TO KEEP HER OUT AND FAR, FAR AWAY FROM ME! I FEEL LIKE I NEVER SEE MY BABY BOY ANYMORE. I ONLY SEE HIM ON WEDNESDAYS AND EVERY SATURDAY FOR HIS FOOTBALL GAME. WELL, LAST SATURDAY WAS HIS LAST GAME. IT WAS SO SAD! THEY DIDN'T MAKE IT TO THE PLAYOFFS. MAS DID ABSOLUTELY FANTASTIC THIS LAST GAME, THOUGH. HE PLAYED BETTER THAN I'D EVER SEEN HIM PLAY BEFORE. I WISH THE REST OF HIS TEAM DID THE SAME. HE MADE 2 TOUCHDOWNS AND PLAYED ALMOST THE ENTIRE GAME! I WAS SO SUPER PROUD OF HIM. YOU CAN SEE HOW PASSIONATE HE IS EVERY TIME HE PLAYS FOOTBALL. I JUST HOPE HE STICKS WITH IT. I KNOW HE CAN MAKE IT INTO THE NFL IF HE WORKS AS HARD AS HE HAS BEEN WORKING!!

TUESDAY, OCTOBER 29, 2013:

JUST GOT DONE AT ADI'S CHOIR CONCERT. THE NIGHT WAS GOING JUST FINE, AND PAUL AND I HAD AN AWESOME MORNING TOGETHER, AND THEN ON THE WAY HOME, HE STARTED ON ME AGAIN. ASKING ME WHO I LET IN HIS HOME WHILE I LIVED

THERE. HE SAID HE FOUND SOMETHING THAT WASN'T HIS, AND THAT HE KNEW I HAD SOMEONE COME OVER AND TAKE A SHOWER. HOW ABSOLUTELY ABSURD IS THAT? NOBODY *EVER* CAME INTO HIS HOUSE AND SHOWERED! I WOULD NEVER LET THAT HAPPEN! I DON'T KNOW WHY HE LIKES FIGHTING WITH ME!! I HATE IT! ADI DID AWESOME ON HER CONCERT. IT WAS SO STINKIN' LONG, THOUGH. SO, MY KITTY WAS OUT OF CAT FOOD, SO I TOLD PAUL I WAS GOING TO GET CAT FOOD AND HE SAID IF YOU LEAVE, DON'T COME BACK. SO, NOW I'M STUCK AT MOTEL 6 WITH THIS GUY I JUST MET TODAY, AND I WANT TO GET THE FUCK OUT OF HERE! HE NEEDED ME TO GET HIM A ROOM 'CAUSE HE HAD NO ID. WELL, I GOT OUT OF THERE, THANK GOD! I WENT AND GOT SOME KITTY FOOD AND NOW I'M BACK AT MY BABY'S HOUSE, BUT HE DEFINITELY IS NOT HAPPY WITH ME AT ALL. HE THINKS I WENT TO MAKE A DRUG RUN. I TOLD HIM HE NEEDS TO HAVE A LITTLE MORE FAITH IN ME. I'M NOT GOING TO BE DECEITFUL IN ANY WAY AT ALL, BUT I CAN'T BE COMPLETELY HONEST WITH HIM, 'CAUSE IF I WAS, HE WOULD BOOT ME IN A SECOND. I JUST NEED TO CHANGE! I KNOW I KEEP SAYING IT AND NOT DOING A THING ABOUT IT, BUT I HAVE A GOAL. THAT'S MORE THAN WHAT I'VE HAD IN A VERY LONG TIME! MY *NEW YEAR'S RESOLUTION* IS TO GET 100% CLEAN FOR THE NEW YEAR AND TO STAY CLEAN! I'M STRONG ENOUGH, I KNOW I AM. I JUST NEED TO STOP BEING SO DAMN SCARED! IT IS SCARY AND IT'S GOING TO BE A COMPLETE LIFE CHANGING EXPERIENCE, BUT IT'S FOR THE BEST. IT WILL BE ONE OF THE MOST IMPORTANT, BEST THINGS I COULD EVER DO FOR ME AND MY FAMILY! I DESERVE IT AND MY AMAZING INNOCENT CHILDREN DESERVE IT. AND, PAUL AND HIS KIDS DESERVE IT. MY LOVED ONES NEED TO SEE THE REAL *NATALIE* AGAIN!

THURSDAY, OCTOBER 31, 2013:

HAPPY HALLOWEEN! JALA LOOKED SO SUPER CUTE TONIGHT! SHE DRESSED UP AS FRANKIE FROM MONSTER HIGH. SHE LOOKED ABSOLUTELY ADORABLE. SHE WENT WITH JAY TONIGHT OVER TO HIS FRIEND'S HOUSE SO JALA COULD TRICK OR TREAT WITH HIS DAUGHTER. I CAME OVER TO PAUL'S AND WE JUST STAYED IN TONIGHT. IT WAS SUCH AN AWESOME NIGHT, WE WATCHED PARANORMAL ACTIVITY, WHICH FREAKED THE FUCK OUT OF BOTH OF US, THEN JUST HUNG OUT. BUT THE NIGHT WASN'T OVER YET, AROUND 11:30 P.M. WE GOT INTO A CONVERSATION THAT LIT HIM UP...AGAIN! LAST NIGHT, HE GOT PHYSICAL WITH ME AGAIN, AND I LEFT AND SAID I WAS NEVER COMING BACK. HE TEXTED ME AND CALLED ME ALL NIGHT LONG SAYING TO COME HOME. I DIDN'T ANSWER HIS TEXTS OR HIS PHONE CALLS. I WAS GONE PRETTY MUCH THE REST OF THE NIGHT, BUT 5:00 A.M. ROLLS AROUND AND I AM MISSING HIM SO BAD, SO I CAME BACK, STUPID ME! HE WAS BEING SO STINKIN' GOOD TO ME. WE WENT TO BREAKFAST TOGETHER AND WERE TOGETHER TILL ABOUT 2:00 P.M. WELL, HE FREAKED OUT AGAIN TONIGHT. THREW THE LIVING ROOM TABLE ACROSS THE ROOM, BROKE A LOT OF MY NAIL STUFF, AND YELLED AT ME FOR A VERY LONG TIME WHILE I LAID ON THE COUCH CRYING. HOW CAN HE TREAT ME THIS WAY IF HE REALLY LOVES ME? HE IS A HARD ONE TO FIGURE OUT! I PRAY IT GETS BETTER, 'CAUSE I DO LOVE HIM!

FRIDAY, NOVEMBER 1, 2013:

DEFINITELY *NOT* DOING GOOD AT ALL! THIS IS THE WORST DAY EVER! PAUL LEFT ALL MY STUFF THAT WAS IN HIS HOUSE ON HIS PORCH AND HAS NOT SPOKE TO ME FOR OVER A WEEK. *(She was with him the day before).* I AM DYING! JUST HAD SURGERY, ANOTHER FUCKING ABSCESS, AND HE DIDN'T EVEN RESPOND TO ME WHEN I TOLD HIM THAT I WAS IN THE

HOSPITAL! HE'S DONE, AND I AM SO *NOT!* I AM TOTALLY AND COMPLETELY IN LOVE WITH HIM. WHAT AM I GOING TO DO? I AM NOT AT ALL GOING TO BE OKAY! MY LIFE JUST KEEPS GETTING WORSE AND WORSE AND I DON'T DO A THING ABOUT IT! I KNOW WHAT I NEED TO DO, BUT I JUST DON'T DO IT. WHY AM I SUCH A LAZY ASS? I LOVE MY KIDS AND PAUL MORE THAN ANYTHING IN THIS ENTIRE WORLD AND I LOST ALL OF THEM.

Two weeks later…

<u>11-14-2013:</u> <u>Dr. Note</u>–120 lbs. Prescribed Suboxone.

Three weeks later…

<u>MONDAY, DECEMBER 2, 2013</u>:

I AM AT THE WORST POINT IN MY ENTIRE LIFE! IT'S DECEMBER 2ND AND I AM NOW LIVING IN CATHERINE'S BASEMENT AGAIN WITH MARY, ANTHONY AND DAVID. I HAVE NEVER IN MY LIFE BEEN THIS DEPRESSED. PAUL HASN'T TALKED TO ME IN OVER A WEEK AND A HALF, HE WANTS NOTHING AT ALL TO DO WITH ME. I LOST MY CAR, MY MAZDA 3, THE ONE THING I DID NOT WANT TO LOSE! *(Her car was repossessed.)* I HAVE ABSOLUTELY NOTHING RIGHT NOW AND CHRISTMAS IS COMING UP AND I HAVE NO IDEA WHAT TO DO! I HAVE NO WAY OF GETTING AROUND, NO FRIENDS EXCEPT MARY AND ANTHONY, AND I HATE MYSELF MORE THAN ANYONE COULD EVER IMAGINE. ANTHONY AND I CAN *NEVER, EVER* GET ALONG, AND MARY AND I ARE NOT ALWAYS ON THE BEST OF TERMS EITHER! I HONESTLY DON'T KNOW WHAT THE *HELL* TO DO! I WANT TO BE WITH PAUL MORE THAN ANYTHING IN THIS WORLD, AND I DON'T KNOW IF HE WILL EVER BE WITH ME AGAIN. I'M COMPLETELY HEARTBROKEN. ALL I HAVE BEEN DOING ALL DAY, EVERY DAY IS CHASING DOPE *(looking for drugs)*! I AM SO SICK OF IT! I CAN'T STAND IT ANYMORE! I WANT TO BE DONE SO BAD! NOT BEING ABLE TO SEE MY KIDS TODAY REALLY FUCKED ME UP! I MISS THEM ALL SO STINKIN' MUCH! I COMPLETELY FUCKED UP ON THANKSGIVING! I WAS 2 HOURS LATE 'CAUSE I WAS CHASING DOPE, THEN WHEN I GOT THERE, I WAS FADING THE ENTIRE TIME! I ACTUALLY FELL ASLEEP AND NOBODY COULD WAKE ME UP! MY KIDS TRIED.

Six days later...

SUNDAY, DECEMBER 8, 2013:

SITTIN' HERE, IT'S ABOUT 8:30 A.M., WITH GARY. MARY AND I HAVE BEEN STAYING HERE WITH GARY 'CAUSE WE HAVE HAD NOWHERE ELSE TO GO. I SLEEP ON GARY'S BED WITH HIM WHILE MARY SLEEPS ON THE FLOOR. I HAVE NO CAR, NO HOME, AND NOW, NO FAMILY. MY FAMILY HAS COMPLETELY WROTE ME OFF AGAIN. IT'S SUCH BULLSHIT! MY MOM TOLD ME IF I EVER WANTED TO COME OVER AGAIN THAT I HAD TO BE CLEAN, NOT STINK (LIKE SMOKE), NOT FALL ASLEEP AT ALL WHILE I'M THERE, AND TO SPEND TIME WITH MY KIDS, ONLY MY KIDS, AND NOT COME AND GO! I WANTED TO BEAT HER ASS WHEN I READ THAT. I DON'T STINK, I FELL ASLEEP THE OTHER DAY 'CAUSE I WAS STINKIN' TIRED. *(In the last entry, she admitted to fading from dope when she was at my mom's; she couldn't remember what happened from day to day),* I NEVER COME AND GO WHEN I'M THERE, AND I AM ALWAYS JUST WITH MY KIDS WHEN I'M OVER THERE. *(She was always in and out of the house, and she never sat still unless she was sleeping).* IT'S CHRISTMAS TIME AND I CAN'T EVEN SPEND TIME WITH MY FAMILY OVER THE HOLIDAYS. JAY WON'T LET ME SEE OR TALK TO JALA AT ALL! IT'S ABSOLUTELY KILLING ME! I HONESTLY NEVER THOUGHT HE WOULD DO THIS AGAIN TO ME, AND HE HAS. PAUL WON'T SPEAK TO ME AT

ALL, I HAVE TRIED AND NO RESPONSE AT ALL. IT'S BREAKING MY HEART INTO A MILLION PIECES! I LOVE THAT MAN MORE THAN ANYTHING IN THIS WORLD! I HAVE NEVER IN MY LIFE BEEN IN LOVE WITH A MAN LIKE I AM WITH PAUL. I HOPE AND PRAY THAT HE WILL ONE DAY LOVE ME FOR WHO I AM AND ACTUALLY REALLY LOVE ME, REALLY, REALLY LOVE ME! I CAN'T EVEN LOOK AT ANOTHER MAN AT ALL, HE IS ALWAYS ON MY MIND, ALL THE DAMN TIME! I CAN'T GET HIM OR MY KIDS OFF MY MIND 24/7, AND IT'S REALLY, REALLY KILLING ME! LITERALLY KILLING ME! IT'S THE CHRISTMAS HOLIDAYS AND I AM MORE MISERABLE THAN I EVER HAVE BEEN BEFORE IN MY LIFE!!

12-12-2013: Dr. Note–116 lbs. Prescribed Suboxone. *Once again, I do not know why this doctor is prescribing her Suboxone without drug testing her.*

A week later...

This is the last time Paul was mentioned and this is the last journal entry she made until May, 10, 2014.

FRIDAY, DECEMBER 13, 2013:

SITTIN' HERE WITH GARY RIGHT NOW, LIKE I HAVE BEEN FOR THE PAST COUPLE WEEKS. HE IS SO GROWING ON ME...*BAD!* HE HAS DEFINITELY KEPT MY MIND BUSY AND OFF OF PAUL. EVEN THOUGH I STILL MISS PAUL MORE THAN ANYTHING IN THIS WORLD. GARY HAS HELPED ME SO MUCH. I HAVE BEEN LIVING HERE WITH HIM FOR THE PAST 2 WEEKS. ME AND MARY BOTH CAME OVER HERE AFTER ANTHONY AND DAVID KICKED US BOTH OUT OF CATHERINE'S HOUSE. HOW FUCKED UP IS THAT? I CALLED GARY AND HIM AND NICHOLAS WERE THERE IN 20 MINUTES TO PICK ME UP. THEY DIDN'T KNOW MARY WAS COMING, SO THEY WEREN'T TOO HAPPY AT FIRST, BUT

THAT BITCH IS GONE! SHE WAS HERE FOR ABOUT 4 DAYS, AND THAT WAS LONG ENOUGH FOR ALL OF US. SHE ENDED UP STEALING FROM GARY AND TALKED A WHOLE BUNCH OF SHIT ON ME, GO FIGURE! I AM SO COMPLETELY *DONE* WITH HER. MY LIFE WILL BE SO MUCH BETTER WITHOUT HER IN IT! SHE IS NOT EVEN ALLOWED OVER HERE AND THAT DEFINITELY PUTS MY MIND AT EASE. I SAW JALA AND MAS WEDNESDAY AND IT WAS AWESOME! GOT TO HANG OUT WITH THEM FOR ABOUT 3 HOURS. THEY DESERVE A LOT BETTER MOM THAN ME. WAY BETTER! I NEED TO GET MY SHIT TOGETHER AND SHOW THEM HOW MUCH THEY REALLY MEAN TO ME!!!

• • •

CHAPTER 11

2014

IN 2014, NAT TURNED *thirty-five, Adi eighteen, Mas fifteen, and Jala eight.*

This was the year that Mas found out the truth, and he really struggled to grasp the reality of his mom's life.

1-10-2014: Dr. Note–115 lbs. Prescribed Suboxone.

2-13-2014: Dr. Note–120 lbs. Prescribed Suboxone. Had dental work done in last two weeks, more than expected. Prescribed Percocet, said she took 2 then got back on Suboxone.

3-13-2014: Dr. Note–119 lbs. Prescribed Suboxone. Says she is taking no other meds. Pending dental work.

4-14-2014: Dr. Note–122 lbs. Prescribed Suboxone and Trazadone *(sleeping medication).*

There was an incident at my mom's house on Easter Sunday, April 20, 2014. Nat was outside on a chair with Mas, and her eyes were closed and she looked frozen. My brother-in-law said something was wrong with her, and someone got Adi from inside the house. They were able to get Nat to wake up for a few minutes, and she went in the house and sat on the couch and started rocking back and forth. Adi went through her mom's purse and found needles, a spoon, and other drug paraphernalia. Adi called the cops, and Mas was really upset. She told the cops she'd found drugs, and at that point, Nat woke up and got her purse and left the house on foot. The cops arrested her a few doors down from my mom's. I cannot even start to comprehend how hard this must have been for Adi to call the cops on her own mother and at the same time upsetting her brother. She is a very strong girl. Nat was arrested and booked in jail.

***ARREST:* April 20, 2014–April 21, 2014**
West Bountiful Police Department
Charged with Narcotic Equipment–Possession
Marijuana–Possession
Marijuana–Possession
Heroin–Possession

Ryan bailed her out. She was only in for one day.

She was arrested again on May 1st after a Heroin bust in Salt Lake City's Pioneer Park, where she was selling and using. That time, she was in for twenty-two days.

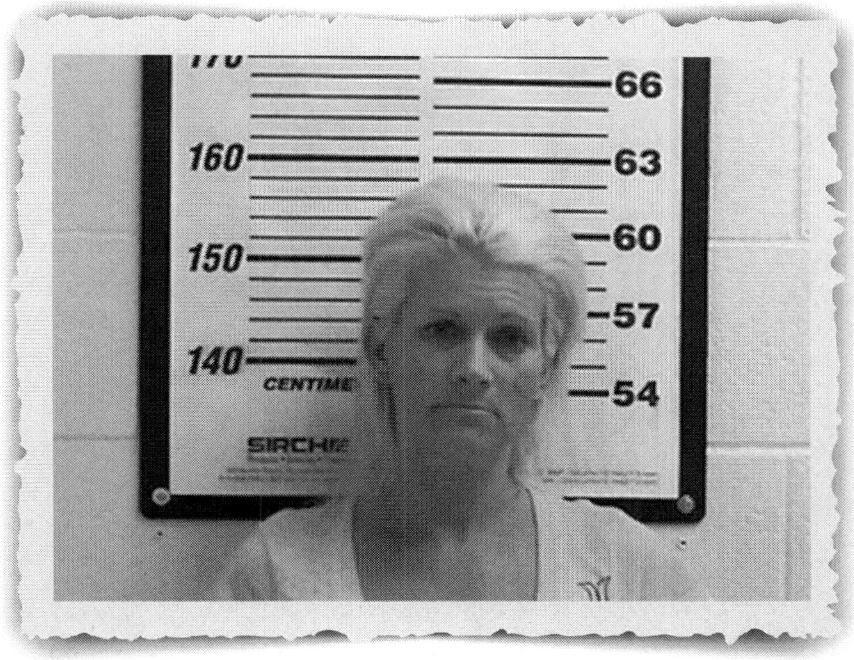

ARREST: May 1, 2014–May 22, 2014
Davis County SO
Charged with Marijuana–Possession
Amphetamine–Possession
Marijuana–Possession
Narcotic Equipment–Possession
Amphetamine–Sell

SATURDAY, MAY 10, 2014, LDS ADDICTION RECOVERY PROGRAM JOURNAL FROM JAIL:

WELL, I'M HERE IN KILO IN DAVIS COUNTY JAIL AND IT'S BEEN OVER A WEEK AND A HALF. TODAY WAS THE VERY FIRST DAY THAT I HAVE FELT AT PEACE. I HAVE COURT ON TUESDAY AT 1:30 AND I'M PRAYING TO GOD THAT HE RELEASES ME, BUT IF HE DOESN'T, I KNOW GOD HAS A BETTER PLAN FOR ME. I HAVE TOTALLY CHANGED IN HERE. *THIS IS THE FIRST TIME IN OVER EIGHT YEARS THAT I HAVE BEEN COMPLETELY CLEAN.* I NEEDED THIS TIME IN JAIL, AS MUCH AS I ABSOLUTELY *HATE* TO SAY IT. I DESPERATELY NEEDED THIS. I AM FINALLY, IN YEARS, TALKING TO MY SISTERS AGAIN AND GETTING MY FAMILY BACK. I CAN'T EVEN THINK OF A BETTER MOTHER'S DAY GIFT TOMORROW THAN BEING CLEAN FOR ME AND MY FAMILY.

SUNDAY, MAY 11, 2014:

WELL, IT'S MOTHER'S DAY TODAY AND I'M SICK HERE, STUCK IN JAIL. NOT FUN, BUT DEFINITELY PROMISING. I JUST GOT BACK FROM AN AA MEETING AND IT'S TIME TO LOCK DOWN, AND I AM SO READY FOR BED. TODAY WAS A VERY, VERY, VERY LONG DAY. NO ONE CAME TO SEE ME. I DIDN'T GET AHOLD OF MY MOM, AND I'M JUST WAITING FOR COURT ON TUESDAY. I BETTER BE OUT BEFORE ADI'S GRADUATION, BUT I DON'T THINK I WILL. *(She missed Adi's high school graduation.)*

Ten days later...

WEDNESDAY, MAY 21, 2014:

LOCKED DOWN RIGHT NOW AND HAVE BEEN FOR A COUPLE HOURS NOW. IT'S ABOUT 10:30 A.M. AND I HAVE BEEN UP PRETTY MUCH ALL NIGHT LONG! IT'S SO STINKIN' HARD TO SLEEP HERE. I WENT TO COURT FOR THE THIRD TIME YESTERDAY

AND IT WENT ABSOLUTELY HORRIBLE! I THOUGHT IT WAS GOING TO BE A GOOD OUTCOME, BUT NOT WITH MY DISTRIBUTION CHARGE NOW. I'M OKAY, THOUGH! ALL I THINK ABOUT IS RYAN *(Our family didn't know much about him at the time),* MY KIDS, AND MY SWEET PUPPY *(Sydka, which Ryan got her).* I JUST GOT A LETTER, ACTUALLY TWO LETTERS, FROM RYAN WITH SOME PICTURES AND IT MADE MY ENTIRE DAY. SO, MY MOM ACTUALLY SHOWED UP IN COURT YESTERDAY WITH ADI, JAY, AND ANGIE. IT WAS SO STINKIN' HARD TO SEE HER. WROTE HER A LETTER AND ADI AND ANGIE SAID SHE WOULDN'T EVEN OPEN IT. IT BREAKS MY HEART THAT I HURT HER SO BADLY. SO, MY NEXT COURT DATE IS NOT UNTIL JUNE 3, TWO WEEKS AWAY. BUT MY HONEY RYAN IS COMING TO BAIL ME OUT IN THE MORNING. I CAN'T WAIT TO SEE HIM. I'M JUST SO SCARED FOR MY NEXT COURT DATE. I COULD BE FACING PRISON TIME, BUT I SURE HOPE NOT. HEAVENLY FATHER IS ON MY SIDE THIS TIME 'CAUSE I HAVE FAITH, SO I KNOW I WILL BE OKAY. I HAVE A FRIEND IN HERE NAMED CYNTHIA, AND WE CLUNG TO EACH OTHER FROM THE SECOND DAY I WAS HERE. I ABSOLUTELY LOVE HER AND KNOW WE WILL ALWAYS BE FRIENDS. SHE IS ONE OF THE REASONS I AM MAKING IT IN HERE. ANGIE AND MICHELLE AND ADI HAVE BEEN GREAT! ACTUALLY, THE VERY FIRST PERSON TO COME AND SEE ME IN HERE AND PUT MONEY ON MY BOOKS WAS ERIC (EX BROTHER IN LAW). BLESS HIS HEART. THE FIRST WEEK I WAS HERE, HE CAME TWICE TO SEE ME AND PUT $50 ON MY BOOKS. HE CAME THE SECOND TIME AND READ ME A BOOK, *I AM SPECIAL.* HE MADE ME CRY. I ABSOLUTELY ADORE THAT MAN, HE HAS TAUGHT ME A LOT! ADI, ANGIE, AND JAY HAVE WENT TO EVERY COURT HEARING THAT I HAVE HAD. I HAVE TALKED TO JAY ONCE ONLY FOR A COUPLE MINUTES THROUGH THE MONITOR, OTHER THAN THAT, IT HAS BEEN ANGIE AND ADI THAT HAVE CAME EVERY TIME TO SEE ME. ADI GRADUATES NEXT WEEKEND, AND I AM SO HAPPY FOR HER AND I WILL BE THERE TO SUPPORT HER. I PRAY EVERY SINGLE DAY AND NIGHT FOR MY 3 BEAUTIFUL

KIDS, THAT I CAN'T EVEN TALK ABOUT OR I WILL LOSE IT, AND FOR MYSELF THAT I WILL BE BACK OUT THERE WITH THEM VERY SOON. LIKE TOMORROW! I HAVE REALLY BEEN HERE WAY TOO LONG, BUT, I DEFINITELY NEEDED IT WITHOUT A DOUBT, BUT, IT'S TIME TO GET OUT NOW AND SEE MY HONEY THAT HAS SUPPORTED ME THE ENTIRE TIME I HAVE BEEN IN HERE AND SEE MY ALMOST PERFECT KIDS AGAIN AND BE A GREAT MOTHER TO THEM AGAIN. A MOTHER THAT THEY HAVE WAITED FOR, FOR WAY TOO LONG NOW. I AM SO THANKFUL FOR EVERYTHING THAT I HAVE, AND I AM GRATEFUL FOR LIFE! MICHELLE HAS PUT LOTS OF MONEY ON MY BOOKS, SO HAS ANGIE, AND I HAVE TALKED TO SHALL A COUPLE TIMES FOR THE FIRST TIME IN YEARS. I FEEL ABSOLUTELY AWESOME, I CAN'T WAIT TO HAVE MY FAMILY AND SISTERS BACK AGAIN! I AM GAINING LOTS OF WEIGHT, THOUGH, IN HERE, BUT IT'S OKAY. I'M HEALTHY. I CAME IN AT 103LBS, SKINNY, SKINNY, SKINNY, BUT LET'S SEE WHAT I COME OUT AS!

ARREST: *June 14, 2014–June 16, 2014*
Bountiful Police Department
Amphetamine–possession

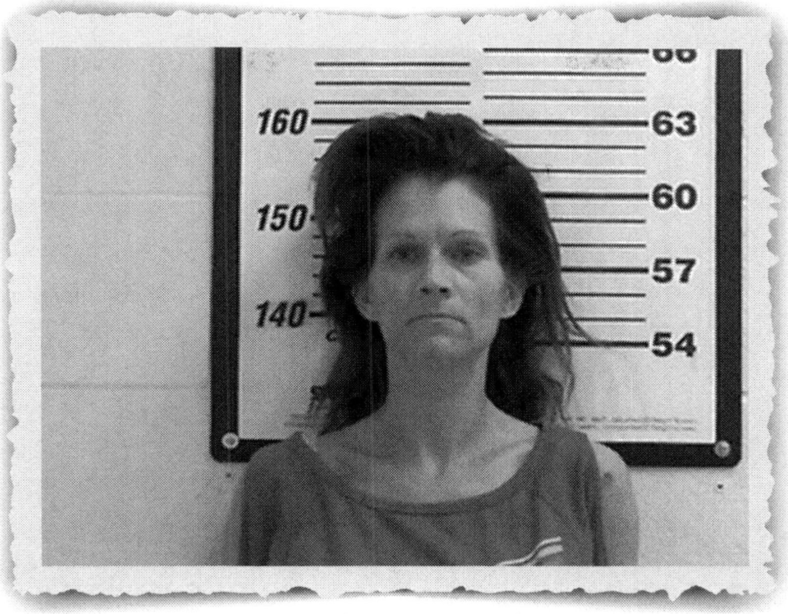

ARREST: July 9, 2014–August 20, 2014
Davis County
Narcotic Equipment–possession
Heroin–possession
Marijuana–possession
Heroin–sell
Marijuana–possession

Nat was ordered to complete Drug Court at this time. As soon as she left jail, she had to be in an outpatient program at the Women's Recovery Center for an extended period of time. She also had a Parole Officer who tracked her, and she had to have random drug tests done and appear in court often to speak to the judge. This went on for fifteen months, until she was successfully released from Drug Court. I was able to attend a few of her court hearings and her graduation from Drug Court. I was always so proud of her at her hearings because the judge always complimented her on being the "model student."

The following are Nat's step notes from her time in the WRC.

WRC (WOMEN'S RECOVERY CENTER) AFTER-JAIL OUTPATIENT TREATMENT 2014 STEP NOTES:

STEPS 1 & 2: Missing.

STEP 3: "We made a decision to turn our will and our lives over to the care of God as we understand Him."

Why is making a decision central to working this step? Because I am opening my mind to a different way of thinking. Turning my decisions and thoughts over to my higher power.

Can I make this decision just for today? Do I have any fears or reservations about it? What are they? Yes, absolutely, that's all I need to do, make a decision just for today. Yes, I have fears that I may have a moment of weakness and of the unknown. I have fear for tomorrow.

What action have I taken to follow through on my decision? I have opened my mind to the possibilities of my higher power.

What areas of my life are difficult for me to turn over? Why is it important that I turn them over anyway? Opening up to other people or absolutely anything in my life. To allow people or my higher power in to help me and give me different thought patterns.

How have I acted on self-will? What were my motives? I put myself and my addiction before absolutely everything. I put my addiction before my kids all the time and my needs were always met first, not theirs. About two years ago, I was at Jay's apartment with Jala while Jay was at work, and I was in the bathroom smoking bath salts and shooting up heroin. I was in there for longer than 30 minutes while Jala was standing outside of the bathroom crying. I just kept telling her to hold on. I didn't come out until I hit a vein. Jala was sobbing when I got out. My motives were always the same thing, day after day, to get high. Never thought about anything else. My drugs were the only thing on my mind.

How has acting on self-will affected my life? How has my self-will affected others? Acting on my self-will turned my life completely upside down. I lost my self-esteem, myself, and the absolute most important thing to me, my three children. My self-will affected my loved ones and my kids to the point that they were no longer in my life anymore.

My parents and my sisters and my kids, after 10 years, had finally had enough. This last time I was in jail, they completely wrote me off. No letters, phone calls, or visits. They didn't attend my court hearings. They told me I had one last chance and that was it, this time they were done. I didn't hear or talk to my family or kids for months.

Will pursuing my goals harm anyone? How? Absolutely not because my goals are to stay away from the drug world entirely. This means NO ASSOCIATION with past "so called friends" and not putting myself anywhere near drugs or people that use. My biggest goal (future goal) is to have a strong, healthy support system to lean on and be completely honest and have healthy people in my life. My goals for the future are to finish Davis County Drug Court, stay connected with my sponsor and meetings, and take my life a day at a time. And, most importantly, stay close to my kids and always have a strong, healthy connection with them.

In the pursuit of what I want, is it likely that I will end up doing something that adversely affects others or myself? My goals that I want for my future will be nothing but happiness for me and my loved ones. If I achieve my goals as I plan on doing, it will affect me and my life and others in a healthy way. I will have respect for myself and from others.

Will I have to compromise any of my principles to achieve this goal? I want to practice honesty every day of my life from this point on because it is very important to me and my recovery. I will not have to compromise any of my principles.

Describe the times when my will has not been enough. About 3 years ago, I wanted to get clean and tried to do it on my own but failed. This was the second time I tried to get clean on my own. Went about 24 hours being sick from withdrawals and just couldn't do it, so I got on Methadone. I did this two times within 10 years of my addiction.

What is the difference between my will and God's will? I couldn't do it with my own will, I never turned my will over to my higher power until this last time. Now that I have turned it over to God's will, I am staying clean and I definitely see the difference. Every time I tried on my own, I did not succeed, now that I have it in God's hands, I am finally doing it.

Have there been times in my recovery when I have found myself taking back my will and my life? What alerted me? What have I done to recommit myself to the Third Step? Yes, in the beginning of my recovery and treatment I got a little too confident and I found myself taking a couple steps back. My fear is what alerted me, I got too confident and I was faced with certain situations, like Mary stopping by my house and old friends contacting me. This put fear in me, which alerted me that I needed something more, or different. I have finally opened my mind up and turned myself over to my higher power and listened more instead of being too confident and thinking I could do it on my own.

Does the word "God" or even the concept itself make me uncomfortable? What is the source of my discomfort? It did at first, but not anymore. Now that I have started to listen to my higher power and praying and asking for help and receiving answers very clearly, I feel anything but uncomfortable. I have seen a huge change in the way I think and handle certain situations now that I have let God in. I don't have any discomfort with the word "God." It's the exact opposite and I have not had this feeling of being comfortable and safe for I don't know how long.

Have I ever believed that God caused horrible things to happen to me or was punishing me? What were those things? Yes, when I was active in my addiction, I thought God was punishing me when I got my kids taken from me. Also, when my family disowned me and I had no place to live and was feeling all alone. I thought I was being punished because of what I was doing.

What is my understanding of a Power greater than myself today? How is my Higher Power working in my life? My understanding of a power that is greater than myself today is Heavenly Father and I believe and trust that he is working every day, every moment in my life today because of the changes I have made. He has taken over me and I recognize it every day. I feel very blessed and safe. Something that I have longed for, for a very long time now.

How do I communicate with my Higher Power? Through prayer and I receive answers through listening to my instincts when they are very strong.

How does my Higher Power communicate with me? What feelings do I have about my Higher Power? The most important thing and the way I have found answers to my prayers and receive communication from my higher power is through my family members and my kids. He talks through them to me.

Am I struggling with changing my beliefs about the nature of my Higher Power? No, my beliefs are getting stronger every day about my higher power. I communicate with him more every day than I have in many years. I am receiving answers, which I never have before, or at least can remember, and I am getting closer to him every day.

Is my current concept of a Higher Power still working? How might it need to change? Yes, I notice a lot more now than I ever have before that He is present in my life and listening to my prayers. I only hope it stays this strong in my life and I stay this connected with my higher power.

What does "to the care of" mean to me? It means letting someone (higher power) have complete control over me.

What does it mean for me to turn my will and my life over to the care of the God of my understanding? To completely trust in him in every aspect of my life. I will give myself to him completely. To have complete faith in him, listen to him, even if I don't agree.

How might my life be changed, if I make the decision to turn it over to my Higher Power's care? I will make better decisions in my life. I will stay clean, always be connected to my loved ones and kids, and have complete peace.

How do I allow my Higher Power to work in my life? Listen and have faith. Stay connected with Him through communication daily.

How does my Higher Power care for my will and my life? Gives me only what he knows I can handle and helps me each step of the way. Teaches me the things I need to learn to have a clean and happy life. He is always there for me, He never leaves me.

Have there been times when I have been unable to let go and trust God to care for the outcome of a particular situation? Yes, when I was using, I tried twice to get clean on my own and couldn't do it. I didn't have my higher power in my life at all and didn't trust anyone but myself. I didn't even make it 24 hours going through withdrawals without giving up. Another time was when I lost my kids in court to my ex-husband. I left the court room thinking I could get myself clean without any help from anyone. I failed and became worse into my drug addiction.

Have there been times when I have been able to let go and trust God for the outcome? Yes, when I entered treatment and was there for about a week, I finally completely let go and I trusted my higher power and let him take control. I have been succeeding and have found a new way of life, finally. This is the very first time in my life where I have trusted and had faith in something much bigger than me.

How do I take action to turn it over? Are there any words I say regularly? What are they? Continuing treatment, talking with Kathleen, talking to my sponsor on a regular basis, and praying daily asking Heavenly Father each morning to help me make it through the day clean. Also, thanking him for each day that I get through and for being healthy and clean.

What am I doing to reinforce my decision to allow my Higher Power to care for my will and my life? Staying connected each day with my higher power, staying close to my kids and my family, and opening my mind more and more every day to healthy possibilities and patterns.

How does the Third Step allow me to build on the surrender I have developed in Steps One and Two? It has helped me get closer to my higher power and opened me up to new and better ways of looking at my life. I pray every morning and night, which I didn't used to do, and I am a much more spiritual person after doing this step.

In what ways have I demonstrated willingness in my recovery so far? Doing the work that needs to be done for treatment and my recovery. Processing my steps honestly and openly. Trusting in myself and my treatment.

Am I fighting anything in my recovery? What do I think would happen if I became willing to let recovery prevail in that area of my life? Yes, my guilt that I have held onto. I think it would become a big weight lifted off my shoulders and I could focus on my goals for the future instead of feeling like I'm still being held back from all the guilt I carry.

How have hope, faith, and trust become positive forces in my life? I have made it through some of the toughest experiences that I never thought I could. I am staying clean, making it through treatment and becoming the mother that I know I can be. Having faith that I haven't had much of before and trusting my higher power that I never thought I could have in my life again has given me the chance to make this important decision in my life happen.

What further action can I take to apply the principles of hope, faith and trust in my recovery? Attend some church meetings at least a couple times a month and sharing my experiences with others that might need the help. Helping others helps me and my recovery and gives me more hope, faith, and better self-esteem.

What evidence do I have that I can trust confidently in my recovery? That I am clean today and I am the mother that I know I can be. A good example to my kids and the people around me. I have become an honest, trustworthy person that perseveres each day in my recovery. And the love and faith in me from my family and loved ones.

What have I done recently that demonstrates my commitment to recovery and to working a program? I have completed the steps that I have been given that I thought I could do. I have opened up in meetings, which is really hard for me, and shared my story, and I have been completely honest with my counselor and sponsor, even when it was extremely difficult.

Do I have any reservations about my decision to turn my will and my life over to God's care? At times, I thought I did, like when I needed to start this step. I procrastinated and didn't think I would have the knowledge or memory to complete it. But each time I went to do it, I prayed and got through it very well and learned a lot more about myself and my higher power than I ever thought I would.

Do I feel that I am now ready to turn it over? Absolutely, I have shown myself and my loved ones that I trust my higher power to help me and take control of my recovery.

How does my surrender in the First Step help me in the Third Step? I started the process, became honest with myself, my treatment providers, and my peers in the program. Faced my past that I didn't want to face, shared my story that could help others, and it has helped me get to the point that I am at now in recovery.

What action do I plan to take to follow through on my decision? How does working the remainder of the steps fit into this? Staying connected to my higher power, being honest with myself and my loved ones, and taking this a day at a time and continuing with my goals that I have for my future. They open my mind to a different and new way of life and healthier possibilities for my future.

STEP 4: "We made a searching and fearless moral inventory of ourselves."

Do I have any reservations about working this step? What are they? No, I am ready to move on and get to know myself better so I can be at peace with myself.

What are some of the benefits that could come from making a searching and fearless moral inventory of myself? I will get a better understanding of the things I need to work on and work through and become a stronger person for me and my kids. And hopefully let go some or all of this guilt that I am carrying.

Why shouldn't I procrastinate about working this step? What are the benefits of not procrastinating? Because I can find more out about myself, my addiction and learn from it. Getting this step done will help my self-esteem and let me know the areas of myself that I need to work on. A better understanding of the things I really need to work on and help me make future goals.

Am I afraid of working this step? No, I am excited to reveal more of myself and work through more of my issues.

What does it mean to me to be searching and fearless? To dip deep into myself and have the courage and strength to do the things in recovery that I have always been afraid to do, find more out about myself that I have never known.

Am I disturbed by thinking about society's expectations and afraid that I cannot, and never will be able to conform to them? Yes, because for the longest time I have not felt good enough for my family, my kids or anyone else. I am hoping and praying that through my recovery and working my steps that I can feel better about myself and have more confidence and better self-esteem.

What value and principles are important to me? Being a genuine and honest person. Always having a healthy and good support system. Being connected to my higher power and being a good example to my kids and people around me. Staying away from unhealthy people and situations. Being a good mother that I know I can be.

How is my decision to work Step Four a demonstration of courage? Faith? Honesty? Willingness? Because I am facing my deepest darkest secrets about me and my life. It's showing me that opening up with myself and my past fears that I can work these things out and trust that I will get through them. That I am writing and sharing with myself and my counselor the things that I never wanted to reveal and putting through my best effort and ability in pulling everything up in my past and working through them no matter how hard it is.

Who are the people that I resent? Explain the situations that led to the resentment. My Ex for taking my kids from me. His new wife for not allowing him to talk to me for all these years, becoming closer to my kids in the past 10 years, more than I have been. Mary and David for introducing me into the drug world, giving me drugs for the first time and allowing me to get close to them while they were putting me in dangerous situations and being around harmful people. Never letting me go, even when they know I am doing well and they know I care about them. By still trying to keep in contact with me when they know I am in recovery doing well and it's hard for me to keep them at a distance. Past drug friends because they acted like they cared about me and they didn't call. Jennifer, introduced me to Mary and David. Paul, he gave up on me when I needed him the most, won't have anything to do with me and won't forgive me.

What institutions do I resent? Explain the situations that led to the resentment. The legal system taking my kids from me and giving my ex full custody.

What was my motivation, or what did I believe, that led me to act as I did in this situation? I gave up completely on myself and all my values. Turned all my emotions and feelings into hatred. I believed that it was everyone else's fault that these situations happened. Not because of me or my actions. I believed I was being punished.

How has my dishonesty contributed to my resentments? Because I was dishonest with myself and blamed everyone else, but me.

How has my behavior contributed to my resentments? Never looked at my own actions and behavior, always put blame on all these people. It definitely pushed my addiction further and further.

Am I afraid of looking at my part in the situations that caused my resentments? Why? Some of them because I made the choices that I did and could have filtered people out of my life before it got to the point that it did.

How have my resentments affected my relationships with myself, with others and with a Higher Power? It has put negative and hatred thoughts in my mind. Guilt that I have a hard time of letting go and I have a very hard time getting close to anyone other than my family. I have thought for the longest time that my Higher Power was punishing me daily because of the things I was doing, until recently.

What recurring themes, thoughts, or responses do I notice in my resentments? Jealousy, anger, anxiety, not letting go and pure guilt.

How do I identify my individual feelings? Acknowledging them and dealing with them. I cry when I am emotional and I cry when I am angry too at times. I make sure that now I am not shutting them down, I am very aware of my feelings today and deal with them the best I can.

What feelings do I have the most trouble allowing myself to feel? Self-worth and trust in other people or faith.

Why have I tried to shut off my feelings? To get rid of my pain and guilt of the past. That is the only time I have shut down my feelings since I have been clean. When I was using I shot them down all the time to not feel all the pain and hurt and complete sadness.

What means have I used to deny how I really felt? Being sarcastic and not dealing with those feelings at all. Avoidance.

Who or what triggered a feeling? What was the feeling? What were the situations? What was my part in each situation? Seeing or hearing from old friends. My feelings were sad, angry, hurt, jealous, lost, wishy-washy. Mary stopping by my house or leaving notes on my front door. Thought about her and David a lot. More than I wanted to. Remanising old memories and getting very emotional over it. Wanting to call her and talk to her again cause I missed her.

What was my motivation, or what did I believe, that led me to act as I did in these situations? My thought or belief was that I could never let either one of them go and they would be in my life forever. Because I care about them way more that I want to. I think of them sometimes as my family. (My past family cause they were all I had). My emotions and sadness always take over involving these 2 and I have a very hard time blocking them out of my mind.

What do I do with my feelings once I have identified them? Since I have been clean I talk a lot with my family and am more open with them especially when I am having a hard time. I also am around my kids a lot and it opens my eyes to what's the most important to me in my life.

Who or what do I feel guilty or ashamed about? Explain the situations that led to these feelings. I feel guilt about my addiction and the length of my addiction. For putting my addiction before my kids. The loss of my kids and the length of time I lost with my kids. For using in the bathroom when my kids were under the same roof. For taking Jala on drug runs and around dangerous people. For lying to my family and kids for so long. For putting my family and kids through complete hell for so many years. For putting Mary and David and friends before my kids and family. For losing sight of what mattered to me most in life and losing my whole values system and morals. And for giving up and losing myself, my kids and my family.

Which of these situations have caused me to feel shame, though I had no part in creating them? I don't think I feel any shame, just severe guilt and I had every part in creating these situations.

In the situations, I did have a part in, what was my motivations or belief that led me to act as I did? My belief was that I couldn't function properly being off the drugs. I thought I was a better mother at times because I had more energy and no cares. I never thought I would make it through the withdrawals and being that sick.

How has my behavior contributed to my guilt and shame? I acted like I never thought I would. I lied, cheated, stole and only thought and did things for myself. All my morals were discontinued as if I had none at all. I was a mean and manipulative person that didn't care about anyone, or myself in any way.

Who or what do I fear and why? I fear that I won't ever let go of my guilt and I will carry and remember it always. It's difficult for me to move forward in my life and to feel comfortable with myself carrying this guilt. I fear it won't ever go away. I fear of being alone the rest of my life because I am a drug addict and have kids and getting older everyday. I fear that I won't get my self-worth or self-esteem back the way it used to be before I started using and if I do it will be a long time from now. I have a fear of relapsing in my future and I don't ever want to go back to that horrible life I had.

What have I done to cover up my fear? Focused on the most important things to me in my life time with kids and being a good mother and example to them. Thought positive instead of negative and taking my life one day at a time.

How have I responded negatively or destructively to my fear? I haven't been, I have been facing my fear and conquering it so far. I get anxiety at times but use some tools that I have learned to get rid of that anxiety quickly.

What do I most fear looking at and exposing about myself? What do I think will happen if I do? Some of the things in my addiction, what I did and my family or kids finding out about those things. I am afraid of losing their trust, respect, or them. Especially since I just got them back in my life.

How have I cheated myself because of my fear? Because I have lost my confidence, self-esteem, good judgement and my complete self-worth and respect. The things in my life that I have always wanted to accomplish, like being successful and a good mother to my kids. And I have cheated myself out of happiness.

What conflicts in my personality make it difficult for me to maintain friendships and/or romantic relationships? People pleasing, not trusting in anyone, selfishness, dishonesty.

How has my fear of being hurt affected my friendships and romantic relationships? My fear of being hurt in my friendships either caused me to not make relationships with good and healthy friends and was not able to let go of dangerous friends. And with romantic relationships it made me settle with someone that was not good for me. Pretty much all of my relationships in my life I settled out of fear. Was afraid of financially supporting myself and always relied on a man even If I didn't want to be with him, or because I was terrified of being alone.

How have I sacrificed platonic (nonsexual) friendships in favor of romantic relationships? A lot, never became friends with the men I was in relationships, 1st it just always ended up and began in romantic. If I would of become friends with these men 1st, then things might have been different.

In what ways did I compulsively seek relationships? Went from man to man cause I was never satisfied. My expectations were always too high and I always ended up resenting a lot of the men I was with in the end. But I was always searching for "Mr. Perfect" and never found him. I just jumped from guy to guy and I never thought they were good enough or perfect enough.

In my relationships with family, do I sometimes feel as though we are locked into repeating the same patterns repeatedly without any hope of change? What are those patterns? What is my part in perpetuating them? I felt like when I was growing up I had to be the perfect child. I have always had a great relationship with my family other than I have always felt like they expected too much out of me. My relationship with my little sister was the only problem I had with my family. We never got along growing up because she felt like she was ignored because my mom was so involved in my life. I just felt like I was being pushed everyday to be little miss perfect. And I was a good kid, always made them proud, but for me I felt like it still wasn't good enough for them. I always did what was expected to do from my parents.

How have I avoided intimacy with my friends, partners or spouses and family? I haven't been honest with anyone for so long, it was normal for me to hide everything from absolutely everybody, my husband, kids, sister's, mom and dad and friends. I have not let myself get close to anyone for over a decade or as long as I remember. My 2 older sisters I have always looked up to, idolized and thought they were perfect in everyway, so I tried to be like them always but never felt like I measured up to them or could ever be as perfect as them. I feel like that to this day, so it has made me very closed off to everyone in my life.

Have I had problems making commitments? Describe. Yes, I tried to always make a commitment to myself a number of times that I was going to stop using and never once followed through with it until I was forced by the law to do so. I also have never committed to any man that I have ever been with, my husbands, boyfriends or any man I have ever been with I never was faithful to any of them. And for as long as I can remember the one thing I have always heard in my life from everyone is that I never follow through with anything I say to anyone. Whether it be calling someone back, following through with plans or following through with any commitment I gave to anyone, including myself.

Have I ever destroyed a relationship because I believed I was going to get hurt anyway so I should get out before that could happen? Describe. Yes, my marriage with Jay. Except I didn't get out, I just put him through hell because I wouldn't leave, but I always thought he was going to either hurt me or cheat on me someday. From the day I met Jay, I always thought he was too good for me and that he would hurt me so I sabbotaged our relationship and I was the one that hurt him because I was always so scared.

To what degree do I consider the feelings of others in my relationships? Equal to my own? More important that my own? Of minor importance? Not at all? With my kids up to the day I started using I always considered their feelings more important than mine. When I started using, mine were more important than anyone's. In my relationships with men, even when I wasn't using, my feelings were always more important. With my family when I wasn't using, I usually put theirs first, but when I was using, it was always my feelings 1st.

Have I felt like a victim in any of my relationships? Describe. Yes in my first marriage because I got married at 16 years old and I wasn't ready. I was disappointed the entire marriage and was not happy. I felt like I was a victim because I felt forced into a marriage I didn't want to be in. And with Jay because I was the bread winner for about a year and I resented him for that and I felt like a victim because I was making all the money and being a new mother to Jala and I didn't think it was fair.

What have my relationships with my neighbors been like? Do I notice any patterns appearing that carried through no matter where I lived? Yes, got really close 3 times in the places I lived the longest and started using with all of them and spent everyday high with them.

How do I feel about the people with and for whom I have worked? How have my thinking, beliefs and behaviors caused problems for me at work? With pretty much all my jobs in the past I had problems with people telling me what to do. Whether they were my boss or not. While I did nails, I worked for myself, paying rent at 3 different salons which was great because I made my own schedule and came and went as I pleased, but as soon as the owner's got on me for anything at all, I wasn't okay with it and I would do my own thing anyways. When I worked at Iggy's I made myself high in the company pretty quick, opened and closed the restaurant and was over all the servers and I did this by manipulating the GM and the manager. I did a good job there, but as soon as they started catching on 2 years later that I was using, they started telling me what to do more, I no longer had my free reign so I quit on them with no word at all. Just didn't show up. I have regretted it since that day cause that was my favorite job I have ever had. I have a huge problem with authority when it comes to jobs.

How do I feel about people I went to school with? Did I feel less than or better than the other students? Did I believe I had to compete for attention from the instructor? Did I respect authority figures or rebel against them? I always felt better than people I went to school with when growing up, but I was very respectful to my instructors and students in school. I got along with pretty much everyone.

Have I ever joined any clubs or membership organizations? How did I feel about the other people in the club? Have I made friends in these organizations? Have I joined clubs with high expectations, only to quit in a short time? Yes, I have joined AA, NA and CA and go to at least 2 times every week. I have liked the majority of the people in every meeting. I have felt safe and not judged while I am there. I have felt pain, sadness and happiness for others in my meetings. I also have felt very motivated by other's in these meetings. I have made lots of friends but I keep them at a distance because I don't quite trust them or anyone but my family right now. My expectations have definitely been fulfilled by joining these meetings. I learn and take something very important from each person that shares. I enjoy going more and more each time I attend a meeting and leave feeling very good every time.

Have I ever been in a mental hospital, jail, prison, or otherwise been held against my will? What effect has that had on my personality? What were my interactions with the authorities like? Did I follow the rules? Did I ever break the rules and then resent the authorities when I was caught? Yes, it has made me a lot less judgmental about other people. It has softened me a lot. I look at people in a much different way, usually for the better. I don't judge many people at all anymore. My interactions with the authorities were always good. I always followed the rules and did what I was suppose to. Never got in trouble while I was in jail, got along with the guards really well.

Did early experiences with trust and intimacy hurt me and cause me to withdraw? Describe. No, I have only withdrawled the past ten years because of my own actions and drug use.

Have I ever let a relationship go when the potential existed to resolve conflicts and work through problems? No.

Did I become a different person depending on who I was around? Yes, especially when I was using because I didn't want anyone to see through me so I faked everything. And, I am a little bit of a people pleaser so depending on who I am around, I act different to avoid conflict or any problems. And, I like to be liked.

Have I discovered things about my personality that I did not like, and then found myself overcompensating for that behavior? Yes, I don't like that I can't be faithful to anyone, so I was rarely nice to my partners at times because I felt so bad for what I was doing to them. I don't like how dishonest I have been around people either and became overly nice after lying and putting them through hell.

What defects are most often at play in my relationships (dishonesty, selfishness, control, manipulations)? Dishonesty, selfishness, control, manipulation, non-caring. I play victim a lot. Untrustworthy, disrespectful, mean and stubborn.

How can I change my behavior so that I can begin having healthy relationships? Practice honesty, have boundaries and follow through with them. Listen and be compassionate. Also being a team player and completely trustworthy is what I am striving for.

Have I had any kind of relationship with a Higher Power? How has this changed in my lifetime? What kind of relationship do I have with my Higher Power now? Yes I did growing up, then when I got into using I didn't at all. I now have a great relationship with my Higher Power and it gets stronger every day.

Has my sexual behavior been based in selfishness? Yes, because I usually only did it to get something I wanted.

Have I confused sex with love? What were the results of acting on that confusion? I have never been a very sexual person and the men I was with I didn't want to be with, so it was awful for me to be sexual. But with Paul, the sex was so great that I think it blinded me because I had never experienced sex like that before or enjoyed it as much with anyone but him. I think it made me believe I was in love with him only because I actually enjoyed it with him.

How have I used sex to try to avoid loneliness or fill a spiritual void? I haven't, never used sex to avoid loneliness or a spiritual void.

In what ways did I compulsively seek or avoid sex? I completely avoided sex as much as I could by faking that I was asleep.

Have any of my sexual practices left me feeling ashamed and guilty? What were they? Why did I feel that way? Yes, many of them. During my drug use I slept with a lot of men for drugs and compromised my values and morals and it left me with so much guilt, even to this day.

Have any of my sexual practices hurt others or myself? Yes, because I slept with about 4 married men and their wives found out, which hurt them terribly, and over the years it also hurt me.

Am I comfortable with my sexuality? Yes.

What does a healthy relationship mean to me? Two people that are 100% honest with each other. Someone to have fun with, respect each other, no drugs or harmful people around that could cause dangerous situations. Two people that love each other, care for each other, work together, as a team with absolutely everything. Two people that can communicate with each other well and have the same morals and values.

Have I ever been abused? By whom? What feelings did I, or do I now have about it? Yes, emotionally and physically a couple times by Paul, my ex-boyfriend. I felt like I deserved it because I was lying, cheating and using him through our relationship. And the times he got physical with me, I started it, so I thought I deserved it. Now, I do know it absolutely was not right, not because I was doing what I was doing it was no excuse for him to physically or emotionally abuse me in any way, he could have just left me.

Has being abused affected my relationships with others? Yes, because I feel a lot lower than people. My self-worth has been destroyed and I feel like I can never find anyone again in my life that will love me for me. I don't feel good enough for anyone.

If I have felt victimized for much of life because of being abused in childhood, what steps can I take to be restored? I never got abused in my childhood, had a great childhood.

Have I ever abused anyone? Who and how? Yes, my kids, my family (emotionally), my husbands, got physical with both of them a couple times during fights and emotionally a lot. Past boyfriends, Ryan, physically during three fights and always emotionally abused him, with Paul too.

What was I thinking and feeling right before I caused the harm? Complete anger, selfishness and no care at all.

Did I blame my victim or make excuses for my behavior? I always made excuses by telling them they didn't know me at all or anything about me. And I always blamed drugs on my abusive personality. I blamed them for all of it because I was never wrong.

Do I trust my Higher Power to work in my life and provide me with what I need so I do not have to harm anyone again? Am I willing to live with the painful feelings until they are changed through working the steps? Yes, and I believe while I am clean and not using drugs that I won't harm anyone at all. The painful feelings that I have been feeling are fading away more and more each day and soon I believe I will be over them completely.

What qualities do I have that I like? Those others say they like? That work well for me? How have I shown concern for others and myself? Caring, respectful, loving, helpful, trustworthy, fun personality, friendly and loyal and a good mom. I have shown concern for others and myself by staying clean, doing the right things, helping others in need and being there for anyone that needs me, it helps me and them.

Which spiritual principles am I practicing in my life? How has doing so changed my life? I practice praying every day and night and sometimes more during the day, going to church on occasions and making the right choices daily. It has changed my life in many ways, I am happy, I receive blessings every single day and I see them very clearly and most important it has changed my relationships with my loved ones in ways I never thought possible.

How has my faith and trust in a Higher Power grown? It has grown more than I ever could have imagined and it's growing more and more each day.

Do I have a current relationship with my sponsor? How do I see that positive experience translating into other relationships? Yes, because I believe someday I can be that person that my sponsor is for me by helping someone else out. It also has humbled me a lot. Seeing what she does for me and others inspires me and makes me want to be a better person.

What goals have I accomplished? Do I have other goals I am taking action to reach? What are they and what action am I taking? A lot. I got my kids and family back in my life. I'm a great mother today, good daughter, sister and friend. I live alone, completely independent, have a job, staying clean each day. Doing well in treatment and drug court, and being an example to others. My only goal is to be happy and to stay clean and get healthier and healthier each day. I am doing treatment drug court and being a good mom to my kids, those are the actions I am taking.

What are my values? Which ones have I committed to living by and how? To be a good example to others, be a good mom, a good daughter and sister, stay clean and sober, have a strong bond with my Higher Power and be a hard and honest worker in everything that I do. I have committed to staying clean by working my treatment to the best of my ability, being an example to others by doing the right things and being an honest and caring person. Staying in touch with my Higher Power by praying and having faith and being a good mother by putting my kids and me first before anyone or anything else. Being honest with them and being with them as much as I possibly can.

How am I showing gratitude for my recovery? By staying clean each day, working my treatment and drug court honestly and the best that I can and by working hard every day at the most important things in my life, such as my kids, my family, myself and my job. By thanking my Higher Power each day.

LETTER FROM NAT TO MARY:

I HAVE NEVER HAD THE CHANCE TO TELL YOU EXACTLY HOW I FEEL. YOU HAVE BEEN SUCH A HUGE PART OF MY LIFE, BUT I AM REALIZING NOW THAT IT HAS NEVER BEEN FOR THE GOOD. I LOVE YOU BUT I HATE YOU AT THE SAME TIME. I MISS YOU SO MUCH AND HONESTLY I HAVE NO IDEA WHY. THE MAJORITY OF OUR TIME TOGETHER WE WERE EITHER GETTING OUR HOTEL ROOM DOORS KICKED DOWN BY THE SWAT TEAM, RUNNING FROM THE POLICE, STEALING FROM STORES OR PEOPLE, HANGING AROUND DANGEROUS PEOPLE, GUNS PUT TO OUR HEADS A NUMBER OF TIMES AND HUSTLING FOR MONEY. THAT WAS OUR LIFE FOR 10 YEARS. YOU PUT ME IN THE MOST DANGEROUS PLACES THAT I HAVE EVER BEEN. YOU INTRODUCED ME TO METHADONE, METH AND DAVID INTRODUCED ME TO HEROIN. YOU EVEN PUT A NEEDLE IN MY ARM. WHAT KIND OF FRIEND DOES THAT? YA, YOU WERE THERE FOR ME WHENEVER I WAS GOING THROUGH SURGERIES OR HOSPITALIZED AND YOU TOOK CARE OF ME AFTER EVERY TIME TOO, BUT I WAS THERE BECAUSE OF WHAT WE WERE DOING TOGETHER. YOU PUT ME IN THE WORST ENVIRONMENTS AND SITUATIONS THAT I HAVE EVER BEEN IN IN MY LIFE. I WILL NEVER FORGET THAT FIGHT WE HAD WHERE YOU PICKED ME UP AND THREW ME ACROSS THE ROOM. IF IT WASN'T FOR DAVID STOPPING YOU PHYSICALLY, I THINK YOU MIGHT HAVE KILLED ME, OR AT LEAST COME CLOSE! AND WE CAN'T FORGET THE DAY YOU TOOK MY BRAND NEW CAR THAT

I WORKED SO HARD FOR, WRECKED IT AND ASKED ME TO COVER FOR YOU TO THE COPS SO YOU WOULDN'T GO TO JAIL BECAUSE YOU HAD A WARRANT. I DID, AND LOOK WHAT IT COST ME. MY CAR WAS ALMOST TOTALED, MY BRAND NEW CAR THAT I LOVED AND PAID FOR EACH MONTH AND AT THE END OF THE YEAR I LOST MY LICENSE BECAUSE YOU DIDN'T PAY THE FINE AND I ENDED UP PAYING FOR IT. AND AFTER ALL THAT IT ENDED UP GETTING REPOED BECAUSE YOU SAID YOU MADE TWO PAYMENTS FOR ME CAUSE YOU OWED ME AND YOU REALLY DIDN'T. THE LIES, DECEIT AND BRUTAL REVENGE THAT YOU TOOK ON ME WAS UNFORGIVABLE. YOU WENT TO MY FAMILY, MY HUSBAND AND ANYONE ELSE THAT YOU KNEW WOULD HURT ME THE MOST AND TOLD THEM EVERYTHING AND LIES TOO. YOU WERE THE ONE PERSON THAT KNEW JUST HOW MUCH MY KIDS, MY HUSBAND AND MY FAMILY MEANT TO ME. I CAN'T EVEN SAY YOUR NAME AROUND MY FAMILY OR KIDS WITHOUT TERRIFYING THEM BECAUSE THEY KNOW HOW TOXIC AND DANGEROUS YOU ARE FOR ME. AND I PUT YOU AND OUR FRIENDSHIP BEFORE ANYONE FOR 10 SOLID YEARS. I STILL TO THIS DAY HAVE NO IDEA WHY. AFTER EVERYTHING YOU HAVE PUT ME THROUGH AND THE PAIN YOU HAVE CAUSED ME FOR SO MANY YEARS, I AM RACKING MY BRAIN TO TRY TO FIGURE OUT WHY I CARE ABOUT YOU AT ALL! BUT YOU KNOW I DO AND YOU KNOW HOW HARD IT IS FOR ME TO SAY GOOD-BYE TO YOU AND DAVID. THAT'S WHY I HAVEN'T YET. SO THAT IS WHY I AM WRITING YOU THIS LETTER. YOU KNOW I WILL ALWAYS LOVE YOU, I WILL NEVER FORGET EITHER ONE OF YOU, BUT I NEED TO LET GO. I RESENT YOU THE SAME TIME THAT I CARE ABOUT YOU AND LOVE YOU. BUT NOW THAT I AM DOING WELL, HAVE MY KIDS, MY FAMILY AND MYSELF WORTH BACK, I DON'T NEED YOU ANYMORE. I NEED TO LET GO AND SAY GOODBYE FOR GOOD. I CAN'T HAVE YOU IN MY LIFE ANYMORE. MY KIDS ARE MY NUMBER 1 PRIORITY AND MY SOBRIETY AND I KNOW YOU DON'T EVER LEAVE UNLESS I TELL YOU TO AND I STILL DON'T KNOW IF YOU WILL, BUT

I AM. I AM DONE MARY. I DON'T EVER WANT TO SEE YOU OR HEAR FROM YOU AGAIN. YOU WILL ALWAYS HAVE A PLACE IN MY HEART BUT I CAN'T HAVE YOU IN MY LIFE AGAIN. GOODBYE MARY AND DAVID. I HOPE SOMEDAY YOU CAN FINALLY GET CLEAN AND TURN YOUR LIFE AROUND. IT'S WORTH IT!
NATALIE

STEP 5: This step is missing.

STEP 6: "I become entirely ready to have God remove all of these defects of character."

List a defect I have and the ways I act on it: I am very OCD and I like it to a point but I definitely think it's a defect. I like everything to be as perfect as possible, my house has to be spotless and it's really hard to keep it up, but if I don't, then I'm really stressed out. I am also a people pleaser, let people walk all over me in certain situations. I like that I am a friendly person, but it's a defect that I can't be completely honest to some people because of the way they might react. And I like to be taken care of by a man.

Have I changed so far? Every day I am getting stronger, more aware and more willing to fix my defects. I think I am finding my defects more and more and trying to fix them so every day I am working on a better me.

Can I see the principles of 12 Step recovery as being the opposite of my character defects? Absolutely 100%! I have already done a complete turn around and I am a totally different person today. I think I still have some changing to do and some growing, but I do believe I have changed for the better and my recovery is what has made me the person that I am today.

What action can I take that shows that I am entirely ready? I believe in myself, when I never did before. I am humble, caring and a trustworthy person now. I am a fantastic mother today and a hard worker. Everything that I hold most precious to me in my life like my kids and my family I have back now. I don't have to act on being around dangerous people and possibly hurting myself or family because of the friends I was around. I am honest with people now and don't need to cover up lies anymore. I no longer depend on a man to take care of me.

What defects do I no longer have to act on? I have defects, but I believe with time and recovery that they can all be removed.

How may I practice the principle of self-acceptance, even when once again I act on a defect against my will? By reminding myself the person I am today vs. the person I was in the past. Being honest with myself and everybody else. Surrounding myself with only good influences, my kids and family. And trying to be a good example every day for my kids and people I may be around and also being aware of my defects daily and working on fixing them. I am a good mother today, a trustworthy person, a hard worker, and a much better person overall.

How may I demonstrate my commitment to persevere in my recovery today? Trusting in myself and my Higher Power to guide me through this process. And by talking to my counselor on help that I think I might need.

Which of my unwanted defects are still there? Dependent. I want a man to take care of me. People pleaser. I don't like tension or disappointment from anyone. Thrill seeker. I enjoy living on the edge. Selfish. I like things my way. OCD. I like everything as perfect as can be. Judgmental. I judge people before I get to know them. Materialistic. I like to always have nice things, or I feel ashamed and embarrassed. Impatient. I am not a patient person at all.

Am I entirely ready to let my Higher Power remove my character defects? Yes, I am very aware of them and have been working on them daily. Since I have been in recovery they have gotten a lot better and hopefully someday soon I can have them removed.

How do I feel when I act out on each defect? It makes me feel very guilty and brings my self-esteem down and it makes my relationships with others harder.

What feelings do my defects help me change or avoid? Guilt, sadness, anger, anxiety, low self-esteem (mostly guilt).

What would my life be like without each defect? Less guilt, anxiety, better self-esteem, being humble.

How does my surrender deepen this step? Working my steps honestly, staying only around the people that support my recovery and having a strong connection with my Higher Power.

Can I relax since I do not do it alone? Absolutely! Because it will get easier each day by working this quality with my recovery. And I believe it will keep me clean and more humble.

How may I let go through prayer and meditation and reflect on my Higher Power? Working everyday as hard as I can with my recovery and removing my defects. Being very spiritually connected with my Higher Power, praying and listening to Him.

How may I increase my trust in God? By being completely honest, praying before working this step and listening to His guidance.

How am I willing to act differently? My willingness to become a better person and be an example to my kids and people around me. I also like that I am a very caring person and want to help others. I also like the fact that I am a good mom and am in my kids life now more than I ever have been and I am clean!

STEP 7: Missing.

STEP 8: "I make a list of persons that I have harmed and become willing to make amends to them all."

My children. Adi I emotionally lost time and lied. Mas I emotionally lost time and lied. Jala I emotionally lost time and lied. (Was not there as a mother). Michelle, my oldest sister I lost time, lied to her over and over, emotionally harmed her, borrowed money from her for drugs and never paid it back. Angie, I lost time, lied, borrowed and never paid back and emotionally harmed her. Emily, my younger sister I lied, lost time, emotionally harmed her. Mom I lied, borrowed money and never paid back, emotionally harmed her. Took advantage of her and her help. Dad I lied, borrowed and never paid back, emotionally harmed him, took advantage of him and his help. Put them through hell. Jay I lied, cheated, emotionally abused him, left him, stole from him, completely bailed on him and our marriage. Took complete advantage of him. My ex-husband I lied, cheated, emotionally abused him, left him and our marriage, took advantage of him. Nieces and nephews I lied and emotionally harmed all of them. Paul I lied, cheated, emotionally abused, abandoned. Ryan

I lied, stole, used and emotionally abused him. Grandparents I lied and emotionally harmed them. Friends I lied, used and treated badly.

STEP 9, 10, 11: Missing.

STEP 12: "Having had a spiritual awakening as a result of these steps, we tried to carry this message to addicts, and to practice these principles in all our affairs."

What is my overall experience as a result of working the steps? I have become a humble person, a better mother than I ever thought I could be, a trustworthy person, more knowledge about myself and the person I want to be. I now have a strong connection with my Higher Power which I never thought could happen. I am a very spiritual person and a completely different person! The kind of person people want to be around and kids look up to.

What has my spiritual awakening been like? Describe. My spiritual awakening has been shocking to me. I have never been a very spiritual person and now I am and I love it. I have so much faith that my Higher Power is working in my life daily and guides me each day. I feel protected and peace now more than ever.

What lasting changes have resulted from my spiritual awakening? My connection with my Higher Power, my faith in Him and a result of this is I am a completely different person, a much better person.

What spiritual principles have those contributed to my spiritual awakening? I am an honest, caring and humble person now. Something I haven't been for a very long time and actually have never been till now.

What does the phrase "spiritual awakening" mean to me? Finally being aware of my spirituality, feeling my Higher Power with me and having complete faith in Him, listening to Him and following His guidance.

What are the different ways in which I have experienced the message? Through watching others and hearing different people in treatment and meetings. But the message was mainly carried to me within myself and my own experiences. My life has changed 100% and I have received blessings that I never would have dreamed of having in my life and it has changed me and I still receive messages daily because of this.

What kind of service work am I doing to carry the message? Approaching new comers at meetings that I attend and welcoming them and letting them know I am there if they ever needed anything and sharing my story and experiences with as many people in need that I can.

What are some of the ways of carrying the message? In which ones do I personally participate? Sharing at meetings, reaching out to others in need. Both.

What is my personal style of sponsorship? Sharing my story and being there to help for someone that needs me.

What is the difference between attraction and promotion? We share our message freely instead of trying to force another person to receive the message.

What does it do for me to carry the message? It helps my own recovery get stronger each time I do and makes me feel better about trying to help someone else. It fulfills me when I carry the message to others and makes it easier to approach each time and try to help.

What keeps me coming back and trusting the AA/NA/or CA 12 step program? Because I learn something that I need each time I go to a meeting, when I leave I always feel a sense of freedom and peace and it makes me feel comfortable being around people that know where I am coming from and don't judge.

What is selfless service? How do I practice it? Putting other people's needs before my own. Being a friend to another addict in need and talking to them when they need someone to talk to and just simply helping anyone with whatever I can when they need it. I am also helping my sister with a special needs pageant twice a year.

Why was an AA/NA/ or CA member able to reach me in a way that no one else ever had? Describe the experience. Because she welcomed me with open arms, never judged and was there for me when she didn't even really know me. Became a good friend that made me feel so welcome every time I walked in the room. And I heard her story and it was similar to mine and she is now an amazing person, someone I look up to.

What is the therapeutic value of one addicted/dependent person helping another? Because we are so similar and been through the same things. We help each other by being there for each other sharing our experiences in life and learning from one another.

Why do I find it difficult to practice principles? When dealing with miserable/mean people, like my old boss. When I am depressed and angry.

Which spiritual principles do I have a particularly hard time practicing? Opening up spiritually in meetings. I keep them to myself.

How am I practicing the principle of unconditional love with the addicted/dependent persons I am trying to help? I am not around any dependent/addicted person other than at meetings. And when I am there I am very friendly, very welcoming to them and sometimes offer my number to them if they need anything or just someone to talk to.

What is my attitude about sponsorship? I would love to someday sponsor someone and I am very willing to share my story.

What is my attitude about this service? I would help absolutely anyone in need unless it compromised my recovery somehow.

Am I committed to my recovery? What am I doing to maintain it? Yes, staying around healthy people, going to meetings, praying and staying very connected to my higher power.

How will I express my gratitude? Staying clean each day for myself and my kids, help in any way that I can people who are in need and showing my compassion and humility to others.

THOUGHTS ABOUT RYAN AND WHY THE BREAKUP IS STRESSFUL FOR ME. (REASONS FOR BREAKUP): It stresses me out when I think about ending it with Ryan because I have tried a couple times and he tried to commit suicide. He tells me if I leave him, then he has nothing to live for, and it scares me he will do something to himself. I am also afraid of losing my security and I am comfortable, but not happy. I have plenty of reasons for the breakup: I am not in love with him, I don't find him attractive in any way, so when he tries to hold my hand or come near me, I cringe, he bothers me really bad and embarrasses me in public. I feel bad for saying when I don't want to be with him, but I am scared to leave.

This next section is meant for Nat to list her fears and then list a different way of thinking of each fear in a positive way.

10 THINGS THAT MAKE ME ANXIOUS AND CHANGING MY THOUGHT PROCESS:

Testing at C&D, I hate peeing in front of someone. Sometimes I can't pee, or if I can't pee, I always have a couple more chances to do it.

Being late for treatment, it will ruin my entire day. I might get an occurrence if I'm late or I might not, and by lunch, I will forget about the whole thing.

Going to my self-help meetings at night, don't know who I am going to see there, there might be someone there that I used to use with and it might trigger me, or I will take something from the meeting that will really help my recovery and only leave with that in mind.

Being house manager for the week, too much needs to be done and it all falls on me, if I don't do things right, I might get an occurrence, but I'm doing my best and I have the girls to support me and help me, it gives me a chance to help the new people, show them around, and it will make me more comfortable in the end.

Completing Davis County Drug Court, it's for 15 months and I'm scared of not completing it. If I don't, I have a chance to go to prison but I am learning every day being in Drug Court, especially because of day treatment, and I will learn the tools more and more each day to stay clean and strong so I can make it and graduate from drug court. (*Nat did complete drug court.*)

Giving feedback to peers in treatment, I might offend them and they will take it wrong and hold it against me, they might dislike me after that and we might have problems from then on out, or they will take it the right way, the way I was presenting it for their benefit, and they will realize that, and it might help her and we could become closer because of it.

Breaking up with Ryan, how can I support myself, he will do something to himself or he might not, it's not my problem if he does, I will be much happier.

Being independent (all on my own), how am I going to financially do it, trying to do it can get me overwhelmed, could cause a relapse, or I will gain better self-esteem and confidence.

Not having enough money for drug court or testing, I will miss a test, possibly get kicked out of drug court, or I could call Shirley if I have an issue with money and we could possibly figure something out.

Getting final answer on going to Idaho this week, I need to be there for my little sister, can't miss it, fear that not being there again for my little sister when she really needs me will have a huge impact in her life or a negative impact might set us backwards again, whether I am there or not she is gonna know I really wanted to be, and I know whatever decision Shirley and WRC staff makes, it's the best for me and it will be better for me in the long run.

RELAPSE PREVENTION PLAN:

My friend called me, someone I used to use with, and he wanted to see me.

Mary called me to see how I was doing, and she told me she missed me and wanted to see me.

Picked up Ryan from work and drove down State Street on the way home by one of my old dealers' houses.

Heard a song while driving that brought up past using memories.

Mary showed up at my door in the middle of the night.

Knowing that Mary and David live right down the street from me.

Driving past Iggy's in Centerville brings up past using memories.

Having using nightmares and waking up remembering the nightmare very clearly.

Call someone for distraction, my mom, my sister Michelle. Call someone to talk about urges or desires, sponsor, counselor, tracker, peers at WRC.

THOUGHT TRIGGERS:

1. I feel overwhelmed and anxious when I think about breaking up with Ryan, but it will be nice to finally be alone and find myself.
2. When Bath Salts get brought up in treatment, like working on my assignments or hearing from peers on their assignments, but I can focus more on treatment and recovery rather than the past.
3. My weight, I have gained at least 40 pounds, but I'm getting healthier.
4. R&R class is too long and too hard, but I'm learning more about myself and how to stay clean and it's helping my recovery to dig deep. I can do hard things.
5. When I get bored and start thinking about the past, I need to keep busy so my head doesn't take over (especially negatively).
6. When I think about Mary and David and how I miss them, but I would relapse if I saw them and go right back downhill.
7. Listening to songs when I was using, and it brings back those memories, but I can turn the song off—turn the station.
8. When I get angry at somebody (got an occurrence for I don't believe the right reasons), I can let it go, they know what's best, and learn from it.
9. Looking at myself in the mirror, I'm healthy and alive and am okay with it.
10. Having Ryan's son living with us now, he needs us, maybe he can help us with some things like the house and Sydka.
11. Thinking about doing drug court for 15 months, that's way too long, but the longer I do this, the more knowledge I will have and it will help my recovery.

12. Getting kicked out of WRC 'cause now I have 2 occurrences, so I don't get a third one and learn from the two that I got.
13. That I am not in IOP *(Intensive Out-Patient)* yet (I get anxious and angry), but everyday I'm learning more and it helps my recovery.
14. Trying to sleep at night and staying asleep, but I can watch TV to get my mind off things and focus on something else while relaxing (get in the bath right before bed).
15. When I am in horrible pain and over the counter pain killers do nothing, I can self soothe, bath tub, hot pad, massage.

BRIEF THOUGHT OR MANTRA:

1. I am better than that
2. Don't go there, Nat
3. It's not worth it
4. NO!
5. Adi, Mas, Jala!

EMOTIONAL TRIGGERS:	EMOTIONAL STRATEGIES:
1. When I am lonely	Interact with healthy people
2. Boredom	Exercise or read
3. Depression	Self talk or talk to Sponsor
4. Financial Problems (stressed)	Meditation
5. Being independent	Balanced sleep, take a nap
6. Missing my old friends	Go to a meeting, make new ones
7. Music	Change the music, pray

ADDITIONAL COPING STRATEGIES:

1. Trampoline at Mom's house, looking at stars with kids.
2. Being in my mom's living room with my kids in front of fire.
3. Laying on the beach with the one I love in the sun.

LETTING GO OF THE NEED FOR CERTAINTY:

Get Deliberate about my little sister that everything will work out for her. Putting my plans into motion about recovery so I can go be with her and help her. Staying clean. Praying for her and me daily.

Get Inspired: Focusing on my recovery so I can get through treatment so I can go be with her and help her. Checking in with her often, calling her.

Get Going: Getting my release prevention plan done. Graduate from treatment. Moving forward with drug court.

• • •

CHAPTER 12

2015–2016

IN 2015, NAT TURNED *thirty-six, Adi nineteen, Mas sixteen, and Jala nine.*

Nat finished drug court on December 22, 2015. She appeared to be clean while she was attending, but not long after, she relapsed. She was living in her own apartment our parents helped her get.

In 2016, Nat turned thirty-seven, Adi twenty, Mas seventeen, and Jala ten.

She worked at the University of Utah in a cafe where she was hired by one of her old managers from Iggy's. Her boss at the U held her job for her while she went to treatment in Idaho.

We held an intervention at my mom and dad's house in February 2016, Nat went to the University of Utah Detox Center to detox. After a few days, she was taken by a driver to a treatment center in Idaho Falls. She only lasted a month. She reached out to Ang and Em to come and get her because everyone in the house she was in was using. She used the entire time she was there. Ang and Em dropped her off to Ryan in Utah and he had heroin waiting for her.

INTERVENTION LETTER FROM MAS TO NAT:

DEAR NATALIE,
I DON'T KNOW WHAT TO SAY. I'M SO DISAPPOINTED. THAT'S BASICALLY IT. YOU HEAR MY FRIEND DIED AND NOW YOU BASICALLY KILL YOURSELF. I'M NOT GONNA CALL YOU MOM UNTIL YOU APOLOGIZE, BUT HERE IS THE CATCH, I DON'T WANT TO SEE YOU, HEAR FROM YOU OR ANYTHING FOR AT LEAST HALF A YEAR TO 1 YEAR. THAT'S ONLY IF YOU GO TO IDAHO WITH THE GUY TONIGHT AND STAY CLEAN. IF YOU DON'T GO THEN I NEVER WANT YOU AROUND, BROUGHT UP, I DON'T WANT TO SEE YOU, HEAR FROM YOU EVER. I AM SO MAD BECAUSE YOU LIED TO ME. AGAIN. I CAN'T TRUST YOU ANYMORE. I WOULD SAY I'M SORRY BUT I DON'T WANT TO BECAUSE I DON'T NEED TO. YOU SHOW TO ME YOU LOVE ME AND I WILL SHOW TO YOU HOW MUCH YOU MEAN TO ME. NATALIE JUST BE SMART IF YOU EVER WANT TO SEE ME AGAIN OR TALK TO ME THEN LEAVE AND COME BACK CLEAN (AGAIN) THEN I WILL.
GO, AND I'LL SEE YOU SOON.
SINCERELY,
MASON ALLEN UZELAC

NAT'S AUTOBIOGRAPHY FROM RENAISSANCE RANCH TREATMENT FACILITY IN IDAHO:

Describe the primary relationships in your life, how do you feel about each member of your family? Why do you feel that way? The 3 most important people in my life are my kids. We are all super close and I am usually never without them. My mom and dad are the best people I know, very supportive of me and always have been. And my 3 sisters are my best friends, when I wasn't using we were all together all the time with our kids. And Jay my ex *(still married)* is always there for me and always has been, we are best friends.

Describe a meaningful event or interaction that you remember with each of your family members. When I got pregnant at 16 years old all 3 of my sisters were there with me through my entire pregnancy and after. Adi, my oldest daughter, moved in with me about a year ago and I loved being with her every day. My 17 year old son Mason never left my side as a baby and toddler, he's always had to be with his mom. A couple weeks ago I took Jala, my 10 year old with her friend to Lava Hot Springs for a couple days and went 4 wheeling. Jala always wants to be with me. Mom and dad were the best parents I could ever have asked for!

Describe the way you feel being part of your family. I am very close with each person in my family, even when I was using I talked to my sisters almost every day and I am the favorite aunt to both my nieces. I have never felt like an outsider even when my family needed space while I was using. They were always trying to get me help.

Write about the happiest moment you remember in your life and the saddest moment of your life. The happiest moments in my life were the birth of each of my children. The saddest moment was when I got them taken away because of my drug use.

Describe events from your school experiences. When I was in High School I got to go to California and compete with the varsity cheerleading squad as a sophomore. They only picked me from the sophomore squad and I was the only one that got to be with varsity my entire sophomore year. That was the funnest part of my High School life.

Share how you feel about God, religion, spirituality and the dark power and why you feel this way. I am LDS, grew up LDS, believe in mostly everything in the Mormon religion, I am just not active. I pray every night and am a very spiritual person. I feel like God has always been there for me even when I was at my worst, I just didn't realize it at the time.

Describe three things you like about yourself or you are proud of, and three things you want to change about yourself. I am very kind to others and have a big heart for others, I am a very sociable person and when I am not using, I am a really good mother. I am not a patient person, I am a procrastinator, I am a drug addict.

Describe your best friend. Somebody that is always there for me, never judges me and supports me no matter what. Someone I can completely trust and rely on. Someone that loves me unconditionally.

What do you want in the future? What are two of your goals? Do you see yourself as happy or sad? Why? What are your dreams and visions of the future? To stay clean and close to my family and kids. I see myself as a happy person, and it takes a lot to really make me mad. To stay clean, be a good mom, and maybe someday find someone to spend my life with.

Why are you here? My family and kids did an intervention on me and my main reason for coming and motivation was my kids.

How are you feeling about your treatment right now? Wishy washy, want to go home to my kids. Overwhelmed, there is so much to do! Grateful that I decided to take the first step and move out here.

What do you think could be different about you or your life after treatment? I believe this is the last chance I have and if I don't stay clean and finish this program I will lose my kids and family or even my life. I have no more chances at this.

Are you more interested in working the treatment program for yourself or someone else? Right now my motivation was my kids, but I do completely believe that if I don't have a change of heart and do this for myself, I won't get through it successfully.

What do you want to get out of treatment? How to stay clean, learn more about myself and learn tools to keep me healthy and with healthy relationships.

Provide three examples of "insane" things you did while you were using. Selling and distributing drugs. Stealing from friends. Had my kids around drug addicts, including myself.

How do you behave when you are being sneaky or when you are scamming? When I worked at Iggy's, I kept 2 syringes in my apron with me of Heroin and Meth so that I could use on my break. I took a syringe with me in my purse everyday to work at the U and used in the bathroom. I kept my drugs under my dresser at home so my daughter wouldn't find it and used every chance that she was gone or went into the bathroom when she was home.

What kind of excuses do you use when you are being sneaky? I never admitted to my drug use until this last intervention. I always denied my drug use to everyone. I was a very functional addict, worked and took care of my kids the best I could for years and years while I used.

What does it mean to "work a recovery program"? To be completely honest and open to feedback and advice. Staying away from unhealthy people and being motivated to stay clean for myself and not somebody else.

What does honesty mean to you? Being completely trustworthy.

What would you accomplish by being honest? It helps people support me and help me in my recovery the best they can, so I can stay clean.

How does lying affect your treatment? It will put me in the exact place I have always been, back using. Hard to get help from others.

What do you need to do to be "working a recovery program"? Being 100% honest. Being open to healthy feedback from peers. Have a healthy support system. Staying away from people I used with (no contact).

Are there parts of your story that are more difficult to own than others? Of course, because there are more hard times in my life than other times. Some are a lot more traumatizing than other times.

What would reclaiming those orphaned stories mean for you? Learning experiences for me, more knowledge about life whether they were good or bad.

What is the fable you were told? "Black or white" I either go to church and live by my parent's and Utah's morals, or I was a complete rebel.

What does it feel like when your life does not match the story you were told you should have? I feel like an absolute disappointment, failure, not worthy for anyone, a rebel, horrible bad person.

Who are you afraid of disappointing? My loved ones and myself.

Who will hold space for your full story? My loved ones, people that genuinely care about me.

What does it look like for you when you hustle for worthiness on the outside of your story? I try way too hard, get overwhelmed and then I fail. Too fake.

How has who you are become secondary? I have failed myself horribly because I never felt important enough to put my true beliefs and self-esteem first. I gave up and didn't care.

What does your hustle look like? Pleasing, always being right, being fake, perfectionism, needing to be in the spotlight, was not humble in any way shape or form.

What parts of your story first comes to mind when you think about the tension of wanting to feel worthy and being afraid to feel worthy? Embarrassed of my actions and trying so hard for the respect and attention of my sisters, mom and dad and other loved ones, especially my kids.

Thinking about your goals and dreams, do you know "how" to achieve them? Yes, I need to stay sober and learn really what I need to in treatment to stay sober without relapses.

What's getting in the way? Nothing as of today but it was usually my guilt and the people I was around.

What persons in your life live wholeheartedly? My daughter Adi, my son Mason, my youngest daughter Jala. They all three are the most compassionate, genuine people in my life or that I know. (Very humble too).

What struggles are you most likely to numb? The temporary loss of my kids, the loss of the man I love, the loss of my family.

What are you grateful for? My children, my life, my loved ones, my sobriety, my knowledge today, my treatment and myself.

NAT'S JOURNAL FROM RENAISSANCE RANCH IDAHO TREATMENT CENTER:

I left after a month because I just wasn't ready and I was just getting high up there too, wasn't a good place for me at all!

This is an article she copied in her journal. It was part of an assignment in the treatment center. These are not her words:

Written by Dr. Michael Bihari
Addiction and Free Choice…

I continue to hear from people in the community, many of them well educated as well as reading commentary and survey results, which indicate that Drug/Addiction is a choice and addicts should have the same respect or benefits enjoyed by people who "choose" not to use. Recently, a close friend shared with me that the drug problem was the "fault" of the court system, which is too lenient on addicts. Fortunately, he listened to the facts and has a better understanding of the complexity of managing drug addiction and greater appreciation for the reality that addiction is a "DISEASE".

Dr. Nora Volkow, director of the National Institution on Drug Abuse (NIDA) which supports most of the world's research on the health aspects of drug abuse and addiction, wrote the following in her blog on the NIDA website, which was published earlier this year in 2016.

The recent death of Phillip Seymour Hoffman as a result of Drug Addiction had provoked many thoughtful, sympathetic responses in the media from people in recovery who understand how hard it is to wrestle with addiction, as well as from scientifically informed journalists who understand that addiction is a disease, but it has also prompted others to express the age-old motion that drug use is a choice and that those who die as a consequence of their drug use are just reaping the consequences of their freely chosen action. It is unfortunate that the view persists in our society, despite the decades of scientific research soundly disproving it. Choices do not happen without a brain—it is the mechanism of choice. The quality of a person's choices depends on the health of that mechanism. However, as much as we may wish that a person's choices were free in all instances. It is simply a fact that an addicted person's failure's in the realm of choice are a product of a brain that has become greatly compromised—it is readily apparent when we scan their brains, even if taking a drug for the first time it is a "free choice". The progression of brain changes that occur after that involves the weakening of the circuits in the prefrontal cortex and elsewhere that are necessary for exerting self-control and resisting the temptations of drug use. Once addiction takes hold, there is greatly diminished capacity, no one's own, to stop using. This is why the psychiatry recognizes addiction as a disease of the brain, and why professional intervention is needed to treat it in most instances. Moreover, even the "freely" willed first choice to take a drug cannot be the basis for judgment and stigma against people suffering from addictions. Matters of choice and lifestyle, what you eat, how active you are, where you live—may contribute to the risk for, or even directly cause a wide range of medical conditions, including chronic diseases, type 2 diabetes and several cancers. We do not withhold or impede treatment of people suffering from these conditions. Even if their health may have turned out differently had they made different choices at various points in their lives. There is no way of precisely predicting which freely chosen adolescent drink, or cigarette, or experimentation with an illegal substance, opened the door to a later loss of free choice capacity in a person who has become addicted. But once addiction is established, the sufferer from this disease cannot will themselves to be healthy and avoid drugs any more than a person with heart disease can will their heart back to perfect functioning, or a person with diabetes can will their bodies insulin response to return to normal. Thus, those that say "it is their own choice" after a person dies of an overdose, fail to grasp that an addicted person's brain has a disrupted choice mechanism. And as revealed by Hoffman's tragic, ultimately fatal relapse into drug taking the neurological disruptions in the brain of an addicted person can persist even after decades of sobriety. Speaking of "free choices" is simply not useful when trying to understand an individual's addiction or its consequences as addiction is precisely a disease that disrupts the neuronal circuits that enable us to exert free choice. Opiate addiction is a treatable brain disorder, it is absolutely NOT a character flaw or a moral problem, it is a disease that can be treated and managed over time.

She was out of the Idaho Treatment Facility in March, 2016.

In December of 2016, Nat's good friend Michael offered to pay for her to complete his outpatient drug program called Renaissance Ranch in Utah. She ended up going.

• • •

CHAPTER 13

2017

IN 2017, NAT TURNED *thirty-eight, Adi twenty-one, Mas eighteen, and Jala eleven.*

This was the year that things really went downhill and never came back. She realized her addiction had complete control of her life and that her body was starting to deteriorate rapidly.

TUESDAY, JANUARY 3, 2017, NAT'S JOURNAL:

JUST STARTED MY FOURTH WEEK IN RENAISSANCE RANCH OUTPATIENT PROGRAM WITH THE HELP OF MY GOOD FRIEND MICHAEL. COULDN'T HAVE DONE IT WITHOUT HIM. I HAD NO MONEY AND COULDN'T GET ANY HELP FROM FAMILY ANYMORE AFTER COMING HOME FROM IDAHO FALLS (TREATMENT). I WAS ABSOLUTELY MISERABLE UP THERE AND AM VERY COMFORTABLE IN THIS NEW TREATMENT CENTER. I FEEL VERY LUCKY AND LOVE THIS PROGRAM. IT'S LIKE NO OTHER TREATMENT I HAVE EVER BEEN TO. I LOVE THE STAFF AND AM SO GRATEFUL I GET TO DO THIS. I AM JUST PRAYING THAT THIS TIME IT WILL WORK FOR ME. I AM STILL STRUGGLING EVERY DAY AND HAVE RELAPSED TWICE, RIGHT BEFORE CHRISTMAS AND THEN AGAIN

Nat at work at the U of U Café

A DAY BEFORE NEW YEAR'S EVE. I HAVE THREE DAYS CLEAN TODAY. I AM STILL REALLY RESTLESS AND CAN'T SLEEP AT NIGHT AT ALL. I JUST GOT HOME ABOUT THREE HOURS AGO AND AM HAVING A REALLY HARD TIME, SO I TOOK A 1/2 OF A SUBOXONE, NOT SUPPOSED TO BE TAKING ANYTHING AT ALL, BUT I AM REALLY STRUGGLING. I JUST NEED TO REMEMBER TO TAKE IT A DAY AT A TIME, SO I DON'T GET OVERWHELMED. I START MY JOB AGAIN AT THE U ON MONDAY AND I'M EXCITED BUT NO ENERGY AT ALL. I AM HOPING THINGS GET BETTER REALLY SOON.

WEDNESDAY, JANUARY 4, 2017:

TODAY HAS NOT BEEN A VERY GOOD DAY. I STILL CANNOT SLEEP AT ALL AT NIGHT, SO I WAS TOSSING AND TURNING ALL NIGHT LONG. AT NIGHT IS MY BIGGEST TRIGGER, 'CAUSE I CAN'T SLEEP. I JUST DON'T SEE MYSELF NOT USING HEROIN EVER AGAIN. I WISH I WAS AT THAT POINT, BUT I'M NOT. I WANT SOME SO BAD! MICHAEL CHECKED UP ON ME THIS MORNING AND THAT MAKES ME FEEL REALLY GOOD, BUT I AM REALLY STRUGGLING BAD RIGHT NOW. WENT TO TREATMENT AND THAT WAS OKAY BUT STARTED GETTING A HEADACHE HALFWAY THROUGH GROUP, SO I GOT REALLY IRRITATED 'CAUSE I WAS IN PAIN. DROVE HOME IN A COMPLETE SNOWSTORM AND DIDN'T MAKE IT HOME UNTIL 9 P.M. NOW, I AM LITERALLY IN SO MUCH PAIN FROM MY HEADACHE AND ALL I CAN THINK ABOUT IS USING. I AM NOT GOING TO, THOUGH. I AM IN BED AND

HOPING I CAN FINALLY SLEEP TONIGHT. I HOPE AND PRAY THAT THESE CRAVINGS SUBSIDE A BIT SOON 'CAUSE IF THEY DON'T, I WILL USE AGAIN!

It is apparent how she struggled from minute to minute of every day to fight this demon. I can't imagine the inner turmoil she went through every day.

Five days later...

MONDAY, JANUARY 9, 2017:

I HAD A HORRIBLE WEEKEND THIS PAST WEEKEND. I WAS SO SUPER RESTLESS AND LOTS OF ANXIETY AND WANTED TO USE SUPER BAD, BUT I DIDN'T. INSTEAD, I CALLED JOHNATHAN AND HE TALKED ME THROUGH IT, HE IS AMAZING. I DID TAKE A SUBOXONE, THOUGH, BECAUSE I WAS GOING CRAZY, BUT AT LEAST I DIDN'T GO GET ANY HEROIN. TODAY, I STARTED WORK AGAIN AT THE U AND IT WAS OKAY. REALLY SLOW, BUT I AM GLAD TO HAVE MY JOB BACK. JASON TOLD ME THIS IS MY LAST CHANCE WITH HIM, AND I TOTALLY UNDERSTAND. I PRAY I DON'T FUCK IT UP, 'CAUSE I USUALLY DO. JUST GOT HOME FROM TREATMENT AND I REALLY DO LOVE IT THERE. IT'S HARD GOING EVERY DAY, ESPECIALLY AFTER WORKING ALL DAY, BUT WHEN I GET THERE, I FEEL SO MUCH BETTER. I STILL HAVE A LONG WAYS TO GO WITH TREATMENT AND RECOVERY. I JUST PRAY THAT I GET IT THIS TIME. I DON'T WANT TO DIE, AND I DO *NOT* WANT TO LOSE MY KIDS AGAIN!

Six days later...

JANUARY 15, 2017:

IT'S SATURDAY NIGHT AND I FUCKED UP AGAIN! I HAD 14 DAYS CLEAN AND I JUST MESSED UP. I HAVE HAD ANXIETY SO SUPER BAD LATELY AND I JUST WANTED ONE GOOD NIGHT

TO SLEEP. I MADE A HORRIBLE DECISION TONIGHT AND GOT ME A 20 *(mg)* OF HEROIN. I USED IT TWICE, THEN THREW THE REST DOWN THE TOILET. I CAN'T EVEN PUT INTO WORDS THE GUILT AND SHAME I FEEL RIGHT NOW, AND THAT HAPPENS EVERY TIME I USE. WHY DO I DO THIS TO MYSELF? FOR ONLY THE RELIEF AND PLEASURE FOR MAYBE A COUPLE HOURS, THEN I LITERALLY PUT MYSELF THROUGH HELL AFTERWARDS! I'M REALLY NERVOUS ABOUT GOING TO GROUP ON MONDAY AND LETTING EVERYONE THERE KNOW I RELAPSED AGAIN, THIS IS THE THIRD TIME SINCE I HAVE BEEN THERE. I PRAY TO GOD THAT THEY WILL STILL WORK WITH ME BECAUSE I ABSOLUTELY *LOVE* THIS GROUP AND STAFF, I WILL NOT GO ANYWHERE ELSE, THAT'S WHY I NEED TO FIGURE THIS SHIT OUT AND CHANGE EVERYTHING IN MY LIFE. I KNOW THIS IS MY LAST CHANCE, SO WHY THE HELL DO I KEEP DOING WHAT I'M DOING? FOR ONE NIGHT OF RELIEF OR PLEASURE?! IT'S SO NOT WORTH IT! I KNOW I CAN DO THIS, I PRAY TO GOD THAT I WILL GET THIS, THIS TIME!!

MONDAY, JANUARY 16, 2017:

TOMORROW IS MY BABY GIRL'S BIRTHDAY! SHE WILL BE 11. SHE IS THE SWEETEST LITTLE GIRL IN THE WORLD, AND SHE LOVES ME SO MUCH. SHE ALWAYS WANTS TO BE WITH ME AND TELLS ME ALL THE TIME THAT NO MATTER WHAT I DO AND EVEN THOUGH I HAVE MADE MISTAKES, SHE WILL ALWAYS LOVE ME. I LOVE THAT LITTLE GIRL! WELL, I WENT TO TREATMENT TONIGHT THINKING I WAS GOING TO BE KICKED OUT 'CAUSE I HAVE RELAPSED 3 TIMES ALREADY AND I HAVE ONLY BEEN THERE FOR A MONTH. THEY DIDN'T AND I AM SO GRATEFUL! THEY ARE GIVING ME ANOTHER CHANCE, BUT IF I USE AGAIN, THEY RECOMMEND INPATIENT *(which means she would live in a treatment facility rather than just go to meetings every day).* I CAN'T DO THAT, SO I BETTER GET MY SHIT TOGETHER AND THIS RECOVERY THING. IT'S SO DAMN HARD, THOUGH! I HAVE SO MUCH ANXIETY ALL THE DAMN TIME. I AM GOING TO SEE THE DOCTOR NEXT WEDNESDAY AND GETTING THE VIVITROL SHOT. THAT WILL HELP ME A TON, BUT IT'S VERY EXPENSIVE. BUT I NEED TO DO WHATEVER IT TAKES TO KICK THIS LIFE THREATENING DISEASE IN THE BUTT! I PRAY TO GOD I CAN DO THIS AND I CAN FINALLY BREAK FREE FROM THESE DEMONS IN MY HEAD THAT KEEP MAKING ME GO BACK TO HEROIN! IT'S THE DEVIL!!

The Vivitrol shot is a nonaddictive, once-monthly treatment proven to prevent relapse in opioid-dependent patients when used with counseling following detoxification. The shot was paid for by a grant. I remember her calling me after she received this shot and she was really depressed. I went to Salt Lake to see her, and she was in the apartment where she lived with Ryan. We sat on her couch, and it was obvious she was so depressed and depleted of energy. She told me one of the side effects of the shot was depression, which she already had. She had to stick it out for a month, because that was when it would wear off. At the time, I believed her depression was worse than normal because of the Vivitrol shot. But more than the shot, it was a side effect of using drugs.

1-25-2017: Dr. Note–123 lbs. IV Heroin dependency, panic attack, anxiety, insomnia. At Renaissance Ranch Intensive Out-Patient in Farmington. Detoxed at U. Clean for 8 days off Heroin. Used Tylenol with Codeine. Here for Vivitrol Injection. Renaissance Ranch referred her to get Vivitrol injection. She's clean and wants injection. Gave her 380 mg injection today. Next injection 4 weeks. Seroquel and Trazadone don't work—side effects. Prescribed Amitriptyline for sleep, Propranolol for panic attacks and Buspirone for anxiety.

A couple of weeks later...

MONDAY, JANUARY 30, 2017, NAT'S JOURNAL:

JUST FOUND THIS BOOK LAST NIGHT AND I USED IT WHEN I WAS REALLY HEAVY IN MY ADDICTION. STILL ACTIVE IN MY HORRIBLE ADDICTION BUT NOT AS BAD AS I WAS BACK THEN. I'M ACTUALLY IN A TREATMENT (OUTPATIENT) PROGRAM RIGHT NOW, BUT I HAVE RELAPSED 4 TIMES NOW AND DON'T KNOW HOW MUCH LONGER I WILL BE IN THERE. I WENT TO THE DR. WEDNESDAY AND TODAY IS MONDAY AND I GOT THE VIVITROL SHOT. I ABSOLUTELY *HATE* IT! IT HAS MADE ME SO SUPER DEPRESSED THAT I DON'T CARE ABOUT A FUCKING THING! WENT AND SMOKED SOME METH YESTERDAY AND I HAVEN'T DONE THAT FOR MONTHS AND MONTHS! THAT'S ABOUT THE ONLY THING I CAN USE 'CAUSE THE SHOT BLOCKS ALL OPIOIDS, WHICH IS GOOD, BUT I FEEL REALLY, REALLY TRAPPED RIGHT NOW! I'M AT WORK RIGHT NOW AND I DON'T CARE ABOUT A FUCKING THING! I FEEL WORTHLESS AND UGLY, UGLIER THAN EVER. I HAVE TO BREAK THIS CYCLE! I JUST DON'T KNOW HOW, IT'S NOT A CHOICE ANYMORE! THIS ADDICTION HAS ME! IT'S NOT LETTING GO! GOD, PLEASE HELP ME OR I AM GOING TO DIE!

IT'S ABOUT 1:00 A.M. MONDAY MORNING AND I AM A COMPLETE IDIOT! SO, I GOT THE VIVITROL SHOT ON WEDNESDAY AND THE DR. GAVE ME SOME MEDS THAT I ABSOLUTELY *HATE!* I GOT SO STINKIN' DEPRESSED AND FELT LIKE I WAS FLOATING AND DIDN'T KNOW WHICH WAY WAS UP OR DOWN!! I'M GLAD THAT I CAN'T USE HEROIN, BUT I FEEL TRAPPED AND 100% DEPRESSED. SO, I GOT SOME VALIUM SATURDAY NIGHT, THEN I COULDN'T FUNCTION SUNDAY AT ALL. THAT LED ME TO METH! I HAVEN'T DONE METH FOR SO, SO LONG, SO I AM SO UPSET WITH MYSELF. THAT'S WHY IT'S 1:00 A.M. AND I AM STILL AWAKE! I HAVE TO WORK IN THE MORNING TOO. I'M JUST PRETTY MUCH SCREWED. AND TREATMENT TOMORROW, I

HAVE TO BRING IN SOME PEE SO I DON'T GET KICKED OUT *(which meant she had to buy urine in a bag off the streets to pass off as her own so they can't trace what she's been using).* I OBVIOUSLY NEED TREATMENT MORE THAN I EVER THOUGHT. I NEED TO GET THROUGH THIS. I HOPE GOD CAN GUIDE ME AND GET ME THROUGH THIS. I WANT TO FEEL NORMAL AGAIN OR AT LEAST WHERE I CAN LIVE LIFE LIKE NORMAL PEOPLE DO!!

TUESDAY, JANUARY 31, 2017:

IT'S ABOUT 10:30 A.M. AND I AM AT WORK. I ACTUALLY SLEPT LAST NIGHT BUT USED A LITTLE METH AGAIN THIS MORNING. I NEED TO STOP. I HAD TO TAKE SOME PEE IN WITH ME LAST NIGHT SO THEY WOULDN'T KNOW. THAT FELT LIKE COMPLETE SHIT! THEY DID TELL ME THAT MY EYES LOOKED REALLY DILATED, BUT I BLEW IT OFF! I DON'T LIKE BEING DISHONEST AT ALL, BUT I NEED TO BE THERE. THIS IS MY VERY LAST CHANCE. I CAN SLOWLY SEE MYSELF GOING BACK DOWNHILL, AND I DON'T WANT TO!!! I HATE BEING AN ADDICT. IT'S SUCH A DAMN STRUGGLE EVERY WAKING MOMENT.

Same day, different journal…

I AM SUCH A FUCKED UP PERSON! WHY CAN'T I MAKE THE RIGHT CHOICES?? I PAID $600 FOR THE VIVITROL SHOT SO I COULDN'T USE HEROIN…AND WHAT DO I DO…I START USING METH AGAIN, FUCK, FUCK, FUCK! I STAYED UP ALL NIGHT LAST NIGHT AND WENT TO WORK THIS MORNING. I HAVEN'T EATEN ANYTHING FOR OVER A DAY AND A HALF. I FEEL LIKE SHIT! I WAS DEBATING ALL DAY LONG IF I SHOULD GO TO TREATMENT TONIGHT OR NOT 'CAUSE IF THEY FOUND OUT, I WOULD BE OUT! I DON'T WANT TO DO THAT TO MY KIDS, MICHAEL, OR MYSELF. SO, I WENT AND TOOK SOME PEE WITH ME AND CHEATED. I FEEL HORRIBLE, BUT I WILL HAVE TO DO IT ALL WEEK. I HATE BEING DISHONEST MORE THAN

ANYTHING, BUT I NEED THIS TREATMENT. I MADE ANOTHER MISTAKE AND DO *NOT* WANT TO GET KICKED OUT! THIS IS AN AWESOME GROUP I'M WITH RIGHT NOW, AND I CAN'T LEAVE THEM! AND THE STAFF IS SUPER FANTASTIC! I'M ASKING AND PLEADING AGAIN, GOD, PLEASE TAKE CONTROL OF MY LIFE AND LEAD ME IN THE RIGHT DIRECTION. I NEED MY LIFE BACK!

ADDICTION IS BY FAR THE HARDEST THING IN THE WORLD!

I include some of the text messages between me and Nat.

TEXT FROM NAT TO ME: How are you doing?

ME: I'm doing good! How are you? How are the meds working? What did you decide to do? *(She had told me about the medications the doctor had given her to help with the depression from the Vivitrol shot; that is what I was referring to.)*

NAT: I'm so glad your doing better, I got off my meds, I couldn't do it anymore. Waiting for Dr. to call me back. I'm so depressed.

ME: Oh shoot! Are you going to try Prozac? *(I did not know she was using again. She did tell me about one of the relapses she had in this program, but I believed she was just struggling with depression at this point.)*

NAT: I will try anything at this point Shall. I'm not okay.

ME: When did you call him?

NAT: This morning. They are probably at lunch.

ME: K make sure to call them back if they don't call you and make sure to let them know how bad you really are. Then let me know k? You can do this I promise. Remember this is a moment and it will pass. I love you.

NAT: Thanks Shall! I needed to hear that. Love you!!

ME: Did you hear from the Dr.?

NAT: He wasn't in today so the nurse told me he would call me tomorrow.

ME: Are you going to be ok?

NAT: Ya, just really depressed.

ME: I'm so sorry.

NAT: Thanks Shall. I just hope this passes soon.

ME: Me too.

NAT: Thank you for checking on me Shall. I really needed that. Love you.

ME: Love you call me tomorrow.

<u>WEDNESDAY, FEBRUARY 1, 2017</u>:

IT'S 8:30 A.M. WEDNESDAY MORNING AND I AM AT WORK FEELING LIKE SHIT! I WOULD GO HOME, BUT I WOULD PROBABLY LOSE MY JOB. HAVEN'T EATEN IN TWO DAYS. I FEEL LIKE I AM GOING TO FAINT. DIDN'T GO TO GROUP LAST NIGHT AND EVERYONE TEXTED ME SAYING HOW MUCH THEY MISSED ME.

I LOVE THEM ALL SO MUCH! SO, I NEED TO GET MY SHIT TOGETHER AND WORK ON MY RECOVERY HONESTLY AND THE BEST THAT I CAN. THIS IS MY LAST CHANCE!!! USED AGAIN THIS MORNING JUST TO WAKE MYSELF UP, THEN I GOT RID OF THE REST! IT MAKES ME FEEL LIKE COMPLETE SHIT. MAYBE THIS WAS A GOOD LESSON FOR ME SO IT WILL KEEP ME AWAY FROM IT. EVERY TIME I GET UP, I FEEL LIKE I'M GOING TO FAINT. I REALLY DON'T KNOW HOW I'M GOING TO MAKE IT THROUGH THIS DAY. I AM GOING TO GROUP TONIGHT, AND I HOPE IT ALL GOES WELL 'CAUSE I NEED THIS MORE NOW THAN I EVER THOUGHT AND I NEED THOSE PEOPLE IN MY LIFE, THEY MAKE ME HAPPY. GOD, PLEASE BE WITH ME TODAY AND HELP ME GET THROUGH THIS DAY.

<u>FRIDAY, FEBRUARY 3, 2017</u>:

IT'S 10:00 A.M. FRIDAY MORNING AND I'M AT WORK RIGHT NOW. DOING A LITTLE BETTER TODAY BUT STILL PRETTY DEPRESSED. WE WATCHED MY VIDEO LAST NIGHT *(This was the video where I recorded her, years earlier, telling her story for my son's Red Ribbon week at school)* IN TREATMENT, AND THAT WAS REALLY HARD. IT WAS SEVEN YEARS AGO THAT I MADE THAT VIDEO, AND MY LIFE GOT EVEN WORSE. I'M NOT HAPPY WITH ANYTHING IN MY LIFE RIGHT NOW. WORK SUCKS, I HAVE NO ENERGY AT ALL, AND I'M SUPER DEPRESSED. THE DR. CALLED ME IN SOME PROZAC, SO I STARTED TAKING THAT A COUPLE DAYS AGO AND I'M PRAYING THAT THINGS GET BETTER. I MISS HEROIN SO MUCH! I KNOW THAT SOUNDS BAD, BUT I DO. I DON'T MISS HOW BAD MY LIFE WAS ON IT, BUT I MISS THE ACTUAL DRUG. AND BEING WITHOUT IT RIGHT NOW DOESN'T SEEM MUCH BETTER. NO MATTER WHAT I DO OR WHO I'M WITH, I'M JUST SO UNHAPPY, I CAN'T TAKE MUCH MORE OF THIS. DON'T EVEN KNOW HOW TO LIVE LIFE ANYMORE, AND I REALLY DON'T WANT TO. I PRAY IT GETS BETTER BECAUSE I'M REALLY STARTING TO SCARE MYSELF!

SUNDAY, FEBRUARY 5, 2017:

WELL, I HAVEN'T BEEN DOING SO GREAT. USED SALT THIS LAST WEEKEND AND I DON'T KNOW WHY. I AM SO SICK OF BEING AN ADDICT! I WISH THERE WAS A CURE SO *BAD!* IT'S THE SUPER BOWL RIGHT NOW AND I DON'T EVEN CARE! I HAVE BEEN SO DEPRESSED THAT I DON'T WANT TO DO ANYTHING OR TALK TO ANYBODY. THIS IS THE WORST I HAVE BEEN IN SO LONG. KILL ME NOW! I DON'T EVEN CARE ANYMORE! JALA IS SUPER SICK RIGHT NOW, SO I WENT OVER AND TOOK HER A STUFFED ANIMAL AND SOME PICS OF US. I HATE IT WHEN SHE IS SICK, IT BREAKS MY HEART! I HOPE I DON'T GET KICKED OUT OF TREATMENT 'CAUSE I KNOW I NEED IT, BUT I KEEP MESSING UP! WHY DO I DO THIS? I AM ALMOST 38 YEARS OLD, IT'S TIME TO GROW UP, EVEN THOUGH I KNOW THIS IS A VERY NASTY DISEASE. I'M GOING TO BE STRUGGLING THE REST OF MY LIFE! I DON'T KNOW HOW MUCH MORE I CAN TAKE. GOD, HELP ME!

She truly wanted out of this addiction and this life she was living and wanted to get well and complete the treatment program she knew had been handed freely to her, but there was such an inner battle going on. She knew if she didn't get clean through this program, it was her last chance.

FRIDAY, FEBRUARY 10, 2017, NAT'S JOURNAL:

JUST GOT BACK FROM MASON'S BASKETBALL GAME AND THEY KICKED BUTT! I MESSED UP AFTER WORK, THOUGH. WENT BY LARRY'S AND DID SOME METH WITH HIM, THEN HE FIXED MY TATTOOS ON MY WRIST. I REALLY NEED TO GET AWAY FROM HIM *BAD!* I HAVE GOT TO STOP DOING THIS. I WANT RECOVERY AND I WANT IT *BAD!*

SATURDAY, FEBRUARY 11, 2017:

IT'S SATURDAY NIGHT ABOUT 10:00 P.M. AND I JUST GOT OUT OF THE BATH. AND, I AM SO TIRED I CAN'T EVEN SEE STRAIGHT. I HAVE BEEN UP FOR TWO WHOLE DAYS WITH ABSOLUTELY NOTHING TO EAT. THANKS TO METH! I HAVE NOT GONE ON A METH SPREE FOR YEARS. BUT SINCE I HAVE THE VIVITROL SHOT, I FEEL SO TRAPPED AND COMPLETELY DEPRESSED THAT I NEEDED SOMETHING, AND I DIDN'T CARE WHAT IT WAS. I HAVE BEEN SMOKING METH WITH LARRY AND ANNA FOR THE PAST 2 DAYS AND JUST SMOKED CRACK WITH LARRY A COUPLE HOURS AGO. I REALLY FUCKED UP THIS WEEKEND! I DEFINITELY WENT ON A BINGE! FUCK ME!!! LARRY DID FIX MY TATTOO ON MY WRIST AND GAVE ME A NEW TATTOO ON MY LEFT ARM THAT MEANS "NEW BEGINNINGS." WHY CAN'T I CATCH ON TO THAT? I AM NOT A DUMB PERSON, I KNOW I AM VERY SICK WITH THIS DISEASE, BUT I DO BELIEVE WE HAVE CHOICES AT TIMES. I FEEL HORRIBLE RIGHT NOW, JUST LIKE MY OLD DAYS. I CAN'T EVEN SEE STRAIGHT NOW. BUT ON A GOOD NOTE, JAY GOT JALA A PUREBRED WHITE, BLUE EYED HUSKY! JALA DESERVES IT AND SHE IS SO STINKIN' EXCITED, I'M SO HAPPY FOR HER!

Nat was living with Ryan in an apartment and Jala was living with her dad, Jay. Nat and Jay always lived in the same town.

Six days later...

FRIDAY, FEBRUARY 17, 2017:

WELL, I HAVE NOT BEEN DOING GOOD AT ALL! THE VIVITROL SHOT MADE ME SO DEPRESSED THAT I DIDN'T CARE ABOUT A THING. I'M NOT DOING WHAT I SHOULD BE DOING, AND I REALLY WANT TO! WHY IS IT SO DAMN HARD? I'VE BEEN DOING BATH SALTS AND METH AGAIN, HAVEN'T EATEN IN LIKE

4 DAYS, AND I AM SO SUPER SAD ALL THE TIME! I DON'T WANT TO DO ANYTHING, AND I CAN HARDLY SMILE ANYMORE. I REALLY HOPE AND PRAY THAT I CAN STAY IN TREATMENT 'CAUSE I REALLY NEED IT. I'M PRAYING SO HARD THAT I CAN GET THROUGH THIS. I'M ALMOST 38 YEARS OLD AND WHAT DO I HAVE TO SHOW FOR MY LIFE AT ALL, NOTHING EXCEPT MY WONDERFUL KIDS. I NEED TO FIGHT THIS, I NEED STRENGTH AND COURAGE AND CONFIDENCE AND I JUST CAN'T FIND IT!

SATURDAY, FEBRUARY 18, 2017:

BEEN DOING REALLY, REALLY SHITTY! I CAN'T STOP USING METH OR BATH SALTS AND MY ADDICTION IS GOING FULL FORCE AGAIN. I WANT IT TO STOP!! WELL, IT'S ABOUT 3:00 A.M. SO I WILL WRITE AGAIN TOMORROW. GOD HELP ME THIS NIGHT AND TOMORROW!

MONDAY, FEBRUARY 20, 2017:

WELL, I'M PRETTY SURE I JUST FUCKED UP MY LIFE AGAIN! IT'S MONDAY AND I DIDN'T GO TO TREATMENT 'CAUSE I HAVE BEEN USING BATH SALTS AND METH, AND THE LAST COUPLE DAYS HEROIN. *(Her Vivitrol shot had worn off so she could use heroin again).* I'M PRAYING THEY DON'T KICK ME OUT 'CAUSE I THINK I WILL GO OFF THE EDGE IF THEY DO, AND WHAT WOULD MY FAMILY THINK, MY SWEET KIDS AND MICHAEL WHO GOT ME INTO TREATMENT FOR FREE. HOW CAN I BE SOMEBODY LIKE THIS, SUCH A SELFISH PERSON! I AM REALLY SICK RIGHT NOW TOO. HAVEN'T EATEN MUCH OF ANYTHING AT ALL IN THE PAST 5 DAYS. I'M SURPRISED I'M STILL BREATHING. I'M SO DEPRESSED AND DON'T KNOW WHAT TO DO ANYMORE. I'M PRAYING GOD PUTS ME EXACTLY WHERE I SHOULD BE AND I WILL BE OKAY.

TUESDAY, FEBRUARY 21, 2017:

WELL, IT LOOKS LIKE I'M GOING TO GET FIRED FROM MY JOB *(at the U in the cafe).* EVEN THOUGH I DIDN'T REALLY LIKE IT ANYWAYS. BUT IT STILL SUCKS. I FEEL SO LOST RIGHT NOW. I WANT TO KEEP GOING TO TREATMENT, BUT I DON'T KNOW IF THEY WILL LET ME. I'M PRETTY MUCH SCREWING MY LIFE OVER AGAIN! TOMORROW IS A NEW DAY AND I AM NOT GOING TO USE. THIS WAS MY LAST DAY! I HONESTLY CAN'T TAKE IT ANYMORE. IT'S LITERALLY KILLING ME! MY KIDS NEED ME, AND MY FAMILY NEEDS ME. I CAN'T DO THIS TO THEM ANYMORE. I'M PRAYING THAT I CAN DO THIS AND STAY CLEAN AND FINALLY BE HAPPY! IT'S BEEN SO LONG SINCE I HAVE BEEN HAPPY. I NEED TO START MAKING THE RIGHT CHOICES AND THEN I'M PRETTY DAMN SURE I CAN BE HAPPY! GOD, I PRAY YOU HELP ME WITH WORDS THIS WEEK AND ACTIONS. PLEASE GUIDE ME, I CANNOT DO IT WITHOUT YOU!!!

2-22-2017: Dr. Note–115 lbs. Ears hurt. Vivitrol worsened depression. Started Prozac. Denies relapse. Sore throat, ear pain, was with family and they were diagnosed with strep throat. Couldn't afford test so treated with Amoxicillin.

WEDNESDAY, FEBRUARY 22, 2017:

WELL TOMORROW IS MY STINKIN' BIRTHDAY AND I'M GOING TO BE RIGHT IN BED ALL DAY. JUST GOT BACK FROM THE DOCTOR AND I HAVE STREP THROAT WHICH I'M SURE I CAUSED MYSELF FROM THE WICKED BATH SALTS AND METH. WHAT THE FUCK AM I DOING? I KNOW I GOT THIS, I JUST DON'T TAKE THE ACTIONS AND FOLLOW THROUGH WITH THEM. I PRAY SOMEDAY I WILL QUIT BEING SO SELFISH, EVEN THOUGH I KNOW IT'S A VICIOUS DISEASE, AND FINALLY START TO HELP OTHER PEOPLE THAT ARE IN NEED FROM DRUG ADDICTION! THAT IS

MY DREAM, I JUST NEED TO CATCH ON TO IT FIRST. I FEEL LIKE SHIT, I'M 38 TOMORROW AND OTHER THAN MY BEAUTIFUL KIDS, WHAT IN THE HELL DO I HAVE TO SHOW FOR IT? I 100% FUCKED UP MY LIFE AND IT'S SO STINKIN' HARD TO GET IT BACK TOGETHER. I FEEL LIKE A KID AGAIN BECAUSE I HAVE NO IDEA HOW TO LIVE LIFE CLEAN! I PRAY TO GOD THIS HORRIBLE DISEASE DOESN'T KILL ME, 'CAUSE THAT'S HOW IT'S LOOKING SO FAR! I WANT TO BE THE OLD, FUN, ENERGETIC *NATALIE* BACK!

Six days later…

<u>TUESDAY, FEBRUARY 28, 2017</u>:

WELL, IT'S BEEN A REALLY, REALLY SHITTY PAST WEEK AND A HALF. I LOST MY JOB, EVEN THOUGH I DIDN'T REALLY LIKE IT ANYWAYS, BUT THE FACT THAT I LOST IT REALLY PISSES ME OFF! HAVEN'T BEEN GOING TO TREATMENT EITHER 'CAUSE I HAVE BEEN SO SICK. I HOPE THEY LET ME COME BACK. SHALL WANTS ME TO COME TO SAINT GEORGE THIS WEEKEND AND I WANT TO BAD, BUT I DON'T KNOW IF MY TREATMENT CENTER WILL LET ME. THIS REALLY, REALLY SUCKS! I DON'T REALLY KNOW WHAT TO DO RIGHT NOW. STAY IN TREATMENT OR DON'T, I DON'T KNOW! ALL I KNOW IS THAT I WANT TO STAY CLEAN MORE THAN ANYTHING! I PRAY IT ALL WORKS OUT THE BEST FOR ME. I REALLY NEED TO GO TO SAINT GEORGE AND JUST GET AWAY FOR A WHILE, GET AWAY FROM EVERYTHING HERE! I NEED TO START MY LIFE OVER AND IT'S SO STINKIN' HARD! I KNOW I CAN DO IT, THOUGH, I'M A STRONG PERSON!

I remember she was so sick and I was really worried about her because she was down for so long. I didn't realize then that most of the time she was sick with anything it was a result of her drug use.

WEDNESDAY, MARCH 1, 2017:

IT'S ABOUT 10:30 P.M. AND I JUST GOT BACK FROM DINNER WITH JAY AND JALA AT TEXAS ROADHOUSE. JAY REWARDED HER BECAUSE SHE IS DOING REALLY WELL IN SCHOOL. THAT IS A HUGE DEAL! I'M SO PROUD OF HER. SO, I THOUGHT FOR SURE THAT I WAS KICKED OUT OF TREATMENT, BUT I'M NOT, NOT AT ALL! I HAVEN'T BEEN TO GROUP IN 2 WEEKS, AND JOHNATHAN AND I WERE TEXTING AND HE SAID, "OF COURSE YOU CAN COME ON MONDAY," AND HE ASKED IF THERE WAS ANYTHING I NEEDED. HOW SWEET ARE THEY? BEST TREATMENT CENTER I HAVE *EVER* BEEN THROUGH, BY FAR!!! PLANNING ON HEADING OUT TO SAINT GEORGE TOMORROW JUST TO GET AWAY. GET AWAY FROM ABSOLUTELY EVERYTHING HERE FOR A MINUTE. THE BAD THING IS THAT I LOOK HORRIBLE. I HAVEN'T SEEN MY FAMILY IN A COUPLE WEEKS, AND I HAVE BAGS UNDER MY EYES, BRUISES ALL OVER MY ARMS AND MY LEGS AND FEET. THERE IS *NO* WAY OF COVERING THEM, ESPECIALLY OUT THERE 'CAUSE I WILL BE WEARING SHORT SLEEVES INSTEAD OF LONG SLEEVES. I JUST DON'T CARE ANYMORE WHAT PEOPLE THINK, I CAN'T CONTROL HOW THEY FEEL, I CAN ONLY CONTROL MY REACTIONS TOWARDS THINGS!

(GRATITUDE JOURNAL) I AM SUPER GRATEFUL THAT I HAVE A ROOF OVER MY HEAD, FOOD TO EAT, AN APARTMENT OF MY OWN. *(She and Ryan had an apartment together.)* BUT THE 3 BIGGEST BLESSINGS IN MY LIFE ARE ADI, MAS, AND MY SWEET LITTLE JALA! WHAT WOULD I DO WITHOUT THOSE 3? THEY ARE MY WORLD AND MY EVERYTHING!

THURSDAY, MARCH 2, 2017:

I AM SO SICK AND TIRED OF BEING A LIAR OR LYING A LOT. EVERYONE LIES NO MATTER WHAT, WE ARE HUMAN, BUT

THIS KIND OF LYING AND MANIPULATING ARE 2 VERY BIG, VERY IMPORTANT THINGS THAT I HAVE ALWAYS DONE. TRYING TO LIVE LIFE AGAIN, LIVE BEING COMPLETELY HONEST TO MYSELF, MY KIDS, MY FAMILY, AND TO OTHERS. I HAVE NOT BEEN CLEAN FOR A LONG PERIOD OF TIME BESIDES DRUG COURT. I HAD A LOT OF RULES THAT *HAD* TO BE MET OR I WOULD END UP BEING SANCTIONED "GOING BACK TO JAIL"...SO I PLAYED THE JUDGES STUPID, INTENSE, AND SO NOT WORTH IT RULES FOR 15 MONTHS! BUT I GOT THROUGH THAT, THE *HARDEST* 15 MONTHS OF MY LIFE (OR AT LEAST ONE OF THEM). RYAN IS NEXT TO ME RIGHT NOW TRYING TO SLEEP, BUT I AM DEFINITELY KEEPING HIM AWAKE AND IT'S 4:45 A.M. (YES, IN THE MORNING). GOD, WHEN AM I GOING TO FINALLY GET MY SHIT TOGETHER? HOW PATHETIC AM I? I JUST TURNED 38 LAST WEEK AND I WAS IN BED ALL DAMN DAY! WHAT A BIRTHDAY, HUH? GOING TO SLEEP AT 5:00 IN THE MORNING.

(GRATITUDE JOURNAL) TODAY I AM VERY THANKFUL THAT MY SISTER IS BACK IN MY LIFE AND THAT WE GET TO SPEND TIME TOGETHER THIS WEEKEND. AND I'M GRATEFUL I HAVE THE OPPORTUNITY TO GET AWAY FOR A COUPLE DAYS AND GO DO SOME RELAXING IN THE SUN. GOD, HELP ME STAY CLEAN TODAY!!

SURRENDERING TO DRUGS (RENAISSANCE RANCH NOTEBOOK):

I AM SURRENDERING TO YOU BY NOT MAKING YOU MY TOP PRIORITY. I AM SURRENDERING TO YOU BY GOING TO TREATMENT DAILY AND PARTICIPATING IN GROUP. I AM SURRENDERING MYSELF WITH HEALTHY PEOPLE. I AM SURRENDERING TO YOU TO GET CLOSER TO MY HIGHER POWER. I AM SURRENDERING TO YOU BY REACHING OUT AND ASKING FOR HELP WHEN I NEED IT. AND...I AM SURRENDERING TO YOU BY COMPLETELY STAYING AWAY FROM YOU. I AM SURRENDERING TO YOU BY

GOING TO MEETINGS AS MUCH AS I CAN. AND…I AM SURRENDERING TO YOU BY TELLING OTHERS MY STORY SO IT CAN HELP OTHER ADDICTS.
I PRAY EVERY DAY THAT I CAN GET THROUGH THIS AND START HELPING OTHERS IN NEED.–THAT IS MY DREAM –

FRIDAY, MARCH 3, 2017:

IT IS LITERALLY 2:15 A.M. FRIDAY MORNING AND I AM LEAVING AT 9:30 A.M. AT THE LATEST TO GO DOWN TO SAINT GEORGE AND SPEND SOME TIME WITH SHALL AND A CHANCE FOR ME TO GET AWAY FROM THIS *HELL HOLE* THAT I HAVE BEEN LIVING IN. I'M SO SUPER EXCITED TO GET AWAY FOR A FEW DAYS BUT AT THE SAME TIME, I'M COMFORTABLE HERE IN MY LITTLE APARTMENT! BUT IF I DON'T START GETTING OUT MORE, TRYING NEW THINGS, CHALLENGE MYSELF EVERY ONCE IN A WHILE, THEN WHAT GOOD ARE OUR LIVES? I HAVE NOT BEEN DOING GOOD AT ALL THE PAST 2 WEEKS. HAVEN'T BEEN TO TREATMENT IN A LITTLE OVER 2 WEEKS AND I HAVE BEEN USING EVERY SINGLE DAY. MY ARMS, FEET, AND HANDS HAVE BRUISES ALL OVER THEM FROM TRYING TO HIT *(injecting the drugs with a needle).* SHALL IS NOT GOING TO LIKE THAT AT ALL! I WENT TO ADI'S SCHOOL TONIGHT AND SHE DID MY NAILS. IT WAS FUN! ADI AND I ARE SUPER CLOSE AND WHEN I DON'T TALK TO HER AT LEAST 3 TIMES A DAY, THEN SOMETHING IS NOT RIGHT. I FREAKING LOVE THAT DAUGHTER OF MINE AND SO STINKIN' PROUD OF HER. LET'S JUST FACE IT…I HAVE THE MOST BEAUTIFUL THREE KIDS IN THIS ENTIRE WORLD!

(GRATITUDE JOURNAL) I AM GRATEFUL TODAY BECAUSE I GET TO GO TO MY SISTER'S TOMORROW. RIDING WITH ANGIE AND STAYING WITH SHALL IN SAINT GEORGE. IT WILL BE GOOD FOR ME, REALLY GOOD FOR ME! I NEED TO GET AWAY FOR

A MINUTE AND NOT WORRY ABOUT ANYTHING THAT'S GOING ON HERE, I'M GOING TO DO JUST THAT! TODAY I AM VERY THANKFUL THAT MY SISTER IS BACK IN MY LIFE AND THAT WE GET TO SPEND TIME TOGETHER THIS WEEKEND. AND I'M GRATEFUL I HAVE THE OPPORTUNITY TO GET AWAY FOR A COUPLE DAYS AND GO DO SOMETHING IN THE SUN. GOD, HELP ME STAY CLEAN TODAY!!

SATURDAY, MARCH 4, 2017:

(GRATITUDE JOURNAL) I AM THANKFUL AND VERY GRATEFUL FOR RYAN. HE IS SUCH AN AMAZING MAN AND THE KINDEST HEART THAT I HAVE EVER SEEN IN ANYONE BEFORE. I DON'T TREAT HIM THE WAY I SHOULD, AND EVERYONE POINTS THAT OUT TO ME. I NEED TO TREAT HIM BETTER, FIGURE OUT WHAT THE *HELL* I WANT, AND GO GET IT! WILL I *EVER REALLY* EXPERIENCE REAL LOVE?

SUNDAY, MARCH 5, 2017:

JUST GOT BACK FROM SAINT GEORGE A COUPLE HOURS AGO! I JUST WANTED TO GET AWAY AND CHILL, AND FOR THE MOST PART I DID, BUT I AM HAPPY TO BE HOME. SHALL AND I WENT TO A MOVIE YESTERDAY, JUST HER AND I, AND WE SAW *A DOG'S PURPOSE.* THAT'S BASICALLY THE ONLY ONE THAT WAS OUT AND THAT WE COULD GO SEE BECAUSE SHALL WON'T WATCH RATED R MOVIES. THE SHOW WASN'T THAT GREAT BUT ME AND SHALL HAD FUN BECAUSE WE WERE TOGETHER. I HAVE BEEN REALLY HONEST WITH HER LATELY. SOMETHING THAT I HAVE *NEVER, EVER* DONE AND THE REACTION THAT I GOT FROM HER (AND EMILY) WAS SOMETHING THAT I NEVER THOUGHT WOULD HAPPEN. THEY BOTH PRETTY MUCH EMBRACED ME AND WAS THERE FOR ME AND TOLD ME THAT AS LONG AS I WAS HONEST WITH THEM THAT THEY BOTH WOULD ALWAYS BE THERE TO SUPPORT ME. IT'S VERY HARD TO BE COMPLETELY

HONEST WITH ANYONE ABOUT THIS KIND OF STUFF, BUT EVEN HARDER WITH FAMILY MEMBERS (MY SISTERS). I'M JUST BARELY ACTUALLY REALIZING AND TRY TO DEAL WITH ON MY OWN THAT THIS STRUGGLE, THIS DEMON IN MY HEAD IS NEVER GOING AWAY AND I HAVE TO LEARN HOW TO DEAL WITH IT IN A HEALTHY WAY. SUPER HARD, I'M SCARED, I AM SUPER DEPRESSED 'CAUSE I'M STARTING MY LIFE ALL OVER AGAIN AT 38 YEARS OLD. I FEEL LIKE A CHILD AGAIN THAT'S LEARNING EVERYTHING FOR THE FIRST TIME AND IT'S SUPER SCARY AND I DON'T KNOW AT ALL HOW TO LIVE MY LIFE CLEAN. AND JUST RECENTLY THAT HAS HIT ME LIKE A TON OF BRICKS! I'M STARTING *ALL OVER AGAIN!* I AM SO STINKIN' SCARED AND DON'T THINK I AM STRONG ENOUGH TO DO THIS! I DON'T KNOW ANYTHING RIGHT NOW, NOR HOW I FEEL ABOUT ANYONE. I AM SO 100% COMPLETELY LOST AND AM SO AFRAID TO FAIL. I WANT TO BE A BETTER MOTHER, SISTER, DAUGHTER, AND FRIEND TO THE LOVED ONES IN MY LIFE. SYDKA IS BARKING OUT OF CONTROL RIGHT NOW AND I THINK IT'S BECAUSE I AM NOT GIVING HER ANY ATTENTION. SHE IS THE MOST SPOILED DOG *EVER,* SHE RULES THIS HOUSEHOLD AND I AM JUST FINE WITH THAT. SHE IS MY BABY AND MAKES ME SO HAPPY! WHAT I HAVE WITH MY DOG IS PURELY UNCONDITIONAL LOVE THAT GETS STRONGER EVERY SINGLE DAY. *I LOVE MY PUPPY SO, SO MUCH!

(GRATITUDE JOURNAL) JUST GOT HOME FROM SAINT GEORGE AND I WAS VERY THANKFUL THAT I HAD AN APARTMENT (MY HOME) TO COME HOME TO! RYAN AND HIS SON ARE ALWAYS SUPER GOOD TO ME AND I FELT VERY LOVED WALKING THROUGH THE DOOR TONIGHT. AND, OF COURSE, MY SYDKA BABIES WAS HERE TOO!!

MONDAY, MARCH 6, 2017:

WELL, I DON'T QUITE KNOW RIGHT NOW WHAT THE HELL TO DO ABOUT TREATMENT. 'CAUSE I KEEP RELAPSING, AND THEY TOLD ME THE NEXT TIME I RELAPSE AGAIN, THEN I WOULD BASICALLY GET KICKED OUT! THEY DON'T USE THOSE WORDS, BUT WE ARE NOT STUPID. SO, PRETTY MUCH, IF I DON'T TAKE PEE (CLEAN PEE) WITH ME, THEN I'M SCREWED! I DON'T WANT TO LIE TO ANYONE IN MY GROUP, BUT IF I TELL THE TRUTH, THEN I *WILL* GET KICKED OUT! AND I NEED THIS TREATMENT *BAD!* I GOT HOME FROM SAINT GEORGE, WAS AT THE APARTMENT FOR MAYBE 20 MINUTES, THEN WENT OVER TO LARRY'S AND SMOKED SOME SALT RIGHT AWAY AND BOUGHT SOME MORE BLACK! I CAN'T DO THIS AGAIN OR ANYMORE OR I *WILL* END UP DEAD. I FOUND SOME VEINS IN MY FEET THAT AREN'T BATTERED UP TOO MUCH LIKE MY ARMS AND NOW I CAN'T STOP! ONCE I START, I TELL MYSELF I WILL ONLY DO ONCE, BUT THAT *NEVER EVER* HAPPENS. I HOPE AND PRAY THAT THINGS WILL GO WELL TONIGHT AND I WILL STAY…IF THINGS GO BADLY, THEN I GUARANTEE I WILL LEAVE. PLEASE HELP TONIGHT THAT THINGS WILL GO SMOOTHLY.

TUESDAY, MARCH 7, 2017:

IT'S ABOUT 6:00 P.M. AND I SHOULD BE IN GROUP RIGHT NOW, BUT INSTEAD I DID THE EXACT OPPOSITE, I GOT HIGH INSTEAD. WHAT IS WRONG WITH ME??? I CAN'T KEEP LIVING THIS WAY. I HAVE BEEN DOING THIS SHIT WAY TOO LONG! BUT I FEEL LIKE I CAN'T LIVE MY LIFE CLEAN. I'M AFRAID OF *EVERYTHING!* SO, I JUST STAY IN THIS COMFORTABLE BUBBLE OF MINE AND NEVER CHALLENGE MYSELF. I NEED TO DO SOMETHING WITH MY LIFE! IT'S NOT OVER YET, BUT I ACT LIKE IT IS. I JUST DON'T KNOW WHAT TO DO NEXT! I HAVE EVERYTHING I NEED, SO WHY AM I SO STINKIN' DEPRESSED? I HATE FEELING THIS WAY! IT IS THE WORST

FEELING IN THE WORLD! I *CANNOT* LET THIS DRUG ADDICTION TAKE MY LIFE. IT HAS TAKEN TOO MANY PEOPLE THAT I KNOW, AND I AM STILL HERE! WHY??? I KNOW THERE IS SOMETHING IMPORTANT I NEED TO DO WITH MY LIFE BUT I HAVE NO IDEA WHAT THAT IS. *(I believe she lived as long as she did to finish journaling her story so others could learn from her life.)* I JUST WANT TO FEEL OKAY, FEEL OKAY AND NOT USE DRUGS. I KNOW WHAT I NEED TO DO, I JUST DON'T DO IT! I COULD HAVE AN AMAZING, HAPPY LIFE IF I STOPPED USING AND FOCUSED ON MY FAMILY (KIDS) AND MYSELF IN A HEALTHY WAY. THIS IS JUST SO DAMN HARD! I WISH I KNEW HOW TO START OVER! I DON'T EVEN KNOW WHAT THE NEXT STEP IS THAT I SHOULD TAKE. *(Whenever she would tell me she didn't know where to start, I always told her to pray for help and listen and she would know. She was trying to get clean on her own, and she desperately needed professional and heavenly help.)* I HOPE TOMORROW NIGHT IN GROUP GOES WELL, I'M SCARED!

WELL, THEY ARE LETTING ME COME TO GROUP TOMORROW NIGHT, SO AS FAR AS I KNOW, THEY ARE NOT KICKING ME OUT, BUT IF THAT IS THE CASE, THIS DEFINITELY IS MY LAST CHANCE. AND...TO MAKE THINGS BETTER IN MY LIFE, RYAN STARTED USING AGAIN, AND I KNEW HE HAD, BUT I HAD NO IDEA HOW MUCH. WELL, APPARENTLY, IT'S BEEN A LOT, 'CAUSE HE HAS A HABIT AGAIN. HE CAN'T EVEN GO ONE DAY WITHOUT IT. I'M SO SCARED BECAUSE I HAVE HAD HIM TO RELY ON WHEN THINGS IN MY LIFE AREN'T GOING GOOD, AND NOW I DON'T! I'M SO UPSET THAT HE HAS A HABIT AGAIN! I LOST MY JOB AND THAT'S SCARY AS IT IS, BUT IF RYAN LOSES HIS, WE ARE COMPLETELY FUCKED! AND, I HATE IT THAT I HAVE TO WORRY ABOUT THIS, WHILE I'M TRYING TO FIX MY OWN LIFE. HAVEN'T SEEN JALA AT ALL OTHER THAN RIGHT BEFORE I WENT TO SAINT GEORGE, AND SHE IS HAVING A REALLY HARD TIME NOT SEEING ME A LOT. IT'S 10:45 P.M. RIGHT NOW AND I JUST GOT OFF THE PHONE WITH MASON, WE TALKED FOR ALMOST 30 MINUTES. I

FREAKING LOVE THAT KID! HE IS PLANNING ON GOING ON A MISSION *(for our church)* STILL, AND HE SAYS HE IS TURNING IN HIS PAPERS PRETTY SOON. SO PROUD OF HIM, BUT I AM GOING TO HAVE A HARD TIME 'CAUSE 2 YEARS IS TOO DAMN LONG!

(GRATITUDE JOURNAL) IT'S 6:00 P.M. AND I SHOULD BE IN A GROUP TONIGHT, BUT INSTEAD I DID THE EXACT OPPOSITE. I FEEL LIKE MY WORLD IS IN A HUGE WHIRLWIND RIGHT NOW! I LOST MY JOB, NOT DOING WELL WITH TREATMENT AT ALL, AND I FEEL LIKE A COMPLETE FAILURE. I'M LITERALLY STARTING ALL OVER AGAIN. I NEED TO MAKE IT WORK THIS TIME.

<u>WEDNESDAY, MARCH 8, 2017</u>:

IT'S ABOUT 11:15 P.M. AND I JUST GOT BACK FROM GROUP A COUPLE HOURS AGO. I AM SO SUPER SHOCKED THAT THEY DIDN'T KICK ME OUT! I AM SUPER LUCKY AND I HAVE ANOTHER CHANCE, *AGAIN!* I NEED TO BE A LITTLE MORE GRATEFUL FOR THE 2ND, 3RD, OR EVEN 4TH CHANCE THAT I HAVE. THIS TREATMENT CENTER THAT I'M IN RIGHT NOW IS AMAZING! AND THEY ARE NOT AT ALL ABOUT THE MONEY LIKE MOST TREATMENT CENTERS ARE. I AM GOING THROUGH THIS PROGRAM COMPLETELY FREE BECAUSE OF MICHAEL. I NEED TO REMEMBER THAT EVERY TIME I WANT TO USE AGAIN (WHICH IS EVERY SECOND OF EVERY DAY). NOBODY ELSE GETS THIS CHANCE LIKE I HAVE. THEY KICKED 2 OTHER PEOPLE OUT WHILE I WAS GONE. I HAVE RELAPSED A LOT MORE THAN ONE OF THEM. I HAVE BEEN GONE FOR A LITTLE OVER 3 WEEKS, TONIGHT WAS MY FIRST NIGHT BACK. WE GOT 4 NEW PEOPLE AND LOST 2 PEOPLE. I'M STILL IN SHOCK THAT THEY DIDN'T BOOT ME OUT! I AM SO LUCKY AND NEED TO REMEMBER THAT AND GIVE THIS RECOVERY THING MY ALL!!! I PRAY WITH ALL MY HEART THAT I WILL GET THROUGH THIS AND SOON

BE AN EXAMPLE TO OTHERS THAT ARE GOING THROUGH THIS *HELL* OF ADDICTION TOO. I'M STRONG ENOUGH, *I JUST NEED TO DO IT!!*

(GRATITUDE JOURNAL) TONIGHT WAS MY FIRST NIGHT BACK IN TREATMENT AFTER BEING GONE FOR A LITTLE OVER THREE WEEKS. I THOUGHT FOR SURE I WAS GOING TO GET KICKED OUT, BUT I DIDN'T AND NOW I HAVE *ANOTHER* CHANCE TO DO THIS. I JUST HOPE AND PRAY THAT I WILL DO EVERYTHING I CAN TO STAY CLEAN THIS TIME. I WANT IT MORE THAN ANYTHING IN THIS WORLD. I JUST NEED TO DO THIS 100% THIS TIME!

<u>THURSDAY, MARCH 9, 2017</u>:

IT'S ALMOST 11:00 P.M. AND RYAN AND I JUST GOT BACK FROM WALKING OVER TO LEE'S 'CAUSE I NEEDED CHOCOLATE. I WENT TO GROUP TONIGHT AND IT'S JUST DIFFERENT. WE GOT 4 NEW PEOPLE. I AM NOT LIKING IT AT ALL AS OF RIGHT NOW! AND LIKING MY GROUP IS A HUGE DEAL IN MY RECOVERY. IF I DON'T LIKE THE PEOPLE IN MY GROUP, THEN IT'S VERY HARD FOR ME TO GET MOTIVATED TO GO. THAT'S HOW IT IS RIGHT NOW. I LOVED MY OLD GROUP, DON'T REALLY LIKE THE ONE WE HAVE NOW. I JUST PRAY TO GOD THAT I GET THROUGH IT AND DON'T GIVE UP, CAUSE AS OF RIGHT NOW, I TOTALLY WANT TO GIVE UP. I FEEL SO LOST RIGHT NOW! MY LIFE IS UP IN THE AIR AND I DON'T KNOW HOW TO FIX IT AND IT DOESN'T HELP AT ALL THAT RYAN HAS A HABIT AGAIN 'CAUSE HE CAN'T STOP RIGHT NOW WITHOUT GETTING REALLY SICK AND HE CAN'T MISS ANY WORK, AND WE ARE RELYING ON HIS INCOME ALONE RIGHT NOW. *(Nat and Ryan were in the habit of telling family members like his mom, my mom, me, and Ang that they were out of money and couldn't pay for Nat's Suboxone to stay clean, so we would all help. They would also switch it around and say they didn't have money for rent because they paid for the Suboxone, so my mom and his mom would pay for rent quite often, as well as groceries.)* I JUST HATE THIS FEELING...OF BEING COMPLETELY TERRIFIED AND NOT KNOWING. WHY DOES LIFE HAVE TO BE *SO DAMN HARD?* AND AM I GOING TO MAKE IT THROUGH IT? SOMETIMES I REALLY WONDER!

(GRATITUDE JOURNAL) I AM GRATEFUL TODAY THAT I AM ALIVE, BUT THESE DAYS, SOMETIMES I WISH I WASN'T. THIS JOURNAL IS SUPPOSED TO BE WRITING DOWN EVERYTHING THAT I AM GRATEFUL AND THANKFUL FOR, BUT IT'S GETTING HARDER AND HARDER TO DO THAT LATELY. THIS DRUG ADDICTION IS TAKING ME DOWN. I'VE BEEN ABLE TO BEAT IT THIS FAR AND IT'S BEEN VERY DIFFICULT. NOW I JUST DON'T KNOW HOW MUCH FIGHT I HAVE IN ME ANYMORE!

It's so awful to read how she was slowly starting to shut down and lose her fight.

FRIDAY, MARCH 10, 2017:

JUST GOT BACK FROM MASON'S LAST BB *(basketball)* GAME FOR THE YEAR. THEY LOST, BUT MASON PLAYED A GOOD GAME, AS HE ALWAYS DOES. EVEN THOUGH HE IS SHORT (TAKES AFTER ME), HE PLAYS SPORTS SO WELL! FOOTBALL, BB, HOCKEY, ETC.! HE JUST ROCKS! ADI HAS JALA AT DISNEY ON ICE RIGHT NOW. HOW SWEET IS THAT? I AM SITTING AT HOME JOURNALING BECAUSE I HAVE NOTHING BETTER TO DO. EVEN THOUGH I WAS SO READY TO GET AWAY FROM THAT CAFE, I WAS WORKING UP AT THE UNIVERSITY, I FEEL LIKE A COMPLETE FAILURE. I GOT LET GO BECAUSE I WAS SICK! I COULD SUE JOHNATHAN SO EASY, BUT WHY? IT WAS TOTALLY NOT RIGHT WHAT HE DID TO ME BY LETTING ME GO, EVEN AFTER SHOWING HIM A DOCTOR NOTE. HAVE ABSOLUTELY NO IDEA WHAT I AM GOING TO DO NOW, AND I'M SO SCARED.

I'M JUST PLAIN OUT SCARED OF LIFE! I FEEL LIKE I HAVE DONE EVERYTHING WRONG IN MY LIFE, EXCEPT MY KIDS. THEY WERE SOMETHING I ACTUALLY DID RIGHT. BUT EVERYTHING ELSE, I'M 38 YEARS OLD, DIVORCED TWICE *(once)*, HAVE NO JOB, HAVE NO MEDICAL INSURANCE, AND I JUST SIGNED A YEAR LEASE WITH MY APARTMENT COMPLEX AND HAVE TO COMPLETELY RELY ON RYAN RIGHT NOW, AND THAT DOESN'T HELP ME AT ALL, THOUGH, I'M FUCKING TERRIFIED!!

(GRATITUDE JOURNAL) I KNOW I HAVE SAID THIS BEFORE, BUT I AM SO STINKIN' GRATEFUL FOR MY 3 KIDS! THEY ARE ABSOLUTELY INCREDIBLE KIDS.

Six days later...

<u>THURSDAY, MARCH 16, 2017</u>:

IT'S ABOUT 8:45 P.M. AND I MISSED TREATMENT TONIGHT BECAUSE I JUST DIDN'T WANT TO GO, AND I WAS AT LARRY'S HOUSE INSTEAD. WHY? WHY DO I DO THIS? I KNOW THIS IS A SICK DISEASE THAT I HAVE, BUT WHY CAN'T I PULL MYSELF OUT OF IT? OTHER PEOPLE HAVE, AND I HAVE ONCE BEFORE, SO WHY CAN'T I DO IT NOW? JEFFREY TEXTED ME TODAY AND I HAVEN'T HEARD FROM HIM IN MONTHS. HE IS CLEAN STILL! AND STILL GOING TO CHURCH. IF JEFFREY CAN DO IT, THEN SO CAN I!! SO, FOR GROUP LAST NIGHT, WE WENT TO THE FARMINGTON POND AND ROASTED HOT DOGS AND S'MORES.

(GRATITUDE JOURNAL) I AM VERY GRATEFUL TODAY THAT I AM ALIVE AND BREATHING! I AM STILL IN TREATMENT AND I NEED TO REMEMBER HOW LUCKY I AM THAT I WAS ABLE TO GET TREATMENT WITHOUT PAYING FOR IT. I TAKE IT FOR GRANTED AND I NEED TO DO MY VERY BEST TO STAY CLEAN

BECAUSE THAT IS WHAT I WANT. EVEN THOUGH MY LIFE SUCKS RIGHT NOW…I HAVE EVERYTHING I NEED!

MONDAY, MARCH 20, 2017:

Nat must have had a conversation with me and told me about some relapses…

TEXT FROM ME TO NAT: Thank you Nat for being honest with me. It helps so much. I am so proud of you and your desire to get clean. Instead of focusing on the relapses look at all the days you DON'T use. I love you so much and you will get through this! You are a very strong person.

NAT: Thank you Shall!! That means so much to me to hear that. And I can promise you this, I won't stop fighting this horrible disease, and I will always be honest with you! Thank you for being here for me and supporting me, I know I can't do this alone. Love you Shall!!

TUESDAY, MARCH 21, 2017:

IT'S ABOUT 7:15 P.M. AND I SHOULD BE IN GROUP RIGHT NOW, BUT I DROPPED OUT OF TREATMENT. I FEEL LIKE SUCH A FAILURE. THEY WOULD HAVE KICKED ME OUT EVENTUALLY 'CAUSE I KEPT RELAPSING. EVEN THOUGH THEY HAVEN'T ALREADY, IT'S AMAZING HOW THE STAFF AT R&R IN FARMINGTON WERE PULLING FOR ME AND GAVE ME MANY, MANY CHANCES THAT I DID NOT DESERVE. PAMELA IS ABSOLUTELY AMAZING, SHE IS A GENUINE, AUTHENTIC, GREAT WOMAN. I WILL MISS HER SO MUCH! I WISH I COULD GO BACK AND DO IT SO DIFFERENTLY. I HAD AN AMAZING OPPORTUNITY TO CHANGE MY LIFE AROUND AND GET THE HELP THAT I NEED. INSTEAD, I FUCKED IT UP! THIS CHANCE WAS LITERALLY JUST HANDED TO ME AND I COULD HAVE REALLY CHANGED MY

LIFE AROUND AND BECOME THE PERSON THAT I KNOW I CAN BE. I FUCKED IT UP! I THREW IT ALL AWAY, FOR WHAT?? TO CONTINUE TO GET HIGH? I FEEL COMPLETELY WORTHLESS AND THE BIGGEST FAILURE. HOW COULD I LET THIS HAPPEN? I WISH I COULD GO BACK AND DO IT ALL OVER AGAIN AND TAKE THE CHANCE THAT I DESERVE TO CHANGE MY LIFE!

IT'S ABOUT 11:30 P.M. AND I HAVE RYAN ASLEEP NEXT TO ME, HIS SON IS IN HIS ROOM ASLEEP, AND I HAVE CARL SLEEPING OVER TONIGHT ON THE COUCH 'CAUSE HE DIDN'T HAVE ANYWHERE TO GO TONIGHT. I MET HIM AT THE U IN DETOX. NOW WE ARE GOOD FRIENDS. HE IS HAVING A HARD TIME RIGHT NOW 'CAUSE HE RELAPSED AND HIS FAMILY HAS PRETTY MUCH TURNED AWAY FROM HIM. I'M NOT DOING MUCH BETTER AT THE MOMENT. I AM SO STINKIN' DEPRESSED, IT'S HARD FOR ME TO GET UP AND OUT OF BED EVERY MORNING. SOMETHING NEEDS TO CHANGE, I JUST WON'T LET IT, APPARENTLY. I DROPPED OUT OF R&R OUTPATIENT 'CAUSE I COULDN'T STAY CLEAN, I LOST MY JOB UP AT THE U AND I AM BACK ON HEROIN AGAIN, EVERY DAY. HOW DID I GET HERE AGAIN? AND SO *FAST?* LIFE IS HARD ENOUGH AS IS, MIX IN A DRUG ADDICT, IT GETS 10 TIMES BETTER. I REALLY CAN'T TAKE THIS LIFE ANY LONGER. IF I DIDN'T WAKE UP IN THE MORNING, I WOULD BE OKAY WITH THAT. MUCH EASIER THAN TRYING TO GO THROUGH ANOTHER DAY LIKE THIS. I HATE MY LIFE RIGHT NOW AND I DON'T KNOW WHAT THE HELL TO DO!!!

(GRATITUDE JOURNAL) IT'S VERY HARD TO WRITE DOWN THINGS I AM GRATEFUL FOR WHEN I AM SO EXTREMELY DEPRESSED. I NEED TO REMIND MYSELF THAT THERE ARE PEOPLE OUT IN THE WORLD THAT ARE GOING THROUGH THINGS THAT ARE FAR WORSE THAN WHAT I AM COMPLAINING ABOUT TODAY. I HAVE A PLACE TO LIVE, I HAVE A CAR TO DRIVE *(our parents bought her another car),* I HAVE FOOD IN MY FRIDGE, I HAVE MY FAMILY IN MY LIFE, AND I AM *ALIVE!*

<u>WEDNESDAY, MARCH 22, 2017</u>:

I'M AT MASON'S CHOIR CONCERT RIGHT NOW AT BOUNTIFUL HIGH WITH MY MOM. THESE CONCERTS ARE ALWAYS WAY TOO LONG! JUST SAW JAY 'CAUSE HE WAS PICKING UP JALA AND HE TOLD ME I LOOKED STUNNING TONIGHT, HOW SWEET IS THAT? CARL IS SLEEPING OVER AT OUR HOUSE RIGHT NOW 'CAUSE HE HAS NO PLACE TO GO. I'M REALLY NOT HAPPY ABOUT IT AT ALL. HE IS USING REALLY HEAVILY, AND I DON'T TRUST HIM AT ALL! WHY DO I PUT MYSELF IN THESE POSITIONS? I HELP SOMEONE IN NEED 'CAUSE I DON'T WANT HIM TO BE LEFT IN THE STREETS, AND NOW I'M BUGGED 'CAUSE HE IS TAKING FULL ADVANTAGE OF ME! WHY DON'T I EVER THINK FIRST BEFORE I OPEN MY MOUTH AND GET MYSELF IN THESE SHITTY SITUATIONS! FRANK AND BRENDA TEXTED ME A LOT TONIGHT SAYING THEY MISS ME AND THEY WANT ME BACK IN GROUP. THEY SAID IT'S NOT THE SAME WITHOUT ME THERE. THAT MADE ME FEEL GOOD. I HAVEN'T TOLD MY KIDS OR MY FAMILY YET THAT I DROPPED OUT OF TREATMENT. I'M SCARED TO TELL THEM. SUPER, SUPER SCARED!

Same day, different journal...

IT'S ABOUT 11:15 P.M. AND I GOT BACK FROM MASON'S CHOIR CONCERT ABOUT AN HOUR AND A HALF AGO. I DROPPED OUT OF TREATMENT, WHICH WAS THE STUPIDEST THING I EVER COULD HAVE DONE. I DIDN'T WANT TO, BUT I KNOW THEY WOULD HAVE WANTED ME TO GO TO RESIDENTIAL *(live-in)* R&R BECAUSE OF ALL MY RELAPSES...I WAS DOING OKAY, BUT RYAN STARTED USING AGAIN AND A LOT MORE THAN WHAT HE WAS TELLING ME, SO I STARTED AGAIN *(on heroin)* BECAUSE IF I KNOW IT'S HERE, THEN I DON'T HAVE A CHOICE ANYMORE, I JUST DO IT. WELL, I'M NOT SAYING IT'S RYAN'S FAULT AT ALL, BUT I KNEW HE HAD IT HERE, SO I USED IT! I'M NOT BLAMING HIM AT ALL. I AM THE ONE WHO INTRODUCED

RYAN TO HEROIN IN THE FIRST PLACE. I AM JUST *NOT* IN A GOOD PLACE RIGHT NOW AT ALL. CARL IS STAYING WITH US RIGHT NOW BECAUSE HE HAD NOWHERE TO GO. WHY DO I GET MYSELF IN THESE HORRIBLE SITUATIONS? I HAVE NO JOB, I STARTED USING AGAIN, I LIVE WITH RYAN AND HIS SON, EVEN THOUGH THIS IS MY APARTMENT, 'CAUSE I CAN'T AFFORD IT ON MY OWN. RYAN IS NOT MAKING GOOD ENOUGH MONEY TO TAKE CARE OF THE BOTH OF US AND WE ARE BOTH USING AGAIN AND THAT PRETTY MUCH TAKES THE MAJORITY OF HIS PAYCHECKS. HOW DID I GET HERE AGAIN? IN THIS COMPLETE *HELL HOLE* OF A LIFE? I WAS DOING GOOD FOR A MINUTE AND COULD ACTUALLY SEE A BRIGHT FUTURE FOR MYSELF AND THEN I END UP HERE…*AGAIN!* A WORTHLESS JUNKIE! I HATE THAT WORD MORE THAN ANYTHING AND I HATE PEOPLE SAYING THAT WORD, BUT HOW I'M LIVING MY LIFE RIGHT NOW FITS THAT WORD PERFECTLY. I KNOW I'M BETTER THAN THIS AND I KNOW I CAN FIGHT AND NOT GIVE UP ON SOMETHING, BUT WHY CAN'T I BEAT THIS STUPID DISEASE? OR AT LEAST JUST GET ON TOP OF IT? MY KIDS DESERVE BETTER, THEY DESERVE A MOM THAT'S HEALTHY AND STABLE, NOT SOMEONE LIKE ME. I NEED TO *FINALLY* PULL MY HEAD OUT OF MY ASS AND MAKE THIS LIFE OF MINE WORTH LIVING, BECAUSE IF I KEEP GOING ON LIKE THIS, I WILL BE DEAD IN MONTHS! MY KIDS NEED ME, AND I NEED TO BE AN EXAMPLE TO THEM, NOT HOW I HAVE BEEN THE LAST 10 YEARS. I PRAY I WILL BEAT THIS DISEASE AND I WILL GIVE MYSELF A BETTER LIFE, A MUCH BETTER LIFE, FOR ME AND MY KIDS!

FRIDAY, MARCH 24, 2017:

IT'S ABOUT 1:59 A.M. AND I'M JUST GETTING IN BED. RYAN IS UPSET RIGHT NOW 'CAUSE I AM KEEPING HIM UP AND HE HAS TO GET UP EARLY FOR WORK. I DON'T BLAME HIM AT

ALL FOR BEING UPSET. IF IT WAS THE OTHER WAY AROUND, I WOULD BE LIVID AND DEFINITELY THROWING A *HUGE* FIT! WELL, I HAVE COMPLETELY FUCKED UP MY LIFE...*AGAIN!* IT ONLY TOOK LIKE THREE DAYS, AND MY WHOLE WORLD SPIRALED OUT OF CONTROL!!! AND THAT IS AN UNDERSTATEMENT. I SHOULD BE GRATEFUL BECAUSE I STILL HAVE MY APARTMENT AND I STILL HAVE RYAN BY MY SIDE, I STILL HAVE MY KIDS IN MY LIFE, BUT I AM COMPLETELY *MISERABLE!* AND THAT IS DEFINITELY AN UNDERSTATEMENT. I WAS DOING OKAY, AND MY LIFE WAS GOING IN THE RIGHT DIRECTION, AND ONLY IN A MATTER OF A COUPLE DAYS, I MANAGED TO RUIN IT ALL! I'M 38 YEARS OLD AND HAVE MANAGED TO 100% FUCK UP MY LIFE. HOW IN THE *HELL* AM I GOING TO PULL MYSELF OUT OF THIS ONE? I HONESTLY DON'T REMEMBER EVER IN MY LIFE FEELING THIS WORTHLESS AND THIS DEPRESSED. IT'S *BAD!* IT'S REALLY, REALLY *BAD!!* I NEED TO FIND JUST A SPEC OF HOPE, SOMETHING THAT GIVES ME A REASON TO GET OUT OF BED EVERY MORNING. I LOST MY JOB, DROPPED OUT OF TREATMENT, STARTED HANGING AROUND DRUG DEALERS AGAIN. I *HATE* MY LIFE RIGHT NOW AND SO DESPERATELY NEED SOMETHING TO CHANGE THIS TIME. I WANT TO BE CLEAN, I DON'T WANT TO BE IN THE DRUG WORLD ANYMORE AT ALL! IT JUST KEEPS PULLING ME BACK IN. PAMELA TEXTED ME TODAY SAYING SHE LOVES ME AND SHE KNOWS HOW STRONG I AM AND BELIEVES I WILL GET THROUGH THIS. SHE SAID TO LET HER KNOW WHEN I AM REALLY READY, AND SHE WILL BE THERE FOR ME. SHE IS ABSOLUTELY AMAZING. I AM SO THANKFUL SHE CAME INTO MY LIFE. I HAVE A DOCTOR APPOINTMENT IN THE MORNING, AND I AM HOPING HE WILL PUT ME ON SUBOXONE! THAT IS THE ONLY THING LEFT THAT I BELIEVE JUST MIGHT WORK! I AM PRAYING THAT HE WILL HELP ME WITH WHAT I NEED, AND I CAN FINALLY GET CLEAN AND START TO MEND MY LIFE BACK TOGETHER. PRAY, PRAY, PRAY!!!

3-24-2017: Dr. Note–114 lbs. No repeat Vivitrol shot. Relapsed on Heroin and Meth. Working with Renaissance Ranch. Lost job and relapsed using Heroin and Meth. Using $60 per day using IV injection. Prescribed Suboxone.

March 25, 2017–Nat at my house in Saint George

WEDNESDAY, MARCH 29, 2017:

IT'S ABOUT 9:30 P.M. AND I JUST GOT HOME FROM LARRY'S HOUSE. GOT HOME FROM SAINT GEORGE, GOT IN THE CAR FIRST THING AND WENT TO LARRY'S. WHY? I HAVE SUBOXONE WITH ME AND I AM DOING GOOD. WHY DID I FUCK UP, AGAIN? I WANT TO STAY CLEAN MORE THAN ANYTHING, BUT MY ADDICTED BRAIN WANTS SOMETHING DIFFERENT. I WAS IN SAINT GEORGE FOR 5 DAYS WITH MY MOM, EMILY AND HER KIDS, AND JALA. I DID GREAT WITHOUT USING, BUT THE MINUTE I GET BACK, EVERYTHING TOTALLY CHANGED. I NEED TO GO LIVE IN SAINT GEORGE FOR A WHILE, KEEP MYSELF CLEAN. WE HAD FUN, BUT THE FIRST DAY I WAS THERE, SHALL AND EM TOOK ME ASIDE AND ASKED ME IF I BROUGHT ANY DRUGS WITH ME BECAUSE OF HOW I LOOKED. I LOST 10 POUNDS IN THE PAST FEW WEEKS AND I GUESS IT WAS NOTICEABLE. I TOLD THEM I DIDN'T AND AFTER BEING THERE AND AROUND THEM FOR THE PAST 5 DAYS, THEY KNEW I WASN'T USING. I AM GOING TO BE QUESTIONED THE REST OF MY LIFE! BETTER GET USED TO IT!

(GRATITUDE JOURNAL) NOW THAT I'M BACK, I HAVE TO APPLY TO PLACES TO GET A JOB 'CAUSE WE AREN'T OKAY WITH JUST

RYAN'S INCOME. BUT I AM THANKFUL I GOT TO BE WITH MY BABY GIRL IN SAINT GEORGE FOR 5 DAYS.

THURSDAY, MARCH 30, 2017:

IT'S ABOUT 1:00 IN THE MORNING AND I CAN'T SLEEP. I JUST GOT BACK FROM SAINT GEORGE TONIGHT AFTER BEING THERE FOR 5 DAYS. IT WAS FUN, BUT I'M GLAD TO BE HOME. WHILE I WAS THERE, JAY ASKED ME IF I WOULD CONSIDER DATING HIM AGAIN AND GIVING OUR MARRIAGE ANOTHER SHOT, *WOW!!!* IT COMPLETELY CAME OUT OF THE BLUE HE HAS MENTIONED IT BEFORE, BUT HE HAS NEVER STRAIGHT OUT ASKED IF I WOULD GIVE "US" ANOTHER CHANCE. I LOVE HIM AS A PERSON AND AS MUCH AS I WOULD LOVE TO GIVE JALA A STABLE HOME WITH HER MOM AND DAD BACK TOGETHER, I JUST CAN'T DO IT. WE GET ALONG GREAT RIGHT NOW, AND I DON'T WANT TO MESS OUR FRIENDSHIP UP IN ANY WAY. RYAN IS ASLEEP RIGHT NEXT TO ME AND I DON'T KNOW WHAT TO DO ABOUT THAT SITUATION EITHER. I LOVE HIM AS A PERSON TOO, BUT NOT AT ALL IN LOVE WITH HIM. I WISH I WAS IN LOVE WITH HIM BECAUSE HE IS THE BEST GUY I HAVE EVER KNOWN. I DON'T KNOW HOW I WOULD LIVE WITHOUT HIM. I NEED TO MAKE UP MY MIND, THOUGH, AND QUICK. I'M OLD, 38 YEARS OLD!

IT'S ABOUT 2:15 A.M. AND I CAN'T SLEEP AT ALL! AS ALWAYS, I AM SO SUPER DEPRESSED AND HAVE FAILED AT BEING A GOOD MOTHER TO MY 3 BEAUTIFUL KIDS, FAILED AT MY JOB, FAILED AT BEING A GOOD GIRLFRIEND, AND FAILED AT MY LIFE!! I DON'T KNOW HOW TO FIX IT AND I AM COMPLETELY MISERABLE. I'M 38 YEARS OLD AND I HAVE NOTHING TO BE PROUD OF OTHER THAN ADI, MAS, AND JALA. IT HAS *FINALLY* HIT ME THE LAST COUPLE WEEKS THAT I WILL BE STRUGGLING TILL THE DAY I DIE WITH HORRIBLE ADDICTION. WHY ME? I WANT TO MAKE SOMETHING OF MY LIFE, I WANT TO BE HEAD OVER HEELS IN LOVE WITH SOMEBODY AND

I WANT TO BE A GOOD EXAMPLE TO MY KIDS. SOMEONE THAT THEY COULD LOOK UP TO. DON'T KNOW WHERE TO START AND I FEEL OVERWHELMED WHEN I THINK ABOUT WHAT I NEED AND WHAT I WANT TO DO IN MY LIFE. I DO KNOW ONE THING...I *DO NOT* WANT TO LIVE LIKE THIS. I WANT OUT OF THE DRUG WORLD FOREVER!!! (EASIER SAID THAN DONE).

A little over an hour later...

(GRATITUDE JOURNAL) IT'S ABOUT 3:25 IN THE MORNING AND I JUST WANTED TO WRITE DOWN HOW THANKFUL I AM FOR THE LIFE I HAVE. I HAVE MADE *A LOT* OF MISTAKES, BUT I AM TRYING EACH DAY TO NOT MAKE THOSE MISTAKES AGAIN. I AM SO BLESSED FOR 3 VERY IMPORTANT PEOPLE IN MY LIFE...ADI, MAS, AND JALA. I COULDN'T ASK FOR BETTER KIDS THAN THESE 3. I LOVE THEM SO MUCH!

<u>FRIDAY, MARCH 31, 2017</u>:

(GRATITUDE JOURNAL) IT'S ABOUT 4:45 P.M. AND I CAN HEAR MY BABY GIRL'S SHOUTING AND PLAYING, IT PUTS A SMILE ON MY FACE AGAIN. LATELY I HAVEN'T HAD MUCH TO SMILE ABOUT, BUT WHEN I'M WITH JALA AND I HEAR HER LITTLE VOICE, MY SMILE IS RIGHT BACK ON! THAT LITTLE GIRL OF MINE IS ABSOLUTELY INCREDIBLE! JUST GOT BACK FROM GOING TO LUNCH WITH JAY AND JALA. NOW WE ARE HOME TRYING TO HAVE FUN!

IT'S ABOUT 9:35 AT NIGHT AND RYAN AND I ARE SITTING AT LARRY'S HOUSE GETTING READY TO DO ANNA'S NAILS. YAY!! I AM ABSOLUTELY MISERABLE WITH MY LIFE RIGHT NOW, I CAN HARDLY STAND IT! RYAN AND HIS SON LIVE WITH ME IN *MY* APARTMENT BECAUSE I HAVE NO JOB RIGHT NOW 'CAUSE JASON LET ME GO, SO I COULDN'T AFFORD MY PLACE ON MY OWN. I AM SO SUPER UNHAPPY, STARTED USING AGAIN

AND DROPPING WEIGHT WAY TOO FAST. STOPPED GOING TO TREATMENT AND PRETTY MUCH JUST LET MYSELF GO. I LOOK LIKE SHIT! THAT'S THE FIRST THING MICHELLE AND EMILY SAID WHEN I GOT TO SAINT GEORGE, THEY SAID I LOOKED DARK AND HOLLOW LIKE I DID WHEN I WAS CRACKED OUT ON METH REALLY BAD! I JUST DON'T CARE RIGHT NOW. I DON'T CARE ABOUT A DAMN THING! I AM SO NOT OKAY AND JUST WANT TO NUMB MYSELF OUT. I DON'T THINK I HAVE EVER BEEN THIS UNHAPPY IN MY ENTIRE LIFE! KILL ME NOW!!! SOMETIMES I WISH I WOULD FALL ASLEEP AND NOT WAKE UP. I HAVE NEVER BEEN THIS LOST AND MISERABLE BEFORE. I PRAY IT GETS BETTER!

SATURDAY, APRIL 1, 2017:

IT'S 1:00 A.M. SATURDAY MORNING AND I HAVE BEEN UP FOR THREE DAYS STRAIGHT! NOT BECAUSE I WANT TO, 'CAUSE I *CANNOT* SLEEP AND IT'S LITERALLY KILLING ME! I HAVE LOST A LITTLE OVER 10 POUNDS WITHIN THE LAST 3 WEEKS AND I LOOK HORRIBLE! I NEED TO PULL MYSELF TOGETHER. JALA IS RIGHT NEXT TO ME IN BED AND I HAVE NOT BEEN ABLE TO HAVE HER SLEEP OVER IN MONTHS. I AM COMPLETELY LOST AND COMPLETELY MISERABLE. I AM HAVING A REALLY HARD TIME PULLING MYSELF OUT OF THIS ONE. I PRAY TO GOD THAT THIS ROUND ISN'T GOING TO KILL ME…BECAUSE THAT IS REALLY HOW IT'S LOOKING SO FAR. I AM TERRIFIED RIGHT NOW! MY ENTIRE BODY IS TREMBLING AND EVERY TIME I STAND UP, I FEEL LIKE I AM GOING TO FAINT. HOW IN THE *HELL* DID I GET HERE…*AGAIN?* I CAN'T EVEN SWALLOW RIGHT. I CHOKE EVERY TIME I DRINK SOME WATER. I AM FUCKED AND REALLY WANT TO BE CLEAN, BUT I'M STARTING TO THINK THIS IS THE END FOR ME, AND I AM PETRIFIED!

JUST ANOTHER DAY IN MY HORRIBLE, AWFUL LIFE. I REALLY DON'T THINK I HAVE BEEN *THIS* DEPRESSED LIKE I AM NOW. THIS REALLY, REALLY SUCKS! DON'T WANT TO GET

OUT OF BED AND I HAVE ABSOLUTELY NO DESIRE TO GET READY AND GO SOMEWHERE. I DON'T KNOW HOW MUCH MORE OF THIS HORRIBLE LIFE THAT I CAN TAKE. NOTHING MAKES ME HAPPY ANYMORE, NO MATTER HOW HARD I TRY, AND I WANT TO BE CLEAN MORE THAN ANYTHING IN THIS WORLD AND STAY CLEAN...BUT UNFORTUNATELY, IT'S NOT AT ALL WORKING OUT FOR ME THE WAY I WAS HOPING AND PRAYING. I AM SO SUPER SAD EVERY MINUTE OF EVERY FUCKING DAY. I DON'T KNOW WHAT TO DO, WHO TO TALK TO AND COMPLETELY TRUST, HOW TO GET UP TOMORROW MORNING, AND THE MOST CHALLENGING THING OF ALL...STAYING CLEAN! SO MUCH WORK, I FEEL SO DRAINED *ALL THE TIME!* SOMETHING HAS GOT TO CHANGE, OR I MIGHT NOT BE HERE TO START OVER AND TRY TO LIVE A HAPPY SOBER LIFE! *GOD, HELP ME!*

(GRATITUDE JOURNAL) IT'S 9:48 P.M. SATURDAY NIGHT AND I HONESTLY DON'T FEEL LIKE I HAVE MUCH TO BE GRATEFUL FOR LATELY. I KNOW THAT SOUNDS REALLY NEGATIVE AND SELFISH, BUT I AM NOT DOING VERY GOOD LATELY. BUT I NEED TO KEEP TELLING MYSELF THAT THERE ARE PEOPLE OUT THERE WHO HAVE IT MUCH WORSE THAN ME–I AM THANKFUL FOR MY KIDS, SYDKA, AND A HOME TO LIVE IN.

<u>SUNDAY, APRIL 2, 2017</u>:

I DON'T THINK MY LIFE COULD GET ANY WORSE THAN IT IS RIGHT NOW! OKAY, THAT'S A BIG EXASPERATION! I'M JUST REALLY MISERABLE RIGHT NOW. I DROPPED OUT OF TREATMENT THAT I WAS GETTING FOR FREE, I'M USING AGAIN, EVERY DAY. I HAVE BEEN DOING HEROIN, METH, BATH SALTS, AND CRACK COCAINE PRETTY MUCH DAILY. HOW DID I GET BACK DOWN HERE IN THIS SHIT HOLE DRUG WORLD AGAIN? ALL MY MORALS, VALUES, AND ANY PASSION, ALL THAT I HAVE FOR LIFE...COMPLETELY DOWN THE DRAIN! GONE! I DON'T EVEN KNOW WHO I AM RIGHT NOW, AND I *DO NOT* LIKE THIS

GIRL THAT I HAVE BECOME LATELY. I WANT A LIFE AGAIN! A LIFE THAT I AM HAPPY IN. A LIFE THAT I ACTUALLY LOVE AND MAYBE SOMEDAY HAVE THAT SOMEONE THAT MAKES ME HAPPY AND THAT I AM ACTUALLY IN LOVE WITH. I TOLD RYAN YESTERDAY I DON'T KNOW HOW LOVE FEELS WITH THAT SPECIAL SOMEONE 'CAUSE I HAVE NEVER BEEN IN LOVE WITH ANYONE BEFORE. I PRAY THAT I WILL IN THIS LIFETIME!

MONDAY, APRIL 3, 2017:

IT'S 9:51 P.M. AND I AM JUST GETTIN' SETTLED IN FOR BED. I HAVE A DOCTOR APPOINTMENT IN THE MORNING ABOUT HOW I'M DOING WITH THE SUBOXONE. WELL, I WAS DOING GREAT, I WAS ON IT THE ENTIRE TIME IN SAINT GEORGE AND DID GREAT. I TOOK 2 A DAY, THE DOCTOR ONLY WANTED ME ON 1 1/2 BUT I TOOK 2 'CAUSE I DIDN'T WANT *ANY* WITHDRAWALS AT ALL!

4-4-2017: Dr. Note–116 lbs. Has a recovery coach *(I believe she is talking about Pamela from Renaissance Ranch she had in the past).* Prescribed Suboxone, Fluoxetine *(antidepressant)*, and Zofran *(nausea).*

TUESDAY, APRIL 4, 2017:

IT'S 8:45 TUESDAY NIGHT AND I AM OUT ON THE BALCONY SMOKING AND REALIZING WHAT DAY IT IS TOMORROW. IT IS MASON'S 18TH BIRTHDAY AND HE IS IN SAN DIEGO WITH HIS CHOIR GROUP FROM SCHOOL. MY MOM IS WITH HIM BEING A CHAPERONE. I HAVE *NEVER* BEEN WITHOUT ANY OF MY THREE CHILDREN ON THEIR BIRTHDAYS! EVEN WHEN I WAS USING HEAVILY, I STILL GOT TO BE WITH THEM ON THEIR BIRTH-DAYS. I WENT TO THE DOCTOR TODAY AND HE PRESCRIBED ME 8 MORE SUBOXONE FOR THE NEXT TWO WEEKS TILL I SEE HIM AGAIN. NOW I JUST NEED TO GET OFF THE HEROIN FOR 24 HOURS BEFORE I CAN START TAKING THEM. RYAN

STARTED ON THEM, THOUGH, WHICH MAKES ME VERY HAPPY. IT BUGS ME THAT I HAVE TO SUPPLY HIM AND TAKE CARE OF THE BOTH OF US SO WE CAN STAY CLEAN. WHY COULDN'T HE FIGURE THIS OUT ON HIS OWN? I JUST FEEL LIKE WITH RYAN THAT I AM TALKING TO A BOY. TEENAGE BOY! IT'S SO FUCKING FRUSTRATING. I WANT TO BE WITH A MAN! *A REAL MAN* THAT CAN TAKE CARE OF WHATEVER COMES OUR WAY AND THAT CAN COMPLETELY TAKE CARE OF ME!!!

Two days later...
This entry does not make sense...

<u>THURSDAY, APRIL 6, 2017</u>:

WELL, TODAY WAS FILLED WITH A WHOLE LOT OF NOTHING. IT WAS REALLY JUST A LAX DAY, I HAVE BEEN A BIT UNDER THE WEATHER. WE WERE TALKING ABOUT SOMETHING WITH THE KIDS AND THEY CAME AROUND IT AND ASKED IF WE WOULD GO TO THEIR BED. APRON, COOKIES, CANDLES, AND COLOGNE. (I HONESTLY HAVE NO IDEA WHAT I WAS WRITING. I HAVE BEEN COMPLETELY CHECKED OUT SINCE WE PULLED UP HERE). I CAN'T EVER SLEEP AT NIGHT AND THE CRYS *(meth)* I HAVE SMOKED HERE AND THERE HAS DEFINITELY NOT HELPED ME OUT WITH THAT SITUATION. IT'S ALMOST 1:00 A.M. AND I AM THE MEANEST MOTHER *EVER!* NOWADAYS EVERYTHING HAS 100% CHANGED. ADI I WOULD NOT SAY THIS ANYMORE. WELL, I AM LITERALLY FALLING ASLEEP RIGHT NOW. TALK TO YOU TOMORROW, SUNSHINE. I LOVE YOU, BUDDY. I THOUGHT I WAS TALKING TO MASON. I LOVE ALL THREE OF MY ABSOLUTELY BEAUTIFUL, AMAZING KIDS. NIGHT, NIGHT.

<u>FRIDAY, APRIL 7, 2017</u>:

ANOTHER ABSOLUTELY DEPRESSING DAY IN NATALIE'S WORLD. DIDN'T SLEEP AT ALL LAST NIGHT, SO I HAVE BEEN UP FOR

MORE THAN 24 HOURS...AGAIN. GOT UP, WENT TO LARRY'S AND GOT MY TATTOO FINISHED, THEN CAME HOME AFTER SMOKING METH WITH LARRY AND ANNA, AND SALT, GOT IN THE SHOWER, PICKED UP CARL 'CAUSE HE HAD NOBODY TO TAKE HIM TO PICK UP HIS CHECK. TOOK HIM CLEAR OUT TO LEHI TO PICK UP HIS $180 CHECK, AND HE TOLD ME IT WAS A $400 CHECK AND HE WOULD PUT GAS IN MY CAR AND HELP ME OUT A BIT! HE DIDN'T! AFTER PICKING UP HIS CHECK, WE MET UP WITH LARRY AND ANNA AGAIN AND GOT SOME SALT AND BLK. CAME HOME, DID A SHOT, LEFT CARL HERE AND I WENT TO JAY'S TO HANG OUT WITH JALA, JAY, AND ADI. ADI CAME OVER TO DO MY EYELASHES AT JAY'S BUT GOT TORN AWAY BECAUSE OF WORK! CARL LEFT AND I'M BACK AT HOME WITH JALA SLEEPING OVER HERE. I AM THE WORST MOTHER IN THE WORLD, AND I AM SO SICK OF IT! ADI, MAS, AND JALA DESERVE SO MUCH BETTER, SO, SO MUCH BETTER! THEY ARE THE BEST 3 KIDS *EVER,* ESPECIALLY AFTER EVERYTHING I HAVE PUT THEM THROUGH. THEY ARE ABSOLUTELY *AMAZING* KIDS AND THEY DESERVE TO HAVE A GOOD MOM IN THEIR LIFE. IT'S TIME TO DO A COMPLETE CHANGE OF MY LIFE AND I AM SO, SO READY. I JUST HOPE AND PRAY THAT I PULL THROUGH. I HAVE SUBOXONE WITH ME TO WEAN OFF THE BLK AND I DON'T REALLY CARE ABOUT METH AS MUCH AT ALL. I CAN DO THIS!!! I AM 38 YEARS OLD, JALA IS 11, MASON JUST TURNED 18, AND ADI IS ALMOST 21. THEY DESERVE TO HAVE THEIR MOM COMPLETELY IN THEIR LIVES FOR A CHANGE, NOT A MOM THAT COMES AND GOES. A MOM THAT IS A GOOD EXAMPLE AND TAKES CARE OF HER CHILDREN. I PRAY TO GOD THAT I WILL PULL THROUGH AND DO THIS, 'CAUSE IF I DON'T, I WILL END UP DEAD. THAT IS THE NEXT TURN IN MY LIFE IF I DON'T CLEAN UP!

JUST WHEN I THOUGHT I HAD MY LIFE A BIT FIGURED OUT, AT LEAST MORE THAN I HAVE IN A LONG TIME, *BAM!* IT'S RIGHT BACK TO THE SHITTY OLD DRUG LIFE I KEEP TRYING TO GET AWAY FROM. I WAS DOING SO GOOD, I WAS

IN TREATMENT, HAD A GOOD JOB, AND HAD MY KIDS EVERY DAY. BUT TODAY...I HAVE BEEN IN BED ALL DAY, WAITING TO GET MORE BLACK, AND HAVE NO MONEY TO MY NAME AT ALL! WE DID GET RENT PAID, THOUGH, *BARELY!* I SAW THE DOCTOR YESTERDAY *(three days before)* AND HE CALLED IN SUBOXONE FOR ME AGAIN, THIS TIME I ACTUALLY NEED TO TAKE IT. MY FRIEND CARL CAME OVER TODAY AND HE ASKED ME FOR A LITTLE SHOT, THEN HE WAS GOING TO PICK UP MORE FOR US. WELL, APPARENTLY, HE OVERDOSED AND DIED AT ONE POINT TODAY WHILE HE WAS GETTING *US* STUFF AND ENDED UP GETTING REVIVED BY THE AMBULANCE AND ENDED UP IN LAKEVIEW HOSPITAL. THAT IS GOING TO BE ME IF I DON'T CHANGE MY LIFE AROUND! I KNOW I SAY THAT EVERY TIME, BUT IT'S GETTING CLOSER TO ME EACH DAY THAT GOES BY. PRAY FOR ME TODAY AND EVERY DAY THAT I CAN BEAT THIS DEMON, BEAT THIS HORRIBLE, HORRIBLE ADDICTION!

(GRATITUDE JOURNAL) I AM SO STINKIN' GRATEFUL THAT I GET TO HAVE MY DARLING LITTLE JALA SPEND THE NIGHT WITH ME TONIGHT! I AM SITTING OUTSIDE RIGHT NOW ON THE BALCONY WITH RYAN, SYDKA, AND KORA *(Adi's dog),* WATCHING JALA PLAY WITH HER FRIENDS. IT'S ABOUT 8:00 P.M. SO IT'S GETTING A LITTLE DARK, SO I AM WATCHING JALA PLAY 'CAUSE IT MAKES ME FEEL BETTER WATCHING HER.

<u>SATURDAY, APRIL 8, 2017</u>:

ONCE AGAIN...FUCKED EVERYTHING UP! I AM STRONGER THAN THIS. GROW UP, NAT! THAT IS WHAT *EVERYONE* HAS BEEN TRYING TO TELL ME FOR YEARS. I WISH I WOULD HAVE LISTENED YEARS AGO, AND MAYBE I WOULDN'T BE IN THIS *HELL HOLE* OF A LIFE I AM IN. I HAVE THE PILLS THAT I NEED TO TAKE TO GET OFF THIS SHIT, I JUST NEED TO BE CLEAN 24 HOURS BEFORE I TAKE MY FIRST DOSE. AND SO FAR, I HAVEN'T BEEN ABLE TO DO IT! WELL, NOW I

AM FORCED TO. WE HAVE NO MONEY! AND I MEAN 0 MONEY! RYAN'S PAYCHECK WAS $300 WHEN IT IS USUALLY $900. WE ARE LITERALLY SCREWED! I GET SICK EVEN THINKING ABOUT IT. PAMELA CALLED ME THE OTHER DAY AND ASKED ME IF I WOULD CONSIDER HER BEING MY SPONSOR, I WAS *SO HAPPY* TO HEAR THAT 'CAUSE I HAVE WANTED HER TO BE MY SPONSOR EVER SINCE I FIRST MET HER. SO, OF COURSE, I SAID YES! JALA IS SLEEPING OVER HERE WITH ME TONIGHT AND I AM SUPER EXCITED TO HAVE HER HERE WITH ME, BUT I FEEL LIKE SHIT, AS *ALWAYS!* AND I LOOK EXACTLY HOW I FEEL!!!

Same day, different journal…

JALA SLEPT OVER, WHICH I LOVE EVERY SINGLE TIME, EXCEPT I *DO NOT* GET ANY SLEEP AT NIGHT AT ALL. SHE SLEEPS IN THE SAME BED AS ME WHEN SHE STAYS OVER NOW 'CAUSE RYAN'S SON TOOK OVER HER BEDROOM. SHE WAS EXTREMELY PISSED OFF WHEN SHE SAW THAT FOR THE FIRST TIME. RYAN SLEEPS ON THE COUCH, WHICH ISN'T VERY UNUSUAL FOR HIM, 'CAUSE WHEN JALA DOES NOT STAY OVER, HE ENDS UP ON THE COUCH ANYWAYS. WE ARE HAVING MASON'S BIRTHDAY DINNER AT MY MOM'S TOMORROW AT 2:30 P.M. I GET SO SCARED SOMETIMES GOING OVER THERE NOW, ESPECIALLY WHEN EVERYONE IS THERE, BECAUSE THE LAST TIME WE *ALL* GOT TOGETHER AT MY MOM'S, EVEN SHALL WAS THERE, THEY HAD MY INTERVENTION. ADI ALSO TEXTED RYAN A COUPLE DAYS AGO AND ASKED HIM NOT TO TELL ME THAT HE WAS TEXTING YOU AT ALL…BUT, SHE ASKED HIM IF I USED OVER THE WEEKEND. OF COURSE, HE SAID NO, AND SHE SAID, "ARE YOU POSITIVE?" AND HE WROTE BACK, "YES." AND WHO ELSE IS TRYING TO FIGURE OUT WHETHER I RELAPSED OVER THE WEEKEND OR NOT? SO, I TEXTED ADI TONIGHT AND TOLD HER IF SHE THOUGHT SOMETHING WAS UP WITH ME, NOT TO BE AFRAID AND COME TALK TO ME HERSELF. SHE WROTE BACK AND JUST SAID THAT SHE THOUGHT IT WAS WEIRD THAT I

CAME HOME AND WAS SICK *AGAIN*. JUST AS BAD AS A COUPLE WEEKS AGO. I DON'T BLAME HER AT ALL, AND I NEVER WILL. I TRY TO PUT MYSELF IN MY SISTER'S OR FAMILY'S SHOES AND JUST TRY TO IMAGINE JUST HOW TRAUMATIZING I HAVE MADE THEIR LIVES. I HONESTLY CAN'T IMAGINE!! SO, I AM PRAYING I DON'T EVER HAVE TO GO TO ONE OF THOSE INTERVENTIONS EVER AGAIN...IF IT WERE MINE. I AM REALLY, REALLY STRUGGLING LATELY WITH DEPRESSION AND GUILT AND SHAME...I HAVE NEVER IN MY LIFE BEEN SUICIDAL, BUT IF I EVER HAD BEEN, IT WOULD WITHOUT A DOUBT BE THE LAST COUPLE MONTHS. I HAVE CAUSED *SO MUCH* HURT AND TURMOIL IN MY LIFE WITH MY FAMILY THAT I AM NEVER SHOCKED AT ANY REACTION THEY GIVE ME NOW. I HAVE PUT THEM THROUGH *HELL* AND BACK! AND MY POOR KIDS...THAT'S WHERE I CAN'T EVEN THINK ABOUT IT WITHOUT WANTING TO PUT A GUN TO MY FUCKING HEAD!

MY BRAIN IS A BIT FRIED, SO I FEEL PRETTY STUPID ALL THE TIME. WHICH IS REALLY SAD BECAUSE GROWING UP I ALWAYS GOT AS AND BS IN ALL MY CLASSES! I AM SITTING OUT ON THE BALCONY WHILE IT IS POURING RAIN AND IT FEELS *ABSOLUTELY AMAZING!* I JUST GOT OUT OF THE BATH 'CAUSE A CERTAIN LITTLE DOG...BRATTY BEAUTIFUL LITTLE DOG COVERED ME IN MUD TODAY! I WAS IN HYSTERICS AT THE TIME BUT NOW, LOOKING BACK, IT WAS ACTUALLY PRETTY DAMN FUNNY. MIA *(Jala's dog)* TRAUMATIZED ME TODAY. I HAD TO GO LET HER OUT A COUPLE TIMES TODAY WHILE JAY AND JALA WERE IN LOGAN WITH JAY'S DAD AND IT WAS A COMPLETE NIGHTMARE FOR ME AND MIA! SHE IS STILL JUST A PUPPY AND NOT AT ALL TRAINED, AND SHE IS TWICE THE SIZE OF SYDKA AND SHE IS NOT EVEN A YEAR OLD YET. SHE GOT ME ALL MUDDY AND FRAZZLED TODAY. I WAS BAWLING MY EYES OUT. SO, NOW I AM SO EXTREMELY TIRED. JUST GOT

OUT OF THE BATH, GOING TO JUMP IN BED AND CUDDLE MY DOG WHILE I GO TO SLEEP!

(GRATITUDE JOURNAL) IT'S ABOUT 9:00 P.M. AND I JUST GOT OUT OF THE BATH AND NOW IN BED CUDDLING WITH THE BEST DOG *EVER!* I LOVE MY FREAKING DOG MORE THAN ANYTHING! EVERYONE KNOWS IT TOO. MY KIDS SAY THAT I LOVE SYDKA MORE THAN I LOVE THEM! SYDKA IS THE BEST THING THAT HAS EVER CAME INTO MY LIFE, BESIDES MY KIDS, OF COURSE.

SUNDAY, APRIL 9, 2017:

TODAY WAS ACTUALLY A PRETTY GOOD DAY. IT'S VERY HARD FOR ME TO HAVE THESE TYPES OF GOOD DAYS AND I'M TRYING TO BE POSITIVE ABOUT ME SLEEPING THROUGH THE NIGHT TONIGHT. I WOULD GIVE ANYTHING AT THIS POINT TO BE ABLE TO HAVE A GOOD DAY AND ACTUALLY HAVE A GENUINE SMILE ON MY FACE. WE HAD MASON'S BIRTHDAY DINNER AT MY MOM'S TODAY, SO IT WAS MOM AND DAD, OMI, ANGIE'S FAMILY, KAILEE AND JASON AND MY 3 KIDS (WHICH ARE ALWAYS PRETTY GREAT FREAKING KIDS!). I COULDN'T BE BLESSED MORE THAN ADI, MASON, AND JALA. THEY ARE MY *ABSOLUTE* CHERISHED THINGS THAT I HAVE IN MY LIFE AND WILL ALWAYS BE WITH ME. THAT DEFINITELY PUTS A GREAT *BIG* SMILE ON MY FACE…OH AND I CAN'T FORGET TO MENTION MY LITTLE PRINCESS *SYDKA!* THE *BEST* DOG ANYONE COULD EVER ASK FOR. HEAVENLY FATHER BROUGHT ALL FOUR OF THEM INTO MY LIFE AND I FEEL COMPLETE AND TRULY, TRULY BLESSED! GETTIN' TO BED EARLY TONIGHT SO I CAN *FINALLY* GET SOME GOOD SLEEP. I HONESTLY CANNOT REMEMBER BEING ASLEEP FOR AN ENTIRE NIGHT. GOOD LUCK!

Eleven days later...

THURSDAY, APRIL 20, 2017:

IT'S 11:32 P.M. THURSDAY NIGHT. JUST ANOTHER SHITTY DAY IN MY SHIT LIFE! I FEEL LIKE I HAVE PRETTY MUCH GIVEN UP. I DON'T WANT TO, BUT I HAVE NO MOTIVATION AT ALL TO DO ANYTHING WITH MYSELF OR MY LIFE. HOW PATHETIC IS THAT? AND HOW SAD FOR MY 3 AMAZING KIDS TO HAVE SUCH A DEAD BEAT JUNKIE AS A MOM. IT BREAKS MY HEART AND MAKES ME PHYSICALLY SICK IF I REALLY LOOK AT HOW I HAVE TREATED MY KIDS. BUT YET, I DON'T DO *A THING* TO CHANGE IT! I WANT TO, MORE THAN ANYTHING IN THIS WORLD, BUT JUST HAVEN'T DONE IT. I AM ONLY 38 YEARS OLD AND I LITERALLY FEEL LIKE I AM 80 YEARS OLD. MY IMMUNE SYSTEM AND BODY IN GENERAL ARE TOTALLY FEELING LIKE THEY ARE SHUTTING DOWN. I AM ALWAYS SICK AND ALWAYS DEPRESSED FOR THE PAST COUPLE YEARS. WELL, IT'S BEEN LONGER THAN A COUPLE YEARS, BUT IT'S BEEN WAY WORSE THAN I EVER COULD HAVE IMAGINED. IS THIS IT? IS THERE SOMETHING MORE FOR ME TO DO...'CAUSE I ALWAYS THOUGHT THERE WAS, THAT'S WHY I AM STILL HERE AND NOT DEAD. BUT LATELY, I HAVE A REALLY HARD TIME BELIEVING AND TRUSTING THAT THERE IS MORE TO MY LIFE THAN JUST THIS. 'CAUSE THIS SUCKS!

FRIDAY, APRIL 21, 2017:

IT'S ABOUT 12 MINUTES TILL MIDNIGHT AND I AM SITTING IN MY CLOSET WHERE THERE IS LIGHT TRYING NOT TO WAKE UP A PRETTY LITTLE 11-YEAR-OLD THAT'S IN MY BED NEXT TO ME. SHE WENT TO A BIRTHDAY PARTY TONIGHT AT ONE OF HER FRIEND'S, THEN GOT DROPPED OFF HERE AROUND 8:00 P.M. 'CAUSE SHE WANTED TO SLEEP AT HER MAMA'S HOUSE! SHE HAS BEEN VERY, VERY CLINGY LATELY, ACTUALLY THE

PAST COUPLE YEARS, AND WANTS TO BE WITH ME NONSTOP, WHICH I ABSOLUTELY LOVE, BUT IT GETS A BIT DRAINING BECAUSE I WENT FROM RARELY SEEING HER EACH WEEK AND THEY HAD TO BE SUPERVISED VISITS WHEN I SAW HER, TO ALMOST AN EVERYDAY THING NOW, WHICH AGAIN...I ABSOLUTELY LOVE...I JUST GET A BIT OVERWHELMED. I LOVE THIS BEAUTIFUL LITTLE GIRL! FOR ME...I AM STILL USING 'CAUSE I WON'T GO 24 HOURS WITHOUT USING AND IT HAS GOTTEN MUCH WORSE. WENT FROM DOING MAYBE A 40 EACH DAY, TO NOW ALMOST A GRAM A DAY, I'M FUCKED! THIS IS NOT GOING TO BE FUN!

A week later...

4-28-2017: Dr. Note–118 lbs. Relapsed 2 days ago on Heroin due to lack of sleep. Insomnia is a huge trigger. Ambien worked in the past. Starting her new job in two weeks. *(I don't know what she was referring to here.)* Still at Renaissance Ranch. *(She stopped going to treatment.)* Prescribed Ambien *(for sleep)* and Suboxone.

Two weeks later...

SUNDAY, MAY 14, 2017:

IT'S 1:00 A.M. AND I AM NOT A BIT TIRED. STORY OF MY LIFE. MY DOCTOR EVEN PUT ME ON AMBIEN TO SLEEP AT NIGHT AND THAT'S ONE OF THE STRONGEST NIGHT MEDS THAT'S OUT THERE AND IT DIDN'T EVEN FAZE ME AT ALL! I TOOK 2 TOGETHER ONE NIGHT AND IT STILL DIDN'T TOUCH ME. I NEED TO FIGURE THIS SHIT OUT 'CAUSE I CANNOT LIVE OR FUNCTION NORMALLY WITHOUT ANY SLEEP. IT HAS BEEN MONTHS (MAYBE EVEN YEARS) THAT I HAVE SLEPT THROUGH THE NIGHT. IT IS DEFINITELY CATCHING UP TO ME AND KNOCKING ME RIGHT THE FUCK OVER!! I AM NOT EVEN LIVING AT ALL RIGHT NOW. I AM COMPLETELY MISERABLE.

WE ARE BROKE 'CAUSE I STILL DON'T HAVE A JOB AND RYAN'S CHECKS KEEP GETTING GARNISHED. WE ARE *HELLA* STRUGGLING RIGHT NOW. I AM STILL USING, BUT I HAVE A WHOLE SCRIPT OF SUBS *(Suboxone)* AND THEN SOME. I JUST NEED TO GO 24 HOURS WITHOUT USING AND I COULD TAKE ONE. HAVEN'T MADE IT TO THAT POINT YET, I'M *SO* READY TO CHANGE MY LIFE AROUND, BUT AM SO SCARED OF CHANGE, AND JUST TO MAKE THAT FIRST STEP. I KNOW I CAN DO THIS, I HAVE ABSOLUTELY EVERYTHING I NEED... JUST NEED TO *DO IT!*

(GRATITUDE JOURNAL) IT'S ABOUT 1:00 A.M. AND RYAN JUST BROUGHT ME IN A BIG BOWL OF CHOCOLATE AND PEANUT BUTTER ICE CREAM WITH *ALOT* OF HOT FUDGE ON TOP! MMMMMMM! THIS DEFINITELY PUTS A *BIG* SMILE ON MY FACE. WENT AND WATCHED MASON DANCE HIP-HOP ON THE STAGE OF BOUNTIFUL HIGH SCHOOL 'CAUSE THEY DID A TRIBUTE FOR A YOUNG GIRL THEY KNEW WHO DIED. MY BABY HAS RHYTHM! LOVED IT!

Three weeks later...

SATURDAY, JUNE 10, 2017:

(GRATITUDE JOURNAL) IT'S ABOUT 3:10 A.M. SATURDAY MORNING AND I NEED TO REMEMBER TO WRITE IN THIS BOOK DAILY 'CAUSE I TEND TO HAVE A PITY PARTY ON A REGULAR BASIS. IT'S SOOO HARD TO FIND ANY HAPPINESS LATELY. I'M HAVING A REALLY HARD TIME THIS PAST YEAR. BUT I AM SO HAPPY AND THANKFUL THAT I HAVE MY 3 KIDS, MY FAMILY, JAY, AND RYAN. I AM VERY LUCKY!

WELL, THIS NEW YEAR HAS STARTED OUT ABSOLUTELY HORRIBLE AND IT JUST KEEPS GOING ON THAT WAY. YES, STILL USING, BUT WANT TO STOP *BADLY.* I GOT OFF LAST WEEK,

TOOK A SUBOXONE AND GOT THROWN INTO WITHDRAWALS, NO FUN! SO, OF COURSE, I HAD TO GET MORE *(heroin)* TO GET THE WITHDRAWALS UNDER CONTROL. WE ARE COMPLETELY OUT OF MONEY, COMPLETELY! RYAN IS BRINGING HOME 300-DOLLAR PAYCHECKS. I AM ONLY DOING ABOUT A 30 A DAY AND I HAVE WEANED A LOT *(off heroin)*. MY PLAN IS TO DETOX THIS WHOLE NEXT WEEK STARTING TOMORROW. I'M SO STINKIN' SCARED, BUT IT'S THE BEST TIMING. ADI AND MAS ARE GOING ON A CRUISE FOR THE NEXT WEEK, LEAVING TOMORROW, AND JALA HAS PLAY DATES WITH HER FRIENDS ALL WEEK. *PERFECT!* I HAVEN'T HAD A CHANCE TO DETOX BECAUSE EVERY TIME I DO, ADI OR JALA NEED SOMETHING. BLESS THEIR HEARTS, I KNOW THEY WANT ME AROUND ALL THE TIME, BUT I *HAVE* TO DO THIS FOR ME AND FOR THEM. I JUST HOPE I DON'T GIVE UP. I PRAY I MAKE IT THROUGH AND THAT I CAN STAY OFF AND NEVER RELAPSE AGAIN! THIS IS MY GOAL AND DREAM!

The next day...

<u>SUNDAY, JUNE 11, 2017</u>:

DEFINITELY DIDN'T MAKE ANY CHANGES THAT I WANTED TO THIS PAST WEEKEND. ACTUALLY, DID THE COMPLETE *OPPOSITE* OF WHAT I WANTED TO DO THIS WEEKEND. IT'S 3:00 A.M. SUNDAY MORNING. I WANTED TO COMPLETELY DETOX THIS PAST WEEKEND 'CAUSE JALA HAD PLANS AND WAS GOING TO BE WITH HER DAD AND COUSINS AND ADI AND MAS WENT ON A CRUISE WITH THEIR DAD YESTERDAY AND ARE GOING TO BE GONE TILL THIS COMING UP SUNDAY, SO...GENIUS ME DECIDES TO POKE A BUNCH OF SALT WITH BENJAMIN LAST NIGHT, SO IT KEPT ME UP ALL NIGHT AND ALL DAY. STARTED SMOKING AGAIN EARLY THIS MORNING 'CAUSE I STILL HAD A BIT OF SALT LEFT. SO, I HAVE BEEN UP FOR 2 NIGHTS AND ALMOST 2 DAYS NOW. YA, I'M NOT USED TO DOING THIS *SHIT* ANY-MORE, SO I AM A TAD BIT DELIRIOUS! NOT COOL AT ALL, SO

NOT COOL! I NEED AND WANT MORE THAN ANYTHING TO KICK THIS *SHIT!* I AM DEFINITELY NOT OFF THE CHAIN AND NOT OUT OF CONTROL LIKE I USED TO BE AT ALL! SO, UPSIDE, I KNOW I HAVE AT LEAST GOTTEN SOMEWHERE. I WILL *BEAT* THIS, I KNOW I CAN, I JUST NEED TO STOP TALKING AND ACTUALLY DOING!

At this point, she was still unemployed.

Over a month later...

<u>SUNDAY, JULY 23, 2017</u>:

IT'S ABOUT 1:00 A.M. SUNDAY MORNING AND I AM *FINALLY* WRITING IN MY JOURNAL FOR THE FIRST TIME IN MONTHS. WELL, I WISH I COULD SAY I HAVEN'T BEEN WRITING LIKE I USUALLY DO BECAUSE I HAVE BEEN BUSY OR HAVING FUN, BUT IT'S THE TOTAL OPPOSITE! I AM *ABSOLUTELY MISERABLE!* IT'S THE END OF JULY AND I HAVEN'T DONE A DAMN THING ALL SUMMER LONG. I DON'T KNOW THE LAST TIME I ACTUALLY GOT READY FOR THE DAY. I JUST WAKE UP LATE AND STAY IN LEGGINGS AND T-SHIRTS ALL DAY! AND YEP, I'M BACK USING, *AGAIN*. AM I *EVER* GOING TO BE ABLE TO BREAK THIS VICIOUS CYCLE I KEEP DOING? I'M NOT DOING ANY METH OR SALT DAILY, JUST HEROIN. I HAVE DONE METH AND SALT A COUPLE TIMES IN THE LAST 5 MONTHS, BUT THAT'S ALL! *(She wrote in previous entries that she had been using meth and bath salts daily.)* I JUST CAN'T SEEM TO STAY AWAY FROM THE HEROIN, I ALWAYS THINK I CAN CONTROL IT BY USING 1 TIME AND THEN WAIT...BUT I CAN'T EVER DO THAT! I USED ONCE AND THAT WAS IT FOR ME. I DON'T EVEN DO IT TO GET HIGH, I DON'T WANT THAT LIFESTYLE ANYMORE AND I DON'T MISS IT AT ALL! I AM JUST DOING IT NOW TO STAY WELL. AND, OF COURSE, WE ARE COMPLETELY BROKE, BARELY MAKING RENT EACH MONTH BECAUSE I AM USING AGAIN EVERY

DAY. WE HAVE ABSOLUTELY NO FOOD IN OUR FRIDGE AND CUPBOARDS, NO GAS IN OUR CARS, AND NO MONEY AT ALL! WE ARE BARELY SCRAPING BY. I AM SO EXTREMELY THANKFUL FOR BEING ABLE TO STAY IN THIS APARTMENT STILL. THIS HAS BEEN THE WORST SUMMER I HAVE HAD IN A LONG TIME. ADDICTION HAS TAKEN OVER ME AND HAS A HOLD ON ME THAT I DON'T THINK I AM EVER GOING TO BREAK. IT MAKES ME SO SAD AND SO NERVOUS FOR MY FUTURE, IF I EVEN HAVE ONE. MASON GOT HIS MISSION CALL *(where he goes to a different state or country to teach our religion for two years)* AND HE IS GOING TO ORLANDO, FLORIDA, IN THE BEGINNING OF SEPTEMBER 2017. I AM GOING TO MISS THAT KID SO MUCH! HAVEN'T TALKED TO MICHELLE IN MONTHS AND I HAVE ONLY SEEN EMILY A COUPLE TIMES IN A COUPLE MONTHS. I USUALLY SEE ANGIE EVERY SUNDAY. MY MOM AND DAD ARE THE *BEST* PEOPLE I KNOW! THEY HAVE DONE SO MUCH FOR ME AND MY KIDS AND STILL DO. I FEEL SO AWFUL LYING TO THEM OR KEEPING THIS SECRET, BUT I DON'T WANT TO HURT THEM AGAIN. I NEED TO GET CLEAN ON MY OWN, THAT IS THE ONLY WAY I WILL BE ABLE TO STAY CLEAN. I CAN'T KEEP DOING IT FOR EVERYONE ELSE. IT OBVIOUSLY HASN'T WORKED. I WANT TO BE CLEAN MORE THAN ANYTHING AND HAVE A LIFE AGAIN, I JUST GET TERRIFIED OF GOING THROUGH THE HORRIBLE WITHDRAWALS. I PRAY THAT I CAN GET MY LIFE BACK AND BECOME THE MOTHER, DAUGHTER, AND SISTER THAT I KNOW I CAN STILL BE!!

A couple of weeks later…

WEDNESDAY, AUGUST 2, 2017:

IT'S ABOUT 4:00 A.M. WEDNESDAY MORNING, AND OF COURSE, I HAVEN'T BEEN ABLE TO SLEEP AT ALL! IT'S BEEN A PRETTY BUSY MONTH FOR ME AND MY FAMILY. MY BABY BOY IS GOING ON A MISSION! I'M SO STINKIN' PROUD OF HIM, BUT AT

THE SAME TIME, I AM GOING TO FREAK OUT 'CAUSE 2 YEARS IS A *LONG DAMN TIME!* HE IS SO SUPER EXCITED, AND I KNOW HE WILL BE A GREAT MISSIONARY. HE WAS MEANT FOR THIS. HE LEAVES IN A LITTLE OVER A MONTH TO ORLANDO, FLORIDA. HOW COOL IS THAT? I'M SUPER RELIEVED HE IS IN THE STATES STILL AND NOT OUT OF THE COUNTRY. WELL, WHILE HE IS GONE, HOPEFULLY BEFORE HE LEAVES, I WANT TO GET COMPLETELY CLEAN!!! I KNOW I HAVE SAID THIS ALL BEFORE OVER AND OVER AND OVER AGAIN, BUT I BELIEVE THIS TIME WILL WORK. I DON'T KNOW WHY, I JUST DO! I WANT MASON TO COME HOME TO A MOTHER HE ALWAYS DESERVED. A MOTHER HE CAN BE PROUD OF, A MOTHER THAT IS CLEAN AND HAPPY! I'M DEFINITELY BEING CHALLENGED RIGHT NOW IN A LOT OF WAYS. ADI IS WORKING HER LITTLE ASS OFF AND GOING TO SCHOOL, AND SHE IS KICKING ASS AT SCHOOL! SO PROUD OF HER FOR KEEPING THAT GOING. AND ME, ON THE OTHER HAND...I AM GETTING REALLY SCARED ABOUT SO MANY THINGS AND IT'S ALL HITTING ME AT ONCE. THE ONE THING I AM SO MAD AT MYSELF FOR IS LETTING JENNIFER, ANTHONY, NICOLE, BENJAMIN AND RUTH FOR A MINUTE, BACK IN MY LIFE. THEY ARE JUST GOING TO DRAG ME DOWN AGAIN, THEY ALREADY HAVE. I'M USING A LOT MORE NOW THAN I HAVE IN A VERY LONG TIME. BENJAMIN AND RUTH I KICKED OUT OF HERE BECAUSE THEY WERE NOTHING BUT *TROUBLE!* THAT'S AN UNDERSTATEMENT, BUT ANTHONY AND JENNIFER THINK WE ARE BEST FRIENDS AGAIN AND I AM FREAKING THE FUCK OUT! I CAN'T AND DON'T WANT THEM IN MY LIFE ANY LONGER! I JUST DON'T KNOW HOW TO GET RID OF THEM AND NOT FEEL BAD ABOUT IT. I KNOW I NEED TO DO WHAT'S BEST FOR ME, I JUST NEED TO DO IT! I PRAY THAT I CAN CONQUER THIS DISEASE AND FINALLY HAVE A LIFE THAT I CAN ENJOY INSTEAD OF FEELING LIKE TRAILER TRASH ALL THE TIME. I REALLY NEED TO WORK ON ME AND GET *CLEAN, DAMN IT!!!*

(GRATITUDE JOURNAL) I AM SO EXTREMELY GRATEFUL FOR THE PAST COUPLE WEEKS I HAVE HAD. I HAVE NOT BEEN ABLE TO SAY THAT FOR A LONG TIME NOW. MAS IS GETTING READY FOR HIS MISSION TO ORLANDO, FLORIDA, AND I COULDN'T BE HAPPIER FOR HIM. I AM SO STINKIN' PROUD OF THAT KID! HE WENT THROUGH THE TEMPLE *(a place where missionaries are prepared for their mission)* 2 DAYS AGO AND HE IS HAVING HIS FAREWELL *(where missionaries speak at church before they leave on their missions)* IN A COUPLE WEEKS AT CHURCH. HE HAS A MONTH TILL HE LEAVES. I'M HAPPY BUT SAD!

THURSDAY, AUGUST 3, 2017:

THIS HAS BEEN A COMPLETELY HORRIBLE DAY! I GOT NO SLEEP LAST NIGHT AND AT 7:00 A.M., ANTHONY OF ALL PEOPLE CAME KNOCKING ON MY DOOR ALL *FUCKED* UP! I HAVE NEVER SEEN HIM LIKE THAT! AND I DON'T WANT TO EVER AGAIN! HE DID TOO MANY DRUGS LAST NIGHT AND LOST HIS CAR, HAD NO IDEA WHERE HE PUT IT, AND I DIDN'T WANT HIM IN MY HOUSE AND HE KNOWS THAT, SO AT 7:00 A.M. (AND REMEMBER, I HAD 0 SLEEP LAST NIGHT), I TOLD HIM HE HAD TO LEAVE. I DROVE HIM AROUND FOR ABOUT 4 1/2 HOURS AND I HAD LOST IT AT THAT POINT. IT WAS TOTALLY NOT WORTH IT. I WILL NEVER EVER DO THAT AGAIN. I HAD THOSE PEOPLE OUT OF MY LIFE FOR GOOD, AND NOW I KNOW WHY! NOTHING BUT DRAMA AND PUT STRAIGHT INTO A HORRIBLE NIGHTMARE!

IT'S ABOUT 7:30 P.M. AND I AM EXHAUSTED! I CAN'T EVEN KEEP MY EYES OPEN. I NEED TO GET RID OF THESE PEOPLE THAT KEEP POPPING INTO MY LIFE FROM MY HORRIBLE PAST! I HAVE CHANGED A LOT AND I KNOW THAT, SO I WILL NOT HAVE A PROBLEM GETTING RID OF THEM, ESPECIALLY WHEN IT INTERFERES WITH MY KIDS, LIKE IT DID TODAY. MY KIDS COME FIRST BEFORE ANYONE! I KNOW I HAVEN'T BEEN THE *BEST* MOTHER THAT THOSE WONDERFUL

KIDS DESERVE, BUT I DO KNOW THEY STILL LOVE ME. ADI AND I ARE SUPER, SUPER CLOSE! AND I ABSOLUTELY LOVE IT! SHE CAN'T BE WITHOUT ME MORE THAN ONE DAY. I LOVE IT AND HAVE BEEN WAITING FOR THIS FOR SO, SO LONG! SO, I WENT AND GOT SOME XANAX BECAUSE I AM VERY SERIOUS ABOUT QUITTING THIS DEVIL DRUG. I AM NOT GOING TO DIE FROM THIS AND LEAVE MY KIDS. HOW SELFISH WOULD THAT BE? BUT IT IS VERY POWERFUL, THAT'S AN UNDERSTATEMENT, AND IT'S SO HARD TO KEEP IT UNDER CONTROL, BUT I AM PRETTY SURE I CAN DO IT! I DESERVE BETTER, MY KIDS DESERVE A MUCH BETTER MOTHER, AND I WANT MORE THAN ANYTHING TO BE AN EXAMPLE TO PEOPLE AROUND ME. SO, IN THE NEXT COUPLE DAYS (SCARY), I AM GOING TO GET OFF THIS DEVIL HEROIN! I HAVE THE MOTIVATION MORE THAN *EVER!* EVEN THOUGH IT'S VERY STRONG AND POWERFUL, AND HOPING AND PRAYING IT DOESN'T PULL ME BACK. I HAVE *FAITH!* MY SISTERS ARE ALL BEING REALLY GOOD TO ME, TELLING ME THEY WOULD ALWAYS BE THERE FOR ME WHILE I WAS TRYING. THEY MEAN SO MUCH TO ME AND SO DOES MY PRINCESS LOVER BUMS! JUST PICKING UP MY BABY NOW AND TAKING HER TO GET SOMETHING TO EAT. TILL NEXT TIME… THINK POSITIVE THOUGHTS AND DO THE BEST THAT YOU CAN DO, ONE DAY AT A TIME!!

(GRATITUDE JOURNAL) TODAY, I AM EXTREMELY GRATEFUL FOR A PLACE TO LIVE, TO LAY DOWN AT NIGHT, AND SLEEPING IN A COMFORTABLE BED. I WENT DOWNTOWN TODAY AND I HAVEN'T BEEN THERE IN A VERY LONG TIME, AND IT IS SO STINKIN' SAD! I WANTED TO TAKE THEM *(homeless people)* ALL HOME AND FEED THEM AND SHOW THEM WHAT LIFE IS ALL ABOUT! YEAH, IT'S *EVIL* RIGHT NOW, BUT IT IS ALSO VERY WONDERFUL AND BEAUTIFUL. I HAVE BEEN ON BOTH SIDES. I GREW UP WITH WHATEVER I WANTED, THEN STARTED USING DRUGS AND ENDED UP WITH NOTHING AND OUT ON THE

STREETS. I HAVE CHANGED FOR THE BETTER, BUT STILL HAVE A LONG WAYS TO GO!

Five days later...

TUESDAY, AUGUST 8, 2017:

WELL, THIS IS WHAT MY LIFE HAS FINALLY COME TO? I'M SO READY TO BE DONE WITH IT! MY KIDS ARE EVERYTHING TO ME AND I CAN'T STRESS THAT ENOUGH, BUT NOW I BELIEVE THAT THEY WOULD BE MUCH BETTER WITH ME GONE. I DON'T WANT TO HURT THEM IN ANY WAY AT ALL, THAT IS THE LAST THING I WANT, BUT RIGHT NOW I CAN'T GIVE THEM THE MOTHER THEY DESERVE. I HAVEN'T BEEN ABLE TO FOR A VERY LONG TIME NOW. IT'S ADI'S 21ST BIRTHDAY TODAY AND INSTEAD OF SPENDING ONE OF THE BIGGEST DAYS OF HER LIFE, I WAS IN BED ALL DAY WITHDRAWING. HOW EXTREMELY PATHETIC IS THAT? I HAVE NEVER IN MY LIFE CONSIDERED SUICIDE UNTIL NOW. I CAN'T TAKE THIS LIFE ANYMORE. RYAN, THE ONE AND ONLY MAN I TRUSTED WITH ALL MY HEART, I FEEL IN MY HEART THAT HE IS DONE, HE DOESN'T LOVE ME ANYMORE, AND I CAN'T TRUST HIM AT ALL! IF I CAN'T TRUST HIM, WHO CAN I POSSIBLY TRUST?! ABSOLUTELY NOBODY! I'M DEAD INSIDE, I DON'T WANT TO BE AROUND ANY LONGER! I'M DONE!

IT'S 4:00 A.M. RIGHT NOW AND I HAVE NOT SLEPT IN 2 DAYS. MY LIFE JUST KEEPS GETTING WORSE AND WORSE EVEN WHEN I TRY MY HARDEST! ACTUALLY, THAT'S A LIE. I WANT IT TO CHANGE NOW MORE THAN I EVER HAVE BEFORE, BUT I DON'T DO ANYTHING TO FIX IT OR CHANGE IT. SO, I STAY MISERABLE! I'M SO LAZY AND HAVE NEVER FELT SO LONELY, UGLY, AND NOT WORTHY OF ANYONE THAN I HAVE THIS PAST YEAR! THIS HONESTLY HAS BEEN THE WORST SUMMER I HAVE EVER HAD! I HAVE NOT DONE A DAMN THING! I AM SO EXTREMELY MISERABLE, AND I KNOW THE ONE AND

ONLY THING THAT WILL CHANGE THAT FOR ME IS TO STOP USING COMPLETELY, NO RELAPSES, AND *GET OUT* AND MEET NEW, HEALTHY PEOPLE TO BE AROUND. I AM 38 YEARS OLD AND OTHER THAN MY 3 BEAUTIFUL KIDS, I HAVE ACCOMPLISHED ABSOLUTELY NOTHING! I FEEL LIKE MY LIFE IS OVER ALREADY AND SO I HAVE COMPLETELY GIVEN UP. I WANT TO BE CLEAN MORE THAN I EVER HAVE BEFORE, AND THIS TIME, I MEAN IT WITH ALL OF MY BEING. I AM JUST SO SCARED TO GO THROUGH THE WITHDRAWALS AGAIN AND FEEL *ALL* MY EMOTIONS DEEPER THAN I AM NOW!

<u>FRIDAY, AUGUST 11, 2017</u>:

*WELL, I'M NOT GOING BE WRITING VERY MUCH TODAY BECAUSE IT'S 4:30 A.M. AND I'M SO STINKIN' TIRED! I LITERALLY HAVE BEEN UP FOR 5 DAYS STRAIGHT! I HAVE *NEVER* BEEN SUICIDAL BECAUSE I THINK IT'S COMPLETELY 100% SELFISH! BUT AFTER THINKING ABOUT IT, I ALMOST THREW UP! I WOULD *NEVER* HURT MY BABIES LIKE THAT. I HAVE ALL THAT I NEED RIGHT NOW, A NICE PLACE TO LIVE, GETTING ALONG REALLY WELL WITH MY FAMILY AND KIDS, AND OF COURSE, JAY. ME AND HIM ARE *BEST FRIENDS* AND I WOULDN'T GIVE HIM UP COMPLETELY FOR ANYTHING. AND IT MAKES JALA SO EXTREMELY HAPPY THAT WE ARE SO CLOSE AND GET ALONG VERY, VERY WELL. WELL, A LOT HAS BEEN GOING ON, NOT GOOD THINGS, BUT I *FINALLY* FEEL TIRED SO I'M HITTING THE BED NOW (AFTER) I FOLD THE CLOTHES OUT OF THE DRYER AND I WILL VENT IN MY JOURNAL TOMORROW OR I WILL GO INSANE NOT TALKING ABOUT IT OR WRITING ABOUT IT. * I'M PRAYING TOMORROW WILL BE A MUCH BRIGHTER AND BETTER DAY THAN IT HAS BEEN THE PAST COUPLE WEEKS! PEACE OUT! HA HA

Four days later...

TUESDAY, AUGUST 15, 2017:

WELL, I'M AT JENNIFER'S RIGHT NOW WAITING FOR NICOLE TO COME BACK TO HELP US. I HAVE BEEN SICK ALL DAY LONG. I CAN'T STAND THIS ANY LONGER! I NEED TO QUIT, AND I AM SO TERRIFIED! IT'S THE WORST! MAS LEAVES IN A MONTH AND I AM HAVING SUCH A HARD TIME WITH IT! I'M GOING TO MISS MY BOY SO MUCH!

BACK AT HOME NOW, JUST GOT OUT OF THE BATH WITH RYAN WITH CANDLES, AND HE MASSAGED MY BACK WHILE WE WERE IN THERE. IT WAS JUST WHAT I NEEDED. I REALLY NEED TO START TREATING HIM BETTER 'CAUSE I HONESTLY HAVE NEVER IN MY LIFE BEEN TREATED LIKE A PRINCESS LIKE HE TREATS ME. I THINK I'M STARTING TO FALL IN LOVE WITH HIM. ALL I KNOW IS, IF I LOST HIM, I WOULD ABSOLUTELY *NOT* BE OKAY. AND ME AND JENNIFER HAVE BEEN TOGETHER ALMOST EVERY DAY FOR THE PAST 2 WEEKS. IT'S BEEN GREAT! JUST LIKE OLD TIMES, BUT WE DO NEED TO STOP USING, AND QUICK!!! WE ARE BOTH ABSOLUTELY MISERABLE!

WEDNESDAY, AUGUST 16, 2017:

I AM GOING TO MAKE SURE TODAY IS GOING TO BE A GREAT DAY, 'CAUSE I HAVEN'T HAD ONE FOR A LONG TIME NOW!

WELL, IT DEFINITELY DIDN'T WORK OUT LIKE I HAD WANTED IT TO! IT WAS, ONCE AGAIN, A HORRIBLE DAY. PRETTY MUCH SLEPT THE ENTIRE DAY, OTHER THAN TAKING JALA TO LUNCH. I KEEP SAYING I AM GOING TO MAKE THINGS BETTER, AND I DON'T. JUST MAKE IT HAPPEN, *NAT!* I KNOW I AM MUCH STRONGER THAN THIS! I LITERALLY HATE MYSELF RIGHT NOW, AND I HAVE FOR A LONG TIME NOW!

IT'S RYAN'S DAY OFF TODAY AND WE ARE SITTING OUTSIDE ON THE GRASS WITH SYDKA, JUST RELAXING IN THE SUN. JUST GOT DONE TAKING JALA TO CHICK-FILET 'CAUSE

THAT'S HER FAVORITE PLACE TO EAT. I'M STILL PRETTY SICK, EVERY SINGLE DAY, AND I HATE MY LIFE RIGHT NOW. JENNIFER AND I HAVE GOTTEN REALLY CLOSE AGAIN, BUT UNDER (NOT GOOD) CIRCUMSTANCES. MASON LEAVES IN ABOUT 4 WEEKS AND I AM HAVING A VERY HARD TIME WITH IT! HAVEN'T SPENT AS MUCH TIME WITH HIM AS I HAVE WANTED TO BEFORE HE LEAVES. I'M JUST ABSOLUTELY MISERABLE! AND I KNOW HOW TO MAKE MY LIFE BETTER, I'M JUST TERRIFIED TO GO THROUGH WITHDRAWALS *AGAIN!!* BUT I NEED TO DO IT. WELL, WANTED TO WRITE SOME MORE, BUT I NEED TO GO IN 'CAUSE I FEEL LIKE I AM GOING TO PUKE. PEACE OUT ONCE AGAIN!

IT'S 11:00 P.M. NOW AND I'M SITTING ON THE PORCH SMOKING, WAITING FOR ANDREW TO CALL. I'M SICK OF THIS. I JUST TALKED TO DAVID, HE IS IN PRISON STILL, AND CATHERINE IS IN THE HOSPITAL DYING. PROBABLY WON'T MAKE IT TILL THE END OF THIS MONTH. SAD. I HONESTLY DON'T THINK I HAVE EVER BEEN THIS DEPRESSED WHEN I HAVE ABSOLUTELY EVERYTHING I NEED. IT NEEDS TO CHANGE, AND QUICK!

A couple of weeks later...

THURSDAY, AUGUST 31, 2017:

IT'S LATE AND I'M JUST GETTING IN MY BED. MASON LEAVES ON HIS MISSION IN LESS THAN A WEEK. I AM FREAKING OUT! I HAVE TO SAY GOODBYE TO MY ONLY SON FOR 2 YEARS, THAT IS SUCH A LONG TIME. HE IS SO SUPER EXCITED, THOUGH, AND THAT MAKES ME HAPPY. HE WILL BE A GREAT MISSIONARY. JAY IS TAKING JALA AND I TO DISNEYLAND FOR A WEEK IN LESS THAN A MONTH. SHE IS STOKED, AND HONESTLY, SO AM I. I HAVEN'T BEEN ON VACATION IN A VERY LONG TIME. IT SHOULD BE SUPER FUN. IT WILL BE VERY HARD FOR ME TO LEAVE MY BABY SYDKA FOR THAT LONG. SHE IS NOT OKAY

WHEN I AM NOT WITH HER. SHE IS MY LITTLE SHADOW. I LOVE THAT DOG MORE THAN ANYTHING. DON'T KNOW WHAT I WOULD DO WITHOUT HER.

FRIDAY, SEPTEMBER 1, 2017:

IT'S ABOUT 1:00 A.M. AND WE JUST GOT SYDKA OUT OF THE BATH. SHE IS MY BABY. I FREAKING LOVE THIS DOG MORE THAN ANYTHING (BESIDES MY KIDS, OF COURSE), EVEN THOUGH THEY ALL SAY I LOVE MY DOG MORE THAN I LOVE THEM. HA HA!! SYDKA HAS LITERALLY SAVED ME, THOUGH. SHE HAS BEEN THROUGH SO MUCH WITH ME, SHE IS MY LITTLE SHADOW. I DON'T KNOW WHAT I WOULD DO WITHOUT HER. MASON LEAVES IN LESS THAN A WEEK NOW TO FLORIDA ON HIS MISSION. I AM SO HAPPY FOR HIM AND HE IS SO EXCITED AND SO READY TO LEAVE, BUT I AM GOING TO MISS HIM. THIS IS GOING TO BE ONE OF THE HARDEST THINGS I WILL GO THROUGH, I THINK. SAYING GOODBYE TO MY ONLY SON FOR 2 YEARS. JAY IS TAKING JALA AND I TO CALIFORNIA IN A COUPLE WEEKS AND WE ARE GOING TO DISNEYLAND AND WE ARE GOING TO DO LOTS OF FUN STUFF. WE WILL BE GONE FOR A WEEK. I'M SUPER EXCITED AND SO IS JALA. SHE CAN'T WAIT! I JUST NEED TO GET MYSELF CLEANED UP BEFORE I LEAVE, AND I AM COMPLETELY TERRIFIED. BUT I HAVE TO GO THROUGH IT EVENTUALLY, SO IT HAS TO BE NOW, GOOD LUCK, ME!

A few days later...

TUESDAY, SEPTEMBER 5, 2017:

WELL, IT'S LABOR DAY TODAY AND ME, RYAN, AND SYDKA JUST GOT BACK FROM CAMPING FOR THE NIGHT. I WANTED TO GO SO BAD, SO WE PACKED UP AND WENT UP TO MONTE CRISTO (BY PINEVIEW) AND JUST CAMPED FOR THE NIGHT. MY

PARENTS BORROWED US THEIR TENT, COOLER, AND $160.00, HOW SWEET IS THAT? I LOVE MY MOM AND DAD! I NEED TO CLEAN MYSELF UP!!! I AM SO STINKIN' TERRIFIED, THOUGH, 'CAUSE I WILL HAVE TO DO IT ALONE 'CAUSE RYAN WORKS EVERY DAY. IT IS SO HARD TO WITHDRAWAL WITHOUT ANY HELP FROM ANYONE. BUT IT HAS TO BE BEFORE THE END OF THIS MONTH, 'CAUSE I'M GOING TO DISNEYLAND WITH JALA AND JAY. THIS IS GOING TO BE *HARD!!* I AM GOING TO MAKE SURE I DO IT, THOUGH. I KNOW I CAN DO IT! MASON WAS SUPPOSED TO LEAVE ON HIS MISSION TOMORROW AND IT'S BEING POSTPONED. I HAVE BEEN THINKING HARD AND A LOT LATELY ABOUT GETTING BACK IN THE CHURCH. I KNOW IT'S WHAT I WANT, I JUST HAVE TO CHANGE ABSOLUTELY *EVERYTHING* IN MY LIFE, AND THAT'S GOING TO TAKE A LOT OF TIME AND HARD WORK. I JUST KNOW HOW UNHAPPY I AM NOW, SO I WANT TO CHANGE THAT, AND I BELIEVE GETTING BACK INTO THE CHURCH WILL HELP ME AND MAKE ME HAPPY. WELL, ANYTHING WILL BE BETTER THAN WHAT I HAVE BEEN GOING THROUGH THE PAST COUPLE YEARS! GOOD LUCK, NAT, YOU CAN DO IT!

(GRATITUDE JOURNAL) TODAY, I AM GRATEFUL I AM ALIVE! I REALLY NEED TO THANK MY HEAVENLY FATHER THAT I AM STILL HERE WITH MY 3 BEAUTIFUL KIDS. WITH THE CHOICES I HAVE MADE, I AM A VERY LUCKY WOMAN AND I NEED TO REMEMBER THAT ON MY DOWN DAYS, WHICH ARE A LOT LATELY. BUT WHEN I THINK ABOUT ADI, MAS, AND JALA, I ALWAYS GET THE BIGGEST SMILE ON MY FACE! I LOVE THEM!!

<u>WEDNESDAY, SEPTEMBER 6, 2017</u>:

I CAN'T BELIEVE I'M ABOUT TO SAY THIS, BUT I AM THINKING REALLY HARD LATELY ABOUT GETTING BACK INTO CHURCH. MY LIFE IS NOT WORKING AT ALL LIKE I WANT IT AND I KEEP DIGGING MYSELF A BIGGER AND BIGGER HOLE. I HAVE NOT

BEEN HAPPY FOR SO LONG NOW SO WHY NOT TRY SOMETHING NEW? SOMETHING THAT I HAVE SEEN FOR MYSELF THAT MAKES OTHERS HAPPY. I AM A SPIRITUAL PERSON, I JUST HAVE A HARD TIME SHOWING IT. I HOPE I FOLLOW THROUGH WITH IT AND MAKE MY LIFE A BIT BETTER!

THURSDAY, SEPTEMBER 7, 2017:

HANGIN' OUT WITH MY NICOLE TODAY. IT'S ABOUT 9:30 A.M. AND WE ARE JUST PICKING UP *(getting drugs)* IN LAYTON 'CAUSE I HAVE BEEN SO SICK ALL NIGHT LONG. BEEN UP ALL NIGHT LONG, SICK AS HELL.

ANOTHER ONE OF MY SHITTY DAYS DOING NOTHING AT ALL! I WANT TO CHANGE MY LIFE MORE THAN ANYTHING, BUT JUST DON'T DO IT! I'M SO TERRIFIED OF ABSOLUTELY EVERYTHING THAT I AM JUST NOT LIVING. I SIT AT MY APARTMENT EVERY SINGLE DAY AND FIGURE OUT HOW TO STAY WELL EVERY DAY. *(Staying well meant getting the drugs she needed each day.)* IT'S NOT A LIFE AT ALL!

FRIDAY, SEPTEMBER 8, 2017:

WELL, DEFINITELY HAD A NERVOUS BREAKDOWN LAST NIGHT AND TODAY. I HAVEN'T HAD ANYTHING *(drugs)* FOR A WHILE, SO THAT DEFINITELY SETS THINGS IN MOTION. *(She just said she picked up drugs in Layton the day before; her concept of time was getting increasingly distorted.).* I HAVEN'T SLEPT OR EATEN A THING IN 2 DAYS, NOT THAT I PLANNED TO STARVE MYSELF OR DEPRIVE MYSELF OF SLEEP, I JUST COULDN'T DO EITHER ONE. *(This is what happened when she would use meth, bath salts, or cocaine.)* SO, TODAY, FULL BLOWN BREAKDOWN! BEEN CRYING ALL DAY LONG! JAY HAS BEEN TAKING CARE OF ME THROUGH IT A LOT, THOUGH. BLESS HIS HEART. LOVE THAT GUY. I NEED TO DETOX, AND I CAN'T DO IT ALONE, SO HIS FRIEND SAMANTHA THAT IS ABSOLUTELY WONDERFUL TO

HIM AND JALA OFFERED TO HELP ME. HOW SWEET IS THAT? IT WILL BE WEIRD, BUT I HAVE TO DO SOMETHING BEFORE I DIE! I AM NOT IN A GOOD PLACE AT ALL AND HAVEN'T BEEN FOR A VERY LONG, LONG TIME NOW. I JUST WANT TO BE HAPPY AGAIN. I DON'T WANT TO SETTLE 'CAUSE I HAVE DONE THAT MY ENTIRE LIFE, AND LOOK WHERE IT'S GOTTEN ME. I WANT TRUE HAPPINESS, AND THE WAY I'M LIVING MY LIFE NOW, I'M SURE IT'S NOT GOING TO HAPPEN. SO, I NEED TO FACE MY FEARS, TAKE SOME RISKS, AND TURN MY LIFE AROUND, AT LEAST FOR MY BEAUTIFUL LITTLE JALA. SHE DESERVES MUCH, MUCH BETTER THAN THIS, A BETTER MOM THAT IS A GOOD EXAMPLE TO HER. I LOVE THAT LITTLE GIRL SO MUCH!

<u>SATURDAY, SEPTEMBER 9, 2017</u>:

DEFINITELY BEEN AN INTERESTING PAST COUPLE DAYS. I HAD A COMPLETE NERVOUS BREAKDOWN LAST NIGHT AND I STILL AM TODAY! I CAN'T STOP CRYING, SO JAY CAME TO PICK ME UP AND TAKE ME TO HIS HOUSE TO TALK TO HIM AND SAMANTHA AND TRY AND CALM ME DOWN. WELL, THEY DID. THEY FED ME DINNER (EVEN THOUGH I ATE MAYBE 4 BITES OF IT). I HAVEN'T EATEN OR SLEPT IN OVER 2 DAYS. I FEEL LIKE MY LIFE HAS BEEN STANDING STILL FOR THE PAST 4 YEARS. I HAVE ACCOMPLISHED ABSOLUTELY NOTHING! THAT IS NOT ME! I FEEL LIKE MY LIFE IS NEVER GOING TO GET ANY BETTER THAN IT IS NOW, SO WHY TRY? SO, I GUESS SAMANTHA WANTS TO COME HELP ME DETOX FOR THE WEEKEND 'CAUSE RYAN WORKS, AND EVEN WHEN HE IS HERE, HE IS SLEEPING ALL THE TIME, SO HE CAN'T HELP ME AT ALL. I NEED SOMEONE BY MY SIDE AT ALL TIMES WHILE I AM DETOXING. IT'S NOT A PRETTY SIGHT, I'M ABSOLUTELY TERRIFIED. I HAVE FUCKED UP MY BODY SO BADLY THE PAST COUPLE DAYS TRYING TO HIT, 'CAUSE I KNEW THESE WERE

GOING TO BE THE LAST FEW DAYS OF USING. WELL, I DID QUITE A NUMBER ON MY POOR BODY. BRUISES ABSOLUTELY EVERYWHERE! BLACK AND BLUE UP AND DOWN MY LEGS, AND EVEN ON MY BOOBS. I'M A DISGUSTING MESS, JUST HOW MY LIFE FEELS!

A few days later...

WEDNESDAY, SEPTEMBER 13, 2017:

SITTIN' AT MY BESTIE'S RIGHT NOW, JENNIFER AND CHILLIN' WITH CHRISTINE AND A GUY NAMED KEITH. I HAVE BEEN TRYING TO WITHDRAWAL THIS ENTIRE WEEK AND IT'S NOT WORKING SO WELL. SAMANTHA, JAY'S FRIEND, HAS BEEN TRYING TO HELP ME ALL WEEK AND I FEEL LIKE I'M GETTING NOWHERE. I NEED TO GET MY SHIT TOGETHER AND *BAD!*

(GRATITUDE JOURNAL) IT'S ABOUT 5:30 P.M. AND TODAY I AM SO EXTREMELY GRATEFUL FOR THE WOMAN I HAVE IN MY LIFE TODAY. IT'S JAY'S GIRLFRIEND AND SHE HAS BEEN AN ANGEL TO ME. SHE IS HELPING ME DETOX OFF THE HEROIN (EVEN THOUGH SHE THINKS IT'S SUBOXONE), BUT SHE HAS BEEN HERE EVERY DAY THE PAST 4 DAYS HELPING ME. I AM SO LUCKY TO HAVE THIS WOMAN IN MY LIFE. I WILL DEFINITELY KEEP HER AROUND!

THURSDAY, SEPTEMBER 14, 2017:

OKAY, I AM MAKING MYSELF A PROMISE HERE AND NOW. I AM USING ONE MORE TIME THIS MORNING BECAUSE THAT'S ALL I HAVE LEFT, AND I *AM NOT* USING AGAIN! I DON'T WANT TO DIE! HOW SELFISH HAVE I BEEN? ADDICTION IS BY FAR THE HARDEST THING I HAVE EVER GONE THROUGH AND I CAN'T SEEM TO BEAT IT, BUT I AM SO DETERMINED NOW,

I DO NOT WANT TO DIE! I LOVE MY THREE KIDS MORE THAN ANYTHING IN THIS WORLD AND I CAN'T DO THIS TO THEM ANYMORE. I'M STRONGER THAN THIS!

FRIDAY, SEPTEMBER 15, 2017:

JUST ANOTHER SHITTY, SHITTY DAY IN NATALIE'S WORLD! I HAVEN'T SLEPT FOR 2 DAYS NOW AND I FEEL LIKE COMPLETE *SHIT!* I DID GET UP, GOT READY, AND WENT WITH SAMANTHA AND HER DAUGHTER AND JALA TO FARMINGTON STATION AND SHE BOUGHT ME A PHONE CASE AND LUNCH. GOT REALLY SICK FROM EATING, SO I AM BACK HOME NOW FEELING LIKE COMPLETE *SHIT!* I SWEAR THIS HORRIBLE LIFE IS NEVER GOING TO *END!* I HAVE NEVER BEEN THIS LOW AND DEPRESSED IN MY ENTIRE LIFE. I DON'T KNOW HOW TO GET OUT OF IT. GOD HELP ME, PLEASE, BECAUSE I'M AFRAID DEATH IS COMING UPON ME.

SATURDAY, SEPTEMBER 16, 2017:

IT'S ABOUT 4:00 A.M. AND I'M SITTING OUTSIDE ON MY BALCONY AT FOXBORO APARTMENTS (WHERE I HAVE LIVED FOR ABOUT 2 1/2 YEARS NOW). YA, DEFINITELY TIME TO MOVE. I JUST GOT THIS JOURNAL TONIGHT BECAUSE I USED TO, NO MATTER WHAT, EVERY SINGLE DAY WRITE IN A JOURNAL. WELL, I HAVEN'T FOR A LONG TIME NOW AND I NEED TO GET BACK INTO IT. *(It sounds like she didn't even remember writing yesterday).* SO, UPDATE ON MY WONDERFUL LIFE, IT HONESTLY COULDN'T BE WORSE. THIS PAST YEAR, I LOST MY JOB, GOT HOOKED BACK ON HEROIN, TRIED TO STOP, I DON'T KNOW HOW MANY TIMES NOW, AND I HAVE LITERALLY *HAD IT!* IT IS AN ABSOLUTE *MIRACLE* THAT I AM STILL ALIVE! JAY AND I ARE SUPER CLOSE AND GET ALONG GREAT, AND HE KNEW I CAN'T AFFORD ANYTHING (ESPECIALLY TAKING JALA SOMEWHERE FUN), SO HE IS TAKING JALA AND

I TO CALIFORNIA IN 2 WEEKS ABOUT, AND I HAVE TO BE CLEAN. I JUST *HAVE TO!* SO, JAY AND MY FAMILY THINK I AM DETOXING OFF SUBOXONE THIS WEEK. I HATE LYING TO THEM MORE THAN ANYTHING, BUT I JUST DON'T THINK ANYBODY WANTS TO REALLY KNOW ANYMORE. THEY ALL KNOW THEY HAVE DONE EVERYTHING THAT THEY CAN POSSIBLY DO AND SO MUCH MORE, SO NOW IT'S UP TO ME AND ONLY ME! JAY ACTUALLY HAS A REALLY GOOD FRIEND NAMED SAMANTHA THAT IS ABSOLUTELY *AMAZING!* I HAVE NEVER MET ANYONE LIKE HER. SHE JUST WENT THROUGH A DIVORCE AND HAS 3 KIDS, BUT THEY ARE ALL OLDER. SO, SHE HAS BEEN HELPING ME DETOX THIS WEEK, AND LIKE I SAID, SHE THINKS IT'S SUBOXONE I AM COMING OFF OF, I JUST DON'T HAVE THE COURAGE TO TELL HER THE TRUTH. ESPECIALLY IF IT GOT BACK TO MY FAMILY, AND THE LAST THING I WANT TO DO IS HURT THEM MORE. I WAS DOING GREAT THE FIRST COUPLE DAYS, THEN I FUCKED UP AGAIN, THEN AGAIN, AND THEN AGAIN. SHE DOESN'T KNOW THAT, THOUGH. SO, I HAVE FUCKED UP ALL MY OPTIONS, AND NOW I HAVE TO DO THIS THE *HARD* WAY. I AM ABSOLUTELY *TERRIFIED!* OH, ANOTHER THING THAT WASN'T THE BRIGHTEST ON MY PART...I'M TALKING AND HANGING OUT WITH JENNIFER AGAIN. WOW, I KNOW IT'S BEEN YEARS *(it had been months)*, AND SHE IS OFF THE *RAIL!* SHE DOES SO MUCH HEROIN EVERY DAY THAT SHE DOESN'T *EVER* LEAVE HER HOUSE (AND SHE STAYS AT HER MOM'S) AND SHE IS LITERALLY IN BED ALL DAY, EVERY DAY. PROBABLY NOT THE BEST PERSON TO BE HANGING AROUND WHILE I AM TRYING TO GET CLEAN. IT'S GOING TO BE A ROUGH ONE, BUT I NEED TO DO THIS. I AM 38 FUCKING YEARS OLD, AND AT THIS POINT, ALL I'M HEADED FOR IS DEATH. AND I AM *NOT* GOING TO DO THIS TO MY 3 BEAUTIFUL KIDS THAT I KNOW LOVE ME SO MUCH AND THEY FORGIVE ME AFTER ALL THAT I HAVE PUT THEM THROUGH. I AM VERY, VERY LUCKY AND I NEED TO REMEMBER THAT BECAUSE NOBODY GETS THIS MANY CHANCES AT LIFE AND WITH THEIR KIDS LIKE I HAVE.

SO, WAKE THE FUCK UP, *NAT,* YOU ARE STILL HERE FOR A REASON...*FIND IT! I AM STRONGER THAN I THINK!!! I CAN DO THIS!*

SUNDAY, SEPTEMBER 17, 2017:

ANOTHER SHITTY, SHITTY DAY! IT SEEMS TO BE THAT WAY EVERY DAMN DAY NOW. WELL, JENNIFER IS OUT OF MY LIFE NOW, THAT WAS A SHORT FRIENDSHIP (AGAIN). SHE WENT OFF ON ME THIS MORNING, AND I WON'T TAKE IT. I DON'T NEED PEOPLE LIKE THAT IN MY LIFE AT ALL! AND I HAVE NO IDEA WHAT IN THE HELL TO DO ABOUT RYAN ANYMORE. HE LIES TO ME ALL THE TIME ABOUT THE DUMBEST THINGS AND SAYS HE DOESN'T REMEMBER. I CAN'T LIVE WITH HIM, AND I CAN'T LIVE WITHOUT HIM. I HONESTLY *DO NOT* KNOW WHAT TO DO! I AM A COMPLETE MESS AND A CRAZY PERSON RIGHT NOW. I HAVEN'T SLEPT IN 4 DAYS NOW AND I AM 100% DELIRIOUS! I KNOW I HAVE SAID THIS BEFORE, BUT I AM SO COMPLETELY DONE WITH THE FUCKING DRUG WORLD! I AM GETTING MYSELF CLEAN, I DON'T CARE WHAT IT TAKES! I GO TO DISNEYLAND IN 14 DAYS WITH JAY AND JALA, AND I HAVE TO BE CLEAN BY THEN. I NEVER TALK WITH MY SISTERS ANYMORE, AND MY KIDS VERY RARELY. I TALK TO JALA EVERY DAY, AND ADI, BUT NOT MASON VERY MUCH AT ALL. I NEED TO SPEND SOME TIME WITH HIM, BUT HE IS ALWAYS BUSY WITH HIS FRIENDS. I PRAY TO GOD THAT I CAN FINALLY, ONCE AND FOR ALL, KICK THIS STUPID DEATHLY HABIT OF MINE. MY BODY IS COMPLETELY FUCKED UP RIGHT NOW! I HAVE BRUISES ALL OVER MY LEGS, IT'S RIDICULOUS! SYDKA IS SITTING BY ME RIGHT NOW OUTSIDE ON THE BALCONY, AND I AM SO EXTREMELY LUCKY TO HAVE THIS PUPPY OF MINE. SHE MAKES ME WANT TO BE A BETTER PERSON, ALONG WITH MY KIDS. WELL, I DON'T KNOW WHAT RYAN IS GOING TO DO 'CAUSE I KICKED HIM OUT LAST NIGHT AND HE SLEPT IN HIS CAR. I JUST CAN'T HANDLE HIM LATELY. HE EVEN CALLED

JENNIFER, MY FRIEND, AND TOLD HER THAT I KICKED HIM OUT. WHAT THE HELL? I DON'T KNOW WHY HE DOES THAT. YA, THE MAN PAYS FOR EVERYTHING FOR ME RIGHT NOW 'CAUSE I DON'T HAVE A JOB. BUT HE DOESN'T TREAT ME GOOD LIKE *EVERYONE* THINKS HE DOES. HE ACTS LIKE A VICTIM ALL THE DAMN TIME AND MAKES ME LOOK LIKE A TOTAL *BITCH*. AND EVERYONE THINKS THAT. THE ONLY PERSON THAT REALLY KNOWS HOW HE IS TO ME IS JAY. AND JAY IS TRYING TO GET ME TO MOVE INTO SAMANTHA'S HOUSE AND GET AWAY FROM HIM. BUT THIS IS MY HOME AND I DON'T WANT TO LEAVE, EVEN THOUGH RYAN MAKES ME A PERSON I DON'T WANT TO BE! JAY WAS SO SWEET TO ME YESTERDAY, HE TOOK ME AND JALA SHOPPING AND BOUGHT ME A PAIR OF BOOTS AND SOME CONVERSE. OH, AND MY STINKIN' CAR BROKE DOWN TODAY, WHAT MORE CAN GO WRONG?

MONDAY, SEPTEMBER 18, 2017:

IT'S ABOUT 1:30 P.M. AND I'M SITTING DOWNTOWN ON THE SIDE OF THE STREET WAITING FOR ANTHONY AT THE BLOCK *(in Salt Lake City, where she got drugs).* THAT'S HOW DESPERATE I HAVE BECOME. I HAVE 13 DAYS UNTIL I GO TO DISNEYLAND WITH JAY AND JALA AND I NEED TO MAKE SURE I AM OKAY. WE WILL BE GONE FOR AN ENTIRE WEEK, SO I NEED TO BE OKAY *(meaning she needed a big enough supply to last her the week she would be gone).* I PRAY TO GOD THAT BY THE TIME I LEAVE, I WILL BE OKAY. RYAN AND I ARE NOT GETTING ALONG AT ALL. THIS IS THE FIRST TIME I HAVE EVER HAD HIM TREAT ME BADLY. THAT'S WHAT BLK DOES TO PEOPLE, THOUGH, TURNS THEM INTO A COMPLETELY DIFFERENT PERSON! JAY WANTS ME TO MOVE IN WITH SAMANTHA AND I HAVE DEFINITELY THOUGHT ABOUT IT A LOT, BUT IT'S MY APARTMENT, IT'S MY HOME, AND I'M NOT READY TO LEAVE IT UNTIL I FIND SOMETHING OF MY OWN. I ONLY HAVE TILL JANUARY TO BE IN MY APARTMENT 'CAUSE I AM NOT GOING

TO SIGN ANOTHER LEASE. I HAVE BEEN THERE FOR 3 YEARS. I NEED TO GET A JOB, LIVE ON MY OWN WITH SYDKA AND MY KIDS EVERY ONCE IN A WHILE, AND THEN I THINK I WILL BE HAPPY. RIGHT NOW, THERE IS ABSOLUTELY NOTHING THAT MAKES ME HAPPY 'CAUSE I AM SO COMPLETELY DEPRESSED!

Same day, different journal…

IT'S ABOUT 4:00 P.M. AND ALL I HAVE DONE TODAY IS WAKE UP AND THEN GO WITH ANTHONY TO THE BLOCK 'CAUSE I HAVE NOTHING AT ALL AND I'M GETTING REALLY SICK. HE WAS CONFRONTED BY A COP, SO HE SWALLOWED HIS BALLOON *(a "balloon" is an unfilled water balloon that dealers use to put heroin in),* AND WE ONLY HAD ENOUGH MONEY TO GET ONE. YEP, SO IT'S IN HIS BELLY AND HE CAN'T THROW IT UP. THAT WAS ALL THE MONEY I HAD! SO, I'M PRETTY MUCH SCREWED TODAY. I HAVE TO GET CLEAN, THOUGH, 'CAUSE WE ARE LEAVING TO DISNEYLAND IN 13 DAYS. YEP, I BETTER START KICKING! BUT I AM COMPLETELY TERRIFIED 'CAUSE I WILL HAVE TO DO IT COMPLETELY ALONE 'CAUSE RYAN WORKS EVERY DAY AND SO DOES EVERYBODY ELSE. IT IS THE WORST THING IN THE ENTIRE WORLD TO TRY AND WITHDRAW BY YOURSELF. YOU CAN'T DO ANYTHING FOR YOURSELF AND YOU ARE CONSTANTLY IN THE BATHROOM THROWING UP AND HAVING DIARRHEA. THEN YOU (I) ALWAYS FAINT 'CAUSE I HAVE NOTHING IN MY BODY AT ALL. FUN STUFF! I'M JUST LAYING ON MY BED RIGHT NOW WITH SYDKA, WAITING FOR ANTHONY TO COME BACK 'CAUSE HE WENT TO JENNIFER'S TO SEE IF SHE HAD ANYTHING. WE AREN'T TALKING RIGHT NOW 'CAUSE SHE WENT OFF ON ME THE OTHER DAY. PLUS, SHE IS *NEVER* GOING TO GET CLEAN. SHE LIKES DRUGS TOO MUCH AND STAYING IN HER ROOM ALL DAY, EVERY DAY, IN HER BED. I'M NOT OKAY WITH ANY OF THIS! I AM SO SICK OF THE FUCKING DRUG WORLD, I COULD JUST SCREAM. AND I REALLY DON'T WANT TO ASSOCIATE WITH ANYONE ANYMORE

THAT DOES DRUGS. I WANT TO BE WITH MY KIDS MORE AND HAVE A NORMAL LIFE. IT'S ABOUT TIME ALL MY DRAMA GOES AWAY. I'M 38 YEARS OLD, FOR GOD'S SAKE. GROW THE FUCK UP, NAT! TAKE CONTROL OF YOUR LIFE AND BE HAPPY FOR ONCE! I HONESTLY DON'T KNOW THE LAST TIME I WAS TRULY HAPPY. IT'S BEEN DECADES PROBABLY, OR EVEN LONGER. I ALWAYS SETTLE AND TRY TO TAKE THE EASY WAY OUT! I NEVER USED TO BE LIKE THIS. I ABSOLUTELY HATE THE PERSON I HAVE BECOME, AND I WANT TO CHANGE SO BADLY BUT DON'T KNOW HOW. I HAVE BEEN SO LAZY FOR SO LONG NOW THAT IT SCARES THE SHIT OUT OF ME TO DO ANYTHING AT ALL. ESPECIALLY FINDING A NEW JOB, WHICH I REALLY NEED TO DO SOON. I FEEL LIKE I HAVE COMPLETELY WASTED MY LIFE AWAY, AND I FEEL SO BAD FOR MY KIDS THAT THEY HAVE ME AS A MOTHER. THEY DESERVE SO MUCH BETTER, THEY ARE AMAZING AND I LOVE THEM MORE THAN ANYTHING IN THIS ENTIRE WORLD. I JUST WISH THIS ADDICTION DIDN'T HAVE SUCH A POWERFUL, STRONG HOLD ON ME. IT RUNS MY LIFE AND I KNOW THAT, AND I *HATE* IT! I WANT TO BE THE MOTHER MY KIDS DESERVE SO STINKIN' *BAD!* I JUST CAN'T GET OUT OF THIS HOLE OR AWAY FROM THIS POWERFUL ADDICTION.

A few days later…

<u>THURSDAY, SEPTEMBER 21, 2017</u>:

IT'S 11:00 P.M. AND I HAVE BEEN ON THE PHONE FOR THE PAST HOUR WITH SAMANTHA (JAY'S SORT-OF EX). SHE IS HYSTERICAL BECAUSE JAY SAID HE DOESN'T WANT TO SEE HER ANYMORE, AND ME AND HER HAVE BECOME REALLY, REALLY GOOD FRIENDS. SO, I AM PRETTY MUCH STUCK IN THE MIDDLE. IT'S REALLY SAD, THOUGH, 'CAUSE JALA REALLY LIKES HER A LOT AND SO DO I, BUT JAY JUST DOESN'T. HE IS NEVER GOING TO LET ANY WOMAN IN HIS LIFE AGAIN, I REALLY

THINK THAT. I ABSOLUTELY LOVE HOW ME AND JAY ARE RIGHT NOW, THOUGH. HE IS LITERALLY MY BEST FRIEND AND I PRETTY MUCH CAN TELL HIM ANYTHING. NOT *EVERYTHING,* BUT PRETTY MUCH. WE GET ALONG REALLY WELL AND I LOVE IT, AND IT'S SO GOOD FOR JALA. HE IS TAKING JALA AND I TO DISNEYLAND IN ABOUT A WEEK AND A HALF. I'M SUPER EXCITED, BUT SUPER SCARED TOO, BECAUSE I HAVE TO BE OKAY BY THEN, I HAVE TO BE, AND I DON'T KNOW HOW I AM GOING TO DO IT. I WISH MORE THAN ANYTHING IN THIS WORLD THAT SOMETHING SO *EVIL* DIDN'T HAVE THIS MUCH CONTROL OVER ME. I HATE IT AND I ALWAYS FEEL LIKE A WORTHLESS PIECE OF SHIT EVERY DAY! I FEEL *BAD* THAT MY THREE ABSOLUTELY WONDERFUL, AMAZING KIDS HAVE A JUNKIE MOTHER LIKE ME. I WANT THEM TO HAVE THE BEST LIFE POSSIBLE AND I FEEL LIKE I HAVE COMPLETELY RUINED IT FOR THEM. I WISH I COULD GO BACK IN TIME AND CHANGE SO, SO MUCH OF MY LIFE. AND I WANT TO DO BETTER, MORE THAN ANYTHING IN THIS WORLD, BUT I DON'T KNOW HOW. THIS DEVIL HAS COMPLETE CONTROL OVER ME. MY BODY LOOKS SO FUCKED UP RIGHT NOW. I HAVE BRUISES UP AND DOWN MY LEGS AND ANOTHER ABSCESS THAT I'M FREAKING OUT ABOUT RIGHT NOW. I JUST DON'T KNOW WHAT TO DO. I HAVE GROWN A LOT MORE FEELINGS FOR RYAN THAN I EVER HAVE, BUT I'M STILL NOT HAPPY. I DON'T THINK HE IS RIGHT FOR ME, I'M JUST REALLY COMFORTABLE WITH HIM. BUT, I CAN'T LET HIM GO, IT'S SO FUCKED UP. I WOULD DIE (NOT REALLY) IF HE LEFT ME, BUT I DON'T KNOW IF THIS IS WHAT I WANT! I THINK I AM JUST SETTLING (AGAIN) BECAUSE I DON'T THINK I COULD GET ANYONE BETTER. I HONESTLY DON'T THINK I COULD GET ANYONE RIGHT NOW, THE WAY I AM. AND I HAVE FELT LIKE THAT FOR A VERY, VERY LONG TIME NOW, THAT'S WHY I STAY. I AM JUST SO SUPER UNHAPPY I CAN'T STAND IT, AND I DON'T WANT TO DIE, BUT THIS LIFE IS SO HARD AND I DON'T KNOW HOW TO LIVE IT ANYMORE AT ALL! IT WAS MY DAD'S BIRTHDAY

YESTERDAY AND SHALL IS COMING INTO TOWN TOMORROW FOR MY DAD'S BIRTHDAY DINNER ON SUNDAY, AND I GET SO SCARED TO GO AROUND MY FAMILY ANYMORE BECAUSE I FEEL SO EXTREMELY GUILTY. AND THEY ARE THE PEOPLE I WANT TO BE AROUND THE MOST!! PRAY, PRAY, PRAY!!!

IT'S ABOUT 5:30 AND I AM SITTING AT A PARK WAITING FOR ANDREW *(to pick up drugs).* I AM SO STUPID. WHY DO I KEEP DOING THIS TO MYSELF? I HAVE 12 DAYS TILL I GO TO CALIFORNIA AND I HAVE TO BE OKAY BY THEN. HOW IN THE *HELL* AM I GOING TO DO IT? I HAVE NO FUCKING CLUE! SO, I HAVE BEEN SITTING HERE FOR OVER A HALF HOUR NOW. THIS IS RIDICULOUS, BUT I DON'T WANT TO LEAVE NOW. I AM SO SUPER UNHAPPY AND I NEED TO DO SOMETHING ABOUT IT, AND QUICK. MY KIDS ARE MY ENTIRE LIFE AND I ALWAYS SAY THAT…SO WHY CAN'T I PUT THEM FIRST? THIS DISEASE IS SO POWERFUL AND SOMETIMES, ACTUALLY ALWAYS, FEELS IMPOSSIBLE TO OVERCOME. BUT, I HAVE TO SOMEHOW, AND QUICK, OR I WILL DIE AND I *CANNOT* DO THAT TO MY 3 KIDS. THEY ARE ABSOLUTELY EVERYTHING TO ME, I CAN'T STRESS THAT ENOUGH. THEY ARE MY ONLY REASON FOR LIVING. IF IT WASN'T FOR THEM, I WOULD HAVE BEEN DONE WITH LIFE A LONG TIME AGO. THIS IS WAY TOO HARD AND I CAN'T STAND IT ANYMORE. I WISH I KNEW HOW TO OVERCOME THIS DISEASE. I WISH SO BADLY WITH ALL MY HEART AND SOUL THAT I COULD BE DONE WITH IT!

FRIDAY, SEPTEMBER 22, 2017:

IT'S ABOUT 9:00 P.M. AND I JUST GOT BACK FROM JALA'S CARNIVAL AT HER SCHOOL. IT WAS SO CUTE. ME, JAY, AND JALA WENT. WE WENT TO STARBUCK'S FIRST, THEN TO THE CARNIVAL. JALA ROCK CLIMBED AND DID AWESOME AND SHE WON 2 GOLD FISH! JAY WAS REALLY HAPPY ABOUT THAT ONE! I JUST GOT HOME ABOUT A HALF HOUR AGO AND NOW I AM JUST DOING LAUNDRY AND SITTING ON MY BED WRITING. FUN

STUFF! MICHELLE AND HER FAMILY CAME TONIGHT, BUT I PROBABLY WON'T SEE THEM TILL TOMORROW OR SUNDAY FOR DAD'S BIRTHDAY DINNER. I GET SO NERVOUS TO SEE SHALL 'CAUSE SHE IS ALWAYS THE ONE TO QUESTION ME AND I HATE LYING TO HER. MY FAMILY ARE THE PEOPLE I WANT TO BE AROUND THE MOST, AND RIGHT NOW, THEY ARE THE LEAST. AND IT'S 100% MY FAULT! I MISS THEM ALL SO MUCH. WE NEVER TALK ON THE PHONE OR ANYTHING ANYMORE. I TALK TO MY MOM BUT HARDLY EVER SEE MY SISTERS UNLESS IT'S A HOLIDAY OR SOMETHING IS GOING ON WITH THE FAMILY. ME AND MY SISTERS USED TO TALK EVERY SINGLE DAY AND NEVER SKIPPED A DAY, *EVER!* NOW, I HAVE NO IDEA WHAT IS GOING ON IN ANY OF THEIR LIVES AND IT MAKES ME WANT TO CRY. THEY ARE ALL THREE MY VERY BEST FRIENDS AND ALWAYS WILL BE. I WISH MORE THAN ANYTHING THAT I COULD HAVE THE RELATIONSHIP LIKE I USED TO HAVE WITH THEM, AND I KNOW IT'S MY FAULT. HOW DO I GET THAT CLOSENESS BACK WITH THEM WHEN I KNOW THEY WILL *NEVER* TRUST ME AGAIN? I SAY THIS ALL THE TIME, BUT I WISH EVERY DAY THAT I COULD TURN BACK TIME AND DO EVERYTHING ALL OVER AGAIN. I HAVE TOTALLY RUINED MY LIFE, AND I ONLY GET ONE. FREAKING ANTHONY SHOWED UP HERE AT MY HOUSE WITHOUT CALLING OR ANYTHING TWICE THIS WEEK. I NEED TO MOVE, TOO MANY PEOPLE KNOW WHERE I LIVE AND I DON'T THINK IT'S SAFE ANYMORE. MY LEASE IS UP IN JANUARY, BUT I DON'T WANT TO WAIT THAT LONG. BUT, I DON'T REALLY HAVE A CHOICE AT ALL. SAMANTHA HAS ASKED ME TO MOVE INTO HER HOUSE WITH HER, BUT I HONESTLY CAN'T LEAVE RYAN. MY FEELINGS FOR HIM HAVE GOTTEN A LOT STRONGER OVER THE PAST YEAR. I STILL TREAT HIM AWFUL AND I FEEL BAD FOR THAT, BUT HE JUST DOES THINGS SOMETIMES (MOST OF THE TIME) THAT JUST DON'T MAKE SENSE, TO ANYBODY. THE ONE THING THAT REALLY BOTHERS ME, THOUGH, IS THAT *EVERYONE* (LIKE MY FAMILY), AND EVERYONE ELSE THAT KNOWS US, THINKS HE

IS AN ANGEL AND I AM THE DEVIL...ONLY IF THEY REALLY KNEW WHAT WAS GOING ON BEHIND CLOSED DOORS. NOT THAT HE TREATS ME BAD OR ANYTHING, BUT HE IS AN ADDICT, JUST LIKE ME, AND NOBODY, ABSOLUTELY NOBODY KNOWS THAT. HE WAS THE ONE THAT ACTUALLY GOT ME BACK ON IT WHEN I WAS CLEAN, WHEN I CAME HOME FROM IDAHO FALLS. BUT IN EVERYONE'S EYES, HE IS A COMPLETE ANGEL AND I AM A BITCHY JUNKIE!! IT SUCKS!!! *(Most of the family was convinced that Ryan was clean and always wondered about their relationship. It wasn't until she passed away that we found out the truth about him, which was that he was an addict and had been for years. I remember one Christmas asking her why he looked high and she said he had something in his eye.)*

<u>SATURDAY, SEPTEMBER 23, 2017</u>:

THIS JOURNAL IS AT ITS LAST PAGES, SO I THOUGHT I'D WRITE ABOUT MY DAY TODAY. IT HASN'T BEEN TOO BAD ACTUALLY, *WOW,* I KNOW! I AM GETTING READY TO GO TO A WOMEN'S CONFERENCE *(a church meeting)* IN ABOUT AN HOUR WITH MY MOM, SHALL, AND ANGIE. YEP, THEY TALKED ME INTO IT. I JUST GOT BACK FROM PICKING SAMANTHA UP AT THE AIRPORT, AND THE ENTIRE WAY HOME, ALL SHE DID WAS COMPLAIN ABOUT THINKING THAT SHE HAS LOST JAY. AT FIRST, I WAS FINE LISTENING TO HER CRY ABOUT JAY, BUT NOW IT'S GETTING COMPLETELY RIDICULOUS! SHE IS A COMPLETE WRECK! SHE THINKS THERE IS NO LIFE WITHOUT JAY IN IT! I REALLY CAN'T TAKE LISTENING TO IT ANYMORE. I WILL BE HER FRIEND 'CAUSE SHE IS A GREAT FRIEND (SO FAR), BUT I CAN'T LISTEN TO HER CRY ABOUT MY EX EVERY TIME I TALK TO HER. WELL, THIS IS IT, MY LAST PAGE, I PRAY MY NEXT JOURNAL WILL BE A LOT MORE HAPPY AND I HAVE MY PATHETIC LIFE TURNED AROUND. I HOPE! I CAN ALWAYS START OVER, IT'S NOT TOO LATE, I NEED TO REMEMBER THAT! BYE FOR NOW!

Same day...

WELL, ALMOST DONE WITH THIS JOURNAL AND I CAN'T EVEN GO BACK AND READ SOME OF WHAT I WROTE, 'CAUSE I GET TOO *DAMN* DEPRESSED! I AM 38 FUCKING YEARS OLD AND HAVE NOTHING TO SHOW FOR MY LIFE, EXCEPT MY 3 BEAUTIFUL KIDS. THAT IS ABSOLUTELY THE *ONLY* GOOD THING THAT I HAVE DONE IN MY LIFE. HOW EXTREMELY PATHETIC IS THAT?! I JUST DON'T CARE ANYMORE...I DON'T WANT TO DIE (WELL NOT SERIOUSLY) 'CAUSE I WOULDN'T DO THAT TO MY KIDS, BUT I FEEL LIKE I HAVE COMPLETELY GIVEN UP. I WISH I COULD GET THE MOTIVATION AND THE FUN AND ENERGETIC SPIRIT THAT I USED TO HAVE, BUT THAT IS LONG GONE. I HAVE NO IDEA HOW TO GET IT BACK. I'M JUST GOING TO BED RIGHT NOW AND IT'S A LITTLE OVER MIDNIGHT AND RYAN IS ALMOST ASLEEP RIGHT NEXT TO ME. IT BUGS ME *SO BAD*...HE LAYS DOWN AND HE IS OUT...NO MATTER WHAT... ME, I WILL BE UP ALL NIGHT LONG, JUST LIKE I AM EVERY DAMN NIGHT, STRESSING MY LIFE AWAY. I HAVE COMPLETELY RUINED MY LIFE AND IT MAKES ME SO SAD BECAUSE I HAD LOTS OF GOOD GOALS AND DREAMS THE WHOLE TIME GROWING UP, AND I DIDN'T ACCOMPLISH A SINGLE ONE! I FEEL LIKE A PATHETIC JUNKIE ALL THE TIME!

SUNDAY, SEPTEMBER 24, 2017:

SITTIN' OUTSIDE ON MY BALCONY IN THE POURING RAIN, JUST GOT HOME FROM DAD'S BIRTHDAY DINNER. IT WAS NICE EXCEPT FOR THE FACT THAT SYDKA TRIED TO ATTACK ZORRO *(my dog).* THAT WAS THE FIRST TIME THEY HAD MET, IT DIDN'T GO OVER TOO WELL. MY DOG IS A LITTLE BRAT, BUT I WOULDN'T TRADE HER FOR ANYTHING! SHE IS MY BABY, I LOVE THAT DOG MORE THAN ANYTHING IN THIS WORLD (EXCEPT MY KIDS, OF COURSE), EVEN THOUGH THEY ALL THINK I LOVE MY DOG MORE THAN I LOVE THEM. I CAN'T COMPLAIN

ABOUT MY DAY, THOUGH, IT WAS GOOD. SHALL LEFT TODAY, BUT LAST NIGHT WAS AWESOME. ME, SHALL, MOM, AND ADI WENT TO WOMEN'S CONFERENCE, THEN WENT TO EAT AT CHINA PLATTER AND AUSTIN MET US THERE. IT WAS FUN. SO, I HAVE AN ABSCESS ON MY UPPER RIGHT LEG AND I DO NOT WANT TO GO TO THE HOSPITAL AND GET IT CUT OUT. I HAVE BEEN CUT OPEN WAY TOO MANY TIMES AND I CAN'T TAKE IT ANYMORE. RYAN IS MAD 'CAUSE HE SAYS WE REALLY NEED TO GO AND I KNOW WE DO 'CAUSE THE RED STREAK IS GOING DOWN TO MY KNEE, BUT I JUST CAN'T DO IT! I'M LEAVING IN 6 DAYS TO GO TO CALIFORNIA AND I CAN'T EVEN WALK RIGHT NOW. GOD, DID I GET MYSELF INTO A MESS!

MONDAY, SEPTEMBER 25, 2017:

WELL, COULDN'T FINISH LAST NIGHT, SO NOW IT'S MONDAY NIGHT AT 9:00 P.M. HAD ANOTHER SHITTY, SHITTY DAY, AS ALWAYS! I'M SITTING ON MY BED AND RYAN JUST GOT HOME FROM ANDREW'S HOUSE. HE FRONTED HIM A BALL, CAN YOU BELIEVE THAT? A BALL! *(A "ball" is an amount of heroin.)* HE LOVES RYAN, BUT I DIDN'T KNOW THAT MUCH! HOLY SHIT! JENNIFER TRIED TO GIVE ME A 10 TONIGHT THAT WASN'T EVEN SHIT…I HAVE NO IDEA WHAT IT WAS, BUT IT WASN'T SHIT. I HAVEN'T EATEN ANYTHING ALL DAY LONG. WE DON'T HAVE SHIT TO EAT IN THIS HOUSE AND NO MONEY TO GET ANYTHING, SO I AM COMPLETELY STARVING TO DEATH. THIS SUCKS SO BAD!!! MY DAD CALLED ME TODAY, HE GOT HIMSELF AN IPHONE. HE WANTED TO MAKE SURE HE KNEW HOW TO USE IT, SO HE CALLED ME, AND TO THANK ME FOR ALWAYS HELPING AROUND HIS HOUSE WHEN I AM THERE. I LOVE THAT MAN SO STINKIN' MUCH! MY DAD IS TRULY MY HERO! ALWAYS HAS BEEN. WE HAVEN'T ALWAYS GOT ALONG, BUT THAT'S ALL ON ME, 'CAUSE I HAVE PUT HIM THROUGH HELL AND BACK. BUT HE HAS BEEN THERE FOR ME ALWAYS, EVEN WHEN I DIDN'T THINK HE WAS. I'M SCARED 'CAUSE HE IS SO UNHEALTHY,

AND I WOULD LITERALLY DIE IF I LOST MY DAD. HE IS THE GREATEST MAN I HAVE EVER KNOWN IN THIS ENTIRE WORLD! MY SWEET SYDKA IS SITTING RIGHT NEXT TO ME RIGHT NOW, SHE NEVER LEAVES MY SIDE, SHE'S LIKE MY LITTLE SHADOW, I ABSOLUTELY LOVE IT! MY DAD ALWAYS SAYS HOW SWEET IT IS THAT SHE NEVER LEAVES MY SIDE, SHE IS ALWAYS WITH ME, NO MATTER WHAT. I WOULDN'T HAVE IT ANY OTHER WAY!!

TUESDAY, SEPTEMBER 26, 2017:

IT'S ABOUT 9:00 P.M. AND ME, RYAN AND HIS SON AND ADI JUST GOT BACK FROM DINNER AT PROPER BURGER IN SALT LAKE. IT WAS PRETTY FUN, NEVER BEEN THERE BEFORE, IT WAS REALLY GOOD. WELL, ADI AND DAKOTA ARE MOVING THIS WEEKEND OUT OF THEIR FIRST APARTMENT AND THEY ARE MOVING RIGHT DOWN THE STREET FROM JAY AND JALA. JALA IS SO EXCITED ABOUT IT! WELL, WE LEAVE SATURDAY FOR CALI. I'M SUPER SCARED ABOUT THE WHOLE SITUATION BUT SUPER EXCITED AT THE SAME TIME. MY FINGERS ARE ALL SO SWOLLEN LATELY THAT I CAN BARELY WRITE. I TRY TO HIT *(shoot up)* IN MY FINGERS 'CAUSE THAT'S THE ONLY PLACE I CAN HIT, AND IT LITERALLY BLOWS MY FINGERS UP. HOW STUPID AM I? I'M PRETTY TIRED, WENT TO MY MOM'S EARLIER AND SAW MASON FOR A SPLIT SECOND AND CLEANED UP MY MOM'S KITCHEN WHILE SHE IS GONE, THEN GOT KORA *(Adi's dog)*, THEN WENT TO JALA'S FOR A WHILE AFTER SHE GOT HOME FROM SCHOOL TO SEE HER FOR A LITTLE BIT, AND SHE ENDED UP GOING TO HER FRIEND'S HOUSE, SO I CAME BACK HOME. WELL, LATER, MY FINGERS ARE HURTING WAY TOO BAD TO WRITE.

WEDNESDAY, SEPTEMBER 27, 2017:

IT'S 10:50 P.M. AND I JUST GOT OUT OF A NICE, HOT, HOT BATH. IT WAS AN OKAY DAY UNTIL ABOUT A 1/2 HOUR AGO.

I GOT A PHONE CALL AND I DIDN'T ANSWER IT, SO THEY LEFT A VOICEMAIL SAYING, "THIS IS CLARK'S WIFE AND HE JUST WANTED ME TO LET YOU KNOW HE WAS IN JAIL." FIRST OFF, I ALREADY KNEW THAT, SECOND OFF, I DIDN'T WANT MY NAME COMING OUT OF HIS MOUTH, *EVER!* AND NOW I'M GETTING CALLS FROM WHO KNOWS WHO THAT WAS ABOUT HIM! I'M FREAKING THE FUCK OUT NOW AND I ACTUALLY HAD A PRETTY GOOD DAY UNTIL THAT PHONE CALL. NOW THERE IS NO WAY IN *HELL* I'M SLEEPING TONIGHT. MY NAME SHOULD NOT BE ASSOCIATED WITH THAT MAN AT ALL! I PRAY NOTHING COMES OF IT, 'CAUSE I HONESTLY BARELY KNOW THE GUY. ANOTHER REASON HAVING JENNIFER BACK IN MY LIFE IS A BAD IDEA. EVER SINCE I STARTED HANGING OUT WITH HER AGAIN, IT'S BEEN NOTHING BUT HORRIBLE THINGS HAPPENING ALMOST ON A DAILY BASIS. WHEN SHE WASN'T IN MY LIFE, NONE OF THIS WAS HAPPENING, ABSOLUTELY NONE OF IT! BUT I DO CARE ABOUT HER A LOT. IT'S JUST LIKE MARY THEY GET UNDER MY SKIN IN A BAD WAY AND IN A GOOD WAY. THEY GET INTO MY HEART AND THEN THEY KNOW I CAN'T LET THEM GO. I CARE TOO MUCH! I CAN'T JUST HAVE PEOPLE COME IN AND OUT OF MY LIFE AND BE OKAY WITH IT! AND THEY BOTH KNOW THAT. THEY ARE 2 GIRLS THAT DEFINITELY KNOW HOW TO PLAY WITH MY HEART. WELL, CALIFORNIA IS GOING TO HAPPEN WITH ME, JALA, AND JAY. THIS HAS BEEN SOMETHING MY LITTLE MISS JALA HAS BEEN WAITING A VERY LONG TIME FOR. NOBODY BETTER SCREW THAT UP FOR ME. IT WAS RYAN'S DAY OFF TODAY AND WE WENT TO MY MOM'S THIS MORNING AND MADE MASON LUNCH ON HIS LUNCH BREAK. THEN CAME HOME, HUNG OUT A BIT, THEN I WENT TO JENNIFER'S, SHE GAVE ME A BIG SHOT THAT MADE ME PRETTY SICK, AND OF COURSE, ANTHONY SHOWED UP 'CAUSE HE HAS NOWHERE TO GO NOWADAYS, SO I BAILED AS SOON AS HE GOT THERE. I WENT TO JAY'S HOUSE 'CAUSE JALA WAS ALONE AND A MESS 'CAUSE HER 2 GOLDFISH HAD DIED WHEN SHE GOT HOME FROM SCHOOL TODAY. CAME BACK

HOME, COLORED A BIT *(She was always writing or coloring)*, AND GOT IN THE BATH, DOING LAUNDRY, AND NOW I'M SITTING HERE WRITING AND STILL FREAKING OUT. PLEASE GOD, LET ME BE DONE WITH ALL THE BAD AND NOT GOOD PEOPLE IN MY LIFE AND HELP ME MAKE GOOD CHOICES AND BE AN EXAMPLE THAT MY KIDS CAN FINALLY LOOK UP TO. PLEASE HELP THAT OUR TRIP TO CALI WILL BE COMPLETELY, FOR ALL 3 OF US, SOMETHING THAT JALA CAN REMEMBER FOREVER AND CHERISH THE REST OF HER BEAUTIFUL LIFE!

THURSDAY, SEPTEMBER 28, 2017:

OF COURSE, EVERYONE IN THIS HOUSE (RYAN AND HIS SON) ARE OUT COLD ASLEEP AND I AM SITTING HERE WITH MY HEAD LAMP ON FREAKING THE FUCK OUT ABOUT ABSOLUTELY *EVERYTHING!* I JUST LITERALLY HATE (DESPISE) MY LIFE RIGHT NOW! I HATE EVERYTHING ABOUT IT EXCEPT FOR MY 3 BEAUTIFUL KIDS. HOW IN THE HELL DID THEY TURN OUT THE WAY THEY ARE AFTER THE HELL I PUT THEM THROUGH? THEY ARE ABSOLUTELY AMAZING KIDS, AND I'M NOT JUST SAYIN' THAT 'CAUSE THEY ARE MY KIDS, PEOPLE TELL ME THAT ALL THE TIME. I HAVE TO GIVE ALL THE CREDIT TO MY PARENTS. THEY ARE SERIOUSLY THE MOST GENUINE, BEST PEOPLE I HAVE EVER KNOWN. IF I WAS HALF THE MOTHER TO MY KIDS THE WAY MY MOM IS TO ME, THEY WOULD NEVER HAVE WENT THROUGH THE TORTURE THAT THEY DID BECAUSE OF ME. I WISH I COULD TURN BACK TIME. I WOULD HAVE DONE SO MANY THINGS DIFFERENTLY. ONE THING I REGRET AMONG MANY…IS FALLING AWAY FROM THE CHURCH LIKE I HAVE. I AM A MUCH MORE SPIRITUAL PERSON THAN PEOPLE THINK I AM. WHEN I DO GO TO CHURCH, I ALWAYS LEAVE FEELING LIKE A MUCH BETTER PERSON AND USUALLY FEEL LIKE THE SPIRIT IS WITH ME. IT IS SUCH AN AWESOME FEELING AND I LOVE IT, SO WHY DON'T I GO MORE? I HAVE NO IDEA…I HONESTLY FEEL LIKE I AM SABOTAGING MY OWN LIFE, NOT

KNOWING IT. HOW SAD AND PATHETIC IS THAT? I HAVE A STRONG FEELING THAT AFTER THIS TRIP WITH JALA AND JAY, THINGS IN MY LIFE ARE GOING TO BE DIFFERENT FOR THE BETTER. I THINK THIS WILL JUMPSTART THINGS FOR ME, GET ME UP, OUT OF THE HOUSE, GETTING READY EVERY DAY, AND START MAKING NEW AND BETTER CHOICES BECAUSE I WILL FINALLY HAVE THE MOTIVATION AND CONFIDENCE THAT I NEED. I KNOW I CAN DO THIS, I JUST NEED TO START TRYING. I FEEL LIKE I HAVE GIVEN UP ON EVERYTHING THIS PAST YEAR. THAT'S WHY CALIFORNIA WITH MY 2 BEST FRIENDS AND ONE OF THE 2 MOST AMAZING PEOPLE IN MY LIFE IS GOING TO BE A VERY GOOD THING FOR ME. I CAN FEEL IT...AND I HAVEN'T BEEN ABLE TO FEEL FOR SUCH A LONG TIME NOW. I WISH I COULD FALL IN LOVE, I MEAN REALLY, ACTUALLY FALL IN LOVE. NOT JUST LUST AND NOT JUST SETTLE LIKE I HAVE ALWAYS DONE, BUT ACTUALLY FALL IN LOVE WITH SOMEONE. I WOULDN'T EVEN KNOW WHAT THAT FELT LIKE. I LOVE RYAN AS A PERSON, BUT I'M NOT IN LOVE WITH HIM...ACTUALLY I WOULDN'T EVEN KNOW 'CAUSE I HAVEN'T EXPERIENCED IT YET. I WANT TO GROW OLD WITH SOMEONE THAT LOVES ME MORE THAN ANYTHING IN THIS WORLD AND ME LOVE HIM THE SAME. IS IT POSSIBLE FOR ME? I PRAY TO GOD IT IS, AND THAT I AM NOT TOO LATE!

SATURDAY, SEPTEMBER 30, 2017:

GETTING READY AND PACKED FOR CALI! YEAH! WE LEAVE REALLY EARLY THIS MORNING (LIKE 4 A.M.). I'M SUPER EXCITED! IT'S ABOUT 5:30 P.M. AND I'M GOING TO BE HEADING OVER TO JAY'S HERE IN A LITTLE BIT. WE HAVE TO GET TO BED EARLY 'CAUSE WE ARE LEAVING AT THE CRACK OF DAWN. I'M SO SUPER EXCITED BUT SCARED AT THE SAME TIME. I CAN'T GET SICK WHILE I'M THERE, SO I HAVE TO CONSERVE LIKE I NEVER HAVE BEFORE. I CAN DO IT, I KNOW I CAN. THIS TRIP IS FOR THE LITTLE MISS AND IT HAS

TO GO GREAT FOR HER. SHE HAS BEEN WAITING TO GO ON A VACATION WITH JAY AND I FOR SUCH A LONG TIME NOW, WE ARE GOING TO HAVE A *BLAST*, I KNOW IT! I ABSOLUTELY *HATE* LEAVING MY DOG, THOUGH. IT IS SO SUPER HARD BEING GONE SUCH A LONG TIME WITHOUT MY BABY. SYDKA IS MY SHADOW, SO SHE DOESN'T LIKE IT WHEN I'M GONE EITHER. KORA *(Adi's dog)* IS HERE WITH SYDKA, RYAN HAS HER TILL WEDNESDAY, TILL ADI AND DAKOTA CAN MOVE INTO THEIR NEW PLACE. I HAVEN'T EVEN SEEN IT YET. I FEEL SO BAD, I COULDN'T EVEN HELP ADI MOVE THIS WEEKEND 'CAUSE I HAD SO MUCH GOING ON. I'M HERE AT JAY'S HOUSE NOW, IT'S ABOUT 6:50 P.M. AND WE ARE GOING TO GO TO BED PRETTY SOON. SAMANTHA JUST LEFT WITH MIA *(Jala's dog)* AND SHE WAS NOT OKAY AT ALL. PROBABLY 'CAUSE JAY IS LEAVING FOR A WEEK, WHO KNOWS, I LOVE THE GIRL BUT SHE IS OBSESSED WITH JAY, AND THAT'S PROBABLY AN UNDERSTATEMENT. WE ARE JUST WATCHING TV NOW. JUST GOT DONE PACKING JALA. SHE WASN'T PACKED AT ALL. I PRAY THIS WEEK WILL BE AWESOME! WE ALL DESERVE IT, ESPECIALLY MY LITTLE PRINCESS. SHE DESERVES THIS TRIP MORE THAN ANYONE. JALA IS SUCH A GOOD LITTLE GIRL. AND I'M NOT JUST SAYING THAT 'CAUSE SHE IS MY DAUGHTER, SHE REALLY IS THE *BEST* LITTLE GIRL. SO CARING OF OTHERS, AND LOVES HER FAMILY AND HER SISTER AND BROTHER SO MUCH! SHE HAS A FUN AND SWEET PERSONALITY AND IS SO GOOD TO HER FRIENDS. HOW DID I END UP WITH SUCH GREAT KIDS? THEY ARE ALL 3 ABSOLUTELY AMAZING!!!

TEXT FROM ME TO NAT: Tye just texted me this (it's from an Apostle of the Church): "I don't know who in this vast audience today may need to hear the message of forgiveness inherent in this parable, but however late you think you are, however many chances you think you have missed, however many mistakes you feel you have made or talents you think you don't have, or however far from home and family and God you feel you have traveled, I testify to you that you have *not* traveled beyond the reach of divine love. It is not possible for you to sink lower than the infinite light of Christ's Atonement shines." I Love you.

SUNDAY, OCTOBER 1, 2017:

GETTING READY TO HEAD ON OUT TO CALIFORNIA THIS MORNING WITH JAY AND JALA AND I'M SUPER EXCITED, WE ARE GOING TO HAVE A *BLAST!* WE ARE STAYING ALL WEEK ACROSS THE STREET FROM DISNEYLAND. I CAN'T REMEMBER THE LAST TIME I WENT TO DISNEYLAND. THIS WAS ALL JAY'S IDEA, HE WANTED JALA AND I TO FINALLY HAVE A VACATION TOGETHER. HOW SWEET IS THAT? HE IS PAYING FOR ABSOLUTELY EVERYTHING 'CAUSE I HAVE NO MONEY. WHAT EX-HUSBAND *(they never divorced.)* WOULD EVER DO THIS FOR THEIR EX-WIFE? I FEEL SO LUCKY TO HAVE HIM AS MY EX AND MY LITTLE GIRL'S DAD. JAY IS SERIOUSLY MY BEST FRIEND AND HAS BEEN FOR YEARS NOW. I TELL HIM ALMOST EVERYTHING. HE KNOWS ME BETTER THAN ANYONE EVER HAS. HE NEVER JUDGES ME AND IS ALWAYS PRAISING ME INSTEAD OF PUTTING ME DOWN. I'M SO GLAD HE IS WHO HE IS. MY OLDER KID'S DAD AND I STILL HAVEN'T SPOKEN FOR PROBABLY ALMOST 15 OR PLUS YEARS. HE WILL *NEVER* GET OVER WHAT I DID TO HIM (AND THAT IS HIS WORDS), I DOUBT HE WILL EVER TALK TO ME AGAIN. I WISH HE WOULD GET OVER IT ALREADY 'CAUSE IT MAKES THINGS WITH ADI AND MASON VERY HARD AND UNCOMFORTABLE. ADI IS CLOSER WITH ME AND MASON IS CLOSER WITH HIS DAD. ADI IS VERY CLOSE TO ME AND I ABSOLUTELY LOVE IT! I LOVE BEING THIS CLOSE TO HER, I JUST REALLY NEED TO WORK ON MASON 'CAUSE HE STILL HAS A REALLY HARD TIME WITH ME AND I DON'T KNOW IF HE WILL EVER FULLY GET OVER IT. I PRAY HE DOES. *(Mason was still trying to process what was really going on with his mom.)* JALA IS REALLY CLOSE TO ME ALSO.

I GOT SUPER LUCKY WITH THE KIDS THAT I HAVE AND THE RELATIONSHIP I HAVE WITH THEM AFTER EVERYTHING I PUT THEM THROUGH. I AM SO BLESSED, AND I NEED TO REMEMBER THAT ON MY BAD DAYS (WHICH IS EVERY DAY FOR THE PAST YEAR). I REALLY DO TAKE A LOT OF THINGS FOR GRANTED. I NEED TO OPEN MY EYES AND LOOK AT THE THINGS I DO HAVE IN MY LIFE. ESPECIALLY AFTER THE HORRIBLE LIFE I HAVE LIVED FOR SO LONG. I HAVE HAD SO MANY CHANCES AND A LOT OF PEOPLE DON'T EVEN GET A SECOND CHANCE. I REALLY AM BLESSED AND LOOKED AFTER. I HAVE AN ABSOLUTELY AMAZING FAMILY THAT WOULD DO ANYTHING FOR ME, AND THEY SHOULDN'T EVEN BE TALKING TO ME AFTER EVERYTHING I HAVE PUT THEM THROUGH AND FOR SO MANY DAMN YEARS. I AM *TRULY BLESSED!*

NOPE, STILL NOT ASLEEP! IT IS NOW 1:08 A.M. AND WE ARE LEAVING IN 3 FREAKING HOURS. I NEED TO GET SOME SLEEP. I HAVE BEEN GETTING MAD, THOUGH, LATELY, 'CAUSE RYAN IS AN ANGEL IN EVERYONE'S EYES, AND I AM THE *DEVIL!* BELIEVE ME, RYAN IS NO ANGEL. YES, HE IS A GREAT MAN, BUT HE DOES HAVE HIS FLAWS AND HE DOES MAKE MISTAKES, IT'S JUST NOBODY EVER SEES IT OR HEARS ABOUT IT AT ALL. HE IS REALLY GOOD TO ME, LIKE I'VE SAID, BUT HE ALSO LIES A LOT TO ME. I HAVE CAUGHT HIM SO MANY TIMES, AND HE HASN'T STOPPED. I DON'T KNOW WHETHER HE GETS SCARED OR WHAT, BUT THAT IS ONE OF HIS MAJOR, MAJOR FLAWS! BUT I DO FEEL A LOT FOR THE GUY.

WE MADE IT! SAFE AND SOUND, BARELY! WE GOT HERE ABOUT 3:30 P.M. CALIFORNIA TIME. SO, WE GOT HERE A LOT EARLIER THAN WE THOUGHT, BUT WE WERE STUCK IN TRAFFIC FOR ABOUT 3 HOURS. IT SUCKED SO BAD! SO, NOW WE ARE ALL SO EXTREMELY EXHAUSTED. JAY IS ALREADY ASLEEP ON THE OTHER BED, WHILE ME AND JALA ARE IN OUR BED WRITING IN OUR JOURNALS! WE WERE PLANNING ON GOING TO THE BEACH TODAY, BUT I REALLY DON'T KNOW IF THAT

IS GOING TO HAPPEN. WE ARE ALL SO TIRED, ESPECIALLY SINCE WE WOKE UP AT 4:00 A.M. TO START DRIVING HERE. I HAVE ONLY TALKED TO RYAN A COUPLE OF TIMES 'CAUSE HE SAYS HE IS SICK. THAT MAKES ME SO WORRIED THAT MY BABY SYDKA ISN'T GETTING TAKEN CARE OF. I MISS HER SO MUCH ALREADY AND I HAVE ONLY BEEN GONE NOT EVEN A FULL 24 HOURS. I HATE LEAVING MY PUPPY. SHE IS LITERALLY MY LIFE, MY LITTLE SHADOW, MY BABY GIRL! WELL, I'M GOING TO RELAX FOR A MINUTE 'CAUSE I KNOW JALA WILL TALK US INTO GOING TO THE BEACH STILL.

IT'S 7:30 P.M. AND I JUST GOT OUT OF THE SHOWER HERE IN CALIFORNIA AT THE CASTLE INN HOTEL RIGHT ACROSS THE STREET FROM THE ONE AND ONLY DISNEYLAND! JALA IS SO SUPER EXCITED TO GO, SHE CAN'T SIT STILL! ME AND JAY ARE ABOUT READY TO PASS OUT 'CAUSE WE GOT UP SO DAMN EARLY, BUT LITTLE MISS JALA SLEPT THE ENTIRE WAY HERE! WE JUST GOT BACK FROM TONY ROMA'S AND WE HAD A GREAT DINNER, SO NOW TIME FOR BED SINCE WE ARE GETTING UP AT THE CRACK OF DAWN TO GO TO DISNEYLAND! I AM SO STINKIN' TIRED, AND WE ARE WAKING UP AT 7:00 A.M. TO GO TO DISNEYLAND IN THE MORNING, AND I CANNOT SLEEP! I FEEL HORRIBLE! I MADE IT SUCH A HUGE DEAL THAT I WAS COMING TO CALIFORNIA AND I COULDN'T GET SICK AT ALL, THAT WE SPENT RYAN'S LAST DIME ON MAKING SURE I TOOK WHAT I NEEDED TO COME HERE. I LEFT HIM WITH ABSOLUTELY NOTHING AND NO MONEY AT ALL! HE IS SUPER SICK RIGHT NOW AND HAS TO GO TO WORK TOMORROW, BUT I AM IN CALIFORNIA AND GOING TO DISNEYLAND FOR THE NEXT 4 DAYS, AND I HAVE MORE THAN ENOUGH TO TAKE CARE OF ME THE WHOLE TIME I AM OUT HERE. HOW EXTREMELY SELFISH AM I? I THOUGHT ABOUT IT A COUPLE OF TIMES BEFORE I LEFT BUT DIDN'T DO ANYTHING ABOUT IT. ALL I THOUGHT ABOUT AND CARED ABOUT WAS ME, ALL ME! MAKING SURE THAT I HAD WHAT I NEEDED SO I WOULDN'T GET SICK, NOW RYAN IS AT HOME TAKING CARE OF MY BABY SYDKA AND HE

IS SICK AS HELL AND HE CAN'T GET A FRONT FROM ANYONE 'CAUSE WE ALREADY OWE PEOPLE FROM ALL THE SHIT THAT HE GOT ME! I CAN'T BELIEVE HOW SELFISH I AM! I FEEL SICK ABOUT IT. HOW COULD I DO THIS TO HIM? HE TAKES CARE OF ME EVERY DAY AND ALWAYS MAKES SURE I AM TAKEN CARE OF AND HAVE EVERYTHING I NEED. HE ALWAYS HAS. I AM NOT GOING TO BE ABLE TO ENJOY MYSELF NOW, KNOWING THAT I LEFT RYAN WITH ABSOLUTELY NOTHING JUST SO THAT I WAS TAKEN COMPLETELY CARE OF WHILE I WAS ON VACATION WITH MY DAUGHTER AND JAY. HOW FUCKING CRUEL AM I? I REALLY NEED TO TAKE A GOOD LOOK IN THE MIRROR AND REALLY LOOK AT WHAT I SEE, 'CAUSE IT IS A SELFISH PIECE OF SHIT THAT ONLY CARES ABOUT HERSELF! I AM GOING TO CHANGE THAT! I DON'T CARE WHAT IT TAKES, I AM GOING TO MAKE SURE FOR NOW ON THAT I TREAT RYAN THE WAY HE DESERVES TO BE TREATED! MAYBE THIS WAS ALL A LESSON FOR ME TO BE LEARNED!

Ten days later…

WEDNESDAY, OCTOBER 11, 2017:

WELL, WE ARE BACK TO THE REAL, DEPRESSING, STRESSFUL WORLD. WE HAD FUN IN CALIFORNIA, BUT I DIDN'T REALIZE HOW MUCH FUN WE HAD TILL WE GOT HOME. I WANT TO GO BACK. I WAS READY TO COME HOME, HELL, WE WERE THERE FOR 5 DAYS, BUT NOW THAT I'M HOME, I DEFINITELY WANT TO GO BACK. JALA HAD A BLAST AND THAT WAS THE PURPOSE OF THE TRIP. JAY AND I GOT ALONG GREAT, WHICH IS AWESOME. I MISSED RYAN *BAD,* MORE THAN I THOUGHT I WOULD. HE WAS ONE OF THE REASONS I WAS SO EXCITED TO COME HOME TO. BUT NOW I AM JUST DEPRESSED AS FUCK LIKE I HAVE BEEN FOR A LONG, LONG TIME NOW AND HATE HOW I AM LIVING! I HAVE WASTED SO MUCH OF MY LIFE ALREADY, I JUST WANT TO START COMPLETELY OVER…BUT I

JUST DON'T DO IT! MY SELF-ESTEEM THE PAST YEAR HAS GOTTEN SO BAD, I FEEL LIKE I AM WORTH NOTHING AND I WILL NEVER TRULY BE HAPPY AGAIN. AND, I DON'T THINK I DESERVE HAPPINESS. I WISH I COULD GET OVER THAT AND THINK BETTER OF MYSELF. I JUST CAN'T GET MYSELF UP AND START SOMEWHERE. IT'S SO HARD WHEN YOU'RE SO UNHAPPY AND DEPRESSED. I FEEL SO BAD THAT MY KIDS HAVE A MOTHER LIKE ME, THEY DESERVE SO, SO MUCH BETTER! I PRETTY MUCH HAVE FELT LIKE MY LIFE IS OVER AND IT WILL NEVER GET ANY BETTER, SO I JUST GO THROUGH EACH DAY TRYING TO GET THROUGH THAT DAY. I NEVER DO ANYTHING ANYMORE, I RARELY GET READY ANYMORE, 'CAUSE I DON'T GO ANYWHERE OR SEE ANYONE, SO WHY GET ALL DOLLED UP FOR NOTHING? I HATE MY BODY MORE THAN EVER, MY HAIR, AND PRETTY MUCH EVERYTHING ABOUT ME. DRUGS TOOK ME OVER, AND NO MATTER HOW MUCH I HAVE TRIED, THEY ALWAYS HAVE TOO MUCH CONTROL OVER ME, AND THEY RUINED ME IN EVERY WAY. THEY FUCKED UP MY BODY AND I LOOK A LOT OLDER THAN I REALLY AM. I'M JUST FUCKED! I HAVEN'T GIVEN UP COMPLETELY, BUT I'M NOT FAR OFF OF JUST BEING DONE WITH LIFE. I HOPE I CAN CHANGE MY LIFE SOMEDAY AND FIND THE TRUE HAPPINESS THAT I HAVE ALWAYS BEEN SEARCHING FOR. EVERYONE DESERVES AT LEAST A SHOT!

THURSDAY, OCTOBER 12, 2017:

IT'S 9:00 P.M. AND I AM SITTING OUT ON THE BALCONY OF MY APARTMENT SMOKING, ABOUT READY TO TOTALLY BREAK DOWN. I HAVE BEEN COMPLETELY BETRAYED BY THE ONE PERSON I TRUSTED COMPLETELY IN THIS WORLD. RYAN HAS LIED TO ME BEFORE, AND I CONFRONTED HIM WHEN I FOUND OUT AND I TOLD HIM NEVER AGAIN WILL I BE LIED TO OR I WOULD BE GONE. WELL, I CAN'T EVEN COUNT HOW MANY TIMES HE HAS LIED TO ME SINCE THEN. I DIDN'T EVEN

DEAL WITH IT BECAUSE IT WAS HAPPENING SO OFTEN, AND I JUST BLEW IT OFF. THEY WEREN'T HUGE LIES, BUT THEY WERE STRAIGHT UP LIES. NO RELATIONSHIP WILL EVER WORK WITHOUT 100% HONESTY. WELL, I HAVE HAD ENOUGH OF IT, AND I WILL NOT BE LIED TO AGAIN. WHILE I WAS IN CALI, RYAN WENT OVER TO MY BEST FRIEND'S HOUSE (JENNIFER) AND SAT THERE PRETTY MUCH TALKING SHIT ON ME, AND HE TOLD HER NOT TO TELL ME. I CONFRONTED RYAN AND HE DIDN'T DENY IT ONCE. HE JUST DID WHAT HE ALWAYS DOES, BECAME COMPLETELY MUTE, TURNED THE TV ON, AND NOT TALKING TO ME AT ALL! NOTHING AT ALL! HE WILL NOT *EVER* COMMUNICATE WITH ME. BELIEVE ME, I HAVE TRIED! I HONESTLY THINK HE JUST DOESN'T KNOW HOW. I FEEL BETRAYED, HURT, AND VERY STUPID THAT I HAVE ALLOWED THIS TO CONTINUE. I'M NOT SAYING THAT I AM A SAINT AT ALL, 'CAUSE I AM FAR FROM, BUT I DON'T MAKE EVERYONE AROUND BELIEVE AND THINK THAT I WAS SOMEBODY THAT I AM NOT. THAT IS RYAN. HE PLAYS THE INNOCENT MARAUDER SO WELL IT FOOLS ABSOLUTELY EVERYONE. HE EVEN HAS MY ENTIRE FAMILY FOOLED AND CONVINCED THAT HE IS AN ANGEL AND I AM A BITCH THAT TREATS HIM HORRIBLY AND TAKES EVERYTHING THAT HE HAS. I ADMIT, I HAVE DONE THOSE THINGS, BUT I DON'T MAKE OTHER PEOPLE THINK I AM SOMETHING THAT I'M NOT, SOMEONE COMPLETELY FAKE! WHAT YOU SEE IS WHAT YOU GET WITH ME. I WAS VERY, VERY BRUTAL TO RYAN FOR A LONG TIME, WHICH HE DID NOT DESERVE, BUT I HAVE CHANGED FOR THE GOOD AND HOW I TREAT HIM OVER THE PAST FEW YEARS. I STILL HAVE SO MUCH TO WORK ON, AND I STILL AM RUTHLESS WITH HIM AT TIMES, BUT I AM TRYING VERY, VERY HARD. WELL, WHILE I AM DOING MY BEST BY TREATING HIM BETTER AND NOT ALWAYS TAKING, TAKING, TAKING FROM HIM, HE HAS BEEN PULLED BACKWARDS AND TREATING ME MUCH, MUCH WORSE! WE BOTH ARE GOING COMPLETE OPPOSITE DIRECTIONS. AT LEAST I CAN

SAY THAT I AM TURNING INTO SOMEONE BETTER AND HE IS TURNING INTO SOMEONE THAT I NEVER THOUGHT HE WOULD. I NEVER THOUGHT RYAN, OF ALL PEOPLE, COULD EVER HURT ME 'CAUSE I HAVE NEVER CARED ENOUGH. BUT, HE DID IT! HE HAS DEFINITELY HURT ME AND MADE MY SELF-ESTEEM EVEN WORSE THAN IT ALREADY IS, AND THE THING THAT JUST PUTS ME IN TOTAL RAGE AND GOING TO CAUSE ME TO HAVE A NERVOUS BREAKDOWN IS THAT HE, OF ALL PEOPLE, HURT ME AND GOT ONE OVER ON ME! AND LET'S NOT FORGET THAT HE HAS WASTED ALMOST 4 YEARS OF MY LIFE NOW. HOW DOES THAT HAPPEN AND HOW IN THE HELL DID I LET IT GO ON FOR THIS LONG WHILE I WAS FULLY AWARE!! WELL, I DON'T THINK I WILL BE ABLE TO *EVER* TRUST ANOTHER MAN AGAIN. IF I CAN'T TRUST RYAN, OF ALL PEOPLE, AND ALLOW HIM TO DO THIS TO ME MORE THAN ONCE, WHO CAN I TRUST?!? I HAVE A HORRIBLE SELF-ESTEEM NOW AND KNOWING THAT SOMEONE LIKE RYAN GOT THE CHANCE TO ACTUALLY HURT ME AND DO WHAT HE HAS DONE TO ME MAKES ME FEEL EVEN WORSE, AND SO, SO STUPID! I STILL JUST DON'T KNOW HOW THIS HAPPENED AND HOW I COULD LET THIS HAPPEN. I AM SO MUCH BETTER THAN THIS MAN AND HE HURT ME, AND I AM SO LIVID ABOUT IT! MAYBE THIS IS MY KARMA AND WHAT I GET FOR BEING SO ABSOLUTELY HORRIBLE TO HIM IN THE BEGINNING AND AT ALL. I FEEL SO ALONE, SO UNWANTED, AND SO COMPLETELY WORTHLESS. JUST KILL ME NOW, 'CAUSE I HONESTLY CANNOT TAKE MUCH MORE!!

(GRATITUDE JOURNAL) WELL, IT'S ABOUT 11:30 P.M. ON A THURSDAY NIGHT AND THE WAY THINGS HAVE BEEN GOING IN MY LIFE LATELY, IT'S REALLY HARD TO WRITE ANYTHING THAT I AM GRATEFUL FOR. BUT TONIGHT, I WAS REMINDED WHILE I HAVE BEEN SUPER DEPRESSED THAT I HAVE ONE SPECIAL SOMEONE THAT MAKES ME HAPPIER THAN ANYTHING IN THIS WORLD! MY BABIES SYDKA, SHE IS MY ANGEL!

Same day, different journal...

WELL, THIS WAS AN ABSOLUTE HORRIBLE FUCKING DAY! I HAVE LITERALLY BEEN IN BED CRYING AND WITHDRAWING ALL DAMN DAY! I CAN'T TAKE THIS SHIT ANYMORE. I HAVE A DEMON THAT I CANNOT GET RID OF AND IT'S LITERALLY TAKING MY LIFE, ONE DAY AT A TIME. I THINK I HAVE GIVEN UP AT THIS POINT. I CAN'T DO IT ANY LONGER! I CANNOT LIVE THIS LIFE AND I'M SO FUCKING SAD, LOST, AND ALONE THAT I AM A COMPLETE FUCKING MESS!

IT'S 1:00 A.M. AND I AM FINALLY FEELING OKAY (OTHER THAN WANTING TO CRY ALL NIGHT) 'CAUSE ANTHONY OF ALL PEOPLE, WORKED ON GETTING ME WELL ALL DAMN DAY! HE ACTUALLY WENT UP TO PARK CITY LATE TONIGHT TO GET SOME MONEY TO GO GRAB *(get drugs)* SO I COULD GET WELL. IN THE MEANTIME...RYAN WAS LITERALLY SLEEPING ALL DAY 'CAUSE IT WAS HIS DAY OFF AND HE SAID HE WAS SICK, SO HE DIDN'T GET UP AT ALL THE ENTIRE DAY, AND WHEN I GOT HOME TONIGHT AFTER FINDING OUT FROM ANTHONY AND JENNIFER TONIGHT THAT HE HAS BEEN LYING TO ME FOR QUITE A WHILE, HE WAS STILL OUT COLD AND I HAD TO SHAKE HIM TO WAKE HIM UP. BUT, OF COURSE, I'M NOT HEARTLESS, I GOT HIM WELL TOO *(gave him a shot of drugs)*. I JUST DON'T KNOW WHAT TO DO ANYMORE!

Three days later...

<u>SUNDAY, OCTOBER 15, 2017</u>:

WELL, THIS IS NEW...I'M SITTING IN MY LIVING ROOM RIGHT NOW AND IT'S ABOUT 10:30 P.M., RYAN IS IN OUR BED IN THE BEDROOM AND I'M SITTING OUT HERE WITH ANTHONY, YES, ANTHONY OF ALL PEOPLE. HE HAS NOWHERE TO STAY RIGHT NOW, AND HE HAS BEEN STAYING AT JENNIFER'S MOSTLY EVERY NIGHT, BUT JENNIFER'S MOM IS GETTING PRETTY MAD

ABOUT THE SITUATION. I DON'T LIKE HIM HERE AT ALL AND NEITHER DOES RYAN, 'CAUSE MY KIDS COULD SHOW UP AT ANY TIME, BUT TONIGHT I DIDN'T REALLY HAVE A CHOICE. I COULDN'T LEAVE HIM SLEEPING IN HIS CAR. MICHELLE AND KIERRA WERE HERE FOR A COUPLE DAYS AND I DIDN'T EVEN GO SEE THEM. I LOOK LIKE HELL STILL 'CAUSE KIERRA WAS GOING TO DO MY HAIR, AND AT THE LAST MINUTE, SHE SAID I NEEDED TO PAY HER. SYDKA IS LAYING ON THE COUCH WITH ANTHONY RIGHT NOW, AND IT'S SUPER CUTE. WE ARE COMPLETELY OUT OF MONEY TILL THURSDAY NIGHT 'CAUSE RYAN TOOK 3 DAYS OFF THIS PAST WEEK, AND I HAVE NO IDEA WHAT WE ARE GOING TO DO. IT'S SUNDAY AND WE HAVE TILL THURSDAY TO MAKE IT WITH ABSOLUTELY NO MONEY. ANTHONY SAYS HE IS GETTING A CHECK, A BIG CHECK, ON TUESDAY AND THAT HE WILL HELP ME. I REALLY HOPE HE IS TELLING ME THE TRUTH 'CAUSE THAT WOULD SAVE ME. I HAVE NO GAS IN MY CAR AND NOT EVEN MONEY FOR SMOKES! THINGS HAVE GOT TO CHANGE. I HAVE GOT TO CHANGE MY LIFE, AND I MEAN *BIG* CHANGES IF I WANT ANY CHANCE TO ACTUALLY MAKE IT THROUGHOUT EACH DAY. I DID METH A COUPLE TIMES THIS WEEK AND IT FUCKED ME UP FOR 3 OR 4 DAYS.

WELL, STUPID ME, JUST DID A LITTLE BIT A COUPLE HOURS AGO, SO OF COURSE, I AM GOING TO BE UP ALL NIGHT LONG. THIS IS GOING TO SUCK BECAUSE I HAVE TO PICK JALA UP FROM SCHOOL TOMORROW AND I AM GOING TO BE SO OUT OF IT. WHEN AM I JUST GOING TO SAY *NO?!?* AND START LIVING MY LIFE THE WAY I WANT TO…WITH NO DRUGS AT ALL, AND NOT ASSOCIATE WITH ANYONE THAT USES DRUGS. I WILL GET THERE, I KNOW I WILL, I JUST HOPE IT'S SOONER THAN LATER, 'CAUSE I DON'T WANT TO LOSE ANYONE IMPORTANT IN MY LIFE. I HAVE ALREADY DONE THAT MORE THAN I WOULD LIKE TO REMEMBER. I HAVE AN AWESOME RELATIONSHIP WITH MY PARENTS RIGHT NOW, BETTER THAN I EVER HAVE, AND I DON'T WANT TO RUIN THAT AT ALL! IT

MEANS A LOT TO ME, MORE THAN ANYTHING IN THIS WORLD, BESIDES THE RELATIONSHIP WITH MY KIDS.

MONDAY, OCTOBER 16, 2017:

IT'S ABOUT 4:00 P.M. AND I JUST PICKED JALA UP FROM SCHOOL AND I AM HANGING OUT AT HER HOUSE WITH HER FOR A LITTLE BIT. MIA *(Jala's dog)* IS COMPLETELY OUT OF CONTROL! I DON'T KNOW HOW THEY DEAL WITH THIS DOG. ANTHONY IS AT MY HOUSE RIGHT NOW 'CAUSE THERE IS NOWHERE FOR HIM TO GO AND IT'S STRESSING ME OUT SO SUPER *BAD!* HE DRIVES ME NUTS, LIKE SO *SUPER BAD!* I ACTUALLY DID SLEEP LAST NIGHT, THOUGH. I DON'T EVEN WANT ANTHONY IN MY LIFE AT ALL, BUT RIGHT NOW, SINCE JENNIFER IS TRYING TO HELP HIM, I GOT CAUGHT IN THE MIDDLE SOMEHOW. JENNIFER IS A HARD FRIEND TO DEAL WITH, I THINK THAT'S WHY WE STOPPED BEING FRIENDS, BUT WHEN WE ARE TOGETHER, WE HAVE SO MUCH FUN! SHE ALWAYS COMPLIMENTS ME IN FRONT OF OTHER PEOPLE, WHICH IS SO SUPER SWEET, BUT SHE LIES A LOT AND I CATCH HER LIES ALL THE TIME. SO, THIS IS THE SECOND TIME I HAVE SEEN JALA SINCE WE GOT BACK FROM CALIFORNIA. I AM SO NOT OKAY WITH THAT, BUT I NEED TO FIGURE THINGS OUT IN MY LIFE AND GET MY LIFE STRAIGHTENED UP IN A BAD WAY BEFORE I AM AROUND JALA A LOT. SAMANTHA IS WITH HER EVERYDAY ANYWAYS RIGHT NOW. I AM OKAY WITH IT, BUT IN WAYS, I GET JEALOUS TOO! SAMANTHA IS WAY GOOD TO HER AND ME, AND OF COURSE JAY, BUT SHE TRIES WAY TOO HARD! SHE IS OBSESSED OVER JAY, SO THAT MEANS SHE IS REALLY INTO ME ALSO. TEXTS ME AND CALLS ME EVERY SINGLE DAY. IT'S SWEET, BUT IT'S TOO MUCH AND IT'S REALLY WEIRD, IT'S JAY'S GIRLFRIEND! SO, I HAVE TO FIND A WAY TO GET RID OF ANTHONY FOR GOOD. HE IS NOT SOMEONE I WANT IN MY LIFE. EVERYTHING ABOUT HIM BUGS ME. RYAN AND I AREN'T GETTING ALONG AT ALL RIGHT NOW. HE IS STILL

LYING TO ME ALL THE TIME AND I ALWAYS CATCH HIM, AND HE IS OUT OF CONTROL WITH USING NOW! I THINK HE MIGHT EVEN BE USING MORE THAN ME NOW. I DON'T KNOW HOW IN THE HELL HE CAN SUPPORT THE TWO OF US WITH SUCH BIG HABITS, AND THAT'S WHY WE ARE BROKE ALL THE DAMN TIME! I HAD TO ASK MY MOM AGAIN FOR MONEY TODAY, AND BLESS HER HEART, SHE ALWAYS HELPS ME, BUT I ALWAYS PAY HER BACK NO MATTER WHAT, THAT'S WHY SHE DOESN'T HAVE A PROBLEM HELPING ME, BUT I STILL HATE ASKING. *(My mom believed she was clean at this time.)* I ABSOLUTELY HATE IT! I HAD TO ASK JAY LAST NIGHT IF HE WOULD BUY ME SMOKES, AND HE DID, BUT IT'S SO EMBARRASSING ASKING PEOPLE FOR HELP. I HONESTLY DON'T KNOW WHAT I AM GOING TO DO ABOUT RYAN, IF HE IS LYING TO ME NOW WITH LITTLE LIES, THEN WHO KNOWS HOW HE WILL BE IN THE FUTURE. HE WILL BE MUCH, MUCH WORSE. AND, I DON'T WANT HIM TO EVER THINK HE CAN GET AWAY WITH LYING TO ME AND HE STILL GETS TO BE IN MY LIFE. I WILL NOT LET THAT HAPPEN, NOBODY TREATS ME LIKE THIS!!

<u>TUESDAY, OCTOBER 17, 2017</u>:

WELL, HAVEN'T ACCOMPLISHED MUCH AT ALL FOR THE BEGINNING OF THE WEEK. I WISH I HAD MORE MOTIVATION AND ENERGY AND A LITTLE BIT OF HAPPINESS TO GET MYSELF GOING EACH DAY. I HATE GETTING UP IN THE MORNING 'CAUSE I HAVE ABSOLUTELY NOTHING TO LOOK FORWARD TO. I HAVEN'T GONE ANYWHERE AT ALL IN THE PAST YEAR. I HAVE ACTUALLY JUST BEEN GOING DOWNHILL, AND EACH DAY GETS WORSE AND WORSE. IT HONESTLY COULDN'T GET ANY WORSE THAN THIS. I JUST FOUND OUT RECENTLY THAT THE ONE MAN I THOUGHT I COULD TRUST MORE THAN ANYONE IN THIS WORLD AND I KNEW LOVED ME MORE THAN ANYONE OR ANYTHING HAS BEEN LYING TO ME FOR QUITE SOME TIME NOW. IT'S LITTLE STUPID LIES, BUT IT'S LIES. WE HAVE

COMPLETELY DRIFTED APART, AND WE ARE TOTALLY DETACHED FROM EACH OTHER. AND THIS IS THE MAN I LIVE WITH AND COMPLETELY RELY ON FINANCIALLY. IT'S A COMPLETE JOKE. WE DON'T GET ALONG AT ALL, WE DON'T FIGHT 'CAUSE HE NEVER TALKS AT ALL, BUT WE NEVER COMMUNICATE AT ALL. I AM ABSOLUTELY MISERABLE! I FEEL LIKE A WORTHLESS PIECE OF SHIT THAT IS GOING TO BE ALONE THE REST OF MY LIFE. I FEEL SO ALONE ALL THE TIME. JAY IS ACTUALLY MOVING ON WITH SAMANTHA WHICH IS GOOD, I REALLY LIKE HER, BUT I THOUGHT FOR SURE I WOULD FIND SOMEONE BEFORE JAY, BUT NOPE, I HAVEN'T AND I DON'T THINK I EVER WILL. MY EXPECTATIONS ARE WAY TOO HIGH FOR SOMEONE LIKE ME. I AM A WORTHLESS JUNKIE THAT HAS GIVEN UP AND DON'T EVEN KNOW IF I WANT TO GO ON ANYMORE. THANK GOD FOR MY KIDS BECAUSE IF IT WASN'T FOR THEM, I WOULD DEFINITELY BE GONE BY NOW. I HAVE NOT DONE ANYTHING IN MY LIFE TO BE PROUD OF AND HAVE NEVER BEEN A GOOD EXAMPLE TO MY KIDS. THEY NEED A BETTER MOTHER THAN ME, I FEEL SORRY THEY ENDED UP WITH ME. THOSE 3 DESERVE SO MUCH BETTER! WHY CAN'T I START OVER AND HAVE THE MOTIVATION TO MAKE MY LIFE BETTER? I FEEL LIKE IT'S TOO LATE AND THAT THERE IS NOTHING LEFT OUT THERE FOR ME ANYMORE. I DON'T GET EXCITED ABOUT ANYTHING, I NEVER WANT TO DO ANYTHING, I NEVER WANT TO GET READY ANYMORE, I NEVER WANT TO SEE ANYONE AT ALL. I AM COMPLETELY MISERABLE AND HAVE BEEN FOR A VERY, VERY LONG TIME NOW. I JUST FEEL LIKE MY LIFE IS OVER. I WANT EXCITEMENT, I WANT SOMEONE TO LOVE, I WANT TO BE A GOOD EXAMPLE TO MY KIDS, BUT I HONESTLY DON'T THINK IT'S EVER GOING TO HAPPEN FOR ME. I SCREWED MY LIFE UP AND THIS IS THE KARMA I GET, AND I DON'T KNOW IF ALL THESE BAD THINGS IN MY LIFE ARE EVER GOING TO END. HOW FREAKING PATHETIC AM I? I AM EMBARRASSED ABOUT THE PERSON I HAVE BECOME. I

HOPE IT'S NOT TOO LATE TO CHANGE IT, BUT I FEEL LIKE MY LIFE IS OVER!

A few days later...

<u>FRIDAY, OCTOBER 20, 2017</u>:

IT'S ABOUT 6:00 P.M. AND I AM JUST SITTING ON MY BED ACTUALLY RELAXING FOR A MINUTE 'CAUSE I AM ALWAYS STRESSED OUT AND ON THE VERGE OF A MENTAL BREAKDOWN, AWESOME, AWESOME!!! NOT MUCH OF AN EXCITING DAY AT ALL. I WOKE UP AND LAID IN BED FOR A WHILE 'CAUSE I WAS SUPER NAUSEATED. ANTHONY CAME OVER AROUND NOON AND I GOT IN THE SHOWER, GOT READY, AND WE WENT OUT TO SALT LAKE, PLANNING ON GOING TO THE MALL, INSTEAD WENT TO A BOUTIQUE HOME STORE AND I FOUND A REALLY COOL OTTOMAN FOR REALLY CHEAP, LOVE THAT! THEN WE RUSHED HOME 'CAUSE JENNIFER WAS COMPLAINING AND SAYING SHE REALLY NEEDED OUR HELP, SO WE RUSH HOME AND SHE LEAVES TO SALT LAKE! THAT WOMAN IS REALLY PISSING ME OFF LATELY! ANTHONY HAS HELPED ME OUT A LOT THIS PAST WEEK. HE HAD SOME MONEY COME IN, SO HE HELPED ME GET BETTER AND I WILL STAY OKAY FOR A WHILE 'CAUSE OF HIM, BOUGHT US GROCERIES, GOT ME SMOKES, WHATEVER I HAVE NEEDED THE PAST COUPLE DAYS, ANTHONY HAS TAKEN CARE OF. IT IS REALLY SWEET OF HIM, BUT I STILL LET HIM KNOW THERE WILL BE ABSOLUTELY NOTHING BETWEEN US *EVER*, 'CAUSE I WANT TO BE VERY CLEAR WITH HIM SO HE DOESN'T EVER THINK THAT I AM LEADING HIM ON. I TELL HIM STRAIGHT UP, ON MORE THAN ONE OCCASION, THAT WE WILL NEVER, EVER BE ANYTHING OTHER THAN CLOSE FRIENDS! BUT I STILL FEEL LIKE HE GETS HIS HOPES UP. I DON'T KNOW WHY, BUT I HAVE A FEELING THIS MAN WILL *NEVER* GIVE UP, NO MATTER HOW STRAIGHT I AM. HIM AND JENNIFER

BOTH HAVE BEEN STRESSING ME OUT SO BAD LATELY, BUT SO HAS RYAN AND EVERYONE ELSE, SO MAYBE IT'S JUST ME. I'M JUST A MISERABLE, LONELY, DEPRESSED WOMAN THAT CAN'T GET HER SHIT TOGETHER AND HAS ALMOST COMPLETELY GIVEN UP ON HERSELF. IT'S SUPER SAD! ANYONE THAT KNOWS ME KNOWS THAT THIS IS SO NOT ME. I AM USUALLY A FUN, EXCITING, RISK TAKING, SOCIABLE PERSON THAT ALWAYS HAS PEOPLE WANT TO BE AROUND ME...WELL, NOT ANYMORE. I DON'T WANT TO BE AROUND ANYONE AT ALL, I DON'T WANT TO GET OUT OF BED IN THE MORNINGS ANYMORE, I DON'T WANT TO GET READY FOR THE DAY, DOLL MYSELF AT ALL, DON'T CALL OR TALK TO ANYONE, OR TEXT (I HATE FUCKING TEXTING). I AM JUST ABSOLUTELY MISERABLE, AND I NEVER THOUGHT IN A MILLION YEARS THAT I WOULD EVER BECOME THIS PERSON THAT I HAVE BECOME. IT'S SUPER, SUPER SAD AND A WASTE OF A GOOD LIFE! I PRAY TO GOD SOMETHING CHANGES, 'CAUSE I'M TERRIFIED THAT IF IT DOESN'T, I WON'T BE AROUND MUCH LONGER, AND THAT SCARES ME TO DEATH!!!

<u>SATURDAY, OCTOBER 21, 2017</u>:

DON'T KNOW EXACTLY WHAT'S GOING TO HAPPEN TODAY. HOPEFULLY SOMETHING WITH MY KIDS 'CAUSE I MISS ALL OF THEM SO STINKIN' MUCH! THEY ARE LITERALLY RIGHT DOWN THE STREET FROM ME, AND I TOTALLY TAKE THAT FOR GRANTED 'CAUSE I DON'T SEE THEM HALF AS MUCH AS I SHOULD! THESE NEW (OLD) FRIENDS THAT STARTED COMING AROUND ME AGAIN WON'T TAKE A FREAKING HINT! JENNIFER AND ANTHONY CAME BACK INTO MY LIFE AND IT WAS SO NOT A GOOD IDEA! THEY WON'T GO AWAY NOW, AND I DON'T WANT EITHER OF THEM IN MY LIFE ANYMORE AT ALL! AND IT'S SO HARD FOR ME TO TELL THEM, SO I JUST IGNORE THEM, BUT WHEN I DO THAT, THEY TRY EVEN HARDER TO GET IN TOUCH WITH ME. TAKE A FREAKING HINT! I SHOULD HAVE NEVER

LET THEM BACK IN MY LIFE AT ALL, WHAT IN THE HELL WAS I THINKING?!? RIGHT NOW, AT THIS VERY MOMENT, I AM SO STRESSED OUT, I FEEL LIKE I AM GOING TO HAVE A PANIC ATTACK. THIS IS DEFINITELY MY SIGN TO CHANGE THINGS, COMPLETELY CHANGE THINGS. I DON'T WANT MY OLD LIFE BACK, OR ANYBODY THAT WAS IN IT! IT MAKES ME CRY OF PANIC EVEN THINKING ABOUT IT! I DON'T WANT TO THINK OF, REMEMBER, OR HAVE ANYTHING TO DO WITH OR REPEAT ANYTHING IN MY PAST. IT WAS HORRIBLE AND IT RUINED MY ENTIRE LIFE, AND MY PAST HAUNTS ME AND PUTS ME THROUGH COMPLETE HELL EVEN UP TO THIS VERY DAY! *(Nat never opened up completely to me about what haunted her so much about her past.)* THINKING ABOUT MY PAST AND REMEMBERING WHAT A HORRIBLE PERSON I HAD CHANGED INTO HAUNTS ME EVERY DAY. I HAVE TRIED SO HARD GETTING RID OF THAT PERSON I HAD BECOME FOR MANY YEARS NOW, AND I KNOW I HAVE CHANGED, COMPLETELY CHANGED FOR THE BETTER, BUT THAT PERSON THAT I HATE COMES OUT IN ME EVERY ONCE IN AWHILE AND IT MAKES ME SO SICK! I KNOW I AM A MUCH BETTER PERSON TODAY AND I WILL NEVER BECOME THAT HORRIBLE SELFISH PERSON AGAIN, BUT SOME TRAITS COME OUT AND I NOTICE THEM AND AM VERY AWARE WHEN THEY DO, AND I SHUT THEM DOWN FAST! I AM PROUD OF MYSELF FOR TOTALLY TURNING MY LIFE AROUND AND BECOMING A BETTER PERSON, BUT I AM TERRIFIED OF EVERYTHING PRYING ITS WAY BACK INTO MY LIFE, AND GETTING CAUGHT UP TOO QUICKLY THAT IT WILL BE TOO LATE. I AM STILL WORKING HARD EVERY DAY ON KEEPING THAT OLD PART OF ME FAR, FAR AWAY, BUT I AM NOT DOING AS GOOD A JOB AS I KNOW I CAN. I KNOW I AM MUCH STRONGER THAN THIS AND I CAN CONQUER ALMOST ANYTHING. I HAVE PROVEN THAT. I AM JUST SO MAD AT MYSELF FOR BEING SO LAZY AND ALMOST GIVING UP COMPLETELY AFTER EVERYTHING I HAVE DONE THE PAST 3 YEARS TO TURN MY LIFE AROUND AND BECOME A MUCH BETTER PERSON THAN I WAS. *(When Nat wrote that she had turned her life around and evolved into a much better person, I believe she was comparing herself to the dark past that she never talked about.)*

This next entry was on the same day.

(GRATITUDE JOURNAL) I AM SUPER HAPPY AND SUPER ALIVE STILL. I HONESTLY CAN'T BELIEVE THAT I AM STILL ALIVE. EVERYONE ELSE (WELL, A LOT OF THEM) HAVE DIED AND I AM STILL HERE. APPARENTLY, THERE IS SOMETHING I STILL HAVE TO DO AND I'M THINKING IT'S PRETTY IMPORTANT 'CAUSE FOR EVERYTHING I HAVE DONE TO MYSELF, I SHOULD DEFINITELY BE DEAD. BUT I'M NOT AND I'M SO GRATEFUL FOR THAT, SO I NEED TO *STOP* TAKING MY LIFE FOR GRANTED AND *START OVER!*

<u>SUNDAY, OCTOBER 22, 2017</u>:

SO, I WANT TO PUT TOGETHER A DETOX PLAN. I DON'T KNOW WHAT, HOW, OR WHEN JUST QUITE YET, ALL I KNOW IS THAT I AM NOT GOING TO BUY ANYMORE! THIS WAS THE VERY LAST TIME I WAS BUYING BLACK. I GOT PLENTY OF IT LAST TIME I PICKED UP, SO I WON'T BE OUT FOR A MINUTE, ACTUALLY A WHILE, SO IT GIVES ME PLENTY OF TIME TO COME UP WITH A GOOD DETOX PLAN. ONE THAT I WILL MAKE IT ALL THE WAY THROUGH, NOT GIVE UP, AND FINALLY, ONCE AND FOR ALL, I CAN BE CLEAN AND START MY LIFE OVER AND BECOME THE PERSON I KNOW I CAN BE. MY MAIN PURPOSE…MY KIDS! THEY HAVE ALWAYS BEEN MY MOTIVATION TO GET CLEAN AND STAY ON THE RIGHT TRACK. IF IT WASN'T FOR THEM, I PROBABLY WOULD HAVE BEEN FOUND DEAD A VERY LONG TIME AGO. THEY HAVE DEFINITELY SAVED MY LIFE MORE THAN ONCE. THEY ARE MY REASON FOR LIVING, MY REASON I HAVEN'T COMPLETELY GIVEN UP, AND THE REASON I WANT TO GET CLEAN, START OVER, AND BECOME A NEW ME. A BETTER ME! THAT'S NOT

A LOT TO ASK OF MYSELF, AND IT'S VERY DOABLE. I JUST NEED TO STICK WITH IT AND NOT TALK TO ANYONE AT ALL THAT COULD TAKE ME BACK DOWN THAT ROAD AGAIN, AND TAKE EACH DAY ONE AT A TIME INSTEAD OF LOOKING TO THE FUTURE LIKE I ALWAYS DO AND LETTING PEOPLE PRY THEIR WAY BACK INTO MY LIFE! I NEED TO STAY CLEAN, STRONG, AND I KNOW I CAN DO THIS! I AM READY FOR THIS, MORE THAN READY FOR THIS!!! I HAVEN'T SLEPT IN 2 DAYS NOW, PROBABLY EVEN LONGER THAN THAT, I CAN'T KEEP TRACK ANYMORE. I FEEL LIKE COMPLETE *SHIT!* I AM ALWAYS SICK TO MY STOMACH, FEELING LIKE I AM GOING THROW UP. IT'S SO NOT FUN. I WANT TO BE NORMAL AGAIN, DO NORMAL EVERYDAY THINGS, HANG OUT WITH MY KIDS MORE OFTEN, TAKE SYDKA TO THE PARK OR ON WALKS, GO TO A MOVIE, GO OUT TO DINNER, GO DO ANYTHING AT ALL. I JUST WANT MY NORMAL EVERYDAY LIFE BACK, 'CAUSE AT LEAST IT'S A LIFE. THIS IS NO LIFE…THIS IS TRYING TO SURVIVE EACH DAY AND EVERY DAY, TRYING TO SURVIVE THE NEXT HOUR THAT GOES BY. THIS IS ABSOLUTELY NO LIFE. I REALLY DON'T KNOW WHAT TO DO ABOUT RYAN, 'CAUSE NOWADAYS WE ARE PRETTY MUCH POISON TO EACH OTHER. HE USED TO BE A TOTALLY DIFFERENT GUY THAT WOULD DO ANYTHING FOR ME. HE DOESN'T DO ANYTHING ANYMORE. HE WON'T TALK TO ME AT ALL, SO I CALL HIM MUTE, HE WORKS AND SLEEPS AND THAT IS LITERALLY IT! I CAN'T REMEMBER THE LAST TIME HE TOOK ME OUT. IT HAS PROBABLY BEEN OVER A YEAR OR SO. WE NEED TO END.

(GRATITUDE JOURNAL) RYAN JUST CAME UP TO ME AND GAVE ME THE BIGGEST HUG AND KISS AND TOLD ME HOW MUCH HE LOVES ME. THAT IS WEIRD FOR HIM LATELY, 'CAUSE HE HAS BEEN PRETTY MUCH A MUTE AND HASN'T TALKED TO ME FOREVER. SO, THAT JUST MADE ME VERY HAPPY AND ACTUALLY MADE ME FEEL WANTED, WHICH I HAVE NOT FELT IN A VERY

LONG TIME. I AM GRATEFUL TO BE ALIVE AGAIN TODAY AND I AM GRATEFUL FOR RYAN FOR BEING IN MY LIFE.

MONDAY, OCTOBER 23, 2017:

I NEED TO GET A DETOX PLAN DONE *ASAP.* I HAVE TO HAVE IT WRITTEN DOWN AND IT NEEDS TO BE COMPLETELY DETAILED, HOUR BY HOUR, DAY BY DAY. I AM COMPLETELY TERRIFIED, BUT IT NEEDS TO BE DONE...AND I AM GOING TO DO IT! NO MORE EXCUSES AND NO MORE GIVING UP. I AM STRONG ENOUGH TO DO THIS. I MEAN, LOOK AT HALF THE SHIT I HAVE GONE THROUGH IN MY LIFE. THIS SHOULD BE A CAKE WALK FOR ME, EVEN THOUGH WHEN I AM ACTUALLY GOING THROUGH IT I WOULD RATHER DIE! THE MOST INTENSE EMOTIONAL AND PHYSICAL PAIN ANYONE COULD EVER GO THROUGH. YES, GOING THROUGH IT, YOU WOULD RATHER BE DEAD. I HAVE ACTUALLY, IN THE PAST, ACTUALLY A LOT, PRAYED FOR GOD TO TAKE ME AND THOUGHT OF WAYS TO COMMIT SUICIDE GOING THROUGH HEROIN WITHDRAWALS. IT'S NO JOKE, IT IS THE *HARDEST* THING I HAVE EVER WENT THROUGH IN MY LIFE AND GET TERRIFIED AND BAD ANXIETY EVEN THINKING ABOUT IT! BUT, I GOT THIS...I AM ONE STRONG LITTLE BITCH! I'M SITTING OUTSIDE ON THE GRASS IN THIS OCTOBER HEAT, WHICH IS OUTRAGEOUS. IT'S GOTTA BE 65 DEGREES OUT THERE TODAY. SUN SHINING, IT'S PRETTY WARM, GOT SYDKA OUT HERE WITH ME AND SHE ABSOLUTELY LOVES TO BE OUTSIDE. SHE IS BLEEDING RIGHT NOW, SO SHE IS NOT A HAPPY PUPPY. IT MAKES ME SO SUPER SAD WHEN HER BLEEDING IS SO BAD LIKE THIS. SHE HAS TO WEAR A DIAPER AND IT IS THE SADDEST THING EVER! SHE IS SUCH A GOOD DOG, I DON'T KNOW WHAT I WOULD DO WITHOUT HER. WHEN SHE GOES, I AM SERIOUSLY GOING TO LOSE IT. THAT WILL DEFINITELY PUT ME OVER THE EDGE. IT'S ALMOST LIKE SHE IS ONE OF MY KIDS. SHE IS NEVER WITHOUT ME AND WHEN SHE IS, SHE CRIES. SHE IS MY LITTLE SHADOW PUPPY. I LOVE HER

SO MUCH! PROBABLY EVEN MORE THAN MY KIDS! HA, HA, HA (NOT REALLY)! I REALLY HAVE A LOT OF CHANGING TO DO IN THE NEXT FEW MONTHS. FIND ANOTHER PLACE TO LIVE, GET COMPLETELY CLEAN, FIGURE OUT WHAT I AM GOING TO DO ABOUT RYAN AND TURN MY LIFE COMPLETELY AROUND. NOT MUCH, JUST LITTLE THINGS! (YA, RIGHT.) THESE ARE LIFE CHANGING DECISIONS AND TO MAKE THESE KINDS OF DECISIONS, I NEED A CLEAR HEAD, NOT A MESSED UP ONE. WE KNOW HOW THAT TURNS OUT WHEN I MAKE BIG CHOICES WHEN I'M ON DRUGS, IT DOES NOT TURN OUT WELL AT ALL!!! I THINK THE FIRST PERSON I AM GOING TO SIT DOWN AND TALK TO AND MAYBE GET SOME GOOD ADVICE IS JAY. HE DOESN'T JUDGE ME, AND HE DEFINITELY WILL NOT LIE TO ME, AND HE USUALLY HAS GOOD IDEAS AND I KNOW HE WILL HELP ME. I'M SO SUPER LUCKY TO HAVE JAY AS MY VERY BEST FRIEND, 'CAUSE I KNOW HE WILL *ALWAYS* BE HERE FOR ME!

(GRATITUDE JOURNAL) I AM VERY GRATEFUL FOR THIS EXPENSIVE LITTLE APARTMENT THAT I HAVE BEEN LIVING IN FOR THE PAST 3 YEARS NOW. I LIVED ALONE WITH SYDKA AT FIRST, THEN ADI MOVED IN, ALONG WITH JALA SPENDING ALMOST EVERY WEEKEND WITH ME, THEN ADI MOVED OUT AND RYAN AND HIS SON MOVED IN WITH ME. IT HAS BEEN A PERFECT LITTLE PLACE FOR ME AND SYDKA. IT HAS BEEN OUR HOME. BUT IN A COUPLE MONTHS, MY LEASE IS UP, AND I WANT TO MOVE. DON'T KNOW WHERE YET. BUT THIS PLACE HAS BEEN HOME TO SYDKA AND I, AND I HAVE LOVED IT! THE ONE THING THAT I AM GRATEFUL FOR MORE THAN ANYTHING IN THIS ENTIRE WORLD IS THAT I HAVE MY KIDS AND MY FAMILY BACK IN MY LIFE. I GOT THEIR FORGIVENESS AND THAT IS BY FAR THE MOST IMPORTANT THING TO ME, AND I *NEVER* WANT TO TAKE THAT FOR GRANTED, *EVER!* I AM VERY, VERY LUCKY TO HAVE MY KIDS AND MY FAMILY! I AM ALSO VERY EXTREMELY GRATEFUL TO HAVE MY EX-HUSBAND ON MY SIDE AND AS MY VERY BEST FRIEND. JAY AND I ARE

SO SUPER CLOSE AND THAT MEANS EVERYTHING TO ME. JAY WOULD DO ANYTHING FOR ME, AND I TRUST HIM MORE THAN ANYONE IN THIS WORLD! I AM SO GRATEFUL AND SO LUCKY TO HAVE MY EX AS MY BEST FRIEND. I AM EXTREMELY GRATEFUL FOR ANYONE THAT IS STILL BY MY SIDE TODAY THAT WAS AROUND WHILE I WAS USING. IF THEY ARE STILL IN MY LIFE, THEN I AM TRULY GRATEFUL BECAUSE IF THEY KNEW ME AT ALL BACK THEN, THEN I MUST HAVE DONE SOMETHING TO HURT THEM IN ONE WAY OR THE OTHER. I THANK THEM FOR BEING HERE WITH ME TODAY BECAUSE THEY KNOW THAT WAS NOT THE REAL ME.

TUESDAY, OCTOBER 24, 2017:

EVEN THOUGH I HAVE A SHITTY, SHITTY LIFE RIGHT NOW, I AM GOING TO TRY MY VERY HARDEST TO HAVE A GOOD DAY TODAY 'CAUSE I HAVEN'T HAD ONE OF THOSE IN A VERY LONG TIME. I DON'T REMEMBER THE LAST TIME I COULD SAY THAT I HAD A GOOD DAY. GOOD LUCK! I HAVE WRITTEN DOWN A DETOX PLAN, I'M NOT DONE WITH IT YET, BUT IT MAKES ME FEEL BETTER THAT I HAVE AT LEAST STARTED ONE. I AM GOING TO MAKE IT WORK THIS TIME, NO DOUBT IN MY MIND, I AM SO SUPER READY! HEROIN IS NOT GOING TO CONTROL ANYMORE OF MY LIFE, IT HAS ALREADY STOLEN THE PAST 10 YEARS OF MY LIFE, I'M NOT GOING TO LET IT TAKE ANY MORE OF ME! THIS IS MY LIFE AND I NEED TO TAKE CONTROL OF IT, AND STOP SITTING AROUND WAITING FOR SOMETHING THAT I DON'T KNOW IS EVEN THERE. I HAVE COMPLETELY WASTED, I MEAN *WASTED,* THE PAST YEAR AND A HALF. WORST LAST YEAR AND A HALF I THINK I HAVE EVER HAD. I FEEL LIKE I AM 95 YEARS OLD. I'M SCARED MY BODY IS GOING TO SHUT DOWN ANY DAY NOW. IT SCARES ME TO DEATH 'CAUSE I KNOW I AM NOT MOTHER OF THE YEAR AND MY KIDS HAVE GONE THROUGH *HELL* 'CAUSE

OF ME, BUT THEY DO LOVE ME, I KNOW THAT FOR SURE, SO IF ANYTHING WAS TO HAPPEN TO ME, MY KIDS WOULD BE ABSOLUTELY DEVASTATED! I DON'T EVER WANT TO SEE MY KIDS HURT, SO I AM NOT READY TO LEAVE THIS EARTH QUITE NOW EITHER. I COMPLAIN A LOT, I KNOW A LOT, BUT I AM SO SUPER GRATEFUL TO BE ALIVE TODAY. I KNOW THERE IS SOMETHING REALLY IMPORTANT I'M SUPPOSED TO DO, OR I WOULD HAVE BEEN DEAD A LONG, LONG FUCKING TIME AGO. I JUST DON'T KNOW EXACTLY WHAT IT IS QUITE YET.

I AM SO NOT DOING OKAY TODAY AT ALL! WELL, I HAVE DONE CLEAR *(Meth)* THE PAST 4 DAYS, ALONG WITH MY BLACK, OF COURSE, SO I HAVE BEEN UP FOR AT LEAST 4 DAYS NOW. I DON'T DO THAT STUFF AT ALL ANYMORE, SO WHEN I DO, IT HITS ME SUPER, SUPER HARD (HENCE THE NOT SLEEPING FOR 4 DAYS). I REALLY HATE THIS FEELING TOO. I DON'T KNOW WHY I HAVE BEEN DOING IT THE LAST LITTLE BIT. I HAVE PLENTY OF ANXIETY ON A REGULAR BASIS, THERE IS NO WAY I LIKE, OR COULD HANDLE, ANY MORE LIKE I USED TO BE ABLE TO DO, TWEAKING ALL DAY. IT'S SO NOT FUN TO ME *EVER,* AND WE WENT THROUGH 4 BALLS OF BLACK IN 4 DAYS, HOW FUCKING RIDICULOUS IS THAT? I AM NOT AN ENERGETIC, HEALTHY GIRL THAT I ALWAYS USED TO BE, I HAVE TORN MY BODY APART, THAT'S WHY EVERYONE ELSE THAT KNOWS ME IS SHOCKED THAT I AM STILL ALIVE. WELL, I'M DEFINITELY FEELING WHAT ALL THE YEARS OF PARTYING PUT MY POOR BODY THROUGH NOW. I AM SUPER UNHEALTHY, AND I AM ALWAYS SO SICK, CONSTANTLY SICK, EVERY SINGLE DAY!

WHAT A DAY FROM HELL!!!

SO, I AM OUTSIDE ON THE BALCONY WRITING WHILE ANTHONY IS IN THE FRONT ROOM ON THE COUCH AND RYAN IS IN OUR BED THROWING A COMPLETE FIT 'CAUSE ANTHONY IS HERE. KILL ME NOW, *PLEASE!* THEY BOTH DESPISE EACH OTHER, AND THEY WANT TO KILL EACH OTHER, BUT ANTHONY HAD

ABSOLUTELY NOWHERE TO GO TONIGHT, HIS CAR IS NOT WORKING, AND IT'S COLD OUTSIDE. AFTER EVERYTHING ANTHONY HAS DONE FOR ME AND RYAN LATELY, I COULDN'T LET HIM BE OUT ON THE STREET. HE LITERALLY HAS BEEN TAKING COMPLETE CARE OF ME THE PAST COUPLE WEEKS AND THANK GOD HE HAS, 'CAUSE RYAN'S PAYCHECKS HAVE BEEN SHIT 'CAUSE HE KEEPS MISSING DAYS 'CAUSE HE IS "SICK." I THINK ANTHONY HAS SPENT OVER $1,500 ON ME AND RYAN THE PAST WEEK AND A HALF. SO, THERE IS ABSOLUTELY NO WAY, AFTER EVERYTHING HE HAS DONE, THAT I WOULD LET HIM BE OUT ON THE STREETS IN THE COLD. THAT WOULD JUST BE HEARTLESS, AND I HAVE A HUGE HEART. I DON'T LIKE SEEING ANYONE HURT OR ON THE STREETS IN THE COLD. BUT THIS HAS DEFINITELY BEEN AWKWARD AS FUCK FOR ME. THAT'S WHY I AM OUTSIDE RIGHT NOW BEING AWAY FROM BOTH OF THEM AND DOING MY OWN THING, AND I CAN ONLY TAKE SO MUCH BEFORE I BREAK OR FALL! MY LIFE IS LITERALLY SPINNING OUT OF CONTROL AND IT JUST KEEPS GETTING WORSE EVERY STINKIN' DAY! A GIRL CAN ONLY TAKE SO MUCH TILL SHE SNAPS, WELL, NATALIE HAS SNAPPED!

(GRATITUDE JOURNAL) TODAY, I AM GRATEFUL FOR NOT COMPLETELY LOSING MY MIND AND BEING ABLE TO PULL EACH DAY OFF, ACTING SOMEWHAT NORMAL AFTER BEING UP FOR 3 CONTINUOUS DAYS. NOT THAT I MEAN TO BY ANY MEANS, BUT I DID, AND I CAN STILL FUNCTION (BARELY) AND STILL GO OUT INTO THE PUBLIC. I FUCKING ROCK! NOT REALLY, BUT I AM DELIRIOUS.

<u>WEDNESDAY, OCTOBER 25, 2017</u>:

IT'S ABOUT 7:00 P.M. AND I'M SITTING OUTSIDE IN THE DARK ON THE GRASS IN FRONT OF MY APARTMENT WITH SYDKA WRITING, FEELING LIKE COMPLETE SHIT! I HAD BEEN UP FOR ALMOST 6 DAYS STRAIGHT TILL LAST NIGHT. *(The day before, she said she had been up for 3 days. Her sense of time was really off.)* I FINALLY PASSED OUT TILL ABOUT AN HOUR AGO. I HAVE BEEN LIVING LIKE SHIT THE PAST WEEK. I HAVE DONE CLEAR *(meth)* EVERYDAY 'CAUSE ANTHONY HAS HAD IT (STUPID ME) AND THAT HAS BEEN KEEPING ME UP. ANTHONY HAS STAYED HERE ABOUT 3 OR 4 TIMES AND HE ALWAYS HAS CLEAR ON HIM. I HAVEN'T BEEN INTO IT AT ALL, BUT WHEN IT IS IN FRONT OF MY FACE, I CAN'T SAY NO. WELL, NOW I AM NOT OKAY AT ALL! IT HAS CAUGHT UP WITH ME AND I AM SO SICK NOW. NEVER DOING THAT AGAIN, THAT'S FOR DAMN SURE. ANTHONY AND JENNIFER AND ME HUNG OUT AT JENNIFER'S LAST NIGHT ALL NIGHT LONG DOING STUPID SHIT! I NEED TO STAY AWAY FROM THESE PEOPLE! AND I KNOW THIS, BUT THEY KEEP PRYING THEIR WAY INTO MY LIFE AND I AM A SOFTIE AND VERY LONELY, SO I CONTINUE TO ALLOW THEM AROUND ME. I HAVE NOT BEEN OKAY FOR THE PAST MONTH NOW, AND IT DEFINITELY CAUGHT UP WITH ME! I NEED TO STAND UP FOR MYSELF AND STOP DOING WHAT I HAVE BEEN DOING OR I AM GOING TO DEFINITELY DIE THIS TIME. I NEED TO BE AROUND FOR MY KIDS AND FINALLY ACT LIKE THEIR MOTHER. I HAVE SAID THIS MORE THAN ONCE, I HAVE GOT TO CHANGE MY LIFE!!!

WELL, WENT INSIDE FOR A MINUTE, GOT IN A HOT BATH AND SOAKED IN SOME LAVENDER, THAT IS JUST WHAT I NEEDED 'CAUSE I AM *ALWAYS* STRESSED AND EDGY LATELY, ACTUALLY FOR WAY TOO LONG NOW!! HOPEFULLY, I'M PRAYING THAT I CAN FALL ASLEEP AND ACTUALLY STAY ASLEEP, I NEED THAT *BAD!* I NEED SLEEP MORE THAN I HAVE IN A VERY LONG TIME NOW! I *DO NOT* LIKE THIS PERSON I HAVE BECOME AND I'M ALMOST POSITIVE THAT THE PEOPLE AROUND ME OFTEN DON'T LIKE IT AT ALL, EITHER! JEFFREY HAS BEEN CALLING ME ALL NIGHT LONG AND NOT LEAVING ANY VOICEMAILS, SO IT MUST NOT BE TOO IMPORTANT.

WELL, ENDED UP FALLING ASLEEP AFTER BEING UP FOR 6 DAMN DAYS. I WAS A MESS. I WAS COMPLETELY DELIRIOUS

AND NOT AT ALL MYSELF. I DIDN'T GO AROUND MY FAMILY AT ALL OR THEY WOULD HAVE NOTICED RIGHT AWAY. I DON'T KNOW WHAT TO DO ABOUT ANTHONY, HE WON'T GO AWAY NO MATTER WHAT I DO OR WHAT I SAY, HE JUST DOESN'T GET IT! HE PAYS HIS WAY INTO MY LIFE, AND HE IS THE *LAST* PERSON I WANT IN MY LIFE. I NEED TO GET THE GUTS TO JUST TELL HIM, BUT THEN I AM AFRAID OF RETALIATION. WHAT DID I GET MYSELF INTO THIS TIME?

Three days later...

SATURDAY, OCTOBER 28, 2017:

IT'S ABOUT 6:30 P.M. AND I'M SITTING OUTSIDE ON THE GRASS IN THE DARK IN FRONT OF MY APARTMENT WITH SYDKA. IT WAS A WEIRD DAY TODAY. ANTHONY WAS HERE MOST OF THE DAY 'CAUSE HE HAD NOWHERE TO GO AND IT MAKES ME EXTREMELY UNCOMFORTABLE, SO I KICKED HIM OUT AROUND 3. RYAN GOT HOME AT 4, SO IT WAS GOOD THAT HE WAS GONE 'CAUSE THEY DO NOT GET ALONG AT ALL! I FEEL LIKE ANTHONY IS A KID I HAVE TO TAKE CARE OF RIGHT NOW 'CAUSE HE HAS NO HOME AND NOBODY TO HELP HIM. BUT I CAN'T DO IT ANYMORE. HE IS A GROWN MAN AND NEEDS TO TAKE CARE OF HIMSELF. HE DID GIVE ME A LOT OF MONEY, THOUGH, LAST WEEK, SO I FELT LIKE I OWED IT TO HIM TO GIVE HIM A PLACE TO STAY FOR THE NIGHT. HE REALLY STRESSES ME OUT, THOUGH, *BAD!* I HAVEN'T SEEN MY KIDS OR MY FAMILY IN A VERY LONG TIME, AND I DON'T LIKE IT AT ALL. I HAVE NO IDEA WHAT IS HAPPENING WITH ME AND RYAN. HE IS ALWAYS GONE, BUT WHEN I DO SEE HIM, HE DOESN'T TALK TO ME AT ALL. I AM JUST COMPLETELY LOST IN THIS WORLD RIGHT NOW. I DON'T KNOW WHETHER I AM COMING OR GOING. I HATE IT! I HAVE HATED MY LIFE FOR A VERY LONG TIME NOW, AND I HAVEN'T DONE ANYTHING ABOUT IT. I JUST DON'T KNOW WHERE TO START AND GET

MY LIFE GOING AGAIN. I DON'T KNOW WHAT TO DO OR WHO TO BE AROUND. THIS IS THE MOST UNCOMFORTABLE I HAVE EVER BEEN IN MY LIFE!!! I'M TRYING TO FIGURE OUT AND PUT TOGETHER A DETOX PLAN, BUT I DON'T KNOW WHO TO TELL AND WHO TO HAVE HELP ME. BUT I HAVE GOT TO DO IT. I AM SO SICK OF HAVING SOMETHING RUN MY LIFE, IT HAS ALL POWER OVER ME AND I CAN'T CONTROL IT! I KNOW I AM MUCH BETTER THAN THIS AND I KNOW HEAVENLY FATHER HAS A PLAN FOR ME, A BIG PLAN, AND I WANT TO FIGURE OUT WHAT THAT IS AND DO IT. I WANT TO HELP PEOPLE BECAUSE THAT MAKES ME HAPPY, BUT I HAVE TO HELP MYSELF FIRST. MY KIDS DESERVE TO HAVE A GOOD MOTHER, A MOTHER THAT IS *ALWAYS* THERE FOR THEM, A MOTHER THAT IS A GOOD EXAMPLE TO THEM, A MOTHER THAT THEY ARE PROUD OF AND A MOTHER THAT IS SPIRITUAL AND GOOD. I WANT TO BE THAT MOTHER FOR MY KIDS. EVEN THOUGH THEY ARE GETTING OLDER, THEY STILL NEED ME, AND JALA IS ONLY 10 *(she was actually eleven at this time),* I STILL HAVE TIME TO TURN MY LIFE AROUND AND BE A GOOD MOTHER TO HER, ACTUALLY RAISE HER AND BE THERE FOR HER WHENEVER SHE NEEDS ME. I'M SO GRATEFUL FOR JAY AND HOW AWESOME HE HAS BEEN RAISING HER, BUT I WANT A BOND WITH HER LIKE HE DOES. SHE IS MY BABY, I STILL HAVE A CHANCE WITH HER, AND I WANT TO RAISE HER MORE THAN ANYTHING IN THIS WORLD, SO I NEED TO GET CLEAN, BUT I DON'T KNOW HOW TO GO ABOUT IT JUST QUITE YET, AND WHO TO TELL AND WHO TO HAVE HELP ME...IT'S BIG DECISIONS!!!

SUNDAY, OCTOBER 29, 2017:

IT'S 12:30 AND IT'S HOTTER THAN HELL OUTSIDE RIGHT NOW. I'M SITTING OUTSIDE ON THE GRASS WITH MY FAVORITE PUPPY AND RYAN. I DIDN'T GET ANY SLEEP LAST NIGHT AT ALL. I'M WAITING FOR JALA TO GET HOME FROM HER GRANDMA'S SO I CAN FINALLY SEE HER, HAVEN'T SEEN HER FOR A COUPLE

DAYS NOW AND SHE DOESN'T DO SO GOOD WHEN WE GO THAT LONG WITHOUT SEEING EACH OTHER. I'M A COMPLETE MESS RIGHT NOW, I HAVEN'T EATEN OR SLEPT IN OVER 24 HOURS NOW. I'M GONNA TRY AND TAKE A NAP BEFORE I SEE JALA SO I WILL BE SOMEWHAT NORMAL! I HAVEN'T HEARD FROM ANTHONY AT ALL, WHICH MAKES ME VERY HAPPY AND RELIEVES A LOT OF STRESS. HE HAS ABSOLUTELY NOWHERE TO GO, BUT IT'S NOT MY RESPONSIBILITY TO TAKE CARE OF HIM AND HE HAS BEEN ACTING LIKE IT IS LATELY. I CAN'T EVEN TAKE CARE OF MYSELF RIGHT NOW, LET ALONE A 60-YEAR-OLD MAN! I NEED TO CLEAN UP, THAT'S JUST ALL THERE IS TO IT. I THOUGHT ABOUT CALLING PAMELA *(from Renaissance Ranch),* BUT SHE WILL JUST TELL ME TO GET INTO A REHAB, AND WE KNOW HOW THAT ALWAYS WORKS OUT FOR ME. PLUS, I DON'T HAVE A DIME FOR SOMETHING LIKE THAT AND MY FAMILY HAS ALREADY PAID WAY TOO MUCH, TOO MANY TIMES, TRYING TO HELP ME. I'M ON MY OWN THIS TIME, THAT'S WHY IT'S SO HARD TRYING TO PUT A DETOX PLAN TOGETHER, BUT I'M READY, AND I WILL FIGURE SOMETHING OUT ON MY OWN THIS TIME. AND IT WILL WORK THIS TIME, I KNOW IT AND I FEEL IT, AND I AM SO STINKIN' READY FOR IT!!! SO, I JUST GOT READY FOR THE DAY AND I FEEL LIKE I LOOK PRETTY GOOD, AND THAT'S REALLY HARD FOR ME TO SAY, AND I WAS HEADING OVER TO JAY'S TO SEE MY BABY GIRL AND THEY ARE AT LAGOON *(an amusement park)* RIGHT NOW, GLAD I CALLED FIRST. TODAY IS THE LAST DAY LAGOON IS OPEN AND JALA ALWAYS GETS SEASON PASSES, SO I GUESS SHE HAD TO GET THAT LAST DAY IN. I DON'T BLAME HER, SHE LOVES LAGOON. SHE IS A DIE HARD, NOT AFRAID OF ANYTHING! SHE WILL GO ON ANY AND EVERY RIDE THERE IS. SHE WAS ABSOLUTELY FEARLESS IN CALIFORNIA. THERE WAS SOME RIDES I DIDN'T EVEN DARE TO GO ON, AND JALA HAD NO PROBLEM AT ALL.

SO, I'M SITTING OUTSIDE AGAIN, AND IT IS LITERALLY PROBABLY 60 OR 70 DEGREES AND IT'S 4:00 P.M., END OF

OCTOBER, AND IT'S THIS WARM, IT'S CRAZY! RYAN JUST WENT AND MET UP WITH ANDREW SO WE ARE TAKEN CARE OF FOR THE NEXT COUPLE DAYS, ANOTHER $150 DOWN THE DRAIN, AND I MEAN IT GOES DOWN THE DRAIN. IT MAKES ME PHYSICALLY AND MENTALLY SICK HOW MUCH MONEY WE SPEND ON THIS SHIT! IT'S FUCKING RIDICULOUS! BUT, IF WE DON'T DO IT, THEN WE CAN'T PHYSICALLY MAKE IT THROUGH THE DAY. IT KILLS ME THAT SOMETHING HAS THIS MUCH CONTROL OVER ME AND MY LIFE! NOT FOR VERY MUCH LONGER, I WON'T TAKE IT ANYMORE!

MONDAY, OCTOBER 30, 2017:

IT HAS BEEN A HORRIBLE DAY TODAY! I KNOW I SAY THAT A LOT BECAUSE MY LIFE DOES SUCK RIGHT NOW, BUT LAST NIGHT AND TODAY DEFINITELY TOPPED IT. SYDKA STARTED COUGHING LAST NIGHT AROUND 4:00 P.M. AND IT JUST KEPT GETTING WORSE AND WORSE. ME AND RYAN WERE UP ALL NIGHT WITH HER 'CAUSE SHE KEPT COUGHING SO MUCH THAT SHE WAS CHOKING AND COULDN'T BREATHE. IT WAS THE SCARIEST THING *EVER!* SHE HAS NEVER BEEN SICK BEFORE, SO I DIDN'T KNOW WHAT IN THE HELL TO DO. WELL, I CALLED THE VET FIRST THING THIS MORNING AT 6:30 A.M. AND THEY LET ME BRING HER IN AT 9:00. SHE GOT EXAMINED AND SHE HAS KENNEL COUGH. IT'S A VERY CONTAGIOUS SICKNESS THAT DOGS GET AND IT'S AIRBORNE. THEY GAVE ME 2 DIFFERENT ANTIBIOTICS AND SOME COUGH MEDS, BUT IT'S THE SADDEST THING EVER! I CAN'T STAND HAVING MY PUPPY HURTING OR UNCOMFORTABLE IN ANY WAY. I JUST CAN'T TAKE IT! IT COST ME $200 THIS MORNING AT THE VET AND RENT IS DUE IN 2 DAYS. YA, WE ARE DEFINITELY FUCKED THIS MONTH!

(GRATITUDE JOURNAL) IT'S 2:30 A.M. AND THIS IS THE THIRD NIGHT IN A ROW THAT I CANNOT SLEEP! I HAVE INSOMNIA SO STINKIN' BAD! BUT, I AM ACTUALLY GRATEFUL THAT

I ACTUALLY HAVE SOMEWHERE TO LAY MY HEAD AT NIGHT. THERE WERE MANY NIGHTS IN MY LIFE THAT I DIDN'T HAVE ANYWHERE TO SLEEP AT NIGHT. SO, I AM SO THANKFUL FOR THIS BED, THIS ROOM, MY CUTE APARTMENT, AND MY FAVORITE PUPPY IN THE WORLD THAT I HAVE TODAY. THINK I CAN GET SOME SLEEP NOW, GOOD LUCK, ME!

Almost two weeks later...

SUNDAY, NOVEMBER 12, 2017:

IT'S ABOUT 10:00 P.M. AND I JUST GOT OUT OF THE BATH AND AM GETTING READY TO GO TO BED. I WENT OVER TO MY MOM'S TODAY AND SPENT SOME GOOD QUALITY TIME WITH MASON BECAUSE HE WAS THE ONLY ONE THERE. HE IS WATCHING MY PARENTS' HOUSE, SO HE SAYS, WHILE MY PARENTS ARE IN ST. GEORGE. THEY WON'T BE BACK TILL TUESDAY, SO MASON IS ALL ALONE TILL THEN. HE TOTALLY OPENED UP TO ME TODAY AND REALLY TALKED TO ME, IT WAS GREAT. RYAN AND I HAVEN'T BEEN DOING GOOD LATELY. HIS PAYCHECKS HAVE BEEN ABSOLUTELY HORRIBLE, SO WE BARELY MADE RENT. I STILL OWE MY PARENTS $200 FOR RENT. IT'S BEEN REALLY BAD! WE NEVER HAVE ANY MONEY ANYMORE. WE HAD TO PAWN HIS LAPTOP THE OTHER DAY JUST SO WE COULD SURVIVE. HOPEFULLY, IT WON'T BE LIKE THIS MUCH LONGER. I ACTUALLY APPLIED ONLINE TODAY AT TARGET. HOPEFULLY, I GET A CALL BACK FROM THEM. I NEED TO DO SOMETHING, 'CAUSE ME NOT WORKING IS JUST NOT CUTTING IT ANYMORE. IT SCARES ME TO DEATH TO START WORKING AGAIN, BUT WE CAN'T SURVIVE ANYMORE WITH RYAN BEING THE ONLY ONE THAT IS MAKING MONEY. I FINALLY GOT ANTHONY OUT OF MY LIFE. HE IS ABSOLUTELY CRAZY AND COMPLETELY OBSESSED WITH ME, SO I HAD TO GET RID OF HIM. NOW HE IS THREATENING ME AND HARASSING ME, HE NEEDS TO GET A LIFE!

(GRATITUDE JOURNAL) I AM EXTREMELY GRATEFUL FOR THIS HANDSOME MUTE MAN THAT I HAVE RIGHT NEXT TO ME. HE IS ABSOLUTELY AMAZING TO ME AND MY KIDS. IF I SABOTAGE WHAT I HAVE RIGHT NOW WITH HIM (WHICH IS VERY LIKELY WITH ME), I KNOW I WILL REGRET IT FOR THE REST OF MY LIFE. I THINK I WILL KEEP HIM, EVEN THOUGH HE DRIVES ME COMPLETELY NUTS AT TIMES, HE IS BY FAR THE BEST THING THAT HAS HAPPENED TO ME. I CANNOT SCREW THIS ONE UP!!

MONDAY, NOVEMBER 13, 2017:

WELL, IT'S ABOUT 5:00 P.M. AND I AM AT THE CHIROPRACTOR WITH OMI FOR HER BACK 'CAUSE MY MOM IS IN ST. GEORGE. KEITH AND ROGER ARE AT MY HOUSE WAITING FOR ME AND I'M NOT VERY COMFORTABLE WITH IT. I REALLY NEED TO GET HOME, JENNIFER AND KEITH AND ROGER HAVE BEEN AT MY PLACE ALL DAY LONG AND IT'S BEEN A VERY INTERESTING DAY. ANTHONY HAS BEEN HARASSING ME AGAIN TODAY, SO I HAD TO CALL ETHAN AND TALK TO HIM AND TELL HIM EVERYTHING ABOUT HIS SUPPOSEDLY BEST FRIEND. HE HAS BEEN LYING TO ETHAN ALSO. HE HAS BEEN LYING TO ABSOLUTELY EVERYONE. WELL, HE'S NOT ALLOWED AT CATHERINE'S, NOT ALLOWED AT JENNIFERS, AND NOT ALLOWED AT MY MOM'S HOUSE. I WILL NOT LET HIM AROUND ME AGAIN, HE IS AN *EVIL* MAN THAT WILL ALWAYS BE OBSESSED WITH ME, AND IT REALLY SCARES ME TO DEATH. THAT MAN IS CAPABLE OF ANYTHING, BEATING, KILLING, WHATEVER, HE DOES NOT CARE WHEN HE GETS THIS WAY. I AM NOT OKAY RIGHT NOW AT ALL, I HAVE THE WORST MIGRAINE, I FEEL LIKE I AM GOING TO THROW UP AND POSSIBLY FAINT AT ANY TIME NOW. I DID 2 REALLY GOOD SHOTS OF CRYS *(crystal meth)* TODAY, AND I NEVER DO IT. SO, I HAVEN'T EATEN A SINGLE THING TODAY, OF COURSE, AND HAVEN'T SLEPT FOR OVER 2 DAYS. I AM A MESS RIGHT NOW AND CAN'T EVEN SEE STRAIGHT. I HATE METH, THAT'S WHY I NEVER DO IT!

IT'S ABOUT 8:30 P.M. AND I AM AT JENNIFER'S HOUSE HANGING OUT. I WENT TO JALA'S TONIGHT AND HUNG OUT WITH JALA, JAY, AND SAMANTHA FOR A WHILE. I FINALLY BROKE DOWN AND TOLD JAY THAT I WAS USING AND WANTED SOME HELP. HE WAS SO GOOD ABOUT IT AND TOLD ME HE WOULD DO ANYTHING HE COULD TO HELP ME. I EVEN TOLD HIM THAT I BROUGHT A SHITLOAD TO CALIFORNIA WITH ME. HE SAID HE WOULD HAVE BEEN FINE WITH THAT IF I WOULD HAVE TOLD HIM. I KNEW I SHOULD HAVE. I CALLED SHALL AND TOLD HER, AND I ALSO TOLD ADI. THEY WERE ALL SO GOOD ABOUT IT AND TOLD ME THAT THEY WILL HELP ME WITH ANYTHING I NEED. IT WAS THE BIGGEST BURDEN OFF MY SHOULDERS! SO, I HAVE AN APPOINTMENT IN THE MORNING AT TARGET FOR AN INTERVIEW FOR CASHIER. I'M SUPER EXCITED, BUT AT THE SAME TIME, I AM REALLY, REALLY NERVOUS. AFTER I GO, I AM GOING TO MAKE PLANS TO GO OUT OF TOWN FOR A COUPLE WEEKS TO GET CLEAN WITH PROBABLY MICHELLE AND SAMANTHA. I WANT THIS MORE THAN ANYTHING. I CAN'T LIVE THIS LIFE ANYMORE. WE NEVER HAVE MONEY ANYMORE, AND WE CAN'T EVEN LIVE ANYMORE. SO, IT'S DEFINITELY TIME! I WANT TO BE CLEAN SO BAD AND I AM SO SUPER READY. I DON'T KNOW WHERE WE ARE GOING TO GO YET, BUT IT WILL BE WORTH IT! I NEED THIS BEFORE I DIE!

TUESDAY, NOVEMBER 14, 2017:

(GRATITUDE JOURNAL) WELL, I MADE A HUGE, HUGE STEP TODAY! I CALLED SHALL AND TOLD HER I WAS USING AND NEEDED SOME HELP. I WAS ABSOLUTELY TERRIFIED, BUT SHE WAS AWESOME AND SO WILLING TO HELP. I TALKED TO JAY AND SAMANTHA LAST NIGHT TOO, AND THEY JUST HUGGED ME AND CRIED AND SAID THEY WOULD HELP ME IN ANY WAY THAT THEY POSSIBLY COULD. I FEEL SO MUCH BETTER!!

11-21-2017: Dr. Note–132 lbs. With Jay and Samantha they are supporting her. Has a sponsor and is in contact with Renaissance Ranch *(She is talking about Pamela from Renaissance Ranch).* Has been using Heroin the past 6 months, ready to start Suboxone. Starts job at Target *(she was never hired at Target because they do a background check and she had a criminal record).* Jay is managing all meds. Prescribed Xanax, Ambien, Zofran and Suboxone.

Nine days later...

THURSDAY, NOVEMBER 23, 2017:

IT'S THURSDAY MORNING AT 3:00 A.M. AND IT'S THANKSGIVING TODAY. I AM AWAKE IN MY ROOM WITH RUTH SLEEPING IN MY BED NEXT TO ME, BENJAMIN ON THE FLOOR, AND RYAN OUTSIDE ON THE COUCH. HOW MEAN AM I? WELL, RUTH IS 7 MONTHS PREGNANT, SO SHE NEEDS A BED. ME, RUTH, AND SYDKA ARE COMFORTABLE IN THE BED, EVEN THOUGH I HAVE THE WORST HEADACHE I THINK I HAVE EVER HAD, IT IS ABSOLUTELY POUNDING! IT HURTS! WELL, I FINALLY MADE A MOVE, CALLED THE DOCTOR, MADE AN APPT., AND I'M GETTING CLEAN! YAY! I WANT THIS MORE THAN ANYTHING IN THIS ENTIRE WORLD! I SAW THE DR. YESTERDAY MORNING AND HE GAVE ME ALL THE THINGS TO GET BETTER AND KICK THIS STUPID ADDICTION. WELL, I MADE IT THROUGH THE 24 HOURS AND I JUST TOOK MY FIRST SUBOXONE. I FEEL LIKE A HUGE BURDEN HAS BEEN LIFTED OFF MY SHOULDERS. I AM SO DONE WITH HEROIN, I CAN'T EVEN STAND IT! THE DAY BEFORE THANKSGIVING, ACTUALLY IT IS THANKSGIVING, THE DAY I GET CLEAN! THANKSGIVING 2017! NOW, I JUST NEED TO STICK IT OUT AND NOT GIVE IN TO MY TEMPTATIONS! I AM DONE WITH THE PATHETIC DRUG WORLD AND I OWE THE WORLD TO JAY, WHICH IS MY BEST FRIEND IN THE ENTIRE WORLD, AND HIS NEW GIRL SAMANTHA THAT I ABSOLUTELY

ADORE. SHE PAID FOR EVERYTHING FOR ME YESTERDAY. THE DR., PRESCRIPTIONS, FOOD, ETC. SHE PROBABLY SPENT $450. SHE IS AN ABSOLUTE ANGEL! I COULDN'T HAVE DONE IT WITHOUT HER. GOD DEFINITELY BRINGS PEOPLE IN OUR LIVES WHEN WE LEAST EXPECT IT AND THEY BECOME JUST WHAT WE NEED. I AM SO GRATEFUL FOR JAY. HE HAS BEEN MY ROCK AND BEST FRIEND FOR ABOUT 4 YEARS NOW OR EVEN LONGER. HIM AND SAMANTHA SAVED MY LIFE THIS TIME AND I WILL NEVER, EVER FORGET IT. I AM SUPER BLESSED AND HAVE PEOPLE THAT LOVE ME, I JUST NEED TO REMEMBER THAT!!!

THIS IS DEFINITELY THE WORST THANKSGIVING I HAVE EVER HAD. I AM DETOXING TODAY, AND IT'S DAY 3, SO I FEEL LIKE COMPLETE SHIT! I HAVE BEEN UP FOR 3 DAYS STRAIGHT. I HAVE A HEADACHE FROM HELL, MY STOMACH HURTS, MY WHOLE BODY HURTS! I COULDN'T GO TO MY MOM'S AND HAVE EVERYONE SEE ME THIS WAY. THIS IS ABSOLUTELY MISERABLE! MY MOM AND FAMILY JUST THINK I HAVE THE STOMACH FLU, BUT SHALL AND ADI ARE THE ONES THAT KNOW, AND OF COURSE, SAMANTHA AND JAY. SPEAKING OF SAMANTHA AND JAY…I AM SO THANKFUL TO HAVE BOTH OF THEM IN MY LIFE. THOSE TWO PRETTY MUCH JUST SAVED MY LIFE. I DIDN'T HAVE THE MONEY TO GO TO THE DR. AND THAT IS THE ONLY WAY FOR ME TO CLEAN UP, SO SAMANTHA (YES, JAY'S GIRL) PAID FOR MY DR. APPT., WHICH WAS PRETTY PRICEY, AND ALL MY MEDICATION AND A BUNCH OF GROCERIES FOR MY HOUSE. THEY BOTH EVEN CAME INSIDE MY APARTMENT AFTER WE WENT TO THE PHARMACY, AND THEY DID MY DISHES AND THEY CLEANED UP WHAT THEY COULD. I AM SO THANKFUL FOR JAY, HE IS MY BEST FRIEND IN THE WHOLE WORLD AND WE GET ALONG SO GREAT, AND LITTLE MISS JALA SURE LIKES HOW WE ARE TOWARDS EACH OTHER. WHENEVER WE TAKE HER TO SCHOOL FUNCTIONS, BIRTHDAY PARTIES, ETC., SHE ALWAYS GETS SUPER EMBARRASSED OF JAY AND I BECAUSE WE ARE USUALLY DOING STUPID AND

CRAZY THINGS TO TRY AND EMBARRASS HER. WE DON'T DO IT ANYMORE LATELY BECAUSE SHE STARTED GETTING EXTREMELY MAD AT US. JAY AND I ARE FUN!

ALMOST 3 FULL DAYS SINCE I HAVE USED! I GOT THROUGH THE WORST PART, EVEN THOUGH I FEEL LIKE I AM GOING TO DIE RIGHT NOW, I'M PRETTY SURE I'M A BIT BETTER THAN A COUPLE DAYS AGO. WITHDRAWING SUCKS SO *BAD!* I DIDN'T EVEN GET TO SEE MY KIDS TODAY FOR THANKSGIVING. SAW ADI FOR 2 MINUTES BUT HAVEN'T GOT TO SEE JALA OR MASON. IT BREAKS MY HEART COMPLETELY IN HALF, THEY DESERVE MUCH BETTER THAN ME, THEY ARE GREAT KIDS, AND EVERYONE TELLS ME THAT. THEY ARE THE LOVE OF MY LIFE AND MY ABSOLUTE EVERYTHING! I AM SO DEPRESSED THAT I DIDN'T GET TO SEE THEM TODAY, BUT ON THE BRIGHT SIDE, I'M CLEAN OFF HEROIN!! THAT'S THE BIGGEST RELIEF OFF MY SHOULDERS. AND, I COULDN'T HAVE DONE IT WITHOUT JAY AND SAMANTHA, THEY HAVE BEEN MY ANGELS! I ABSOLUTELY LOVE JAY AND HIS GIRLFRIEND!

Six days later…

11-29-2017: Dr. Note–127 lbs. Has anxiety. Has not started job yet, waiting on background check. Prescribed Suboxone film.

WEDNESDAY, NOVEMBER 29, 2017:

TEXT FROM NAT TO ME: It seems like the more I try and the better I am doing, my life is going backwards and being more messed up.

ME: Why do you say that?

NAT: Cause we can't afford rent and it's due on Friday, and I just got a notice on my door that the gas is getting shut off tomorrow and Ryan's check was only 250 and I have to use 100 of it for the Dr. today and our rent is 900$. We are screwed and I am doing absolutely everything I CAN TO MAKE THINGS WORK AND THEY JUST AREN'T!! Ryan said it has been slow at work but he didn't tell me how bad it really was. So I might be homeless as of Sat and that I can't do!! Sorry just in a huge bind and I'm freaking out!!!

ME: Oh my gosh Nat. All you can do is keep pushing forward and take things minute by minute. Just try not to throw away the progress you've made the last 6 days because you've done incredible. Things will be ok even if it doesn't seem that way right now. Pray.

NAT: I will thanks Shall!! You always know what to say to make me feel better. I love you. And I won't give up....

ME: I'm so proud of you. Read that book that mom gave you it will help a TON! I love you.

Four days later...

SUNDAY, DECEMBER 3, 2017:

IT'S ABOUT 2:00 A.M. AND I AM JUST GETTING IN BED, READY TO GO TO SLEEP. RYAN AND I JUST GOT DONE SETTING UP AND DECORATING THE CHRISTMAS TREE. IT ACTUALLY LOOKS FABULOUS! WELL, I'M VERY HAPPY TO SAY THAT THINGS HAVE COMPLETELY CHANGED AND TURNED AROUND FOR ME THE PAST MONTH! I DECIDED I WAS *DONE*, AND I MEAN *DONE!!* I JUST COULDN'T DO THE DRUG WORLD ANY LONGER. SO, I TOOK THE INITIATIVE AND MADE A CALL

TO MY DOCTOR AND GOT IN THE VERY NEXT DAY. JAY AND SAMANTHA PAID FOR IT, BLESS THEIR HEARTS, 'CAUSE THEY KNEW HOW BAD I WAS STRUGGLING AND THEY SAW ME GOING DOWNHILL QUITE FAST. THAT SCARES JAY REALLY BAD! AND I STARTED TO GET REALLY SCARED. I'M SO SICK OF WASTING MY LIFE BEING AROUND OTHER DRUG ADDICTS THAT DON'T GIVE A FUCK ABOUT ME AND THAT STEAL FROM ME AND I WANT TO RAISE MY BABY GIRL AND IT WAS GETTING TOO LATE. I MADE MY FINAL DECISION AND I WAS DONE WITH DRUGS AND THE PEOPLE! I AM 9 OR 10 DAYS CLEAN NOW AND DOING FABULOUS! I HAVEN'T BEEN ABLE TO SAY THAT FOR SO LONG! I AM SO SUPER HAPPY, A WHOLE NEW PERSON! MASON, DILLON, JALA, AND HER 3 FRIENDS ALL SLEPT HERE LAST NIGHT AND IT WAS A *BLAST!* MASON AND I HAVE GOTTEN SUPER CLOSE THE PAST COUPLE WEEKS AND HE COMES OVER ALL THE TIME NOW! I AM IN HEAVEN AND I PLAN ON KEEPING IT THIS WAY!

TUESDAY, DECEMBER 5, 2017:

TEXT FROM ME TO NAT: You ok?

NAT: Not at all. I'm having a nervous breakdown and want to go to the hospital but I can't because I can't rack up another hospital bill. I'll be OK I'm just going through a lot right now. And on top of it all I'm sitting in my house and my internets not working so I can't watch TV, I can't get on my phone I can't get on my laptop and I'm going crazy. I know that sounds stupid sorry but Ryan got paid today but I have no gas to go get money from him to pay the $50 bill to get my internet back on and I don't have a credit card to do it so I'm just stuck and going absolutely crazy. I'm losing my mind. I'm just sitting on my bed crying and I don't know what to do…Kill me now.

Three days since last entry...

WEDNESDAY, DECEMBER 6, 2017:

I DON'T EVEN KNOW WHERE TO START TONIGHT AT 11:30 P.M., SO *MUCH* HAS HAPPENED SINCE I WROTE LAST! WELL, I DID IT! I HAVE BEEN TALKING ABOUT GETTING MYSELF CLEAN FOR OVER 6 MONTHS NOW. I ACTUALLY CAN'T BELIEVE IT MYSELF, BUT I DID IT! AND I DID IT ALL ON MY OWN!!! I GOT TO MY BREAKING POINT A COUPLE WEEKS AGO AND I MADE THE FIRST STEP AND ACTUALLY FOLLOWED THROUGH THIS TIME! I'M SHOCKED STILL THAT I DID IT. WENT FROM USING 3 OR 4 GRAMS OF HEROIN A DAY, SHOOTING UP, TO BEING AT LEAST 12 DAYS CLEAN NOW! THIS TIME I HAD HAD ENOUGH AND WAS FINALLY READY! IT WAS SO *HARD,* OF COURSE, BUT I DID IT. THANKSGIVING REALLY SUCKED, THOUGH. I WAS BY MYSELF ALL DAY IN BED KICKING HEROIN WITH ABSOLUTELY NO HELP FROM ANYONE. IT FEELS SO MUCH DIFFERENT THIS TIME BECAUSE I WAS REALLY FINALLY READY. BUT I AM SUPER PROUD OF MYSELF, I JUST WISH I DID IT A LONG TIME AGO. BUT AT LEAST I DID IT! THE ONLY PEOPLE THAT I TOLD AND KNEW ABOUT IT WAS ADI, SHALL, AND JAY, AND HAVING THEIR SUPPORT, WHETHER THEY WERE RIGHT NEXT TO ME OR NOT, HELPED ME SO MUCH AND IT FELT SO GOOD TO BE 100% HONEST WITH THEM. HONESTY IS WHAT MAKES THINGS HAPPEN, NO MATTER WHAT! SO, ME AND RYAN ARE NOT DOING GOOD AT ALL! WE HAVE NEVER BEEN THIS *BAD!* I DON'T EVEN KNOW HIM ANYMORE. HE HAS CHANGED SO EXTREMELY MUCH THE PAST COUPLE MONTHS THAT I DON'T KNOW WHO THIS MAN IS THAT IS LIVING WITH ME ANYMORE! HE HAS COMPLETELY BROKEN ME! I THINK WE ARE DONE FOR GOOD THIS TIME. HE HAS BEEN LYING TO ME CONSTANTLY AND FOR NO REASON AT ALL! HE HAS *NEVER* BEEN THIS WAY TO ME BEFORE. I'M SO ALONE AND SO EXTREMELY SCARED! I'M SO HURT! HE HAS HURT ME SO BAD AND I REALLY DIDN'T DESERVE IT THIS

TIME! I HAVE TO LET HIM GO, I HAVE TO, WE CAN'T BE TOGETHER ANY LONGER, WE ARE TOXIC TO EACH OTHER AND I NEVER IN A MILLION YEARS THOUGHT THAT RYAN AND I WOULD *EVER* REACH THIS POINT. IT'S LIKE HE TURNED OFF ALL HIS FEELINGS AND EMOTIONS FOR ME. I'M A MESS, AND THAT'S AN UNDERSTATEMENT. THIS IS HONESTLY THE VERY FIRST TIME IN MY ENTIRE LIFE THAT I AM COMPLETELY ALONE WITHOUT A MAN. I'M SUPER SCARED. I DECIDED TO PUT MYSELF IN GOD'S HANDS 'CAUSE HE IS THE ONLY ONE THAT KNOWS WHAT'S BEST FOR ME, ESPECIALLY SINCE MY LEASE IS UP HERE AFTER CHRISTMAS AND I HAVE NO IDEA WHERE I AM GOING TO GO. I'VE NEVER COMPLETELY GIVEN MYSELF TO GOD BEFORE, SO I HOPE HE KNOWS WHAT HE IS DOING WITH ME, AND I AM PRAYING I CAN HANDLE WHATEVER PLAN HE HAS FOR ME! (SCARY.)

12-13-2017: Dr. Note–125 lbs. Mom is helping her. Has not relapsed since 11-21-2017. Has significant anxiety and needs higher dose of Suboxone film. Prescribed Suboxone, Ambien, and Xanax.

12-17-2017: Dr. Note–125 lbs. Prescribed Suboxone and Ambien.

• • •

CHAPTER 14
2018

IN 2018, NAT TURNED THIRTY-NINE, *Adi twenty-two, Mas nineteen, and Jala twelve. This was the last year of her life.*

January 14, 2018 at my house in Saint George

1-8-2018: Dr. Note–125 lbs. Leaving to Saint George for 2–3 weeks. Denies relapse. Prescribed Suboxone and Ambien.

Nat must have come to visit me in Saint George somewhere between the 8th and the 16th of January. I don't remember any details of this visit, but she never stayed more than a few days other than years earlier, when she stayed to try to get clean.

My mom had called and told me that Nat was in the hospital and that she had MRSA in her mouth. She had MRSA in the past. She ended up having Cellulitis in her mouth from smoking Bath Salts. (Cellulitis is a bacteria infection involving the inner layers of the skin.)

2-4-2018: Dr. Note–123 lbs. Has Cellulitis on face. Treated with antibiotic and pain meds. Relapsed on Heroin. Taking Xanax. Mom and Fiance helping her. They knew about relapse. Prescribed Ambien.

First journal entry in two months...

SUNDAY, FEBRUARY 18, 2018:

IT'S ABOUT 10:30 P.M. AND I JUST GOT OUT OF THE BATH AND I AM GOING TO FALL OVER ANY MINUTE NOW AND FALL RIGHT TO SLEEP. I HAVE BEEN UP FOR 2 STRAIGHT DAYS NOW, AND I *NEVER* DO THIS STUPID SHIT ANYMORE (USING METH AGAIN)! I'M TURNING 39 IN A COUPLE DAYS AND I STILL AM DOING STUPID SHIT! *WHEN AM I EVER GOING TO TRULY GROW THE FUCK UP* AND STAY AWAY FROM THE PEOPLE THAT I KNOW BRING ME DOWN??? DON'T GET ME WRONG, I AM DOING A LOT, ACTUALLY A LOT BETTER, BUT I JUST DON'T WANT ANY OF THIS LIFESTYLE IN MY LIFE ANYMORE, AND IT SEEMS TO ABSOLUTELY FOLLOW ME *EVERYWHERE!* I AM OUT ON THE BALCONY, STILL AT FOXBORO, AND IT'S SNOWING OUTSIDE! WE HAVE TO BE OUT OF THESE APARTMENTS AT THE END OF THIS MONTH. I HAVE NO IDEA WHERE WE ARE GOING YET. I HAVE BEEN RIGHT DOWN IN BED FOR ALMOST 2 1/2 WEEKS BECAUSE I HAVE CELLULITIS IN MY FACE. HOW FUCKING FREAKY IS THAT? THE ONLY TIME I SMOKE BATH SALTS IN A LONG TIME AND THAT'S WHAT I GET. KARMA IS A *BITCH!* WE WENT WEDDING DRESS SHOPPING YESTERDAY FOR ADI'S WEDDING DRESS AND WE HAD A *BLAST!* I WANT HER TO HAVE THE WEDDING OF HER DREAMS. I LOVE THAT GIRL OF MINE. I KNOW I HAVE SAID THIS WAY MORE THAN JUST A COUPLE TIMES, BUT I *HONESTLY HAVE THE BEST KIDS EVER!!!* I COULDN'T BE MORE PROUD OF ANY 3 OF THEM. THEY ARE AMAZING KIDS AND THEY ARE THE BIGGEST BLESSING IN MY LIFE! I AM SO STINKIN' LUCKY! WELL, AFTER I HAD THAT HORRIBLE INFECTION IN MY FACE, I RELAPSED 'CAUSE I

WAS IN SO MUCH DAMN PAIN (NOT THAT I CAN USE THAT AS AN EXCUSE), BUT I DID, AND I AM SO MAD AT MYSELF FOR IT 'CAUSE I WAS DOING SO WELL! BUT I AM NOT WORRIED AT ALL, I'M ACTUALLY TRANSITIONING BACK OVER TO MY SUBOXONE TOMORROW. I WANT TO BE CLEAN AND STAY CLEAN AND BE MORE INVOLVED IN ALL 3 OF MY KIDS' LIVES LIKE I SHOULD HAVE BEEN WHILE THEY WERE GROWING UP. I MISSED OUT ON SO MUCH...WELL, NOT ANYMORE! I AM HERE AND AM EXCITED TO BE AROUND MY WONDERFUL, BEAUTIFUL KIDS ALL DAY, OH, AND MY SYDKA BABIES. SO, BENJAMIN IS STAYING WITH RYAN AND I RIGHT NOW 'CAUSE WE ARE MOVING IN A WEEK ANYWAYS AND RUTH IS IN JAIL. SHE HAD HER BABY, AND 2 DAYS LATER, THEY THREW HER IN JAIL. HOW SAD IS THAT? BUT, SHE DID IT TO HERSELF. BENJAMIN HAS CHANGED A LOT NOW THAT THE BABY IS HERE. HE IS SO STINKIN' GOOD TO HIM AND HAS TO GO SEE HIM EVERY DAY AT LAKEVIEW HOSPITAL. BENJAMIN ASKED ME TO BE THE BABIES GODMOTHER! I STARTED BAWLING MY EYES OUT. I WAS SO SUPER EXCITED, AND OF COURSE, I SAID YES!

Nat's birthday was the 23rd and everyone met up in Salt Lake at her favorite restaurant to eat. At the same time, I was in Salt Lake meeting with the wedding planner to make plans for my daughter's wedding and had to miss Nat's dinner. It was the last birthday dinner I would have had with her. I deeply regret not being there. I met up with her at a gas station when she was heading home from Kaysville the next day and she asked me to put gas in her car because she didn't have money, and I did. That was the only time I saw her while I was in town.

<u>3-1-2018:</u> <u>Dr. Note</u>–124 lbs. Has not made transition to Suboxone yet. Mom has been in hospital *(not true)*. She is stressed. Prescribed Ambien.

Almost two weeks later...

FRIDAY, MARCH 2, 2018:

WELL, TODAY WAS ACTUALLY AN OKAY DAY. I CAN'T THINK OF ANYTHING AT ALL THAT WENT WRONG FOR ME TODAY, AND THAT IS A HUGE ACCOMPLISHMENT ON MY PART 'CAUSE I CAN TAKE A PERFECTLY GOOD DAY AND SABOTAGE AND RUIN IT ALMOST ALL THE TIME. BUT, I'M TRYING TO STAY POSITIVE INSTEAD OF NEGATIVE WITH EVERYTHING I DO DURING THE DAY AND IT'S ACTUALLY BEEN WORKING. WELL, I DON'T BELIEVE I DESERVE IT RIGHT NOW, BUT I RECEIVED THE BIGGEST BLESSING THAT IS GOING TO COMPLETELY CHANGE MY LIFE AND I'M SUPER, SUPER EXCITED! WE FOUND A NEW PLACE TO LIVE! IT'S SO NICE, IT'S EAGLEWOOD LOFTS AND IT'S PERFECT! IT'S JUST A ONE BEDROOM BUT THAT'S ALL WE NEED RIGHT NOW! NOBODY KNOWS WHERE WE LIVE, AND WE ARE KEEPING IT THAT WAY. *(My mom helped Nat and Ryan get into this apartment.)* I JUST WENT TO THE DR. YESTERDAY, GOT MY MEDS, IN MY NEW PLACE, HIDDEN FROM ANYONE, AND I'M GETTING MYSELF CLEAN. I'VE DONE IT BEFORE, I CAN DO IT AGAIN. GOD WAS 100% WATCHING OVER ME WITH THIS SITUATION 'CAUSE BY GETTING OUT OF MY OLD APARTMENT AND HOW MANY PEOPLE KNEW WHERE I LIVED. I FEEL SO STINKIN' SAFE HERE! ADI, DAKOTA, AND THEIR FRIENDS ALL CAME OVER TONIGHT AND GOT IN THE HOT TUB! HOW CUTE IS THAT? THEY LOVE MY NEW PLACE, AND SO DO I, FRESH START, HERE I COME!

Eight days later...

SATURDAY, MARCH 10, 2018:

WELL, WE MOVED, *FINALLY DID IT!* AND WE ARE SO SUPER DUPER BLESSED, AND I DON'T KNOW WHY BECAUSE I KNOW I CAN BE A MUCH BETTER PERSON THAN I AM TODAY. I AM THRIVING ON BEING THAT WOMAN, MOTHER, DAUGHTER, SISTER

THAT I KNOW I CAN BE, I HAVE A HUGE HEART AND I CARE SO DEEPLY, SOMETIMES I CARE A LITTLE TOO MUCH. IT'S ABOUT MIDNIGHT RIGHT NOW AND I HAVE MY BABY SYDKA NEXT TO ME AND RYAN NEXT TO ME IN BED. IT WAS A FUN NIGHT. THE APARTMENTS WE MOVED INTO, I COULDN'T BE HAPPIER, AND SO ARE MY KIDS. WE HAVE 2 BIG POOLS AND 2 BIG HOT TUBS. SO, OF COURSE, ADI, DAKOTA, AND THEIR FRIENDS CAME OVER AND SAT IN THE HOT TUB FOR HOURS. THEY GOT A BIT TIPSY! SO RYAN AND I HAD TO DRIVE THEM HOME. SILLY KIDS! I HAVE A LOT OF REALLY BAD THINGS THAT I NEED AND WANT TO CHANGE IN MY LIFE MORE THAN ANYTHING. THIS MOVE, I BELIEVE, IS A NEW BEGINNING FOR ME. START OVER, COMPLETELY OVER, AND THAT IS WHAT I AM STRIVING TO DO. I HAVE BEEN SO EXTREMELY BLESSED LATELY AND HEAVENLY FATHER HAS GOT ME THROUGH SOME SCARY AND TOUGH TIMES, BUT IT WAS SO OBVIOUS TO ME THAT IT WAS HIM BY MY SIDE THE ENTIRE TIME. I'M CHANGING MY LIFE, THE WAY I LIVE, AND AM GOING TO BE A MOTHER THAT MY KIDS ARE PROUD OF, AND A SISTER THAT EVEN EMILY WANTS TO BE AROUND ME. I WANT THIS MORE THAN I HAVE EVER WANTED ANYTHING SO BAD! I WILL SUCCEED!

SO, WHY CAN'T I DO THIS AND BE THE WOMAN I KNOW I CAN BE? I KNOW I AM STRONGER THAN I GIVE MYSELF CREDIT FOR, BUT *DAMN,* THIS LIFE IS *HARD!* I HAVE BEEN SETTLING (VERY LAZY) THE PAST COUPLE YEARS OR MORE AND THIS IS SO NOT WHO I AM. I CAN'T GET MYSELF OUT OF THIS DARK HOLE THAT HAS TAKEN ME DOWN SO FAR AND FOR SO LONG. I HAVE LITERALLY WASTED SO MANY YEARS OF MY LIFE WITH THIS HORRIBLE AND DEADLY ADDICTION. MY ADDICTION WINS EVERY TIME! I WANT TO STAY CLEAN *FOREVER,* BUT I CAN'T SEEM TO DO IT! WHEN I WANT SOMETHING BAD ENOUGH, THEN I CAN USUALLY MAKE IT HAPPEN, BUT THIS HAS ME ON A LEASH AND DRUG ME DOWN FOR SO MANY YEARS, I FEEL LIKE I DON'T EVEN HAVE THE SLIGHTEST CLUE HOW TO LIVE LIFE ANYMORE. I'M SO LOST AND

I HAVE BEEN FOR OVER A DECADE. THANK GOD FOR MY 3 BEAUTIFUL AND AMAZING CHILDREN THAT I ADORE MORE THAN ANYTHING IN THIS ENTIRE WORLD OR I WOULD BE DEAD. MY KIDS, AND OF COURSE MY SWEET LITTLE SIDEKICK SYDKA, DEFINITELY KEEP ME GOING. THEY ARE 4 OF THE BIGGEST BLESSINGS I HAVE EVER RECEIVED!

3-15-2018: Dr. Note–125 lbs. Transferred to Suboxone for 3 days then lost meds in move and relapsed on Heroin. Prescribed Suboxone. Mom is in hospital, stress, moved in new apartment. Prescribed Ambien and Xanax.

Six days later...

SUNDAY, MARCH 25, 2018:

IT'S ABOUT 11:59 SUNDAY NIGHT AND I AM WIDE FUCKING AWAKE. I'M REALLY STRESSING OUT ABOUT A JOB. I NEED TO GET ONE, ESPECIALLY 'CAUSE MY BABY IS GETTING MARRIED AND I NEED TO HELP OUT WITH AT LEAST SOME OF HER WEDDING. I'M SO STINKIN' EXCITED FOR HER! *(Adi got married in December of this year.)*

When she was looking for a job, she had no idea how to apply for one and asked for my help. The most common everyday things were really hard for her; she used to say she felt like a little kid relearning things when she was trying to get clean.

MONDAY, MARCH 26, 2018:

SITTIN' AT MARY AND DAVID'S RIGHT NOW! WHAT IN THE HELL AM I DOING? CAN'T DO THIS LIFE AGAIN. NOW, I AM AT DAVID'S FRIEND'S HOUSE AND I AM NOT COMFORTABLE AT ALL. BUT...I DID JUST GET MY OLD JOB BACK AT TOP STOP *(gas station)*, JEAN JUST HIRED ME ON THE SPOT AND WANTS ME THERE TOMORROW. ALICE WAS THERE TOO, AND THEY

BOTH WERE BEING SO GOOD TO ME! NOW, I HAVE TO WORK TOMORROW ALREADY...PROBLEM IS, THEY RANDOM DRUG TEST NOW, AND IF THEY TEST ME THIS WEEK, I'M FUCKED! I AM PRAYING THAT THEY DON'T. I NEED THIS JOB TERRIBLY. I NEED TO GET CLEAN AGAIN SO STINKIN' BAD, AND I WANT IT MORE THAN ANYTHING. I LOVE MY KIDS MORE THAN LIFE ITSELF! SO, THIS KID JUST GRABBED MY NOTEBOOK AND WROTE DOWN HIS # IN IT! HOW FUNNY IS THAT? I'M NEVER GOING TO USE IT. THAT'S SUPER SAD, BUT *NO, HELL NO!* HE DID JUST HOOK ME UP WITH SOME CLONAPIN *(antianxiety medication)*. I REALLY NEED TO SLEEP TONIGHT SO I CAN FUNCTION ON MY 1ST DAY TOMORROW. PRAY NO DRUG TEST!

Three days later...

3-29-2018: Dr. Note–125 lbs. Had abscess went to ER had I&D *(incision and drainage)*. Has not transitioned to Suboxone. Needs more Xanax, prescribed. Started new job.

THURSDAY, MARCH 29, 2018:

IT'S ABOUT 2:00 A.M. THURSDAY MORNING AND I JUST WOKE UP IN A PANIC, HAVE NO IDEA WHY. HAVEN'T WRITTEN IN QUITE A WHILE *(three days ago)*, PROBABLY BECAUSE I AM TOO EMBARRASSED TO WRITE DOWN HOW MY MISERABLE LIFE IS RIGHT NOW. AND I SHOULDN'T BE COMPLAINING, THERE ARE SO MANY PEOPLE OUT THERE THAT ARE FAR BEYOND NEED OF HELP, I'M JUST BITCHIN'. WE LIVE AT EAGLEWOOD LOFT APARTMENTS NOW, WHICH I AM VERY, EXTREMELY HAPPY ABOUT! THEY ARE REALLY NICE, AND WE ARE SO SUPER HAPPY HERE. THEY HAVE ABSOLUTELY EVERYTHING HERE, 2 POOLS, 2 HOT TUBS, BIKES YOU CAN RIDE FOR THE DAY, FISHING POND, AND ABOUT 4 PARKS AND LOTS OF FIELDS TO RUN AROUND IN. JALA IS IN HEAVEN HERE. I LOVE IT SO MUCH. IT'S JUST ME AND RYAN HERE, AND JALA, OF COURSE, WHEN SHE

STAYS OVER, WHICH IS ALL THE TIME NOW! I LOVE IT! I JUST GOT MY OLD JOB BACK AT TOP STOP (CHEVRON) AND I DON'T KNOW HOW HAPPY I AM ABOUT THAT. BUT, I NEEDED A JOB DESPERATELY AND NOBODY WOULD HIRE ME BECAUSE OF MY BACKGROUND. AT LEAST JEAN IS BEING NICE RIGHT NOW, AND I HOPE IT STAYS THAT WAY. EVERYONE IS SUPER HAPPY I'M BACK! ALL THE USUAL PEOPLE THAT USED TO COME IN STILL DO AND THEY WERE ALL HAPPY I WAS BACK. IT MADE ME FEEL REALLY, REALLY GOOD! MY ONLY PROBLEM RIGHT NOW, WHICH IT'S ALWAYS THE SAME DAMN PROBLEM, IS THAT I STARTED USING AGAIN! I GO TO THE DR. EVERY TWO WEEKS AND GET A SCRIPT FOR SUBOXONE, BUT MY HABIT IS SO BAD AGAIN ALREADY THAT I CAN'T EVEN GO THE 24 HOURS TO GET BACK ON THE SUBS. I WAS DOING SO GOOD TOO. I'M SO DISAPPOINTED IN MYSELF. I'M GOING TO ST. GEORGE FRIDAY TILL TUESDAY AND I HAVE NO IDEA WHAT IN THE HELL I'M GOING TO DO. WE ARE STAYING AT A HOTEL AND IT'S ME, MOM, ADI, AND MAS IN A ROOM TOGETHER. THERE IS NO WAY IN HELL I CAN HIDE THAT FROM THEM. I'M SO SCARED, I'M TOTALLY IN A BIND. I HATE SO BAD THAT I LET MY LIFE GET THIS WAY AGAIN. BUT, I *WILL CHANGE IT!* THAT IS A GUARANTEE. I HATE BEING AND FEELING LIKE THIS. WE ARE TALKING TO MARY AND DAVID AGAIN, AND THAT IS THE STUPIDEST THING WE COULD BE DOING. BUT I DID MISS THEM SO MUCH, SEEING THEM BRINGS BACK SO MANY MEMORIES THAT ARE NOT ALL BAD. WE DEFINITELY HAD SOME FUN TIMES. RYAN LIKES THEM BOTH A LOT AND LOVES TO GO OVER THERE AND HANG OUT WITH THEM, BUT HE DOESN'T REALIZE JUST HOW *HOT* MARY AND DAVID ARE AND THAT HOUSE IS, ESPECIALLY NOW THAT CATHERINE IS DEAD AND DAVID HAS THE HOUSE TO HIMSELF, IT'S A TOTAL DISASTER! THEY ARE RIGHT BACK DOING THE SAME OLD THING, DEALING AND HAVING LOTS OF TRAFFIC THROUGH THAT HOUSE. DAVID JUST GOT OUT NOT EVEN A MONTH AGO. I WILL PRAY FOR THEM, WHILE I'M PRAYING FOR MYSELF!

(GRATITUDE JOURNAL) I AM SO SUPER GRATEFUL FOR THIS NEW PLACE RYAN AND I JUST GOT INTO. IT'S THE NICEST PLACE THAT I HAVE LIVED IN A VERY, VERY LONG TIME. WE LIVE AT EAGLEWOOD LOFTS IN NSL AND THEY ARE SUPER NICE WITH LOTS OF FUN STUFF TO DO. I'M SUPER HAPPY AND I JUST GOT MY OLD JOB BACK AT CHEVRON, DON'T KNOW HOW HAPPY I AM ABOUT THAT, BUT IT'S A JOB FOR NOW. WE HAVE TO STAY ABOVE WATER NOW, BECAUSE WE HAVE BEEN DROWNING LATELY. NO MONEY COMING IN AT ALL, THINGS ARE TURNING AROUND.

About a week later…

THURSDAY, APRIL 5, 2018:

YEP, TODAY IS MASON'S BIRTHDAY AND I ONLY GOT TO SEE HIM FOR MAYBE 10 MINUTES AT LUNCH. I HAVE BEEN UP FOR 2 DAYS AND WORKING OVERTIME AT CHEVRON AND 89. IT'S ABOUT 3:00 P.M. RIGHT NOW, AND LIKE I SAID, HAVEN'T SLEPT IN 2 WHOLE DAYS AND I HAVE TO GO CLOSE TONIGHT BEING TRAINED BY ALICE AT THE 89 STORE FROM 6 P.M. TILL ABOUT MIDNIGHT. HOW IN THE LIVING HELL AM I GOING TO PULL THIS OFF? I *DO NOT* LIKE AT ALL WHERE I HAVE BEEN HEADING LATELY IN MY LIFE…AND THERE ARE 2 REASONS BRINGING ME DOWN! MARY *AND* DAVID!!!! I NEVER THOUGHT I WOULD LET THEM IN AGAIN, AND NOW I HAVE, AND I HAVE NOT BEEN MYSELF AT ALL!! I AM TRYING SO HARD TO STAY CLEAN AND BECOME A BETTER MOTHER AND AN ALL AROUND BETTER WOMAN, WELL, I SHOT THAT TO HELL! AND I REALLY WAS DOING REALLY GOOD FOR A LONG TIME, THEN I SLIPPED, THEN I LET DAVID AND MARY BACK IN MY LIFE. I CAN'T BELIEVE HOW MUCH MY LIFE HAS SPIRALED OUT OF CONTROL THE PAST FEW MONTHS. I'M DONE WITH ALL THIS SHIT! I WANT TO BE CLEAN SO BAD AND I KNOW EXACTLY WHAT I WANT OUT OF MY LIFE, I JUST HAVE THE

HARDEST TIME GETTING THERE. I KNOW I CAN DO THIS, I AM ONE STRONG WOMAN!!!

Nine days later...

SATURDAY, APRIL 14, 2018:

I HONESTLY DON'T REMEMBER HOW LONG AGO I ACTUALLY WROTE IN MY JOURNAL. IT MAKES ME SAD 'CAUSE I USED TO WRITE EVERY SINGLE NIGHT, I WOULD *NEVER* MISS A DAY. I WAS VERY DEVOTED. NOW, I HAVE PRETTY MUCH FUCKED EVERYTHING OFF AND I REALLY DO FEEL LIKE EVERYTHING. I'M NOT SAYING I'M GIVING UP BY ANY MEANS, LIFE IS JUST FUCKING BRUTAL AND WAY TOO HARD TO DO! IT'S ABOUT 4:45 A.M., AND OF COURSE, I HAVE ANXIETY (AS ALWAYS) AND CAN'T SLEEP. IT'S SATURDAY MORNING AND MY LITTLE PRINCESS HAS A SOCCER GAME AT 9:00 A.M. HOW IN THE *HELL* AM I SUPPOSED TO FUNCTION AT THAT? THEN, RIGHT AFTER, I AM GOING TO A BRIDAL SHOW WITH ADI, MOM, KAILEE, AND I DON'T KNOW WHO ELSE. THEN, RIGHT AFTER THAT, I WORK 6 TO MIDNIGHT AGAIN. I JUST STARTED BACK AT TOP STOP A WEEK AND A 1/2 AGO AND SHE IS ALREADY SCHEDULING ME EVERY STINKIN' DAY. I AM SO STINKIN' BURNED OUT. DON'T GET ME WRONG, I AM VERY THANKFUL I GOT THE JOB BACK, I JUST HOPE IT BENEFITS US MUCH MORE THAN IT IS. I HAVE FALLEN BACK INTO THE HOLE AND NEED TO GET BACK OUT FAST! I CAN ALREADY SEE MYSELF GOING DOWN THAT HORRIBLE ROAD AGAIN AND IT COMPLETELY TERRIFIES ME!

SUNDAY, APRIL 15, 2018:

IT'S ABOUT 4:30 A.M. SUNDAY MORNING AND I STILL CAN-NOT SLEEP! I HAVE BEEN UP FOR 3 STRAIGHT DAYS NOW. I HATE METH! WHY IN THE HELL DO I SMOKE IT EVERY TIME

I SEE MARY AND DAVID? I DON'T EVEN NOTICE WHEN I'M DOING IT 'CAUSE WE ALWAYS DID IT TOGETHER. WELL, MY BODY IS NOT AT ALL USED TO IT ANYMORE. IT KEEPS ME UP FOR DAYS AND I START MOVING MY MOUTH A LOT! JUST LIKE EVERYDAY TWEAKERS DO THAT I HAVE MADE FUN OF WHEN I SEE IT. BUT TODAY WAS *NOT THE DAY* MY MOUTH SHOULD HAVE STARTED TWEAKER SHIT! WENT TO JALA'S SOCCER GAME, AND YES, SHE KICKED ASS AGAIN, AND THE GAME WAS REALLY CRAZY EARLY. THEY DID WIN, YAY! AFTER THAT, WENT HOME FOR AN HOUR TO HOP IN THE SHOWER AND GET READY TO GO WITH ADI AND GRANDMA TO THE BRIDAL SHOW AT SOUTH TOWNE. WELL, AT THIS POINT, I HAD BEEN UP FOR 2 SOLID DAYS, SO ADISON LOOKS IN HER REAR VIEW MIRROR WHILE WE WERE DRIVING OUT THERE AND SAID, "MOM, STOP DOING THAT WITH YOUR MOUTH...YOU'RE ACTING LIKE YOU'RE ON DRUGS, YOU'RE ACTING LIKE A TWEAKER." I WAS SO SHOCKED 'CAUSE I HONESTLY DIDN'T KNOW I DID THAT WITH MY MOUTH ANYMORE. I REPLIED BY SAYING, "I'M JUST SO TIRED AND MY JAW HAS BEEN HURTING." I PRAY TODAY WILL BE A MUCH BETTER AND BRIGHTFUL DAY.

4-19-2018: Dr. Note–127 lbs. Working a lot, has not relapsed in 3 weeks. Wants Vivotrol Shot again. Prescribed Suboxone and Xanax.

A few weeks later...

THURSDAY, MAY 3, 2018:

IT'S ABOUT 11:25 P.M. AND MY LITTLE BABY DOLL IS LAYING RIGHT NEXT TO ME IN BED AND I'M HAVING A TOUGH TIME FALLING ASLEEP. I'M TAKING HER TO SCHOOL TOMORROW 'CAUSE JAY CAN'T DRIVE RIGHT NOW. HE TORE HIS TENDON ON HIS ANKLE SO HE MIGHT HAVE TO GET SURGERY. SO, LUCKY JALA GETS TO SLEEP HERE AGAIN TONIGHT. SHE HAS BEEN LOVING IT, ACTUALLY. SHE HAS BEEN STAYING OVER HERE

ALMOST ALL WEEK AND WAS OVER ALL WEEKEND. SHE LOVES IT HERE. IT MAKES ME SUPER HAPPY! I LOVE IT WHEN MY BABY GIRL IS WITH ME. I'M NOT IN A GOOD PLACE RIGHT NOW EMOTIONALLY AT ALL. I'M TRYING TO KEEP ON MY GAME FACE LIKE EVERYTHING IS FINE AND I'M HAPPY AND OKAY. I NEED TO FOR AT LEAST MY KIDS. EVEN THOUGH ADI CAN SEE RIGHT THROUGH ME, BUT I TELL HER EVERYTHING ANYWAYS. I MEAN ABSOLUTELY EVERYTHING. BEING COMPLETELY HONEST WITH ADI IS THE BEST WAY TO GO WITH HER. SHE CAN TAKE IT AND IS ALWAYS BY MY SIDE, I LOVE THAT GIRL SO MUCH! SHALL KNOWS EVERYTHING TOO. THOSE TWO, SHALL AND ADI, KNOW EVERYTHING AND I WILL NEVER LIE TO THEM. FOR THE OTHERS, WE JUST DON'T TALK ABOUT IT. AS FOR RYAN HE IS DRIFTING AWAY FROM ME A LITTLE BIT, DON'T KNOW WHY?

Six days later…

WEDNESDAY, MAY 9, 2018:

SO, I MET THIS 67-YEAR-OLD MAN AT MY OLD WORK (TOP STOP) AND HE IS NOW ABSOLUTELY OBSESSED WITH ME. HOW IN THE HELL DO I GET THESE OLDER MEN TO FALL FOR ME? THEN I HONESTLY CAN'T GET RID OF THEM, NO MATTER HOW HARD I TRY. HE IS SPENDING LOTS OF MONEY ON ME, AND I HAVE BEEN BROKE FOR SO LONG NOW THAT IT'S NICE TO BE PAMPERED BY SOMEONE, BUT IT'S ALSO VERY, VERY WRONG. I CAN'T BE MEAN TO HIM 'CAUSE HE IS SERIOUSLY THE NICEST GUY EVER, BUT HE IS A 67-YEAR-OLD MAN THAT WANTS A RELATIONSHIP WITH ME. HE IS OLDER THAN MY OWN FATHER! OH, AND HE LIVES IN CAMELOT (A TRAILER PARK), TO TOP IT OFF. THE GUY HAS LOTS OF MONEY BUT LIVES IN A TRAILER, GO FIGURE! I REALLY DON'T KNOW WHAT TO DO. I'M KIND OF SCARED THAT IF I TELL HIM TO

BACK OFF OR IN A TACTFUL WAY SAY I NEED SOME SPACE, I THINK HE MIGHT DO SOMETHING CRAZY OR REVENGEFUL. HE'S SWEET AS HELL, BUT HE DOES HAVE A REVENGEFUL SIDE TO HIM. OH, AND I FORGOT TO MENTION, HE ONLY GOES AFTER VERY YOUNG GIRLS. THE LAST GIRLFRIEND HE HAD, AND HE WAS WITH HER FOR 2 YEARS, IS 26 YEARS OLD. HOW DISGUSTING IS THAT! HELP ME, I'M LITERALLY FUCKED!

Adi, Jala Nat and Mas

Ang, Adi Nat and Kailee

Declan and Nat

My daughter got married in Saint George on May 12th. The whole family came down for it and stayed in a hotel, including Nat. I didn't have any one-on-one time with Nat at all during this time because it was busy for me, and because she stayed very distant from me while she was here.

Eight days later...

THURSDAY, MAY 17, 2018:

IT'S ABOUT 5:00 P.M. AND I AM ABOUT READY TO COMPLETELY LOSE MY MIND!!! I HAVE BEEN UP FOR 48 HOURS WITHOUT ANY SLEEP AT ALL AND AM COMPLETELY DELIRIOUS. I CAN'T EVEN SEE STRAIGHT. SYDKA AND I ARE OUTSIDE IN FRONT OF THE POOL ENJOYING THE SUNLIGHT. WE JUST GOT BACK FROM ST. GEORGE A COUPLE DAYS AGO 'CAUSE KIERRA GOT MARRIED. HOW ABSOLUTELY INSANE IS THAT? CLOUDS ARE DEFINITELY COMING OUT RIGHT NOW, WATCH, I JUST GOT OUT HERE AGAIN AND IT'S GONNA START POURING ON ME. STORY OF MY LIFE! I HONESTLY AM SO STINKIN' LOST RIGHT NOW. I DON'T KNOW WHICH WAY IS UP OR DOWN HALF THE TIME. WE LIVE IN AN APARTMENT THAT WE CAN'T AFFORD AT ALL! SO, EVERY TIME RENT IS ALMOST DUE, RYAN AND I GO INTO A COMPLETE PANIC. I DON'T KNOW WHAT'S GOING ON IN MY LIFE ANYMORE, ALL I KNOW IS THAT I AM SO DAMN *UNHAPPY!* I JUST WANT TO BE HAPPY AGAIN, FEEL LOVED AGAIN, FEEL WANTED AGAIN, AND I AM SO EXTREMELY AFRAID THAT I WILL *NEVER* FIND TRUE HAPPINESS. I ALREADY FUCKED UP MY LIFE PRETTY DAMN GOOD AND I CAN'T GO BACK AND FIX IT. WHAT'S DONE IS DONE, AND RYAN AND I ARE *NOT* GETTING ALONG AT ALL LATELY. I DON'T KNOW WHAT'S GOING ON WITH HIM, 'CAUSE HE *NEVER* TALKS TO ME, BUT THERE IS SOMETHING DEFINITELY WRONG...I CAN FEEL IT MORE THAN I EVER THOUGHT I COULD SOMETHING LIKE THAT! NOW WHAT THE HELL DO I DO? I HAVE ABSOLUTELY *NO IDEA* AND IT SCARES ME TO DEATH!! I DON'T KNOW IF HE IS JUST COMFORTABLE OR WHAT...OR IF HE HAS COMPLETELY FALLEN OUT OF LOVE WITH ME, 'CAUSE IT'S DEFINITELY WHAT HE IS SHOWING! I REALLY DON'T KNOW WHAT THE HELL I AM GOING TO DO...BUT, I PRAY I MAKE THE RIGHT CHOICE. I

HAVE FUCKED UP FOR WAY TOO LONG NOW! I PRAY THIS TIME I CAN FIGURE THINGS OUT...'CAUSE WE REALLY DON'T KNOW HOW MUCH TIME WE HAVE!!!

A few weeks later...

6-6-2018: Dr. Note–136 lbs. Struggling financially, lost job *(at Top Stop).* Relapsed has been off all meds. Wants Xanax, Ambien, and Zofran. Used Heroin last night. Mom and sister are aware of her relapse and helping her. Prescribed Prozac, Xanax, and Suboxone.

WEDNESDAY, JUNE 6, 2018:

WELL, IT'S ABOUT 9:00 P.M. AT NIGHT AND I HAVE RYAN IN THE HOSPITAL. HE HAS BEEN SICK WITH SINUS PROBLEMS FOR OVER A MONTH. WELL, HE GOT HOME FROM WORK TONIGHT AND WAS FREAKING OUT 'CAUSE HE COULDN'T BREATHE AT ALL. IT REALLY SCARED ME. I DON'T KNOW WHAT IN THE HELL IS GOING ON WITH HIM, BUT SOMETHING *BAD* IS. I HAVE *NEVER* SEEN HIM LIKE THIS BEFORE. AND IF HE SCARED ME, THEN WE KNOW IT'S SOMETHING *BAD!* I JUST WISH I COULD DO SOMETHING FOR HIM. HE ALWAYS TAKES CARE OF ME, AND I CAN'T DO ANYTHING FOR HIM RIGHT NOW. I FEEL SO HELPLESS. IT'S SO SUPER SAD TO SEE HIM LIKE THIS. I CAN'T DO A THING BUT SIT HERE AND WATCH HIM IN PAIN! THIS IS SO AWFUL! I JUST WISH I COULD TAKE ALL HIS PAIN AWAY. I FEEL SO BAD FOR HIM. I HAVE SEEN HIM BAD, BUT NEVER THIS BAD. I PRAY HE FINDS SOME SORT OF RELIEF HERE PRETTY QUICK. AND, OF COURSE, WE WENT TO THE CLOSEST HOSPITAL, AND OF COURSE, THIS WAS A HUGE MISTAKE. THEY HAVEN'T CHECKED ON HIM FOR 20 MINUTES NOW WHILE HE IS GASPING FOR AIR. I'M GETTING PRETTY LIVID! I'M ABOUT READY TO GO OUT AND CAUSE SOME DRAMA TILL THEY GET THEIR ASS IN HERE!

Twelve days later...

MONDAY, JUNE 18, 2018:

IT'S ABOUT 7:30 A.M. AND I AM SITTING OUTSIDE ON A BLANKET WITH SYDKA, UP BY THE POOL AT MY APARTMENTS. I HAVE BEEN UP FOR 2 1/2 DAYS WITHOUT ABSOLUTELY *NO SLEEP AT ALL!* RYAN AND I HAVE NOT BEEN DOING GOOD AT ALL FOR QUITE A WHILE NOW. WE CAN'T SEEM TO GET OFF THE HORRIBLE HEROIN. WE HAVE TRIED AND TRIED, AND IT HAS COMPLETELY CONSUMED US. WE JUST MOVED IN TO EAGLEWOOD LOFTS (WHICH I *LOVE*) ABOUT 3 MONTHS AGO. EVERY MONTH, WE HAVE STRUGGLED SO BAD TRYING TO COME UP WITH RENT BECAUSE WE SPEND LITERALLY ALMOST ALL OUR MONEY ON HEROIN. WE ARE 2 1/2 WEEKS LATE RIGHT NOW AND STILL HAVEN'T PAID RENT. WE ARE DEFINITELY SCREWED! I HAVE WANTED TO STOP USING FOR SO LONG NOW. I WENT TO THE DR. AND GOT SOME SUBOXONE AND XANAX TO TRANSFER OVER, BUT RYAN HAS BEEN TAKING THEM AND NOW I DON'T KNOW IF I WILL HAVE ENOUGH TO GET CLEAN. HE HAS BEEN IN BED THE PAST TWO DAYS KICKING. MY DAD AND MASON ACTUALLY CAME OVER LAST NIGHT AND GAVE US BOTH A BLESSING *(a church ordinance)*. IT MEANT THE ABSOLUTE WORLD TO ME. RYAN AND I HAVE NOT BEEN DOING GOOD AT ALL FOR A LONG TIME NOW, I DON'T KNOW IF WE WILL BE ABLE TO WORK THIS OUT OR NOT. I'M SO SCARED ABOUT ABSOLUTELY EVERYTHING *(paranoia and depression are side effects of the drug use)*. I PRAY THINGS GET BETTER AND I CAN FINALLY FIND SOME HAPPINESS IN MY LIFE...'CAUSE IT'S BEEN A VERY, VERY LONG TIME SINCE I HAVE BEEN HAPPY!

6-20-2018: Dr. Note–140 lbs. Relapsed wants more Xanax. Mom and sister are caring for her *(not that they remember)*. Prescribed Xanax, Suboxone, and Zofran.

Six days later...

SUNDAY, JUNE 24, 2018:

WELL, IT'S EXACTLY 2:04 A.M. AND I CANNOT FALL ASLEEP! BOY, THAT'S A SHOCKER! MY PRINCESS BABY GIRL IS LAYING IN BED WITH ME RIGHT NOW AND SHE IS OUT COLD! I LOVE THIS LITTLE GIRL! I HAVE ALWAYS HAD DEPRESSION ON AND OFF, BUT RIGHT NOW, IT'S OUT OF CONTROL! I STARTED HAVING FEELINGS FOR RYAN (WHICH I *NEVER* THOUGHT I WOULD), BUT WE HAVE BEEN LIVING TOGETHER FOR (I THINK) OVER 3 YEARS AND HE HAS ALWAYS BEEN VERY GOOD TO ME AND I WAS COMPLETELY AWFUL, BUT NOW, THE ROLES HAVE COMPLETELY REVERSED! ONE THING I CAN SAY, I HAVE *NEVER* LIED TO RYAN! WELL, NOWADAYS HE CAN'T KEEP HIS LIES STRAIGHT. HE ACTS LIKE HE WANTS ABSOLUTELY NOTHING TO DO WITH ME AND IT'S BEEN GOING ON FOR A WHILE NOW. I DON'T REMEMBER THE LAST TIME I HAD SEX. MY LIFE IS ABSOLUTELY HORRIBLE NOW. RYAN TREATS ME LIKE CRAP (IF HE EVEN TALKS TO ME, WHICH IS VERY RARELY). I HAVE NO IDEA WHO RYAN IS ANYMORE. AND I'M STUCK! WE JUST GOT INTO THIS APARTMENT ABOUT 3 MONTHS AGO AND WE SIGNED A YEAR LEASE. I'M HAVING A HELL OF A TIME GETTING A JOB 'CAUSE MY BACKGROUND CHECK, AND ON TOP OF IT ALL, I'M STILL USING. I GO TO THE DOCTOR EVERY TWO WEEKS FAITHFULLY AND I'M TRYING SO *DAMN HARD,* BUT THIS LIFE DOESN'T SEEM WORTH IT ANYMORE.

MONDAY, JUNE 25, 2018:

WE HAVE SOME VERY DISTURBING AND BAD, BAD NEWS TODAY. I CAN'T STOP CRYING. I'M IN COMPLETE SHOCK. MY LITTLE 23-YEAR-OLD COUSIN STEVEN TOOK HIS LIFE LAST NIGHT. *(Steven lived with my parents for years while he was growing up. He was my cousin Arlo's son, and my cousin Arlo had also lived with us while he was growing up. Steven grew up with our children and was more like a cousin to all of our kids.)* HE SHOT HIMSELF AND I AND EVERYONE ARE ABSOLUTELY DEVASTATED. I KNEW HE WAS A LITTLE DEPRESSED, BUT I HAD NO IDEA JUST HOW BAD HE REALLY WAS. BREAKS MY FREAKING HEART! HIS MOM AND ARLO ACTED LIKE THEY DIDN'T EVEN CARE...IN FACT, STEVEN'S REAL MOM IS NOT HAVING ANYTHING TO DO WITH THE MEMORIAL SERVICE OR ANYTHING. SO, OF COURSE, MY WONDERFUL MOTHER IS DOING IT. MY DAD IS A MESS RIGHT NOW. HE THOUGHT HE HELPED RAISE HIM OKAY, BUT NOW I THINK MY DAD IS PUTTING SOME BLAME ON HIMSELF. JUST LIKE HE DOES WITH ME BEING AN ADDICT. WHICH COULD BE *SO FAR* FROM THE TRUTH! MY DAD WAS AN AWESOME FATHER! I DON'T HAVE ONE BAD MEMORY GROWING UP WITH HIM. HE WAS AN ABSOLUTELY AMAZING FATHER. I FREAKING LOVE MY DAD WITH ALL MY HEART AND I AM SO STINKIN' SCARED THAT HE DOESN'T HAVE MUCH LONGER. I HOPE I'M WRONG, 'CAUSE I WILL DIE WITHOUT MY DAD. HE IS SO SUPER GOOD TO ME AND I WOULD DIE WITHOUT HIM!

Five days later...

SATURDAY, JUNE 30, 2018:

IT'S SATURDAY NIGHT AND IT'S ABOUT 8:40 P.M. JALA, HER FRIEND AND SYDKA, AND I ARE OUTSIDE ON THE LAWN WAITING FOR JAY TO GET HERE 'CAUSE HE IS ABOUT 2 HOURS LATE. NICE, HUH? AND, OF COURSE, IT HAS NOT BEEN THE BEST DAY. GOT DONE AT STEVEN'S MEMORIAL SERVICE A COUPLE HOURS AGO AND I AM A MESS AND I JUST WANT TO GO TO BED! ARLO *(Steven's father, our cousin)* ENDED UP SHOWING UP... AND I 100% LOST IT! HE IS A SPITTING IMAGE OF STEVEN. *(We had not seen Arlo in a few years; he would show up at our family Christmas party randomly, but it had been a while).* I JUST WISH I WOULD HAVE TALKED TO HIM MORE AND TRIED

TO MAKE A DIFFERENCE. HE WAS A GREAT KID WITH A VERY SAD AND MESSED UP LIFE! I FEEL LIKE THAT RIGHT NOW! EVERY STINKIN' DAY! I FEEL LIKE AN ABSOLUTE HORRIBLE PERSON THAT JUST KEEPS GOING DOWNHILL! IT'S SO HARD TO GET UP IN THE MORNINGS 'CAUSE I AM SO DEPRESSED. I WOULD *NEVER* DO ANYTHING TO MYSELF 'CAUSE I THINK THAT IS SO SELFISH, ESPECIALLY TO THE PEOPLE YOU LOVE. BUT I DO FIND SOMETIMES, ACTUALLY A LOT OF THE TIME, WISHING I COULD GET INTO A CAR ACCIDENT OR COME DOWN WITH A HORRIBLE SICKNESS. *I FEEL READY TO GO. (She was gone seven months later).* IF IT WASN'T FOR MY 3 BEAUTIFUL KIDS, I WOULD DEFINITELY BE GONE ALREADY! AND SPEAKING OF RYAN...HE HAS TURNED INTO A COMPLETELY DIFFERENT PERSON THAT I DON'T KNOW ANYMORE. HE PUTS ME IN TEARS EVERY DAY!

I came to Bountiful for Steven's memorial service. The service was Saturday and we had to leave right after to get back to Saint George. Nat showed up to the service and could hardly keep her eyes open and was slurring her words. She came in with fake eyelashes on that were glued upside down and backward. Adi and Kierra took her to the bathroom to help her fix them and she was asking them what they were laughing at. She told them she took too much Xanax and also told me and Austin she was on it, but the amount varied from person to person.

A week later...

We had a sisters' weekend at our cabin. Nat didn't come at the last minute.

<u>SATURDAY, JULY 7, 2018</u>:

IT'S ABOUT 6:00 P.M. AND I'M SITTING OUTSIDE BY THE POOL WITH SYDKA AND RYAN, JUST SMOKING AND DOING ABSOLUTELY NOTHING AT ALL. I WAS SUPPOSED TO BE WITH ALL THE ALLEN GIRLS UP AT SHALL'S CABIN, BUT OF COURSE,

I COULDN'T GO 'CAUSE I WAS TOO SICK! ALL I EVER DO ANYMORE IS LAY IN BED, SUPER, SUPER DEPRESSED AND TRYING TO FIGURE OUT A WAY TO GET CLEAN AND STAY CLEAN. THIS LIFE IS *NOT* ME, AND I DON'T WANT IT, I NEVER DID! WHY CAN'T I STOP? I WOULD GIVE ANYTHING TO NOT BE AN ADDICT. IT'S THE WORST THING ANYONE COULD EVER GO THROUGH AND IT'S A LIFELONG THING. I WOULD RATHER DIE THAN TO KEEP GOING ON LIKE THIS. SO, ADI, JALA, AND DAKOTA JUST SHOWED UP AT MY DOOR AND CONFRONTED ME ABOUT USING. *(Adi asked Dakota to go with her because she had a bad feeling about Mark, she didn't trust his reaction to Nat being confronted. This is the first time she felt nervous about him.)* I DIDN'T LIE TO THEM AND TOLD THEM I HAD BEEN 'CAUSE I DIDN'T HAVE THE MONEY FOR MY SUBOXONE. JALA HAD A PRETTY HARD TIME HEARING IT, BUT ADI AND I EXPLAINED IT TO HER AND SHE WAS BETTER WHEN SHE LEFT.

Almost a month later...

<u>8-1-2018:</u> <u>Dr. Note</u>–138 lbs. Relapsed on Heroin couldn't afford Suboxone, used this morning. Wants more Xanax. Looking for financial assistance program for Suboxone. Prescribed Xanax, Suboxone, and Zofran. (*The amount of Xanax and other medications he kept filling for her is shocking to me.)*

<u>WEDNESDAY, AUGUST 8, 2018</u>:

IT'S MY BABY GIRL'S 22ND BIRTHDAY TODAY! TIME GOES BY WAY TOO DAMN FAST. ME, ADI, MY MOM, EMMY, AND JALA ARE ALL GOING TO BREAKFAST FOR ADI IN THE MORNING. OH, AND MY SWEET MAS TOO! I MISS ADI SO MUCH, I HAVEN'T BEEN ABLE TO SEE HER A LOT ANYMORE. WE WENT FROM SEEING EACH OTHER EVERY SINGLE DAY TO MAYBE ONCE EVERY OTHER WEEK. IT'S NOT OKAY, I MISS MY BABY GIRL. BUT I AM SO PROUD OF HER AND HOW GREAT HER LIFE HAS

TURNED OUT SO FAR. SAME WITH MY OTHER TWO. THEY ARE ALL COMPLETE ANGELS AND DAMN GOOD KIDS. I'M STARTING TO GO DOWNHILL AGAIN AND IT'S SCARING THE SHIT OUT OF ME. I CAN'T DO THIS AGAIN. I PRAY THAT I WILL BE STRONG ENOUGH TO GET THROUGH THIS ONE LAST TIME AND STAY CLEAN AND FINALLY BE THE MOTHER THAT I KNOW I CAN BE. MICHELLE ISN'T TALKING TO ME AGAIN AND I HAVE BEEN COMPLETELY HONEST WITH HER. *(When I knew she was lying to me, I would back away to keep my sanity. Sometimes, I was just so exhausted from worrying about her but I thought about her every day.)* I WON'T LIE TO MY FAMILY AND KIDS ANYMORE AT ALL, SO I'M HOPING THEY WILL STAY BY MY SIDE WHILE I STRIVE TO GET THROUGH THIS.

Nat was starting to slowly withdraw from the family and her children more than usual.

Two days later...

FRIDAY, AUGUST 10, 2018:

MY GOALS FOR THE WEEK!

THE VERY 1ST THING I NEED AND HAVE AND WANT TO DO MORE THAN ANYTHING IS TO GET COMPLETELY CLEAN! I KNOW I CAN DO IT, I HAVE DONE IT MANY TIMES BEFORE, BUT THE REASON I HAVEN'T YET IS JUST BECAUSE OF MONEY. THAT IS HONESTLY THE ONLY THING KEEPING ME FROM BEING CLEAN RIGHT NOW. BUT GOD DEFINITELY ANSWERED MY PRAYERS THIS PAST WEEK. MY DOCTOR HAS 2 PEOPLE OUT OF ALL OF HIS PATIENTS THAT HE CAN PICK TO HAVE THE SUBOXONE COMPANY PAY FOR THESE 2 PATIENTS FOR AN ENTIRE YEAR OF THEIR SUBOXONE! HOW INCREDIBLE IS THAT? HE CHOSE ME! GOD IS DEFINITELY LOOKING OUT FOR ME AND ANSWERING MY PRAYERS AS CLEAR AS DAY. THIS IS GOING TO SAVE ME OVER $400 A MONTH AND NO MORE DRUGS! I JUST WANT OUT...I

ALWAYS DO, I JUST ALWAYS GET STUCK. WELL, I JUST GOT MY WAY OUT. *YAY!* SO, THIS WEEKEND IS DEFINITELY GOING TO SUCK 'CAUSE I HAVE TO KICK FOR AT LEAST 24 HOURS. I KNOW THAT DOESN'T SEEM VERY LONG, BUT IT FEELS LIKE A WHOLE MONTH. IT'S ABSOLUTELY HORRIBLE! BUT, I AM SO MOTIVATED AND HAVE HEAVENLY FATHER GUIDING ME.

BY SATURDAY...START WEENING OFF, THEN GO MY 24 HOURS. I CAN DO THIS! I KNOW I CAN!

Four days later...

TUESDAY, AUGUST 14, 2018:

MY GOALS FOR THE WEEK!
GET CLEAN AND STAY CLEAN!

NAT, I HAVE TO DO THIS AND STICK WITH IT! THERE IS MORE FOR ME IN THIS LIFE AND I CAN'T GIVE UP YET. BELIEVE ME, I WANT TO EVERY DAY, BUT THEN I PICTURE ADI, MAS, AND JALA, AND HOW COULD ANY MOTHER DO THAT TO THEIR KIDS???

STAY AWAY, FAR AWAY FROM ANYONE THAT USES OR THAT HAS EVER USED. ESPECIALLY MARY AND DAVID, EVEN THOUGH IT'S GOING TO BE VERY HARD. I DO LOVE THEM IN A WEIRD KINDA PSYCHO WAY. FOCUS ON ME AND MY KIDS AND DOING WHAT'S RIGHT, THEN THINGS WILL FALL INTO PLACE.

Same day, different journal...

I HONESTLY THOUGHT FOR SURE I WOULD BE IN A BETTER PLACE @ THIS TIME IN MY LIFE. I MEAN FOR *HELL'S SAKE,* I AM ALMOST 40! I DID SO EXTREMELY GOOD IN DRUG COURT, BY THE TIME I WAS FINISHED, I THOUGHT I'D NEVER USE AGAIN! BUT AFTER A COUPLE MONTHS, I THOUGHT IF I JUST TRIED ONE TIME, THEN I WOULDN'T DO IT AGAIN. WELL,

THAT IS ALL IT TOOK! I WAS COMPLETELY HOOKED AFTER ONE TIME AFTER BEING COMPLETELY CLEAN FOR 19/20 MONTHS. DRUG COURT DID CHANGE ME ABSOLUTELY, BUT I AM A MUCH WORSE DRUG ADDICT THAN I EVER COULD IMAGINE. I COULD DO A BIG SHOT OF HEROIN EVERY HOUR OF THE DAY AND IT STILL WOULDN'T DO A THING, KEEPS ME WELL BUT I HONESTLY DON'T HAVE ANY IDEA THE LAST TIME I GOT HIGH. SO, WHY DO IT? THE WORST PART OF IT IS THAT I STARTED HANGING AROUND MARY AND DAVID AGAIN. I KNOW I MAKE MY OWN CHOICES AND I KNOW THAT I SHOULDN'T BE AROUND THEM 'CAUSE THEY HONESTLY WILL *NEVER* QUIT USING. A WEEK AFTER DAVID GOT OUT OF PRISON, HE STARTED SELLING AGAIN, AND OF COURSE, I WANTED TO SEE HIM 'CAUSE HE WAS IN PRISON A LITTLE OVER 3 YEARS. I JUST CAN'T SEEM TO GET THOSE TWO OUT OF MY LIFE FOR GOOD. I LOVE THEM AND I HATE THEM. BUT THEY ARE LIKE FAMILY TO ME. A VERY, VERY DYSFUNCTIONAL FAMILY, BUT THEY ARE FAMILY. RIGHT NOW, I HAVE MEGAN AND HER BOYFRIEND SLEEPING OVER TONIGHT AND MARY *HATES* MEGAN! SHIT WOULD HIT THE FAN IF MARY KNEW SHE WAS HERE! I JUST GOT BACK FROM CONNING AN OLD MAN INTO GIVING ME $ SO I COULD GO GET DOPE AND HOPEFULLY PAY OUR RENT TOMORROW, 'CAUSE IT'S 2 WEEKS LATE.

I JUST GOT BACK A COUPLE HOURS AGO FROM BUYING A BALL OF BLACK, $175. INSANE, RIGHT? I WANT OUT, I WANT OUT, I WANT OUT! I WISH I HAD *NEVER* BECOME A JUNKIE DRUG ADDICT!

<u>WEDNESDAY, AUGUST 15, 2018</u>:

WELL, IT'S 3:45 A.M. RIGHT NOW AND I AM WIDE AWAKE WHILE RYAN IS COMPLETELY OUT COLD. THIS IS MY 3RD OR 4TH DAY UP NOW AND I AM SO UPSET WITH MYSELF. I'M NOT PUTTING BLAME ON ANYONE BUT MYSELF, BUT I DEFINITELY

STARTED TO ASSOCIATE WITH PEOPLE THAT ARE VERY TOXIC TO ME AND CONSTANTLY GETTING THEMSELVES INTO A LOT OF TROUBLE...AND THE SUPER SAD THING IS THAT THEY *NEVER LEARN* OR THEY JUST PLAIN DON'T CARE. THEY HAVE BEEN GETTING INTO TROUBLE THEIR ENTIRE LIVES AND IN AND OUT OF JAIL A LOT. A LOT MORE THAN YOU CAN IMAGINE FOR HOW OLD THEY ARE. THEY (DAVID AND MARY) ARE THE TWO THAT INTRODUCED ME TO THE LEGIT DRUG WORLD. THEY WERE BOTH DEALERS. THEY ARE MY VERY BEST FRIENDS, ACTUALLY, THEY ARE CONSIDERED FAMILY HERE. I GOT INTO EVERY DRUG THAT IS OUT THERE (ALMOST) WITH THEM. AT FIRST, I WAS LOVING LIFE BUT THEN COMPLETELY FUCKED UP. DRUGS FUCKED UP MY ENTIRE LIFE SINCE THE 1ST TIME I TRIED THEM. WELL, MARY AND DAVID HAVE BEEN AROUND DRUGS THEIR ENTIRE LIFE. I BELIEVE DAVID STARTED EXPERIMENTING WITH DRUGS IN HIS TEENAGE YEARS AND MARY HAS BEEN SMOKING WITH HER OWN MOTHER SINCE SHE WAS 13 YEARS OLD. WELL, WHEN I 1ST STARTED HANGING OUT WITH THEM, A FEW KIDS AT SCHOOL THAT ARE THAT WERE VERY BRATTY GIRLS ... *(The entry ends here).*

A week later…

WEDNESDAY, AUGUST 22, 2018:

IT'S ABOUT 10:45 P.M. AND INSTEAD OF GETTING READY FOR BED, I'M WRITING A LOT 'CAUSE MY MIND IS GOING CRAZY! SO, STEVEN DIED A COUPLE WEEKS AGO AND THAT WAS SO HARD FOR OUR FAMILY, ESPECIALLY 'CAUSE MY PARENTS RAISED HIM FOR 10 YEARS OF HIS LIFE. WELL, A COUPLE NIGHTS AGO, I GOT A TEXT FROM MY MOM LATE AT NIGHT AND SHE SAID THAT ARLO *(Steven's dad)* HAD HUNG HIMSELF THAT NIGHT. THAT ONE REALLY GOT TO ME. I DIDN'T GET TO LIVE WITH STEVEN, BUT I LIVED WITH ARLO FOR A VERY LONG TIME. HE WAS JUST LIKE A BIG BROTHER FOR

YEARS. ACTUALLY, I CONSIDERED HIM MY BROTHER WHILE HE LIVED WITH US. THIS ONE IS REALLY KILLING ME. I'M A MESS RIGHT NOW AND HAVE BEEN PLANNING ON KICKING FOR THE PAST 2 WEEKS BUT HAVEN'T BEEN ABLE TO 'CAUSE OF EVERYTHING THAT HAS HAPPENED THE PAST COUPLE WEEKS. SO MANY PEOPLE ARE DYING, AND IT'S ALWAYS MY DAD'S SIDE, AND I'M SUPER, SUPER WORRIED ABOUT MY DAD…AND MY MOM. ALL MY DAD HAS LEFT ARE HIS TWO SISTERS. HE HAS LOST SO MANY PEOPLE AND IT BREAKS MY HEART AND I WISH I COULD DO SOMETHING FOR HIM. I PRAY TO GOD THAT MY DAD MAKES IT THROUGH ALL THIS. I WOULD LITERALLY DIE IF I LOST MY DAD RIGHT NOW. THINGS BETTER START LOOKING UP IN LIFE, I DON'T KNOW HOW MUCH MORE I CAN TAKE.

These two deaths, Arlo and Steven, were devastating for our entire family. Arlo's father (my dad's brother) also took his own life when Arlo was five years old. Three generations in suicide.

MY THOUGHTS AND GOALS FOR THE WEEK!

WELL, IT'S BEEN A VERY SHITTY LAST COUPLE WEEKS. IT FEELS LIKE EVERYONE AROUND ME IS DYING. WE 1ST LOSE STEVEN, WHICH WAS COMPLETELY SHOCKING AND HEARTBREAKING, ESPECIALLY 'CAUSE HE WAS SO DAMN YOUNG. HE HAD HIS WHOLE LIFE AHEAD OF HIM. THEN MY MOM TEXTED ME AND THE GIRLS (MY SISTERS) A COUPLE NIGHTS AGO REALLY LATE TELLING US THAT ARLO HAD HUNG HIMSELF THAT NIGHT AND HE WAS GONE. THAT ONE HIT ME VERY, VERY HARD. HE WAS JUST LIKE MY BROTHER. I HAVE SO MANY MEMORIES WITH HIM GROWING UP. IT'S JUST HEARTBREAKING. AND ON TOP OF ALL THIS, I'M TRYING MY HARDEST TO GET BOTH RYAN AND I CLEAN 'CAUSE WE *CANNOT* AFFORD IT AND I'M GETTING CLOSER AND CLOSER TO DYING EACH DAY THAT I USE. I REALLY DON'T WANT TO BE THE NEXT ONE THAT

GOES. *(She was the next one to pass).* I WANT TO RAISE MY BABY GIRL AND SEE MY GRAND BABIES AND WATCH MASON GO ON HIS MISSION AND RETURN IN A COUPLE YEARS. I WISH SO BADLY I WAS NOT AN ADDICT. IT RUINED MY LIFE AND I'M SUPER LUCKY THAT I AM STILL ALIVE AFTER ALL THAT I HAVE BEEN THROUGH. THERE IS A DAMN GOOD REASON I'M STILL HERE, I JUST NEED TO GET MOTIVATED TO FIND OUT WHAT IT IS. I WANT WHAT I WENT THROUGH TO HELP AT LEAST ONE PERSON IN NEED. HOPEFULLY MANY MORE. *(That is why this book exists, to help others and to honor her life and the battle she fought.)* WELL, I'M PRAYING EVERY DAY THAT I CAN GET BETTER AND HELP OTHERS THAT ARE IN NEED. THAT IS WHAT I WANT TO DO WITH THE REST OF MY LIFE. BUT, OF COURSE, BOND WITH MY KIDS MORE. BUT I NEED TO GET MY SHIT STRAIGHT OR I CAN NEVER HELP OTHERS IN NEED. I PRAY I CAN STAY STRONG AND DO THE THINGS I NEED TO DO TO KEEP ME AND MY 3 BEAUTIFUL KIDS HAPPY AND SAFE. GOOD LUCK, NAT!

8-29-2018: Dr. Note–143 lbs. Trying to get Suboxone through program. Relapsed on Heroin because of money. Wants Xanax, needs to get mother involved. Waiting on Suboxone card for help. Prescribed Xanax and Zofran.

Eight days later...

THURSDAY, AUGUST 30, 2018:

THINGS ARE FINALLY STARTING TO LOOK UP 4 ME! YAY! YAY! YAY! IT'S ONLY ABOUT 9:00 A.M. AND I ALREADY GOT READY, CLEANED MY HOUSE, AND WENT OVER TO THE GAS STATION BY MY HOUSE AND ASKED FOR AN INTERVIEW, AND HE HIRED ME ON THE SPOT! I'M SO SUPER EXCITED! I NEED THIS JOB SO MUCH! AND I CAN WALK THERE EVERY

DAY AND VISIT SYDKA LOTS AND MAKE SURE SHE IS OKAY. IT'S ABSOLUTELY PERFECT! I ACTUALLY START TODAY AT 1-4:30, PROBABLY JUST GETTING ME SET UP AND GET MY SCHEDULE. AND...I WENT TO THE DOCTOR YESTERDAY AND GOT ALL MY SCRIPTS AND I AM TRANSITIONING TONIGHT AFTER WORK AND I KNOW I CAN DO IT! I WANT MY LIFE BACK AND I AM GOING TO GET IT!!

Same day...

MY GOALS AND THOUGHTS!

IT'S SERIOUSLY 3:45 A.M. AND I'M WIDE AWAKE 'CAUSE I HAVE SO MUCH GOING ON IN MY HEAD AND I CAN'T GET IT UNDER CONTROL! I'M EXTREMELY DEPRESSED AND IN A HOLE THAT I SEEM TO KEEP GETTING IN DEEPER AND DEEPER AND I HAVE *EVERY* OPPORTUNITY RIGHT NOW TO COMPLETELY CHANGE MY LIFE FOR THE GOOD. I JUST HAVE TO DO IT! IT REALLY IS MUCH HARDER THAN PEOPLE THAT DON'T KNOW ABOUT ADDICTION, THAN YOU COULD IMAGINE. I WOULD RATHER DIE SOMETIMES...ACTUALLY, EVERY TIME WHEN I'M KICKING AND DETOXING. I JUST WANT MY KIDS TO BE PROUD OF ME ONE DAY AND I CAN BE A GOOD INFLUENCE, A ROLE MODEL FOR THEM TO LOOK UP TO. ESPECIALLY THE GIRLS! WELL, JALA IS IN JR. HIGH AS OF A COUPLE DAYS AGO AND SHE LOVES IT, I KNEW SHE WOULD. WELL, I'M NOT WASTING ANYMORE PRECIOUS TIME THAT WE ALL DO HAVE LEFT WITHOUT RAISING JALA. I STILL HAVE A CHANCE TO FINISH RAISING HER WITH JAY. YAY! SO, I WENT TO MY DOCTOR TODAY, GOT ALL MY MEDS, AND I AM GOING TO TRANSITION THE NEXT COUPLE DAYS ONTO SUBS. THE DOCTOR CHOSE ME OUT OF 2 PATIENTS A YEAR THAT HE WOULD GET MY SUBOXONE PAID FOR A FULL YEAR! I WAS DEFINITELY BLESSED IN MORE WAYS THAN ONE.

I AM GOING TO DO THIS, I WANT IT MORE THAN ANYTHING I HAVE *EVER* WANTED IN MY LIFE. BUT IT IS DEFINITELY

HARDER THAN HELL! I PRAY TO GOD THAT I WILL HAVE THE COURAGE AND STRENGTH TO DO THIS AND FINALLY GET MY LIFE BACK WITH MY BEAUTIFUL AND ABSOLUTELY AMAZING CHILDREN...SOMETIMES, HAHAHA!

A couple of days later...

SUNDAY, SEPTEMBER 2, 2018:

MY LOVELY WEEKEND!
WELL, I AM IN THE PROCESS OF GETTING CLEAN AS WE SPEAK. I HAVE ONLY HAD ABOUT 3 SHOTS IN THE PAST 3 1/2 DAYS. I CAN TAKE MY 1ST SUBOXONE TOMORROW AT NOON. I JUST REALLY HOPE I CAN HOLD OUT TILL THEN. RYAN IS A COMPLETE MESS! HE *CANNOT* HANDLE WITHDRAWALS AT ALL! I THOUGHT I WAS BAD, HE IS A FREAKING BABY. NOT TO BE RUDE, BUT IT'S *BAD!* JAY AND JALA WANTED ME TO SLEEP OVER AT THEIR HOUSE TONIGHT, BUT I AM NOT OKAY ENOUGH TO DO THAT! I WANT TO BE CLEAN MORE THAN ANYTHING IN THIS WORLD! I KNOW I CAN DO IT! I HAVE DONE IT MANY TIMES BEFORE, SO I CAN DEFINITELY DO IT AGAIN. I JUST HAVE TO KEEP THINKING POSITIVE. I CAN DO THIS, I CAN DO THIS, I CAN DO THIS! OH, AND ANOTHER THING I NEED TO DO, I NEED TO GET RID OF ALL THE PEOPLE I HAVE BEEN SURROUNDING MYSELF WITH LATELY. THEY ARE NOT GOOD PEOPLE AT ALL AND DON'T GIVE TWO SHITS ABOUT ME AT ALL! ONE GOOD THING HAPPENED THIS WEEKEND, THOUGH...I FINALLY GOT A JOB! YAY! YAY! I WORK AT THE GAS STATION RIGHT BY MY APARTMENT. I CAN WALK THERE EVERY SHIFT. HOW STINKIN' SWEET IS THAT? I ALREADY WORKED ABOUT 4 HOURS A COUPLE DAYS AGO AND THEN I START AGAIN IN A COUPLE DAYS. I GET PAID A LOT MORE THAN JEAN EVER PAID ME AND I'M SUPER EXCITED. I'M TURNING MY LIFE AROUND FOR GOOD THIS TIME AND NEVER

GOING BACK! *NEVER!!* I WANT MY KIDS IN MY LIFE EVERY DAY AND I DON'T WANT TO TELL THEM EVEN ONE MORE TIME THAT I AM SICK! I AM GOING TO DO THIS, I KNOW I CAN! GOOD LUCK, ME, YOU GOT THIS!!

I am amazed by her endless desire to get clean and to be a mother to her children. That never wavered, even though at this point, her body and organs were starting to show signs of shutting down. I think it was the love of her children that gave her this never-ending drive to get clean. She struggled to understand, though, that she couldn't do it on her own and it really was out of her control.

MONDAY, SEPTEMBER 3, 2018:

MY DAY!
WELL, WE CAN DEFINITELY SAY THAT I AM A *FREAKING IDIOT!* I WENT AT LEAST 12 OR 13 HOURS WITHOUT USING AT ALL, THEN I DID THE LAST LITTLE PIECE THAT WE HAD BECAUSE, WELL, THERE WAS NO REASON, I JUST WANTED TO FEEL BETTER. RYAN DID IT, THOUGH. I JUST GAVE HIM A SUB ABOUT AN HOUR AGO AND HE HAD GONE A LITTLE OVER 22 1/2 HOURS. HE DID IT! WE HAVE A FUNERAL TOMORROW NIGHT, SO I USED THAT AS MY EXCUSE TO USE. I WAS SO CLOSE! I AM SO SUPER ANGRY AT MYSELF RIGHT NOW! I WANT TO BE CLEAN MORE THAN ANYTHING IN THIS WORLD! I WANT TO RAISE JALA THE WAY SHE DESERVES TO BE RAISED, AND I WANT MY FREAKING LIFE BACK! BUT, THAT MEANS NO MORE MARY, NO MORE DAVID, NO MORE JENNIFER, AND MANY, MANY MORE! IT MAKES ME REALLY SAD 'CAUSE MARY AND I HAVE GOTTEN SUPER CLOSE AGAIN, EVEN CLOSER THAN WE USED TO BE, BUT SHE IS THE #1 PERSON I WOULD HAVE TO LET GO OF COMPLETELY. NO PHONE CALLS, TEXTS, NOTHING, I WILL HAVE TO GET HER 100% OUT OF MY LIFE, FOR GOOD THIS TIME. IT MAKES ME REALLY SAD 'CAUSE I

ALWAYS HAVE CONSIDERED BOTH MARY AND DAVID PART OF MY FAMILY. THROUGH GOOD TIMES AND BAD, I LOVE THEM BOTH. BUT, THEY ARE TOTALLY TOXIC TO ME AND MY LIFE. THAT WILL BE REALLY HARD LETTING THEM GO AGAIN! BUT, IT IS A MUST FOR SURE IF I WANT TO STAY CLEAN. I HAVE A NEW FRIEND NAMED TERRY AND HE IS 33 YEARS OLD AND ABSOLUTELY DARLING. WE ACTUALLY HAVE BEEN HANGING OUT A LOT LATELY THE PAST 4 DAYS WE HAVE BEEN TOGETHER. IT HAS BEEN FUN! BUT HE IS AN ADDICT TOO. HE HAS THE VIVITROL SHOT, THOUGH, SO HE DOESN'T USE BLACK AT ALL. I THINK I WILL KEEP HIM IN MY LIFE. WE HAVE FUN TOGETHER!

A week later…

MONDAY, SEPTEMBER 10, 2018:

This entry was written while Jala was asleep in bed next to Nat. There were so many situations that Jala was around that were dangerous and toxic. I don't know if this entry is a "code" letter to Mary or if it is even to Mary at all or if she was so out of it she was mixing things up. I've thought about this entry quite often and have drawn some conclusions myself, but of course, I have no proof. We will never know what it is really all about.

WHAT'S BEEN GOING ON WITH NAT LATELY!

WELL, IT HAS DEFINITELY NOT BEEN GOING THE WAY I HAVE PLANNED AND DESPERATELY WANTED LATELY TO BE BETTER, BUT IT'S JUST NOT HAPPENING! I HAVE ALL THESE GOALS EACH WEEK, AND I NEVER HAVE ENOUGH TIME TO DO THEM. I FEEL MY LIFE IS SPINNING OUT OF CONTROL. I AM DEFINITELY TRYING EVERY DAY, THOUGH, BUT IT LOOKS LIKE I NEED TO TRY A BIT HARDER! I HAD A DOCTOR'S APPOINTMENT TODAY AND I FUCKING CAN'T GO 'CAUSE I'M DIRTY AND DON'T HAVE THE MONEY. I HOPE HE STILL KEEPS ME

AS A PATIENT 'CAUSE I HAVE HAD SO MANY MONEY PROBLEMS LATELY AND I KEEP SWITCHING MY APPOINTMENTS. HE LOVES ME, THOUGH. HE HAS ME RUNNING HIS STRIP CLUB AND A COUPLE OTHER BUSINESSES FOR HIM 'CAUSE I AM THE ONLY ONE HE TRUSTS! THAT MAKES ME FEEL REALLY GOOD. I'M DYING, THOUGH, MARY...I GAINED 20 POUNDS IN ABOUT 2 1/2 WEEKS. IT'S SO NOTICEABLE, TOO, I'M ABSOLUTELY ECSTATIC BECAUSE I FOLLOW ALL THE RULES AND EXERCISE A LOT NOW. MAKES ME FEEL SO, SO, SO, SO MUCH BETTER. THIS HAS BEEN GREAT WORKING HERE SO FAR. IT'S PRETTY PRICEY, BUT WE GOT IN ON OUR OWN AND I ABSOLUTELY LOVE THEM! SO DO ALL MY KIDS. HONEY, I HOPE YOU DON'T TAKE THEM TO ANOTHER FAMILY IF IT DOESN'T WORK, THAT WOULD TRAUMATIZE THEM. SO, I GOT A JOB, I WORK RIGHT ACROSS THE STREET (LITERALLY) FROM MY APARTMENTS. COOL, HUH? I DON'T GET PAID A LOT AT ALL, BUT I AM JUST GRATEFUL TO CONTRIBUTE TO THIS FAMILY FINANCIALLY, ALSO, OH NEVER MIND, I FORGOT! I DO GET PAID $2 AN HOUR MORE THAN ANYONE AT MY WORK. I'M SUPPOSED TO KEEP THAT ON THE DOWNLOW. JALA IS HERE FAST ASLEEP IN MY BED, SO I BETTER GO GET SOME MORE REST. IT'S TIRING CHASING BAD PEOPLE, BUT ALSO VERY FUN AND SO EXTREMELY FUN TO WATCH. SO MUCH STUPID DRAMA HA HA HA.

A week later...

<u>MONDAY, SEPTEMBER 17, 2018</u>:

MY FEELINGS & THOUGHTS!
WELL, I HAVEN'T BEEN DOING GOOD AT ALL LATELY. IT'S ABOUT 4:30 IN THE MORNING AND I JUST GOT HOME FROM MARY AND DAVID'S WAITING FOR DOPE! I HATE THIS LIFE MORE THAN I COULD EVER EXPRESS. IT'S JUST SO *DAMN HARD* TO GET OUT OF IT. I HAVEN'T BEEN AROUND MY KIDS LIKE I USUALLY AM AND I'M GOING DOWNHILL *FAST!* BUT,

I DO HAVE ONE GOOD THING THAT HAPPENED IN THE MIDDLE OF MY MESSY LIFE! I GOT A JOB! YAY! I CAN LITERALLY WALK ACROSS THE STREET TO GET TO WORK. I WORK AT THE "STOP" GAS STATION RIGHT ACROSS FROM MY APARTMENT. THEY DON'T PAY TOO BAD AT ALL, A LOT BETTER THAN JEAN EVER PAID ME, AND THEY ARE VERY FLEXIBLE, SO I WORKED TODAY ALL DAY BY MYSELF AND I HAVE ONLY BEEN THERE A COUPLE WEEKS. I GUESS THEY REALLY TRUST ME, BUT I TOOK TOMORROW, MONDAY, TUESDAY, AND WEDNESDAY OFF 'CAUSE I'M PLANNING ON LAYING IN BED AND KICKING, WHICH MEANS I'M GETTING OFF THE DRUGS AND I'M GOING TO BE WITHDRAWING. I WANT THIS SO SUPER BAD! I STILL CAN'T BELIEVE I GOT CAUGHT UP ALL IN IT AGAIN. IT HAPPENED SO FAST, I DON'T REALLY REMEMBER WHEN IT ALL STARTED AGAIN. ALL I KNOW IS I THOUGHT I COULD DO IT ONE TIME AND NEVER DO IT AGAIN. I WAS SO SUPER WRONG. I PRAY I GET THROUGH THESE NEXT COUPLE DAYS OKAY AND I WON'T GIVE UP. I PRAY THAT I STAY STRONG AND CAN OVERCOME THE TEMPTATION. MY LIFE IS WORTH IT! MY KIDS NEED THE MOTHER THAT I KNOW I CAN BE TO THEM. THOSE KIDS ARE MY EVERYTHING AND I HAVE PUSHED THEM ASIDE FOR WAY TOO LONG NOW, JUST BECAUSE OF THIS STUPID, DEADLY, IMPOSSIBLE DISEASE THAT I WILL HAVE THE REST OF MY LIFE. ONE THING I DO KNOW, I'M SUPPOSED TO BE HERE, SO I NEED TO STRAIGHTEN MY ASS UP AND BECOME "NATALIE ALLEN" AGAIN.

<u>9-28-2018:</u> <u>Dr. Note</u>–137 lbs. Rough time, struggling on Heroin again. Wants Xanax. Has job, happy about it. Wants to get back on track. Prescribed Ambien, Xanax, and Zofran.

Almost two weeks later...

SATURDAY, SEPTEMBER 29, 2018:

WELL, IT'S ABOUT 3:10 P.M. AND I AM AT WORK AT THE "STOP" (GAS STATION ACROSS FROM MY APARTMENTS). I REALLY DO LIKE THIS JOB AND I DON'T DREAD IT LIKE I USUALLY DO ALL MY OTHER JOBS AND A BIG REASON FOR THAT IS BECAUSE OF THE PEOPLE I WORK FOR. THEY ARE REALLY GREAT GUYS. BUT TODAY AND YESTERDAY AND THIS ENTIRE WEEK HAS BEEN SO SHITTY FOR ME. I WORKED 11 HOURS YESTERDAY WHEN I WAS ONLY SUPPOSED TO WORK 5 HOURS. YA, THAT'S QUITE A BIT LONGER. WELL, TODAY I AM WORKING ANOTHER 11 HOURS BECAUSE STUPID FUCKING PEOPLE KEEP "NO SHOWING." I'M GOING TO COMMIT SUICIDE TODAY! HA HA HA! I COULD BE DOING A LOT MORE IMPORTANT THINGS, LIKE SPENDING SOME TIME WITH MY SON BEFORE HE LEAVES FOR 2 YEARS IN ABOUT 4 WEEKS! BUT NOPE, I'M STUCK AT FUCKING WORK! KILL ME NOW! I HAVE A MASSIVE HEADACHE FROM HELL, AND I AM IN THE WORST MOOD *EVER!* I JUST MIGHT GO OFF ON ANYBODY SOMETIME SOON! I HATE MY LIFE RIGHT NOW! I'M TRYING TO MAKE IT BETTER AND BE A BETTER PERSON, BUT I'M JUST GOING STRAIGHT DOWNHILL! I DON'T KNOW WHY, I HAVE THE BIGGEST HEART AND WOULD DO ANYTHING FOR ANYBODY IN NEED. I KNOW I MAKE LOTS OF MISTAKES IN MY LIFE, TOO, TOO MANY, BUT IT SHOULDN'T REFLECT ON THE WAY PEOPLE LOOK AT ME. I KNOW I AM A VERY GOOD PERSON, I JUST MAKE STUPID MISTAKES AND OBVIOUSLY HAVE NOT LEARNED FROM THEM AT ALL. OH, AND FYI...MARY IS LIVING WITH ME RIGHT NOW AND I DON'T KNOW WHAT THE HELL TO DO ANYMORE ABOUT ANYTHING!

Nat and I had had a telephone conversation earlier that day because Em had just found out that her second child, Justin, had Type I Diabetes and Celiac Disease. (Her oldest child, Jasa had been diagnosed with the same years earlier.) Nat was very concerned for Em and wanted to know if she should send Em the following text:

TEXT FROM NAT TO ME: Em I can't stop thinking about you and it kills me to think you are doing this all alone. I just want you to know, I'm always here for you, no matter what. That's what sisters are for. If you need anything at all Em, plz don't hesitate to call me, I would drop everything in a heartbeat and come help you. Love you Em

That's what I just sent Em cause I really mean it, even if she's mad at me. I would help her at anytime.

NAT TO ME: My heart hurts for her. I can't imagine doing all that she does on her own. It's Amazing. Thanks for always being there for me Shall, I don't tell you enough. Thank you for always loving me and never giving up on me. I love you!!

Four days later...

TUESDAY, OCTOBER 2, 2018:

I AM A MESS!

IT'S ABOUT MIDNIGHT ON A TUESDAY NIGHT, MARY IS NEXT TO ME. SHE HAS BEEN STAYING WITH ME THE PAST COUPLE WEEKS 'CAUSE SHE HAS A WARRANT AND SHE IS SCARED TO BE AT HOME (AT CATHERINE'S HOUSE). I DON'T BLAME HER AT ALL, BUT I AM GOING CRAZY. WHEN WE ARE TOGETHER FOR TOO LONG, IT BECOMES REALLY BAD. I ALREADY WENT OFF ON HER THE OTHER NIGHT 'CAUSE SHE IS A MESSY PERSON AND LEAVES SHIT EVERYWHERE IN EVERY ROOM IN THE HOUSE. I

AM PICKING UP AFTER HER ALL THE TIME. I FEEL BAD FOR HER, THOUGH, SHE IS MY BEST FRIEND, MY FAMILY, BUT I ALWAYS GET PUT INTO HORRIBLE SITUATIONS WHEN I AM AROUND DAVID AND MARY. I CAN'T KICK HER OUT, THOUGH, SHE IS FAMILY AND I DON'T WANT ANYTHING TO HAPPEN TO HER. I RARELY SEE MY KIDS ANYMORE 'CAUSE I'M EITHER WORKING OR I'M SICK. I WANT TO BE THERE FOR THEM SO BAD. WHY CAN'T I CHANGE MY LIFE AND MAKE IT HAPPEN, THAT'S ALL I WANT TO DO! I WAS PLANNING ON KICKING THESE LAST COUPLE DAYS. I EVEN TOOK WORK OFF FOR IT, BUT IT'S HARD CAUSE MARY IS HERE, AND I KNOW SHE HAS HEROIN. I REALLY NEED TO FIGURE SOMETHING OUT, AND FAST. I NEED MY LIFE BACK, ESPECIALLY 'CAUSE MY BABY BOY IS LEAVING IN LESS THAN 4 WEEKS. OCTOBER 31ST, ON HALLOWEEN DAY. MY BABY BOY IS GOING TO ORLANDO, FLORIDA, ON A MISSION FOR 2 DAMN YEARS! I AM GOING TO MISS HIM *SO MUCH!*

Two days later…

THURSDAY, OCTOBER 4, 2018:

IT'S ABOUT 4:30 AND I HAVE THE DAY OFF TODAY! MARY IS LIVING WITH US RIGHT NOW AND SHE PRETTY MUCH TOOK OVER RYAN'S PART OF OUR ROOM. I MEAN, SHE BROUGHT ABSOLUTELY EVERYTHING OF HERS OVER HERE TO MY TINY APARTMENT AND THE GIRL IS A COMPLETE *HOARDER!* SHE SLEEPS NEXT TO ME IN BED WHERE RYAN IS SUPPOSED TO SLEEP, AND POOR RYAN IS SLEEPING ON THE COUCH EVERY NIGHT. IT'S SAD, BUT AT THE SAME TIME, HE KIND OF DESERVES IT. I DON'T KNOW THE GUY ANYMORE. HE LIES TO ME ALL THE TIME AND I ASK HIM WHY HE LIES ALL THE TIME AND HE SAYS, "I DON'T KNOW," WHAT THE HELL IS THAT ALL ABOUT? I'M SO DEPRESSED AND BACK TO THE SAME HORRIBLE LIFE THAT I USED TO LIVE. MARY HAS A

WARRANT SO SHE CAN'T BE AT HOME, AND SHE REALLY JUST NEEDS TO GO TO COURT AND GET IT TAKEN CARE OF! I WANT TO KICK MORE THAN ANYTHING IN THIS WORLD AND GET MY LIFE BACK, ESPECIALLY BEFORE MASON LEAVES, BUT I CAN'T WITH HER HERE 'CAUSE SHE ALWAYS HAS STUFF AND IS ALWAYS USING. HOW DO I QUIT WHEN I HAVE A DEALER LIVING WITH ME AND SLEEPING RIGHT NEXT TO ME! I REALLY THINK I'M GOING TO HAVE A NERVOUS BREAKDOWN ANY STINKIN' DAY NOW! I HATE MY LIFE RIGHT NOW AND ABSOLUTELY EVERYTHING ABOUT IT!!!

Our family had no idea Mary was living with her during this time or that she even had contact with her and the others. We found out after she passed when we read these journals.

MY THOUGHTS FOR TODAY!

I AM IN A LIVING HELL RIGHT NOW AND DON'T KNOW WHAT TO DO ABOUT IT! I AM MISERABLE, AND I DON'T KNOW HOW TO CHANGE IT! WELL, I DO, BUT IT'S SO HARD FOR ME TO DO. I AM VERY PROUD OF MYSELF FOR GETTING A JOB, THOUGH! IT'S ACTUALLY AN OKAY JOB! I DON'T DREAD GOING INTO WORK LIKE I DID UP AT THE U AND MY OTHER JOBS. THEY ARE VERY LAX THERE AND I FEEL VERY COMFORTABLE WORKING THERE. IT'S SO NICE TOO THAT I JUST WALK ACROSS THE STREET WHEN I GO TO WORK. HOW COOL IS THAT? I JUST HOPE I CAN TURN MY LIFE AROUND VERY SOON 'CAUSE I KNOW I CAN! I'M STRONGER THAN I GIVE MYSELF CREDIT FOR. I NEED TO FOCUS ON THE THINGS THAT MATTER TO ME THE MOST, AND ACTUALLY MAKE IT HAPPEN. I'M ALMOST 40 YEARS OLD, IT'S ABOUT TIME TO GROW THE FUCK UP! I JUST FEEL SO ALONE. I DON'T TRUST RYAN OR ANYONE RIGHT NOW, I HONESTLY TRUST NOBODY IN MY LIFE RIGHT NOW, AND THAT'S REALLY HARD TO LIVE WITHOUT ANYBODY TO VENT TO AND TALK TO! I'M SCARED ABOUT WHAT'S GOING TO

HAPPEN WITH MARY, 'CAUSE I KNOW I AM GOING TO FREAK THE FUCK OUT ON HER ANY DAY NOW!

Eleven days later...

MONDAY, OCTOBER 15, 2018:

MY SHITTY DAY!
IT'S ABOUT 10:00 P.M. AND I HAVE BEEN IN THE CAR CHASING DOPE ALL DAY LONG WITH MARY AND DAVID UNTIL ABOUT A HALF HOUR AGO. WE STARTED AT 8:00 A.M. I AM A COMPLETE MESS RIGHT NOW! I HAVE HAD IT WITH THE BOTH OF THEM, AND THEY ARE SUPPOSED TO BE MY BEST FRIENDS, BUT ALL THEY EVER DO IS BRING ME DOWN. WHY CAN'T I STAY AWAY FROM THEM? MARY HAS BEEN LIVING AT OUR HOUSE FOR THE PAST 3 1/2 WEEKS AND SHE IS STARTING TO FINALLY MOVE OUT! SHE HAS A WARRANT THAT SHE HASN'T TAKEN CARE OF SO SHE DIDN'T WANT TO BE AT HOME 'CAUSE SHE THOUGHT THEY WOULD COME GET HER.

TRUST IN THE LORD WITH ALL OF YOUR HEART AND HAVE FAITH THAT THINGS WILL GET BETTER. I JUST REALLY NEED TO BELIEVE IN MYSELF MORE THAN I DO. I KNOW I AM A STRONG PERSON, I JUST FORGET A LOT! I NEED TO REMIND MYSELF EVERY DAY THAT I AM A STRONG, BEAUTIFUL, AND TRUSTWORTHY PERSON AND I WILL BE ABLE TO GET OUT OF THIS HORRIBLE HOLE THAT I'M IN!

Four days later...

FRIDAY, OCTOBER 19, 2018:

MY DAY!
WELL, MY DAY COMPLETELY SUCKED!! MORE THAN NORMAL, ACTUALLY. I HAVE BEEN WAITING FOR MY PAYCHECK SINCE 7:00 A.M. THIS MORNING 'CAUSE I OWE SO MANY DAMN

PEOPLE AND WE HAVE NO MONEY TILL RYAN GETS PAID NEXT WEDNESDAY. WELL, THEY COULDN'T FIND MY CHECK ALL DAY, FINALLY FOUND IT AT 6:00 P.M., I OPEN IT UP AND ALMOST BURST INTO TEARS (WOULD HAVE IF I WASN'T AT WORK), MY CHECK WAS $110!!! I WAS SO FUCKING SHOCKED. I KNEW IT WASN'T GONNA BE GREAT 'CAUSE I TOOK A LOT OF WORK OFF SO THAT I COULD KICK, WHICH I DIDN'T DO, AND I GET A LOT GARNISHED 'CAUSE OF BACK CHILD SUPPORT! I'M LITERALLY GETTING THREATENED DAILY BY LARRY 'CAUSE I OWE HIM $165. HE WON'T LEAVE ME ALONE! I'M SO FUCKING STRESSED! I WANT TO GET CLEAN MORE THAN ANYTHING BUT CAN'T SEEM TO DO IT. I WANT THE STRENGTH I NEED TO JUST DO IT! LOST TOUCH WITH ALL MY KIDS AGAIN, THAT'S KILLING ME, SO I WANT TO USE MORE. AND TO MAKE MATTERS WORSE, A LOT WORSE, RYAN'S CAR WON'T START ANYMORE AND MINE IS SITTING AT MY MOM'S TILL I GET MY OWN INSURANCE AND REGISTER IT. *(This was the second car my parents had bought her since she lived with Paul. They were paying her insurance until they found out she was still using. Then they took the car and refused to let her drive it until she paid her own insurance. It sat there for a while, but she eventually did get insurance and got it back.)* WE HAVE ABSOLUTELY NO CAR AT THE MOMENT! GOT OVER TO MARY AND DAVID'S TONIGHT FOR A WHILE AND IT WAS A COMPLETE DISASTER. JENNIFER LOST HER DOPE, SO THEY ALL THINK SOMEONE STOLE IT, LIKE ALWAYS (AND THEY ALWAYS JUST MISPLACE IT), BUT IT GOT OUT OF CONTROL OVER THERE. I HAD JENNIFER BRING ME HOME, BUT I'M SHAKEN UP 'CAUSE THEY WERE TRIPPING ABOUT COPS AGAIN, SO IT'S 3:30 IN THE MORNING AND I CAN'T FUCKING SLEEP! KILL ME NOW!

<u>SATURDAY, OCTOBER 20, 2018</u>:

I HONESTLY DON'T THINK I HAVE HAD A SHITTIER DAY AT WORK! I WANT TO KILL MYSELF OR SOMEONE TONIGHT!

IT'S ABOUT 9:00 P.M. AND I STILL HAVE 2 MORE FUCKING HOURS HERE! I CALLED MARY TO SEE IF SHE WOULD COME IN AN HOUR EARLY TO HELP ME 'CAUSE SHE COMES IN AT 11 ANYWAYS, AND WITH ABSOLUTELY ZERO HESITATION, SHE SAID *NO!* *(We had no idea that Mary worked at the gas station with her until we read this journal.)* AM I SURPRISED, NOT AT ALL! BUT I AM *NEVER* DOING A FUCKING THING FOR HER AGAIN. SHE IS NOBODY TO ME, ONCE AGAIN. AND I'M NOT GIVING THAT *EVIL* WOMAN ANY MORE CHANCES. I HAVE HAD MORE THAN ENOUGH! MORE THAN ANYONE SHOULD *EVER* HAVE TO DEAL WITH FROM A SUPPOSED "BFF"!! I'M DONE! 100% DONE!! I KNOW I HAVE SAID THIS BEFORE, BUT AFTER SHE SAID SOMETHING ABOUT JALA, THAT WAS THE *ABSOLUTE* FINAL STRAW! WHO DOES SHE THINK SHE IS??? SHE GIVES HER SON DOPE!!! I KNOW I AM...*(This is how she ended the entry.)*

SUNDAY, OCTOBER 21, 2018:

MY LAST NIGHT AND THIS MORNING!

IT'S ABOUT 1:45 P.M. SUNDAY AND I AM AT WORK RIGHT NOW. GOT HOME FROM WORK LAST NIGHT AT 11:45 P.M. AND HAD A HORRIBLE DAY, BUT TODAY HAS BEEN 100% COMPLETELY DIFFERENT, WHICH IS GOOD! WHEN I CAME INTO WORK TODAY, I WAS DREADING IT BECAUSE OF HOW BAD IT WAS LAST NIGHT. WELL, TODAY IS A BLESSING FOR ME, I WAS ABOUT TO HAVE A NERVOUS BREAKDOWN BUT THANK GOD FOR SWEET, DUMB SEAN (THAT WAS MEAN, I ACTUALLY DO LIKE THE GUY, HE IS JUST A LITTLE KOOKY), HE TOOK ME ASIDE AND TOLD ME JOE WAS LEAVING IN A LITTLE OVER A MONTH AND SEAN IS GOING TO TAKE HIS PLACE AS GENERAL MANAGER, AND HE ASKED ME TO TAKE HIS PLACE AS MANAGER, WITH A $3 RAISE! I ABSOLUTELY SAID YES! THAT WAS A BIG ANSWER TO A LOT OF MY PROBLEMS. BUT IT WON'T HAPPEN FOR AT LEAST A MONTH AND A HALF. I BETTER GET MYSELF RIGHT, AND *FAST!* I AM NOT GOING TO FUCK THIS OPPORTUNITY UP

LIKE I DO EVERYTHING ELSE! I DESERVE THIS! I KNOW I HAVE MESSED UP A LOT LATELY, ACTUALLY FOR WAY TOO LONG NOW, BUT I DO KNOW I AM A GOOD PERSON WITH A VERY BIG HEART! I NEED TO ACCEPT MYSELF AS AN ADDICT, 'CAUSE I NEVER HAVE. THAT DOESN'T MEAN TO USE, IT JUST MEANS I NEED TO FINALLY BE OKAY WITH WHO I AM! I HONESTLY DON'T THINK I EVER HAVE BEEN, WELL AT LEAST THAT I CAN REMEMBER. IT'S TIME TO LIKE MYSELF AND DROP ALL THAT SHAME I HAVE BEEN CARRYING AROUND FOR SO LONG. AND I NEED TO *NOT* CARE AT ALL WHAT ANYONE ELSE THINKS ABOUT ME. I JUST NEED TO TRY MY HARDEST EACH DAY, AND I KNOW EVERYTHING WILL FALL INTO PLACE. IT HAS TO, 'CAUSE IT DEFINITELY COULDN'T GET ANY WORSE.

WEDNESDAY, OCTOBER 31, 2019:

Mas left on his mission to the Missionary Training Center today for a few weeks before he went to Florida for two years. He said he did not think his mom was going to be alive when he returned.

A month later…

TUESDAY, NOVEMBER 20, 2018:

IT'S ABOUT 10:30 P.M. AND I'M SITTING IN BED WIDE AWAKE WITH RYAN, SYDKA, AND DIAMOND *(Mary's dog).* APPARENTLY, WE JUST FOUND OUT TODAY THAT MARY AND DAVID ARE BOTH GOING TO PRISON. MARY HAS BEEN IN A COUPLE WEEKS IN KILO AT DAVIS COUNTY AND SHE FOUND OUT TODAY THAT SHE WILL BE LOCKED UP FOR A WHILE. WELL, I FEEL SO BAD FOR HER LITTLE DOG DIAMOND. SHE IS SO SWEET, AND SHE WAS OVER AT DAVID'S HOUSE WITH JENNIFER WATCHING 5 DOGS. SHE DEFINITELY GETS NEGLECTED. SO, I BROUGHT HER HOME WITH ME TODAY, SHE HAS BEEN GREAT. MASON GOT TO FLORIDA YESTERDAY MORNING, SAFE AND SOUND. I

MISS HIM SO MUCH ALREADY, I DON'T KNOW HOW I AM GOING TO BE OKAY WITHOUT MY SON FOR 2 STINKIN' YEARS! IT'S THANKSGIVING IN A COUPLE DAYS, AND THAT'S GOING TO BE HARD WITH MASON GONE. THE HOLIDAYS ARE DEFINITELY GOING TO SUCK THIS YEAR. I AM SO CONFUSED ABOUT RYAN LATELY. I NEED TO LEAVE HIM, BUT I AM TERRIFIED OF BEING ALONE. I CAN'T SUPPORT MYSELF AT ALL RIGHT NOW. HE HAS BEEN LYING TO ME A LOT LATELY AND HE IS NOT AFFECTIONATE AT ALL! I FEEL SO ALONE ALL THE DAMN TIME. I DON'T WANT TO DATE, BUT IT LOOKS LIKE I'M GOING TO HAVE TO REAL SOON IF I WANT A LIFE AT ALL. I AM SO SUPER DEPRESSED LATELY AND I CAN'T SEEM TO SHAKE IT AT ALL.

WEDNESDAY, NOVEMBER 21, 2018:

IT'S ALMOST MIDNIGHT AND SOON TO BE THANKSGIVING! I'M NOT REALLY LOOKING FORWARD TO THE HOLIDAYS THIS YEAR BECAUSE MY BOY IS GONE. I'M SO SUPER HAPPY THAT MAS DECIDED TO GO ON A MISSION, BUT IT'S JUST SO *DAMN LONG!!* EVERY EMAIL THAT HE HAS SENT SINCE HE HAS BEEN GONE IS NOTHING BUT HAPPY TIMES FOR HIM. SO FAR, HE IS LOVING IT! WHICH IS A HUGE RELIEF FOR ME, 'CAUSE I DON'T WANT HIM TO GET HOMESICK AT ALL. HE IS GOING TO DO GREAT. THAT KID IS ABSOLUTELY AMAZING AND EVERY-ONE THAT KNOWS HIM, ADORES HIM. I LOVE THAT BOY WITH ALL MY HEART AND SOUL. ADI AND DAKOTA GET MARRIED IN LESS THAN 2 WEEKS! I'M SUPER EXCITED FOR THEM. I LOVE DAKOTA AND I BELIEVE THEY WILL MAKE EACH OTHER VERY HAPPY. I WANT GRAND BABIES *SO SUPER BAD!* WELL, IT'S ABOUT 12:15 NOW AND I HAVEN'T SLEPT GOOD AT ALL THIS WHOLE ENTIRE WEEK. RYAN AND I ARE LIVING LIKE ROOMMATES AND I DON'T THINK WE WILL GET ANY BETTER THAN THIS. OH WELL, I AM JUST FOCUSING ON MY KIDS AND WORK RIGHT NOW AND SO SCARED BUT GOING TO DETOX

HERE IN THE NEXT COUPLE WEEKS. JUST WISH MYSELF LOTS AND LOTS OF LUCK!

FRIDAY, NOVEMBER 23, 2018:

IT'S MIDNIGHT RIGHT NOW, WELL, A LITTLE AFTER, AND I AM SITTING IN MY CAR SMOKING AT THE MOMENT 'CAUSE IT'S POURING RAIN RIGHT NOW. IT SOUNDS SO COOL HITTING THE TOP OF MY CAR. IT FEELS LIKE I'M IN A TENT WITH THE RAIN POURING DOWN. THAT'S ONE OF MY FAVORITE THINGS TO DO, SLEEPING IN A TENT, CAMPING WHILE IT'S POURING RAIN. I HAD THE WORST THANKSGIVING YESTERDAY. I WAS HEADING DOWN TO MY MOM'S FOR THANKSGIVING DINNER AND I GOT CALLED INTO WORK 'CAUSE SOME STUPID BITCH DECIDED NOT TO SHOW UP FOR HER SHIFT. SO, I TURNED AROUND AND HEADED TO WORK. I WAS THERE FROM NOON UNTIL 11:15 LAST NIGHT. IT WAS AWFUL. IT WOULD HAVE NOT BEEN A GOOD DAY ANYWAYS 'CAUSE JALA WENT TO JAY'S MOM'S FOR THE DAY AND MASON IS GONE. IT JUST ISN'T THE SAME AT ALL THIS YEAR. I AM NOT EVEN EXCITED WHATSOEVER 'CAUSE FOR THE HOLIDAYS MASON IS NOT HERE WITH US. IT'S GOING TO BE HARD FOR ALL OF US THIS YEAR. ADI AND DAKOTA'S WEDDING DEFINITELY SNEAKED UP ON US, THOUGH, IT'S LESS THAN 2 WEEKS AWAY. I'M SUPER EXCITED FOR THEIR WEDDING. ADI PLANNED HER ENTIRE WEDDING ON HER OWN AND PAID FOR PRETTY MUCH ALL OF THAT BY HERSELF. SHE HAS DONE SUCH A GOOD JOB, HER WEDDING IS GOING TO BE ABSOLUTELY BEAUTIFUL. SHE IS SO GOOD AT PLANNING THINGS AND DECORATING. IT'S DEFINITELY GOING TO BE A DAY TO REMEMBER. I AM SO PROUD OF MY DAUGHTER AND THE WOMAN THAT SHE HAS TURNED OUT TO BE. I AM PROUD OF ALL 3 OF MY KIDS, THEY HAVE TURNED OUT ABSOLUTELY AMAZING! I DON'T WORRY ABOUT ALL 3 OF MY KIDS AT ALL. I HAVE SO MUCH FAITH IN THEM AND THEY ARE ALL 3 SUCH GREAT EXAMPLES TO EVERYONE

AROUND THEM. WELL, I HAVEN'T SLEPT IN 2 DAYS AND I WORK A LONG SHIFT TOMORROW, UNFORTUNATELY AGAIN, SO I NEED TO GET SOME SLEEP OR I WON'T MAKE IT THROUGH MY SHIFT TOMORROW. NIGHT TO MYSELF...SLEEP WELL TONIGHT!

11-26-2018: Dr. Note–140 lbs. Financially she can't make appointments. Having rough time, struggling. Relapsed on Heroin. Working a lot. Wants Xanax. Prescribed Prozac, Xanax, Suboxone, and Zofran. *I can't believe how much this doctor prescribed for her!*

A couple of weeks later...

MONDAY, DECEMBER 3, 2018:

ALMOST TIME FOR ADI'S WEDDING. I CAN'T WAIT 'CAUSE I KNOW HOW HAPPY MY DAUGHTER WILL BE 'CAUSE SHE HAS BEEN WAITING FOR THIS DAY FOR THE PAST 6/7 YEARS! ... AND I ABSOLUTELY LOVE DAKOTA! THEY DEFINITELY HAVE THEIR MOMENTS AND DISAGREEMENTS AT TIMES, JUST AS EVERY COUPLE DOES, BUT THEY BOTH TREAT EACH OTHER VERY GOOD. IT MAKES ME SO STINKIN' HAPPY THAT ADI FOUND SOMEONE LIKE HIM, 'CAUSE THEY ARE SO GREAT TOGETHER... NOT TO MENTION, THE CUTEST COUPLE *EVER!* I DEFINITELY HAVE A DILEMMA NOW, RYAN HAS DONE A COMPLETE 180 FOR THE WORST AND HAS BEEN LYING TO ME CONSTANTLY AND JUST TREATS ME ABSOLUTELY HORRIBLE. I HAVE ACTUALLY BEEN A LOT BETTER, NICER TO HIM, AND NOW I'M GETTING A TASTE OF MY OWN MEDICINE. WELL, AFTER THE WEDDING NEXT WEEK, WHEN EVERYTHING CALMS DOWN, I'M GOING TO ASK MY MOM IF I CAN LIVE THERE JUST FOR A COUPLE MONTHS TO GET BACK ON MY FEET. I'M VERY HESITANT ASKING THEM, THOUGH, 'CAUSE THEY LOVE SYDKA A LOT BUT THEY WON'T WANT A DOG LIVING THERE. WELL, I WILL FIGURE OUT SOMETHING, I ALWAYS DO! I MISS MY BOY SO MUCH THAT I CAN'T EVEN TALK ABOUT IT RIGHT NOW. AND I'M IN THE

WORST POSITION IN MY LIFE RIGHT NOW...WELL, IT'S NOT THE WORST, BUT IT'S PRETTY DAMN BAD. RYAN AND I HAVE BEEN IN EACH OTHER'S LIVES FOR ALMOST 5 YEARS NOW, AND I THINK WE HAVE BOTH JUST HAD ENOUGH. I DON'T LOVE HIM ENOUGH TO BE WITH HIM THE REST OF MY LIFE. AND NOW THAT HE HAS CHANGED SO DRAMATICALLY, THERE IS NO WAY IN HELL I WOULD GET ANOTHER PLACE TO LIVE WITH HIM. HE IS JUST NOT THE RYAN THAT I MET ALMOST 5 YEARS AGO. HE HAS ALWAYS BEEN SO EXTREMELY GOOD TO ME AND I DIDN'T DESERVE HIM...I DID THINGS TO HIM THAT I NEVER THOUGHT IN A MILLION YEARS I WOULD DO. I BROUGHT DRUG DEALERS INTO HIS HOME, WHILE HE WAS WORKING, SO I COULD TAKE CARE OF BUSINESS THERE...AND HANG OUT WITH THEM ONCE IN A WHILE. BUT ONE THING I CAN SAY, I HAVE ALWAYS BEEN UP FRONT WITH RYAN 'CAUSE HE "WAS" A GOOD GUY, SO I BELIEVED HE NEEDED TO KNOW ABOUT A FEW IMPORTANT THINGS. SOMETIMES I REALLY DO BELIEVE THAT I'M TOO HONEST WITH HIM, AND HE LITERALLY GOES INTO A MAJOR DEPRESSION WHEN HE DOESN'T BELIEVE ME. I'M HEADING OFF TO BED 'CAUSE WE WILL BE OUT AND ABOUT DOING WEDDING THINGS. JUST LAST MINUTE THINGS. MY DAUGHTER IS ABSOLUTELY AMAZING AND HAS DONE IT PRETTY MUCH ALL ON HER OWN!

TEXT FROM ME TO NAT: Mom said you're sick! What's going on?

NAT TO ME: Walking Pneumonia. Ya, it's been super fun!! How are you? I miss you!!

ME TO NAT: Oh no! I'm so sorry. I'm good just got here last night.

This was the first time I had heard that Nat had pneumonia. A friend of mine, who lived in Bountiful, texted me and said she saw Nat at work and Nat was really sick. I didn't panic because she was always sick with something from the drug use, but I did know she was really not well from talking to her on the phone. This was when she really withdrew from everyone. She was much sicker than anyone knew.

Nat and Adi on Adi's wedding day

Dakota, Adi and Nat at the wedding

THURSDAY, DECEMBER 6, 2018:

My family was up for Adi and Dakota's wedding. The wedding was beautiful; Adi did an amazing job. Things went pretty smoothly. Nat was with Ryan that night and kept leaving the reception to go either in the bathroom or outside. She missed a lot. It was really hard to watch. At one point, a couple from my parents' neighborhood came up to her, and she was so out of it, I don't think she even recognized them. I could tell they felt uncomfortable, so when Nat walked away, I thanked them for coming and tried to help them feel at ease. It was heart-wrenching to watch. This was such an important day for Adi, and it broke my heart for her that Nat was not really present for it. Knowing what I know now from her autopsy report, it is a miracle she could even attend the wedding. Adi's wedding was the last time I saw my sister alive.

FRIDAY, DECEMBER 7, 2018:

IT'S ABOUT 11:52 P.M. AND IT HAS BEEN A VERY LONG WEEK! I HAVE HAD PNEUMONIA FOR A WEEK NOW, AND ADI AND DAKOTA GOT MARRIED YESTERDAY! IT WAS ABSOLUTELY AMAZING, AND IT TURNED OUT PERFECT! ADI DID EVERYTHING AND IT WAS BEAUTIFUL AND ABSOLUTELY AMAZING! I CAN'T BELIEVE HOW TALENTED MY DAUGHTER IS. MY DAUGHTER IS AN AMAZING YOUNG WOMAN. IT WAS REALLY HARD NOT HAVING MASON THERE, BUT IT WAS SERIOUSLY PERFECT! I'M SITTING AT MY COUNTER RIGHT NOW WRITING IN MY JOURNAL WHILE JALA AND HER FRIEND ARE RIGHT NEXT TO ME, OUT COLD (ASLEEP ON THE BLOWUP MATTRESS). THEY ARE THE SWEETEST GIRLS EVER. I KNOW I SAY THIS A LOT, BUT I REALLY DO HAVE WONDERFUL CHILDREN. I WOULDN'T CHANGE ONE THING ABOUT THEM. ANTHONY IS ACTUALLY ON HIS WAY OVER RIGHT NOW 'CAUSE HE IS BRINGING ME SOME STUFF UNTIL I GET MYSELF TO THE DOCTOR ON MONDAY SO I CAN KICK! I AM SO EXTREMELY READY TO KICK, MORE THAN I EVER HAVE BEEN. I HAVE A SON ON A MISSION, A DAUGHTER THAT JUST GOT MARRIED, AND MY SWEET LITTLE JALA THAT I STILL HAVE TIME TO RAISE. I NEED TO BE CLEAN FOR MYSELF SO I CAN BE THE BEST MOTHER THAT I CAN POSSIBLY BE. I KNOW WHAT KIND OF MOTHER I CAN BE, TOO, AND I AM GREAT AT IT...AS LONG AS I PUT MY KIDS 1ST LIKE I USED TO DO BEFORE I GOT INTRODUCED INTO THE DEATH WORLD (THE DRUG WORLD)! *(She really was an incredible mother and very attentive in the beginning with Adi and Mas.)* I AM SO

READY TO BE DONE AND STAY DONE! I DON'T NEED ANY OF THE SCUMBAGS IN MY LIFE THAT I HAVE ASSOCIATED WITH LATELY. WELL, FOR WAY TOO LONG NOW! MARY IS EVEN ONE OF THEM. I HAVE SAID THIS BEFORE, BUT THIS TIME I MEAN IT, AND I WON'T GO BACK ON MY WORD, SHE IS DEAD TO ME AND ALWAYS WILL BE. SHE IS LOCKED UP RIGHT NOW BUT GETS OUT ANY DAY, AND I ALREADY KNOW I WILL BE ONE OF THE 1ST PEOPLE SHE CONTACTS. WELL, I'M DONE…SHE IS NO LONGER IN MY LIFE, WHATSOEVER! LIKE I SAID…DEAD TO ME, AND IT WILL STAY THAT WAY THIS TIME. I REALLY NEED TO GET RID OF A LOT OF PEOPLE THAT KNOW MY # AND KNOW WHERE I LIVE. THEY ARE DANGEROUS PEOPLE AND I WILL NOT HAVE MY JALA BE IN ANY KIND OF DANGER. AS FAR AS RYAN GOES…I DON'T KNOW. HE IS SO UP AND DOWN, I CAN'T KEEP GOING BACK AND FORTH WITH HIM. HE HAS DEFINITELY GOTTEN A LOT MEANER TO ME, WHICH I NEVER THOUGHT WOULD HAPPEN. I JUST REALLY DON'T KNOW WHAT TO DO WITH HIM AT THIS POINT.

SATURDAY, DECEMBER 8, 2018:

WELL, IT'S ABOUT 2:00 A.M. RIGHT NOW AND I AM SITTING OUT IN MY CAR SMOKING 'CAUSE I CAN'T SLEEP. JALA AND HER FRIEND ARE INSIDE SOUND ASLEEP, AND ANTHONY JUST LEFT BACK TO "THE HOUSE", THE "HORRIBLE HOUSE"! *(I think she was referring to Mary and David's house.)* I'M REALLY WORRIED ABOUT HIM 'CAUSE TERESA IS THERE, AND SHE IS VERY EVIL AND I DON'T KNOW WHAT IN THE HELL SHE IS GOING TO DO. OH WELL, NOT MY PROBLEM. SO, MY MOM GOT REALLY SICK LAST NIGHT AT THE WEDDING AND RYAN HAD TO TAKE HER HOME. I THINK SHE GOT WHAT POOR DECLAN *(our youngest nephew)* HAD. DECLAN HAD BEEN THROWING UP ALL DAY YESTERDAY AND EM HAD TO DRUG HIM *(give him Tylenol)* SO HE COULD WALK DOWN THE AISLE AS THE RING BEARER, BUT HE DID IT! BARELY. I AM GLAD THAT IT'S ALL OVER

AND ADI WAS HAPPY! THAT'S ALL I CARED ABOUT, HER HAPPINESS, AND SHE WAS. DAKOTA AND HER BOTH, THEY WERE ON CLOUD 9! I LOVE THEM BOTH!!

12-9-2018: Dr. Note–140 lbs. States no relapse in 7-10 days. Says she's in a better place, happy about progress. Mother has been more involved. Prescribed Ambien, Zofran, Gabapentin (for back and nerve pain), and Suboxone.

SUNDAY, DECEMBER 9, 2018:

TODAY, I NEED TO HAVE LOTS OF LOVE AND FAITH. TODAY IS MY DAY, DO YOUR ABSOLUTE BEST AND MAKE IT COUNT!!

SO, I GO TO THE DOCTOR TODAY AT 1:45 AND I AM GOING TO GET ALL MY MEDS AND I AM GOING TO KICK THIS SHIT! I HAVE *NEVER* IN MY ENTIRE LIFE BEEN THIS READY. I DON'T WANT THIS SHIT IN ME ANYMORE, NOR DO I WANT TO ASSOCIATE WITH ANYONE AT ALL THAT DOES ANY KIND OF DRUGS! THIS IS JUST IT FOR ME, I HAVE WANTED TO DO THIS FOR QUITE A WHILE NOW, BUT I HAVE NEVER HAD THE CHANCE TO HAVE 3 OR 4 DAYS OFF WORK AND HAVE ALL MY MEDS AT THAT SAME TIME. WELL, THIS IS THE MOST IMPORTANT THING TO ME, AND I AM GOING TO DO THIS! I KNOW HEAVENLY FATHER WILL HELP ME GET THROUGH IT AND HAVE THE STRENGTH TO KEEP GOING. I AM NOT GOING TO GIVE UP THIS TIME! I HAVE MY SON ON A MISSION, ADI AND DAKOTA JUST GOT MARRIED 3 DAYS AGO...AND I GUARANTEE SHE IS GOING TO START POPPING OUT BABIES REAL SOON! AND I AM DEFINITELY GOING TO BE CLEAN FOR THAT! I *WILL NOT* MISS ANY TIME WITH MY GRANDBABIES, AND THAT'S A PROMISE! AND I CAN STILL RAISE MY SWEET LITTLE JALA. I AM GOING TO BE THE *BEST* MOM THAT I CAN BE!

A week later…

SUNDAY, DECEMBER 16, 2018:

IT'S 4:40 A.M. AND RYAN AND I ARE OUTSIDE IN THE JEEP OUTSIDE OUR EAGLEWOOD APARTMENTS 'CAUSE NEITHER ONE OF US CAN SLEEP! I AM REALLY, ACTUALLY, EXTREMELY DEPRESSED RIGHT NOW. ONE OF THE REASONS IS BECAUSE JAY GOT ENGAGED A COUPLE DAYS AGO. I LOVED HOW WE WERE. NOW I GUARANTEE THIS NEW GIRL, THAT I HAVEN'T EVEN MET, IS GOING TO TOTALLY RUIN WHAT JAY AND I HAVE. HE JUST MET THIS GIRL ABOUT 2 MONTHS AGO AND HAS ONLY BEEN DATING HER FOR ABOUT A MONTH. HE DOESN'T EVEN KNOW HER! NOW, JALA IS GOING TO HAVE A FAMILY, JUST LIKE ADI AND MASON DO, AND I AM GOING TO LOSE MY LITTLE GIRL! I HAVE BEEN USING PRETTY HEAVILY THE PAST WEEK BECAUSE OF EVERYTHING THAT IS GOING ON. I ABSOLUTELY *DO NOT* WANT TO GET BACK INTO THE DRUG WORLD. I THINK I MIGHT HAVE LOST MY JOB TOO. I HAVE CALLED IN 3 TIMES THIS WEEK SICK 'CAUSE I WAS USING TOO MUCH AND COULD NOT EVEN FUNCTION THE MAJORITY OF THE WEEK. I AM GOING ABSOLUTELY NOWHERE IN MY LIFE AND I REALLY WOULD RATHER DIE THAN GO ON ANOTHER DAY LIKE THIS. I CAN'T TAKE THIS ANYMORE, AND I'M NOT STRONG ENOUGH TO FIX THIS! I DON'T KNOW WHAT THE HELL TO DO ANYMORE! I MISS MASON SO MUCH IT PHYSICALLY HURTS!!!

There was an incident after the wedding where Adi and Jala called me and told me that Jala had slept over at Nat's house, and when Jala was getting out of the shower and went to grab a towel, a syringe that was full of heroin fell out of it. Jala got really scared because she was old enough to know what it was and what it meant. She had believed her mother was clean for some time, and now she knew she was still using. She went to

Nat and told her, and Nat told her it was medicine for Sydka (the dog). Jala went to school the next day and told her counselor that she didn't feel safe with her mom because she was using again. The school called DCFS (Division of Child and Family Services) and they got in contact with Nat, Jay, and my mom. I don't know how far the investigation went, but I know it was ongoing until she passed because I was in the car with my mom when DCFS called her about it. Jala struggled with emotional issues, as you can imagine. Her counselors at school tried to help, as well as other professionals.

Two days later...

TUESDAY, DECEMBER 18, 2018:

IT'S 5:10 A.M. I CANNOT SLEEP FOR THE LIFE OF ME! I'M SO STRESSED! I FEEL SO SUICIDAL! I DON'T EVER GET THIS BAD—WELL, I DEFINITELY BELIEVE IN KARMA 100%, I ALWAYS HAVE, BUT THIS TIME, IT WAS SO EXTREMELY CLEAR TO ME. I HAVE BEEN USING VERY HEAVILY AGAIN AND AM LYING TO FAMILY ABOUT IT AGAIN BECAUSE I CANNOT LOSE THEM AGAIN. WELL, I THINK I'M TOO LATE, I THINK I LOST THEM ALREADY, AND IT'S A WEEK BEFORE CHRISTMAS! THE ONE HOLIDAY I LOVE SPENDING TIME WITH MY FAMILY, YET I DON'T EVEN KNOW IF I'M ALLOWED TO COME TO THE CHRISTMAS PARTY (ALLEN) PARTY ON THE 21ST, AND THAT PARTY WITH THE ALLEN SIDE IS THE FUNNEST TIME OF THE HOLIDAYS. WELL, I CAN ONLY BLAME MYSELF FOR WHAT I'M GOING THROUGH 'CAUSE I HAVE DONE SOME SHADY SHIT LATELY, SOMETHING AND THINGS I WOULD *NEVER* EVEN THINK ABOUT DOING! SO, ADI GOT HOME FROM HER HONEYMOON CRUISE THIS MORNING AND I CALLED JALA IN THE MIDDLE OF THE DAY AND ASKED HER WHY, AND SHE SAID GRANDMA PICKED HER UP FROM SCHOOL AND SPENT THE DAY WITH HER, AND SO DID ADI AFTER SHE GOT DONE WITH WORK. WELL, APPARENTLY THE SCHOOL COUNSELOR HAD CALLED MY MOM

'CAUSE JALA TOLD THEM TO CALL HER, AND THE COUNSELOR TOLD MY MOM THAT SHE HAS BEEN ON SUICIDE WATCH ALMOST ALL DAY UNTIL GRANDMA PICKED HER UP! SUICIDE WATCH!! THAT DIDN'T EVEN ENTER MY HEAD AT THAT AGE. WELL, ONE OF THE REASONS IS BECAUSE SHE BELIEVES I AM TOTALLY USING 'CAUSE SHE FOUND A RIG *(needle)* IN THE BATHROOM! HOW CARELESS AND STUPID CAN I BE? I WANTED TO GIVE JALA A BETTER YOUNG LIFE THAN I DID ADI AND MAS. AND I HAVE COMPLETELY FAILED! ADI AND I ARE REALLY, REALLY CLOSE NOW, MASON IS OKAY WITH ME, BUT HE JUST LEFT ON HIS MISSION 3 1/2 WEEKS AGO, BUT I MISS HIM LIKE CRAZY! SO ADI TALKED FOR A LITTLE BIT, AND SOME OF IT, ACTUALLY A LOT OF IT, HURTS 'CAUSE I ABANDONED THEM WHEN THEY WERE YOUNG, NOT ON MY OWN BY ANY MEANS, TO GET MYSELF IN TROUBLE SOMETIMES 'CAUSE I GET LIVID AND I DON'T NEED MY DAUGHTER AND I DON'T HAVE TO BE AT WORK ANYMORE 'CAUSE I GOT FIRED... *(This doesn't make sense.)* SEAN, MY BOSS, IS SCREWING HIMSELF 'CAUSE I LITERALLY WAS THE HARDEST WORKER OF A LOT OF PEOPLE. WELL, HE NOTICED TWO WEEKS AFTER WORKING THERE AND ASKED ME TO BE THE ASSISTANT MANAGER. *ANYWAYS!* WELL, I ENDED UP CALLING IN SICK FOR ALMOST A WEEK AND A 1/2 'CAUSE I WENT TO THE HOSPITAL AND I HAD PNEUMONIA. IT WAS REALLY PAINFUL. I AM SO DEPRESSED, I LITERALLY HAVE BEEN CRYING ALMOST ALL DAY! MY BOSS DIDN'T EVEN HAVE THE GUTS TO TELL ME I WAS LET GO UNTIL TONIGHT, AND HE SAID HE NEEDED PEOPLE TO SHOW UP! I DID, AND THE PAY WAS NOT WORTH IT AT ALL! WELL, EVERYONE IN MY FAMILY KNOWS NOW, AND I WAS JUST ABOUT TO KICK!

Jala did talk to her counselor at school and was suicidal. They ended up taking her out of school and took her to the hospital to evaluate her. She came home that same day. Jay, my mom, and Adi were doing everything they could to try and help her. Adi called Nat after this experience and told her that she needed to show up to the Allen party (our extended family

Christmas party) on the 21st even though she was sick, for Jala's sake, and if she let them down, then she needed to stay away from them.

WEDNESDAY, DECEMBER 19, 2018:

I HATE MY LIFE! I HONESTLY DO RIGHT NOW, WORSE THAN I THINK I HAVE *EVER* BEEN IN MY LIFE! I ALREADY WROTE ABOUT THE SUICIDE WATCH YESTERDAY, AND I JUST CAN'T GET THAT OUT OF MY MIND...SHE IS ONLY 12 YEARS OLD, ME AND MY FRIENDS WERE PLAYING KISSING TAG AT THAT AGE, BUT OF COURSE, GRANDMA HAD ABSOLUTELY *NO IDEA!* I AM SO WORRIED AND ABSOLUTELY TERRIFIED FOR MY BABY GIRL RIGHT NOW, IT'S LITERALLY MAKING ME PHYSICALLY SICK. THAT'S WHY I KEPT CALLING INTO WORK SICK (NOT BLAMING IT AT ALL ON JALA OR ANYTHING), BUT THAT WAS THE REASON I LOST MY JOB. I ACTUALLY ENJOYED THAT JOB TOO. I USUALLY NEVER DREADED GOING IN, AND THAT'S PRETTY WEIRD FOR ME. *(Her thoughts were all over the place.)*

IT'S ABOUT 9:00 A.M. IN THE MORNING AND I HAVE BEEN UP FOR 3 OR 4 DAYS. ADI CALLED ME YESTERDAY AND TOLD ME EVERYTHING ABOUT JALA, AND ADI WAS QUITE MAD AT ME HERSELF, WHICH I *DO NOT* BLAME HER AT ALL. SHE SAID WHEN SHE TALKED TO ME, SHE COULD BARELY UNDERSTAND ME 'CAUSE I WAS SO DROWSY THAT I COULDN'T TALK AT ALL AND I SOUNDED LIKE I WAS DRUNK. WELL, I DEFINITELY REASSURED HER THAT I WAS NOT AT ALL DRUNK AND HAD NOT BEEN DRINKING AT ALL. SHE BELIEVED ME, SHE KNOWS I DON'T LIKE *ANY* KIND OF ALCOHOL ANYMORE. SO, IT'S A WEEK AWAY FROM CHRISTMAS AND I HAVE NOT DONE ANY CHRISTMAS SHOPPING WHATSOEVER! CHRISTMAS STRESSES ME OUT NOW THAT I HAVE CHILDREN. IT USED TO BE MY *ABSOLUTE FAVORITE* HOLIDAY EVER, AND NOW ALL IT DOES IS STRESSES ME OUT SO STINKIN' BAD THAT I CAN'T WAIT TILL IT'S OVER AGAIN. I HAVE TURNED INTO A BAH-HUM-BUG!

The Allen Christmas party was held on the 21st of December. Jala waited and waited for her mom, and she never showed. She kept asking me, "Aunt Shall, when is my mom going to be here?" It absolutely killed me to watch her suffer. I had not talked to Nat since we were texting about her being sick, so I only knew what Adi had told me she had said to her mom about showing up to the party. Ryan showed up looking rugged and dirty and grabbed a plate of food for him and Nat, and when we asked where Nat was, he said he was taking her to the hospital because she had pneumonia. We were all pretty upset she wasn't there. She had never missed this party; even our two aunts asked me where she was. That same night, after the party, we all went to my parents' house and exchanged gifts like we do every year. Nat didn't show up for that either. I had bought her a gift and ended up giving it to Adi instead. We had no idea how sick she really was.

Nine days later...

FRIDAY, DECEMBER 28, 2018:

SHITTY, SHITTY CHRISTMAS! I CAN DEFINITELY, 100% SAY THAT THIS WAS BY FAR THE WORST CHRISTMAS I HAVE EVER EXPERIENCED IN MY ENTIRE LIFE. SAD, RIGHT? WELL, 1ST OFF, WE HAD NO MONEY AT ALL FOR ANY OF THE KIDS FOR PRESENTS, SO JENNIFER ACTUALLY HELPED ME CHRISTMAS EVE PUT TOGETHER A COUPLE OF THINGS FOR THE KIDS, BUT IT WAS NOTHIN', ESPECIALLY WHAT THEY USED TO GET FROM ME AT THE HOLIDAYS! A LOT, A LOT, A LOT! EVEN THOUGH I COULD NEVER AFFORD IT, I ALWAYS FIGURED IT OUT SOMEHOW. WELL, NOT THIS YEAR! BUT THERE WAS THE *BEST THING* EVER THAT HAPPENED TO ALL OF US CHRISTMAS DAY...MASON CALLED! WE PUT HIM ON THE BIG SCREEN DOWNSTAIRS AT MY MOM'S SO WE COULD ALL TALK TO HIM. HE LOOKED SO, SO GOOD AND SO SUPER HAPPY! I MISS HIM SO STINKIN' MUCH, AND IT'S ONLY BEEN A COUPLE MONTHS. SO, I HAVE DONE SOME THINGS THIS PAST YEAR THAT I AM SUPER MAD AT MYSELF FOR, THINGS THAT I WOULD *NEVER*

DO, AND I KNOW IT'S BECAUSE OF THE PEOPLE I HAVE BEEN SURROUNDING MYSELF WITH. MARY, DAVID, JENNIFER, ETC. THEY ARE ALL IN JAIL NOW EXCEPT JENNIFER. I KEEP GOING DOWNHILL AGAIN, AND I CAN'T PULL MYSELF OUT OF IT! I'M SO ANGRY WITH MYSELF, BUT ALL I CAN DO NOW IS ASK FOR FORGIVENESS, FORGIVE MYSELF, MOVE ON, AND NEVER MAKE THOSE MISTAKES AGAIN. THIS IS MY ULTIMATE PLAN AND GOALS! SO, JAY IS ENGAGED, I GUESS, THAT REALLY HELPED WITH MY DEPRESSION. I DON'T WANT ANOTHER WOMAN AROUND HIM OR JALA, IT TERRIFIES ME. EVERYTHING IS JUST A MESS RIGHT NOW, TALK TO YA SOON, ME! *(Jay never got married.)*

IT'S 1:25 IN THE MORNING AND I OBVIOUSLY *CANNOT* SLEEP 'CAUSE IT HAS BEEN AN ABSOLUTELY *HORRIBLE* DAY! HAD SYDKA AT THE VET FOR ABOUT 3 HOURS. APPARENTLY, SHE RIPPED HER CLAW CLEAR UP TO THE BONE SO SHE CAN'T WALK TO GO OUTSIDE TO GO POTTY OR ANYTHING. I HAVE BEEN IN TEARS ALMOST ALL DAY. THEY HAD TO PUT HER OUT, THEN CUT THE CLAW ALMOST OFF AND BANDAGED IT UP, AND I HAVE TO GO BACK IN 4 DAYS TO GET IT REMOVED. IT WAS THE SADDEST THING AND VERY TRAUMATIZING TO GO THROUGH, FOR BOTH OF US. RIGHT WHEN WE WALKED INTO THE DOORS TO THE VET, SYDKA STARTED TREMBLING SO BAD THAT WE HAD TO TRY AND GET HER CALMED DOWN. IT TOOK A WHILE. IT WAS JUST AWFUL. AND, OF COURSE, WE DIDN'T HAVE THE MONEY, ESPECIALLY SINCE IT'S JUST A COUPLE DAYS AFTER CHRISTMAS, SO BLESS THEIR HEARTS, MY MOM AND DAD PAID FOR EVERYTHING. THEY ARE 2 OF THE MOST AMAZING PEOPLE IN THIS WORLD. AND I'M NOT JUST SAYING THAT 'CAUSE THEY ARE MY PARENTS OR BECAUSE OF THE MONEY. THEY ARE JUST SO THOUGHTFUL AND CARING. THEY ARE SUCH AN EXAMPLE TO ME, I WISH I COULD BE 1/2 THE MOTHER THAT MY MOM IS, BUT THAT COULD *NEVER* HAPPEN. SHE IS THE *BEST* MOTHER AND ESPECIALLY GRANDMOTHER ANYONE COULD EVER WANT! THE BILL TO THE VET WAS $260.

I WAS FREAKING OUT WHEN THEY TOLD ME THAT, AND MY MOM AND DAD BOTH JUST SAID DO IT, GET SYDKA ALL BETTER, WE DON'T CARE HOW MUCH IT'S GOING TO BE…THAT PUT ME IN TEARS AS WELL…BUT, THOSE WERE HAPPY TEARS. WELL, SHE HAS BEEN ON OUR BED EVER SINCE WE GOT HOME AND HAS NOT MOVED. IT BREAKS MY HEART 'CAUSE I KNOW SHE IS IN PAIN. SHE IS LYING HERE WHIMPERING. AND THEY SAID SHE WOULDN'T BE IN ANY PAIN AT ALL! WHAT THE HELL? SHE IS IN PAIN…*BAD!* I'M JUST SO GLAD I GOT HER IN TODAY, OR I DON'T KNOW WHAT WOULD HAVE HAPPENED TO HER. WE BARELY MADE IT THROUGH CHRISTMAS 'CAUSE WE HAD ABSOLUTELY NO MONEY AT ALL, BUT WE MADE IT. I FELT SO BAD, THOUGH, 'CAUSE MY KIDS, I USUALLY SPOIL, AND THIS YEAR IT WAS REALLY BAD…THEY DIDN'T GET HARDLY ANYTHING FROM ME AT ALL. I KNOW THEY SAY THEY ARE OKAY, BUT I'M NOT…MY GUILT IS LITERALLY KILLING ME, EMOTIONALLY AND PHYSICALLY. WELL, I DON'T KNOW WHAT TO DO, SYDKA IS LYING HERE WHIMPERING AND I JUST DON'T KNOW WHAT THE HELL TO DO! YEP, HERE COME THE TEARS AGAIN…I CAN'T TAKE EVEN ONE MORE THING. I AM GOING TO CUDDLE HER AND TRY AND FIGURE OUT WHAT IN THE HELL TO DO!!

• • •

CHAPTER 15

2019

IN 2019 NAT WOULD HAVE *turned forty, Adi twenty-three, Mas twenty, and Jala thirteen.*

1-1-2019: Dr. Note–137 lbs. Relapsed, lost job. Prescribed Xanax, Suboxone, Zofran, and Gabapentin. *This was her last visit to the doctor.*

Nat's day planner for 2019 had notes for January. She wrote:

1. Change last name!!!
2. Look for jobs
3. Look for cheaper place to live!

Nine days since last entry…

SUNDAY, JANUARY 6, 2019:

IT'S 12:16 AT NIGHT AND I'M SITTING HERE WONDERING WHAT IN THE HELL I AM GOING TO DO WITH MY MISERABLE LIFE! I HAVE DCFS *(Division of Child and Family Services)* POKING AROUND AGAIN BECAUSE JALA TOLD HER THERAPIST AT SCHOOL THAT SHE FOUND A NEEDLE IN MY BATHROOM AND SHE THINKS I'M USING DRUGS AGAIN. THE THERAPIST CALLED DCFS. I HONESTLY CANNOT DEAL WITH ANOTHER ROUND OF

DCFS! I CAN'T BELIEVE THIS IS ALL HAPPENING AGAIN! I SHOULDN'T BE SURPRISED, THOUGH, AT ALL, NOT AFTER ALL THE STUPID THINGS I HAVE BEEN DOING LATELY, JUST TO GET MY STUPID DRUG! HEROIN IS THE *DEVIL!* IT HAS COMPLETE CONTROL OVER ME AND HAS EVERY PART OF ME, EXCEPT MY HEART! I WANT TO QUIT THIS SHIT MORE THAN ANYTHING IN THIS WORLD, BUT I HAVEN'T BEEN ABLE TO YET. HOW CAN SOMETHING HAVE THIS POWER OVER ME, AND IT JUST KEEPS GETTING STRONGER AND STRONGER. IT WON'T LET GO, AND I REALLY AM TRYING SO HARD TO GET RID OF IT, I HAVE TRIED SO MANY TIMES THAT IT'S PATHETIC! COMPLETELY PATHETIC! I AM NOTHING BUT A NO GOOD, MISERABLE JUNKIE! THERE IS NOTHING GOOD ABOUT ME AT ALL ANYMORE. ALL I HAVE EVER WANTED TO BE IS A GOOD MOTHER TO MY 3 WONDERFUL KIDS, THAT DIDN'T DESERVE ANY OF THIS, A GOOD DAUGHTER, A GOOD SISTER TO MY 3 BEAUTIFUL SISTERS, AND A GOOD EXAMPLE TO PEOPLE AROUND ME. I HAVE COMPLETELY FAILED AT ALL OF THOSE THINGS. I KNOW THEY ALL LOVE ME, BUT I DO KNOW THAT THEY HAVE ALL HAD ENOUGH, WHICH I DON'T BLAME THEM AT ALL. I WANT TO CHANGE MY LIFE MORE THAN I CAN EVER EXPLAIN, BUT I JUST KEEP GOING DEEPER AND DEEPER IN THE OTHER DIRECTION. RYAN ISN'T HELPING THE SITUATION NOW EITHER. HE HAS ALWAYS BEEN SO GREAT TO ME, TOTALLY TAKES CARE OF ME, LOVES MY KIDS, SWEETEST MAN THAT I HAVE EVER MET, AND NOW, BECAUSE OF ME, HE HAS TURNED INTO A COMPLETELY DIFFERENT PERSON. I DON'T EVEN KNOW THIS MAN ANYMORE. HE IS A HORRIBLE JUNKIE AND DOES NOT KNOW WHAT IN THE HELL HE HAS GOTTEN HIMSELF INTO. I HONESTLY *DO NOT* KNOW WHAT IN THE HELL TO DO! I DON'T KNOW THE FIRST STEP I NEED TO TAKE, AND I AM LOSING EVERYTHING AS EACH DAY GOES ON. I HAD SUCH A GREAT JOB AT THE GAS STATION ACROSS THE STREET FROM MY HOUSE, AND I FUCKED IT UP AND LOST IT! I HONESTLY

> NEVER THOUGHT I COULD EVER LOSE THAT JOB 'CAUSE THEY LOVED ME OVER THERE, BUT I FUCKED UP FOR THE LAST TIME AND THEY FIRED ME ABOUT A WEEK AGO, AND NOW THINGS ARE GOING DEEPER DOWNHILL, AND *FAST!*

Nat called me on January 7th as I was getting ready to take my son to school. I had been so upset since December about what had happened with Jala and Adi and the Christmas party that I had not reached out to her. When she called me, I answered and asked if I could call her back when I got in the car. I silently prayed that I would say the right things to her and that I would handle the situation in the right way. I felt that if she brought any of the recent situations up, I could tell her how I felt, but if she didn't, I wouldn't bring them up. By then, I knew there were always two ways to react: confront or just listen. Most of the time, I just listened because I had learned that confronting did no good. I ALWAYS told her I loved her and spoke respectfully to her, which I am so grateful for. After my son got out of the car, I called her back and she started talking about how she was struggling financially, and then about Jala and the needle and the suicide watch, and how she didn't feel like our family was close anymore. I responded that the family was very close, we just weren't close to her because she had distanced herself and we were all burned out. I told her we were all exhausted. I also told her that the reason Jala was suicidal was because of what she had put her through, especially lately. I said all of this with love and told her that I loved her, but that that was the reality. Normally, if anyone said anything like this to her, she would cuss at them and hang up on them in a rage. I wasn't trying to fight with her, though; I never was. I was just trying to explain reality to her, which looking back now, I shouldn't have done. However, she only said softly that she knew she shouldn't have called me, and I told her I was glad she did and that I loved her and she could always call me. Then she hung up. I noticed in her voice how weak and tired she seemed. She had no more fight left in her. That was the last time I heard my sister's voice. As I am writing this, it is seven months later and this all still seems like a dream. I felt terrible after she hung up.

Two days later, she texted me a picture of this letter she wrote me:

LETTER FROM NAT TO ME, WEDNESDAY, JANUARY 9, 2019:

SHALL...
HI, HAD TO DOODLE YOUR NAME FOR A MIN. TO GIVE ME SOME TIME TO THINK OF THE RIGHT WORDS TO SAY TO YOU. SORRY IF IT SEEMS CHILDISH.

SHALL, I AM SO SORRY, I CAN'T SAY IT ENOUGH HOW SORRY I AM FOR EVERYTHING I HAVE PUT YOU THROUGH, AND EVERYONE ELSE. YOU DEFINITELY OPENED MY EYES THE LAST TIME I TALKED TO YOU. I WASN'T CALLING FOR MONEY, AND I'M SORRY YOU FEEL THAT THAT WAS THE ONLY REASON I WAS CALLING YOU FOR. I TRIED NOT TO ASK YOU FOR MONEY VERY OFTEN, BUT I AM SORRY. I JUST NEEDED TO TALK TO THE PERSON THAT I IDOLIZE THE MOST AND VENT A LITTLE BIT. I'M VERY SORRY I UPSET YOU, SHALL, I LOVE YOU MORE THAN ANYTHING, BUT I KNOW YOU NEED SPACE, LOTS OF SPACE FROM ME. SO, I WILL GIVE THAT TO YOU. I JUST WANT YOU TO KNOW THAT I WILL PROVE YOU WRONG AND MAKE YOU PROUD OF ME VERY SOON.

I JUST WANTED TO APOLOGIZE FROM THE BOTTOM OF MY HEART. I KNOW OUR RELATIONSHIP WILL NEVER BE THE WAY IT USED TO BE, BUT I WANT YOU TO KNOW JUST HOW SORRY I AM AND JUST HOW MUCH I LOVE YOU. YOU ARE MY IDOL AND ALWAYS WILL BE AND WISH SOMEDAY I CAN BE 1/2 THE WOMAN THAT YOU ARE.
I LOVE YOU, SHALL!
-NAT-

TEXT FROM ME TO NAT: Thank you Nat for the letter, I hoped our conversation would open your eyes by me being honest. I pray every day that you prove me wrong. I love you.

I wish now, looking back, that I would have been kinder. I guess, after years of the same pattern, I just responded not knowing this would be my last interaction with her.

SATURDAY, JANUARY 12, 2019:

IT'S ABOUT 12:35 AT NIGHT, AND APPARENTLY, MY APARTMENT NOW IS A SHELTER FOR PEOPLE THAT DON'T HAVE ANYWHERE TO GO. MARCUS, THERESA AND AMBER ARE ALL HERE. I DON'T MIND EVERY ONCE IN A WHILE PEOPLE STAYING OVER, BUT NOT EVERY NIGHT, LIKE MARCUS HAS BEEN DOING. I HAVEN'T HARDLY BEEN ABLE TO SEE JALA LATELY BECAUSE SHE TOLD HER THERAPIST AT SCHOOL THAT SHE THINKS I AM USING AGAIN, AND THE THERAPIST CALLED DCFS. THEY HAVEN'T FILED ANYTHING ON ME, AND I PRAY IT DOESN'T COME DOWN TO THAT. I AM ACTUALLY DOING PRETTY GOOD THIS WEEK. I AM GETTING OFF THE DEVIL'S DRUG AND HOPEFULLY NEVER GOING BACK TO IT AGAIN. IT HAS RUINED MY LIFE, AND I CAN'T LOSE EVERYTHING ALL OVER AGAIN. MICHELLE IS DONE WITH ME RIGHT NOW. I TALKED TO HER A COUPLE DAYS AGO AND SHE SAID SHE WAS DONE. IT RIPPED MY HEART IN HALF. SHE IS THE CLOSEST PERSON TO ME, AND ALWAYS HAS BEEN. BUT I HAVE TO LET HER GO NOW! IF I THINK ABOUT IT, I ALMOST HAVE A PANIC ATTACK. SHE IS MY SISTER, HOW CAN SHE BE DONE WITH ME? I DON'T UNDERSTAND. I WILL ALWAYS BE HERE FOR ALL MY SISTERS AND I WOULD *NEVER* BE DONE WITH ANY OF THEM. THE ONLY SISTER THAT IS TALKING TO ME RIGHT NOW IS ANGIE. AND I BARELY HEAR FROM HER AT ALL 'CAUSE SHE IS ALWAYS BUSY. IT BREAKS MY HEART 'CAUSE MY SISTERS MEAN SO MUCH TO ME. I NEED TO DO WHATEVER IT TAKES TO GET THEM BACK IN MY LIFE. I WILL SERIOUSLY GO CRAZY WITHOUT THEM! SO, I REALLY NEED TO GET MARCUS OUT OF MY HOUSE, HE IS WAY TOO MUCH DRAMA, I JUST CAN'T HANDLE HIM ANYMORE, AND HIM BEING HERE SCARES THE LIVING SHIT OUT OF ME 'CAUSE I DON'T

KNOW WHAT HE IS CAPABLE OF. HE REALLY DOES HORRIBLE THINGS, ALL THE TIME. HE IS STARTING SOMETHING WITH AMBER RIGHT NOW, AND LIKE I SAID, ALL HE IS, IS DRAMA, DRAMA, DRAMA! AND RYAN HAS COMPLETELY CHANGED TOO. HE HAS TURNED SO MEAN AND HE IS NOT THE SAME PERSON HE USED TO BE. LOVE HIM TO DEATH, BUT ONCE OUR LEASE IS UP NEXT MONTH, I NEED TO FIGURE OUT WHERE TO GO, 'CAUSE I DON'T THINK I CAN LIVE WITH HIM ANYMORE. HE REALLY IS A COMPLETELY DIFFERENT PERSON THAN HE USED TO BE. IT'S REALLY SAD, TOO, 'CAUSE HE USED TO BE A GREAT GUY. HE WAS MY BEST FRIEND AND HE ALWAYS TOOK CARE OF ME, ALL THE TIME. NOW, HE HAS ABSOLUTELY NOTHING TO DO WITH ME, JUST LIKE MY FAMILY RIGHT NOW. I FEEL SO ALONE AND DEPRESSED AND CAN'T GET RID OF THE EMOTIONAL PAIN. I NEED TO SHOW EVERYONE THAT I CAN CHANGE, AND THAT'S EXACTLY WHAT I AM GOING TO DO!!!

Two days later...

I received a phone call from Adi early on the morning of the 14th, and she said her and my mom and Ang were at the hospital and that Ryan had brought Nat in at 10 p.m. the night before because she couldn't breathe and wasn't coherent. Adi had found out that morning and then called me. She said it was bad, then Ang got on the phone and said that when they got there, Nat was intubated and hadn't woken up at all except right before the intubation, when she looked at Adi and said she loved her, then was out again. They ran tests on her and found out that she had multiple drugs in her system and she was septic, a life-threatening complication of an infection (sepsis occurs when chemicals released in the bloodstream to fight an infection trigger inflammation throughout the body, and this can cause a cascade of changes that damage multiple organ systems, leading them to fail and sometimes resulting in death), and an abscess on her upper arm from her elbow to her shoulder, which was where the infection had originated. By the time Ryan had carried her into the hospital that night, she was in heart and kidney failure.

My husband immediately got me and my son packed up and in the car. We arrived at the hospital in the late afternoon. I was in a daze. I had received a call from my mom and Angie during the drive to Salt Lake saying they were told to make a decision about taking her into surgery and trying to remove the abscess (which would probably have ended in amputating her arm), and that she had a 50/50 chance to survive the surgery. If she did, she would be on dialysis for the rest of her life because of kidney failure. I knew in my heart she was done fighting, but I didn't give my opinion. They tried to take her down to surgery, and as they were unhooking her bed, she flatlined, after which she was put on life support. They were able to bring her back, but the family all felt that she was telling us not to do the surgery. When we arrived at the hospital, everyone was there except Jala and Mason, who was on his mission. The first person I saw was Ryan, and he was standing with a social worker and cops in the hall. I had no idea what was going on. There were security guards surrounding her room as well, and I later found out it was because Ryan was apparently so distraught that he threatened to jump off the roof of the hospital and had been locking himself in the bathroom, threatening suicide, and crying and falling all over her, so they had a social worker and security cops with him at all times. (Later in the evening, after she passed, he was escorted out by security.)

I walked in the room and saw my sister lying there, hooked up to multiple machines and tubes. Her head was turned to the side and her eyes were slightly open and empty. They said that when they intubated her, they'd had to administer some medicine to paralyze her face so they could get the tube down, so her eyes would not close. I started shaking immediately and convulsed the entire time I was there. I wanted to be by myself with my sister, I wanted everyone out of the room, and I just wanted to tell her I loved her so much and I was so sorry it was her that had this battle, not me, and that I would help care for her children. Ang and my mom ended up staying in the room with me because I was not able to stand very well. I just sobbed and shook and tried to wrap my head around what I was seeing. Sometime later on, we met with the doctor in a conference room and asked all the questions that we had about her chance of survival and what we should do. It was all explained as I said before, then the doctor left and my father said a prayer that we would all know what to do. My mom, dad, Adi, Ang, Em, and I all knew Nat wanted to be out of this misery and the addiction she had fought for so long. We never even talked about it; we just all knew and were on the same page. The six of us left everyone in the conference room and went to her room. We all stood beside her, holding her hands. Her sweet Adi was the one assigned as the next of kin to make all the decisions. We were all there with her to help her and support her. That was such a burden for a twenty-two-year-old daughter to have. While we were in the room, we told Nat it was okay to go, and my father said another prayer, asking our Heavenly Father to please release her spirit and let her go. She never took another breath. She was gone that fast. We never doubted that we had made the right choice. We knew in our hearts she needed to be released from all her pain.

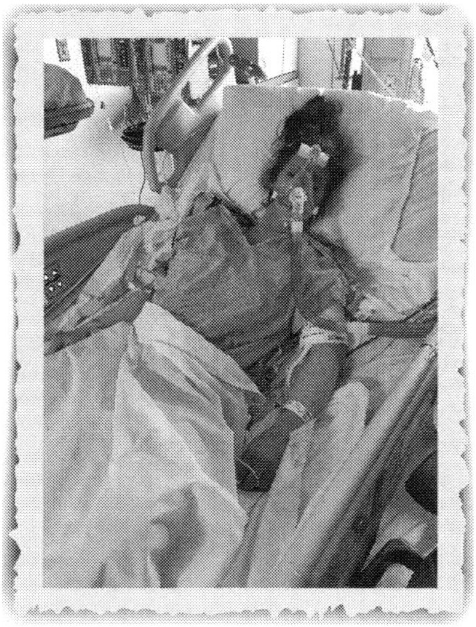

I had feared this day for twenty-three years. I had always imagined that I would get a call that my sister had passed away in a gutter, or even worse, was missing. I believe everything happened just as it should have in that she made sure we were all there, and that she didn't pass until her children were all in a good place in life. Mas had just left on his mission a few months prior, Adi had just

gotten married, and Jala was good with Jay. We all stayed in town until after her services the following Saturday. We spent the week making funeral plans. I remember walking into the mortuary to pick out a casket and I thought, there is no way I can do this, this is not real that we are picking out a casket for Nat. It was the hardest week of my life. Our family was changed forever, as were each of us individually. We had undercover cops at her funeral because there were people from her drug world that were angry with our family because they didn't feel we had fought for her life. We were worried about retaliation. There were so many people that showed up to her viewing that they were lined up in the parking lot, and a lot of people didn't even make it into the viewing because it was so busy. The funeral was so full. There were many people from her drug world that we didn't know. One woman was so high and out of control in the viewing, she had to be escorted out. We all stood by Jala, Adi, and Mas. Mas came home for the funeral and spoke, then flew back out that same evening. We all believe we will be reunited with Nat in the next life, and that brings us so much peace and comfort, but life is not the same without my sister here. I knew after she passed and I went through her apartment and found more journals, that this book needed to be made. I have felt such an urgency to get it out and to let her words, experiences, and her life help others.

It's hard to understand what addiction does to a person, as well as everyone associated with that person. I remember saying for years that she believed at times that it just affected her, but the amount of lives affected by her addiction was endless. I always told her that I had learned more in my life from her than any other person. I have learned what unconditional love is. I have learned patience, forgiveness, understanding, empathy, knowledge, etc. The list could go on. I want to honor her life and give it more meaning than it already has. She lived as long as she did to finish her story so her life would not have been in vain.

Her children are truly the most amazing children. I had the privilege of having Jala live with me and my family in Saint George for six months after Nat's death. I was honored that she chose to live with me. We gave her all the help and love we could for that time. She needed a break from everything and all the memories. After six months, she was ready to be home with her dad, where she remains today.

I am truly honored to be Nat's big sister. I will never know the horrible things she did that she talked about, but I do know who she really was, without the addiction. She was the life of the party, the one that everyone wanted to be around, and she had the biggest heart and loved her family so much. I am so blessed that we were able to have our children together and experience motherhood together. I will forever cherish the memories I have of her and I will never stop missing her.

Sydka, her dog that she adored, went home with Adi after Nat passed. She is so much happier and has other dogs to play with and is well taken care of. We are so happy to still have her around.

TUESDAY, JANUARY 28, 2019, MICHELLE'S JOURNAL:

ON JANUARY 14TH, MONDAY, I GOT A CALL FROM ADI. SHE WAS UPSET AND TOLD ME THAT NAT WAS IN THE U OF U HOSPITAL AND IN CRITICAL CARE. SHE HAD AN ABSCESS IN HER RIGHT ARM FROM HER SHOULDER TO HER ELBOW, AND THE INFECTION WENT TO HER WHOLE BODY AND SHE WAS SEPTIC. HER KIDNEYS WERE ALREADY SHUT DOWN AND SHE WAS NOT RESPONSIVE. TYE PACKED US UP AND WE HEADED FOR SALT LAKE. RIGHT BEFORE WE GOT THERE, THEY HAD TRIED TO TAKE HER TO SURGERY TO REMOVE THE ABSCESS (EVEN THOUGH SHE ONLY HAD A 50 PERCENT CHANCE TO SURVIVE IT), AND SHE FLATLINED BEFORE THEY TOOK HER. WE GOT THERE AFTER THAT AND SHE WAS ON LIFE SUPPORT. MY DAD SAID A PRAYER THAT WE WOULD DO THE RIGHT THING (WE WERE DECIDING ON SURGERY OR REMOVING LIFE SUPPORT), AND AS HE WAS SAYING THE PRAYER, ADI HEARD, "YOU ARE" (DOING THE RIGHT THING). WE ALL KNEW IN OUR HEARTS

THAT NAT DID NOT WANT TO LIVE THROUGH THAT, AND SHE DIDN'T WANT TO BE AN ADDICT ANYMORE. HER BODY AND SPIRIT WERE DONE. AFTER THE PRAYER, ME AND MY PARENTS AND SISTERS AND ADI WENT TO NAT'S ROOM AND MY DAD RELEASED HER IN A BLESSING. I BELIEVE THAT IS WHEN SHE LEFT HER BODY. SHORTLY AFTER, WE REMOVED LIFE SUPPORT, AND SHE NEVER TOOK ANOTHER BREATH. I HAD IMAGINED THIS DAY FOR YEARS. WITH HER DRUG HISTORY, I ALWAYS IMAGINED HER OVERDOSING IN SOME DITCH OR HOTEL ROOM AND US NOT KNOWING AND NEVER HAVING CLOSURE. I ALSO IMAGINED ME CRYING NONSTOP BECAUSE SHE AND I WERE SO CLOSE AND SO CONNECTED. SHE'S ONE OF THE CLOSEST PEOPLE IN MY LIFE AND I COULDN'T EVER IMAGINE LIFE WITHOUT HER, AND I WAS LIKE THAT DURING THE WEEK OF HER DEATH AND FUNERAL. THEN I BECAME NUMB. IT'S SO HARD TO WRAP YOUR BRAIN AROUND IT, EVEN THOUGH I KNOW SHE IS HAPPY AND FREE FROM HER ADDICTION FINALLY. IT'S JUST BEEN THE LAST FEW DAYS THAT I AM REALIZING THAT EVERYTHING HAPPENED AS IT SHOULD. WE WERE SO BLESSED TO ALL BE THERE WITH HER AND THAT SHE WENT SO QUICKLY AND THAT ALL OF THE FAMILY KNEW WHAT DECISION NEEDED TO BE MADE. AND AS I'VE STARTED LOOKING AT THE BLESSINGS, I'VE NOTICED MORE, AND I FEEL NAT SO CLOSE TO ME.

• • •

AUTOPSY

Manner of Death: Accident

Immediate Cause of Death: Complications of Sepsis due to Abscess of Right Arm from Chronic Intravenous Substance Abuse and Drug Intoxication: Morphine, Heroin, Codeine, Methamphetamine, Alprazolam *(Xanax)*.

Diagnosis: Acute Mixed Drug Intoxication, Abscess, Right Arm, History of Clinical Sepsis (including fluid in lungs, puss in abdomen, possible other abscess, inflamed stomach), and Pneumonia and Left Main Coronary Artery Damage.

Toxicology Results: Caffeine, Alprazolam *(Xanax)*, Codeine, Morphine, 6-Momoacetylmorphine *(Heroin)*, Fluoxetine, Norfluoxetine *(In Fluoxetine)*, Diphenhydramine *(Antihistamine)*, Amphetamine, Methamphetamine.

OPINION: This 39-year-old white/female, died as a result of multiple complications of sepsis due to an abscess of the right arm that was a complication of chronic intravenous substance abuse. The dependent came into the hospital on the day prior to death acutely intoxicated and rapidly decompensated. Life-saving efforts were unsuccessful due to the extensive systemic infection from the abscess. Testing of hospital admission blood revealed the decedent was acutely intoxicated by Morphine, Codeine, Methamphetamine, and Alprazolam when admitted. Detection of 6-Momoacetylmorphine in blood indicates that Heroin is the source of the Morphine and Codeine detected. As an acute intoxication contributed to death, the manner of death is accident.

This was sitting next to her bed when we went to clean her apartment out:

Drug Addicts

Drug Addicts are not bad people or just
some junkies and losers that deserve
to die. They're actually good people
who have families that love them,
but just end up being a victim to the disease
of addiction and they can't help it.
So, if you can't help them, don't hurt them.
And instead of judging them, pray for them.
Author Unknown

Tribute at Nat's funeral from Michelle, Angie, and Emily:

Michelle:

We have an abnormally close family and I attribute that to Nat. She loved our family deeply and always told us she loved us every time she saw one of us or talked to one of us. Because of that, everyone of us tells each other we love each other anytime we come and go or talk. I will be forever grateful for that legacy she left behind.

Nat was the whole package. She was beautiful, full of life, and so smart. I loved having her around me, and when she wasn't, our family did not feel complete. Nat always made me feel special when she would call me for advice and help with things.

I remember going to her cheer and dance competitions and being so proud of her and screaming so loud to cheer her on, I would lose my voice. She had so many talents.

My favorite memories with my sister are when we had our oldest two babies together. We had so much fun being pregnant together; we talked every day. We would buy matching jumpsuits and take pictures of ourselves in them. We bought matching clothes for our kids and were together every day with our babies. We would rollerblade around Bountiful while we pushed the babies in their strollers. Our children grew up like siblings, and I couldn't have asked for anything more. We always laughed about how we couldn't believe we would sanitize each toy after the other baby had it in their mouth; by the time we got to our second children, we realized how silly that was!

My greatest memory with my sisters is New Year's, 1998. Our husbands rented a limo and surprised the four of us and took us to the Homestead and we danced all night. I remember all of us slow dancing with our husbands, and I looked at each of my sisters and thought, *this is perfect.*

Nat was my world. I don't think a day went by that I didn't worry about her. I am so grateful she is at peace, but I can't imagine life without her.

Angie:

My life growing up with Nat was always an adventure. She was always my outgoing, spunky little sister. All of my friends that I would bring over loved her. I wish I had her energy when I was little, even though I'm sure my parents don't care that I didn't.

She would always steal my clothes after I left for school and put them back in my closet before I got home. I would always know, being my OCD self, because she never put them back in the right spot.

I will always remember when my guy friends knocked on my window late one night, little did they know, it was actually Nat's room. She was traumatized and ran to my room freaking out. I told her to stop screaming so our parents wouldn't wake up. Needless to say, my dad woke up and chased the boys through the backyard with a baseball bat as they jumped over the fence.

If any of you knew Nat really well, you would know that at any time she didn't like what you were wearing or anything else about you, she would say, "That's butt." It was her favorite phrase, by far, and we will all miss hearing her say it.

Randy *(Angie's husband)* has one of the funniest memories of Nat that I will never forget. These are his words: "One time, we all decided to go horseback riding. Angie was freaked out and got a pregnant horse and tied it to my horse. We all started down the trail. Natalie's horse wasn't really wanting to go anywhere and wouldn't do anything she tried to get him to do. I always joked with her that the horse just didn't like her attitude. About twenty minutes into the ride, Nat got really frustrated and told us all that she just wanted to go home. Apparently, that's what the horse wanted to do as well; it turned around and took off on a full-out sprint. From where I saw, it looked like she was a pro rider. The horse sprinted all the way back to the stables and came to an immediate stop as Nat jumped off in one continuous motion and kept running all the way to the car. It really looked like something you would see a stunt-man do in a movie. Natalie described it as sheer terror and thought she was going to die. She said that she was holding on for dear life and fell off just as the horse stopped. Needless to say, we never went horseback riding again. But we made fun of her every chance we got."

She and I were always so alike, despite the fact that she loved the spotlight and I never did. People would always tell us that we looked alike when we were younger. Probably because of our blond hair. I always took that as a compliment because I knew how beautiful she was.

My life will be forever changed without my little sister. I will miss her forever, but it gives me peace knowing she is no longer in pain. I love you, Nat.

Emily:

Me, being the youngest sister, my memories were not as fond. I remember always crying when my parents left her to tend me because she was mean and would always hit me. I remember how she had boys come over and then she would leave with one of them, which left me alone with some strange boys. I was tortured year after year by being forced to watch all of her dance and cheer competitions. I always wished we were closer, but we never got the chance because she chose a different lifestyle.

Facebook posts from Nat's kids:

Jala:

I cannot explain how amazing you are, and you will always be loved. You will never be forgotten. But you are in a better place now, where you can never, ever get hurt again. So many people love you. You are so amazing. Words cannot explain how amazing you were as a person and as a mom. You never gave up on anyone. You always tried. I love you so much, and you will always be loved. I hope Heaven treats you well; you are so amazing. I love you, Mom.

Adi:

I love you so much, Mom. I feel so much peace and comfort knowing you are no longer in pain. I know you suffered, and I know there were times when you felt like you weren't good enough, but to us, you were. I know you loved each of us kids with the entirety of your heart and would have done anything for us. I know you were suffering and struggled and had a lot on your plate, and I'm so happy that you can finally feel at peace and rest comfortably. I don't know how I'm going to cope without you, but for now, I can say I'll see you soon. Rest easy, Momma, I love you so much.

Mas:

Your only son...

Oh how I will miss you...

The times I haven't had with you and the times I have, you've literally made me the person I am. You thought you were so bad but I can feel your love now more than ever through Heavenly Father's plan. I can't describe anything that is going on and I'm sorry the last time you saw me was on your screen but I can never say I've made the wrong decision coming out *(on his mission)* and asking Heavenly Father to take you from me. You were my biggest sacrifice I needed to give to feel His love. Love you Mom. See you soon.

We put her name on the headstone as Natalie Allen. She said in one of her later journal entries that she wanted to have her maiden name again and in her Planner for 2019 one of her goals was to change her name back to Allen.

• • •

EPILOGUE

WE ARE NOW AT THE END of the 2021 year and we have had so many blessings in the last three years. In November, 2019, my daughter Kierra had our first grandchild, Fenton, who is also the first great-grandchild. Six months later, Adi had Nat's first grandchild, Ryder and a couple of months after that our niece Kailee had Angie's first grandchild, Hagen. In a month Mas will have a son, Nat's second grandchild, and a few months after that my son Austin will have a son, my second grandchild. My parents were blessed with 5 great-grandsons in a little over three years. These sweet babies have given our family such joy and light which were desperately needed after losing Nat. We are all still as close and talk about Nat often. We miss her dearly every single day.

• • •

Made in the USA
Columbia, SC
11 April 2022

58715726R00370